The Early Bronze Age in Western Anatolia

THE INSTITUTE FOR EUROPEAN AND MEDITERRANEAN ARCHAEOLOGY
DISTINGUISHED MONOGRAPH SERIES

Peter F. Biehl, editor-in-chief
Sarunas Milisauskas and Stephen L. Dyson, editors

The Magdalenian Household: Unraveling Domesticity
Ezra Zubrow, Françoise Audouze, and James G. Enloe, editors

Eventful Archaeologies: New Approaches to Social Transformation in the Archaeological Record
Douglas J. Bolender, editor

The Archaeology of Violence: Interdisciplinary Approaches
Sarah Ralph, editor

Approaching Monumentality in Archaeology
James. F. Osborne, editor

The Archaeology of Childhood: Interdisciplinary Perspectives on an Archaeological Enigma
Güner Coşkunsu, editor

Diversity of Sacrifice: Form and Function of Sacrificial Practices in the Ancient World and Beyond
Carrie Ann Murray, editor

Climate and Cultural Change in Prehistoric Europe and the Near East
Peter F. Biehl and Olivier P. Nieuwenhuyse, editors

Water and Power in Past Societies
Emily Holt, editor

Coming Together: Comparative Approaches to Population Aggregation and Early Urbanization
Attila Gyucha, editor

The Early Bronze Age in Western Anatolia
Laura K. Harrison, A. Nejat Bilgen, and Asuman Kapuci, editors

THE EARLY BRONZE AGE IN WESTERN ANATOLIA

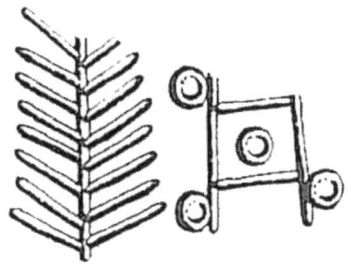

Volume 9

EDITED BY
Laura K. Harrison,
A. Nejat Bilgen,
and Asuman Kapuci

STATE UNIVERSITY OF
NEW YORK PRESS

Logo and cover/interior art: A vessel with wagon motifs from Bronocice, Poland, 3400 B.C. Courtesy of Sarunas Milisauskas and Janusz Kruk, 1982, Die Wagendarstellung auf einem Trichterbecher aus Bronocice, Polen, *Archäologisches Korrespondenzblatt* 12: 141–144.

Published by
State University of New York Press, Albany

© 2021 State University of New York

All rights reserved

Printed in the United States of America

No part of this book may be used or reproduced in any manner whatsoever without written permission. No part of this book may be stored in a retrieval system or transmitted in any form or by any means including electronic, electrostatic, magnetic tape, mechanical, photocopying, recording, or otherwise without the prior permission in writing of the publisher.

For information, contact
State University of New York Press, Albany, NY
www.sunypress.edu

Library of Congress Cataloging-in-Publication Data

Names: Harrison, Laura K., 1985– editor, author. | Bilgen, A. Nejat, editor, author. | Kapuci, Asuman, 1982– editor, author. | University of Buffalo. Institute for European and Mediterranean Archaeology, sponsoring body.
Title: Early Bronze Age in Western Anatolia / Laura K. Harrison, A. Nejat Bilgen, Asuman Kapuci.
Description: Albany : State University of New York Press, [2021] | Series: SUNY series, the Institute for European and Mediterranean Archaeology distinguished monograph series | Includes bibliographical references and index.
Identifiers: LCCN 2020024806 | ISBN 9781438481777 (hardcover : alk. paper) | ISBN 9781438481784 (pbk. : alk. paper) | ISBN 9781438481791 (ebook)
Subjects: LCSH: Turkey—Antiquities. | Excavations (Archaeology)—Turkey. | Bronze age—Turkey. | Material culture—Turkey—History. | Human settlements—Turkey—History. | Turkey—History—To 1453. | Archaeological dating—Turkey.
Classification: LCC DR431 .E36 2021 | DDC 939/.2—dc23
LC record available at https://lccn.loc.gov/2020024806

10 9 8 7 6 5 4 3 2 1

Contents

ILLUSTRATIONS ix

ACKNOWLEDGMENTS xxiii

INTRODUCTION *Laura K. Harrison, A. Nejat Bilgen,*
The Early Bronze Age in Western Anatolia *Asuman Kapuci*
 1

PART I
CHRONOLOGY AND REGIONAL SURVEY

CHAPTER ONE *Turan Efe*
Certain Issues of the Western Anatolian Early Bronze Age
Awaiting Solutions 19

CHAPTER TWO *Rabia Akarsu*
Çivril Plain in the Transition Period from the Early Bronze Age
to the Middle Bronze Age 25

CHAPTER THREE *Ali Umut Türkcan,*
Survey of Kanlitaş Mound and Its Environs (*Eskisehir/Inonu*): *Cansu Topal*
The Settlements and Pottery of the Early Bronze Age 39

CHAPTER FOUR *Tayfun Caymaz*
A Look at the Process of Transition from the Chalcolithic Age
to the Early Bronze Age in Central Western Anatolia in
Light of New Data 49

CHAPTER FIVE *Halime Hüryılmaz*
Northwest Anatolian Influences on Early Bronze Age Cultures
of Gökçeada (Imbros)-Yenibademli Höyük 61

CHAPTER SIX
A New Contribution to the Western Anatolia Early Bronze Age
Chronology: Volute Vessels

Derya Yilmaz

77

CHAPTER SEVEN
Küllüoba Early Bronze Age III Pottery

Murat Türkteki

89

CHAPTER EIGHT
The Figurine/Idol Types of Western Anatolia in the Early Bronze Age
and Their Relationship with Cultural Regions

Deniz Sarı

97

CHAPTER NINE
Distribution and Characteristics of the Beycesultan Early
Bronze Age I Pottery

Sinem Üstün Türkteki

111

PART II
ARCHITECTURE, SETTLEMENT, AND SOCIOPOLITICAL ORGANIZATION

CHAPTER TEN
Urbanism in the Western Anatolian Early Bronze Age

Erkan Fidan

131

CHAPTER ELEVEN
Seyitömer Mound during the Early Bronze Age

A. Nejat Bilgen

145

CHAPTER TWELVE
Power and Ritual Practice in the Early Bronze III Period at
Seyitömer Höyük: An Integrative Analysis of Movement,
Interaction, and Visual Perception

Laura K. Harrison

163

CHAPTER THIRTEEN
On the Perceptions of Sacred Space during the Early Bronze Age:
The Case of Beycesultan

Fulya Dedeoğlu

189

CHAPTER FOURTEEN
Defense Systems Dated to the Early Bronze Age at Liman Tepe

*Ayşegül Aykurt,
Hayat Erkanal*

203

CHAPTER FIFTEEN
Sociopolitical Organization and Territories in Western Anatolia
during the Early Bronze Age

Ralf Becks

217

CHAPTER SIXTEEN
Early Bronze Age Graves from Kubad Abad (Toprak Tol Höyük)

Derya Yalçıklı

229

CHAPTER SEVENTEEN
An Early Bronze Age Cemetery in the Caria Region: Kumyeri

Onur Kara

243

Part III
Material Culture

Chapter Eighteen
Textile Production and Fishing Technologies at Early
Bronze Age I Çukuriçi Höyük

*Barbara Horejs,
Christopher Britsch*
261

Chapter Nineteen
A Preevaluation of Libation Vessels Discovered at Seyitömer Mound
Early Bronze Age Layer III Sanctuaries

Zeynep Bilgen
273

Chapter Twenty
Seyitömer Höyük Early Bronze Age III Platters

Asuman Kapuci
291

Chapter Twenty-One
A Group of Stamp Seals from the İzmir Archaeology
Museum

*Halil Hamdi Ekiz,
Neşide Gençer, Selma Kaya*
303

Chapter Twenty-Two
Acemhöyük Early Bronze Age Pottery

Yalçın Kamış
315

Contributors 327

Index 329

Illustrations

FIGURES

Figure 0.1   Map of Anatolia showing location of sites mentioned in this volume. Credit: Laura K. Harrison.   2

Figure 2.1   Excavation sites in Western and Central Anatolia in the Early Bronze Age III and Middle Bronze Age.   26

Figure 2.2   Aerial photograph of Beycesultan and Çivril Plain.   28

Figure 2.3   Map of Çivril and Baklan plains with Çal Plateau at Upper Meander Basin.   28

Figure 2.4   Architectural ruins in Layers VIII-VI of Beycesultan (Lloyd/Mellaart 1962: Figure 26).   30

Figure 2.5   "Burned Palace" in Layer V of Beycesultan (Lloyd/Mellaart 1965: Figure A.13).   31

Figure 2.6   Examples of ceramic forms from Early Bronze Age III (Lloyd/Mellaart 1962: sheet 7).   32

Figure 2.7   Middle Bronze Age (Lloyd/Mellaart 1965: sheet 1) in Beycesultan.   34

Figure 2.8   Early Bronze Age III and Middle Bronze Age settlements in Çivril Plain.   35

Figure 3.1   KNT'08 21, Illustration 1: Step-sided pot fragment with flaring rim. It has brown-colored thin lining. Its paste includes light brown-colored grit, lime and a trace of mica; KNT'08 20, Illustration 2: Neckless spherical pot fragment. Its fawn-colored surface is burnished and the paste includes grit, calcite and mica; KNT'08

	I 59, Illustration 3: Simple-profiled pot fragment with horizontal handles. It has thin reddish fawn-colored lining. Its paste includes grit, calcite and mica; KNT'08 291, Illustration 4: Concave- necked vessel fragment with a thin grey lining. Its paste consists of brown-colored grit, sand and a trace of mica; KNT'08 41 Illustration 5: Pot fragment with horizontal handles and a flaring rim. It has thin red-colored lining. The clay is made of red-colored sand, mica and a trace of lime; KNT'12 61, Illustration 6: Band handle fragment with incised decoration and a reddish brown-colored lining. The clay is made of calcite, grit and a trace of mica; EYH'08 26, Illustration 7: Bowl fragment with loop handle. Its exterior surface under the lip is reddish brown-colored and it has a thick, burnished lining. The interior surface and rim are glossy black, and the paste is made of grit and sand. Also its cooking quality is good; KNT'09 J 22, Illustration 8: Handle fragment with wreath. It has thin red-colored lining. The paste is made of brown-colored sand with a trace of mica; KNT'08 D 64 K, Illustration 9: Body Fragment (Groove Decoration). It has non burnished thin fawn-colored lining. The paste is made of grey-colored grit and calcite; KNT'08 D-308, Illustration10: Body fragment (Dot pattern Decoration). It has thin non burnished fawn-colored lining. The paste is made of dark grey thin grit and calcite. 43
Figure 3.2	KNT'08 3, Illustration 11: Spherical vessel fragment with flaring rim. It has thin red-colored lining. The clay paste is made of reddish brown-colored grit, calcite and mica; KBY'08 II, Illustration 12: Plate Fragment (A1 Plate). It has red-colored thin lining. The clay paste is made of light red colored sand and a trace of mica; KNT'12 33, Illustration 13: Simple-profiled splay bowl fragment. Its exterior surface is reddish brown-colored. Similarly, its exterior surface has a thin burnished lining. Its interior surface is glossy and black-colored. The clay paste is made of fawn-colored sand, mica and calcite; YKH'09 07, Illustration 14: Simple-profiled deep bowl fragment. It has thin reddish brown-colored lining. The clay paste is made of fawn-colored grit; KNT'08 G 84, Illustration 15: Simple-profiled splay bowl fragment. It has instinctively red-colored lining. The clay paste is made of sand and mica; KNT'08 312, Illustration 16: Splay bowl fragment with flat rim. It has burnished fawn-colored coated face; EYH'08 13, Illustration 17: Pier fragment. Its light red-colored dough involves much stones and lime. 44
Figure 3.3	KNT'08 F 362, Illustration 18: Neck less spherical vessel fragment. It has reddish brown-colored thin lining. The clay paste is made of dark grey-colored thin grit and calcite; KBY'09 6, Illustration 19: Plate Fragment (A1). It has red-colored thick lining. The clay paste is made

of light red-colored sand, mica and calcite; KBY'08 16, Illustration 20: Plate Fragment (A2). Its red-colored exterior surface has thick lining. The clay paste is made of reddish brown-colored sand, calcite and a trace of mica; KNT'A 36, Illustration 21: Splay pot fragment with horizontal handles. It has red-colored thick lining. The clay paste is made of yellowish red-colored sand, calcite and thin grit; KBY'08 II, Illustration 22: Vessel Fragment with flaring rim. It has light red-colored thin lining. The clay paste is made of reddish brown-colored mica, calcite and sand; KBY'08 II 5, Illustration 23: Foot Fragment. It has light red-colored thin lining. The clay paste is made of stones, calcite and mica. 45

Figure 4.1   Map of the Central Western Anatolia Region indicating the primary settlements mentioned in the text. 50

Figure 4.2   Chronological chart. 51

Figure 4.3. Yassıtepe IC3b-f Pottery: Yassıtepe 1c3b-f pottery: 1 Rim diameter 18 cm. Dark brown burnished; 2 Rim diameter 24 cm. Dark greyish brown burnished; 3 Rim diameter 19 cm. Dark brown burnished; 4 Rim diameter 15 cm. Black burnished; 5 Rim diameter 16 cm. Black burnished; 6 Rim diameter 18 cm. Brownish red burnished; 7 Rim diameter 16 cm. Black burnished; 8 Rim diameter 16 cm. Black burnished; 9 Rim diameter 14 cm. Light red plain; 10 Rim diameter 20 cm. Mottled dark greyish brown-black burnished; 11 Rim diameter 15 cm. Dark greyish brown burnished; 12 Rim diameter 18 cm. Grey plain; 13 Rim diameter 10 cm. Purplish brown burnished; 14 Rim diameter 25 cm. Plain, coarse;15 Rim diameter 16 cm. Black burnished, with white filled incision; 16 Rim diameter 12 cm. Very pale brown burnished; 17 Rim diameter 14 cm. Blackish grey burnished; 18 Rim diameter 8 cm. Blackish red burnished; 19 Rim diameter 13 cm. Dark greyish brown burnished; 20 Rim diameter 16 cm. Blackish grey burnished; 21 Rim diameter 25 cm. Pale brown plain; 22 Rim diameter 14 cm. Light red, exterior slightly burnished; 23 Rim diameter 14 cm. Pale brown plain, coarse; 24 Rim diameter 10 cm. Very pale brown plain; 25 Rim diameter 18 cm. Mottled red-brownish yellow burnished; 26 Rim diameter 10 cm; 27 Rim diameter 6.5 cm; 28 Rim diameter 11 cm. Mottled reddish brown-grey burnished; 29 Rim diameter 9 cm. Exterior black burnished, interior coarse; 30 Rim diameter 10 cm. Very pale brown plain, coarse; 31 Rim diameter 13 cm. Exterior black burnished; 32 Neck diameter 4.5–7, belly diameter 16, height 23.5 cm; 33 Neck diameter 7–10 (oval) cm. Brown burnished; 34 Rim diameter 5.5 cm. Light red plain. Coarse; 35 Rim diameter 11 cm; 36 Rim diameter 15 cm;

37 Rim diameter 14 cm. Red plain; 38 Pink plain; 39 Light brown plain; 40 Red slipped; 41 Brown plain.   53

Figure 4.4   Melengiç Sekisi (1–13) and Höyücek (14–21) Pottery: 1 Rim diameter 17 cm. Yellowish red burnished; 2 Rim diameter 18 cm. Black burnished; 3 Rim diameter 16 cm. Black burnished; 4 Rim diameter 20 cm. Red burnished, rim with white filled decoration; 5 Rim diameter 16 cm. Red burnished; 6 Rim diameter 17 cm. Exterior brownish grey, interior grey burnished; 7 Rim diameter 18 cm. Black burnished; 8 Rim diameter 20 cm. Grey burnished; 9 Rim diameter 20 cm. Black burnished; 10 Rim diameter 16 cm. Exterior mottled reddish brown, interior dark grey burnished; 11 Rim diameter 18 cm. Mottled brown and red burnished; 12 Rim diameter 24 cm. Red burnished; 13 Rim diameter 20 cm. Dark reddish black burnished; 14 Rim diameter 20 cm. Semicoarse. Interior very pale brown, slightly burnished; 15 Rim diameter 20 cm. Brown burnished;16 Rim diameter 22 cm. Blackish grey burnished; 17 Rim diameter 20 cm. Brown burnished, rim black; 18 Rim diameter 15 cm. Pale brown slightly burnished; 19 Rim diameter 17 cm. Semicoarse, blackish grey burnished; 20 Reddish brown burnished; 21 With a pinkish brown plain   54

Figure 4.5   Yassıtepe IC3a Pottery: 1 Rim diameter 13–14 cm. Yellowish red burnished. 2 Rim diameter 18 cm. Dark greyish brown burnished. 3 Rim diameter 22 cm. Dark grey burnished. 4 Rim diameter 17 cm. Dark greyish brown burnished. 5 Rim diameter 10–12 cm. Brown burnished, with white filled (?) incision. 6 Rim diameter 25–30 cm. Pale brown burnished. 7 Rim diameter 28–30 cm. Greyish brown burnished. 8 Rim diameter 28 cm. Greyish brown burnished. 9 Rim diameter 16 cm. Black burnished. 10 Rim diameter 10–12 cm. Reddish brown burnished. 11 Rim diameter 18–20 cm. Black burnished. 12 Rim diameter 8–10 cm. Dark grey burnished. 13 Rim diameter 10–12 cm. Interior light grey plain, exterior greyish brown burnished, with white filled (?) incision. 14 Rim diameter 23 cm. Exterior light yellowish brown burnished. 15 Rim diameter 22 cm. Greyish brown burnished. 16 Rim diameter 18 cm. Greyish brown burnished. 17 Rim diameter 14 cm. Dark greyish burnished. 18 Rim diameter 10 cm. Red burnished. 19 Rim diameter 10 cm. Pinkish brown burnished. 20 Rim diameter 18 cm. Dark greyish burnished. 21 Rim diameter 14 cm. Light red plain. 22 Rim diameter 46 cm. Black burnished. 23 Rim diameter 35 cm. Black burnished. 24 Rim diameter 30 cm. Exterior yellowish brown, interior dark grey burnished. 25 Rim diameter 18 cm. Black burnished. 26 Rim diameter 25 cm. Black burnished. 27 Rim diameter 18 cm. Greyish brown burnished. 28 Rim diameter 25 cm. Black burnished. 29 Rim diameter 10 cm. Exterior reddish brown-black, interior coarse. 30 Rim diameter 5.5 cm. 31 Rim diameter 5 cm. 32 Neck diameter 8 cm. Yellowish red plain. 33 Rim diameter 6 cm. Grey plain, semicoarse. 34 Rim diameter 26 cm. Greyish brown burnished. 35 Rim diameter 23 cm. Dark grey burnished. 36 Rim diameter 20 cm. Black burnished. 37 Rim diameter 14 cm. Mottled yellowish brown-black multicolor burnished. 38 Rim diameter 14 cm. Black burnished. 39 Rim diameter 16 cm. Purplish pink plain, coarse. 40 Rim diameter 18 cm. Exterior pale brown, interior black burnished. 41 Rim diameter 8 cm. Yellowish red burnished. 42 Rim diameter 13 cm. Pink plain. 43 Pink plain. 44 Light red plain.   58

Figure 5.1   The location of Yenibademli Höyük in Gökçeada (Imbros).   62

Figure 5.2   The position of Yenibademli Höyük in Büyükdere Valley.   62

Figure 5.3   Yenibademli Höyük. Bowls with sharp carination and horizontal tubular lugs. (EBA II).   64

Figure 5.4   Yenibademli Höyük. Bowl with horizontal tubular lug (1), rim fragment with incised decoration and dot eyes (2), carinated bowl with four strap-handles (3). (EBA II).   65

Figure 5.5   Yenibademli Höyük. Jugs with globular or oblate spherical shapes. (EBA II).   65

Figure 5.6   Yenibademli Höyük. Jug with a small spout on the belly (1), miniature jugs with decorations (2–3). (EBA II).   67

Figure 5.7   Yenibademli Höyük. Jar with collar-neck and plain lip (1), small jar with vertically pierced lugs (2). (EBA II).   68

Figure 5.8   Yenibademli Höyük. Cylindrical lid with flattened top (1), crown-shaped lids (2–4). (EBA II).   69

Figure 5.9   Yenibademli Höyük. Oblate crown-shaped lid (1), lid with two handles (2), lid with rounded corners and four holes (3), disc-shaped knobbed lids with two or four holes (4). (EBA II).   69

Figure 5.10   Yenibademli Höyük. *Pyxis* with incised decoration. (EBA II).   70

Figure 6.1   The map mentioned in the text, showing the points of the volute vessels in the Anatolia and the Aegean World during the Early Bronze Age (Drawing: D. Yılmaz).   79

Figure 6.2   Chronological chart (Drawing: D. Yılmaz).   81

Figure 6.3   A photograph of the volute handles of Maydos Kilisetepe (Photography: D.Ç. Sazcı).   83

Figure 6.4	An illustration of the volute handles of Maydos Kilisetepe (Drawing: A. Ö. Akbaş, S. Yıldız, S. Erol; Preparing: D. Yılmaz). 83
Figure 7.1	Major EB III sites in Western Anatolia. 90
Figure 7.2	A chronological chart synchronizing the stratigraphies of Küllüoba (with calibrated C14 dates) and Troy. 91
Figure 7.3	Percentages of Early EB III Ware Groups. 92
Figure 7.4	Küllüoba EB III Forms (Unscaled). 93
Figure 7.5	Chalice from Küllüoba. 94
Figure 8.1	The Early Bronze Age I Cultural Regions and Pottery Groups of Western Anatolia. 98
Figure 8.2	The Early Bronze Age II Cultural Regions and Pottery Groups of Western Anatolia. 98
Figure 8.3	The Early Bronze Age III Cultural Regions and Pottery Groups of Western Anatolia. 99
Figure 8.4	Western Anatolian figurine/idol types in the Early Bronze Age. 101
Figure 8.5	The distribution of the idol types in the Early Bronze Age I. 102
Figure 8.6	The distribution of the idol / figurine types in the Early Bronze Age II. 103
Figure 8.7	The distribution of the idol types in the Early Bronze Age III. 105
Figure 9.1	1, 2, 7, 10, 12 (Level XX), 6 (Level XXX), 13 (Level XXII)—LC 4; 3, 4, 5, 8, 10 (Level XIX), 11, 14 (Level XVIIb)—EBA I. 114
Figure 9.2	1–3 Beak-spouted jugs; 4–6 jars; 7, 8 pots with incrusted decoration. 115
Figure 9.3	EBA 1 Red-black slipped and brilliant burnished ware with fluted decoration. 116
Figure 9.4	Characteristic pottery forms of EBA 1. 117
Figure 9.5	Distribution area of the Beycesultan EBA 1 cultural region; adapted from J. Mellaart. 119
Figure 9.6	Distribution area of the Beycesultan EBA 1 cultural region; adapted from D. French. 120
Figure 9.7a	Distribution area of the Beycesultan EBA 1 cultural region, around Kütahya; adapted from T. Efe. 121
Figure 9.7b	Distribution area of the Beycesultan EBA 1 cultural region in Western Anatolia; adapted from T. Efe. 121

Figure 9.7c	Distribution area of the Beycesultan EBA 1 cultural region, around Manisa; adapted from T. Efe. 122	
Figure 9.8	Pisidia/Lake District EBA 1 Local Wares. 123	
Figure 9.9	Pisidia/Lake District EBA 1 Form Table. 124	
Figure 9.10	Distribution of area of the Beycesultan EBA 1 Cultural Region in light of recent research, adapted from Akdeniz. 125	
Figure 10.1	Early Bronze Age sites in Western Anatolia. 133	
Figure 10.2	Criteria for urbanism in Western Anatolia. 134	
Figure 10.3	3D plan of Karataş Semayük Central Complex (Drawing by S. Kuşu and E. Fidan). 135	
Figure 10.4	Karataş Semayük EBA I Settlement Plan (Mellink 1974: Fig. 1; Warner 1994: Plan 8). 136–137	
Figure 10.5	Küllüoba EBA II Settlement Plan. 138	
Figure 10.6	Settlement Plan of Troia IIc, Early Bronze Age III (Jablonka 2001: Fig. 437 and 439). 139	
Figure 10.7	Topographical map of Liman Tepe (Drawing by M. Massa). 140	
Figure 11.1	Aerial view of Seyitömer Höyük. 146	
Figure 11.2	Roman period remains from Seyitömer Höyük. 147	
Figure 11.3	Carbonized brain tissue from the Middle Bronze Age at Seyitömer Höyük. 148	
Figure 11.4a	Detail of carbonized brain tissue from the Middle Bronze Age at Seyitömer Höyük. 149	
Figure 11.4b	Detail of carbonized brain tissue from the Middle Bronze Age at Seyitömer Höyük. 149	
Figure 11.5	Location of Middle Bronze Age circuit wall at Seyitömer Höyük. 150	
Figure 11.6	Middle Bronze Age lead figurine. 151	
Figure 11.7	Middle Bronze Age foot rhyton. 151	
Figure 11.8	Selection of seals from Seyitömer Höyük. 152	
Figure 11.9	Sanctuary building at center of mound from Early Bronze Age Phase V-A. 154	
Figure 11.10	Detail of sanctuary building at center of mound from Early Bronze Age Phase V-A. 154	

Figure 11.11   Libation vessels from sanctuary building in Early Bronze Age Phase V-A.   155

Figure 11.12   Evidence for use pottery production, including pottery kilns in houses and moulds for shaping pottery.   155

Figure 11.13   Early Bronze Age pottery from Seyitömer Höyük.   158

Figure 11.14   Terracotta brushes from the Early Bronze Age.   158

Figure 11.15   Metal finds from the Early Bronze Age.   159

Figure 11.16   Figurines and idols from the Early Bronze Age.   159

Figure 11.17   Stone objects from the Early Bronze Age.   160

Figure 11.18   Bone objects from the Early Bronze Age.   160

Figure 12.1a   Calibrated C14 dates from Phase V-A, V-B and V-C plotted in a Bayesian sequence. Credit: Laura K. Harrison.   165

Figure 12.1b   Bayesian phases and interval length from Phase V-A, V-B and V-C. Credit: Laura K. Harrison.   166

Figure 12.2   Plan of Seyitömer Höyük Phase B settlement showing analytical sections. Credit: Laura K. Harrison.   167

Figure 12.3   Aerial photo of Seyitömer Höyük. Credit: A. Nejat Bilgen.   167

Figure 12.4a   Drawing of offset entrances in first use phase and second use phase of Central Megaron Complex. Credit: Laura K. Harrison.   168

Figure 12.4b   Photo of offset entrances in first use phase and second use phase of Central Megaron Complex. Credit: Laura K. Harrison.   168

Figure 12.5   Megaron Front Room and Main Room showing key architectural features: plastered, semi-coursed rubble walls, interior and exterior wall plaster, and yellow clay floor. Credit: Laura K. Harrison.   169

Figure 12.6   Artists' reconstruction of Central Megaron Complex, showing construction technique. Credit: Kristin Donner.   170

Figure 12.7   Photo of Central Megaron Complex with features and in situ deposits labeled. Credit: Laura K. Harrison.   171

Figure 12.8   In situ ritual vessel deposit from northeast corner of Megaron main room. Credit: A. Nejat Bilgen.   172

Figure 12.9   Loomweight found in Room 1 of Central Megaron Complex. Credit: A. Nejat Bilgen.   173

Figure 12.10   Diagrammatic representation of access analysis. On the left, convex interior spaces are represented as nodes, and pathways between them are represented as lines. The graph on the right is justified, and shows the depth of each room from the street. Space syntax analysis quantifies the spatial relationships of these access graphs, in order to reveal how the building configuration shapes movement and interaction. Credit: Laura K. Harrison.   175

Figure 12.11   Viewshed coded for proxemic distance from the entrance to the front room Credit: Laura K. Harrison.   179

Figure 12.12   Viewshed coded for proxemic distance from the hearth in the main room. Credit: Laura K. Harrison.   180

Figure 12.13   Pedestrian route through Central Megaron Complex. Credit: Laura K. Harrison.   182

Figure 13.1a   Early Bronze age "shrines" from Beycesultan Höyük. Layer XVII (adapted by Yakar 1978: Fig. 91).   192

Figure 13.1b   Early Bronze age "shrines" from Beycesultan Höyük. Layer XVI (adapted by Lloyd/Mellaart 1962: Fig. 10).   192

Figure 13.1c   Early Bronze age "shrines" from Beycesultan Höyük. Layer XV (adapted by Lloyd/Mellaart 1962: Fig. 13).   193

Figure 13.1d   Early Bronze age "shrines" from Beycesultan Höyük. Layer XVI (adapted by Lloyd/Mellaart 1962: Fig. 17).   193

Figure 13.2   A different interpretation for architecture of "twin shrines" from Beycesultan Höyük.   195

Figure 13.3   Architectural remains at XXXII-XXXIA-B of Late Chalcolithic from Beycesultan (adapted by Lloyd/Mellaart 1962: Fig. 5).   196

Figure 13.4   The architectural remains of domestic structures at Layer 5b from Beycesultan Höyük.   198

Figure 13.5   Details of horn-shaped ovens and domestic structures at Layer 5b from Beycesultan Höyük.   199

Figure 14.1   A general view of Liman Tepe (Photo: Hakan Çetinkaya).   204

Figure 14.2   Plan of the Early Bronze Age I settlement (LMT VI).   205

Figure 14.3   Early Bronze Age I defensive system (LMT VI).   206

Figure 14.4   Early Bronze Age I city gate (LMT VI).   207

Figure 14.5   Early Bronze Age I houses (LMT VI).   207

Figure 14.6   Plan of the Early Bronze Age II settlement (LMT V.2).   209

Figure 14.7   Early Bronze Age II defensive system (LMT V.2).   210

Figure 14.8	The cell in Early Bronze Age II bastion (LMT V.2).	211
Figure 14.9	Early Bronze Age IIIA ramp (LMT IV.2).	214
Figure 15.1	Frequency of Bronze Age settlement types in Western Anatolia (prepared by the author).	219
Figure 15.2	Distribution of Bronze Age sites (all types) in Western Anatolia (map prepared by the author).	220
Figure 15.3	Excavated sites of the Early Bronze Age in Western Anatolia (map prepared by the author).	220
Figure 15.4	Chronological frequency of Bronze Age sites in Western Anatolia (prepared by the author).	221
Figure 15.5	Frequency of Bronze Age sites according to size categories (prepared by the author).	222
Figure 15.6	Distribution of Early Bronze Age II settlements according to size categories (map prepared by the author).	223
Figure 15.7	Cultural pottery groups of the Early Bronze Age II period in Western Anatolia (map after Efe 2003, Figure 5) combined with Early Bronze Age II settlements according to size categories (prepared by the author).	225
Figure 16.1	Map showing the location of Kubad Abad.	230
Figure 16.2	KubadAbad is situated on the southwest side of Beyşehir Lake.	230
Figure 16.3	Ceramic finds.	231
Figure 16.4	Topographical map of Kubad Abad and Toptak Tol Höyük.	232
Figure 16.5	Ceramic finds from Grave M5.	233
Figure 16.6	Graves, M6, 7, 3.	234
Figure 16.7	Ceramic find from Grave M6.	235
Figure 16.8	Finds from the graves.	236
Figure 16.9	Ceramic finds from Grave M7.	237
Figure 17.1	Aerial photo of Kumyeri showing the EBA cemetery and decoupage area.	244
Figure 17.2	Grave No [KYM 14].	245
Figure 17.3	Pithos burial with burial offering in-sutu, Grave No [KYM 14].	246
Figure 17.4	Grave No [KYM 16].	247
Figure 17.5	EBA II-III graves and architectural remains (EBA III).	247

Figure 17.6	Grave No **[KYM 01]**. 248	
Figure 17.7a–b	Type No: ÇA II.5; Type No: F II.1. 250	
Figure 17.8	Type No: KÇ II.1. 251	
Figure 17.9a–b	Type No: TE III. 1; Type No: TE III. 2. 251	
Figure 17.10	Type No: TA I.1. 252	
Figure 18.1	Selection of spindle whorls of Early Bronze Age Çukuriçi Höyük (Photographer: N. Gail). 262	
Figure 18.2	Typology of spindle whorls of Çukuriçi Höyük phases ÇuHö IV-III (n = 56). 263	
Figure 18.3	Weight of individual spindle whorls (exemplary selection, n = 50, n (g) = 2047.9). 264	
Figure 18.4	Distribution of spindle whorl types within phases ÇuHö III and IV (n = 41). 264	
Figure 18.5	Sites mentioned in the text. 267	
Figure 18.6	Selection of pierced discs of Early Bronze Age Çukuriçi Höyük (Photographer: N. Gail). 286	
Figure 19.1	V-B Phase, Megaron-Planned Sanctuary. 274	
Figure 19.2	V-B Phase, libation vessels. 275	
Figure 19.3	V-A Phase, Megaron-Planned Sanctuary. 277	
Figure 19.4	Double plate from Sanctuary Complex B Phase. 278	
Figure 19.5	Sanctuary Complex B Phase. Double-necked double-spouted pitchers. 279	
Figure 19.6	Sanctuary Complex B Phase. Double-necked double-spouted pitcher. 280	
Figure 19.7	Sanctuary Building B Phase. Double-necked double-spouted pitcher. 280	
Figure 19.8	Sanctuary Complex A Phase. Double-necked double-spouted pitcher. 281	
Figure 19.9	Sanctuary Complex A Phase. Single-necked spouted pitcher. 282	
Figure 19.10	Sanctuary Building A Phase. A spouted-pitcher shaped rython carrying a vessel. 283	
Figure 19.11	Sanctuary Complex B Phase. Human-faced pitcher-shaped rython. 284	

Figure 19.12   Sanctuary Complex B Phase. Human-faced pitcher-shaped rhyton.   284

Figure 19.13   Sanctuary Complex B Phase. Human-faced pitcher-shaped rhyton.   284

Figure 19.14   Sanctuary Building A Phase. Zoomorphic rython.   284

Figure 19.15   Sanctuary Building A Phase. Zoomorphic rython and Zoomorphic/Turtle (?) rython.   284

Figure 20.1   The Platters—Phase VA (Seyitömer Höyük excavation archive).   297

Figure 20.2   The Platters—Phase VB (Seyitömer Höyük excavation archive).   298

Figure 20.3   The Platters—Phase VC (Seyitömer Höyük excavation archive).   299

Figure 20.4   Context of the Platters (Seyitömer Höyük excavation archive).   300

Figure 20.5   Context of the Platters (Seyitömer Höyük excavation archive).   300

Figure 20.6   Context of the Platters (Seyitömer Höyük excavation archive).   301

Figure 20.7   Context of the Platters (Seyitömer Höyük excavation archive).   301

Figure 20.8   Context of the Platters (Seyitömer Höyük excavation archive).   302

Figure 21.1   Inv. No. 24677.   306

Figure 21.2   Inv. No. 26315.   307

Figure 21.3   Inv. No. 26316.   307

Figure 21.4   Inv. No. 3725.   308

Figure 21.5   Inv. No. 5586.   309

Figure 21.6   Inv. No. 21839.   309

Figure 21.7   Inv. No. 3724.   310

Figure 22.1   Topographical map of Acemhöyük.   316

Figure 22.2   Southeastern slope of Acemhöyük.   316

Figure 22.3   Western Anatolian related pottery from Acemhöyük.   319

Figure 22.4   Local EBA III pottery shapes of Acemhöyük.   321

Plans

Plan 11.1   Early Bronze Age Phase V-A settlement at Seyitömer Höyük.   153

Plan 11.2   Early Bronze Age Phase V-A settlement at Seyitömer Höyük.   156

Plan 19.1   Seyitömer Mound, Early Bronze Age III, Phase V-B, Sanctuary and Palace Complex.   274

Plan 19.2   Seyitömer Mound, Early Bronze Age III, Phase V-A, Sanctuary.   276

TABLES

Table 0.1   Relative chronology of Early Bronze Age in Western Anatolia. Credit: Laura K. Harrison.   3

Table 2.1   Comparative chronological table showing the Early Bronze Age III and Middle Bronze Age.   29

Table 12.1   Space syntax measures and their significance. Credit: Laura Harrison, adapted from Hillier and Hanson, 1984).   176

Table 12.2   Space syntax values for the Central Megaron Complex, second use phase. Credit: Laura K. Harrison.   178

Table 13.1   Distribution of finds from Beycesultan "shrines."   197

Table 18.1   Weights and diameters of the groups of net sinkers in phases ÇuHö IV-III.   268

Acknowledgments

The editors wish to gratefully acknowledge the Institute for European and Mediterranean Archaeology, and Peter Biehl in particular, for supporting this project. We wish to express our thanks to the organizers of the Fourth International Archaeology Symposium, held at Dumlupınar University, in Kütahya, Turkey and also to Heather Rosch, who assisted with the preparation of the volume. Finally, we wish to express gratitude to the authors for their insightful and valuable contributions to the field of Anatolian archaeology.

Introduction

The Early Bronze Age in Western Anatolia

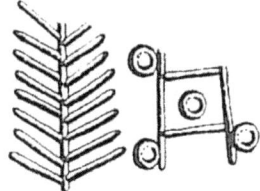

*Laura K. Harrison,
A. Nejat Bilgen, Asuman Kapuci*

The Early Bronze Age in Western Anatolia is a transformative period that witnesses social, political, and economic changes, which reflect the distinctive local character of the region, and document increasing sociopolitical complexity and urbanization over time. The Early Bronze Age falls between the Late Chalcolithic, which is characterized by a tradition of personal and communal symbolism (Kouka 2011:44–45) and proto-urban settlement layouts (Efe and Ay Efe 2007; Erkanal 1996), and the Middle Bronze Age, which is characterized by centralized social and political institutions and trade relations with the expanding Assyrian Empire. Developing a better understanding of the Early Bronze Age—which spans the third millennium B.C.—thus informs our understanding of long-term change, while drawing attention to smaller-scale issues, such as social organization, interregional relations, and political institutions. This volume contains English-language articles about Early Bronze Age Western Anatolia that shed light on the region's material culture, architecture and settlement, regional-scale developments, and trajectories of social and political development. The authors in this volume bring a wide variety of expertise to bear on these key questions, and in doing so, they discuss a great deal of material culture from recently excavated sites (Figure 1.1).

The collective aim of this volume is to gain a broader and deeper understanding of the culture and chronology of Early Bronze Age Western Anatolia. The authors call attention to a number of key issues in the field, which include: the longstanding debate over the timing of the start and the end of the Early Bronze Age; the boundaries of cultural regions in Western Anatolia and their changes over time; the relationship of cultural regions to administrative centers; the characteristics of local pottery traditions; the reconstruction of pan-regional trade routes; the distinctive characteristics of urbanism; the changing role of sacred spaces throughout the Early Bronze Age; and the relationship between cemeteries, settlements, and society.

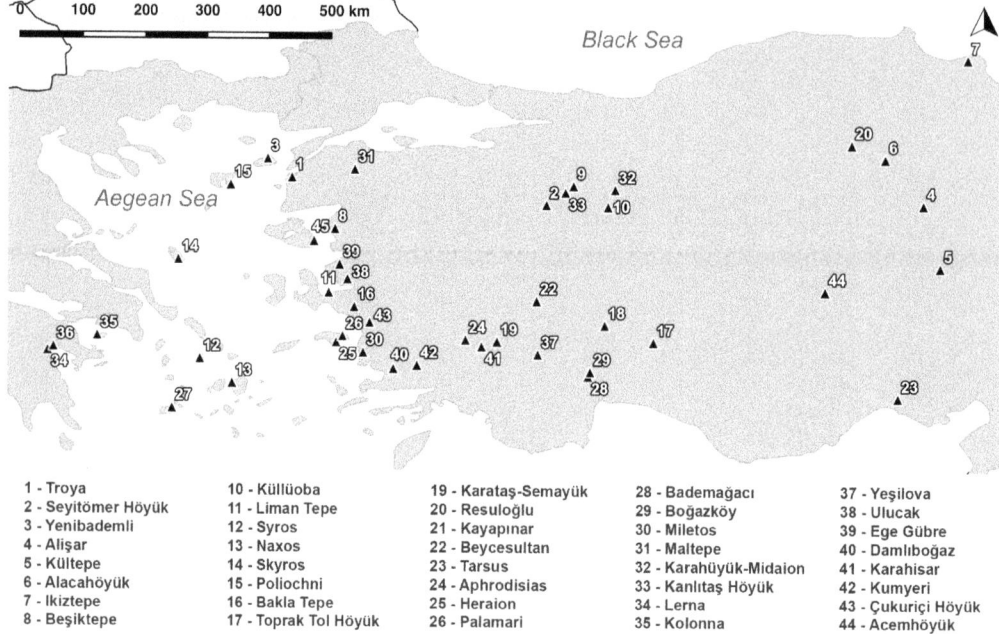

FIGURE 0.1. Map of Anatolia showing location of sites mentioned in this volume. Credit: Laura K. Harrison.

CHRONOLOGY AND REGIONAL SURVEY

Several articles in this volume address issues of Early Bronze Age chronology, the boundaries of regional cultural groups, and the nature of the relationship between them (Table 0.1). Efe's chapter discusses current unresolved issues in Early Bronze Age archaeology in Western Anatolia, and he draws attention to three problems: the imperfect synchronization of local chronologies; gaps in understanding cultural and political developments; and the problematic use of competing or unclear Turkish terminology to describe temporal periods (for example, "İlk Tunç Çağı" and "Erken Tunç Çağı" both mean "Early Bronze Age" in Turkish, and are used interchangeably in publications) (Efe, this volume). Efe argues that more research would clarify these chronological and archaeological issues, and that adopting a standardized terminology would increase the intelligibility of archaeological reports and publications. Efe also calls for the publication of excavation reports from Central Anatolian sites, and highlights a need for research into the absolute and relative chronology of the EBI and EBIII periods in Western Anatolia, which is necessary to clarify the chronology of the start and end of the EBA.

Like Efe, Akarsu points out that a key challenge faced in understanding the shift from the Early Bronze Age to the Middle Bronze Age in Western Anatolia is the limited number of well-stratified, excavated sites in the region (Akarsu, this volume). This

Table 0.1
Relative Chronology of Early Bronze Age in Western Anatolia

	Seyitömer	Troy	Demirchöyük	Küllüoba	Beyçesultan	Poliochni	Thermi	Aegina	Lerna	Aegean
1900	V-A	V								
2000	V-A									
2100	V-B	IV								
2200	V-B	III		IID-E	XII	Yellow		III	IIID	Kastri-Lefkandi I
2300	V-C	IId-h		IIIA						
2400	V-C	IIc		IIIB						
2500	V-C	IIb	Hiatus	IIIC	Hiatus	Red		II	IIIC	
2600		IIa	Q	IV-A	XIIIa		IV			
2700		Id		IV-B	XIIIc-b					
2800			O-P	IV-C	XIV					
2900			N-M							

Credit: Laura K. Harrison.

chapter draws attention to a longstanding debate about whether the changes in material culture and the widespread destruction of sites at the end of EBIII are due to migration, trade relationships, or a crisis brought about by a severe drought (Forsén 1992, Mellaart 1958, Mellink 1986, Staubwasser and Weiss 2006). In order to address this issue, Akarsu analyzes the settlement organization and material culture of EBIII and MBI levels of Beycesultan, and presents a survey of the Çivril Plain that incorporates observations about site number, site size, pottery fabric, and small objects. While noting changes in architecture that suggest cultural and political transformation, and a shift in the regional settlement pattern from EBIII to MBI, Akarsu overall argues for general continuity in the cultural development of Southwestern Anatolia.

Several authors in the volume deal explicitly with pottery assemblages of chronological significance to Early Bronze Age Western Anatolia. Türkcan and Topal argue that there is a similarity in the style and surface treatment of Early Bronze I-II pottery from the Kuzfındık Valley and Phrygia, and that EBII pottery is most ubiquitous (Türkcan and Topal, this volume). They analyze the style and relative frequency of EBI, EBII, and EBIII pottery at six EBA sites: Kanlıtaş Mound, Esnemez's Road Mound, Kuzfındık Dam Mound, Erenköy I, Erenköy II, and Yeniköy Mound. The pottery from the survey area, which is located in the Kuzfındık Valley in the Inonu district of Eskişehir, resembles assemblages from neighboring sites. The authors point out specific parallels with material from Demircihöyük, Küllüoba, Seyitömer, Çukurhisar, Bahçehisar, Aharköy, and Yeniköy. This comparative analysis improves our understanding of the regional chronology of the Kuzfındık Valley, and encourages future research into the dynamic Early Bronze Age occupation of the region.

Caymaz addresses the chronology of the Chalcolithic through the Early Bronze I in Central Western Anatolia with a comparative analysis of pottery from Beycesultan and other sites in the region. One key difference Caymaz highlights between the Late Chalcolithic and the Early Bronze Age is the disappearance of cheese pots and horned handles in the Late Chalcolithic and Early Bronze Age. Caymaz introduces new data for use as comparanda in future relative dating projects and clarifies the Late Chalcolithic/Early Bronze I transition. He argues for the existence of a deeply rooted tradition of Chalcolithic pottery that begins in the mid-sixth millennium B.C. and continues into the Late Chalcolithic and eventually the Early Bronze Age. In addition, Caymaz notes a convergence in styles between the coastal region and the inland region in Early Bronze I, which suggests increased cultural affinity between the two regions.

For more than a century, the pottery sequence of Troy has been fundamental to our understanding of Early Bronze Age chronology (Horejs and Weninger 2016; Ivanova 2016; Pavúk; Yakar 1979). The Trojan sequence remains the longest and most complete in the Western Anatolia region, and remains crucial for cross-dating sequences from neighboring sites. In this volume, two articles deal specifically with the relationship of pottery from the Troad region to local assemblages in Western Anatolia. Hüryılmaz addresses the relationship between pottery styles and cultural groups through an analysis of Yenibademli Early Bronze II pottery, and contextualizes it with assemblages from surrounding Northwestern Anatolian sites, including the Troia I assemblage, Kumtepe IC, Beşik-Yassıtepe, Thermi, and Poliochni (Hüryılmaz, this volume). She suggests that the widespread occurrence of tubular lugs indicates a shared pottery tradition in EBII Northwestern Anatolia, and concludes that overall, the potters of Yenibademli worked under influence and imitated pottery from the Troad region during the Troia I period.

In addition, Yılmaz's chapter suggests using the diagnostic Near Eastern style volute motif as a marker of the late EBIII/early MBI period in Northwestern Anatolia, the northern Aegean, and the Izmir region (Yılmaz, this volume). She argues that this motif originates in Western Anatolia and is important because it is found in distant regions from the eastern Aegean islands to the Balkans and Cilicia, indicating interregional cultural relations. Therefore, it is useful in cross-dating contexts that date to the end of the Early Bronze Age/beginning of the Middle Bronze Age. In addition to showing cultural relations between the Troad and surrounding regions, the volute motif substantiates evidence for long-distance trade between the Anatolian coast and distant areas of Syria, Mesopotamia, the Balkans, the eastern Aegean, Central Anatolia, and Cilicia in EBIII.

Murat Türkteki discusses the pottery of Küllüoba in the EBIII period, makes observations about changes in the pottery repertoire between the Early and Late phases of this period, and proposes a chronological equivalency between Küllüoba IIIC and Troy IIc and Tarsus Phase 3a on the basis of diagnostic pottery forms (M. Türkteki, this volume). He suggests that the potter's wheel expanded the fluidity and plasticity of pottery shapes in the EBIII period, and notes that intensive trade relations with distant regions during this period are responsible for the local appearance of imported goods, including a Syrian bottle and a beaker, at Küllüoba. One of the most significant changes between Early and Late EBIII he observes at Küllüoba is an increase in the use of the potter's wheel in the Late phase, to make vessels such as platters.

Sarı's chapter approaches the question of defining cultural regions in Western Anatolia from an innovative, figurine-based perspective (Sarı, this volume). She outlines the boundaries of five cultural regions in EBA Western Anatolia, and summarizes the diagnostic pottery traditions that characterize each. She then chronologically analyzes the development of various figurine types of the EBA, and maps their geographic distribution, in order to test their adherence to the traditional model based on pottery styles. Her paper demonstrates a strong correlation between figurine traditions, pottery styles, and cultural boundaries, which supports the use of figurines as indicators of group affiliation in future studies of cultural regionalism in the Early Bronze Age.

Sinem Türkteki considers the EBI cultural region surrounding Beycesultan and proposes the existence of a Beycesultan pottery zone that lies within a broader geographical region that encompasses the middle of inland Western Anatolia (S. Türkteki, this volume). This pottery zone highlights the question of whether the developments of this period represent an uninterrupted sequence from the Late Chalcolithic or whether there is a gap between the Late Chalcolithic and EBIA. The chapter combines insights from the distribution and chronology of a diagnostic Beycesultan pottery zone, within a broader geographical region that encompasses the middle of inland Western Anatolia.

Architecture, Settlement, and Sociopolitical Organization

In the Early Bronze Age, fortified citadels with tightly packed rowhouse-style megaron buildings appear throughout Western Anatolia. These megaron buildings are either grouped together in house blocks, as seen in the Aegean littoral sites of Poliochni (Cultraro 2007), and Thermi (Aslan 2006:138) or arranged radially around an open space, often with a freestanding architectural complex at the center, as seen at Demircihöyük (Korfmann 1983), Küllüoba (Efe and Fidan 2008), Seyitömer Höyük (Bilgen 2011; Bilgen and Bilgen 2015; Harrison, 2019), and Troia (Aslan 2006). These changes in the built environment accompany increasing urbanization in the latter half of the third millennium B.C., as the number of sites decreases and their size increases (Bachhuber 2015, Becks, this volume; Çevik 2007).

Population growth during the Early Bronze Age spurred an increase in the number of sites in Western Anatolia during EBII (Dedeoğlu 2008:591–592), and led to transformations in social, political, and economic organization. These changes are reflected in the appearance of elaborate elite architectural complexes (Efe and Fidan 2008, Fidan et al. 2015:70), and planned settlement layouts (Cultraro 2007:63; Efe and Ay Efe 2007:254–256; Korfmann 1983), which reflect the increasing complexity of sociopolitical organization at this time (Dedeoğlu 2008:591–592; Erkanal 1996:79–81). In addition, fortified settlements with upper and lower towns reflect incipient social ranking (Efe and Ay Efe 2007:257; Düring 2011; Fidan et al. 2015:70; Korfmann 1994), and craft workshops and public storage facilities provide evidence for the rise of specialized economies (Harrison 2016:172–179; Korfmann 1983:283; Kouka 2103:577).

This volume adds to our understanding of these changes, with chapters that develop a locally specific working definition of urbanism in Western Anatolia (Fidan, this volume); discuss Early Bronze Age fortifications in light of new data and in the context of extant data from surrounding regions (Aykurt and Erkanal, this volume); and identify regional centers and settlement hierarchies in the EBII period (Becks, this volume). Bilgen evaluates evidence for incipient sociopolitical complexity at an Early Bronze Age production center (A. N. Bilgen, this volume), and Harrison (this volume) and Dedeoğlu (this volume) consider the role of ritual practice in EBA society. Observations by Yalcikli (this volume) and Kara (this volume) add further depth to our understanding of EBA social ranking, as reflected in funerary deposits.

Our knowledge of urbanism in EBA Western Anatolia has grown steadily over the past several decades, raising the issue of whether to investigate these changes in the context of earlier Mesopotamian examples or to view them primarily as a local development. In addressing this issue, Fidan asserts that the criteria normally used to detect urbanism in prehistory are not relevant outside the geographical bounds of Southern Mesopotamia, and stresses that criteria specific to urbanism in Western Anatolia are needed (Fidan, this volume). Fidan points out that Western Anatolia experiences a different cultural trajectory from Mesopotamia, and a unique type of sociopolitical organization characterizes its cities. He suggests narrowing Childe's (1950) list of the ten archaeological criteria that distinguish cities down to just four, which are locally relevant in Western Anatolia: the existence of a ruling class, the emergence of an upper and lower town, the storage of surplus, and the existence of specialized craft industries that are relevant to the specific type of urbanism that develops in third-millennium Western Anatolia.

A. Nejat Bilgen presents a thorough evaluation of the archaeology and chronology of Seyitömer Höyük, and focuses on the character of deposits, architecture, and features, which should form useful comparanda for archaeologists working in this region and time period (Bilgen, this volume). His chapter approaches urbanism at Seyitömer Höyük from a perspective that emphasizes its unique, local expression. This well-preserved settlement is one of the only sites in the inland Western Anatolia region with a well-preserved EBIII occupation. He also discusses changes in settlement organization over time, and their relationship to a proposed Middle Bronze Age migration, which fills a gap in our understanding of the later phases of the Early Bronze Age; a chronological period that is widely recognized as important yet under-studied (Harrison, 2017; Kouka 2013).

Harrison suggests that the architecture, spatial arrangement, and nonverbal cues of a ritual building at Seyitömer Höyük represent a deliberate attempt to organize and control encounters between visitors and residents (Harrison, this volume). This, in turn, reflects a broader development in the Early Bronze Age toward formalizing power relations in increasingly complex, urban societies. Harrison's analysis incorporates quantitative and qualitative methods to reconstruct patterns of movement, interaction, and visibility in a ritual building (also see Harrison 2017). She observes that there are three interior rooms on the main pathway through the building—a courtyard, a front room, and a large main room with a hearth, in which private and exclusive occasions would have taken place. In order to reach the main room, visitors must wait on benches, navigate stepped entrances and changes in direction, and pass through narrow doorways—all of which interrupt movement from the public street space to the private, sacred space. The built environment of this ritual building thus expresses a desire to limit access to the main room through a process of social filtering.

Dedeoğlu posits that domestic worship, centered on the cult of the bull and the oven, was important in the religious system of EBA Beycesultan, rather than formalized public rituals, as is often assumed in the literature. She offers a reassessment of the prevalent assumption that EBA Beycesultan contained a twin shrine with an altar that served as the center of public ritual practice (Dedeoğlu, this volume). In addition, she questions the assumption that the "shrine" at Beycesultan solely served a religious function above a domestic scale, on the basis that the building itself is not built in a unique style but rather conforms to a well-known architectural plan of adjacently built independent buildings that is seen throughout EBA Anatolia. Furthermore, Dedeoğlu asserts that the "altars" within the shrines might well be ovens, based on stylistic parallels with domestic ovens at Seyitömer and Tarsus.

A key contribution of Aykurt and Erkanal's article is its broad temporal scope and focus on the development of fortifications in surrounding regions: the article discusses the Neolithic roots of fortification systems in Western Anatolia, and the possibility that defense systems spread from Western Anatolia to the Aegean in EBII (Aykurt and Erkanal, this volume). They offer a detailed description of the monumental fortifications and associated interior structures at Liman Tepe, an important port city with links to the Aegean and Western Anatolia. The article contrasts the fortifications at Liman Tepe with the more modest defense systems found at other Anatolian and Aegean sites. The discussion chronicles the increasing monumentality of the fortifications from EBI to EBII, and discusses changes in the formal details of construction technique over time.

Becks identifies regional centers and settlement hierarchies that he argues represent distinct territorial units in Western Anatolia (Becks, this volume). These territorial units, he proposes, are representative of an underlying regional expression of sociopolitical organization. He uses a geo-archaeological approach, based on survey reports and satellite images, to measure settlement size and establish settlement hierarchies, in order to better understand different stages and types of sociopolitical organization in western Anatolia. In doing so, he analyzes data from more than 1,000 Early Bronze Age through Late Bronze Age sites that range in size from 1.5 to 40ha, and argues that EBII Western Anatolia is a distinct and homogeneous cultural region that cultivated an individual identity while absorbing cultural influences from all directions.

Synthetic analyses of funerary contexts in Western Anatolia are scarce, with the exception of several key studies: the excavation of Alacahoyuk's Royal Tombs (Koşay 1937); Stech-Wheeler's volume on EBA burial traditions (Stech-Wheeler 1974); and Massa's synthetic study of the graves at Demircihöyük (Massa 2014). This is unfortunate because, as Parker Pearson notes, one of the main ways in which we interpret past societies is through recovering the material traces of those practices associated with the remains of the dead (Şahoğlu and Massa 2011; Parker Pearson 1999:3). Grave goods in funerary contexts include objects that were used by the deceased during life; objects meant to equip the deceased with tools and provisions for the afterlife; reminders of a person's actions or character; or mourners' gifts to the dead (Parker Pearson 1999:9). A detailed analysis of grave goods in burial contexts therefore offers insight into past social organization (Massa 2014:73). Likewise, cemeteries offer insight into social ranking and organization through spatial clustering according to status, age, gender, and family, to name a few (Parker Pearson 1999:11–17).

In this volume, Yalçıklı's chapter investigates social ranking in EBA Western Anatolia through an analysis of funerary deposits from five graves excavated at the site of Toprak Tol Höyük (Yalçıklı, this volume). Yalçıklı identifies parallels between the shapes and relief bands of Toprak Tol Hoyuk grave pottery and those found in the EBIII Harmanören graveyard. She argues that the deposits date to the late third and early second millennium B.C. because the style of the metal objects, such as needles with animal figurines, are found in a number of Anatolian sited during that period. Although the prehistoric settlement associated with the Toprak Tol Höyük funerary site is presently unknown, Yalçıklı persuasively argues that the high number of ornaments of personal adornment and metal objects found in the graves suggest the presence of a local elite class with connections to Central and Western Anatolia, as well as Cilicia.

Kara argues for the existence of a ranked society with a ruling administrative class, based on findings of stamp seals and metal prestige goods in the graves. His chapter demonstrates how a detailed analysis of the spatial location and material culture of funerary contexts can shed light on social organization in the past (Kara, this volume). The article discusses the graves from the cemetery of Kumyeri in order to gain insight into social organization and the cultural and ethnic identity of its EBA residents. He also points out that the material culture from Kumyeri Cemetery has strong parallels in Northwestern Anatolia, the Aegean coast, and the Menderes Basin, and stresses that the Caria region in which the cemetery is located was not isolated, but rather part of a complex regional network of trade and cultural exchange.

Material Culture

There is an increasing recognition among archaeologists in Anatolia that material culture studies are important not just because of their chronological and typological significance but because they offer insight into the practices and activities of individuals living in the past. This volume makes several contributions to this theme, with articles that address a diverse range of topics. Horejs and Britsch reconstruct local economic production based on archaeological evidence for spinning and fishing activities; Z. Bilgen documents the existence of a heretofore unknown type of communal ritual practice based on the use of anthropomorphic and zoomorphic vessels; Kapuci carries out a typological and regional analysis of EBIII dishes from Seyitömer Höyük, Ekiz, Gençer, and Kaya consider the origins of Early Bronze Age administrative practices, through a discussion of group of Late Chalcolithic and Early Bronze Age stamp seals; and Kamış considers how the formal attributes of pottery assemblages reflect production technique and change over time, while contextualizing it with surrounding regions.

Horejs and Britsch identify shape and weight as key indicators of whether a spindle whorl is used to spin wool or plant fibers, and argue that the spindle whorl assemblage from Çukuriçi Höyük reveals a preference for producing wool fibers over plant fibers. The chapter investigates the activities of spinning and fishing at EBI Çukuriçi Höyük by carrying out an analysis of spindle whorls and perforated disks (Horejs and Britsch, this volume). In addition, the weight of the perforated disks suggests they functioned as net sinkers, rather than spindle whorls.

Z. Bilgen interprets a highly symbolic pottery deposit within an EBA sanctuary building as evidence for a heretofore unknown type of ritual practice in Western Anatolia (Z. Bilgen, this volume). Her chapter presents a detailed stylistic analysis of the beakers and libation vessels found in situ at the Early Bronze Age III sanctuary at Seyitömer Höyük, and argues that their technical features, including their mould-based construction, indicate they were produced locally. Z. Bilgen notes that the unique forms of the libation vessels—many of which are anthropomorphic and zoomorphic—do not clearly relate to the cults of the mother goddess or the bull, which are widespread in Anatolia. Her suggestion that they might relate to another, unknown cult is an enticing area for future research.

Kapuci suggests that the deep dishes and shallow dishes from Seyitömer Höyük are similar to examples from Troy, Küllüoba, and Beycesultan, indicating a shared regional pottery repertoire (Kapuci, this volume). Her chapter focuses on utilitarian pottery from the EBIII period, and takes into account the surface properties, inclusions/additives, colors of paste, construction techniques, and decorations of each vessel. On the basis of these observations, Kapuci presents a typology that chronicles the relative distribution of various styles of dishes across three successive phases of the EBIII period.

How, and whether, to study "orphaned" archaeological materials that lack a sound provenance and information about their findspot is an ethical question that is increasingly at the forefront of discussions about twenty-first-century museum practice (Biehl and Harrison 2014, Leventhal and Daniels 2013). Those who argue in favor of acquisition stress that analyzing the archaeological context of an artifact is just one kind of knowledge production, and that other kinds of knowledge production (such as object-based analysis in museums) recontextualize objects and can generate meaningful studies of unprovenanced artifacts (Osborne 2015:243). In this volume, Ekiz, Gençer, and Kaya demonstrate that orphaned objects can benefit from a museum-based kind of knowledge production, by drawing comparanda with objects from secure archaeological contexts (Ekiz et al., this volume). They carry out a study of a group of stamp seals in the Izmir Archaeology Museum, some of which were bought by the museum and others that were brought by means of confiscation. Their chapter presents a catalog of previously unstudied EBA seals from the Izmir museum, and develops a typology based on the stylistic analysis of seal motifs. They suggest dates for each on the basis of extensive comparanda with other Late Chalcolithic and Early Bronze Age seals from Anatolia. The geometric motifs date to the Late Chalcolithic and Early Bronze Age, and the depictions of animals and plants date to the Late Chalcolithic period.

One key research lacuna in the archaeology of Western Anatolia is the relationship between Early Bronze III (Harrison 2019, Harrison 2017, Sari 2013:310–311), and the later Assyrian Trading Colonies period in the second millennium B.C., in which a prosperous trade route stretched from Western Anatolia to Syro-Cilicia. Efe and Fidan have argued for increasing cultural and political alignment of Western Anatolia with Mesopotamia as early as EBIII (Efe and Fidan 2015:83), and Efe suggests that a "Great Caravan Route" that connected these regions in EBIII may have "paved the way for the new trade network of the Assyrian Colony period" (Efe 2007:60). In addition, Kouka discusses cultural aspects of the transition from the EBA to MBA, and argues against the existence of "gaps" in the eastern Aegean and Western Anatolia at this time (Kouka 2013).

The archaeology of Acemhöyük, near Tuz Gölü in Western Anatolia, figures into this debate because previous research at the site has focused on the monumental buildings and rich finds that date to the Assyrian Trading Colonies period in the MBA, and ignored EBA developments—creating a gap in our understanding of the relationship between the two periods. Kamiş's chapter in this volume addresses this gap by introducing new data from excavations carried out on the southeastern slope of the mound, aimed at revealing the stratigraphy from the Early Bronze II through the Assyrian Trading Colonies period

(Kamiş, this volume). He argues that the increase in wheel-made pottery wares occurs later at Acemhöyük than in Central Anatolia, and that moiré painted ware and Konya Plain Painted Ware differentiate the southwestern part of Central Anatolia from the core area of Central Anatolia. These observations contribute to our understanding of how the local pottery production technique at Acemhöyük changes over time, and contextualizes it with developments in Central Anatolia.

Conclusion

The story of the later prehistory of Western Anatolia is a story of great sites, such as Alacahöyük, Beycesultan, and Troia, which captured public imagination and incited archaeological investigations beginning in the nineteenth century. It is also a story of dynamic social transformations. The third millennium B.C. witnesses the emergence of cities and urbanism, the concretization of regular, long-distance trade routes, the rise of an elite social class, the adoption of wheel-made pottery, and the variegation and specialization of economic roles within society. The ascendance of the citadel in the mid-third millennium B.C. transformed the two primary modes of Early Bronze Age power: administrative and ritual (Bachhuber 2015:180). Later in the Early Bronze III period, sociopolitical centralization reached its apex, fueled by urbanization and population agglomeration at larger centers (Harrison, 2019).

These changes clearly distinguish the EBA from the more agrarian and less hierarchical societies of the Late Chalcolithic. They also establish Western Anatolia as a distinct autochthonous cultural landscape, separate from Southeast Anatolia, in which direct influence from Mesopotamia is apparent. Çevik and others have already observed separate trajectories of development in Western Anatolia versus Southeastern Anatolia (Çevik 2007; Sagona and Zimansky 2009). With the exception of Bachhuber's recent book on Early Bronze Age Anatolia, which focuses squarely on the cultural developments of the period (Bachhuber 2015), and Sari's study of EBA cultural groups (Sari 2012), there have been no comprehensive, English-language studies of third-millennium archaeology in Western Anatolia to date. A central goal of this volume is to address this lacuna, by prioritizing EBA Western Anatolia as a vital field of archaeological research.

Throughout history, Anatolia has often been viewed as a bridge between East and West—a place where ideas are transmitted and a stage for cultural encounters among different groups (Özdoğan 2007). This narrative has foregrounded discussions of outside innovations in the prehistory of Anatolia, while diminishing the role of local, endogenous developments, and individual agency. The chapters in this volume call attention to the importance of Western Anatolia as a compelling, local context in its own right, and many of the authors are explicit in ascribing a local impetus for change rather than relying on metanarratives of cultural diffusion. In doing so, the authors offer fresh observations about the chronology and delineation of regional cultural groups in Western Anatolia; the architecture, settlement, and sociopolitical organization of the Early Bronze Age; and the local characteristics of material culture assemblages.

This wealth of new information also invites future research in several areas. Among these are the synchronization of local chronologies, and their association with regional cultural groups, which Efe (this volume) correctly notes is essential to understanding local sociopolitical developments. In addition, while urbanization and the citadel phenomenon in the EBA are well established (i.e., Bachhuber 2105; Korfmann 1983), we lack a clear understanding of the timing and tempo of these changes—for instance, how much time elapsed between EBII destructions and EBIII construction? This is an area currently under investigation by Harrison, and can be addressed with Bayesian dating frameworks (see Harrison, this volume). Methodological advances are also becoming increasingly critical to future research. In addition, quantitative methods of analysis can greatly improve our understanding of cultural processes at regional and local scales, by highlighting nuances of material culture and settlement that might otherwise be lost. This extends to the realm of another key research question—what was the sociocultural landscape of EBIII/MBI Western Anatolia, and how does this relate to the 4.2kya BP aridification event that is attested throughout the eastern Mediterranean (Staubwasser and Weiss 2006). Answering this question will require a combination of archaeological syntheses, regional surveys, and intensive local excavations, in combination with chronometric data and paleoclimactic data. Developing integrated and interdisciplinary research agendas in the future will help enrich our understanding of the EBA in Western Anatolia.

References Cited

Akarsu, R. 2021 Çivril Plain in the Transition Period from the Early Bronze Age to the Middle Bronze Age. In *Early Bronze Age in Western Anatolia*, edited by L. K. Harrison, A. N. Bilgen, and A. Kapuci, pp. 25–38. State University of New York Press, Albany.

Aslan, C. 2006 Individual, Household, and Community Space in Early Bronze Age Western Anatolia and the Nearby Islands. In *Space and Spatial Analysis in Archaeology*, edited by E. C. Robertson, pp. 133–140. University of Calgary Press, Calgary.

Aykurt, A., and H. Erkanal 2021 Defense Systems Dated to the Early Bronze Age at Liman Tepe. In *Early Bronze Age in Western Anatolia*, edited by L. K. Harrison, A. N. Bilgen, and A. Kapuci, pp. 203–216. State University of New York Press, Albany.

Bachhuber, C. 2015 *Citadel and Cemetery in Early Bronze Age Anatolia*. Monographs in Mediterranean Archaeology 13. Equinox Pub, Bristol.

Becks, R. 2021 Sociopolitical Organization and Territories in Western Anatolia during the Early Bronze Age. In *Early Bronze Age in Western Anatolia*, edited by L. K. Harrison, A. N. Bilgen, and A. Kapuci, pp. 217–228. State University of New York Press, Albany.

Biehl, P. F., and L. K. Harrison 2014 University Museums in the Digital Age. In *10 Must Reads: Inclusion—Empowering New Audiences*, pp. 37–63. Museumsetc, Boston.

Bilgen, A. N. 2011 *Seyitömer Höyük Kazisi on Raporu, 2006–2010*. Dumlupinar Universitesi Fen-Edebiyat Fakultesi Arkeoloji Bolumu, Kütahya.

Bilgen, A. N., and Z. Bilgen 2015 Early Bronze Age III Settlement. In *Seyitömer Höyük I*, edited by A. N. Bilgen, pp. 143–204. Dumlupinar Universitesi Fen-Edebiyat Fakultesi Arkeoloji Bolumu, Kütahya.

Bilgen, A. N. 2021 Seyitömer Mound during the Early Bronze Age. In *Early Bronze Age in Western Anatolia*, edited by L. K. Harrison, A. N. Bilgen and A. Kapuci, pp. 145–162. State University of New York Press, Albany.

Bilgen, Z. 2021 A Preevaluation of Libation Vessels Discovered at Seyitömer Mound Early Bronze Age Layer III Sanctuaries. In *Early Bronze Age in Western Anatolia*, edited by L. K. Harrison, A. N. Bilgen, and A. Kapuci, pp. 273–290. State University of New York Press, Albany.

Caymaz, T. 2021 A Look at the Process of Transition from the Chalcolithic Age to the Early Bronze Age in Central Western Anatolia in Light of New Data. In *Early Bronze Age in Western Anatolia*, edited by L. K. Harrison, A. N. Bilgen, and A. Kapuci, pp. 49–60. State University of New York Press, Albany.

Çevik, Ö. 2007 The Emergence of Different Social Systems in Early Bronze Age Anatolia: Urbanisation versus Centralisation. *Anatolian Studies* 57:131–140.

Childe, V. G. 1950 The Urban Revolution. *The Town Planning Review* 21(1):3–17.

Chippindale, C., and D. W. J. Gill 2000 Material Consequences of Contemporary Classical Collecting. *American Journal of Archaeology* 104(3):463–511.

Cultraro, M. 2007 Domestic Architecture and Public Space in Early Bronze Age Poliochni (Lemnos). *British School at Athens Studies* 15:55–64.

Dedeoğlu, F. 2008 Cultural Transformation and Settlement System of Southwestern Anatolia from Neolithic to LBA: A Case Study from Denizli/Civril Plain. In *Proceedings of the 5th International Congress on the Archaeology of the Ancient Near East*, edited by J. M. Cordoba, M. Molist, M. C. Perez, I. Rubio, and S. Martinez, pp. 587–601. Colección Actas (Universidad Autónoma de Madrid), Madrid.

Dedeoğlu, F. 2021 On the Perceptions of Sacred Space during the Early Bronze Age: The Case of Beycesultan. In *Early Bronze Age in Western Anatolia*, edited by L. K. Harrison, A. N. Bilgen and A. Kapuci, pp. 189–202. State University of New York Press, Albany.

Düring, B. S. 2011 Fortifications and Fabrications: Reassessing the Emergence of Fortifications in Prehistoric Asia Minor. In *Correlates of Complexity: Essays in Archaeology and Assyriology Dedicated to Diederik J. W. Meijer in Honour of His 65th Birthday*, edited by B. S. During, A. Wossink, and P. M. M. G. Akkermans, pp. 69–85. Nederlands Instituut voor het Nabije Oosten, Leiden.

Efe, T. 2021 Certain Issues of Western Anatolian Early Bronze Age Awaiting Solutions. In *Early Bronze Age in Western Anatolia*, edited by L. K. Harrison, A. N. Bilgen, and A. Kapuci, pp. 19–24. State University of New York Press, Buffalo.

Efe, T., and D. Ş. M. Ay Efe 2007 The Küllüoba Excavations and the Cultural/Political Development of Western Anatolia before the Second Millennium B.C. In *Ali Dinçol—Belkıs Dinçol Anı Kitabı*, edited by M. Doğan-Alparslan, M. Alparslan, and H. Peker, pp. 251–267. Ege Yayınları, Istanbul.

Ekiz, H. H., N. Gençer, and S. Kaya 2021 A Group of Stamp Seals from the Izmir Archeology Museum. In *Early Bronze Age in Western Anatolia*, edited by L. K. Harrison, A. Nejat Bilgen, and A. Kapuci, pp. 303–314. State University of New York Press, Albany.

Erkanal, H. 1996 Early Bronze Age Urbanization in the Coastal Region of Western Anatolia. In *Housing and Settlement in Anatolia: A Historical Perspective*, edited by Y. Say, pp. 70–82. Turkiey Ekonomik ve Toplumsal Tarih Vakfı, Istanbul.

Fidan, E. 2021 Urbanism in the Western Anatolian Early Bronze Age. In *Early Bronze Age in Western Anatolia*, edited by L. K. Harrison, A. N. Bilgen, and A. Kapuci, pp. 131–144. State University of New York Press, Albany.

Fidan, E., D. Sari, and M. Türkteki 2015 An Overview of the Western Anatolian Early Bronze Age. *European Journal of Archaeology* 18:60–89.

Harrison, L. K. 2016. Living Spaces: Urbanism as a Social Process at Seyitömer Höyük in Early Bronze Age Western Anatolia. PhD dissertation, University at Buffalo, Buffalo.

Harrison, L. K. 2021 Power and Ritual Practice in the Early Bronze III Period at Seyitömer Höyük: An Integrative Analysis of Movement, Interaction, and Visual Perception. In *Early Bronze Age in Western Anatolia*, edited by L. K. Harrison, A. N. Bilgen, and A. Kapuci. pp. 163–188. State University of New York Press, Albany.

Harrison, L. K. 2017 Architecture, Urbanism, and Radiocarbon Dating at Seyitömer Höyük, Turkey. Edited by L. K. Harrison. Released: 2017-05-05. Open Context. http://opencontext.org/projects/347286db-b6c6-4fd2-b3bd-b50316b0cb9f. doi: http://dx.doi.org/10.6078/M76W980X.

Harrison, L. K., and A. N. Bilgen 2019 Emergent Urbanism: Trade, Settlement, and Society at Seyitömer Höyük in Early Bronze Age Western Anatolia. In *Coming Together: Comparative Approaches to Population Aggregation and Early Urbanization*, edited by Attila Gyucha, pp. 189–214. State University of New York Press, Albany.

Horejs, B., and C. Britsch 2021 Textile Production and Fishing Technologies at EBA 1 Çukuriçi Höyük. In *Early Bronze Age in Western Anatolia*, edited by L. K. Harrison, A. N. Bilgen, and A. Kapuci, pp. 261–272. State University of New York Press, Albany.

Horejs, B., and B. Weninger 2016 Early Troy and Its Significance for the Early Bronze Age in Western Anatolia. In *Early Bronze Age Troy: Chronology, Cultural Development, and Interregional Contacts: Proceedings of an International Conference Held at the University of Tubingen May 8–10, 2009*, edited by E. Pernicka, S. Unlusoy, and S. W. E. Blum, 8:123–146. Herausgeber, Bonn. doi:10.1017/CBO9781107415324.004.

Hüryilmaz, H. 2021 Northwest Anatolian Influences on Early Bronze Age Cultures of Gökçeada (Imbros)-Yenibademli Höyük. In *Early Bronze Age in Western Anatolia*, edited by L. K. Harrison, A. N. Bilgen, and A. Kapuci, pp. 61–76. State University of New York Press, Albany.

Ivanova, M. 2016 Stratigraphy and Architecture of Troy I: The Excavations in Schliemann's Trench. In *Early Bronze Age Troy: Chronology, Cultural Development, and Interregional Contacts. Proceedings of an International Conference Held at the University of Tubingen May 8–10, 2009*, edited by E. Pernicka, S. Ünlüsoy, and S. W. E. Blum, pp. 39–48. Verlag Dr. Rudolf Gabelt GMBH, Bonn.

Kamiş, Y. 2021 Acemhöyük Early Bronze Age Pottery. In *Early Bronze Age in Western Anatolia*, edited by L. K. Harrison, A. N. Bilgen, and A. Kapuci, pp. 315–326. State University of New York Press, Albany.

Kara, O. 2021 An Early Bronze Age Cemetery in the Caria Region: Kumyeri. In *Early Bronze Age in Western Anatolia*, edited by L. K. Harrison, A. N. Bilgen, and A. Kapuci, pp. 243–257. State University of New York Press, Albany.

Korfmann, M. 1994 Troia-Ausgrabungen 1993. *Studia Troica* 4 (Band IV). pp. 1–50. P. von Zabern, Mainz am Rhein.

Kouka, O. 2013 Against the Gaps: The Early Bronze Age and the Transition to the Middle Bronze Age in the Northern and Eastern Aegean/Western Anatolia. *American Journal of Archaeology* 117:569–580.

Kapuci, A. 2021 Seyitömer Höyük Early Bronze Age III Dishes. In *Early Bronze Age in Western*

Anatolia, edited by L. K. Harrison, A. N. Bilgen, and A. Kapuci, pp. 291–302. State University of New York Press, Albany.

Leventhal, R. M, and B. I. Daniels 2013 Orphaned Objects, Ethical Standards, and the Acquisition of Antiquities. *Journal of Art, Technology & Intellectual Property Law* 23(2):339–361.

Massa, M. 2014 Early Bronze Age Burial Customs on the Central Anatolian Plateau: A View from Demircihöyük-Sarıket. *Anatolian Studies* 64:73–93.

Massa, M., and V. Şahoglu 2011 Early Bronze Age Burial Customs in Western Anatolia. In *Across the Cyclades and Western Anatolia during the 3rd Millennium B.C.*, pp. 164–171. Sabanci Universitesi, Sakip Sabanci Müzesi, Istanbul.

Osborne, R. 2015 De-Contextualising and Re-Contextualising: Why Mediterranean Archaeology Needs to Get out of the Trench and Back into the Museum. *Journal of Mediterranean Archaeology* 28(2):241–261.

Özdoğan, M. 2007 Amidst Mesopotamia-Centric and Euro-Centric Approaches: The Changing Role of the Anatolian Peninsula between the East and the West. *Anatolian Studies* 57:17–24.

Parker Pearson, M. 1999 *The Archaeology of Death and Burial*. Texas A&M University Press, College Station.

Pavúk, P. 2016 Dating of the Pinnacle in Square E4/5, Dörpfeld Stratigraphy and Formation Processes at Troy. In *Early Bronze Age Troy: Chronology, Cultural Development, and Interregional Contacts: Proceedings of an International Conference Held at the University of Tubingen May 8–10, 2009*, edited by E. Pernicka, C. B. Rose, and P. Jablonka, pp. 49–60. Verlag Dr. Rudolf Habelt GMBH, Bonn.

Sagona, A. and P. Zimansky 2009 *Ancient Turkey*. Routledge, New York.

Sarı, D. 2021 The Figurine/Idol Types of Western Anatolia in the Early Bronze Age and Their Relationship with Cultural Regions. In *Early Bronze Age in Western Anatolia*, edited by L. K. Harrison, A. N. Bilgen, and A. Kapuci. pp. 97–110. State University of New York Press, Albany.

Sarı, D. 2012 İlk Tunç Çağı ve Orta Tunç Çagı'nda Batı Anadolu'nun Kültürel ve Siyasal Gelismi. *Masrop E-Dergi* 7:112–249.

Staubwasser, M., and H. Weiss 2006 Holocene Climate and Cultural Evolution in Late Prehistoric–Early Historic West Asia. *Quaternary Research* 66:372–387.

Türkcan, A. U., and C. Topal 2021 Survey of Kanlitaş Mound and Its Environ (Eskisehir/Inönü: The Settlements and Pottery of Early Bronze Age. In *Early Bronze Age in Western Anatolia*, edited by L. K. Harrison, A. N. Bilgen, and A. Kapuci, pp. 39–48. State University of New York Press, Albany.

Türkteki, M. 2021 Küllüoba Early EBIII Pottery. In *Early Bronze Age in Western Anatolia*, edited by L. K. Harrison, A. N. Bilgen, and A. Kapuci, pp. 89–96. State University of New York Press, Albany.

Türkteki, S. Ü. 2021 Distribution and Characteristics of the Beycesultan Early Bronze Age 1 Pottery. In *Early Bronze Age in Western Anatolia*, edited by L. K. Harrison, A. N. Bilgen, and A. Kapuci, pp. 111–127. State University of New York Press, Albany.

Ünlüsoy, S. 2006 Vom Reihenhaus zum Megaron—Troia I bis Troia III. In *Troia: Archäologie eines Siedlungshügels und seiner Landschaft*, edited by M. Korfmann, pp. 133–144. P. von Zabern, Mainz am Rhein.

Yakar, J. 1979 Troy and Anatolian Early Bronze Age Chronology. *Anatolian Studies* 29:51–67.

Yalçikli, D. 2021 Early Bronze Age Graves from Kubad Abad (Toprak Tol Höyük). In *Early Bronze Age in Western Anatolia*, edited by L. K. Harrison, A. N. Bilgen, and A. Kapuci, pp. 229–242. State University of New York Press, Albany.

Yilmaz, D. 2021 A New Contribution to the Western Anatolia Early Bronze Age Chronology: Volute Vessels. In *Early Bronze Age in Western Anatolia*, edited by L. K. Harrison, A. N. Bilgen, and A. Kapuci, pp. 77–88. State University of New York Press, Albany.

PART I

Chronology and Regional Survey

CHAPTER ONE

Certain Issues of the Western Anatolian Early Bronze Age Awaiting Solutions

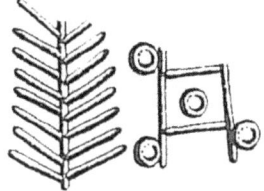

Turan Efe*

Introduction

The foremost questions of the Western Anatolian EBA awaiting solutions are those relevant to chronology. In this respect, the synchronization of local chronologies in the region and their correlations with that of Mesopotamia, as well, have not yet been sufficiently determined. In addition to these, cultural and political development of the region as well as dimensions of cultural interactions and trade relations in interregional and international scale also cannot yet be defined in detail. Yet another group of questions are those related to terminology.

The most important underlying reason for these problems is insufficient research. The completed and ongoing excavations in the region are very few in number. In certain geographical regions no excavations have even been carried out. An important number of sites do not include all the phases of the EBA. Contrary to Mesopotamian cultures, which became—in a great extent or in their entirety—influential in the region, many local cultural formations and pottery zones appeared in the Anatolian Peninsula, mostly due to its mountainous terrain. While this situation hinders a reliable synchronization of local chronologies, no excavation worth mentioning has yet been carried out in the distribution areas of some of these cultural regions or pottery zones. Until recently, the "Western Anatolian EBA chronology" has been based on the long stratigraphies of Tarsus, Kültepe, Beycesultan, and Troy. Since these sites mostly belong to different cultural regions and are located in very distant areas from one other, their stratigraphies could not be sufficiently synchronized and thus no reliable EBA chronology of the Anatolian Peninsula

---

*Prof. Dr. Turan Efe, Bilecik Şeyh Edebali Üniversitesi. E-mail: turan_efe@hotmail.com

has been established. However, the long stratigraphies recently established at Liman Tepe and Küllüoba made an important contribution toward revealing a more reliable chronology. Seyitömer Höyük, which is situated 35 km to the north of Kütahya, provides important clues in terms of revealing the characteristics of the EB III and interregional relations of the region. On the other hand, the publication of the detailed excavation reports of Central Anatolian sites such as Kültepe, Acem Höyük, Ovaören, Kaman-Kalehöyük, Resuloğlu, and Eskiyapar would, no doubt, eventually make an important contribution to the solution of the problems in terms of the Central Anatolian EBA.

Issues Concerning Chronology and Dating

The Early Bronze Age in Anatolia covers approximately a millennium, the timespan stretching between the years 3000/2900–1900 B.C. The term *Early Bronze Age* was used for Anatolia for the first time by C. W. Blegen. Hetty Goldman, who carried out excavations at Tarsus in the '30s and the end of the '40s, separated the EBA stratigraphy of Tarsus—according to the material evidence—into three periods as EB I, EB II, and EB III (Goldman 1956:92). This conventional terminology continues to be used for Anatolia today. H. von der Osten, on the other hand, separated the layers 19-5 corresponding the EBA at Alişar into three phases. These are, from oldest to newest, Chalcolithic, Copper Age, and Early Bronze Age.

In his thesis, which was published toward the end of the 1960s, W. Orthmann adapted Von der Osten's chronology to that of Goldman. He dated the Chalcolithic layers of Von der Osten to the EB I period and suggested Early Bronze Age II for the "Copper Age" (Orthmann 1963a:14–20, Table 2). Furthermore, Orthmann—based especially on the stratigraphies of Kültepe and and Boğazköy—separated the second half of the third millennium B.C. in Central Anatolia into two sub-periods: the EB III and "the Transitional Period into the Middle Bronze Age" (Übergangsperiode) (Orthmann 1963a:13–14, Table 1, 41–44, Table 3; Orthmann 1963b:13–47). These periods are defined as EBA IIIa and EBA IIIb in the southern Aegean coastal regions.

Determination of the Beginning of the Early Bronze Age

Tarsus-Gözlükule always played a key role in the correlation of the chronologies of Mesopotamian Cultural Sphere and Western Anatolia due to its location in the Cilician Plain, which forms the "buffer zone" between the regions in question and has an uninterrupted stratigraphy of Chalcolithic and the Early Bronze Age. Based on the correlations with Syria, H. Goldman dated the lower layers to the Chalcolithic period due to certain parallels with Ubaid and Uruk cultures. An uninterrupted EBA sequence subdivided into EB I, EB II, and EB III periods has been established on top of this. Every period within itself has architectural phases. The EB I pottery yields parallels not only with Syria but also with Western Anatolia. At Tarsus, the architectural layer in which the beak-spouted jug form, characteristic of Western Anatolia, appears for the first time has been considered the beginning of the EBA (Goldman 1956:92) since this form seems to have emerged at the site on the horizon corresponding to the beginning of the EBA in Upper Mesopotamia. From this time on, the beak-spouted jug has been considered one of the most important indicators in the determination of the beginning of the EBA in Western Anatolia.

Especially considering C-14 dates, D. Easton reevaluated the Western Anatolian EBA chronology in the 1970s with quite a radical approach. According to him, the EBA pottery characteristics began to appear in Western Anatolia from the beginning of the fourth millennium B.C. on. For example, he dated the Beycesultan EB I layers to the first half of the fourth millennium B.C. (Easton 1976:145–173). This opinion does not find acceptance anymore. On the other hand, the dates of 3000–2900 B.C. for the beginning of the EBA—based on the many C-14 dates from Demircihüyük, Beşiktepe, and Troy—coincide with the dates for the beginning of the EBA in Southeastern Anatolia (Di Nocera 2000:73–93). Thus, Küllüoba 5-3, Kaklık Mevkii, Beşiktepe IB, and Poliochni Black, which predated this horizon, should then be dated to the Late Uruk and consequently to the pre-Tarsus EB I period. It is most likely that the beginning of this timespan defined as "EBA IA" by Mellink (1992), and "Transitional Period into the EBA" by the author (1994), cannot go back as early as 3500 B.C. as suggested by Easton; instead it might cover the length of time between 3200–3000/2900 B.C. It is controversial to name this timespan EBA IA, in which typical EBA pottery elements began to develop, on the grounds that it corresponds to the Late Chalcolithic in the Mesopotamian cultural sphere.

Determination of the Beginning of the Early Bronze Age III Period

Around the middle of the third millennium B.C., important innovations begin to appear, especially in pottery, marking the beginning of the EB III in Western Anatolia. Rough estimates of this horizon correspond to the timespan between 2500–2400 B.C.; in other words, to Mesopotamian Early Dynastic III or to the beginning of the EB III in Eastern and Southeastern Anatolia. The introduction of the wheel, and certain other forms, are among the most prominent of these innovations which appear as a result of influence from the east. In this context the most characteristic new form is known as the "Trojan plate"; it is either plain wheel-made or red-slipped (hand or wheel-made). Depas, as well, appear at the beginning of this period (see Türkteki 2012 for details on wheel-made pottery in EBIII). While these innovations are also evident at Kültepe near Kayseri, they appear more predominantly along the communication route stretching from Cilicia over the plains of Konya, Akşehir, Eskişehir, and İznik-İnegöl, as far west as the North Aegean (Troy). This route has been referred to as the "Great Caravan Route" (Efe 2007). This event seems to have influenced—to a lesser extent—the Lake District and the close vicinity of Denizli. These innovations appear, at the earliest, around the middle of the EB III period in the northern part of Central Anatolia, the southern Aegean shoreline, and finally in Cyclades in the eastern part of mainland Greece as an extension of this dispersal toward the west. This horizon, known as "Kastri-Lefkandi I" (Broodbank 2000:309–319; Rutter 1979) in the Aegean should correspond roughly to Troy IIg-III; the pottery of Anatolian origin in this area during this period is called "Kastri Group" (Renfrew 1972:Figure 11.2.). Due to the delay in the influx of inland Anatolian EB III pottery elements in the Aegean, the EB II along the southern Aegean coastline and the corresponding Keros-Syros Period in the Cyclades continued longer by comparison to the EB II periods in the Troad and inland Western Anatolia. Thus, the beginning of the EB III in the Aegean is synchronized with Troy IIg-III, instead of Troy IIc. A similar situation is also the case for the EB II period of the northern part of Central Anatolia. There are important chronological/terminological problems that have resulted from this situation which must be resolved.

Issues Concerning the Central Anatolian EBA Chronology

Certain parallels can be traced in the cultural development of Central Anatolia encompassing a large geographical area stretching from the Polatlı-Ankara area in the west into the Kızılırmak bend in the east; from Cappadocia in the south to the shorelines of the Middle Black Sea Region in the north. Unfortunately, no reliable Central Anatolian EBA chronology has so far been established, although excavations carried out in certain areas from the early 1930s on, among these Alişar, Kültepe, Alacahüyük, and İkiztepe, yielded long stratigraphies. One of the most important reasons underlying this is the absence of detailed statistical evaluations of pottery, the materials that are of utmost importance in the establishment of chronology. The chronology of the early periods of the EBA, on which little work has so far been done, is particularly unreliable. The placement of Büyük Güllücek within the chronology is still disputed. In this context we are still not well informed when brilliant red/black burnished pottery (called "Copper Age Pottery") emerges in the chronology. According to current research, the EB III pottery innovations disperse through the north of the region—as was the case in the Aegean—at a later date; in other words this occurred shortly before the Transitional Period into the Middle Bronze Age. This situation makes it even harder to correlate this chronology with that of western Anatolia. Until now, the absence of a tangible EBA stratigraphy in the Konya Plain, which is situated on the crossroads from Cilicia/Mesopotamia and different parts of Western and Central Anatolia, also posed a great hindrance in establishing a more reliable Western Anatolian EBA chronology.

The Issues to Be Solved in the Context of Cultural and Political Development of the Region

In the early 1940s it was Kurt Bittel who mentioned for the first time the existence of certain EBA cultural groups in the Anatolian Peninsula (Bittel 1942). J. Mellaart then reevaluated the topic in the 1960s in light of new research (Lloyd and Mellart 1962). D. H. French preferred to use the definition *pottery zone* instead of *cultural group* in his unpublished dissertation (1969).

The author of this article approached the subject with a slightly different point of view, noting that pottery zones are formed in most of the cultural regions (Efe 20003; see also Sarı 2012 and 2013). It is most likely that they gradually gained a political identity in the later phases of the EBA. We do not yet have enough knowledge of their cultural developments and interrelations due to the lack of sufficient research and the absence of any tangible excavation in the distribution areas of some of these formations. As a result of this, it is not yet possible to adequately analyze the EBA architecture of the Anatolian Peninsula—both locally and in its entirety—in terms of general settlement patterns and the development of urbanism in all aspects. Further clues are vital in order to gain a better perspective on how interregional and international trade networks developed toward the end phases of the EBA.

One of the other important questions awaiting an answer is that of any organic ties between the EBA cultural/political formations and the "lands" mentioned in the Hittite written sources of the second millennium B.C. to determine if they are successors of one another. In this respect the excavation of large sites in the cultural/political regions, which might have functioned as administrative and commercial centers, gains great importance. There are also unanswered questions concerning metallurgy in Western Anatolia in terms of the determination of the developmental stages of metal work, local metal working schools, and the provision of tin.

Terminology Problems

Some of these questions are related to terminology. These are, in fact, valid for all periods. In this context, the questions concerning terminology in pottery are of the greatest priority. Specifically, Carl Blegen (Troy publications), James Mellaart, and David French all made important contributions to the formation of Western Anatolian EBA terminology. However, we still cannot speak of a terminology that finds wider acceptance. For example, there is not yet enough agreement on the naming and descriptions of the ware groups and forms. Here, we should stick to traditional terminology and everything ought to be built on that foundation; local terminologies and radical changes should be avoided.

We are also confronted with some important problems in Turkish terminology specifically. For example: which is more convenient, "*İlk Tunç Çağı*" or "*Erken Tunç Çağı*," for the Early Bronze Age? Or which of the following should be used for pottery: *seramik, keramik, çanak çömlek*? It would be a great benefit to organize workshops in which all these issues are discussed and debated to produce possible solutions.

References Cited

Bittel, K. 1942 *Kleinasiatische Studien* (İstanbuler Mitteilungen 5).
Broodbank, C. 2000 *An Island Archaelogy of the Cyclades*. Cambridge University Press, Cambridge.
Di Nocera, G. M. 2000 Radiocarbon Datings from Arslantepe and Norşun Tepe: The Fourth-Third Millennium Absolute Chronology in the Upper Euphrates and Transcaucasian Region. In *Chronologies des Pays du Caucase et de L'Euphrate aux IV.–III. Millenaires,* edited by C. Marro and H. Hauptmann, pp. 73–93. De Boccard, Paris.

Easton, D. F. 1976 Chronology for the Anatolian Early Bronze Age. *Anatolian Studies* 26:145–173.

Efe, T. 1994 Eskişehir Yöresindeki Bazı Höyüklerde Saptanmış Olan İlk Tunç Çağı'na Geçiş Evresi Çanak Çömleği. *Anadolu Araştırmaları* XIII:17–46.

Efe, T. 2003 Pottery Distribution within the Early Bronze Age of Western Anatolia and Its Implications upon Cultural, Political (and Ethnic?) Entities. In *Archaeological Essays in Honour of Homo amatus:Güven Arsebük,* edited by M. Özbaşaran, O. Tanındı, A. Boratav, pp. 87–104. Ege Yayınları, İstanbul.

Efe, T. 2007 The Theories of the "Great Caravan Route" between Cilicia and Troy: The Early Bronze Age III Period in Inland Western Anatolia. *Anatolian Studies* 57:47–64.

French, D. H. 1969 *Anatolia and the Aegean in the Third Millennium B.C.* Unpublished dissertation, Oxford.

Goldman, H. 1956 *Excavations at Gözlükule, Tarsus* II. Princeton University Press, Princeton.

Korfmann, M., and B. Kromer 1993 Demircihüyük, Beşik-Tepe, Troia-Eine Zwischenbilanz zur Chronologie Dreier Orte in Westanatolien. *Studia Troica* 3:135–171.

Lloyd, S., and J. Mellaart 1962 *Beycesultan* I. British Institute at Ankara, London.

Mellink, M. J. 1992 Anatolian Chronology. In *Chronologies in Old World Archaeology,* edited by R. W. Ehrich, Vol. I–II, pp. 207–220. The University of Chicago Press, Chicago.

Orthmann, W. 1963a Die Keramik der Frühen Bronzezeit aus Inneranatolien. Verlag Gebr. Mann, Berlin.

Orthmann, W. 1963b FrüheKeramik von Boğazköy; Aus den Ausgrabungen am Nordwesthang von Büyükkale. Gebr. Mann, Berlin.

Renfrew, C. 1979 *The Emergence of Civilisation. The Cyclades and the Aegean in the Third Millennium B.C.* Oxbow Books, London.

Rutter, J. 1979 *Ceramic Change in the Aegean Early Bronze Age.* UCLA Institute of Archaeology Occasional Papers 5, Los Angeles.

Sarı, D. 2012 İlk Tunç Çağı ve Orta Tunç Çağı'nda Batı Anadolu'nun Kültürel ve Siyasal Gelişimi. *MASROP* 7:112–249.

Sarı, D. 2013 Evolution culturelle et politique de l'Anatolie de l'Ouest au bronze ancien et au bronze moyen. National Thesis Reproduction Workshop, Lille.

Türkteki, M. 2012 Batı ve Orta Anadolu'da Çark Yapımı Çanak Çömleğin Ortaya Çıkışı ve Yayılışı. *MASROP* 7:45–111.

Weninger, B. 1987 Die Radiocarbon Daten. In *Demircihüyük. Die Ergebnisse der Ausgrabungen 1975–1978. Vol. II. Naturwissenshaftliche Untersuchungen,* edited by M. Korfmann, pp. 4–13. Verlag Philipp von Zabern, Mainz am Rhein.

CHAPTER TWO

Çivril Plain in the Transition Period from the Early Bronze Age to the Middle Bronze Age

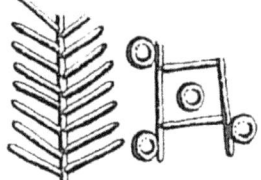

*Rabia Akarsu**

INTRODUCTION

In this study, the developments that occurred in the Western Anatolia Region during the process of transition from the Early Bronze Age to the Middle Bronze Age are discussed, taking the data from the Beycesultan excavation and the Çivril Plain surveys into consideration. The Early Bronze Age III was not a process of the beginning of new cultural developments in just Western Anatolia, but rather a process that affected Anatolia entirely. When the Western Anatolia Region is considered, the major problem would be the limited number of excavation sites offering uninterrupted stratification. One of the most important excavations that offers significant information about the subject is Troy, which shows an uninterrupted stratification (Blegen et al. 1950; Blegen et al. 1951; Blegen et al. 1953; Korfmann 2001:347–354). The ceramic sequence of the Early Bronze Age of Troy is considerably significant for both the comparative and absolute chronology of Western Anatolia. The process of dating other settlements in the region has been done through their connections with Troy. In the excavations of Demircihöyük, which has an important location between Central Anatolia and Western Anatolia, the transition process was determined only on the surface in a mixed form, making it necessary to study other settlements to solve the problem (Efe 1988; Korfmann 1983; Kull 1988; Seeher 1987). The Küllüoba excavations that began by Prof. Dr. Turan Efe to eliminate the lack of knowledge on this subject were successful to arouse interest in archeological environments (Efe and Türkteki 2005). The second-term excavations that were initiated by Prof. Dr. Nejat Bilgen in 2006 on Seyitömer Höyük, located 25 kilometers northwest of Kütahya province, revealed a settlement that measures 150 × 140 meters which had a strategic importance (Figure 2.1; Bilgen 2011; Bilgen 2012).

---

*Rabia Akarsu, Asst. Prof., Faculty of Letters, Department of Archaeology, Atatürk University, Erzurum, 25100, TURKEY.

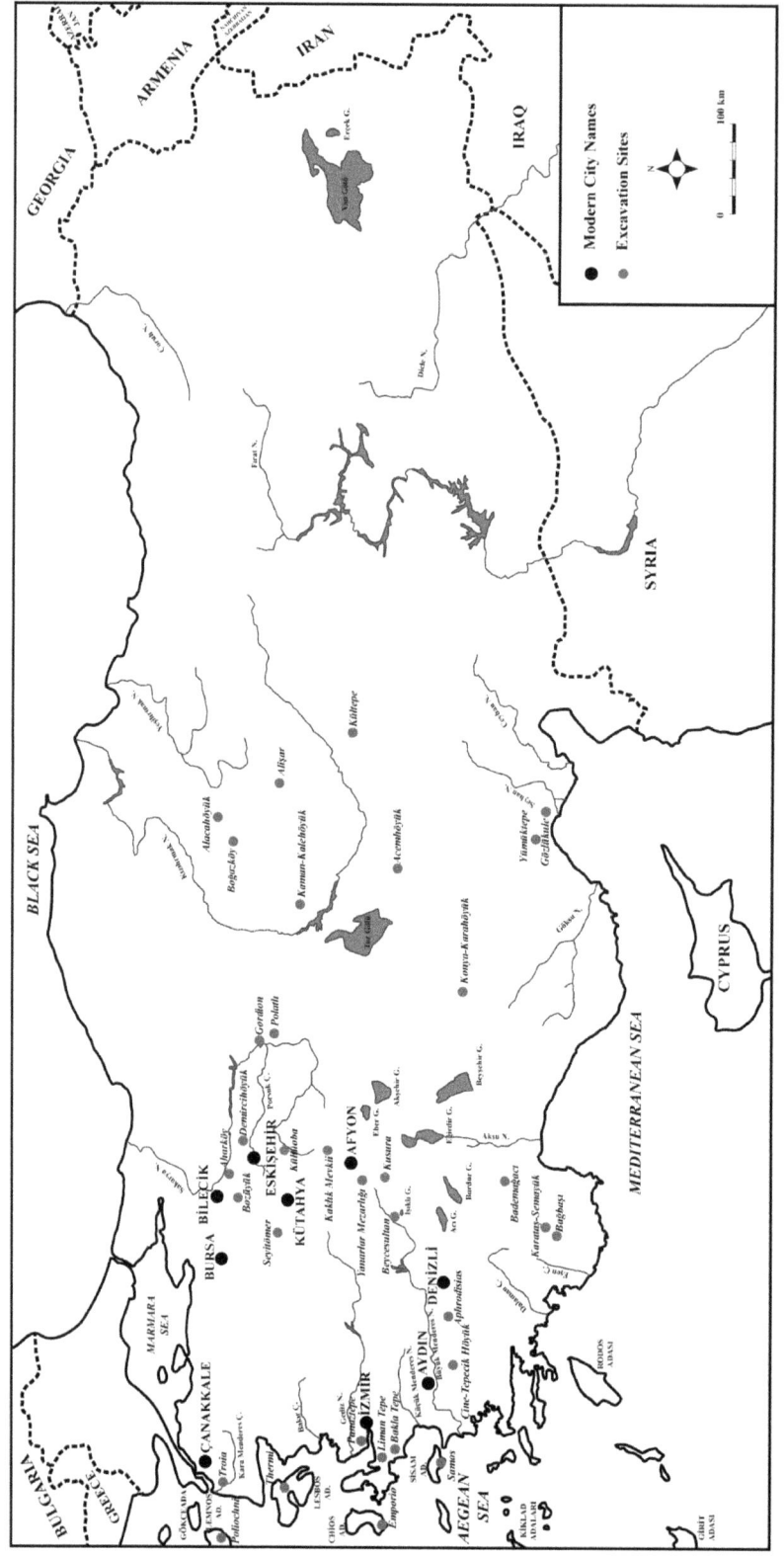

FIGURE 2.1. Excavation sites in Western and Central Anatolia in the Early Bronze Age III and Middle Bronze Age.

At most of the settlements that were excavated in Anatolia there are destruction marks belonging to the Early Bronze Age III. Some cultural changes were detected together with the destruction marks in the settlements that were mentioned.[1] It has been suggested by most archeologists, mainly James Mellaart, Turan Efe, and Vasıf Şahoğlu, that the cultural change in Western Anatolia occurred as a result of new coming communities or trading relations.[2] Even though Mellaart suggested the migration movements of new communities as the reason for cultural change in the Early Bronze Age III, currently this suggestion seems to be kept in the background by long-distance trade models (Mellaart 1981:148). However, it can be understood that these two models are not very different. According to this, there are obvious changes in the elements of material culture in both of them.[3]

At the end of the Early Bronze Age and the Middle Bronze Age, city-states and local kingdoms began to emerge and new developments began to appear. In this period, the emergence of noble classes in regional centers such as Troy, Liman Tepe, Küllüoba, Karataş-Semayük, Tarsus, and Kültepe, comprised of advanced complex structures, powerful defense systems, an administrative system, new settlement organization, and increasing population, specialization in the production of metal products, and new developments in ceramics show us the socioeconomic changes in Anatolia in the second half of the fourth millennium B.C. (Efe 2007; Kouka 2009; Şahoğlu 2005).

For the rest of this study the cultural developments in Beycesultan in the late third millennium B.C. will be discussed and then the conclusions derived from Çivril Plain surveys will be discussed.

Beycesultan in the Process of Transition from the Early Bronze Age to the Middle Bronze Age

The first-term excavations in *Beycesultan,* which took place 5 kilometers southwest of the Çivril district of Denizli province, were performed by English archeologists James Mellaart and Seton Lloyd between 1954 and 1959 (Lloyd 1972; Lloyd and Mellaart 1962; Lloyd and Mellaart 1965; Mellaart and Murray 1995). The second-term excavations have been proceeding under the direction of Prof. Dr. Eşref Abay since 2007 (Figure 2.2) (Abay and Dedeoğlu 2011). Also, under the leadership of Eşref Abay extensive surveys were performed in the Çivril and Baklan plains with Çal plateau at Upper Meander Basin between 2003 and 2011 (Figure 2.3). Thanks to these investigations, 107 archeological places are known from Late Neolithic Period, namely 102 settlements, 3 cemetery areas, and 2 tumuli have been uncovered (Abay 2011; Abay and Dedeoğlu 2005, 2007). Surveys in highland and upland parts of Çal, Baklan, and Çivril districts of the Upper Meander Basin have been carried out since 2011 under the direction of Asst. Prof. Dr. Fulya Dedeoğlu (2013).

Beycesultan Höyük is a settlement excavated in the Çivril Plain that introduces significant information about the Western Anatolian Bronze Age. Beycesultan has an important place in Western Anatolian archaeology with both its architecture and the findings from it. The Early Bronze Age III is divided into two sub-phases, namely IIIa (early) and IIIb (late) in Beycesultan (Lloyd and Mellaart 1962). The Early Bronze Age

FIGURE 2.2. Aerial photograph of Beycesultan and Çivril Plain.

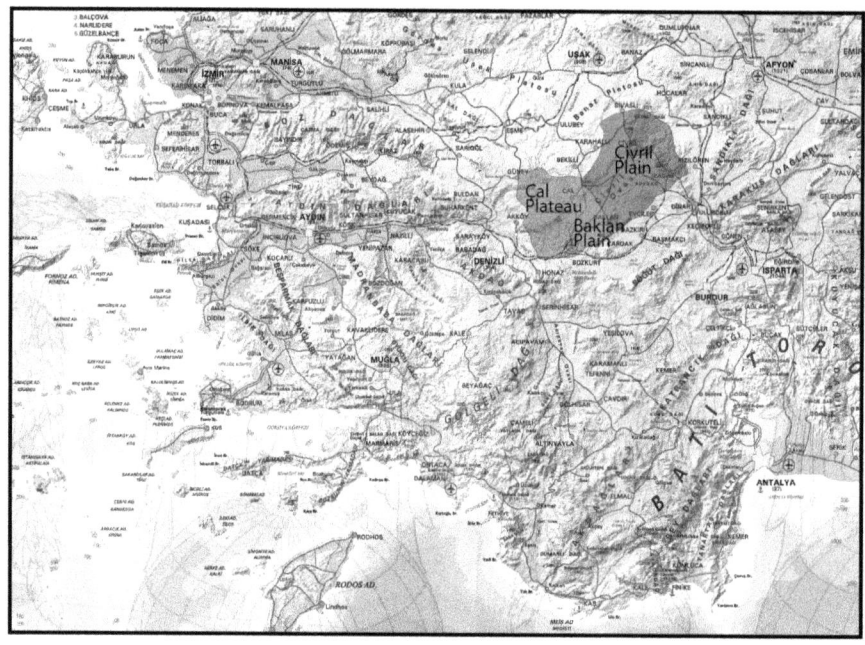

FIGURE 2.3. Map of Çivril and Baklan plains with Çal Plateau at Upper Meander Basin.

IIIb phase signifies the transition to the Middle Bronze Age in Beycesultan, as is the case in all of Western Anatolia. Mellaart dated EBA IIIa phase to 2300–2100 B.C., the EBA IIIb phase to 2100–1900 B.C., and finally the MBA to 1900–1450 B.C. (Table 2.1).[4]

TABLE 2.1
COMPARATIVE CHRONOLOGICAL TABLE SHOWING THE EARLY BRONZE AGE III AND MIDDLE BRONZE AGE

B.C.	Beycesultan	Aphrodisias	Karatas	Seyitömer	Küllüoba	Troy	Liman Tepe	Cyclades	Kültepe	Gözlükule	Period
1450	V-IV	MBA	Bağbaşı MBA	IV	IID-A	Vg-i-VIa-c	III	MC	Kültepe 8-6, Karum II-Ib-a	MBA	MBA
1500											
1600											
1650											
1700											
1800											
1900	VII-VI	Acropolis II-1				IV-Va-f					
1950							IV-1	EC IIIb Phylakopı I	Kültepe 10-9, Karum IV-III	EBA IIIb	EBA IIIb
2000			VI: 1-2	V A-C	IIIC-A	IIb-g-III					
2100	XII-VIII	Acropolis VI-III					IV-2	EC IIIa Kastrı Group	Kültepe 13-11	EBA IIIa	EBA IIIa
2200											
2300											

Architectural ruins belonging to the Early Bronze Age III are only be found in S, SX, and A trenches (Figure 2.4). The structures revealed are mud-brick structures on stone foundations, as is found in the earlier phases of Early Bronze Age. Three structures that belonged to the Early Bronze Age IIIa with megaron plans were revealed (Lloyd and Mellaart 1962). In this period, Beycesultan would have had the appearance of a city consisting of megarons next to one another (Lloyd and Mellaart 1962). Below Layer V at A trench on the east hill, and under the palace and contemporary structures, the walls belonging to quite modest structures from the Early Bronze Age IIIb were discovered. The architecture of Layer VII is composed of two houses that are separated by a narrow street. These houses were used again in the phase of VIb and rebuilt using new stone foundations in Phase VIa (Lloyd and Mellaart 1962).

From Layer V the Middle Bronze Age was marked with new developments both culturally and politically. Beycesultan Höyük, with its large palace structure and other administrative structures from 2000 B.C., and smaller settlements around it show us that there was a complex social organization. Beycesultan Höyük, surrounded with a fortification or periphery wall,[5] is composed of an upper city of 35 hectares, including a palace structure, and a lower city of no more than 70 hectares by current estimates. This means that the settlement is an important city within the context of all of Southwestern Anatolia. The structures revealed during excavations have public features. The palace structure, referred to as "Burned Palace," which was built with a great ordered plan must have had

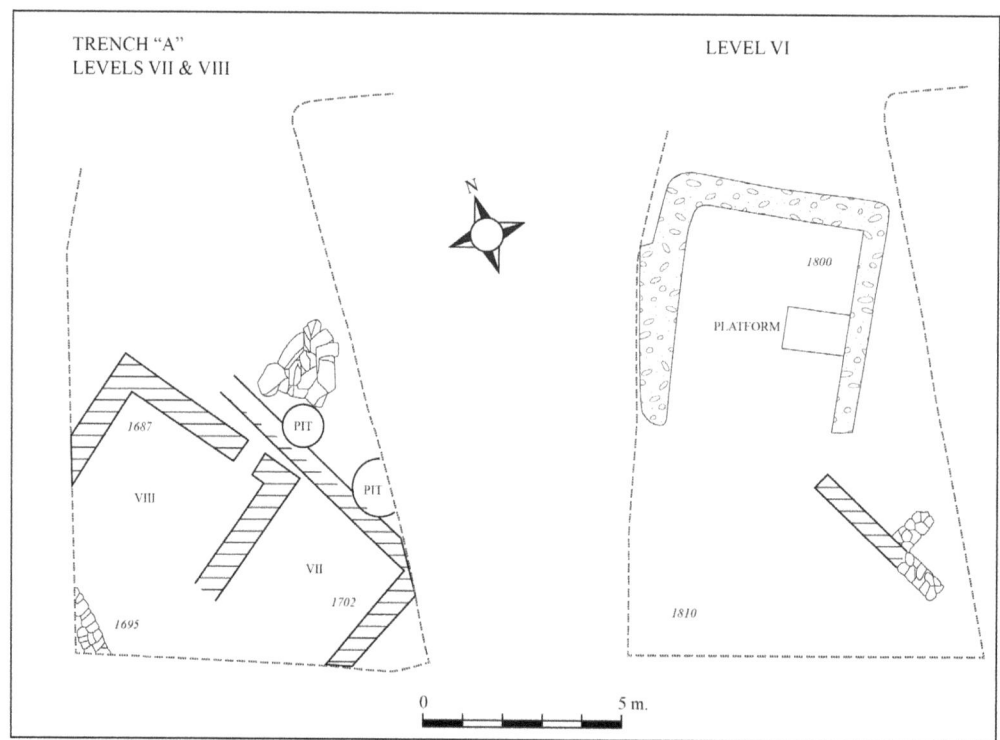

Figure 2.4. Architectural ruins in Layers VIII-VI of Beycesultan (Lloyd/Mellaart 1962: Figure 26).

an ostentatious appearance with its large central courtyard surrounded by wooden columns, ceremonial entrance, acceptance rooms, administrative parts, and storage rooms (Figure 2.5).

The most notable change in Beycesultan Höyük in the Early Bronze Age IIIa as opposed to the Early Bronze Age II is that potter's wheel had arrived in Beycesultan during this phase. Most of the ceramic forms of Beycesultan's Early Bronze Age III have parallels at Troy. Cut spouted jugs, trefoil jugs, and tankards belonging to Early Bronze Age IIIa period, and red cross bowls, inverted rim bowls, horseshoe-shaped handles belonging to Early Bronze Age IIIb period are examples of these (Figure 2.6). The ceramic materials are composed of partly wheel-made, red polished, and slipped bowls (Lloyd and Mellaart

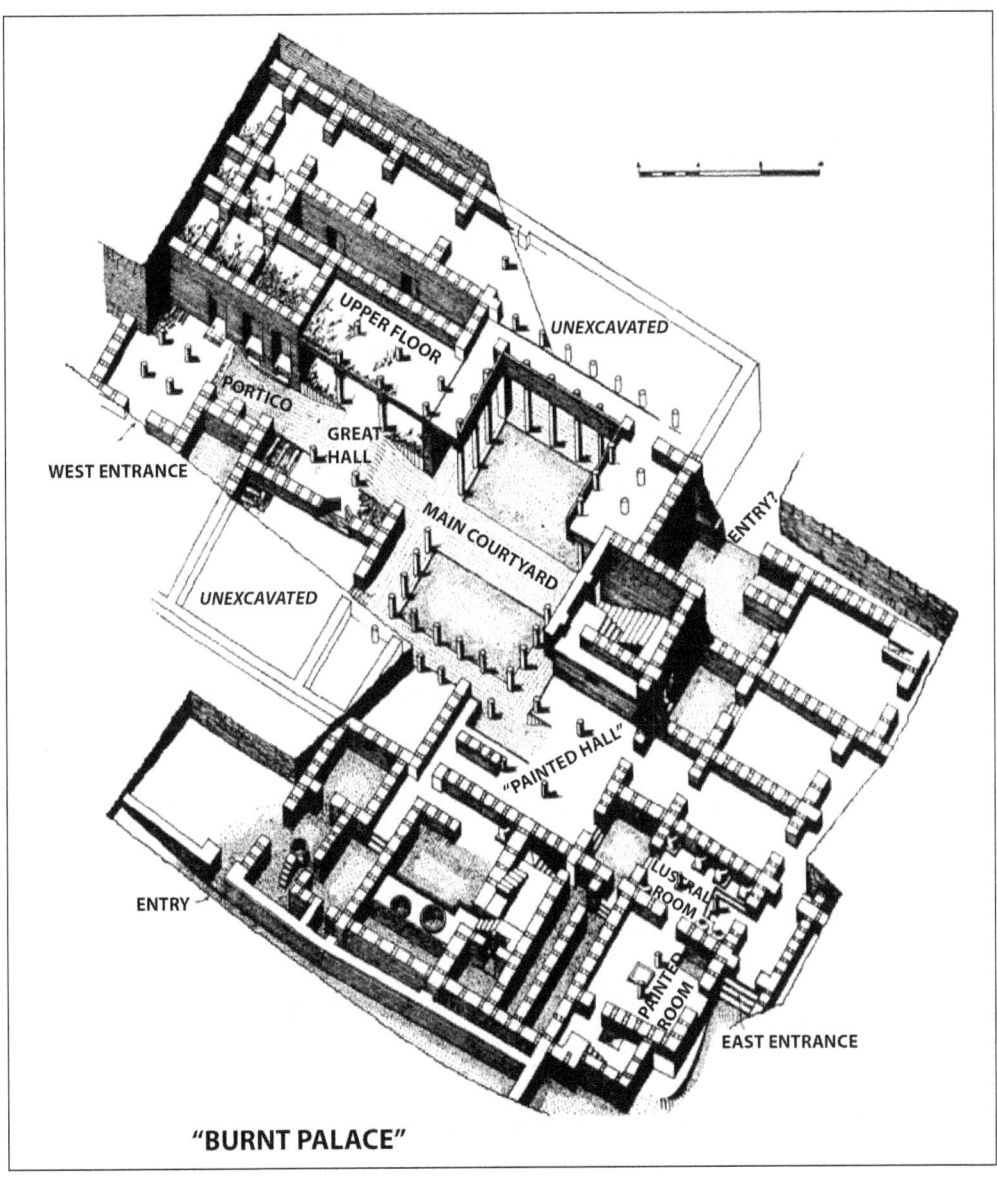

FIGURE 2.5. "Burned Palace" in Layer V of Beycesultan (Lloyd/Mellaart 1965: Figure A.13).

1962). In Layers XII–VI of Beycesultan, inverted rim bowls, red cross bowls, wheel-made plates, depases, tankards, small jars, cut spouted jugs, and cups that all resemble the examples from Troy, Aphrodisias, Seyitömer, and Küllüoba are found (Joukowsky 1986a:389vd).

The Middle Bronze Age ceramic repertoire of Beycesultan was analyzed by Mellaart in four phases (V, IVc, IVb, IVa) (Lloyd and Mellaart 1965). Red and brown wash wares in dark tones remained from the Early Bronze Age III to the end of the Middle Bronze

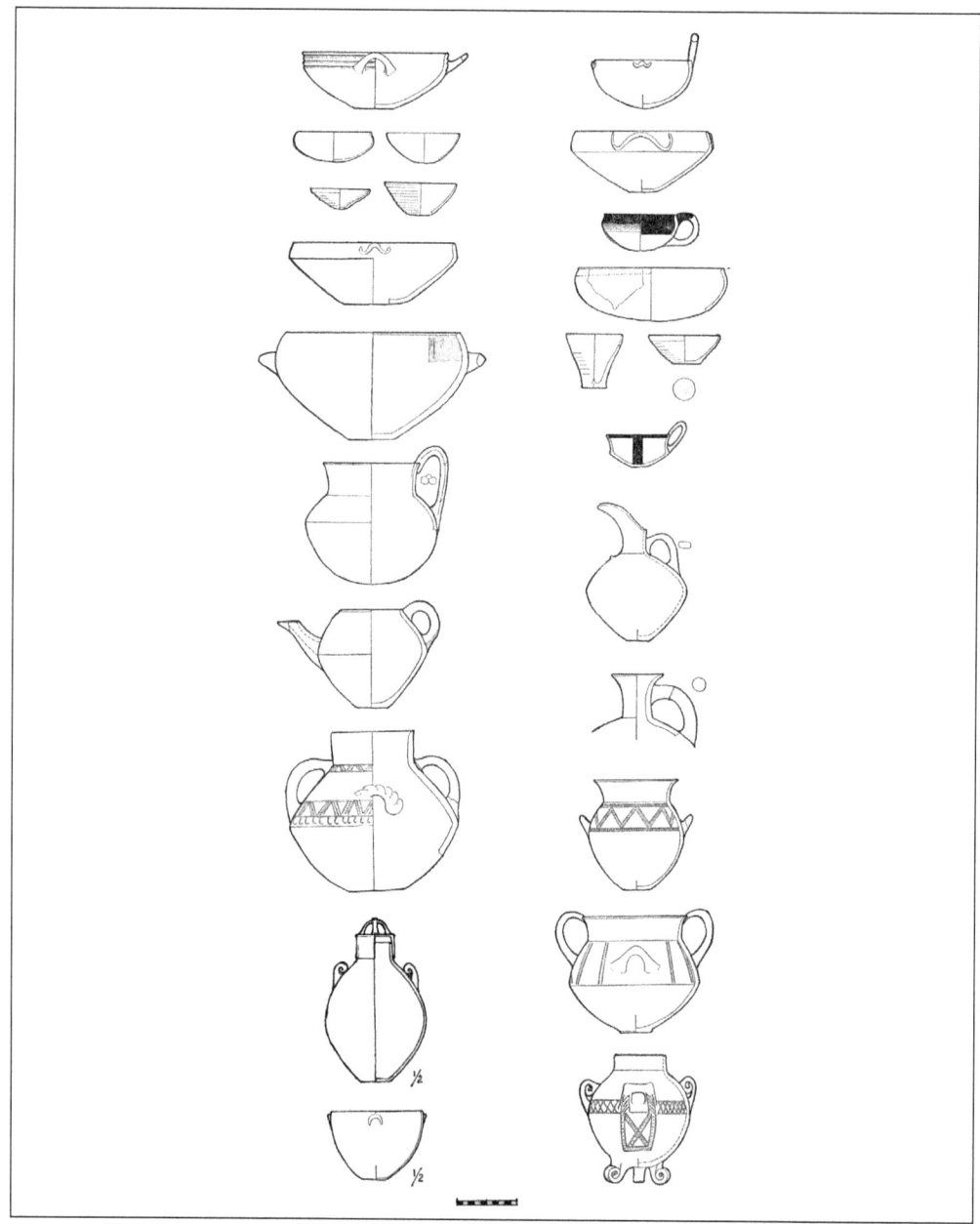

Figure 2.6. Examples of ceramic forms from Early Bronze Age III (Lloyd/Mellaart 1962: sheet 7).

Age. In the Middle Bronze Age the appearance of red and buff wash wares with smooth surfaces began. As the Middle Bronze Age continued, ceramics with carinated and angled profiles, rounded rims, W-shaped relief ornaments, and round bases came into prominence (Figure 2.7). The most characteristic form of the Middle Bronze Age is bead rim bowls (Lloyd and Mellaart 1965:70). Spouted jars and trefoil jugs appear first in this period (Lloyd and Mellaart 1958:126). We can, in general, affirm that the Middle Bronze Age ceramics of Beycesultan were technically more skilled than the Early Bronze Age III wares.

ÇIVRIL PLAIN SURVEY

One of the most significant reasons why the Upper Meander Basin was chosen as a research region is that its geographical conditions and climate are suitable for people to live in. The possibilities for agriculture and animal husbandry caused people to choose the region for settlement continuously. Thirteen of the 26 settlements that were discovered in the Çivril Plain offered information about the Early Bronze Age III, whereas 26 settlements provided information about the Middle Bronze Age (Figure 2.7). According to the surveys in the region, it is understood that settlements of the Early Bronze Age III declined in number as opposed to those in the Early Bronze Age II. In this period, the size of the settlements remained the same but they declined in number. This situation was discovered not only in our research region but also in the surveys in the Eskişehir, Afyon, and Konya provinces (Bahar and Küçükbezci 2011:97–116; Efe 1997:215–232; Koçak 2004). Whereas there were 61 settlements in the Early Bronze Age II, there were only 13 in the Early Bronze Age III. The number of settlements in the region doubled and reached 26 in the Middle Bronze Age. Apart from the number, an increase in the size can also be observed in the settlements. Larger-size settlements remained during the period of complexity that dominated in Anatolia and from the Middle Bronze Age so there must have been another increase in the number of settlements.

Whereas the biggest settlement in the Early Bronze Age III was Beycesultan in Çivril Plain, with 25 hectares, Kepir Höyük on Baklan and Çal region, with 20 hectares on southwest of Upper Meander Basin, is also a large settlement (Abay 2011). The common element of these large settlements, each of which was on a fertile plain, was that there were smaller settlements in their neighborhood. Smaller settlements get closer to central settlements. This can be considered a safety measure.

It is understood that in the Middle Bronze Age, apart from flat plains, there are big settlements located on high mountainous parts, especially on natural gateways. Settlements such as Asar Tepe in Çal region, Höyük Mevkii in the entrance of the plain split by Küfü Çayı, and Belence Höyük are castle-type settlements. It is known that settlements such as Değirmen Höyük and Kepir Höyük are composed of upper and lower cities like Beycesultan (Abay 2011:27).

The number of small objects that were discovered during surveys is minimal in comparison with ceramics. Small objects that are dated to Early Bronze Age III and Middle Bronze Age are composed of clay spindle whorls. The tradition of spindle whorls starts from Early Bronze Age I and continues until the end of Late Bronze Age in Beycesultan

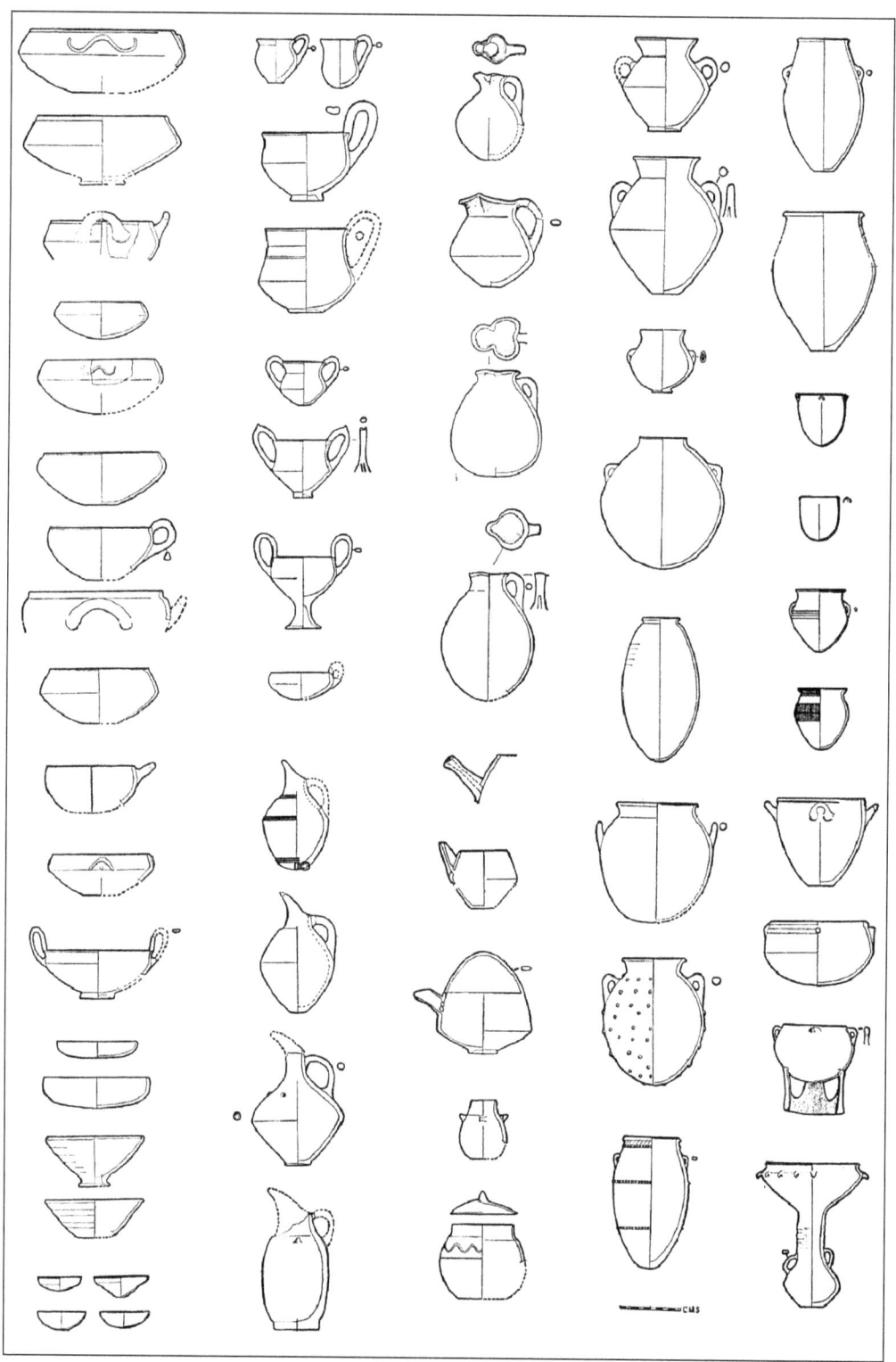

FIGURE 2.7. Middle Bronze Age (Lloyd/Mellaart 1965: sheet 1) in Beycesultan.

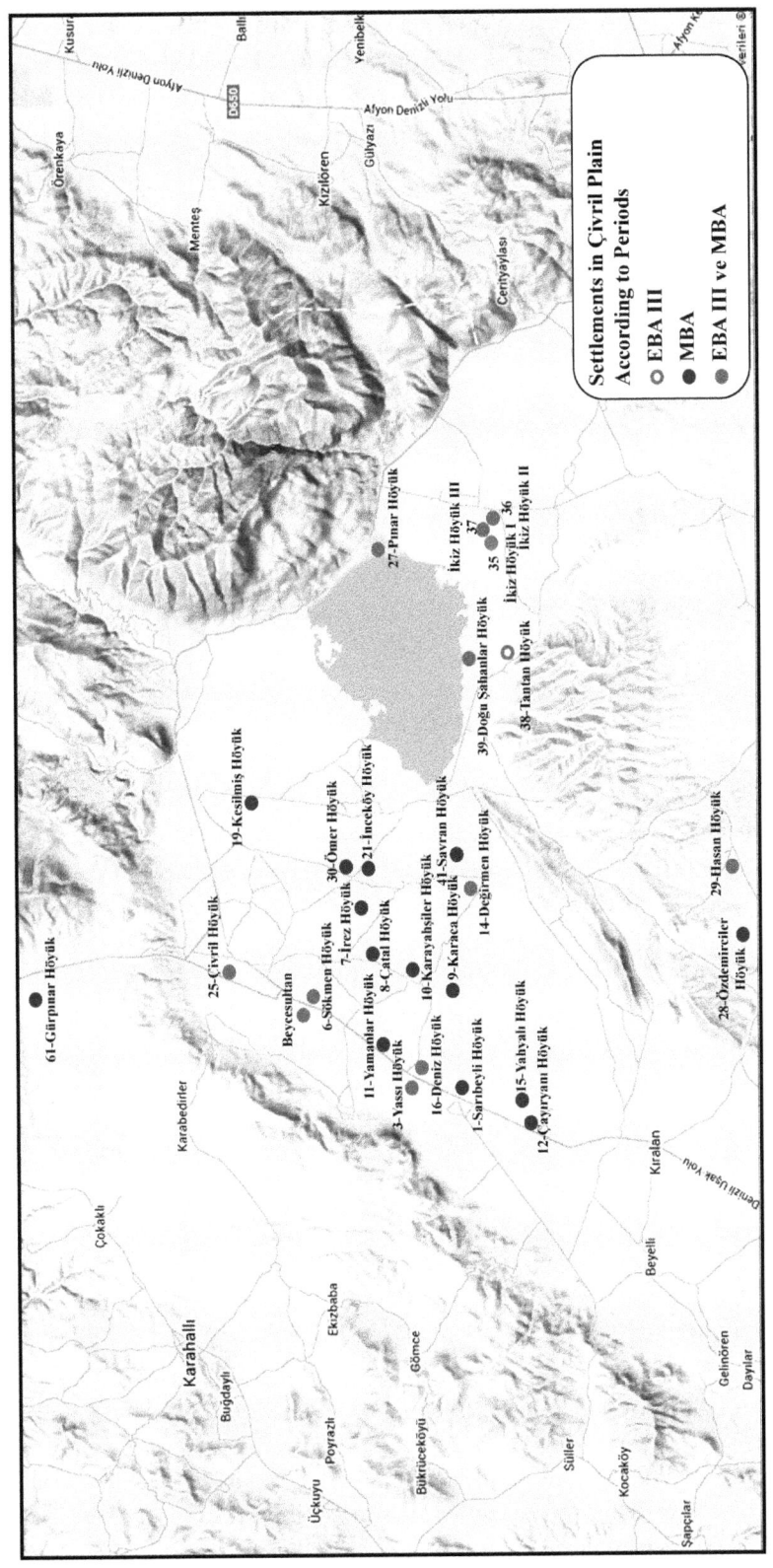

FIGURE 2.8. Early Bronze Age III and Middle Bronze Age settlements in Çivril Plain.

(Murray 1986:348). As can be seen in Beycesultan, there are similarities between Early Bronze Age III and Middle Bronze Age I in terms of form and decoration of the spindle whorls (Lloyd and Mellaart 1962:277). There are examples of spindle whorls both with and without decoration, both made and decorated very carefully. Examples have brown and brown tone–colored clay. Decorations on the spindle whorls were applied only on one side as a specific feature of the Early Bronze Age.

The quantity of temper and surfaces of ceramic material collected from the Çivril Plain allows for a division in classification between fine or coarse ware. The rate of fine ware increases to 68 percent in Middle Bronze Age, while it was 15 percent in Early Bronze Age III. When the ceramic material dated to Middle Bronze Age was analyzed it became clear that the clay fabric is denser and the surface appears matte. The slip on the surface is very small and these wares are called "wash wares." Carinated bowls and bead rim bowls are seen first in the transition period to the Middle Bronze Age, and they increase in number in this period, becoming the characteristic forms of this period. In both periods, brown wash wares are the most common. In the Middle Bronze Age an increase in the number of buff and orange wash wares can be seen. Additionally, a continuity of some forms from former period and replacement by new forms are observed when detailed analyses are done on the goods.

Conclusion

There is no doubt that the importance of the Southwest Anatolia Region, where the Meander River tours from end to end, lies in its geographical circumstances. The Meander River provides intraregional and interregional natural connection between the Aegean basin and interior Anatolia. Intense interregional cultural and trading relations also brought new elements of material culture. Even though a number of cultural developments were discussed, it is apparent that there was no cultural break in the transition from the Early Bronze Age to the Middle Bronze Age in Beycesultan and Çivril Plain. It is not possible to confirm the position of Beycesultan during the political and trading developments since the first term excavations took place in limited fields and the findings are not sufficient. It is important to emphasize that the findings from new excavations will be extremely significant for the archaeology of the region.

Notes

1. The destruction of settlements in Anatolia at the end of EBA II/at the beginning of EBA III is a discussed issue (Ünal 1989:21). The information about settlements such as for Aegean World from Poliochni, Thermi, Emporio; for Anatolia from Beycesultan, Troy, Acemhöyük, Alaca Höyük, Polatlı, Gordion, Kaman Kalehöyük, Tarsus Gözlükule are very important. The changes/developments in these settlements in architecture, ceramics, and other findings tend to be attributed to a newcomer community. However, these destructions and abandonings may have resulted from socioeconomical, climatic, and other reasons as well.
2. Recent studies emphasize that a severe drought period may have had an effect on the abandonment of a number of settlements between 2300–1900 B.C. (Wossink 2009).

3. In Anatolia in the middle of EBA, there was an interregional that reached to Greek continent from Mesopotamia and intra interaction and trading networks in different names, such as Anatolian Trade Network (Şahoğlu 2005:339) and Great Caravan Route (Efe 2007:48).
4. Lloyd and Mellaart 1962:264; Lloyd and Mellaart 1965:73. The dates put by Mellaart for Beycesultan are constituted by comparison of ceramics from that layer with ones from other settlements in Anatolia and the historical facts, since there are not any written documents or radiocarbon dating available (Mellaart 1970:55).
5. The function of the wall that surrounds Beycesultan is not exactly known. (Lloyd and Mellaart 1965: Figure A.13, A.20).

REFERENCES CITED

Abay, E. 2011 Preliminary Report on the Survey Project of Çivril, Baklan, and Çal Plains in the Upper Meander Basin, Southwest Anatolia. *Ancient Near Eastern Studies* 48:1–87.

Abay, E., and F. Dedeoğlu 2005 2003 Yılı Denizli/Çivril Ovası Yüzey Araştırması. 22. *Araştırma Sonuçları Toplantısı* 2:41–51.

Abay, E., and F. Dedeoğlu 2007 2005 Yılı Çivril Ovası Yüzey Araştırması. 24. *Araştırma Sonuçları Toplantısı* 1:277–292.

Abay, E., and F. Dedeoğlu 2011 Beycesultan 2007–2010 Yılları Kazı Çalışmaları Raporu. 33. *Kazı Sonuçları Toplantısı* 4:303–330.

Bahar, H., and H. G. Küçükbezci 2011 2010 Yılı Konya ve Karaman İlleri ile İlçeleri Arkeolojik Yüzey Araştırması. 29. *Araştırma Sonuçları Toplantısı* 1:97–116.

Bilgen, A. N. 2011 *Seyitömer Höyük Kazısı Ön Raporu 2006–2010*. Dumlupınar Üniversitesi Fen-Edebiyat Fakültesi Arkeoloji Bölümü, Kütahya.

Bilgen, A. N. 2012 *Seyitömer Höyük Kazısı Ön Raporu 2011–2012*. Dumlupınar Üniversitesi Fen-Edebiyat Fakültesi Arkeoloji Bölümü, Kütahya.

Blegen, C. W., J. L. Caskey, M. Rawson, and J. Sperling 1950 *Troy. General Introduction. The First and Second Settlements, Vol. I/1: Text, Vol. I/2: Plates*. Princeton University Press, Princeton.

Blegen, C. W., J. L. Caskey, and M. Rawson 1951 *Troy. The Third, Fourth, and Fifth Settlements, Vol. II/1: Text, Vol. II/2: Plates*. Princeton University Press, Princeton.

Blegen, C. W., J. L. Caskey, and M. Rawson 1953 *Troy. The Sixth Settlement, Vol. III/1: Text, Vol. III/2: Plates*. Princeton University Press, Princeton.

Dedeoğlu, F. 2013 Yukarı Menderes Havzası Dağlık Bölge Yüzey Araştırması 2011 yılı Çalışmaları. 30. *Araştırma Sonuçları Toplantısı* 1:215–226.

Efe, T. 1988 Demircihüyük. Die Ergebnisse der Ausgrabungen 1975–1978. Vol. III, 2. Die Keramik 2. C Die frühbronzezeitliche Keramik der jüngeren Phasen (ab Phase H). Verlag von Philipp von Zabern, Mainz am Rhein.

Efe, T. 1997 1995 Yılında Kütahya, Bilecik ve Eskişehir İllerinde Yapılan Yüzey Araştırmaları. XIV. *Araştırma Sonuçları Toplantısı* II:215–232.

Efe, T. 2007 The Theories of the "Great Caravan Route" Between Cilicia and Troy: The Early Bronze Age III Period in Inland Western Anatolia. *Anatolian Studies* 57:47–64.

Efe, T., and M. Türkteki 2005 The Stratigraphy and Pottery of the Period Transitional into the Middle Bronze Age at Küllüoba (Seyitgazi, Eskişehir). *Anatolia Antiqua* XIII:119–144.

Hüryılmaz, H. 1995 Uşak Arkeoloji Müzesinden Bir Grup "Depas Amphikypellon." In *Metin Akyurt ve Bahattin Devam Anı Kitabı*, edited by H. Erkanal, A. Erkanal et al., pp. 177–189. Arkeoloji ve Sanat Yayınları, Istanbul.

Joukowsky, M. S. 1986a *Prehistoric Aphrodisias: An Account of the Excavations and Artifact Studies I.* Brown University, Center for Old World Archaeology and Art, Providence.

Joukowsky, M. S. 1986b *Prehistoric Aphrodisias: An Account of the Excavations and Artifact Studies II.* Brown University, Center for Old World Archaeology and Art, Providence.

Koçak, Ö. 2004 Erken Dönemlerde Afyonkarahisar Yerleşmeleri. Kömen Yayınları, Konya.

Korfmann, M. 1983 Demircihüyük. Die Ergebnisse der Ausgrabungen von 1975–1978. Vol. I. Architektur, Stratigraphie und Befunde. Philip von Zabern, Mainz am Rhein.

Korfmann, M. 2001 Tarih Öncesi Yerleşim Yeri, Hisarlık Tepesi. Düş ve Gerçek. *Troia*:347–354.

Kouka, O. 2009 Cross-Cultural Links and Elite Identities: The Eastern Aegean/Western Anatolia and Cyprus from the Early Third Millennium through the Early Second Millennium BC. *Cyprus and East Aegean: Intercultural Contacts from 3000 to 500 BC, Proceedings of the International Archaeological Symposium 17th–18th October 2008*:31–47. Pythagoreion Samos.

Kull, B. 1988 *Demircihüyük. Die Ergebnisse der Ausgrabungen 1975–1978. Die mittelbronzezeitliche Siedlung. Mit einem Anhang von H. Kammerer-Grothaus und A.-U. Kossatz zu antiken Funden aus Demircihüyük.* Philip von Zabern, Mainz am Rhein.

Lamb, W. 1937 Excavations at Kusura near the Afyon Karahisar. *Archaeologia* 36:1–64.

Lloyd, S. 1972 *Beycesultan Vol. III Part I, Late Bronze Age Architecture.* British Institute of Archaeology at Ankara, London.

Lloyd, S., and J. Mellaart 1958 Beycesultan Excavations: Fourth Preliminary Report, 1957. *Anatolian Studies* 8:93–125.

Lloyd, S. and J. Mellaart 1962 *Beycesultan Vol. I: The Chalcolithic and Early Bronze Age Levels.* British Institute of Archaeology at Ankara, London.

Lloyd, S., and J. Mellaart 1965 *Beycesultan Vol. II: Middle Bronze Age Architecture and Pottery.* British Institute of Archaeology at Ankara, London.

Mellaart, J. 1970 The Second Millenium Chronology of Beycesultan. *Anatolian Studies* 20:55–67.

Mellaart, J. 1981 Anatolia and the Indo-Europeans. *Journal of Indo-European Studies* 9:135–149.

Mellaart, J., and A. Murray 1995 Beycesultan Vol. III Part II, Late Bronze Age and Phrygian Pottery and Middle and Late Bronze Age Small Objects. British Institute of Archaeology at Ankara, Oxford.

Murray, A. 1986 Elazığ ve Pamukkale Müzeleri Çalışmaları. *Araştırma Sonuçları Toplantısı* IV:347–357.

Orthmann, W. 1963 Die Keramik der Frühen Bronzezeit aus Inneranatolien, Istanbuler Forschungen 24. Verlag Gebr. Mann, Berlin.

Özgüç, T. 1999 *Kültepe-Kaniš-Neša Sarayları ve Mabetleri.* Türk Tarih Kurumu Basımevi, Ankara.

Seeher, J. 1987 Demircihüyük. Die Ergebnisse der Ausgrabungen 1975–1978. Vol. III, 1. Die Keramik 1. A Die neolithische und chalkolithische Keramik, B Die frühbronzezeitliche Keramik der älteren Phasen (bis Phase G). Philip von Zabern, Mainz am Rhein.

Şahoğlu, V. 2005 The Anatolian Trade Network and the Izmir Region During the Early Bronze Age. *Oxford Journal of Archaeology* 24(4):339–361.

Ünal, A. 1989 Orta ve Kuzey Anadolu'nun M.Ö. 2. Binyıl İskan Tarihiyle İlgili Sorunlar. *Anadolu* 22:17–37.

Wossink, A. 2009 Challenging Climate Change. Competition and Cooperation among Pastoralists and Agriculturalists in Northern Mesopotamia (c.3000–1600 BC). Sidestone Press, Leiden.

CHAPTER THREE

Survey of Kanlıtaş Mound and Its Environs (*Eskisehir/Inonu*)

The Settlements and Pottery of the Early Bronze Age

Ali Umut Türkcan,* Cansu Topal**

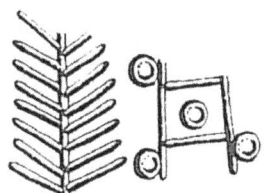

INTRODUCTION

The region analyzed is a pass between main roads that are in the east-west direction and the roads that come from the straits to extend to Syria and Cilicia. The region that includes Inonu Plain is another pass among the important central cities of Early Bronze Age. Bilecik-Demircihöyük is located in the west and Seyitömer is located in the south. The region is important for analyzing Early Bronze Age cultures.

THE SETTLEMENTS AND POTTERY OF EARLY BRONZE AGE

In 2008–2009, the surface analysis of Kanlıtaş Mound was made by the archaeology department at Anatolia University under the supervision of Ali U. Türkcan, who defined an area around Kanlıtaş Mound that is located near Kuzfındık Village, which belongs to the Inonu district of Eskisehir. The diameter of the survey area was seven kilometers and Kanlıtaş Mound was the central point of the research area. Different assemblages from the Paleolithic period to the Early Ottoman period were found in Kuzfındık Valley and its environs, including Kanlıtaş Mound. Material from the Neolithic period could not be found in the region. The pottery of the Early Bronze Age was used by survey research to determine in six settlements. The settlements are Kanlıtaş Mound, Esnemez's Road Mound, Kuzfındık Dam Mound, Erenköy I, Erenköy II, and Yeniköy Mound.

The location of Kanlıtaş Mound was first discovered by Eskisehir Archaeological Museum, and then the mound was documented by Turan Efe in 1989 (Efe 1991). The

---

*Dr. Ali Umut Türkcan, Department of Archaeology, Anadolu University
**Cansu Topal, Anadolu Universitesi, Edebiyat Fakültesi, Arkeoloji Bölümü, Yunus Emre Kampusu 26470. Eskişehir, Turkiye

Kanlıtaş settlement lies adjacent to the north side of a boulder or crag, which stands independently in the center of the valley (Türkcan 2011:303–317). Kuzfındık Valley is located on the heel of the crag. The region is referred to as Kanlıtaş Locality by local people. The height of the mound is 18 meters and the diameter of the mound is more than 100 meters. It is one of the most important Chalcolithic sites in Northwestern Anatolia with material from Early, Middle, and a few from the Late Chalcolithic, along with a sister site Orman Fidanlığı in the Porsuk Basin near Eskişehir, which was first introduced and excavated by Turan Efe (2001). The mound was divided into 12 different survey sectors according mainly to its topographical setting. The segments extend from east to west. All Early Bronze Age material came from the edges of the eastern part of the mound, which was probably inhabited in the EBA period. When the material found by the surface analysis of Kanlıtaş Mound was analyzed according to periodic distribution, it was determined that most of finds belonged to the Early Bronze Age and Chalcolithic Age. Wares of Early Bronze Age comprised 49 percent of the finds, 46 percent of them were wares from Early Bronze Age I, and 5 percent of the wares were attributed to the Early Bronze Age III. The wares of Early Bronze Age I are divided into five main groups. While brown wares make up the largest group, the other groups consist of red-slipped wares, rough wares, grey nonslipped wares, and black-topped wares. The form of the wares include steep-sided pots with flaring, concave-curved, necked, neckless, spherical, and narrow-necked jars with flaring. Additionally, vertical handles, loop handles, strap handles, and horizontal handles that are unconnected from vessels and jar feet were explored. Decoration is divided into four groups. These groups are incised decoration, dimpled decoration, fluted decoration, and pseudo-mesh decoration. Gutter decoration and pseudo-mesh decoration are the fluted decoration types. Pseudo-mesh decoration is on the vertical handles, while fluted decoration is on the strap handles. Incised decoration and dimpled decoration are on the body parts. Much of the pottery that was explored from Kanlıtaş Mound is the pottery of Early Bronze Age II. In addition to the pottery of previous periods, white-burnished wares and orange wares were examined. Similarly, in addition to the forms of previous periods, direct-profile deep bowls and splay bowls were discovered. Furthermore, a disc-base part that has a single form was found among other pottery obtained from all settlements. Splay pots that belong to brown wares of Early Bronze Age, neckless spherical jars, and horizontal handles represented by red coarse wares form the smallest portion of the pottery.

Kuzfındık Dam Mound is located in the west of Kuzfındık Valley inside a dam that at present is located two kilometers to the west of Kanlıtaş Mound. The mound is unconnected from the land because of increasing water levels in the dam over time. Today, the mound is partially under water, and a boat was used to reach the mound. We assume that the mound belongs to the Early Bronze Age because 73 percent of the wares were dated to the Early Bronze Age III, 23 percent of the wares from the Early Bronze Age II, and 4 percent of the total consists of wares from the Early Bronze Age I. One fragment from the Early Bronze Age I was discovered. Neckless spherical jars are represented by brown wares. In Early Bronze Age II, red wares were obtained, but they could not have been obtained from previous period. The forms from this period include wide-necked spherical jars, and spouted pitchers. Also, vertical and horizontal handles that are unconnected from vessels and plates were discovered. In addition to the wares of previous periods, rough wares, imported wares, and plain wares were found from the Early Bronze Age III. In this period, the lid that is represented only in a single form among all wares of Early Bronze Age, was found. In addition, plates and wide-necked jars with flaring rims constitute other forms of the period. Horizontal ledge, loop handles, strap handles, and vertical handles that are unconnected from vessels and jar feet are prevalent among the pottery of the period that was obtained.

Esnemezyolu Dam Mound is located about 10 kilometers southwest of Inonu Town as the crow flies and two kilometers southwest of Esnemez village on the west side of the village road. The mound is 110 meters in diameter and 2.5 meters in height, and was first documented by Turan Efe in 1992 (Efe 1994). The mound that pertains to the Early Bronze Age has disappeared because of agricultural activities. The pottery found on the mound was 64 percent pottery Early Bronze Age II, 27 percent Early Bronze Age III, and 9 percent Early Bronze Age I. Loop-handled bowls, which represent the black-topped wares of Early Bronze Age I, were found. There are five different types of wares in Early Bronze Age II. They include grey unlined wares, rough wares, brown wares, red wares, and plain wares. When we analyzed forms of the wares, we saw that direct profiled bowl, spouted jugs, prominent direct S-profiled bowls, and plates are prevalent form types in Early Bronze Age II. Also, handles and foot fragments that are unconnected from vessels were found. When wares were examined from Early Bronze Age III, brown slipped wares that have brick-colored paste, red slipped wares, and plain wares were uncovered. The form of the wares included direct profiled bowls and wide-necked spherical jars with flaring rims, and an additional fragment. We assume that the fragment belongs to a tray that is represented in a single form among all forms.

Yeniköy Mound, first documented by Turan Efe in 1988, is located 1.5 kilometers to the northwest of Yeniköy Village, which is at the western edge of Upper Porsuk Basin near the hills. The settlement is more than two kilometers from Kanlıtaş Mound in the SW. When we use the plain as a base, the diameter of the mound is 150 meters. The height of the mound is around 10 meters. The mound is mostly comprised of Early Bronze Age II and III (Efe 1990). The wares of Early Bronze Age I have not been found. The pottery of Early Bronze Age II is categorized in two different types; black-topped wares and grey non-slipped wares. The form of the wares are direct profiled deep bowls and direct profiled splay bowls. Splay pots that belong to red-slipped wares of Early Bronze Age III were obtained.

Erenköy I Mound is located on the south side of the Erenköy-Kümbet highway on the west of Inonu Valley and two kilometers distant from Erenköy village. When we use the plain as a base, the diameter of the mound is 100 meters and the height of the mound is 11 meters. The wares of the mound are from the first periods of Early Bronze Age II and III. The wares were documented by Efe Turan in 1988 (1990). Black-topped wares and red wares were found. The form of the wares were neckless spherical pots and loop handles unconnected from the vessels.

Erenköy II Mound is located on the south side of the Erenköy-Kümbet highway west of Inonu Valley and four kilometers from Erenköy village at its southwest. The mound was first documented by Turan Efe in 1988. The mound was visited a second time in 1989 (Efe 1991). The dimensions of the small mound are 35 × 4 meters. Coarse wares, brown wares and red-slipped wares of Early Bronze Age I were found. Forms of the wares include wide-necked spherical jars with flaring, vertical handles, and horizontal handles. In addition to this, brown wares and orange-slipped wares of Early Bronze Age II were uncovered. The form of the wares include splay pots and spherical jars with flaring.

Conclusion

When we analyze the wares that were found in Kuzfındık Valley, we see that the ware types are also included in the pottery of Demircihöyük. Similarly, by analyzing the wares we learn that the pottery of Early Bronze Age I-II resembles, in many aspects, the pottery that was found in Phrygia. Black-burnished pottery and red-slipped burnished pottery were found in the settlements and the pottery group pertains to the region. Many of the black-burnished wares are black-topped bowls. The interior surface of the bowls is black, and the black continues until the bottom of the bowl's rim on the exterior surface. The color of the exterior surface's other parts vary from red to brown (Efe and Ay-Efe 2001:53). While native red-slipped wares are prevalent among all the residential areas, black-topped wares draw considerable attention. On the other hand, wide-necked spouted jugs and cross-taped bottles are not found in the region. Similarly, bottles and jugs that have zigzag and cross-taped decoration have not been found, although they are common forms in the region (Efe and Türkteki 2011:215).

The majority of the wares found in Kanlıtaş Mound and its environment were comprised of wares of the Early Bronze Age II. Black-topped wares that were the main wares of Demircihöyük in Early Bronze Age II (Efe 1998:5) are prevalent among all wares included in the research. While the wares are parallel to those of Küllüoba that represent the pottery of Sakarya's upstream regions located in Phrygia, there are some differences among the two ware groups. The main difference is that black-rimmed wares containing the secondary main ware group of the Kanlıtaş Tumulus and its environment in Early Bronze Age II have only been found in Küllüoba (Efe 1988). Similarly, the imitated wreath-loop handles that comprise the small number of wares of Early Bronze Age II were found in Demircihöyük. Also, in Küllüoba, black-topped bowls that have groove decorations on their interior surface had been explored since the end of Early Bronze Age II (Efe 1988). In Demircihöyük, the groove decorations had been observed since K period. On the one hand, the groove decoration was explored on the body part of a bowl in Kanlıtaş Mound. We suppose that the body part belongs to a bowl. Oval loop handles found in Erenköy 1 Mound and Kanlıtaş Mound have a single form. However, in Demircihöyük, they have different forms in P-Q stage (Efe 1988). They comprise the majority of pottery of Aharköy. Similarly, in this period, simple-profiled deep and shallow bowls that belong to black-topped wares of Kanlıtaş Mound and Yeniköy Mound have similar properties with bowls of Küllüoba (Sarı 2004). In addition to this, simple-profiled bowls and splay pots explored in Esnemezyolu Mound are similar with forms of Küllüoba. Finally, neckless spherical vessels, wide-necked vessels with a flaring rim, simple profiled

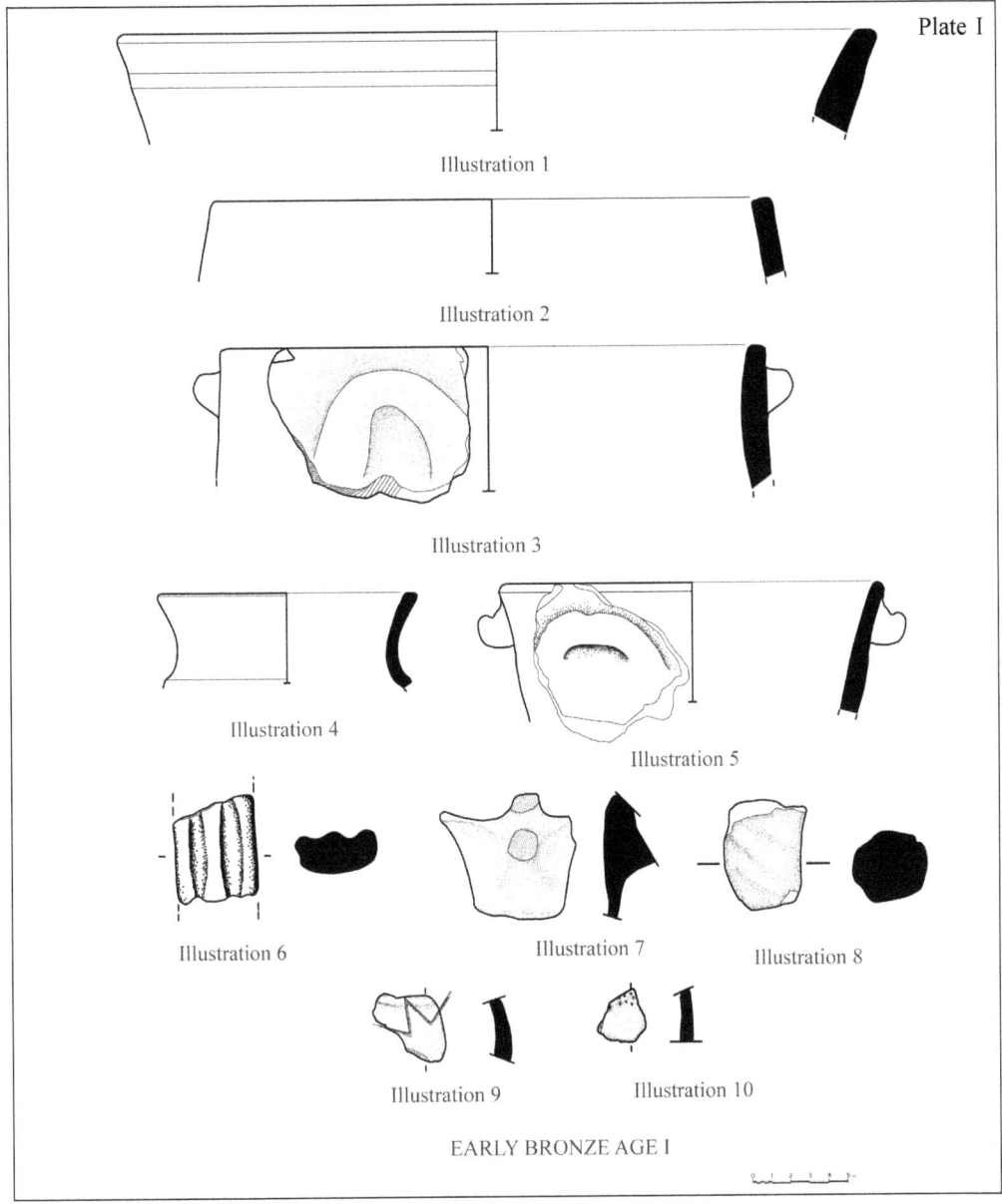

FIGURE 3.1. KNT'08 21, Illustration 1: Step-sided pot fragment with flaring rim. It has brown-colored thin lining. Its paste includes light brown-colored grit, lime and a trace of mica; KNT'08 20, Illustration 2: Neckless spherical pot fragment. Its fawn-colored surface is burnished and the paste includes grit, calcite and mica; KNT'08 I 59, Illustration 3: Simple-profiled pot fragment with horizontal handles. It has thin reddish fawn-colored lining. Its paste includes grit, calcite and mica; KNT'08 291, Illustration 4: Concave- necked vessel fragment with a thin grey lining. Its paste consists of brown-colored grit, sand and a trace of mica; KNT'08 41 Illustration 5: Pot fragment with horizontal handles and a flaring rim. It has thin red-colored lining. The clay is made of red-colored sand, mica and a trace of lime; KNT'12 61, Illustration 6: Band handle fragment with incised decoration and a reddish brown-colored lining. The clay is made of calcite, grit and a trace of mica; EYH'08 26, Illustration 7: Bowl fragment with loop handle. Its exterior surface under the lip is reddish brown-colored and it has a thick, burnished lining. The interior surface and rim are glossy black, and the paste is made of grit and sand. Also its cooking quality is good; KNT'09 J 22, Illustration 8: Handle fragment with wreath. It has thin red-colored lining. The paste is made of brown-colored sand with a trace of mica; KNT'08 D 64 K, Illustration 9: Body Fragment (Groove Decoration). It has non burnished thin fawn-colored lining. The paste is made of grey-colored grit and calcite; KNT'08 D-308, Illustration10: Body fragment (Dot pattern Decoration). It has thin non burnished fawn-colored lining. The paste is made of dark grey thin grit and calcite.

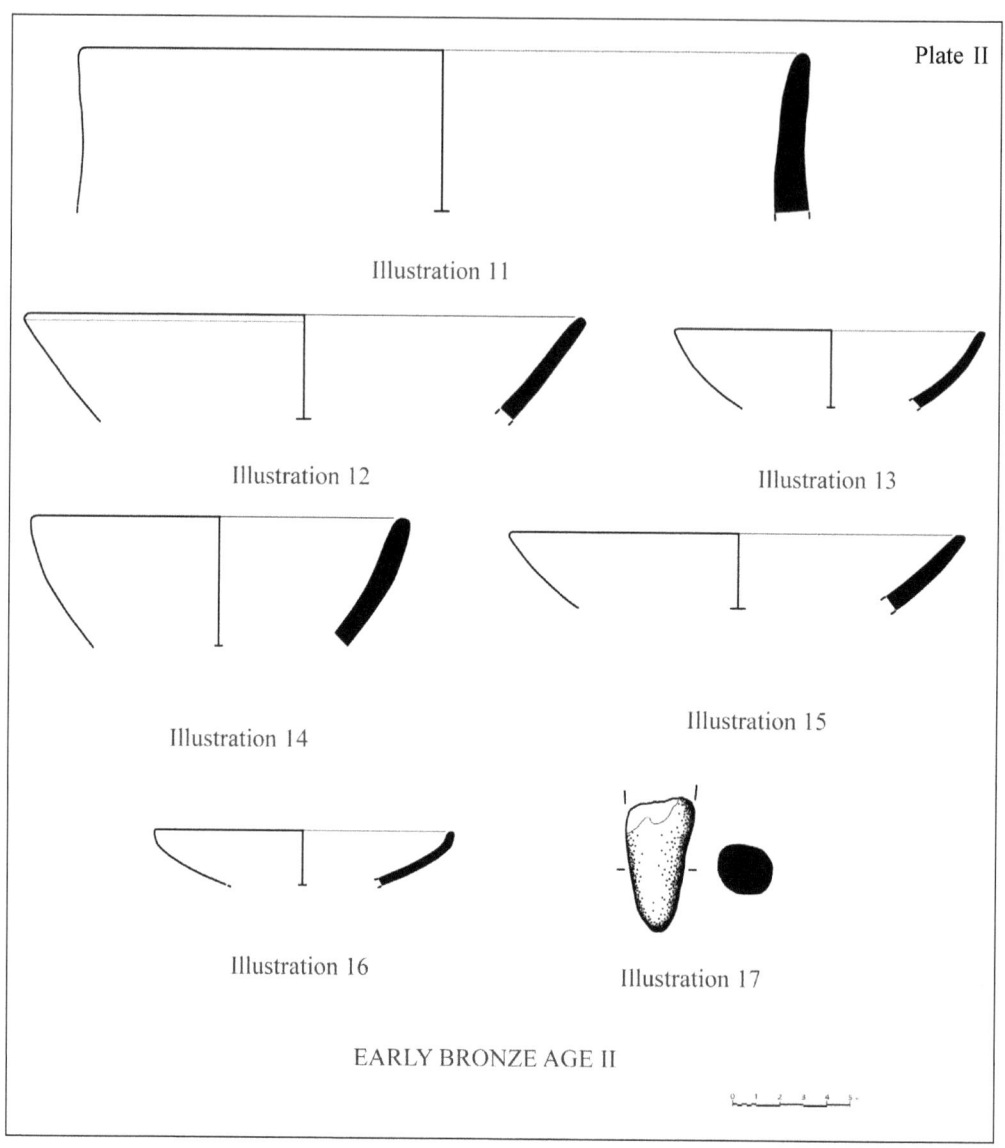

FIGURE 3.2. KNT'08 3, Illustration 11: Spherical vessel fragment with flaring rim. It has thin red-colored lining. The clay paste is made of reddish brown-colored grit, calcite and mica; KBY'08 II, Illustration 12: Plate Fragment (A1 Plate). It has red-colored thin lining. The clay paste is made of light red colored sand and a trace of mica; KNT'12 33, Illustration 13: Simple-profiled splay bowl fragment. Its exterior surface is reddish brown-colored. Similarly, its exterior surface has a thin burnished lining. Its interior surface is glossy and black-colored. The clay paste is made of fawn-colored sand, mica and calcite; YKH'09 07, Illustration 14: Simple-profiled deep bowl fragment. It has thin reddish brown-colored lining. The clay paste is made of fawn-colored grit; KNT'08 G 84, Illustration 15: Simple-profiled splay bowl fragment. It has instinctively red-colored lining. The clay paste is made of sand and mica; KNT'08 312, Illustration 16: Splay bowl fragment with flat rim. It has burnished fawn-colored coated face; EYH'08 13, Illustration 17: Pier fragment. Its light red-colored dough involves much stones and lime.

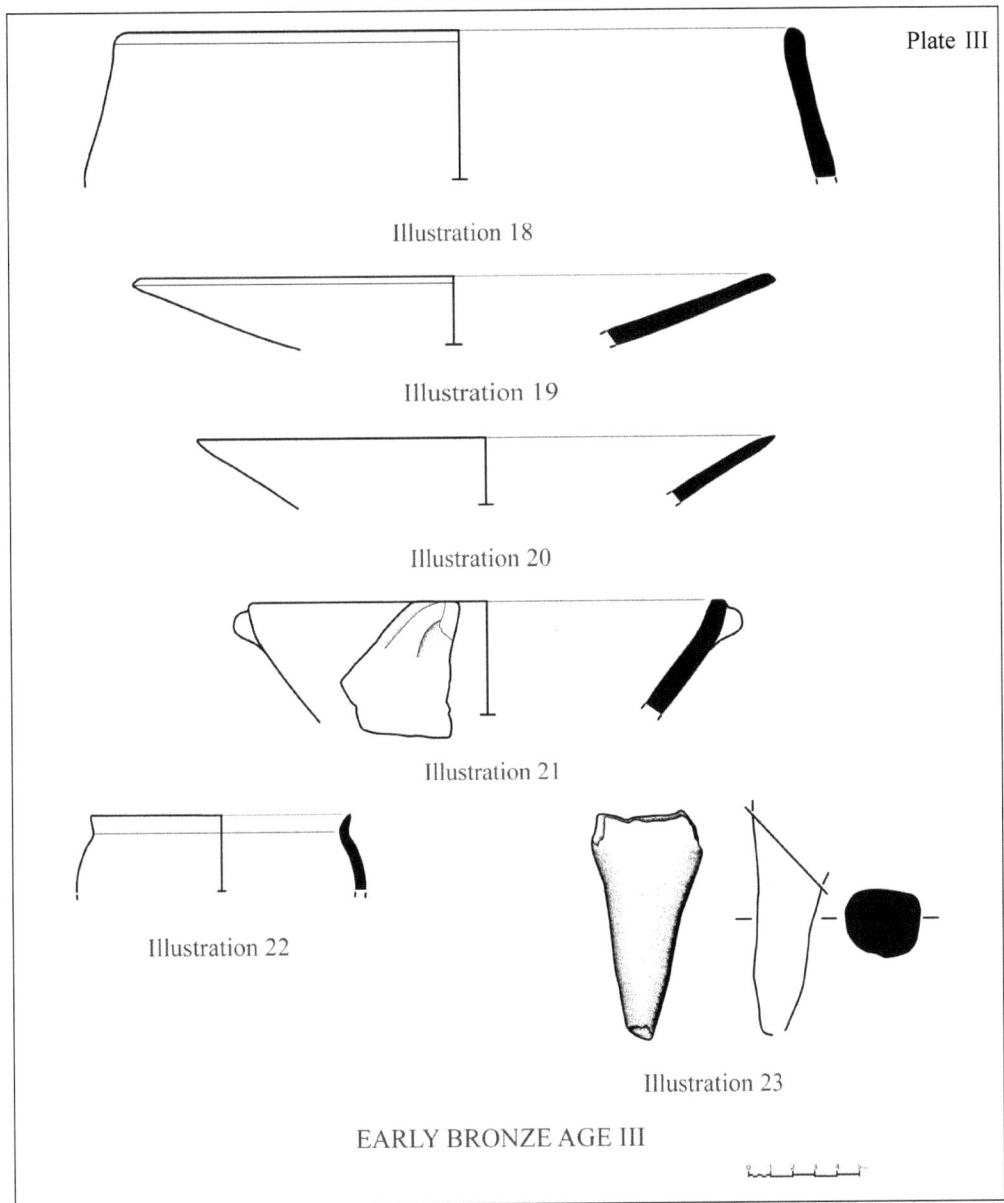

FIGURE 3.3. KNT'08 F 362, Illustration 18: Neck less spherical vessel fragment. It has reddish brown-colored thin lining. The clay paste is made of dark grey-colored thin grit and calcite; KBY'09 6, Illustration 19: Plate Fragment (A1). It has red-colored thick lining. The clay paste is made of light red-colored sand, mica and calcite; KBY'08 16, Illustration 20: Plate Fragment (A2). Its red-colored exterior surface has thick lining. The clay paste is made of reddish brown-colored sand, calcite and a trace of mica; KNT'A 36, Illustration 21: Splay pot fragment with horizontal handles. It has red-colored thick lining. The clay paste is made of yellowish red-colored sand, calcite and thin grit; KBY'08 II, Illustration 22: Vessel Fragment with flaring rim. It has light red-colored thin lining. The clay paste is made of reddish brown-colored mica, calcite and sand; KBY'08 II 5, Illustration 23: Foot Fragment. It has light red-colored thin lining. The clay paste is made of stones, calcite and mica.

splay and deep bowls and flat-bottom forms have similar properties with the forms of Küllüoba (Sarı 2004). Moreover, neckless spherical vessels called Altıntaş were found in Kanlıtaş Mound (Türkteki 2004:18). The vessels are also observed in Beycesultan and its environment. They belong to orange wares.

A1 plates were found in Kuzfındık Mound toward the end of the period. In Early Bronze Age III, A2 plates discovered in Kuzfındık Mound, similar to the forms of Küllüoba plates. While Küllüoba A2 plates belong to plain wares, the plates of Kuzfındık Mound belong to red-slipped wares (Türkteki 2004:23). In addition, their forms are similar with Aharköy and Çukurhisar A2 plates' forms (Efe 1994b). A1 plates are similar to Küllüoba (Türkteki 2004:23) and Bahçehisar (Efe 1994b:14) plates from the points of wares and forms.

Pier fragments were found in Kuzfındık Mound. It is believed that they belong to tripod vessels, and they are similar with pier parts of Küllüoba's vessels. The pier fragments of Küllüoba are sharper and more thin-walled than the fragments of Kuzfındık, but are similar to fragments from Seyitömer (Türkteki 2004). Similarly, wide-necked vessels with flaring rim found in the settlement are similar to the forms of Aharköy and Bahçehisar (Efe 1994b). Moreover, orange-colored body parts called Altıntaş were explored in Esnemezyolu Mound. Models belonging to the ware group were observed in Küllüoba Mound. The pottery of Early Bronze Age III explored in the settlements is similar to red-slipped wares, rough wares, and orange-colored wares of Küllüoba. On the other hand, wash wares, grey wares and red-slipped burnished wares were also present. We have limited knowledge about the Early Bronze Age pottery that was prevalent in Küllüoba Mound, and those at Eskişehir and its environment could not be found (Türkteki 2004:15–18). We suppose that the later stages of the ongoing excavation will help to determine the Early Bronze Age chronology of Western Anatolia.

References Cited

Efe, T. 1990 1988 Yılında Kütahya, Bilecik ve Eskişehir İllerinde Yapılan Yüzey Araştırmaları. *Anadolu Araştırmaları VII*:297–302. Anakara.

Efe, T. 1991 1989 Yılında Kütahya, Bilecik ve Eskişehir İllilerinde Yapılan Yüzey Araştırmaları. *Araştırma Sonuçları Toplantıs VIII*ı:165–167. Ankara.

Efe, T. 1994a 1992 Yılında Kütahya, Bilecik ve Eskişehir İllerinde Yapılan Yüzey Araştırmaları XI. *Araştırma Sonuçları Toplantısı*:578. Ankara.

Efe, T. 1994b Early Bronze Age III Pottery from Bahçehisar: The Significance of the Pre-Hittite Sequence İn the Eskişehir Plain, Northwestern Anatolia. *American Journal of Archaeology* 98(1):5–34.

Efe, T. 1998 Demircihöyük. Band III, Die Keramik 2, C Die Frühebronzezeitliche Keramik der Jüngeren Phasen (ab Phase H). P. Von Zabern, Mainz am Rhein.

Efe, T. 2001 The Salvage Excavations at Orman Fidanlığı. A Chalcolithic Site in Inland Northwestern Anatolia. TASK Vakfı Yayınları, Istanbul.

Efe, T., and D. S. M. Ay-Efe 2001 Küllüoba:İç Kuzeybatı Anadolu'da Bir ilk Tunç Kenti, 1996–2000 Yılları Arasında Yapılan Kazı Çalışmalarının Genel Değerlendirilmesi. *TÜBA-AR* 4:43–78.

Massa, M. 2011 MÖ. III. Bin yılın sonunda Batı ve İç Anadolu'da Yıkımlar, Terk Etmeler, Sosyal Yapıda yeniden Örgütlenme ve İklimsel Değişim. *Arkeolojide Bölgesel Çalışmalar Sempozyum Bildirisi* 4:89–123.

Sarı, D. 2004 *Küllüoba İlk Tunç Çağı II Çanak Çömleği*. Yüksek Lisans Tezi, Üniversitesi Protohistorya ve Önasya Arkeolojisi Bilim Dalı ve Sosyal bilimler Enstitüsü, İstanbul.

Türkcan, A. U. 2011 Kanlıtaş Höyük ve Civarı (İnönü, Eskişehir) Yüzey Araştırması. *Araştırma Sonuçları Toplantısı* (AST) 28:303–328.

Türkteki, M. 2004 *Küllüoba İlk Tunç Çağı III çanak çömleği*. Yüksek Lisans Tezi, İstanbul Üniversitesi, İstanbul.

CHAPTER FOUR

A Look at the Process of Transition from the Chalcolithic Age to the Early Bronze Age in Central Western Anatolia in Light of New Data

*Tayfun Caymaz**

INTRODUCTION

Central Western Anatolia covers a region from the Bakır Çay in the north to Büyük Menderes in the south and from the Aegean Sea in the west to Afyon in the east (Figure 4.1). The west of this region is defined as the coastal or Aegean part, while its east is defined as the interior part. Excavations and research which have intensified for the last 20 years especially have allowed significant clarification of the early prehistory of the region. Within this framework, we understand that the Neolithic culture has parallels with the Lake District in the south, Northwestern Anatolia, and the neighboring islands. The Chalcolithic culture that followed seems to have occurred in a process related to Marmara, Thrace, and the Balkans. The pottery of the new period observed in the settlements of Ulucak and Ege Gübre in the coastal area differ quite particularly in surface treatment from the Neolithic pottery. Shades of grey and brown are common on this pottery, on which burnish rather than slip stands out. Open vessels are a considerable portion of the pottery repertoire. Pattern-burnished decoration, horned handles, and vessels known as *cheese-pots* are the primary characteristic elements. The data obtained from settlements such as Yeşilova 2, Emporio X-VIII, and Tigani II-III show that the above-mentioned features continued by developing in the Middle Chalcolithic Age as well. The Chalcolithic pottery gained an identity as a deep-rooted tradition in the process that commenced around the middle of the sixth millennium B.C. The continuation of this tradition throughout the Late Chalcolithic Age and its reflection on into the Early Bronze Age constitutes the subject of this paper.

---

*Dr. Tayfun Caymaz, Department of Archaeology, Faculty of Arts and Science, Nevşehir Hacı Bektaş Veli University, Nevşehir, 50300, Türkiye, caymaztayfun@gmail.com

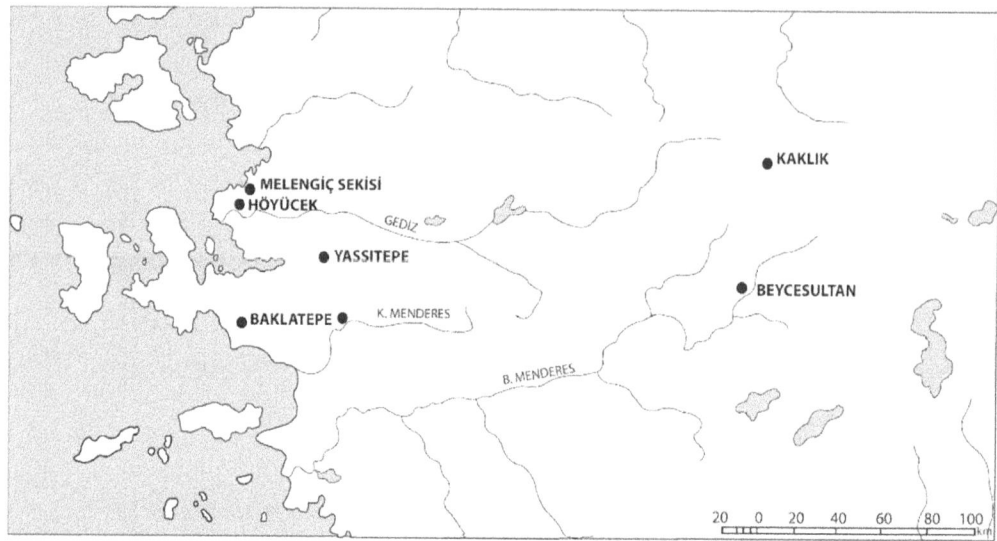

FIGURE 4.1. Map of the Central Western Anatolia Region indicating the primary settlements mentioned in the text.

THE LATE CHALCOLITHIC AGE

The Late Chalcolithic Age in Western Anatolia is considered a process that began circa the fourth millennium B.C. and extended to early Troy I (Figure 4.2). The termination of the process has been established around 2900 B.C. according to the C14 results obtained from Troy (Korfmann and Kromer 1993:165). However, we lack the results that allow dating the commencement of the process. In the coastal part of Central Western Anatolia, Liman Tepe VII reflects a transitional period in which the vessel shapes of the Middle Chalcolithic Age maintained their existence, but shapes of the next period also occurred. It is seen that the old predominant shapes disappeared and new shapes became common at Bakla Tepe Late Chalcolithic Level 4. Containing some parallels with the Middle Chalcolithic shapes of the coastal part, Orman Fidanlığı VII displays a transitional position in the interior part. In this part, Beycesultan is the settlement where the beginning and development of the new period are observed.[1]

In both parts, the pottery maintains the Chalcolithic tradition in terms of surface treatment and colors. The white painted decoration that appeared in the transitional period is the common characteristic feature of both parts. Nevertheless, there are differences in their vessel shapes. Bowls with everted and usually thickened rims are common in the early phase of Beycesultan (Shapes 2–4; Lloyd and Mellaart 1962). However, bowls with interior thickened rims and their variations are the most common and characteristic shapes in Bakla Tepe (Caymaz 2013). White painted decoration was mostly applied to these vessels.

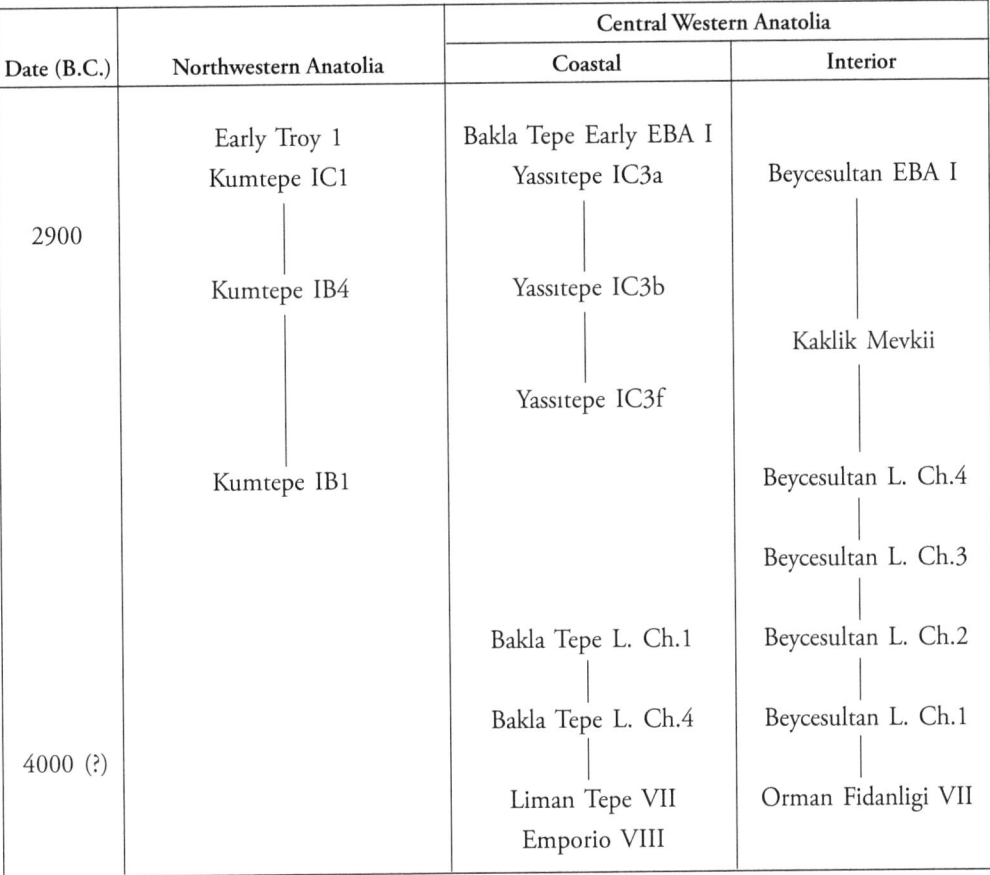

FIGURE 4.2. Chronological chart.

With its 20 meter cultural deposits containing 20 levels, the Late Chalcolithic settlement of Beycesultan doubtlessly reflects a longer process than Bakla Tepe. Likewise, new vessel shapes occurred in this process, whereas some shapes disappeared. Nevertheless, the above-mentioned vessels keep their prevalence in Bakla Tepe throughout the four levels. In this respect, the Late Chalcolithic settlement of Bakla Tepe appears contemporary with the early phases of Beycesultan (Figure 4.2).

THE LATE PERIOD OF THE LATE CHALCOLITHIC AGE

A series of developments, such as the predominance of new shapes, the fact that carinated bowls with concave rims became the most common shape (Shape 19), the appearance of handles on some bowls, and the fact that white painted decoration became very sparse, are seen in the Beycesultan Late Chalcolithic 4 pottery (Lloyd and Mellart 1962:95). Pottery containing parallels with both Late Chalcolithic 4 and Early Bronze Age I of

Beycesultan was detected during the excavations carried out in Kaklık Mevkii, Afyon (Efe et al. 1995:373). So, it is possible to form a sequence extending to the beginning of the new period in the interior region. In addition, in terms of the failure to see characteristic Shape 19 of Late Chalcolithic 4 in Kaklık, the presence of a developmental phase between these two is a great probability (Figure 4.3).

It is understood that Kumtepe IB in Northwestern Anatolia was present in the process following Bakla Tepe (Figure 4.3). However, there has not been any adequate data yet to form a sequence between these two. Promising results on this matter are being obtained at the excavations in Yassıtepe, Bornova. The uppermost level preserved here (IC3a) is contemporary with Kumtepe IC1 and early Troy I. Beneath this level, with long houses located side by side, are building levels (IC3b-f) that display parallels with Kumtepe IB. An unbroken development of pottery extending to early Troy I is followed at these levels, which are being investigated vertically around 2 meters within a narrow area (Derin and Caymaz 2014:422). On the other hand, pottery finds relevant to this period were obtained in two settlements of the İzmir region, in Höyücek, investigated with a trial excavation in 1949, and in Melengiç Sekisi, detected with surveys (Caymaz 2014:160–162). The deposit, which is located farther beneath and has not yet been excavated in Yassıtepe, is expected to provide information on the process extending to late Bakla Tepe.

Pottery of the Late Period

It is seen that the traditional character has been preserved in terms of surface treatment and colors on the Beycesultan Late Chalcolithic 4, Kaklık, and Yassıtepe potteries that we evaluate within the scope of the late period (Derin and Caymaz 2014:422–423; Efe et al. 1995:365; Lloyd and Mellaart 1962:95). Nevertheless, as elaborated below, it is understood that significant developments took place in terms of shapes and some other elements.

Bowls with Interior Thickened Rims

They are common at, and characteristic of, Levels IC3b-f in Yassıtepe (Figure 4.3:1–15). Understood to have been available at the lower levels of Höyücek as well, such bowls (Figure 4.4:14–17) are common in Melengiç Sekisi (Figure 4.4:1–11). These vessels are quite different in both size and types of handles from the bowls with the same name in the development of Bakla Tepe. The bowls of Bakla Tepe are mostly moderate- and large-sized, whereas the bowls of Yassıtepe are particularly small-sized. On the other hand, the trumpet lugs seen on the bowls of Bakla Tepe lost their significance, and the horizontally perforated lugs usually placed between the shoulder and the belly became common.

Bowls with interior thickened rims are particularly parallel with the bowls of Kumtepe IB3 and 4 in terms of their types, sizes, and lug types (Korfmann et al. 1995; Sperling 1976: Figure 14, Figure 15, Figure 19, Figure 20). Those with trumpet lugs are also available at Kumtepe Level IB2 (Sperling 1976:330). Bowls with interior thickened rims are unavailable in the pottery repertoire of the interior region.[2]

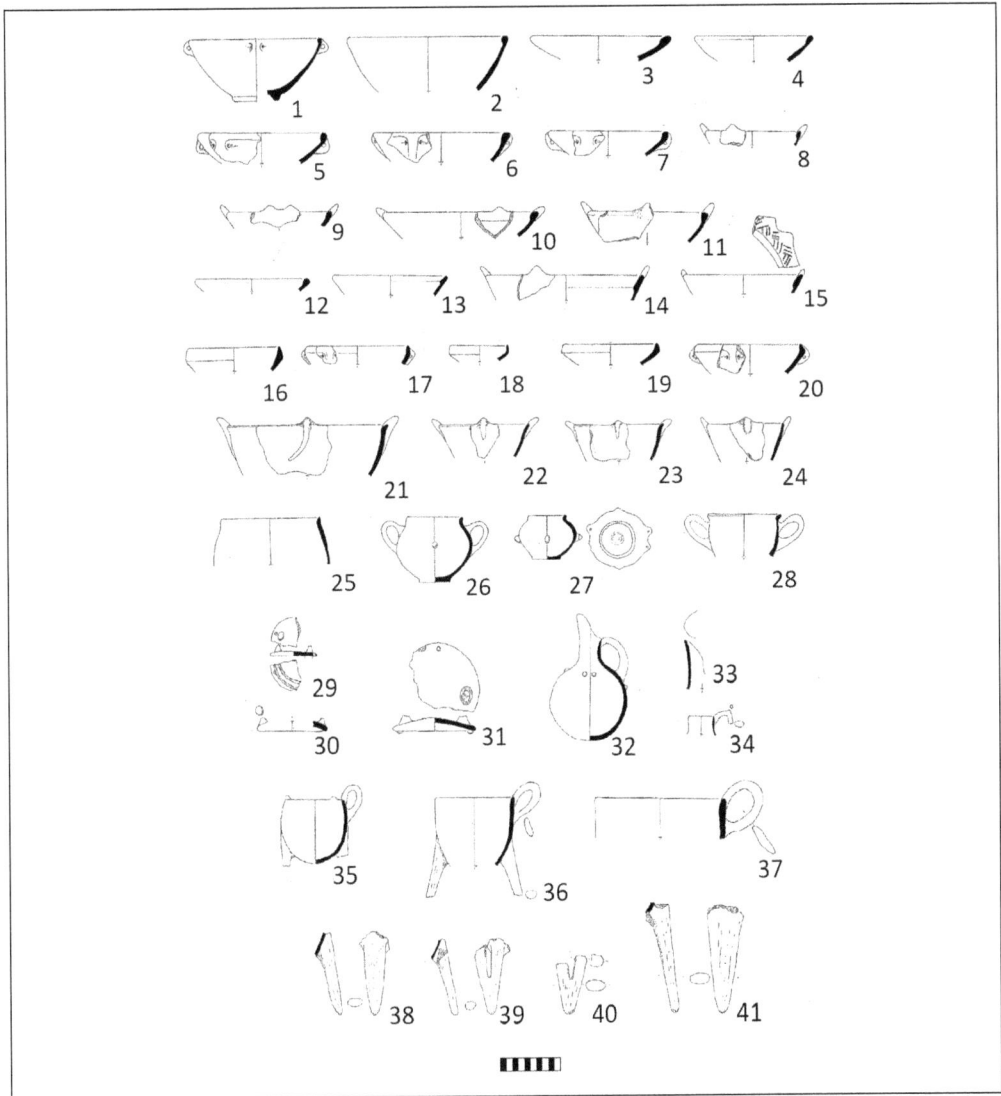

FIGURE 4.3. Yassıtepe IC3b-f Pottery: Yassıtepe 1c3b-f pottery: 1 Rim diameter 18 cm. Dark brown burnished; 2 Rim diameter 24 cm. Dark greyish brown burnished; 3 Rim diameter 19 cm. Dark brown burnished; 4 Rim diameter 15 cm. Black burnished; 5 Rim diameter 16 cm. Black burnished; 6 Rim diameter 18 cm. Brownish red burnished; 7 Rim diameter 16 cm. Black burnished; 8 Rim diameter 16 cm. Black burnished; 9 Rim diameter 14 cm. Light red plain; 10 Rim diameter 20 cm. Mottled dark greyish brown-black burnished; 11 Rim diameter 15 cm. Dark greyish brown burnished; 12 Rim diameter 18 cm. Grey plain; 13 Rim diameter 10 cm. Purplish brown burnished; 14 Rim diameter 25 cm. Plain, coarse;15 Rim diameter 16 cm. Black burnished, with white filled incision; 16 Rim diameter 12 cm. Very pale brown burnished; 17 Rim diameter 14 cm. Blackish grey burnished; 18 Rim diameter 8 cm. Blackish red burnished; 19 Rim diameter 13 cm. Dark greyish brown burnished; 20 Rim diameter 16 cm. Blackish grey burnished; 21 Rim diameter 25 cm. Pale brown plain; 22 Rim diameter 14 cm. Light red, exterior slightly burnished; 23 Rim diameter 14 cm. Pale brown plain, coarse; 24 Rim diameter 10 cm. Very pale brown plain; 25 Rim diameter 18 cm. Mottled red-brownish yellow burnished; 26 Rim diameter 10 cm; 27 Rim diameter 6.5 cm; 28 Rim diameter 11 cm. Mottled reddish brown-grey burnished; 29 Rim diameter 9 cm. Exterior black burnished, interior coarse; 30 Rim diameter 10 cm. Very pale brown plain, coarse; 31 Rim diameter 13 cm. Exterior black burnished; 32 Neck diameter 4.5–7, belly diameter 16, height 23.5 cm; 33 Neck diameter 7–10 (oval) cm. Brown burnished; 34 Rim diameter 5.5 cm. Light red plain. Coarse; 35 Rim diameter 11 cm; 36 Rim diameter 15 cm; 37 Rim diameter 14 cm. Red plain; 38 Pink plain; 39 Light brown plain; 40 Red slipped; 41 Brown plain.

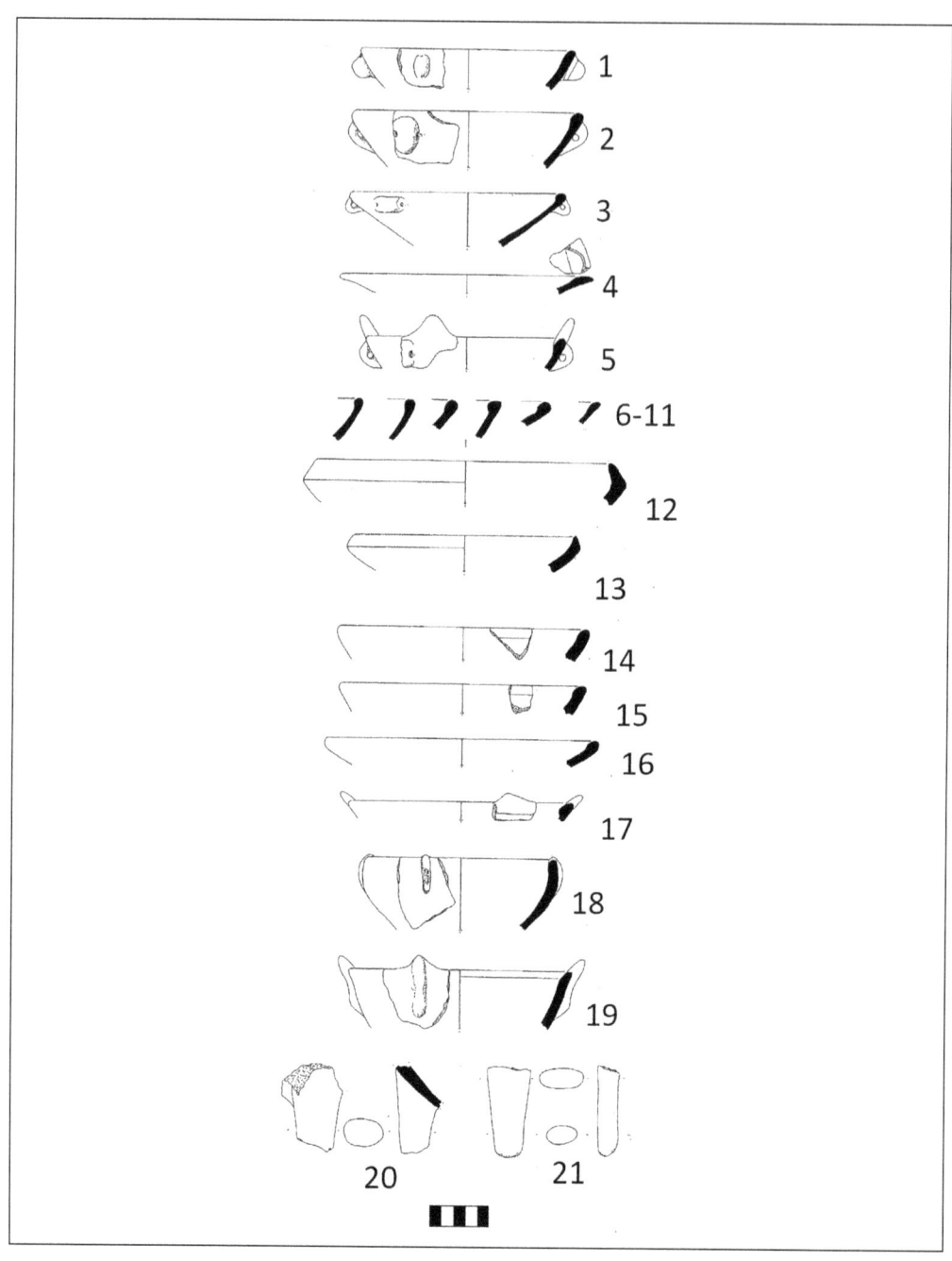

FIGURE 4.4. Melengiç Sekisi (1–13) and Höyücek (14–21) Pottery: 1 Rim diameter 17 cm. Yellowish red burnished; 2 Rim diameter 18 cm. Black burnished; 3 Rim diameter 16 cm. Black burnished; 4 Rim diameter 20 cm. Red burnished, rim with white filled decoration; 5 Rim diameter 16 cm. Red burnished; 6 Rim diameter 17 cm. Exterior brownish grey, interior grey burnished; 7 Rim diameter 18 cm. Black burnished; 8 Rim diameter 20 cm. Grey burnished; 9 Rim diameter 20 cm. Black burnished; 10 Rim diameter 16 cm. Exterior mottled reddish brown, interior dark grey burnished; 11 Rim diameter 18 cm. Mottled brown and red burnished; 12 Rim diameter 24 cm. Red burnished; 13 Rim diameter 20 cm. Dark reddish black burnished; 14 Rim diameter 20 cm. Semicoarse. Interior very pale brown, slightly burnished; 15 Rim diameter 20 cm. Brown burnished;16 Rim diameter 22 cm. Blackish grey burnished; 17 Rim diameter 20 cm. Brown burnished, rim black; 18 Rim diameter 15 cm. Pale brown slightly burnished; 19 Rim diameter 17 cm. Semicoarse, blackish grey burnished; 20 Reddish brown burnished; 21 With a pinkish brown plain

Some bowls with interior thickened rims in the pottery of Yassıtepe, Höyücek, and Melengiç Sekisi contain triangular projections raising from the rim (Figure 4.4:8–11, 14–15; Figure 4.4:17). In the interior part, such lugs are encountered on a wide bowl in Beycesultan Late Chalcolithic 4 (Lloyd and Mellaart 1962: Figure P.12).

CARINATED BOWLS

Bowls of this type are not encountered in the pottery of Bakla Tepe after the disappearance of the types with basket handles unique to the Middle Chalcolithic Age. Vessels of this family are seen in the pottery of Yassıtepe and Melengiç Sekisi (Figure 4.3:16–20; Figure 4.4:12–13). These bowls, not considerable in quantity, are usually small-sized and have horizontally perforated lugs just like the bowls with interior thickened rims. The closest parallels of such bowls again appear in Kumtepe IB pottery (Korfmann et al. 1995). Having occurred in Beycesultan Late Chalcolithic 4, Shape 20 resembles this type (Lloyd and Mellaart 1962: Figure P. 12). This shape is also seen in Kaklık (Shape 7; Efe et al. 1995: Figure 20).

BOWLS WITH PLASTIC LUGS

They constitute a characteristic vessel type obtained in Yassıtepe and Höyücek (Figure 4.3:21–24; Figue 4.4:18–19). These vessels have either a convex profile or an S-profile and are usually of semi-coarse quality and are small-sized. The plastic lugs that provide them with a distinctive feature extend from the triangular projection at the rim to the body with a straight or curved line. Such bowls are not encountered in the interior part, whereas some bowls that one may establish parallels with are available at Kumtepe IB4 (Korfmann et al. 1995).

SMALL SHORT-NECKED JARS

Obtained at Yassıtepe 1C3b-f, such jars have either two vertical handles or perforated lugs (Figure 4.3:25–28). It is understood that they mostly had lids.

LIDS

No element categorized as a lid is available in Beycesultan. There are some shallow bowls, which may have also been used as lids, in Bakla Tepe (Caymaz 2013: Figure 16, Figure 17). The lids are evident in Yassıtepe and Kaklık potteries (Efe et al. 1995: Figure 25). The lids obtained in Yassıtepe IC3b-f are small-sized (Figure 4.3:29–31) and appear to have been used on small short-necked jars.

BEAK-SPOUTED JUGS

In the coastal region, the earliest beak-spouted jugs are seen in the pottery of Liman Tepe VII of the late Middle Chalcolithic Age (Caymaz 2013: Figure 14). Such jugs are in small quantity in Bakla Tepe, which reflects the following process (Caymaz 2013: Figure 16, Figure 18). Various types of jugs, some of which contained white painted decoration, were available in Beycesultan, while no beak-spouted jugs were encountered. Nevertheless, beak-spouted jugs are available in Kaklık (Efe et al. 1995: Figure 21). These jugs increase toward the upper phases in Yassıtepe (Figure 4.3:32–33). The beak-spouted jugs are available in Kumtepe IB3 and IB4 (Korfmann et al. 1995; Sperling 1976: Figure 15).

TRIPOD VESSELS

These vessels are represented at a low percentage in the pottery of Bakla Tepe. However, they exhibit an increase in quantity toward the final level. Tripod vessels are not seen in Beycesultan. Nevertheless, they are available in Kaklık (Efe et al. 1995: Figure 24). These vessels are common in Yassıtepe (Figure 4.3:35–41), Melengiç Sekisi, and Höyücek (Figure 4.4:20–21) potteries in the coastal part. There is also a unique type of leg produced with "ajouré" technique in Yassıtepe (Figure 4.3:39–40).

WHITE PAINTED DECORATION

The portion of vessels with white painted decoration at the early level of the Late Chalcolithic settlement of Bakla Tepe, that is 10 percent, falls to around 3 percent at the final level with a gradual decrease. Having followed a decreasing course in the process in Beycesultan as well, such decoration becomes very rare in the final phase (Lloyd and Mellaart 1962:95). White painted decoration was not encountered at building levels Ic3b-f in Yassıtepe. However, bowl and jug sherds containing such decoration are available in Kaklık Mevkii (Efe et al. 1995: Figure 20, Figure 26, Figure 30). A jug sherd with white painted decoration was obtained in Kumtepe IB4 (Sperling 1976:336).

PATTERN-BURNISHED DECORATION, CHEESE-POTS, AND HORNED HANDLES

They are among the elements that were present since the Early Chalcolithic Age and which characterize this culture. Pattern-burnished decoration is represented by two body sherds obtained in Beycesultan Late Chalcolithic Period 2 (Lloyd and Mellaart 1962:91). Nevertheless, no pattern-burnished vessel was encountered in Bakla Tepe, except for some suspected sherds. It has been observed that the *cheese-pot*s continued to exist throughout the building levels of the Late Chalcolithic Age in Bakla Tepe, although at a low percentage (Caymaz 2013: Figure 15, Figure 16, Figure 17, Figure 18). However, such vessels are not encountered in Beycesultan. Horned handles are very rarely seen in Bakla Tepe (Caymaz 2013: Figure 17). Such handles are presumed to have been unavailable in Beycesultan and that some jar handles contain small decoration-like knobs (Lloyd and Mellaart 1962:108).

No pattern-burnished decoration or *cheese-pot* was encountered in Kaklık and, according to the limited areas excavated, Yassıtepe. At this point, it must be emphasized that few *cheese-pot* sherds were obtained in Kumtepe IB1 and IB3 (Sperling 1976:329, 333, Figure 16, Figure 18). On the other hand, a pattern-burnished jar sherd was found in IB1 (Sperling 1976:316). Horned handles were obtained in a small quantity in Yassıtepe (Figure 4.3:34).

MISCELLANEOUS

Carinated bowls with concave rims constitute the most common and characteristic type of pottery in Beycesultan Late Chalcolithic 4 (Shape 19; Lloyd and Mellaart 1962:95). Such bowls are not encountered in the pottery of Kaklık. Nevertheless, the bowls with everted and interior thickened rims and two handles (Shape 26; Lloyd and Mellaart 1962: Figure P.11) that emerged in the last phase of Beycesultan are also seen in Kaklık (Efe et al. 1995: Figure 20). It is understood that open bowls, some of which contain vertical handles (Shapes 1–3), are common in Kaklık (Efe et al. 1995:367). Some of them have high pedestals and are of fruit-stand type (Shape IB; Efe et al. 1995: Figure 19). All these shapes are elements without any parallel within the coastal region of Central Western Anatolia.

Early Period of Early Bronze Age I

The pottery, which has an uninterrupted progression in Yassıtepe and contains parallels with Kumtepe IB, reaches a stage involving a series of developments at the uppermost level preserved (IC3a; Derin 2012:47–48; Derin and Caymaz 2013:127). Shades of grey and brown are common among the surface colors, while shades of red are seen less. The majority of the open vessels and almost half of the closed vessels are burnished. In this new phase the characteristic bowls with interior thickened rims of the previous period lost their significance and decreased in number (Figure 4.5:1–5); however, carinated bowls became common (Figure 4.5:6–20). The trumpet lugs that were considerably seen in Bakla Tepe but lost their significance in the following phase gained prevalence again and became a characteristic element of carinated bowls (Figure 4.5:6–8, 11). Identified as A12 in Troy, such bowls constitute the most common and characteristic type of vessel of the early period of Troy I (Blegen et al. 1950:60). Another type of vessel that became common is the bowls with interior and widely thickened rims and with rims containing triangular projections that are identified (Blegen et al. 1950:58) as A6 in Troy (Figure 4.5:22–28). The earlier bowls of this type were encountered in Yassıtepe IC3b and d (Figure 4.3:13–15). Possibly a white-filled incision made at the rim is seen on one of them (Figure 4.3:15). A rim with such decoration is also available in Melengiç Sekisi (Figure 4.4:4). The white-filled incision was not very popular on A6-type bowls in the Central Western part, which is not the case in the Northwestern Anatolia region. Bowls with plastic lugs continued to exist (Figure 4.5:21). Small jars and tripod vessels became common (Figure 4.5:29–31, 42–44). Beak-spouted jugs seem to have virtually boomed in this new phase (Figure 4.5:32). Obtained in small quantities in the previous phases,

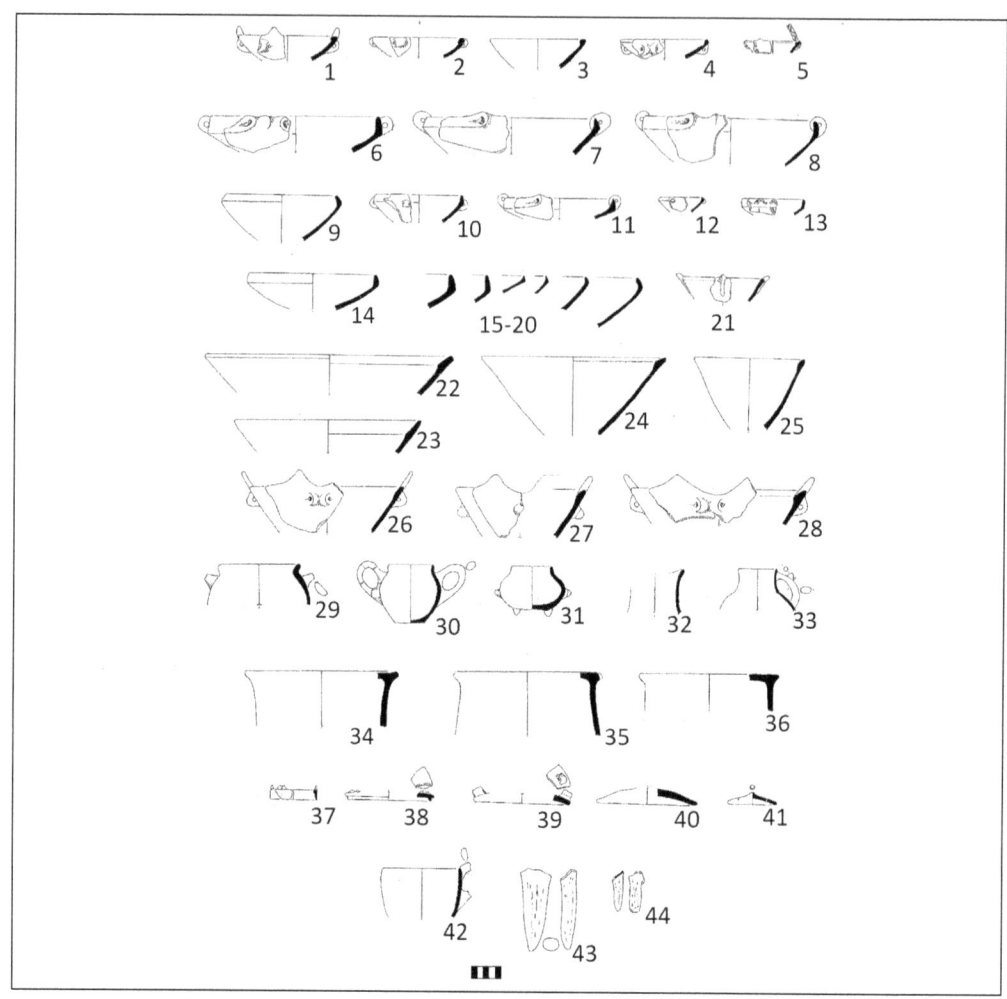

FIGURE 4.5. Yassıtepe IC3a Pottery: 1 Rim diameter 13–14 cm. Yellowish red burnished. 2 Rim diameter 18 cm. Dark greyish brown burnished. 3 Rim diameter 22 cm. Dark grey burnished. 4 Rim diameter 17 cm. Dark greyish brown burnished. 5 Rim diameter 10–12 cm. Brown burnished, with white filled (?) incision. 6 Rim diameter 25–30 cm. Pale brown burnished. 7 Rim diameter 28–30 cm. Greyish brown burnished. 8 Rim diameter 28 cm. Greyish brown burnished. 9 Rim diameter 16 cm. Black burnished. 10 Rim diameter 10–12 cm. Reddish brown burnished. 11 Rim diameter 18–20 cm. Black burnished. 12 Rim diameter 8–10 cm. Dark grey burnished. 13 Rim diameter 10–12 cm. Interior light grey plain, exterior greyish brown burnished, with white filled (?) incision. 14 Rim diameter 23 cm. Exterior light yellowish brown burnished. 15 Rim diameter 22 cm. Greyish brown burnished. 16 Rim diameter 18 cm. Greyish brown burnished. 17 Rim diameter 14 cm. Dark greyish burnished. 18 Rim diameter 10 cm. Red burnished. 19 Rim diameter 10 cm. Pinkish brown burnished. 20 Rim diameter 18 cm. Dark greyish burnished. 21 Rim diameter 14 cm. Light red plain. 22 Rim diameter 46 cm. Black burnished. 23 Rim diameter 35 cm. Black burnished. 24 Rim diameter 30 cm. Exterior yellowish brown, interior dark grey burnished. 25 Rim diameter 18 cm. Black burnished. 26 Rim diameter 25 cm. Black burnished. 27 Rim diameter 18 cm. Greyish brown burnished. 28 Rim diameter 25 cm. Black burnished. 29 Rim diameter 10 cm. Exterior reddish brown-black, interior coarse. 30 Rim diameter 5.5 cm. 31 Rim diameter 5 cm. 32 Neck diameter 8 cm. Yellowish red plain. 33 Rim diameter 6 cm. Grey plain, semicoarse. 34 Rim diameter 26 cm. Greyish brown burnished. 35 Rim diameter 23 cm. Dark grey burnished. 36 Rim diameter 20 cm. Black burnished. 37 Rim diameter 14 cm. Mottled yellowish brown-black multicolor burnished. 38 Rim diameter 14 cm. Black burnished. 39 Rim diameter 16 cm. Purplish pink plain, coarse. 40 Rim diameter 18 cm. Exterior pale brown, interior black burnished. 41 Rim diameter 8 cm. Yellowish red burnished. 42 Rim diameter 13 cm. Pink plain. 43 Pink plain. 44 Light red plain.

horned handles are represented with more finds in this phase (Figure 4.5:33). Various lids, the analogues of which we know from Troy I and its parallel settlements, are another element of development (Figure 4.5:34–41). There is an incised decoration on some lids, jugs, small jars, and bowls. Traces showing that some of them contained white-filled decoration are available (Figure 4.5:5, 13). No white painted decoration was encountered.

Developments parallel with those in the coastal part are also seen at Beycesultan Early Bronze Age I. Carinated bowls (Shape 5) are the most common and characteristic shape here as well (Lloyd and Mellaart 1962:5). Shapes 3 and 4 may also be regarded as the variations of these bowls. The lack of trumpet lugs on carinated bowls is a significant difference compared with those in the coastal part. A rim with white-filled decoration, which might be considered a parallel of the bowls with interior and widely thickened rims (Troy A6), was obtained (Lloyd and Mellaart 1962:123). The beak-spouted jugs, the early specimens of which are seen in Kaklık, are also available at Beycesultan Early Bronze Age I (Lloyd and Mellaart 1962: Figure P.14). Nevertheless, it is stated that they are not very common, unlike those in Yassıtepe (Lloyd and Mellaart 1962:125). However, small short-necked jars constitute a common shape (Lloyd and Mellaart 1962:125). The large shallow bowls with incurving rims (Lloyd and Mellaart 1962:119; Shape 2) and tripod vessels (Lloyd and Mellaart 1962: Figure P.16) in Beycesultan are the shapes known from the phase of Kaklık. White painted decoration is uncommon (Lloyd and Mellaart 1962:116).

Conclusion

The pottery data discussed that develop from the early phases of Bakla Tepe and Beycesultan to early Troy I progressed following the Chalcolithic tradition. Within this framework, burnish is of greater importance than slip in the surface treatment, as in the previous periods. Shades of grey and brown are in demand among the surface colors. Differences in pottery repertoires of the coastal and interior parts are seen in the early phase. Nevertheless, the bowls with interior thickened rims of Bakla Tepe and the bowls with everted and thickened rims of Beycesultan are not highly dissimilar shapes. The pottery features of both parts converge via the white painted decoration applied to the vessels concerned.

Beycesultan reflects a long process involving twenty levels. No significant changes in pottery are seen in the settlement process covering the four levels within a deposit of 1 to 1.5 meters in Bakla Tepe. We lack data to join this process to Kumtepe Period IB. However, we see that the usually medium- and large-sized bowls with interior thickened rims of Bakla Tepe were replaced by mostly small-sized bowls in the late period, and that white painted decoration was no longer applied to them. Beak-spouted jugs, small short-necked jars, lids, and tripod vessels gained importance in this period. These elements are also seen in Kaklık and express that the parallels between the coastal and interior parts increased.

It is understood that pattern-burnished decoration, *cheese-pot*s, and horned handles, which are among the distinctive features of the Chalcolithic pottery, gradually lost their significance in the Late Chalcolithic Age and disappeared or became substantially sparse at the end of the period.

The radiocarbon samples collected from Yassıtepe building levels IC3b-f yielded results that indicated the late fourth millennium B.C. and the early third millennium B.C., that is, immediately before early Troy I (Derin and Caymaz 2014:223). Likewise, the pottery also displays some development that joins Kumtepe IC1–early Troy I. The development in the interior part parallels this. An increase in parallels between both parts can be observed in the Late Chalcolithic period. Carinated bowls became the common and distinctive shape at Beycesultan Early Bronze Age I, which demonstrates that this development reached a broader dimension.

Notes

1. For the process of transition from the Middle Chalcolithic Age to the Late Chalcolithic Age, see Caymaz 2013:65.
2. There is an exceptional specimen which is likely to be considered analogous in Beycesultan Late Chalcolithic 4. This bowl was evaluated as a variation of Shape 22. See Lloyd/Mellaart 1962, 97, Figure P.12: 35.

References Cited

Blegen, C. W., J. L. Caskey, M. Rawson, and J. Sperling 1950 *Troy. General Introduction; The First and Second Settlements*. Princeton. University Press, Princeton.

Caymaz, T. 2014 Menemen Ovası Kuzeyinde Üç Prehistorik Yerleşimve Geç Kalkolitik Çağ'dan Erken Tunç Çağı'na Uzanan Süreçle İlgili Veriler. In *Armağan Erkanal'a Armağan/Compiled in Honor of Armağan Erkanal, Anadolu Kültürlerine Bir Bakış/Some Observations on Anatolian Cultures*, edited by N. Çınardalı-Karaaslan et al., pp. 157–170. Hacettepe Üniversitesi Edebiyat Fakültesi, Ankara.

Caymaz, T. 2013 Yeni Veriler Işığında Orta Batı Anadolu Kalkolitik Çağ Kültürü. (The Central West Anatolia Chalcolithic Culture on the Basis of the New Evidence) *ADerg* XVIII:39–112.

Derin, Z. 2012 İzmir'in Prehistorik Yerleşim Alanı Yeşilova Höyüğü-2010. *Kazı Sonuçları Toplantıları* 33(2):39–56.

Derin, Z., and T. Caymaz 2013 İzmir-Yeşilova Höyüğü 2011 Yılı Çalışmaları. *Kazı Sonuçları Toplantıları* 34(1):119–142.

Derin, Z., and T. Caymaz 2014 İzmir'in Prehistori kyerleşim Alanı Yeşilova Höyüğü 2012 Yılı Çalışmaları. *Kazı Sonuçları Toplantıları* 35(1):419–433.

Efe, T., A. İlaslı, and A. Topbaş 1995 Salvage Excavations of the Afyon Archaeological Museum. Part I: Kaklık Mevkii. A Site Transitional to the Early Bronze Age. *Studia Troica* 5:357–399.

Korfmann, M., and M. B. Kromer 1993 Demircihöyük, Beşik-Tepe, Troia-Eine Zwischenbilanzzur Chronologie Dreier Orte in Westanatolien. *Studia Trioca* 3:135–171.

Korfmann, M., Ç. Girgin, Ç. Morçöl, and S. Kılıç 1995 Kumtepe 1993. Bericht über die Rettungsgrabung. *Studia Troica* 5:237–289.

Lloyd, S., and J. Mellaart 1962 *Beycesultan, I: The Chalcolithic and Early Bronze Age Levels*. British Institute of Archaeology at Ankara, London.

Sperling, J. W. 1976 Kum Tepe in the Troad. *Hesperia* 45(4):305–364.

CHAPTER FIVE

Northwest Anatolian Influences on Early Bronze Age Cultures of Gökçeada (Imbros)-Yenibademli Höyük

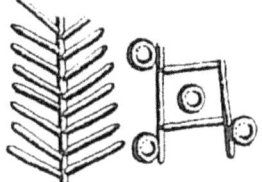

Halime Hüryılmaz*

INTRODUCTION

Yenibademli Höyük is situated 1.7 kilometers to the south of Kale village of Gökçeada district in Çanakkale province, in the lower part of the Büyükdere valley (Figure 5.1, Figure 5.2). The mound starts to rise up on the western edge of a rocky ridge, which originally formed a peninsula and has a very strategic location by controlling the Aegean Sea to the north and inland routes of the island to the south. As the paleogeographical investigations indicate, once the mound was surrounded with a 16 meter deep bay in the north and a ria-type inlet in the west, however, at present day, all the surroundings are filled with alluvial deposits (Öner 2001:789). The mound covers an area of 120 × 130 meters, in East-West and North-South directions respectively and rises 18 meters above the sea level. It is composed of two terraces and a flat hilltop.

Yenibademli Höyük was first discovered in 1964 by N. Fıratlı (1964) and has been continuously excavated since 1996.[1] It plays an important role regarding the research on the cultural history of Imbros Island and provides valuable information to the field of Aegean prehistory. The settlement, which dates back to 5,000 years, not only shows the island's rich cultural history, which remained silent for a long period in archaeological record, but also presents a great amount of data, especially for the Early Bronze Age II period (in terms of Aegean chronology).

---

*Prof. Dr. Halime Hüryılmaz, Hacettepe Üniversitesi, Edebiyat Fakültesi, Arkeoloji Bölümü, 06800 Beytepe-Ankara / Türkiye. halimeh@hacettepe.edu.tr

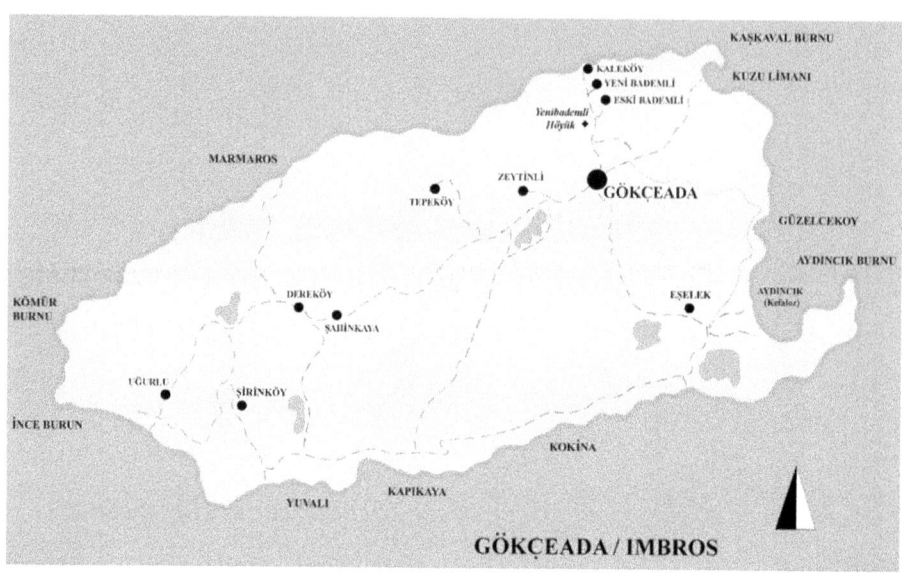

FIGURE 5.1. The location of Yenibademli Höyük in Gökçeada (Imbros).

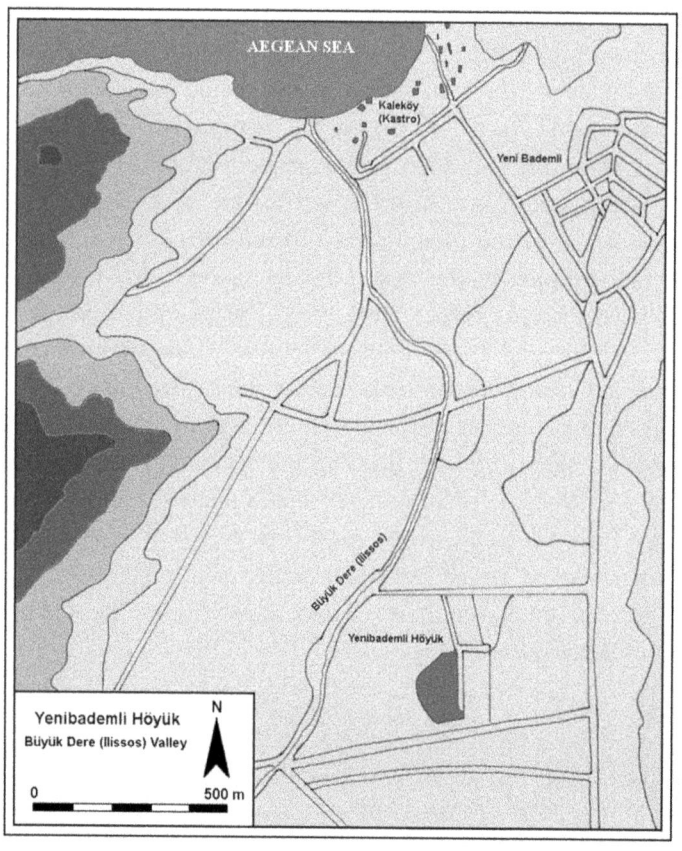

FIGURE 5.2. The position of Yenibademli Höyük in Büyükdere Valley.

Cultural Sequence of the Mound

The systematic excavations conducted between 1996 and 2013 have revealed the presence of three cultural periods at this old settlement. From most recent to the oldest, these can be listed as follows: (1) The culture of the inhabitants with Greek origin, (2) Late Bronze Age culture, (3) Early Bronze Age II culture.

The chapel, which was built as a singular structure on the hilltop about 100 years ago, was used by the inhabitants with Greek origin (Hüryılmaz 2011:47). There have not been any settlement activities around this religious building, which represents the first cultural period at the mound. The second cultural period is made identified by the Mycenaean and Minoanising pottery sherds and small-scale remains of cyclopean masonry. The finds of this period, which represent the Late Bronze Age, are dated between 1400–1060/1040 B.C. (Hüryılmaz 2008:149). The third cultural period is characterized by wide-scale settlement activities and lasted for about 400 years, starting from the beginning of the third millennium B.C., and is represented by eight building levels.

The habitation history of Yenibademli Höyük, which starts with the simple pit of the first settlers, dug into the bedrock (Hüryılmaz 2006:59), transformed into a well-planned settlement layout over time.

Early Bronze Age II Culture

The architectural remains of the Early Bronze Age II period (i.e., Troia I), which represent the genuine character of the mound, have been uncovered at the hilltop and the west terrace (Hüryılmaz 1998:362–365; 2002a:75–76; 2002b:29–31; 2006:57–59; 2013a:2–9; 2013b:169–175). The buildings at the hilltop, which provide comprehensive information on the settlement plan of this period (especially the last three building levels), are composed of rectangular houses with the entrances on their narrow sides and represent a characteristic type for the Aegean world. The houses are built either independently or next to each other with shared long walls, and the upper structures are supported with regularly placed wooden posts. Besides buildings with stone foundations and mud-brick walls, some houses show full stone masonry, and in some houses the upper parts of the stone walls have been built with mud-brick extensions. All of the floors are built of compressed soil. Simple hearths and horseshoe- or pear-shaped ovens discovered within the houses are among the standard household inventories.

The increasing needs, limited space, and precautionary measures for the northern winds resulted in a tight and dense settlement structure of house units, of which inventories are defined by find groups of pottery, bone, and lithic industries. The pottery industry, which has the highest profile on the scale of manufacturing economics, also presents the largest find assemblage of the settlement.

Pottery Industry

As in many other settlements, the majority of the finds, discovered at different building levels of the Early Bronze Age II period at Yenibademli Höyük, are composed of pottery sherds and nearly intact vessels. At a time when the potter's wheel was not in use, handmade vessels were produced within domestic contexts. With their well-polished surfaces and divergent forms, these vessels are products of carefulness and effort in domestic production and they can be classified in two main groups: fine and coarse ware, respectively. The surfaces of elegant fine ware examples in the form of bowls, jugs, jars, lids, and *pyxides* are slipped and polished. Most of them appear in different shades of black, brown, and grey, whereas few items come in reddish color. The coarse ware is represented by large-sized *pithoi* and large jars in red shades, which were used for grain storage. Their surfaces are usually matte or slightly polished, as seen in fewer examples.

The majority of fine-ware examples, which were used for preparation, serving, and consumption of foods and for special purposes, are composed of everted bowls with sharp carination. These have horizontal tubular lugs between the carination and the rim (Figures 5.3:1, 5.3:2, 5.3:3). Long sections of these lugs have either a straight or a concave profile. Oblate knobs between the carination and the rim are placed at equal distances to each tubular lug (Figure 5.3:4). These types of bowls, which represent the most common form at Troia I settlement, resemble the A 12 and A 13 types of Trojan pottery typology (Blegen et al. 1950: Figure 223a). Although Blegen has stated that Trojan bowls have only one tubular lug, the bowls from island settlements such as Yenibademli Höyük (Figure 5.4:1) and Thermi (Lamb 1936:76) may have more than one tubular lug.

FIGURE 5.3. Yenibademli Höyük. Bowls with sharp carination and horizontal tubular lugs. (EBA II).

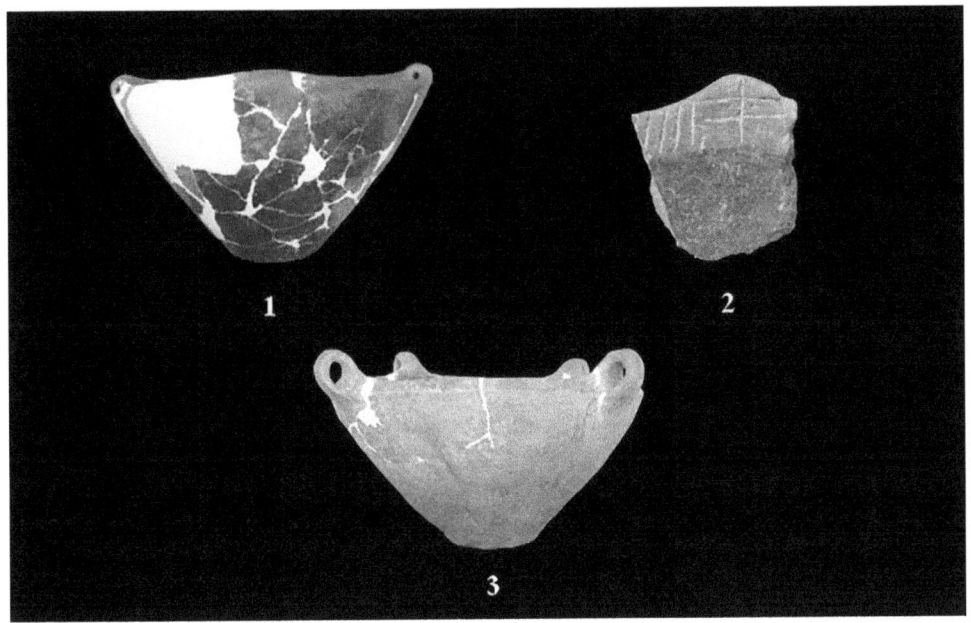

FIGURE 5.4. Yenibademli Höyük. Bowl with horizontal tubular lug (1), rim fragment with incised decoration and dot eyes (2), carinated bowl with four strap-handles (3). (EBA II).

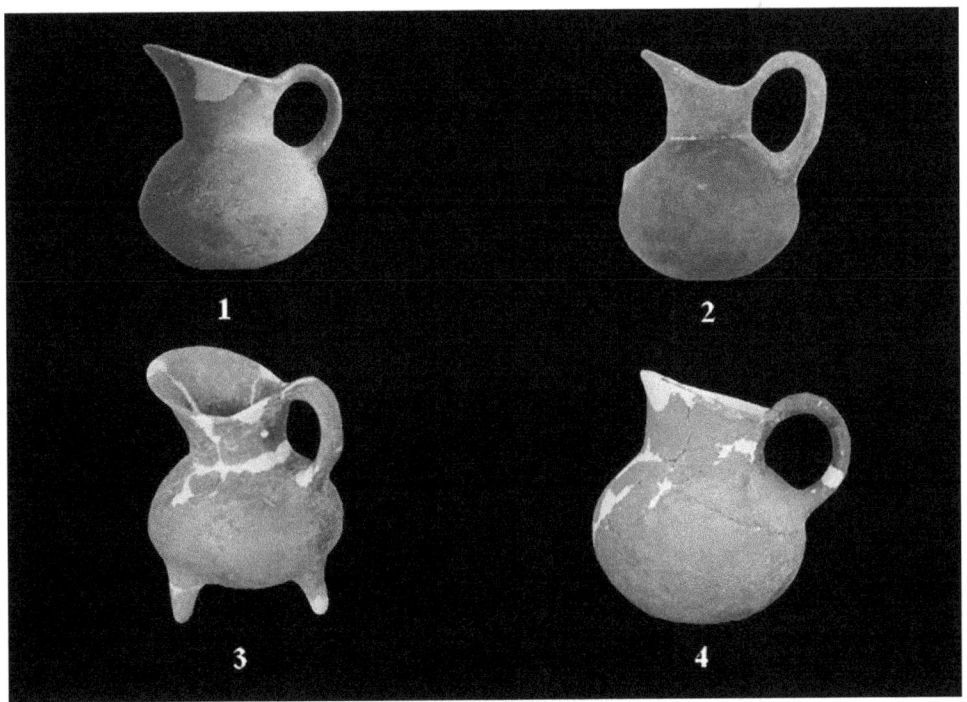

FIGURE 5.5. Yenibademli Höyük. Jugs with globular or oblate spherical shapes. (EBA II).

While these types of lugs placed between the carination and the rim on examples from Yenibademli, Troia I and Kumtepe IC, on the Early Bronze Age II bowls from Thermi (Lamb 1936:159), Protesilaus (Demangel 1926: Figure 52), and Beycesultan (Lloyd and Mellaart 1962: Figure P.23) they appear below the carination.

Carinated bowls, which evolve in terms of rim types and lug shapes at Troia I settlement, have a sharp carination and long, straight tubular lugs with oblique ends during Early Troia I. During Middle Troia I tubular lugs have a slightly concave profile with slightly upraised ends. During Late Troia I period these type of vessels have an everted profile without carination and their lugs appear in more developed forms.

These types of bowls, which start to appear with the beginning of the Early Bronze Age in many settlements as a common form, varied over time and became a dominant form within the Western Anatolian pottery repertoire. Although they represent a similar development pattern in Anatolia (Forsdyke 1925; Garstang 1953; Lloyd and Mellaart 1962; Lamb 1938; Orthmann 1966), the Aegean (Heurtley 1939; Kunze 1934; Wace and Thompson 1912), and the Balkans (Berciu 1961; Popov 1919), it should be noted that there are some regional differences in terms of decoration techniques. For example, in Thrace (French 1964: Figure 5-12, Figure 6-4, Figure 8-10 and 11) they appear with graffiti paintings on the outer surface, whereas in Northwestern Anatolia (Blegen et al. 1950; Lloyd and Mellaart 1962; Mellaart 1954) they are decorated with incised motifs and with white paintings in Central Anatolia.

Bowls with internally thickened rims, which represent the second large group of the Yenibademli pottery assemblage, are among the forms that were adopted during the Early Bronze Age II period. On these examples, the projections above the rim are rendered as a human face, such as the one on the Early Troia I find (Figure 5.4;2; Blegen et al. 1950). Vertical, diagonal, and zigzag lines and lozenge motifs, encountered on most of the bowls as decorative elements, have always been applied on the inner surface and filled with a white substance for visual appeal. Local potters imitated decoration types applied on A6-type bowls of Troia Ia and Ib phases (Blegen et al. 1950) and carried on this tradition for a long time. Similar decoration patterns, which were adopted at Kumtepe IC phase (Korfmann et al. 1995; Sperling 1976), synchronised with Troia I and at Beşik-Yassıtepe (Korfmann 1984), considered as one of Troia's satellite settlements, are undoubtedly important parameters to determine the cultural zones, of which Yenibademli potters were influenced.

Carinated bowls with four strap-handles, which are represented with a singular example at Early Troia I settlement (Blegen et al. 1950: Figure 223a; Podzuweit 1979:112) and limited to a few sherds along with a restored specimen (Figure 5.4:3) at Yenibademli resemble each other in terms of their forms. The fact that these types of vessels remain at a low percentage and do not occur on all building levels at both settlements leads to the conclusion that they were no longer produced due to the lack of functionality.

The jugs that were used for liquids by Yenibademli inhabitants don't reflect a great variety in pottery typology. They usually appear in medium or small sizes and are in black, light grey, brown, beige, and reddish colours. They have a globular or oblate spherical shape where the outer surface is always polished and slipped. Jugs with a round base are dominant at the settlement, where those with a flat base and tripods are represented at lower rates. Yenibademli jugs (Figure 5.5:1; 5.5:2), which are reminiscent of the B 13 Type of Troia I pottery assemblage, in many ways resemble the examples from Early Troia I; levels 3 and 4 of Protesilaus; Kumtepe IC; Thermi Ia, b, II-III, IIIa-c phases; and I, IIa, and IV settlements of Poliochni (Blegen et al. 1950; Podzuweit 1979; Sperling 1976). Although another tripod jug (Figure 5.5:3), similar to the B 14 type known from Troia (Blegen et al. 1950) has been uncovered at Yenibademli, it seems that this type was not a common form at the settlement. Such examples, which have also been produced at IIa phase of Poliochni, are frequently encountered among vessels of Anatolian Yortan culture (Podzuweit 1979:166). It can be said that the jug form listed as B 17 Type in the Troia I pottery assemblage (Blegen et al. 1950) resembles the Yenibademli example with wide and inclined mouth and flat base (Figure 5.5:4). The parallel of the Yenibademli black polished jug with a small spout on the belly (Figure 5.6:1) was found at the 3. building level of Protesilaus (Demangel 1926:57). Spouted jugs, which are not foreign at Thermi in IIa settlement and in Yortan culture (Lamb 1936; Orthmann 1966), were also found at Troia during Schliemann's excavations (Schliemann 1881), however it was stated that it should belong to Troia VI or later periods. Spouted jugs, which are represented in few numbers at the abovementioned centers and Yenibademli, were apparently not a popular form in the Northern Aegean islands and Northwest Anatolia.

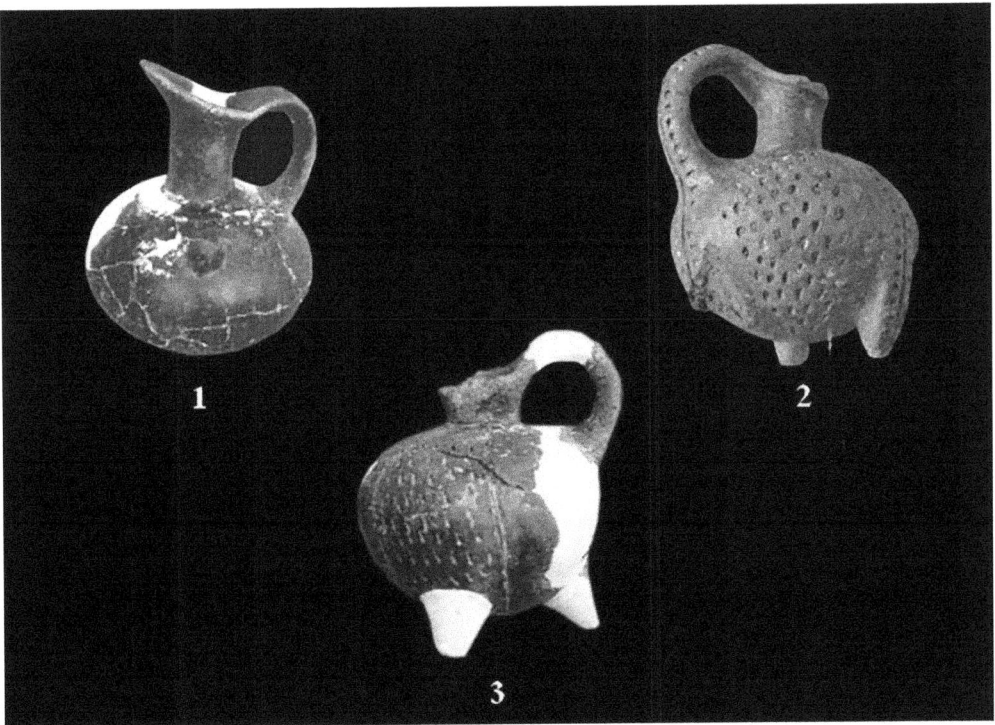

FIGURE 5.6. Yenibademli Höyük. Jug with a small spout on the belly (1), miniature jugs with decorations (2–3). (EBA II).

The miniature jugs of Yenibademli (Figure 5.6:2, 5.6:3) bear attraction with the arrangement of decorations and they show similarities with those uncovered at Troia, at the 1. building level of Protesilaus and at IIa and IIb settlements of Thermi in terms of form and decoration (Demangel 1926:18; Lamb 1936; Schliemann 1881:452). The fact that they were produced in small sizes with a narrow neck and mouth leads to the conclusion that they were most likely used to store perfumed oils, that is, cosmetic substances, rather than functioned as kitchen ware. At Yenibademli, they haven't been found in every house context, which supports the view that they might have been used only by elite families.

Some of the jar-class pottery of Yenibademli has a Northwest Anatolian character. Close parallels are the ledge-handled collared neck jar, which represents the C4 type of Troia I pottery assemblage (Blegen et al. 1950: Figure 223b, Type C4), and is defined according to the example of Kumtepe IC phase. This shape is well adopted at Yenibademli (Figure 5.7:1). These types of jars have been produced during Early and Middle phases of Troia I and several neck and handle fragments have been found also at Poliochni IIb (Bernabò-Brea 1964) and at Thermi IV (Lamb 1936: Figure 29a). The detection of such jars in Northwestern Anatolia and at island settlements should be interpreted as an indicator that a common idea was shared among the potters.

A small jar (Figure 5.7:2), representing a unique form in the Yenibademli pottery assemblage, has four pierced lugs and resembles the C 31 type, which was in use during the Troia I settlement (Blegen et al. 1950). Although they bear some minor differences in detail, such finds occur both at Early Troia I (Blegen et al. 1950), at Ia, IIIa, and IIIb phases of Thermi (Lamb 1936) and within the finds of Yortan, Bayındırköy, and Babaköy, as mentioned by Podzuweit (1979). This type of jar that was uncovered at Yenibademli in fragments gains importance by indicating the distribution limit of this type in the northern part of the Aegean Sea.

The lids of Northwestern Anatolian settlements and of Yenibademli resemble each other in many respects. These appear without grips in cylindrical form, crown-like shaped, and edged or disc-shaped. One of the rare examples at Yenibademli is the cylindrical

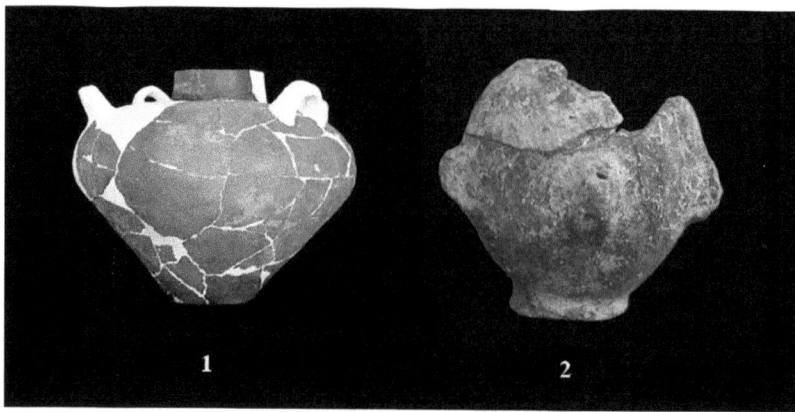

FIGURE 5.7. Yenibademli Höyük. Jar with collar-neck and plain lip (1), small jar with vertically pierced lugs (2). (EBA II).

lid with flattened top and without a grip (Figure 5.8:1), which is known as D1 Type in Trojan pottery typology (Blegen et al. 1950). Such lids, which served at Troia I and later at IIg and IVd phases, show no continuity in the Yenibademli building levels.

The so-called crown-shaped lids, which constitute a rich collection at Yenibademli, are listed in two main groups as high (Figure 5.8:2, 5.8:3) and oblate (Figure 5.8:4, 5.9:1) examples. These may appear with or without knobs and have two or four handles (Figure 5.9:2). They resemble the D 9 and D 10 types of the Troia I period lid assemblage

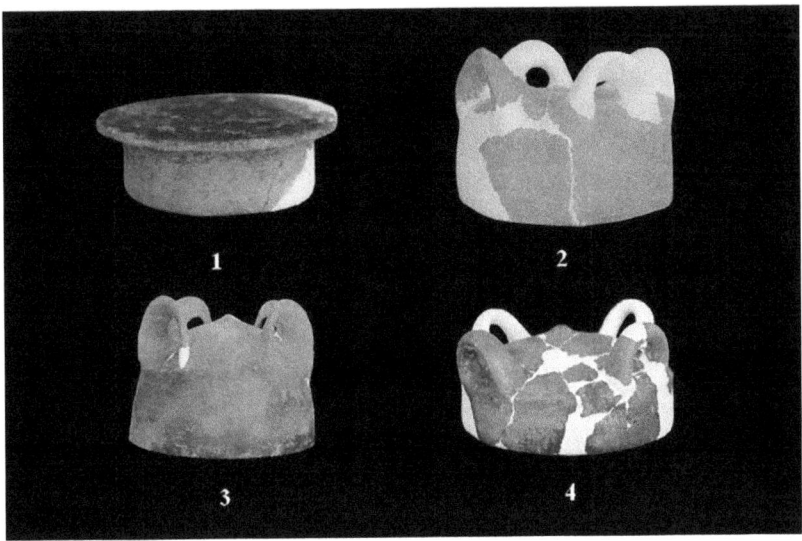

FIGURE 5.8. Yenibademli Höyük. Cylindrical lid with flattened top (1), crown-shaped lids (2–4). (EBA II).

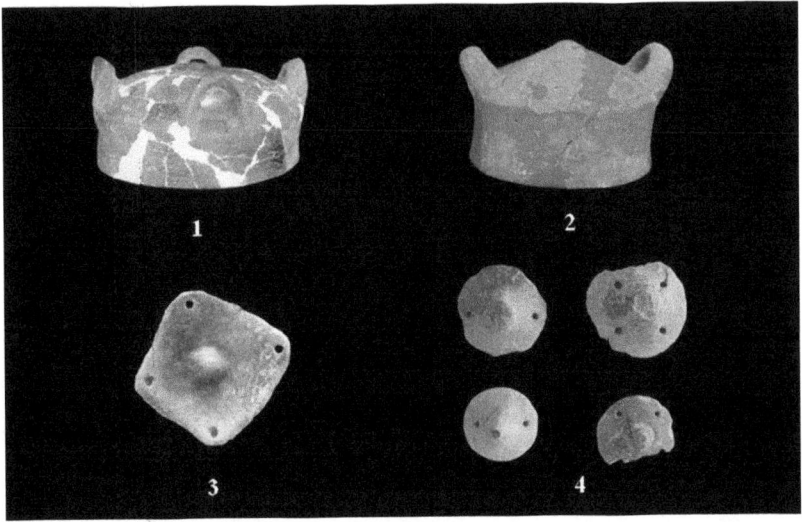

FIGURE 5.9. Yenibademli Höyük. Oblate crown-shaped lid (1), lid with two handles (2), lid with rounded corners and four holes (3), disc-shaped knobbed lids with two or four holes (4). (EBA II).

(Blegen et al. 1950) and are well known from Beşik-Yassıtepe (Korfmann 1984), 1. and 2. building levels of Protesilaus (Podzuweit 1979), Babaköy (Bittel 1939–41) and IIb phase of Poliochni (Bernabò-Brea 1964).

Another group as common as the crowned-shaped lids are those with grips. They are either edged or disc-shaped. One of these (Figure 5.9:3) is slightly raised with rounded corners and has a string hole in each corner. Centrally placed grips taper to the end. Outside Anatolia, close parallels of our example, which fit into D 19 type of Troia I settlement (Blegen et al. 1950), were also produced at Thermi, in I-IV Settlements (Lamb 1936). The bottom surfaces of Yenibademli's disc-shaped knobbed lids with two or four string-holes (Figure 5.9:4) are either flat or slightly hollowed. In most of the examples the grips with tapering points are broken and the outer surfaces left undecorated. Disc-shaped lids with flat bottoms, which are characteristic for the Early and Middle phases of Troia I, are representatives of D 14 Type (Blegen et al. 1950). Decorated examples have been uncovered at Thermi in I-IV Settlements (Lamb 1936), at Ovabayındır (Akurgal 1958) within the Yortan cultural zone, whereas undecorated examples were found at the 1. settlement of Protesilaus (Demangel 1926). Disc-shaped lids of Yenibademli with slightly hollowed bottoms seem to fit more likely into the D 15 Type of Trojan typology. An addition to those at Troia I settlement (Blegen et al.1950: Figure 223b), their counterparts can be seen among finds from Yortan (Forsdyke 1925: Figure 15) and IC2 phase of Kumtepe (Sperling 1976).

Another vessel form, which constitutes a basis for the cultural interactions between Yenibademli and Northwestern Anatolia is the so-called *pyxis*. In Troia I pottery classification, such vessels represent C 37 and D 31 types (Blegen et al. 1950: Figure 223b), as

FIGURE 5.10. Yenibademli Höyük. *Pyxis* with incised decoration. (EBA II).

singular or composite vessels respectively. Yenibademli find (Figure 5.10), similar to Trojan C 37 type *pyxis,* resemble with those examples dated to Troia Ia and Ib phases (Blegen et al. 1950) in terms of its form. Regarding the decoration, it differs from Trojan examples and was probably used to store jewelry items. It represents the singular example at the settlement, which was recovered with its lid. Such finds, which are known from Kumtepe IC1 phase (Sperling 1976: Figure 22), Protesilaus,[2] Yortan find assemblages (Kamil 1982: Figure 91, Figure 33; Orthmann 1966: Figure 7), Panderma (Wiegand 1904:287) and İzmir Archaeological Museum (Özkan 1999: Figure 10), represent a common form in Western and Northwestern Anatolia in the earlier phases of the Troia I period. Although a similar find uncovered at Thermi I was interpreted as a lid by Lamb (1936), Blegen stated that it should be a *pyxis* (1950:72).

Evaluation and Conclusion

As already mentioned above, all of the Early Bronze Age II pottery of Yenibademli is handmade. Apart from the kitchenware, which constitutes a large group, vessels with special functions are well-represented. Carinated bowls with horizontal tubular lugs, which reflect the Northwestern Anatolian pottery influence, seem to be imitations of A 12 and A 13 type bowls of Troia I period and are among the dominant forms at the settlement. Small-sized incised motifs encountered on outer rims of such examples fit in the decoration pattern of Northwestern Anatolia. Such vessels might have been decorated with wide knobs, just like the examples of Troia I period. Bearing a singular or more tubular lug should be associated with the choices of Yenibademli society. The chronological evaluation of tubular lugs, through Early, Middle, and Late phases of Troia I, can also be followed at Yenibademli. The absence of Troia I period bowls with sophisticated tubular lugs among the aforementioned examples does not mean that they didn't exist at the settlement. The presence of such bowls is evidenced, at least, with fragments of highly developed lugs. Placing tubular lugs between the carination and the rim at Yenibademli, Trojan, and Kumtepe bowls is an indicator that potters shared a common idea.

Bowls with internally thickened rims, which form the second large group of the settlement's pottery assemblage, have incised decorations similar to A 6 type bowls, which were starting to be produced during the first phases of Troia I. Human face depictions, which were used to decorate the band inside the rim, and some other geometric motifs have been filled with a white substance for a visual appeal. Such applications have been frequently encountered on incised bowls of the settlements, which fall within the diffusion zone of Maritime Troia culture. Just like the Trojan examples, the decorated bands on Yenibademli bowls are short and have a convex surface. The attachment of the decorated band to the body with a distinct contour, seen on same type bowls, resembles the examples of Troia Ib phase. Such types of bowls and decorations, which have also been found at Kumtepe IC phase and Beşik-Yassıtepe, considered mainland satellites of Troia, are important parameters that show from which region Yenibademli potters were influenced in terms of forms and decorations.

Carinated bowls with strap handles projected from the rim, which represent A 15 type of the Troia I settlement and started to be produced in Northwestern Anatolia and in North Aegean islands at centers such Troia and Yenibademli, do appear in very limited numbers, which makes one think that they were out of production due to their impracticality.

The jugs of Yenibademli, which don't represent a great variety of forms, are usually in small or medium sizes. They appear as globular or oblate spherical bodies, where the round bases are dominant. Yenibademli jugs resemble B 13 type examples of Troia I period in terms of inclined mouths; distinct neck contour and vertical handles slightly rising from the rim; they also resemble examples from Protesilaus, Kumtepe IC, Thermi, and Poliochni. This constitutes a basis for the fact that in Northwestern Anatolia and the islands, similar jugs were adopted for practical manners apart from some minor differences. The distribution area of such jugs is not limited to a narrow region, since they have been found at the XVI level of Beycesultan, at Kusura B phase, at Karataş, and at the V level of Asarcık Höyük, which means that their distribution zone was covering a much wider area.

Although Yenibademli jug, which fits into the B 14 category tripod jug of Troia I typology, recalls the few examples from Poliochni and the unique tripod jugs of Yortan culture, its limited number at the settlement is considered, as they were not so popular in the islands compared to the mainland.

Many parallels of the red jug, which represents a popular shape at Yenibademli and fits into the B 17 category of the Troia I typology, have been found in house contexts in black and brown tones. These are examples of the usual jugs on the mainland and apart from minor details they are known for their wide and inclined mouths, globular bodies, and slightly flattened bases.

Disregarding the rim shape, the restored jug with a spout on the belly is almost the same as that one found at Protesilaus. Such jugs, known from Thermi IIa and the Yortan Culture in the Northern Aegean have not been defined in Troia I pottery typology. These types of spouted jugs, which remain in limited numbers at Protesilaus, Yenibademli, and Thermi, represent an unpopular shape within the pottery industries of Gallipoli peninsula and Northern Aegean island settlements.

Miniature tripod jugs with incised and pierced dot decorations were probably used by elite families. Yenibademli's miniature jugs, which bear attraction with their high quality and decoration designs, come from houses with a rich inventory. These examples recall the finds from Troia, Protesilaus, and Thermi. Since they have been attested in few quantities in the Northern Aegean makes one think that they were not used by each and every family. Since they seem to be impractical for storing food substances, it's possible that they were used for other purposes. Perhaps they were served to store perfumed oils applied to the skin after the bath, as mentioned by Homer in later periods.

The collared neck jar, which represents one of the distinguished vessels of the settlement and has a close parallel at Kumtepe IC phase, is defined as the C 4 type in Troia I typology. This Troia C 4 type jar, which was restored according to the Kumtepe find, is one of the elaborate products at Yenibademli. This form, which was adopted in medium- and large-size vessels, resembles in some ways jars from Poliochni and Thermi. Yenibademli Höyük should also be included among the list of settlements with such finds, which support the view that technological knowledge was shared between Northwestern Anatolia and the island settlements.

Apart from some minor details, the coarse jar of Yenibademli with vertical pierced lugs, which resembles C 31 type of Troia I typology, recalls the jars from the Yortan cultural zone and Thermi. Such examples do not appear in large quantities at the settlement; although their production has started, there cannot be seen any continuity in the manufacture.

Lids of Yenibademli form a rich collection, which were manufactured in the fashion of examples unique to Troad region. These are representatives of the D 1, D 9, and D 10 types, which are known from Troia I period. Among these, D 1 type cylindrical lids with flattened top and without a grip represent a low profile at the settlement. Crown-shaped lids of Yenibademli, which in many ways resemble with D 9 and D 10 types of Troia I, show a great variety with their subtypes. Such examples were manufactured as an inspiration of Northwestern Anatolian specimens and show continuity through the consequent building levels. The fact that they were found utmost at Yenibademli among island settlements, righteously proves the definition of this settlement as the "Oversea Satellite of Troia."

D 19 type lids, known from Troia I and Thermi I-IV, with rounded corners and string-holes in each corner, are very rare at Yenibademli. Even though it's assumed that lids of this type were used with small-sized, edged containers, no such vessel has been found so far at the settlement to prove this hypothesis.

Disc-shaped knobbed lids with two or four string-holes are among the most frequent examples at the settlement and are close parallels of D 14 and D 15 types, which are characteristic for the Early and Middle phases of Troia I. Apart from Thermi, decorated examples of such lids occur also at Ovabayındır within the sphere of Yortan Culture. Such examples were most probably used to cover small, *pyxis* type vessels with a cylindrical body and represent a common form seen in a geographical area extending from Yortan region to the Northern Aegean islands.

The *pyxis*, which supports the view that cultural interactions with Yenibademli were emphasized in Northern Anatolia, resembles the C 37 type of Troia, in terms of both its form and decoration technique. Such finds, which are very common at the first two phases of Troia I, but remain limited at Yenibademli, are also known from Thermi, Kumtepe, Protesilaus, and Yortan find assemblage. Among these centers, Yenibademli marks the westernmost distribution limit of such vessels.

Considering the abovementioned pottery forms in a chronological manner, it can be proposed that these were produced during Troia I period and that during this time interval, elements of the Maritime Troia Culture were dominant in terms of shapes and decoration arrangements. This shows that Early Bronze Age II pottery industry of Yenibademli was under the influence of Northwestern Anatolia. The fact that local potters were under the influence of another region and continued to imitate their forms for a long time period makes one think that a conservative approach predominated the settlement and the personal preferences of the manufacturers of these vessels were omitted. Considering the fact that the pottery assemblage of the settlement shows a character of the Troad region, it should be remembered that this is related to the proximate location of Yenibademli to Northwestern Anatolia.

Notes

1. The excavations at Yenibademli Höyük were conducted by the author as the scientific supervisor (1996–1997) and as the director (1998–2013), with the permission of the Ministry of Culture and Tourism, General Directorate of Cultural Heritage and Museums, on behalf of the Hacettepe University. The excavations are generously supported by the Ministry of Culture and Tourism, DÖSİMM, Institute for Aegean Prehistory (INSTAP), Governorship and Municipality of Gökçeada, Governorship of Çanakkale, Turkish Historical Society, Hacettepe University Scientific Research Unit (Project No: 0202701001 and 013 A 701 001). I want to take this opportunity to express my gratitude to all of the listed institutions and their directors.
2. Demangel 1926: Figure 80, No. 157. Podzuweit (1979: 41, fn. 178) states that the *pyxis* at Protesilaus might have been found at the 4. level.

References Cited

Akurgal, E. 1958 Yortan kultur-Siedlung in Ovabayındır bei Balıkesir. *Anadolu (Anatolia)* III: 156–164.
Berciu, D. 1961 Contributii le probleme neoliticului în Romania în lumina noilor cercetari. Ed. Academiei R.P.R., Bucureşti.
Bernabò-Brea, L. 1964 *Poliochni. Città Preistorica Nell'isola di Lemnos,* Vol. I. L'Erma di Bretschneider, Roma.
Bittel, K. 1939–41 Ein Gräberfeld der Yortan Kultur bei Babaköy. *Archiv für Orientforschung* 13:1–31.
Blegen, C. W., J. L. Caskey, M. Rawson, and J. W. Sperling 1950 *Troy. General Introduction, The First and Second Settlement* Vol. I. Princeton University Press, Princeton.
Demangel, R. 1926 *Le Tumulus dit de Protésilas.* De Boccard, Paris.
Fıratlı, N. 1964 *İmroz ve Bozcaada.* Türkiye Turing ve Otomobil Kurumu Yayını, İstanbul.
Forsdyke, E. J. 1925 Catalogue of the Greek and Etruscan Vases in the British Museum, Vol. I. British Museum, London.
French, D. 1964 Prehistoric Pottery from Macedonia and Thrace. *Prähistorische Zeitschrift* XLII:30–48.
Garstang, J. 1953 Prehistoric Mersin:Yümük Tepe in Southern Turkey. Clarendon Press, Oxford.
Heurtley, W. A. 1939 *Prehistoric Macedonia.* Cambridge University Press, Cambridge.
Hüryılmaz, H. 1998 Gökçeada-Yenibademli Höyük 1996 Yılı Kurtarma Kazısı. *XIX. Kazı Sonuçları Toplantısı,* Vol. I, pp. 357–377. T. C. Kültür Bakanlığı Yayınları, Ankara.
Hüryılmaz, H. 2002a Gökçeada Arkeolojisi /Archaeology of Gökçeada. *Gökçeada.* In *Yeşil ve Mavinin Özgür Dünyası,* edited by B. Öztürk, pp. 69–91. Ser Offset, İstanbul.

Hüryılmaz, H. 2002b Yenibademli Höyük: Kuzeydoğu Ege Denizi'nde Bir Erken Tunç Çağı Yerleşmesi. *Hacettepe Üniversitesi Edebiyat Fakültesi Dergisi* 19(1):27–44.

Hüryılmaz, H. 2006 *Kuzeydoğu Ege Denizi'nin Rüzgârlı Bahçesi: Gökçeada*, edited by B. Uysal. Gökçeada Belediyesi Yayınları, Çanakkale.

Hüryılmaz, H. 2008 Gökçeada-Yenibademli Höyük'te Kent Olgusu ve Sosyokültürel Yaşam. *Batı Anadolu ve Doğu Akdeniz Geç Tunç Çağı Kültürleri Üzerine Yeni Araştırmalar*, edited by A. Erkanal-Öktü, S. Günel, and U. Deniz, pp. 141–150. Hacettepe Üniversitesi Yayınları, Ankara.

Hüryılmaz, H. 2011 Erken Bronz Çağı'nda Gökçeada-Yenibademli Höyük'te Kent ve Kadın. In *VIII. Çanakkale Troas Arkeoloji Buluşması*, edited by S. Yavuz, pp. 42–50. Çabisak, Çanakkale.

Hüryılmaz, H. 2013a Gökçeada-Yenibademli Höyük 2010 Yılı Kazıları. *33. Kazı Sonuçları Toplantısı*, Vol. I, pp. 1–18. T. C. Kültür Bakanlığı Yayınları, Ankara.

Hüryılmaz, H. 2013b Gökçeada-Yenibademli Höyük 2011 Yılı Kazıları. *34. Kazı Sonuçları Toplantısı*, Vol. I, pp. 169–186. T. C. Kültür Bakanlığı Yayınları, Ankara.

Kâmil, T. 1982 Yortan Cemetery in the Early Bronze Age of Western Anatolia. B. A. R., Oxford.

Korfmann, M. 1984 Beşik-Tepe. Vorbericht über die Ergebnisse der Grabung von 1982. Die Hafenbucht vor 'Troja' (Hisarlık), Grabungen am Beşik-Yassıtepe. *Archäologischer Anzeiger* 2:165–195.

Korfmann, M., Ç. Girgin, Ç. Morçöl, and S. Kılıç 1995 Kumtepe 1993 Bericht über die Rettungsgrabung. *Studia Troica* 5:237–289.

Kunze, E. 1934 *Orchomenos. Die Keramik der Frühen Bronzezeit*, Vol. III. Verlag der Bayerischen Akademie der Wissenschaften, München.

Lamb, W. 1936 *Excavations at Thermi in Lesbos*. Cambridge University Press, Cambridge.

Lamb, W. 1938 Excavations at Kusura near Afyon Karahisar: II. *Archaeologia* 87:217–273.

Lloyd, S., and J. Mellaart 1962 *Beycesultan. The Chalcolithic and Early Bronze Age Levels*, Vol. I. British Institute of Archaeology at Ankara, London.

Mellaart, J. 1954 Preliminary Report on a Survey of Pre-Classical Remains in Southern Turkey. *Anatolian Studies* IV:175–240.

Orthmann, W. 1966 Keramik der Yortankultur in den Berliner Museen. *Istanbuler Mitteilungen* 16:1–27.

Öner, E. 2001 Gökçeada Kıyılarında Holosen Deniz Seviyesi ve Kıyı Çizgisi Değişmeleri. In *Türkiye'nin Kıyı ve Deniz Alanları III. Ulusal Konferansı, Türkiye Kıyıları 01 Konferansı Bildiriler Kitabı*, edited by E. Özhan and Y. Yüksel, pp. 779–790. Kıyı Alanları Yönetimi Türkiye Milli Komitesi, Ankara.

Özkan, T. 1999 *İzmir Arkeoloji Müzesi Kataloğu*. İzmir Arkeoloji Müze Müdürlüğü, İzmir.

Podzuweit, C. 1979 Trojanische Gefäßformen der Frühbronzezeit in Anatolien, der Ägäis und angrenzenden Gebieten. Von Zabern, Mainz am Rhein.

Popov, R. 1919 Kodja-Dermenskata Mogila pri grad Şumen. *İzvestiya na Bılgarskoto Arheologiçesko Drujestvo* VI, 1916/1918:71–155.

Schliemann, H. 1881 *Ilios, Stadt und Land der Trojaner*. Brockhaus, Leipzig.

Sperling, J. W. 1976 Kum Tepe in the Troad. *Hesperia* 45(4):305–364.

Wace, A. J. B., and M. S. Thompson 1912 *Prehistoric Thessaly*. Cambridge University Press, Cambridge.

Wiegand, T. 1904 Reisen in Mysien. *Athenische Mitteilungen* 29:254–339.

Chapter Six

A New Contribution to the Western Anatolia Early Bronze Age Chronology

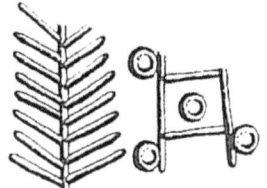

Volute Vessels

Derya Yilmaz*

Introduction

A volute is a Near Eastern motif that was applied to different material groups with different techniques in Anatolia during the Early Bronze Age. It shows up regularly during a very long period, from the Near Eastern cultures to the Classical culture, and even today it can be seen in some modern art works. The volutes were used on the metal and pots of various cultures in the Near East during the Bronze Age. For example, lower volute strap-handles and completely volute handles have been found among the pottery of the city of Hazor, in Palestine, dated to the Middle and Late Bronze Age (Yadin et al. 1961:Pl. CCCXIII 8–10, CXCII, 7). The volute handles, their presence known at Mallia in Crete since the Middle Minoan I period, were also seen on a rhyton of amphora at Pyrgos in Myrtos dated to Late Minoan IB period (Koehl 2006:211; Mellaart 1957:75). Furthermore, it is known that the volutes continued to exist on the metal feet, also known as "Cyprus type," that spread through the eastern Mediterranean coast in the Late Bronze Age (Mazar et al. 1964).

The volutes that appear on the baked clay vessels in Western Anatolia at the end of the Early Bronze Age indicate the existence of a chronologically special group, because they are found only at a limited number of settlements and are used only in approximately the same period. The volute vessels are one of the forms that help us to identify the date, because they generally indicate the time period from the end of the Early Bronze Age III to the beginning of Middle Bronze Age in the north of Western Anatolia. The

---

*Associate Prof. Dr. Derya Yilmaz, Ankara University, Faculty of Language, History and Geography, Department of Archaeology, Protohistory and Near Eastern Archaeology, Sıhhiye, Ankara-Turkey, 06100, d.yilmaz@ankara.edu.tr

handles of a group of basket-handled metal teapots, which were uncovered in Alaca Höyük and Kayapınar in Central Anatolia and linked to Troy and the Troad region in Western Anatolia at the Early Bronze Age III, were volute (Schmidt 1902:no.6147; Bittel 1959:Abb.7, 8a-b; Arık 1937:Pl. CCLXVII:Al. 1746; Koşay 1951 Pl. CLXXVIII: Al.K.41; Temizer 1954:325–326). An Akkadian historical connection may be established with the disk of Enheduanna, which illustrates metal basket-handled teapots of the Anatolian Early Bronze Age IIIA type (Öktü 1973:110–111).

Distribution Area and Chronology of the Volute Vessels

The earliest examples of volute pottery were seen at Troy III and continued until the end of Troy V. The use of the volutes continued during the end of the Early Bronze Age and beginning of the Middle Bronze Age. The volutes in Western Anatolia are generally seen on the handle and foot parts of the vessels in various forms (Blegen et al. 1951). Similar types of volutes were applied to the foot of the tripod vessels in Cilicia, Mersin Kilisetepe, Tarsus Gözlükule, and Mersin Yümüktepe (Garstang 1953; Symington 2007). According to the distribution map of the volutes, published in 1962 (Lloyd and Mellaart 1962), the existence of volute vessels has been known in Troy, Poliochni, Larisa, Heraion, Beycesultan, Tarsus, and Tatarlı Höyük. After quite a long period, the new evidence in Cilicia and Inland Western Anatolia pointed out new locations of the distribution area (Figure 6.1). Also, the volutes from Maydos Kilisetepe carry a significant importance as it is the northernmost point of the distribution area (Figure 6.1).

The volutes uncovered in Troy III-V appeared on both handles and on the feet of many various forms such as Blegen form A21, A37, C29, C35, D3, and Easton form C218.[1] Baked clay vessels with volute handles uncovered at Kumtepe II in the Troad region, dated to the Early Bronze Age III, display characteristics similar to Troy V. The volutes of Kumtepe were placed on the top part of the vertical handle that rises above the rim of the bowl in the form of Troy A18 and on both sides of the handles that rise horizontally from the rim of the bowl in the form of A21 and were probably on the handle of a jar of C29 form (Sperling 1976). A volute handle fragment dated to Period B was found at Hanay Tepe (Lamb 1932:118). One of the earliest examples of volute handle on a Hanay Tepe fragment should be a contemporary of Troy III. A pithos, which was uncovered at Yortan Cemetery, had both handles made with the binding of four cylinder strips and the lower part of the handles, which were connected to the body, and ended with four spiral reliefs (Kamil 1982: Figure 7.57, 22.57). Those four spiral reliefs should be interpreted as another variation of the volute handles uncovered at Maydos Kilisetepe. The other volute handles were uncovered at the prehistoric levels of the ancient city Larisa IB (Buruncuk), which is one of the important Aeolian cities located in coastal Western Anatolia. Those volute handles, which are the contemporary with Troy III-V, are important because they show the connection with the city of Larisa and the Troad region. The volute handles of open vessels are included in the dark red slip pottery group (Boehlau and Schefold 1942). Some fragments of a half-preserved vessel

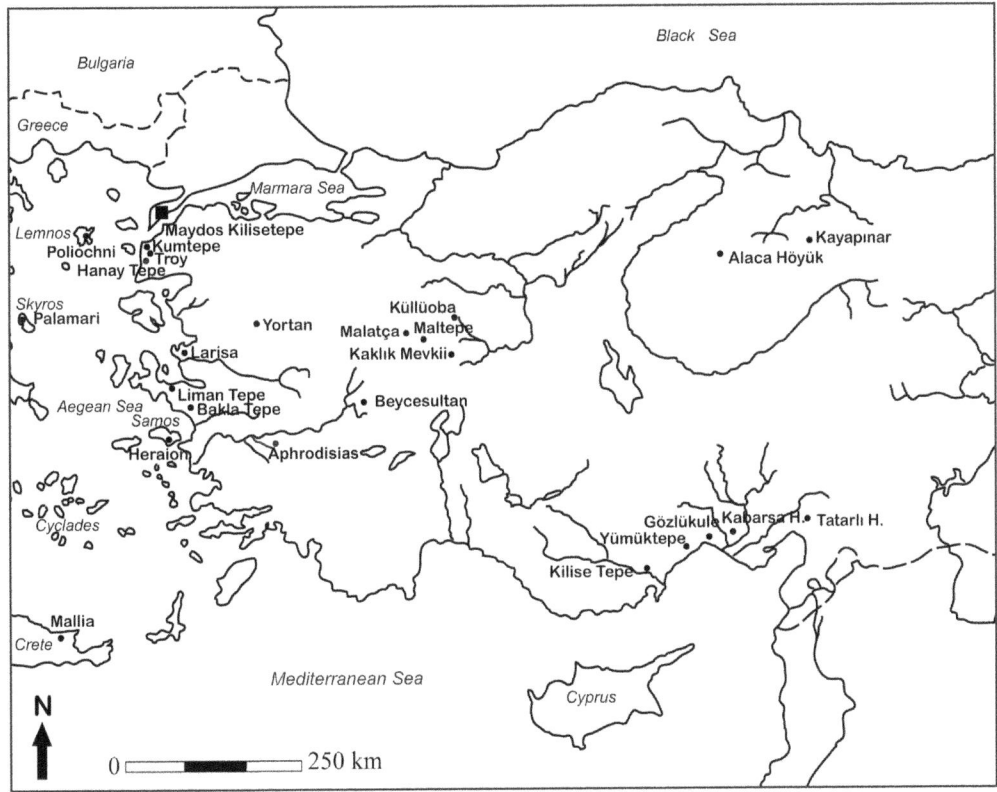

FIGURE 6.1. The map showing sites mentioned in the text, showing the points of the volute vessels in the Anatolia and the Aegean World during the Early Bronze Age (Drawing: D. Yılmaz).

with a volute tripod and with a strap-handle were uncovered at a pithos grave dated to Early Bronze Age III at Afyon Kaklık region (Topbaş et al. 1998:38, 73). This example is important because it shows that the volute vessels are not only found at settlements, but also in grave findings. There is also another volute vessel known from Afyon Maltepe (Lloyd and Mellaart 1962:255). Furthermore, a volute foot sherd dated to the end of the Early Bronze Age III was found in Malatça, near Kütahya, during the survey conducted by T. Efe (Efe 1994:575). With the presence of a volute foot discovered in Küllüoba IIIA, synchronization can be established between Troy III and Beycesultan X (Efe and Türkteki 2005:134, Figure 10). The first volutes appeared Beycesultan X and continue throughout level VII (Lloyd and Mellaart 1962). The volute vessels were included in the list of the vessels of Early Bronze Age character in Beycesultan VI at the Middle Bronze Age transitional period (Lloyd and Mellaart 1956). The volutes dated to Early Bronze Age IIIA and B in Beycesultan were placed on the lid lugs, on both ends of the basket-handles, and on the foot and handles of the vessels (Lloyd and Mellart 1962). At Aphrodisias among the new features of the Early Bronze Age IIIB is the appearance of volute handle, which is synchronizing within Troy III-V and Tarsus Early Bronze Age III (Kadish 1971:138–139).

The volute vessels were found in the eastern Aegean islands, which were culturally connected to Anatolia during the Early Bronze Age (Figure 6.1). Furthermore, several other volute vessels were discovered in the red-slipped vessels at Poliochni VI (Brown Period/*Bruno*), contemporary with Troy V, located at the southeast coast of Lemnos Island, which is across Troy and the Troad region.

There is a hiatus between the Poliochni VI and Poliochni V (Yellow Period/*Giallo*), which is chronologically dated to the Early Bronze Age III (Figure 6.2). The wings jars with spiral reliefs at the connection points are the precursors of volute vessels, and they were uncovered at Poliochni V and were also known from Troy (Bernabò-Brea 1976:319; Blegen et al. 1951:250). Furthermore, a volute vessel in the form of a barrel, in a zoomorphic character resembling a ram's head, was found during this period (Bernabò-Brea 1976:276). Moreover, a small vessel with a volute handle in the form of Troy C35 was found at Heraion II, which is located on the southern coast of Samos Island close to Anatolia (Milojcic 1961:Table 26.1). This vessel, which is contemporary with the period before Troy V, shows the close connection between Troy and Heraion. It is also known that a volute handle was discovered in Palamari, located at the northeast coast of Skyros Island in the middle of the Aegean Sea, and similar ones were discovered at Kumtepe, Troy V, and Poliochni VI (Brown Period/*Bruno*). The volute handle, which was found in Palamari (Theochari et al. 1993:191) and dated to the period between the Early Bronze Age II and beginning of the Middle Bronze Age reflects the pottery tradition in Western Anatolia and shows the connection between Troy and the Aegean world.

A bead rim bowl with volute handles was found at the fourth cultural layer of Liman Tepe, representing the transition from the Early Bronze Age to Middle Bronze Age (Aykurt forthcoming). The Liman Tepe bowl, which is contemporary with Maydos Kilisetepe, is important because it provides evidence that the volute vessels existed in the pottery repertoire around Izmir, a coastal area of Western Anatolia during the transitional period into the Middle Bronze Age.

H. Erkanal stated that a hook-shaped protrusion of a baked clay teapot with a basket-handle, which was uncovered at a grave in the Bakla Tepe cemetery area, dated to the end of the Early Bronze Age II and can be associated with the metal teapots with volute basket-handles dated to the Early Bronze Age III (Erkanal and Özkan 2000:265). The volute vessels that were uncovered at several coastal and inland settlements of Western Anatolia were also known in Cilicia in its contemporary period. Moreover, the red-cross motif that was found in a bowl with volute feet in Tarsus helps us to date the abovementioned bowl. Wheel-made red-cross bowls are the typical pottery group of the transitional phase from Early Bronze Age III to the Middle Bronze Age. The Tarsus Gözlükule bowl is unique both for its red-cross motif and its volute foot. The round-necked jars with volute feet that were found in Gözlükule are typical for Early Bronze Age III (Goldman 1940: Figures 36 and 5). Also, Kabarsa and Tatarlı Höyük were mentioned in the distribution area of volute handle/foot types in Cilicia (Girginer et al. 2010:455;

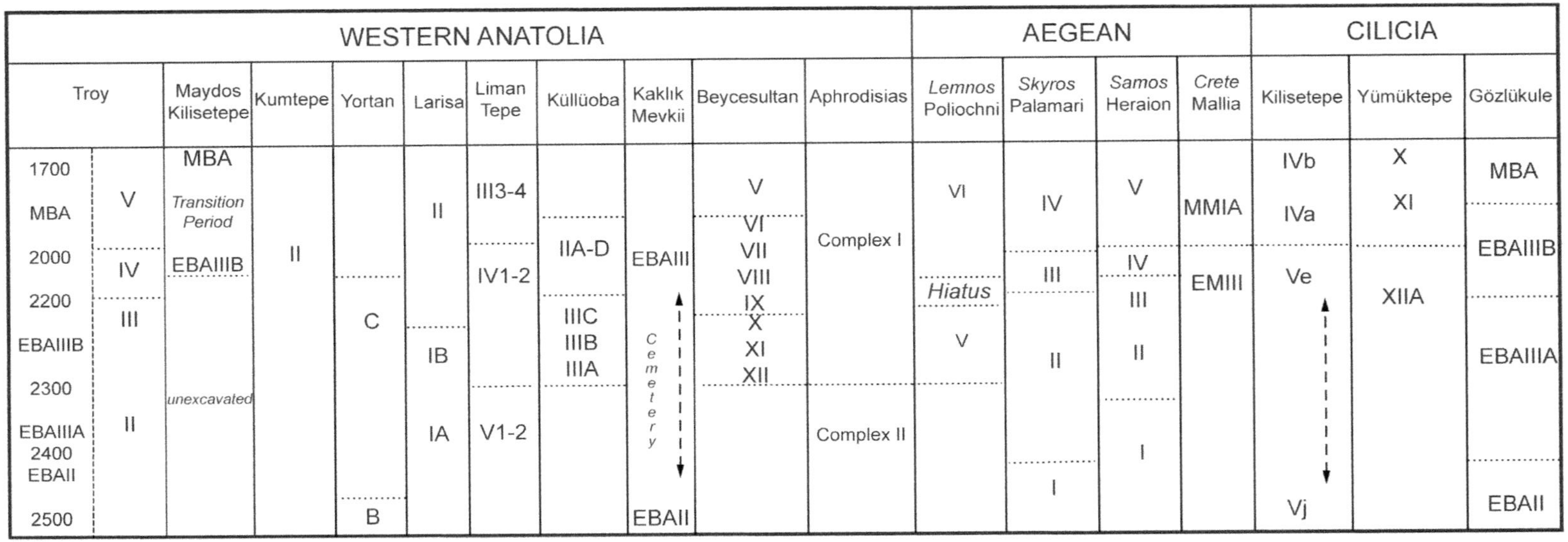

	WESTERN ANATOLIA									AEGEAN					CILICIA		
Troy	Maydos Kilisetepe	Kumtepe	Yortan	Larisa	Liman Tepe	Küllüoba	Kaklık Mevkii	Beycesultan	Aphrodisias	Lemnos Poliochni	Skyros Palamari	Samos Heraion	*Crete* Mallia	Kilisetepe	Yümüktepe	Gözlükule
1700	MBA																MBA
MBA V	*Transition Period*			II	III3-4		EBAIII	V	Complex I	VI	IV	V	MMIA	IVb IVa	X XI	EBAIIIB
2000 IV	EBAIIIB	II			IV1-2	IIA-D	← ─ ─ ─ →	VI VII VIII			III	IV	EMIII	Ve	XIIA	
2200 III			C	IB		IIIC IIIB IIIA	C e m e t e r y	IX X XI XII		Hiatus V	II	III				EBAIIIA
EBAIIIB	*unexcavated*															
2300 II				IA	V1-2				Complex II		I	II		←─ ─ ─→		
EBAIIIA 2400 EBAII			B				EBAII					I		Vj		EBAII
2500																

FIGURE 6.2. Chronological Chart. (Drawing: D. Yılmaz).

Lloyd and Mellaart 1962:257; Seton-Williams 1954:158, 131). In addition, a volute foot was uncovered in Mersin Kilisetepe, within the tradition of Late Early Bronze Age III (Symington 2007:317). A similar volute foot Early Bronze Age III was also found in Mersin Yümüktepe (Garstang 1953:193–194).

The volutes should have a connection with the spiral relief decorations that were seen on the pottery of Troy II-V. The volute motif, which was made by a curling process, must have been repeated on the pottery as a relief decoration. The spiral reliefs must have been a variant of a volute motif (Blegen et al. 1950; Blegen et al. 1951: Figure 81, Figure 164, Figure 244:23; Schliemann 1881: nos. 231, 240, 349). The storage-jar body fragment with a trumpet-shaped handle and a pot sherd with spiral relief decoration were found side by side in the same level (Figure 3b:6, catalog no. 6) contemporary with Troy V at Maydos Kilisetepe, and those findings help us to build a connection.

During the Early Bronze Age, the volutes also emerge in different artifact groups. Some metal razors, which were uncovered in Troy III and the Yortan cemetery, have their ends curled to make volute motifs (Kamil 1982:21–22; Schliemann 1881:965–966). This shows that spiral reliefs and volute motifs were not only used on the handle and feet of the baked clay and metal vessels, but that they also represent a significant trend in Troy. The other samples, uncovered in Cilicia and Western Anatolia prove that this fashion had spread outside of the Troad region. It is known that incised decoration or relief motifs on the pottery in the Balkans occurred as a result of cultural relations with Northwestern Anatolia (Heurrtley 1939:177; Mellaart 1958:11).

The volutes were applied to the pottery in two different forms, either as a foot or as a handle in Anatolia. The vessel forms include bowls with a horizontal volute handle, lids with a volute basket-handle, cooking-pots with volute feet, jars with volute feet, and storage-jars with volute handles. Furthermore, the volute vessels found in Poliochni, Larisa, Troy, and Maydos Kilisetepe show that they were usually included in the pottery group containing vessels that were red-slipped, burnished, and wheel-made. Six volute handles were found inside the same room of a building at the excavations conducted in Maydos Kilisetepe (Figure 6.3). One of them is a bowl with a horizontal handle in the form of Blegen A21 (Figure 6.4; catalog no. 5); the other is a handle of a big closed vessel which can be seen as trumpet-shaped from the outside, and as volute-shaped from the side, and similar to the one found in Beycesultan; two of them are probably in the Blegen C29 form (Figure 6.4; catalog no. 3–4); one of them probably belonged to a closed jar (Figure 6.4; catalog no. 1); and the last one should belong to the vessel in the closed jar-like form (Figure 6.4; catalog no. 2), which is similar to the one was found in Beycesultan (Lloyd and Mellaart 1962). One of the handles that were found in Maydos Kilisetepe appears as trumpet-shaped from the outside (Figure 6.4; catalog no. 6). The tips of the handles of the metal pans that were found in the Troad region of Early Bronze Age III end as trumpet-shaped. Although the pan handle of Eskiyapar pan was not preserved, T. Özgüç suggested that the pan handle was also trumpet-shaped (Bittel 1959; Özgüç and Temizer 1993:625). Similar pans were uncovered in a simple earth grave (Grave No. 20) of the Akkadian Period in the city of Assur in Mesopotamia (Calmeyer 1977:90; Haller 1952:Table 10b). There is great similarity between the trumpet-shaped

Figure 6.3. A photograph of the volute handles of Maydos Kilisetepe (Photography: D.Ç. Sazcı).

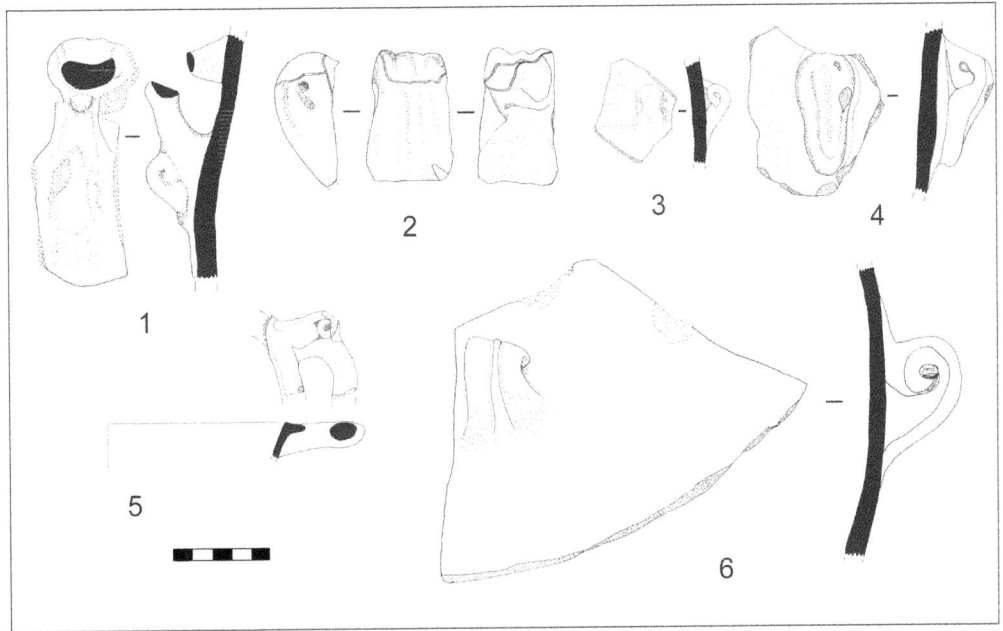

Figure 6.4. An illustration of the volute handles of Maydos Kilisetepe (Drawing: A. Ö. Akbaş, S. Yıldız, S. Erol; Preparing: D. Yılmaz).

metal pans with volute handles and the metal pans of Anatolia (Schliemann 1881: no. 923). The pans, which were dated to Early Bronze Age III, around 2300 B.C., indicate that trade relations between Anatolia and the city of Assur started at the end of the third millennium B.C. It is known that the metal pans with omphalos are an important form, which show the trade relations between Anatolia and Syria (Calmeyer 1977:97; Maxwell-Hyslop 1971:58; Mellaart 1982: Figure 1; Yılmaz 2009:442). Additionally, the trumpet at the tip of the pan-handles of the metal pans appears again on the some of the baked clay volute handles, and it shows that pottery samples were produced as an imitation of metal vessels. Some of the metal spouted basket-handled teapots seen in Western and Central Anatolia in the Early Bronze Age have volutes on both sides of the handles (Bittel 1959). Baked clay volutes that were produced as an imitation of metal vessels are known from the pottery repertoire of Western Anatolia, the eastern Aegean islands, and Cilicia in Early Bronze Age III.

Conclusion

The volute vessels reflect a long tradition in Troy in the chronology of Western Anatolia, and they are also observed in the pottery of Early Bronze Age III and the transitional phase to the Middle Bronze Age (Figure 6.3) (Mellaart 1967:692–694). The volute vessels help us to establish the chronology and are also important because they show cultural relations between regions. All the volute vessels found in Maydos Kilisetepe were uncovered at the level contemporary with Troy V. M. Korfmann defined Troy IV and V as the "Anatolian Trojan Culture." The Troy V period is dated to the end of Early Bronze Age III and the beginning of Middle Bronze Age (Korfmann 2001:203). M. Mellink stated that Western Anatolia, which experienced increasing wealth during the Early Bronze Age III, turned its face to the East, which provided international trade links with Syria and Mesopotamia (Mellink 1986:151). In particular, the uncovered depas and tankard vessels in the region stretching to the Euphrates River prove the existence of cultural relations with Western Anatolia. Findings in Cilicia in Southern Anatolia contained various forms characteristic of Western Anatolia, including volute vessels. On the other hand, the existence of volute vessels in the eastern Aegean islands, which is near the coast of Anatolia, is important because they demonstrate the continuation of cultural unity with Western Anatolia until Early Bronze Age III (Figure 6.2).

The Maydos Kilisetepe volute handles that were introduced in this article are dated to the period from the end of the Early Bronze Age III to the beginning of the Middle Bronze Age, which is the last phase when the use of volute vessels occurred. Volute vessels are important forms that show cultural relations between Western Anatolia and the Balkans, the eastern Aegean islands, Central Anatolia, and even with Cilicia in the last phase of the Early Bronze Age. The Maydos Kilisetepe pottery dated to Early Bronze Age III shows parallels with the Troad region and the eastern Aegean islands. It is suggested that volute vessels, which first appeared with the basket-handled metal teapots in the end of the Troy II Period during Early Bronze Age III, originated from Western Anatolia. The earliest known metal and baked clay volute handles were found in Troy and the

Troad region, and they are especially important as they indicate the starting point of the cultural relations that extend to Cilicia.

Acknowledgments

I am indebted to Dr. G. Sazcı, director of the Maydos Kilisetepe Project, for providing an opportunity to work on this subject, to D. Çalış Sazcı (MA, PhD Candidate) for the photograph, to A. Ö. Akbaş, S. Yıldız, S. Erol (archaeology students) for the first drawings of the artifacts and to A. Ö. Akbaş for rearranging the drawings.

Note

1. H. Schliemann completed the foot of the vessel belongs to Troy I in the volute form. However, there is no other sample that belongs to Troy I, and therefore this sample should be approached with uncertainty. There are some bronze teapots with volute basket handles in Troy II during the Early Bronze Age III. Then plastic volutes first introduced in Troy III pottery repertoire. See Schliemann 1881: nos. 44, 1007, 1009, 1025, 1044, 1049; for A21 see Blegen et al. 1951: Figure 249: 1a, 1b, 2a, 2b, for C 29 form see ibid. Figure 238; for A 37 ibid. Figure 154a; Zimmermann 2006: Abb.2; for C35 see Podzuweit 1979: Taf. 16.1,B IIa2; for C 218 form see Easton 2002: Figure 128; for D3 see Blegen et al. 1951: Figure 59b.

References Cited

Arık, R. O. 1937 *Alaca Höyük Hafriyatı, 1935'deki Çalışmalara ve Keşiflere Ait İlk Rapor*. Ankara.

Aykurt, A. Forthcoming Liman Tepe during the Transition Period from the Early Bronze Age to the Middle Bronze Age. In *The Aegean Early Bronze Age: New Evidence, International Conference*, edited by C. G. Doumas, A. Giannikouri, O. Kouka. Archaeological Institute of Aegean Studies, Athens.

Bernabò-Brea, L. 1976 *Poliochni Città Preistorica Nell'isola Di Lemmos* vol. II. L'Erma di Bretschneider, Roma.

Bittel, K. 1959 Beitrag zur Kenntnis Anatolischer Metallgefässe der Zweiten Hälfte des Dritten Jahrtausends V. Chr. *Jahrbuch Des Deutschen Archäologischen Instituts* 74:1–34.

Blegen, C. W., J. L. Caskey, M. Rawson, and J. Sperling 1950 *Troy General Introduction the First and Second Settlements*, Volume I. Princeton University Press, New Jersey.

Blegen, C. W., J. L. Caskey, and M. Rawson 1951 *Troy The Third, Fourth, and Fifth Settlements*, Volume II. Princeton University Press, New Jersey.

Boehlau, J., and K. Schefold 1942 *Larisa am Hermos, Die Kleinfunde, Band III*. Walter de Gruyter, Berlin.

Calmeyer, P. 1977 Das grab eines altassyrischen kaufmanns. *Iraq* 39(1):87–97.

Easton, D. F. 2002 *Schliemann's Excavations at Troia 1870–1873*. Von Zabern, Mainz Am Rhein.

Efe, T. 1994 1992 Yılında Kütahya, Bilecik ve Eskişehir İllerinde Yapılan Yüzey Araştırmaları. *XI Araştırma Sonuçları Toplantısı*, edited by F. Bayram, H. Eren, N. Ülgen, and A. H. Ergürer, pp. 571–592. T.C. Kültür ve Turizm Bakanlığı, Ankara.

Efe, T., and M. Türkteki 2005 The Stratigraphy and Pottery of the Period Transitional into the Middle Bronze Age at Küllüoba (Seyitgazi, Eskişehir). *Anatolia Antiqua* XIII:119–144.

Erkanal, H., and T. Özkan 2000 1998 Bakla Tepe Kazıları. *21. Kazı Sonuçları Toplantısı*, 1. Cilt, edited by K. Olşen, F. Bayram, A. Özme, K. Ataş, Y. Kepnek, H. Dönmez, and C. Süvari, pp. 263–279. Kültür ve Turizm Bakanlığı, Ankara.

Garstang, J. 1953 Prehistoric Mersin Yümük Tepe in Southern Turkey. Clarendon Press, Oxford.

Girginer, S., Ö. O. Girginer, and H. Akıl 2010 Tatarlı Höyük (Ceyhan) Kazısı: İlk İki Dönem *31. Kazı Sonuçları Toplantısı*, 3. Cilt, edited by H. Dönmez and C. Keskin, pp. 453–476. Kültür ve Turizm Bakanlığı, Ankara.

Goldman, H. 1940 Excavations at Gözlükule, Tarsus, 1938. *American Journal of Archaeology* 44(1):60–86.

Haller, A. 1952 *Die Graber und Grüfte von Assur*. Gebr. Mann, Berlin.

Heurtley, W. A. 1939 Prehistoric Macedonia: An Archaeological Reconnaissance of Greek Macedonia (West of the Struma) in the Neolithic, Bronze, and Early Iron Ages. The University Press, Cambridge.

Kadish, B. 1971 Excavation of Prehistoric Remains at Aphrodisias, 1968 and 1969. *American Journal of Archaeology* 75(2):121–140.

Kamil, T. 1982 Yortan Cemetery in the Early Bronze Age of Western Anatolia. BAR International Series 145, Oxford.

Koehl, R. B. 2006 *Aegean Bronze Age Rhyta*. INSTAP Academic Press, Pennsylvania.

Korfmann, M. 2001 Tarih Öncesi Yerleşim Yeri Hisarlık Tepesi Aşağıdan Yukarıya "Troia'nın On Kenti." In *Troia Düş ve Gerçek*, edited by J. Latacz, pp. 203–204. Homer Kitabevi Yayınları, Istanbul.

Koşay, H. Z. 1951 T. T. K. Tarafından Yapılan Alaca Höyük Kazısı 1937–1939'daki Çalışmalara ve Keşiflere Ait İlk Rapor. Türk Tarih Kurumu Basımevi, Ankara.

Lamb, W. 1932 Schliemann's Prehistoric Sites in the Troad. *Praehistorische Zeitschrift* XXIII:111–131.

Lloyd, S., and J. Mellaart 1956 Beycesultan Excavations, Second Preliminary Report. *Anatolian Studies* 6:101–135.

Lloyd, S., and J. Mellaart (eds.) 1962 *Beycesultan Vol. I, The Chalcolithic and Early Bronze Age Levels*. British Institute of Archaeology at Ankara, London.

Maxwell-Hyslop, K. R. 1971 *Western Asiatic Jewellery c. 3000–612 B.C*. Methuen, London.

Mazar, B., A. Biran, M. Dothan, and I. Dunayevsky 1964 Ein Gev: Excavations in 1961. *Israel Exploration Journal* 14(1–2):1–49.

Mellaart, J. 1957 Anatolian Chronology in the Early Bronze and Middle Bronze Age. *Anatolian Studies* VII:55–88.

Mellaart, J. 1958 The End of the Early Bronze Age in Anatolia and the Aegean. *American Journal of Archaeology* 62(1):9–33.

Mellaart, J. 1967 Anatolia, c. 2300–1750 B.C. In *The Cambridge Ancient History Third Edition* (Vol. 1) *Early History of the Middle East*, edited by I. E. S. Edwards, C. J. Gadd, and N. G. L. Hammond, pp. 681–706. Cambridge University Press, Cambridge.

Mellaart, J. 1982 Archaeological Evidence for Trade Routes between Syria and Mesopotamia and Anatolia during the Early and the Beginning of the Middle Bronze Age. *Studi Eblaiti* V:15–32.

Milojčić, V. 1961 *Samos, Die Prähistorische Siedlung Unter dem Heraion, Grabung 1953 und 1955*. R. Habelt, Bonn.

Öktü, A. 1973 *Die Intermediate-Keramik in Kleinasien*. Inaugural-Dissertation zur Erlangung des Doktorgrades der Philosophie, München.

Özgüç, T., and R. Temizer 1993 The Eskiyapar Treasure. In *Nimet Özgüç'e Armağan Aspects of Art and Iconography: Anatolia and Its Neighbors Studies in Honor of Nimet Özgüç*, edited by M. J. Mellink, E. Porada, and T. Özgüç, pp. 613–628. Türk Tarih Kurumu Basımevi, Ankara.

Podzuweit, C. 1979 *Trojanische Gefäßformen der Frühbronzezeit in Anatolien, der Ägäis und angrenzenden Gebieten*. P. von Zabern, Mainz am Rhein.

Schliemann, H. 1881 *Ilios the City and Country of the Trojans* (reprint edition 1976). Arno, New York.

Schmidt, H. 1902 *Heinrich Schliemann's Sammlung, Trojanischer Altertümer*. G. Reimer, Berlin.

Seton-Williams, M. V. 1954 Cilician Survey. *Anatolian Studies* 4:121–174.

Sperling, J. W. 1976 Kum Tepe in the Troad, Trial Excavation, 1934. *Hesperia* 45(4):305–364.

Symington, D. 2007 The Early Bronze Age Pottery. In *Excavations at Kilise Tepe, 1994–98 from Bronze Age to Byzantine in Western Cilicia*, edited by N. Postgate and D. Thomas, pp. 319–329. McDonald Institute for Archaeological Research, Cambridge.

Temizer, R. 1954 Kayapınar Höyüğü Buluntuları. *Belleten* XVIII/71:317–330.

Theochari, M. D., L. Panama, and E. Hatzipouliou 1993 Kerameike tes Proimes Chalkokratias apo to Palamari tes Skyrou. In *Wace and Blegen: Pottery as Evidence for Trade in the Aegean Bronze Age 1939–1989*, edited by C. Zerner, P. Zerner, and J. Winder, pp. 187–193. Brill, Amsterdam.

Topbaş, A., T. Efe, and A. İlaslı 1998 Salvage Excavations of the Afyon Archaeological Museum, Part 2: The Settlement of Karaoğlan Mevkii and the Early Bronze Age Cemetery of Kaklık Mevkii. *Anatolia Antiqua* VI:21–95.

Yadin, Y., Y. Aharoni, R. Amiran, T. Dothan, I. Dunayevsky, and J. Perrot 1961 The James A. De Rothschild Expedition at Hazor, Hazor III–IV, An account of the Third and Fourth Seasons of Excavations, 1957–1958. The Hebrew University of Jerusalem, Jerusalem.

Yılmaz, D. 2009 Commercial Activities between West and Central Anatolia Regions during the Early Bronze Age. In *SOMA 2007 Proceedings of the XI Symposium on Mediterranean Archaeology*, edited by Ç. Ö. Aygün, pp. 441–448. BAR International Series 1900, Oxford.

Zimmermann, T. 2006 Die Bronze-und früheisenzeitlichen Troiafunde der Sammlung Heinrich Schliemann im Römisch-Germanischen Zentralmuseum. Römisch-German. Zentralmuseum, Mainz.

Catalogue

1. (Fig.6.4:1)Volute handle, moderately fired, wheel-made, tempered with fine sand and few chaff, very fine paste. There is a knob decoration in the middle of the handle. Same knob decoration also affixed to a place immediately below the volute handle. It is in the same shade with the paste, slipped and burnished. Inventory Number: D3/2 245 1 5. Munsell (Munsell soil-color charts, 2009 year revised (2012): Paste 2.5YR 6.6. light red; core 2.5 YR 5.1 reddish gray; inner surface 2.5 YR 6.4 light reddish brown; outer surface 5 YR 6.6 reddish yellow.

2. (Fig.6.4:2)Volute handle, hardly fired, paste tempered with few mica and very few sparse chaff, When viewed from the above, it appears as three paste strips joined together side by side. When viewed from the side, it appears as an inward curled volute. Outer surface is slipped in the same shade with the paste. The handle probably modeled in advance in a mold and then mounted to the vessel. Large size probably belongs to a storage vessel.

Inventory Number: D3/3 21.1 5, paste 2.5 YR 6.6 light red; core 2.5 YR 5.1 reddish gray; inner surface 5YR 6.3 light reddish Brown; Outer surface 5YR 6.3 light reddish brown.

3. (Fig.6.4:3)Volute handle, wheel-made, outer surface slipped, paste tempered with mica, fine chaff and very few sand, hardly fired, very fine paste. Volute handle is shaped by hand and then mounted on the vessel. Inventory Number: D3/2 172.1 2, paste 2.5YR 5.6. red; core 2.5YR 5.6. red; inner surface 5 YR 6.6 reddish yellow; outer surface 7.5 YR 5.6 red.

4. (Fig.6.4:4) Volute handle, wheel-made, very fine paste, tempered with mica, sand, few chaff. It is slipped in the same shape with its paste, unburnished. It has volute handles which were shaped by hand and then mounted on the body. Inventory Number: D3/2 95.1 1, paste 2.5YR 6.4 light reddish Brown; no core; inner surface 5 YR 7.6 reddish yellow; outer surface 7.5 YR 6.4 light Brown.

5. (Fig.6.4:5) Bowl rim fragment with volute handle, diameter (rim) 20 cm, tempered with mica, sand and lime, thick-slipped and burnished. A part of the volute horizontal handle placed right next to the rim has been preserved. The volute handle of the wheel-made bowl was shaped by hand and mounted on the vessel later. Inventory Number: D3/2 162.1 8, paste 2.5YR 6.6 light red; no core; inner surface 10 YR 5.6 red; outer surface 10 YR 5.6 red.

6. (Fig.6.4:6) Trumpet-shaped volute handle, wheel-made, well fired, tempered with few mica, very few chaff and very few grit, fine paste. Outer surface is slipped and burnished. The sherd should belong to a storage vessel. It appears as trumpet-shaped as viewed from the above, volute as viewed from the side, it was made by the help of a mould by hand. Inventory Number: D3/2 310. 1 1, paste 2.5YR 6.6. light red; core 2.5 YR 6.2 Pale red; inner surface 2.5 YR 6.8 light red; outer surface 7.5 YR 6.4 light brown.

CHAPTER SEVEN

Küllüoba Early Bronze Age III Pottery

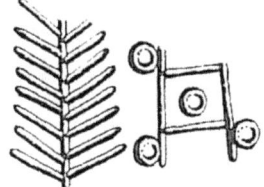

*Murat Türkteki**

The Early Bronze Age III period has not been fully established on the entire Anatolian Peninsula due to an insufficient number of research projects. Unique treasure deposits and burial offerings detected in Anatolia, such as those at Troy and Alacahöyük, or monumental buildings of architecture imply that this period was splendid and also constituted a major step for Anatolia toward urbanization and centralization.

No doubt this is also a result of the effects of the trade network that emerged between Cilicia and Troas. Effects of Syro-Cilicia, and therefore Mesopotamia, reached Troy at the far west of the peninsula over Inland Western Anatolia and even to Thrace and the Aegean world toward the end of the period (Efe 2007; Şahoğlu 2005). Among the characteristic features of this new period are intensified relations with remote regions and innovations in metallurgy and pottery technology.

The chronology of the Western Anatolian EB III could not be fully identified due to lack of a complete correlation between the Tarsus and Troy chronologies, as is the case for the entire EBA chronology. At this point, some important data has been obtained on EB III from Küllüoba (Figure 7.1) excavations under the guidance of Prof. Dr. Turan Efe that has been going on since 1996 in the Eskişehir region, which occupies an important location on a path thought to be a trade route between two remote regions. The excavations in recent years in Kütahya-Seyitömer (Figure 7.1; Bilgen 2011; 2012) as well as the completed salvage excavation in Kaklık Mevkii (Figure 7.1; Efe et al. 1995) in the north of Afyon are also informative on the period.

At Küllüoba the EB III period is divided into two periods, called Early and Late EB III. Early EB III is dated approximately between 2450 and 2200 B.C. and Late EB III is

---

*Associate Professor Doctor Murat Türkteki, Bilecik Şeyh Edebali University, Faculty of Science & Letters, Department of Archeology, Gülümbe Campus, BİLECİK.

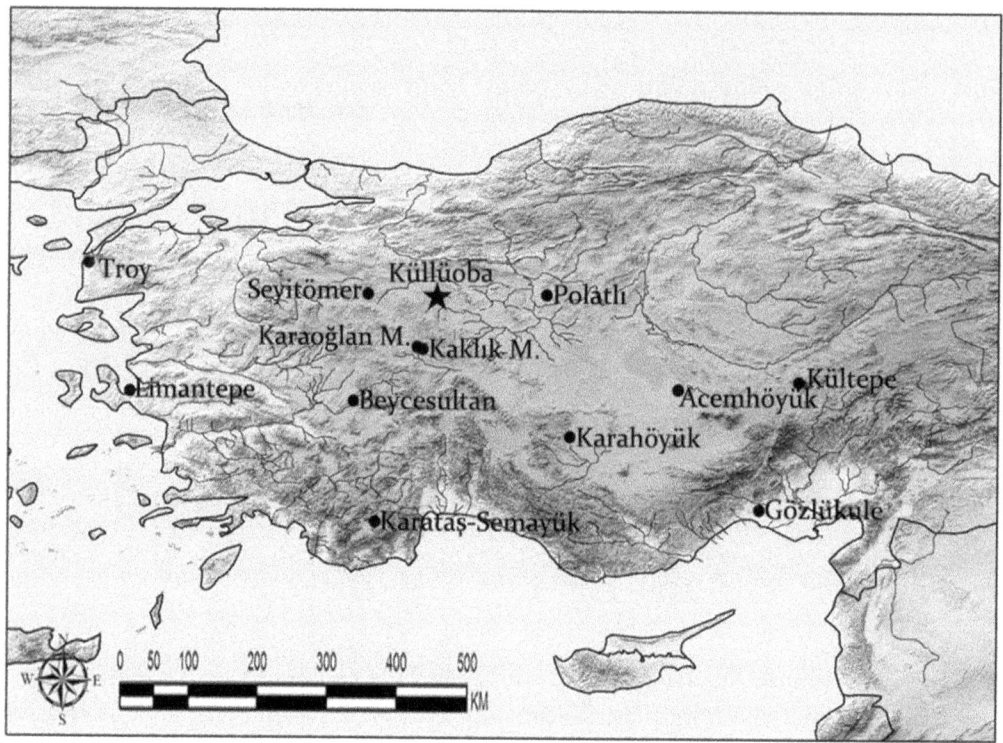

FIGURE 7.1. Major EB III sites in Western Anatolia.

dated between 2200 and 1950 B.C., which is also called transition to the middle Bronze Age period (*Übergangsperiode*) (Figure 7.2). Küllüoba Early EB III is observed stratigraphically in the trenches AA 19 and Z 19 on the empty space that correspond to the yard of the EBA II settlement on the central section of the mound. In the above-mentioned area, layers are clearly separated by floors and fill but with no architectural structures. However, in the Late EB III five phases that have been associated with architecture were discovered. The architectural remains of Early EB III without a plan has been identified in trench AD 18. On the other hand, pottery from EB III is also found in many pits and votive pits all over the settlement. Early EB III is identified in Küllüoba in three phases named as IIIC, IIIB, and IIIA from earliest to latest (Figure 7.2).

In the last phase of the EB II some important changes are observed on pottery forms and ware groups. Incurving rimmed bowls, S-profile carinated bowls, handmade platters, single-handed tankards, and tripod-cooking pots are encountered for the very first time during this period. If we look at ware groups, the prototype of red-coated wares, which will become the characteristic ware of the next phase, and wares named proto-red-coated ware appear.

In phase IIIC, which is the earliest phase of EB III, important changes occurred in ware groups, forms, and most importantly in the technology of pottery manufacture. The

Dates	ANATOLIAN EBA CHRONOLOGY	KÜLLÜOBA			TROY
		Eastern Sector	C 14 Dates	Western Trenches	
2000	Late EB III	IIA	2044-1937 BC		
		IIB	2139-2110 BC		
		IIC	2198-2160 BC		IV
		IID			
2200		IIE			
	Early EB III	IIIA	2314-2197 BC		IIg-III
		IIIB			IIc-f
2400		IIIC			IIb-c
	Late EB II	IVA			IIa
2500		IVB			Ij
		IVC			Ih-i
2600	EB II	IVD	2603-2487 BC		Ig
		IVE			If
2700		IVF		1	Id
	EB I	VA			Ic
2800		VB	2701-2620 BC	2	
		VC	2862-2809 BC		Ib
2900				3	
3000	Transitional Period into the EBA			4	Ia
3100				5	
3200	Late Chalcolithic			6	

FIGURE 7.2. Chronological chart synchronizing the stratigraphies of Küllüoba (with calibrated C14 dates) and Troy.

potter's wheel first started to be used for 3 percent of pottery during the IIIC period, its use increased to 8 percent in the succeeding phase IIIB, and grew to 13 percent in the latest IIIA. The use of this technique of manufacture is of course reflected in forms and ware groups. Specifically, the ware group called plain ware that is the characteristic ware group of this method of manufacture appeared in parallel with the use of the potter's wheel (Figure 7.3). Red-coated wares also appear for the first time during this period. These wares have evolved from proto-red-coated wares, which appeared at the end of the previous Late EB II. Red-coated wares are made of quality paste, are commonly dark red slipped, are well burnished occasionally horizontal or vertical, and are well fired. This ware group is both used for handmade and wheel-made pottery manufacture.

Another ware group appeared during Phase IIIC of Early EB III, a very thin-slipped ware group known as wash ware. Their slip is very thin and in one of two main color tones, red or brown. This ware group is also mostly produced by a potter's wheel.

Along with these ware groups that appeared in the beginning of Early EB III, red-slipped wares that were used since EB II still continue to be used and are now the most widely used ware group in terms of percentage (Figure 7.3). Few examples of grey ware and

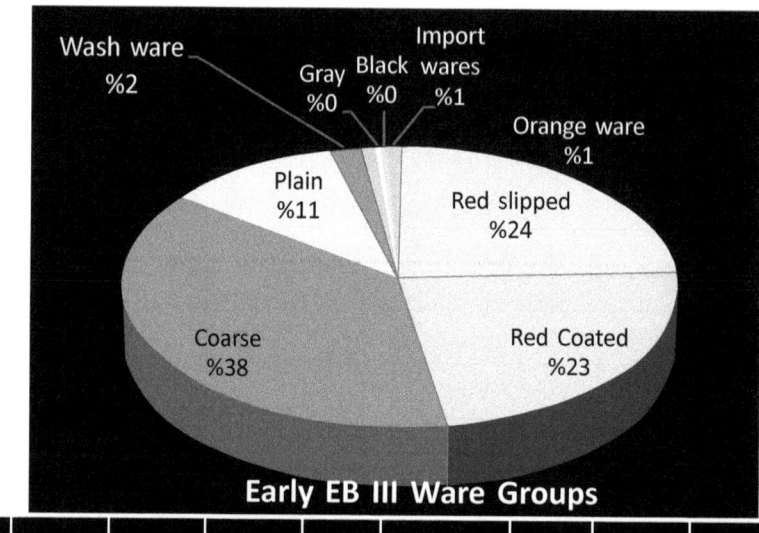

FIGURE 7.3. Percentages of Early EB III Ware Groups.

many orange ware (which are Kütahya-Seyitömer's main ware group and that we associate with the south parts of the region) are found from Early EB III among ware groups that are characteristic of the mentioned period. Coarse ware is commonly used in cooking and storage vessels (Figure 7.3). Therefore, this is the ware group used most commonly.

Some forms are used for the first time during this period, as was the case with ware groups. Sharp S-profile bowls are observed along with incurving rimmed bowls (Figure 7.4e) and slightly S-profile bowls (Figure 7.4c) that persist EB II. Simple profile looped handle bowls decrease (Figure 7.4g). Double-handled deep bowls are horizontally fluted (Figure 7.4h). Slightly carinated bowls (Figure 7.4d), which are characterized with red-coated ware are the characteristic bowl forms of EB III. Examples decorated with red paint also continue to exist during this period. Other decorations of bowls include relief knobs and worm shapes.

Handmade platters are first manufactured during the last phase of Late EB II. Wheel made platters (Figure 7.4a-b) appear for the first time during Phase IIIC. After the potter's wheel started to be used, platters are manufactured increasingly on the wheel. The characteristic ware group of the form named as A2 platter (Figure 7.4b) at Troy is plain ware, while a few slipped versions are found. The flat-profiled platter form, named the A1 platter (Figure 7.4a), can also be counted among the forms that appear in the beginning of the period for the first time.

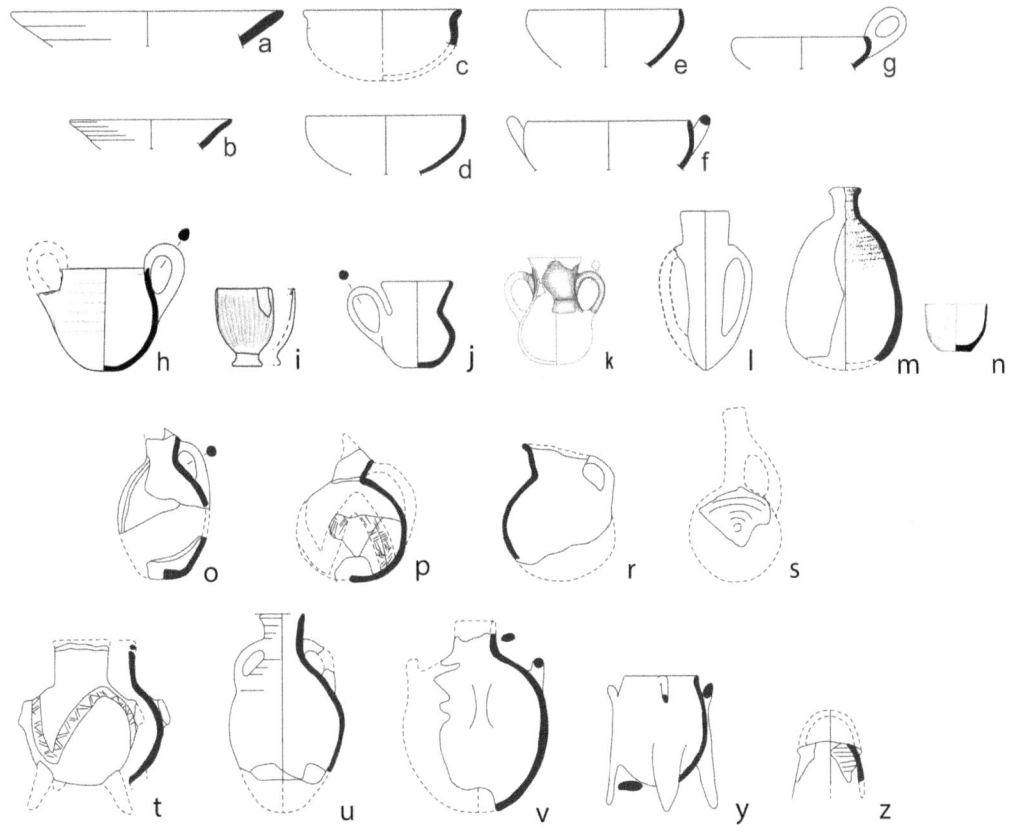

FIGURE 7.4. Küllüoba EB III Forms (Unscaled).

Along with single-handled tankards (Figure 7.4j) present in the latest phase of EB II double-handled examples (Figure 7.4k) are present in EB III. Comparisons with Southeast Anatolia show that the mentioned forms occurred less frequently in the Eskişehir region. Wheel-manufactured versions of the *depa* (Figure 7.4l) that is represented with handmade examples (as opposed to tankard form) in Phase IIIC, which is the earliest phase of EB III, are found often in Küllüoba. The mentioned form is manufactured mostly from red-coated ware in two main types, outturning rims and flat rims. Slips below the rims (*Rim-slip*) are quite characteristic of the *depa* made from red-coated ware. The slip application appeared as a thicker band in the last phase of EB II, but was applied as a thinner band during EB III. One example of a wheel-made *depa* in plain ware and another paint-decorated sample were found.

Another form appearing for the first time in this period is the chalice (Figure 7.4i and Figure 7.5). The metal samples of chalice are also known from Troy. The similar metal examples of this chalice form (especially when decorations are considered) found in Ur kings' tombs suggest that Küllüoba's chalice is manufactured as a metal imitation.

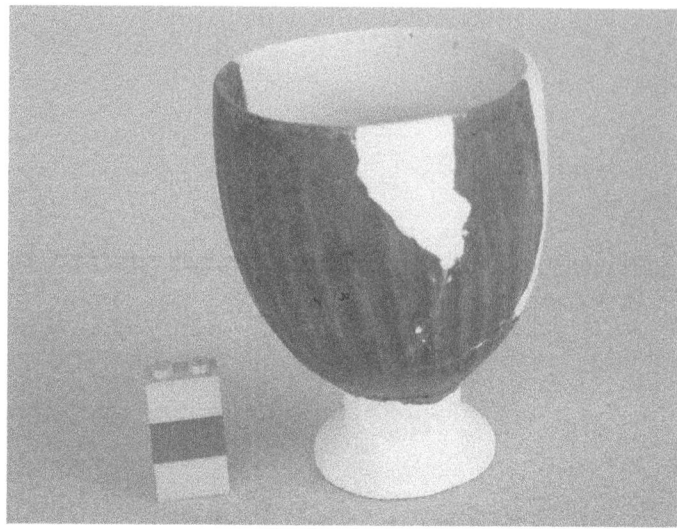

FIGURE 7.5. Chalice from Küllüoba.

Considering this example, we can suggest that some pieces of rims that we believed to be groove-decorated *depa* to date were actually pieces of chalices decorated with horizontal and diagonal flutings.

The change in pottery production, namely, the use of the potter's wheel, had its effects on the forms, which took on more fluent contours and were more plastic in shape. Therefore, the general view of pottery during Early EB III is that rounder and more spherical forms appeared. Wide-necked and cylindrical-necked pots (Figure 7.4t-v) and spherical pots are extensively used. Among handmade pottery forms, the tripod cooking pots (Figure 7.4y) that started to be used from the end of EB II are used frequently during this period. Pieces from bell-shaped (Figure 7.4z), domed, and disc-shaped samples of lids related to the jars are found.

Amphora forms (Figure 7.4u), which were in use since the late Chalcolithic, also started to be produced on the wheel. This form is manufactured in separate pieces on the wheel and then combined, or alternatively only the rim may be shaped on the wheel and then attached to the body. The form took a more elliptical shape in this period.

The beak-spouted jug form that was used in the region since the beginning of the EBA persisted during EBA III, although the number of findings in Küllüoba is not high during this period (Figure 7.4o-s). Also, a few beak-spouted jugs with backward-leaning necks (Figure 7.4p) are found that can be associated with the south of Eskişehir region in the form of concentric shallow flutes and reserved slip with grooved lozenges. The first examples of the wheel-made beak-spouted jug form (Figure 7.4o) also occurred during this period, as well as flask-shaped versions (Figure 7.4s) of the same form.

Some import ware groups and forms arrive in the region for the first time due to intensive relations with remote regions, during EB III. One of these new forms, called a beaker, (Figure 7.4n) originated from Northern Syria. Among those forms found so far in Anatolia only those that are found in Küllüoba are produced from ware groups that are completely foreign to the region.

Another form that points to relations between remote regions are Syrian bottles. Alabastron-shaped (Figure 7.4m), sphere-bodied, slightly out-turning rimmed long-necked versions of the forms are found especially in Northern Syria, especially in the Middle Euphrates Basin. Single- or double-rimmed pieces belonging to Syrian bottles that are encountered in late phases of Early EB III in Western Anatolia are also found in Küllüoba. A piece that is spiral burnished, called a ring burnish and which is possibly a part of the mentioned form, displays similarities with the Tarsus example. It is understood that all pieces of bottles represented imported ware groups.

Conclusion

Küllüoba Early EB III pottery displays important similarities with Troy, especially in the introduction process and phases. Tankards appear in Küllüoba for the first time in Phase IVA at the end of EB II as stated above. Later, the first use of the potter's wheel occurs in Phase IIIC, the first phase of EB III. Also, *depa* appear as handmade for the first time in this first phase. All this information suggests that Troy IIc and Küllüoba IIIC phases are contemporary (Figure 7.2; Blegen et al. 1950; Türkteki 2013). The fact that wheel-made *depa*, amphorae, necked-jars, and Syrian bottles are observed in Küllüoba during Phases IIIB and IIIA suggests that these phases are parallel with Troy IIg and Troy III. Calibrated C14 results for the mentioned Phase IIIA point to the interval between 2314 and 2197 B.C. (Table 8.1). Based on these assessments we can conclude that Tarsus EB IIIA is contemporary with Küllüoba Early EB III layers.

Based on the information obtained mainly from pottery, the socioeconomic order that appeared in Western Anatolia at the end of EB II and the political structure move toward centralization at the end of EBA III. This is demonstrated by the reduced number of settlements and by the increasing concentration of the population in certain centers. On the other hand the cultural regions that are mostly determined by pottery persist during this period almost within the same boundaries (Sarı 2013). The fact that pottery detected in Küllüoba from EB III includes forms and ware groups that persist from the previous period show that there is no interruption in the process. However, the use of potter's wheel technology, imported forms, and ware groups suggest that relations with the remote regions occurred intensely.

The main reason for the organized trade-based relationship between two remote regions of Mesopotamia and Inland Western Anatolia seems to be that in the former no mines existed and there was a developed central Akkadian state formation. Copper, gold, and silver mines in Western Anatolia were probably controlled by regional powers. This fact is the most important reason for the development of urbanization and for the appearance of a new ruling class in Western Anatolia. On the other hand, fulfillment of the needs of the elite class is the reason for more intensive mining activities and use of new techniques in metallurgy.

The coverage of the trade network is extended at the end of the period when imported pottery is found between the east border of Euphrates on the one side and Thrace and the Aegean on the other. The weights found in many settlements during this period (Rahmstorf 2006) show that common metrology was established between regions. For the trade to become possible, the basic needs and security must have been established and interregional political agreements must have occurred. Some statements in Akkad texts verify this situation. All these developments appearing during this period have provided the infrastructure for the political structure and trade routes that took shape during Late EB III.

References Cited

Blegen, C., J. L. Caskey, M. Rawson 1950 *Troy I, General Introduction, The First and Second Settlements*. Princeton University Press, Princeton.

Bilgen, N. 2011 *Seyitömer Höyük Kazısı Ön Raporu (2006–2010)*. Dumlupınar Üniversitesi Fen-Edebiyat Fakültesi Arkeoloji Bölümü, Kütahya.

Bilgen, N. 2012 *Seyitömer Höyük Kazısı Ön Raporu (2011–2012)*. Dumlupınar Üniversitesi Fen-Edebiyat Fakültesi Arkeoloji Bölümü, Kütahya.

Efe, T., A. İlaslı, and A. Topbaş 1995 Salvage Excavations of the Afyon Archaeological Museum, Part 1: Kaklık Mevkii, A Site Transitional to the Early Bronze Age. *Studia Troica* Band 5:357–399.

Efe, T. 2007 The Theories of the "Great Caravan Route" between Cilicia and Troy: The Early Bronze Age III Period in Inland Western Anatolia. *Anatolian Studies* 57:47–64.

Rahmstorf, L. 2006 Zur Ausbreitung vor der asiatischer Innovationen in die Frühbronzezeitlische Agäis. *Praehistorische Zeitschrift* 81:49–96.

Sarı, D. 2013 Evolution culturelle et politique de l'Anatolie de l'Ouest au bronze ancien et au bronze moyen. ANRT, Lille.

Şahoğlu, V. 2005 The Anatolian Trade Network and the Izmir Region during the Early Bronze Age. *Oxford Journal of Archaeology* 24:339–361.

Türkteki, M. 2013 The First Use of Wheel-Made Pottery and Its Distribution in Western and Central Anatolia. In *Soma 2012 Identity and Connectivity, Proceedings of the 16th Symposium on Mediterranean Archaeology, Italy, 1–3 March 2012* Vol. I, edited by L. Bombardieri, A. D'Agostino, G. Guarducci, V. Orsi, and S. Valentini, pp. 193–200. BAR International Series 2581, Oxford.

CHAPTER EIGHT

The Figurine/Idol Types of Western Anatolia in the Early Bronze Age and Their Relationship with Cultural Regions

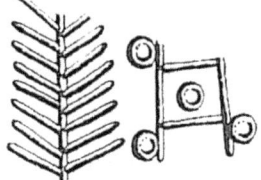

*Deniz Sari**

In Western Anatolia, certain cultural features of the Early Bronze Age begin to occur during the later phases of the Late Chalcolithic Period, the timespan which is called either "EBA IA" or "Transitional Period into the EBA." This becomes especially apparent in the emergence of local pottery distribution areas. It was K. Bittel (1942) and A. Goetze (1950) who first drew attention to the distinct cultural groups in Western Anatolia during the Early Bronze Age. In the 1960s J. Mellaart and D. H. French mentioned the existence of local pottery regions and defined the boundaries of these regions (French 1969; Lloyd and Mellaart 1962). In the light of recent investigations T. Efe (2003), on the other hand, speaks of the existence of "cultural regions," the borders of which were mainly determined by pottery, and within each of these cultural regions there were also closely related "local pottery groups" in the first half of the third millennium B.C. (EBA I-II). The boundaries of these regions in question mostly overlap with the distribution areas of the cultural groups based on the pottery features of the Neolithic and Early Chalcolithic Periods (Efe and Ay Efe 2007:251–268).

The pottery groups have not always had clear-cut boundaries, and often buffer zones are formed along the common borders. Certain pottery groups have more common traits in comparison to the others, and these form larger units, which we call "Cultural Regions." The boundaries of Cultural Regions and pottery groups are primarily determined by pottery and, to a lesser degree, by some small finds such as figurines and idols, as well as certain architectural traditions. These Regions are: "Troy-Yortan," "Bithynia," "Phrygia," "Büyük Menderes–Upper Porsuk," and "Lycia-Pisidia" (Figures 8.1–8.3).

---

*Associate Professor Dr. Deniz Sarı, Bilecik Şeyh Edebali University, Faculty of Science & Letters, Department of Archeology, Gülümbe Campus, BİLECİK.

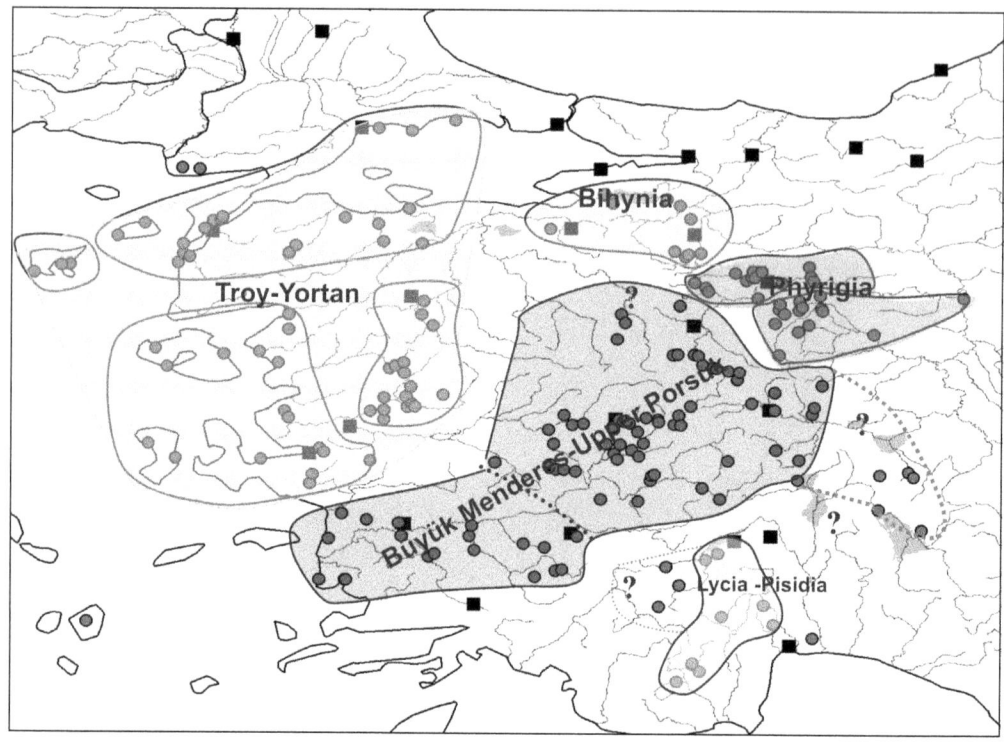

FIGURE 8.1. The Early Bronze Age I Cultural Regions and Pottery Groups of Western Anatolia.

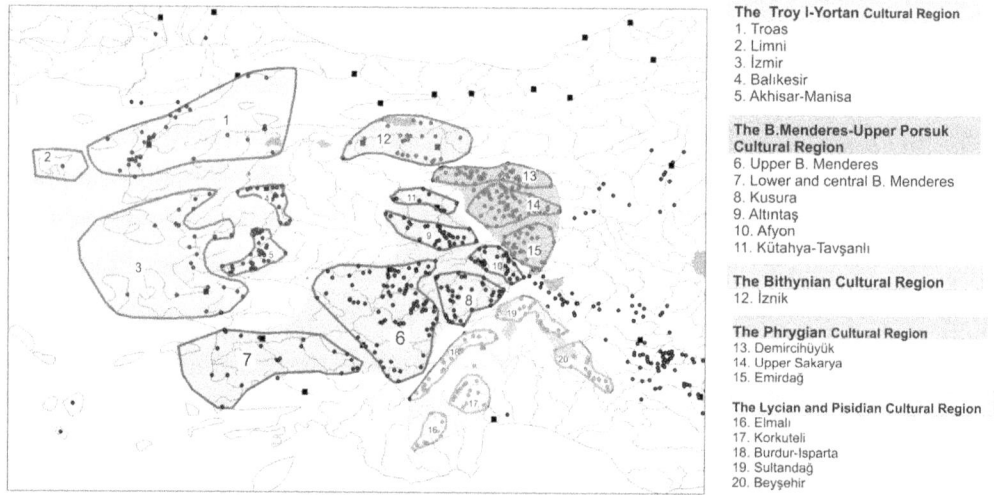

FIGURE 8.2. The Early Bronze Age II Cultural Regions and Pottery Groups of Western Anatolia.

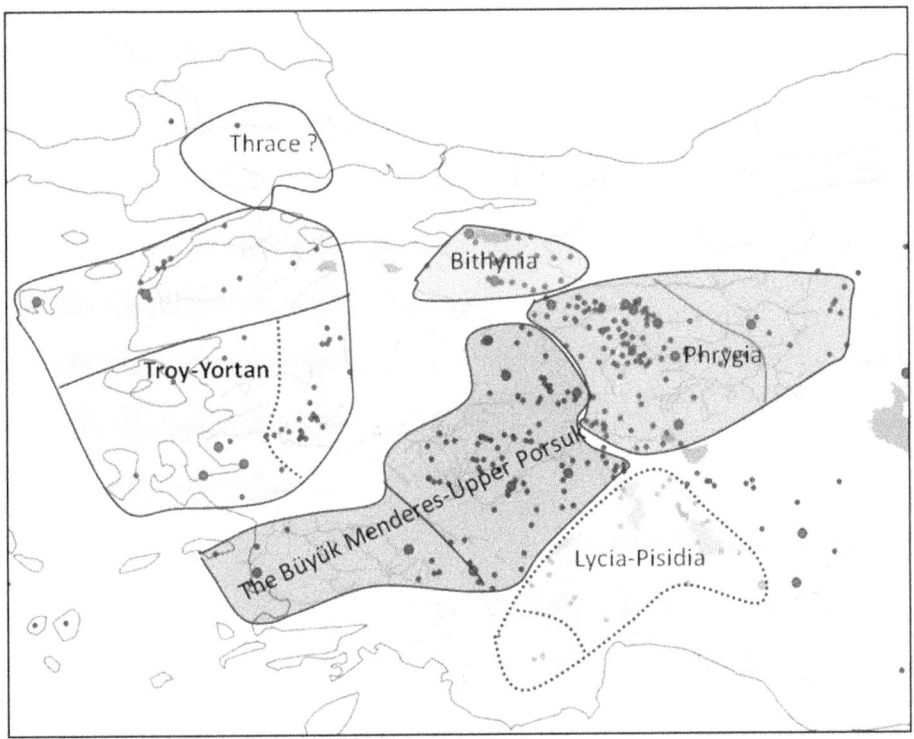

FIGURE 8.3. The Early Bronze Age III Cultural Regions and Pottery Groups of Western Anatolia.

Although we trace certain changes, over time, of the distribution areas of some of these cultural regions, they seem to have survived until the end of second millennium B.C. The best known cultural regions are as follows:[1]

THE TROY-YORTAN CULTURAL REGION

The "Kumtepe IB" culture of the period transitional into the EBA of this region is followed by the "Troy I-Yortan Cultural Region in the succeeding EBA I." Dark-faced burnished wares, bowls with interior-thickened rims (with or without pedestal) and anti-splash bowls often with tubular lugs are the most characteristic features of Troy-Yortan Cultural Region.

The settlement patterns and Trojan-style marble idols are the other common cultural features that prevail throughout the region. The settlement layout consists of adjacent longhouses attached to the defensive wall at their backs. On the other hand, certain pottery wares, forms, and stylistic features help us determine the boundaries of the local pottery groups within this Cultural Region.

The Bithynian Cultural Region

The Bithynian Cultural Region, which is characterized by grey-brown burnished wares and flaring bowls, is a buffer region that contains features specific to both Troia-Yortan and Phrygia Cultural Regions.

The Phyrigian Cultural Region

The Phrygian Cultural Region covers the plains of Eskişehir and Yukarı Sakarya, the highlands of Phrygia, and the area around Emirdağ. These geographical regions overlap with the distribution areas of the pottery groups. Eventually, in the early EB III the Afyon Plain is integrated into the Phrygian Cultural Region. Some of the most characteristic features of the Phrygian Cultural Region are red-slipped and burnished wares, black-topped wares, simple-profile bowls often with loop handles, red cross or multiple cross bowls and cross-band bottles, S-profiled bowls of the late EBA II, and baked clay idols. The Demircihöyük pottery group is particularly characterized by black-topped ware, which is hardly represented in the Yukarı Sakarya group. Red-slipped and burnished ware becomes more and more popular toward the end phases of the EB II. The characteristic settlement layout of this cultural region is defined as "Anatolian Settlement Plan" by Korfmann. This is a layout in which a central court is surrounded by adjacent row-houses which are attached to the defensive wall at their backs.

The Büyük Menderes–Upper Porsuk Cultural Region

The Büyük Menderes–Upper Porsuk Cultural Region covers most of inland Western Anatolia. The Akşehir Plain is also an integral part of this cultural region in the EBA I. The pottery of this vast area is characterized by vessels of fine wares that are generally thin-walled, slipped either black or bright red, and decorated with wide and shallow fluting. This pottery group is also called "Beycesultan EBA I Cultural Region."

In the EBA II period many local pottery groups can be identified within the boundaries of Büyük Menderes–Upper Sakarya Cultural Region, except the Akşehir Plain. These are: Lower and Middle B. Menderes, Upper B. Menderes, Afyon and Kusura, Altıntaş, and Kütahya-Tavşanlı. Over time, at Beycesultan a new pottery tradition emerges within Yukarı B; the Menderes Group, which is completely different from the previous EBA I Cultural Region. Marble or limestone idols are characteristic in the region, different from the Phrygian Cultural Region.

The Lycian-Pisidian Cultural Region

Almost nothing is known—except on the Elmalı plain—about the EBA I pottery tradition of the Lycia and Pisidia Cultural Region. The distribution areas of the pottery groups are more concrete in the EB II. These are: Elmalı, Korkuteli, Burdur, Sultandağ, and Beyşehir. Red or gray-slipped and burnished wares are very characteristic in the region.

Pinkish-red-slipped pottery—often painted in white—is very typical in the Elmalı region. Clay idols and Kusura-type marble idols both occur frequently in the Lake District. Also, the cooking pots with tripods and the vessels with strainer spouts provide analogies with lower Büyük Menderes valley and the Aegean coastal region.

Western Anatolian Figurine/Idol Types, Their Development through the EBA, and Their Relations with the Cultural Regions

Two main statuette types exist during the EBA; one is completely naturalistic and are defined as "figurine," and the other is mostly flat and schematized and called "idols." Figurines are always made of clay while idols are mostly shaped of stone. Bone idol examples appear during the beginning of EBA III, while rare lead examples are encountered during late EBA III. The most common figurine/idol types encountered in Western Anatolia during EBA are Trojan-style stone/marble idols (Figure 8.4:a), Violin-shaped marble idols (Figure 8.4:b), Kusura-type idols (Figure 8.4:c), Beycesultan-Kusura-type idols (Figure 8.4:d), Demircihöyük-type clay idols (Figure 8.4:f), owl-faced idols (Figure 8.4:e), Bone idols (Figure 8.4:j), Çaykenar-type idols (Figure 8.4:g), and disc-faced figurines (Figure 8.4:i).

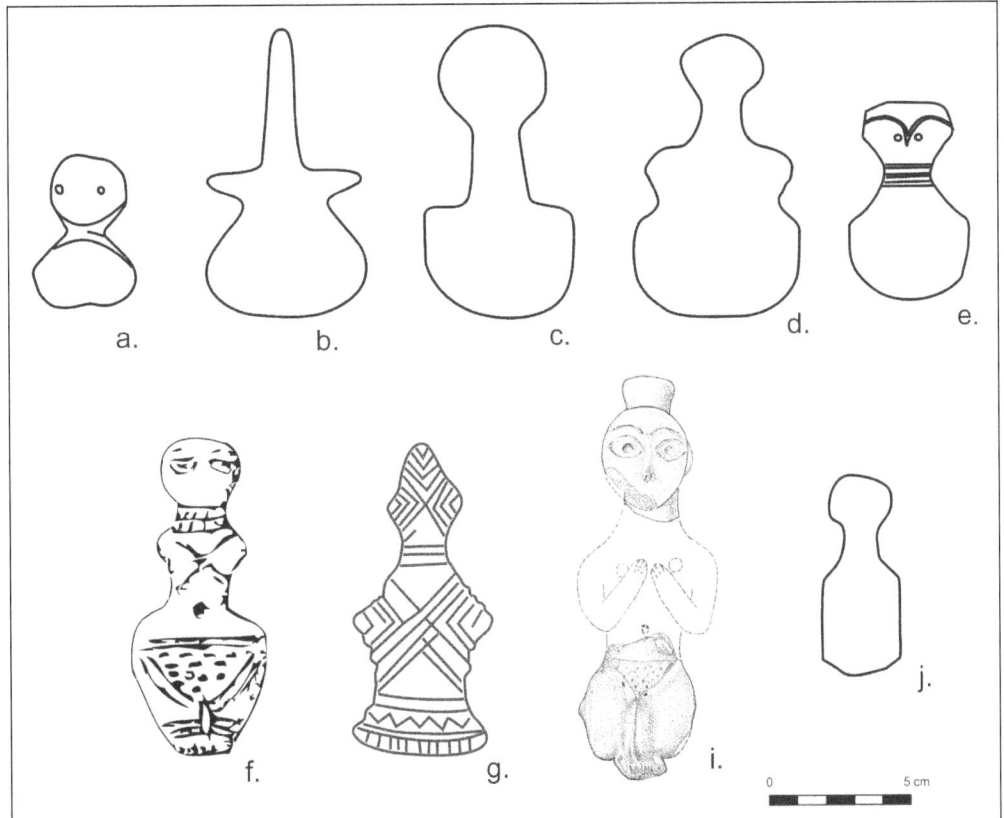

Figure 8.4. Western Anatolian figurine/idol types in the Early Bronze Age.

Transitional Period into the EBA

Clay figurines appear in the Neolithic Period over all of Anatolia while a new group called "Kilia-type Marble idols" is encountered in Coastal Western Anatolia during the Late Chalcolithic Period. These idols are called Kilia type after the site situated in the Gelibolu Peninsula where the first such idol was found. These idols have a thin, flat body and neck, and a large head in contrast with the body. Another, more characteristic feature of these idols is that the arms curl upward from the elbow. Curled arms, as well as legs, are specified with grooves (Takaoğlu 2005:162). The distribution area of the Kilia idols, dated mostly to the Late Chalcolithic Period, covers the coastal region lying on the west of the plateau. The Kulaksızlar marble workshop situated in Manisa is one of these centers where Kilia-type figurines were produced and distributed. The other sites from which other Kilia figurines come are Troy, Beşik-Yassı Tepe, Hanaytepe, Yortan, Aphrodisias, Karain, Çine Tepecik, and Çukuriçi (Takaoğlu 2005:38).

Early Bronze Age I

"Troy-type" marble or limestone idols appear in Northwestern Anatolia, within the distribution area of the pottery groups of Troas, İzmir, and probably Yortan during almost the entire EBA (Figure 8.5). These idols are very small in size and heavily stylized. Only the head and body are distinct, even if crudely. The body is round, shaped like a shovel, or rectangular. The neck is not distinct in many examples; and the details of the body are not clear. Among the sites where these types of idols are encountered are Troy, Aphrodisias, Tepecik Çine, Karataş Semayük, Kusura, and Bakla Tepe.

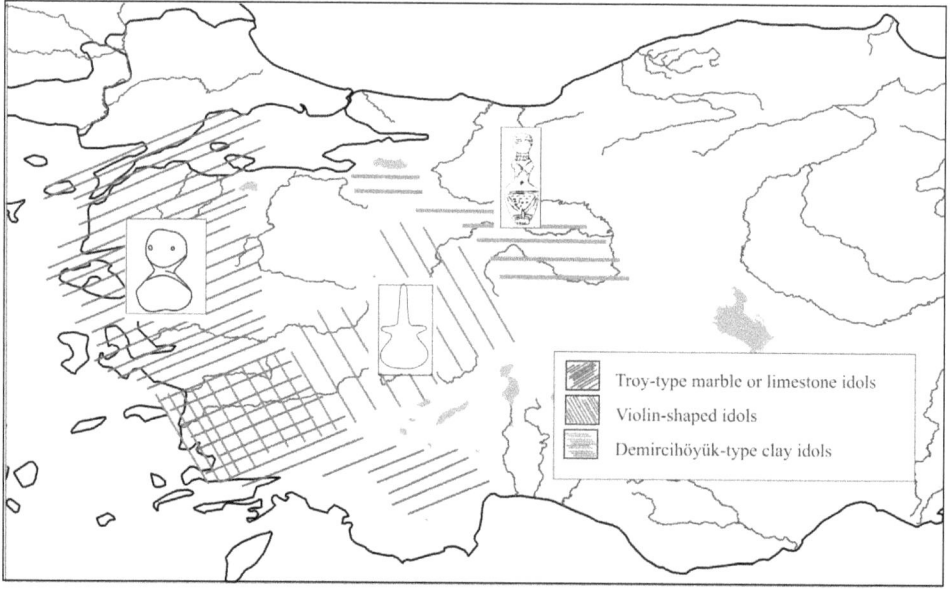

FIGURE 8.5. The distribution of the idol types in the Early Bronze Age I.

However, in Beycesultan "violin-shaped" idols are characteristic in the EBA I. These are commonly round, or round-like, or rectangular-bodied, with a pointed head and with arms in the form of protuberances (Lloyd and Mellaart 1962:Figure F.1). A similar type of idol is found on the surface of Subak Mound in the east of Emet (Efe 1994) and also in the Çine Tepecik Mound (Günel 2007:236; 2008:Figure 1). Thus, we can stress that these types of figurines may spread through the distribution area of the Beycesultan EBA I pottery (Figure 8.5).

Since the EBA I period is not sufficiently investigated in the Lake District in the south, it is difficult to make any concrete statements on the figurine/idol characteristics of the region during the period in question.

There are no stone figurines or idols found in the Phrygian Cultural Region during the EBA I while clay statuettes are mostly shaped as idols, as well known from Demircihöyük (Figure 8.5). The square or triangular pubic areas are always engraved (Obladen-Kauder 1996). A similar development is also observed at Hacılartepe, which represents the Bithynian Cultural Region (Eimermann 2008:412).

Early Bronze Age II

The highest number of figurines and idols comes from the EBA II; therefore, the relationships between the distribution areas of the figurines and idols and that of the Cultural Regions can be established in a more concrete way. During this period, the production of Troy-type idols continued in Northwestern Anatolia (Figure 8.6). However, while stone idols are encountered in Layers I and II in Thermi, Lesbos, baked clay figurines replaced these in Layers III and IV as a part of the local diversity (Lamb 1936:146). The same is

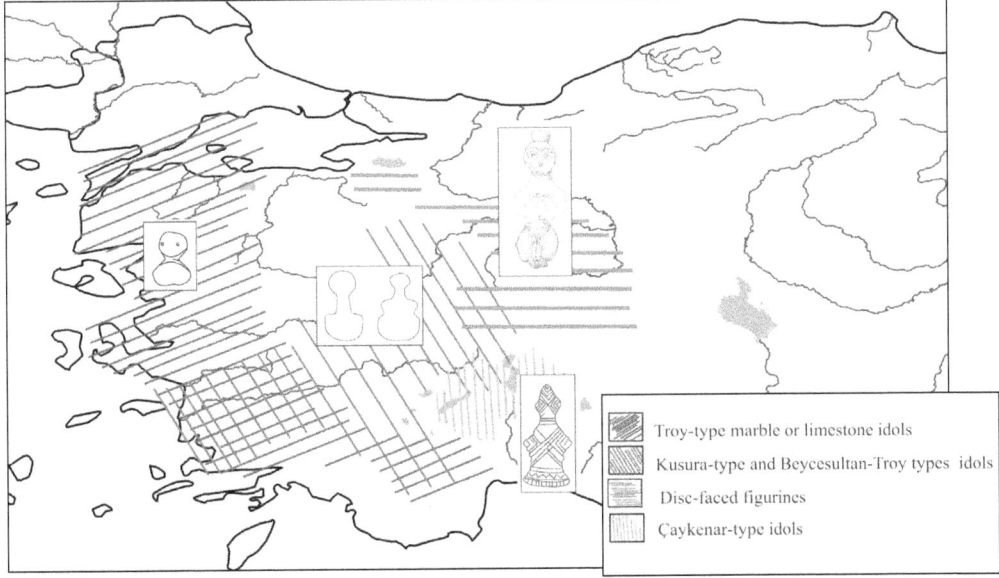

Figure 8.6. The distribution of the idol / figurine types in the Early Bronze Age II.

true for Yenibademli Höyük in Gökçeada where most of the EBA II figurines are made of baked clay with a few stone-made examples (Bülbül Akyol 2006:203). These types of idols appear in Aphrodisias, situated in the Central Büyük Menderes basin, which always constitutes a buffer zone (Joukowsky 1986:212–213).

In the EBA II, the marble idols now known as the "Kusura-type" idols appear in the Büyük Mendres–Upper Porsuk Basins (Figure 8.6; Renfrew 1969:5, 27). These idols have round or triangular heads with bodies that are commonly round, rectangular, or shovel-shaped, and usually have a significantly long neck. A few of these are found in Kusura, from which the type derives its name from (Lamb 1937; 1938). Among other centers where this type is encountered are Beycesultan (Lloyd and Mellaart 1962), Karaoğlan Place (Topbaş et al. 1998), Kaklık Place (Topbaş et al. 1998), Aphrodisias Joukouwsky 1986), and Karahisar (Akdeniz 2002). These also appear in the south in Karataş Semayük (Mellink 1964, 1967) through the EBA II. Stylistically this idol reflects a mix of features of Beycesultan and Troy types and is distributed over a large area from Tavas and Elmalı Plains in the south to Emet and Eskişehir plains in the north (Figure 8.6; Seeher 2000). These types of marble idols also exist in museums in Inland Western Anatolia, obtained through trade. Marble idols are rendered in a mixture of Kusura and Beycesultan types, which mostly have a violin-shaped body, and a disc-shaped head. Some examples contain a *polos* on the rear head, which has been recognized as hair. These types of idols are found mostly from Afyon and Yalvaç surroundings and obtained by purchasing by museums (Bilgi 2013:205, 208).

Baked clay idols having faces decorated with dense, deep grooves are found in the Isparta, Burdur, Bucak, and Korkuteli areas within the Lake District (Figure 8.6). These baked clay idols with flat heads, sack-like bodies, and shoulders represented by protuberances were introduced as the "Çaykenar-type" by T. E. Peet (1909) because they had been found first near the village of Çaykenar in Korkuteli. Frequently, the head and body contain zigzag motifs carved in deep grooves, with occasional diagonal grooved bands on the chest. These types of idols, which are in many national and overseas museums, are also unearthed in Kuruçay and Bademağacı excavations of the region (Duru 1996, 2003, 2005). However, Çaykenar-type idols are also found in Kusura along with Kusura-type idols (Lamb 1937: Figure 11.1); which suggest that these types of idols penetrated into the neighboring region to the north.

The EBA I baked clay idols of the Phrygian Cultural Region gradually develop into the figurines specific to this region during the early EBA II. These figurines, so-called disc-faced (*Scheibengesicht*) figurines, are shaped in a standing or sitting position. They have a round or oval disk-shaped face; with a *polos* behind the head; having eyebrows, eyes, and mouth carved in grooves; commonly having one to four holes for earrings on the ears. Frequently, the hands are placed beneath the chest, while some are placed on the knees. The mostly triangular or squarish pubic area is delineated with grooves and the area inside is filled with dots (Ay Efe 2006:92). Disc-faced figurines from this period are observed in the İznik-İnegöl region having strong influences from the Phrygian Cultural Region in this period, as well as in the distribution area of the Afyon Pottery Group (Figure 8.6). Disk-faced figurines and marble idols are found together in

Karaoğlan Mevkii in the burial tomb 1 of Kaklık Cemetery in the Afyon Plain (Topbaş et al. 1998). The Afyon Pottery Group appears to have been a buffer zone between the regions to the north and south, as we can judge from the pottery itself. The figurine with a disc-face that comes from Isparta Şarkikaraağaç, the so-called Nudra figurine, can also be considered part of this group (Aydıngün 2003:lev 45a).

EARLY BRONZE AGE III

In the succeeding early EBA III, the trade relations between distant regions became more intense. This development led to the gradual disappearance of the local differences between material groups such as pottery and idols. However, the mosaic of cultural regions and pottery groups mostly continues. As a reflection of intensive trade, the potter's wheel is used for the first time and, thus, new wares and forms of pottery appear in regions along the "Great Caravan Route," such as Phrygia and the Troad. Parallel to these developments, the marble idols as well as bone idols are characteristic in the entire region of Western Anatolia. Marble idols from this period along with a few Western Anatolian pottery forms spread throughout Central Anatolia (such as Kültepe marble idols [Bilgi 2013:210–211]) as far east as the Euphrates River in Southeast Anatolia (i.e., Western Anatolian–type marble idols from Titriş Höyük [Algaze et al. 1995:Figure 35]).

While Kusura-type idols continued to be produced in Central Western Anatolia during early EBA III for a little longer (Harmanören [Özsait 2000:Figure 8.7], Küllüoba [Efe-Türkteki 2011:333, 384, 386], Kaklık Place [Efe-Türkteki 2011:346, 476]), Troy-type stone and bone idols (Blegen et al. 1950:Figure 127) penetrate the entirety of Western Anatolia during the later phases of the EBA III (Figure 8.7). Therefore during this period,

FIGURE 8.7. The distribution of the idol types in the Early Bronze Age III.

a development toward cultural homogeneity can be observed in Anatolia, which is a result of intense cultural and trade relations, as can be observed in idols and other find groups. Now the heads and necks of the marble idols are made more distinct and eyebrows, eyes, and noses are frequently specified with grooves. These are defined as "Owl-faced idols" by Schliemann (1875:37). Troy-type idols are found in the tombs dated to Late Troy II at Bakla Tepe in the south of İzmir (Özkan-Erkanal 1999). These types of idols are also found at Seyitömer and Küllüoba in Inland Western Anatolia (Efe-Türkteki 2011). Most of the Seyitömer idols are made locally of marl.

Conclusion

Naturalistic steotopic statuettes, which are associated with the Mother Goddess Cult, are common in Western Anatolia during the Neolithic and Early Chalcolithic Periods. Figurines and idols that are very rare or not found in the settlements from Late Chalcolithic Period appear to have regained importance beginning from the EBA I, parallel with the changes in the cultural developments. These artifacts display some differences over all of the Anatolian Peninsula according to the periods and geographical/cultural regions that are expressed in terms of raw materials, preference of figurines over idols, stylistic features, and decorations.

In this context, the primary shift and regionalization in Anatolian plastic arts must extend into the Late Chalcolithic Period. While entirely clay figurines are observed in the Neolithic Period, a new tradition is encountered during the Late Chalcolithic Period in coastal Western Anatolia named as "Cilia-type Marble idols." Local differences started to emerge gradually during the Late Chalcolithic Period, possibly due to discovery of new sources of raw materials. In this context, mainly marble stone statuettes are frequently encountered in the coastline of Western Anatolia now produced in marble workshops.

Processing marble is much more difficult compared to clay; thus, possibly due to raw material preference, schematized figurines are found more frequently after the Late Chalcolithic compared to the previous period. "EBA Cultural Regions" begin to occur during the last quarter of the fourth millennium B.C., that is, the Transitional Period into the Early Bronze Age. It is not possible to make any solid statements on the traditions of figurines and idols of this period. However, when the Kumtepe IB culture spread in Northwestern Anatolia, the Kilia-type marble idol tradition must have continued from the previous period. No figurines or idols are found in Inland Western Anatolia during this period. The boundaries of the cultural regions appear more distinctively in the next EBA I period. Along with pottery, other finds such as figurines and idols increased in diversity and contribute to the establishment of the boundaries of the cultural regions. This time, the Troy-Yortan and Bithynian Cultural Regions emerge within the distribution area of the Kumtepe IB culture of the previous period. The Troy-type marble and stone idols that characterize the region spread through the Lower and Central Büyük Menderes basins. Meanwhile, the Büyük Menderes–Upper Porsuk Cultural Region (where the Beycesultan

EBA I pottery is characteristic) is represented by violin-shaped idols. The baked clay idol tradition exists in the Phrygian Cultural Region. The relationship between the distribution areas of the figurines/idols and Cultural Regions could be determined in a more concrete way due to the increasing number of statuettes found in the next period, EBA II. Though having more diversity in the forms of Troy-type idols in the Troy-Yortan Cultural Region, baked clay idols appear in Yenibademli and Thermi as a new local variation. At this time Kusura-type marble idols appear in the Büyük Menderes–Upper Porsuk Cultural Region; Disc-faced figurines appear in the Phrygian Cultural Region and Çaykenar idols in the Lycian-Pisidian Cultural Region. However, Çaykenar idols are found in Kusura, while Kusura-type idols are found in Harmanören, and disc-faced figurines are found in the Afyon Plain, which suggest that the interregional relations are intensified at the end of the period, due to cultural and political developments. In the succeeding EBA III, as a result of intensified trade relations between the distant regions, local differences between material groups such as pottery and idols slowly disappear while the earlier mosaic of the Cultural Regions and Pottery Groups mostly persist. While marble and bone idols now become dominant in the entirety of Western Anatolia, baked clay figurines and idols almost disappear. Troy-type idols exist in the Troy-Yortan, Bithynian, and Phrygian Regions, most probably due to the Great Caravan Route. Kusura-type idols are dominant in the Büyük Menderes–Upper Porsuk and Lycian-Pisidian Cultural Regions.

In conclusion, the distribution areas of Western Anatolian figurines and idols is established by taking their types and stylistic features into consideration, mainly overlap with those of the cultural regions determined by pottery distribution areas. This situation supports the hypothesis of "Cultural Regions."

Note

1. For more information on Western Anatolian Cultural Region and Pottery Groups, see Efe 2003; Sarı 2012.

References Cited

Akdeniz, E. 2002 Akdeniz Erken Tunç Çağına Ait Bir Grup İdol. *Anadolu Araştırmaları* XVI:9–18.
Algaze, G., P. Goldberg, D. Honça, T. Matney, A. Mısır, A. Rosen, D. Schlee, and L. Somers 1995 Titris Höyük, A Small Early Bronze Age Urban Center in Southeastern Anatolia: The 1994 Season. *Anatolica* 21:13–64.
Ay-Efe, D. Ş. M. 2006 Küllüoba'da Bulunmuş Olan Pişmiş Toprak Figürinlerden Birkaç Örnek. In *Hayat Erkanal'a Armağan. Kültürlerin Yansıması*, edited by A. Erkanal and S. Günel, pp. 90–94. Homer Bookstore, Istanbul.
Aydıngün, Ş. 2003 *Eski Tunç Çağında Anadolu Pişmiş Toprak Figürin ve İdolleri*, Hacettepe Üniversitesi Sosyal Bilimler Enstitüsü. Unpublished PhD Thesis.
Bilgi, Ö. 2013*Anadolu'dan İnsan Görüntüleri*. Aygaz Yayınları, Istanbul.
Bittel, K. 1942 *Kleinasiatische Studien*. Istanbuler Mitteilungen Heft 5, Istanbul.

Bittel, K. 1945 *Gründgzuge der Vor-und Frügeschichte Kleinasiens*. Verlag Ernst Wasmuth, Tübingen.

Blegen C., J. L. Caskey, M. Rawson, and J. Sperling 1950 *Troy I: General Introduction—The First and Second Settlements*. Princeton University Press, Princeton.

Bülbül Akyol, H. 2006 Gökçeada-Yenibademli Höyük'ten Bir Grup İnsan Figürini. In *Hayat Erkanal'a Armağan; Kültürlerin Yansıması/ Studies in Honor of Hayat Erkanal; Cultural Reflections*, edited by A. Erkanal Öktü, E. Özgen, S. Günel et al., pp. 200–205. Homer Kitabevi, Istanbul.

Duru, R. 1996 Kuruçay Höyük II, 1978–1988 Kazılarının Sonuçları Kalkolitik ve İlk Tunç Çağı Yerleşmeleri. Türk Tarih Kurumu Basımevi, Ankara.

Duru, R. 2003 Bademağacı Kazıları 2000 ve 2001 Yılları Çalışma Raporu. *Belleten* LXVI(246):549–594.

Duru, R. 2005 Bademağacı Kazıları 2002 ve 2003 Yılları Çalışma Raporu. *Belleten* LXVIII(252): 519–560.

Efe, T. 2003 Pottery Distribution within the Bronze Age of Western Anatolia and Its Implications upon Cultural, Political (and Ethnic?) Entities. In *Archaeological Essays in Honour of Homo amatus: Güven Arsebük için Armağan Yazılar*, edited by M. Özbaşaran, O. Tanındı, and A. Boratav, pp. 87–105. Ege Yayınları, Istanbul.

Efe, T. 1994 1992 Yılında Kütahya, Bilecik ve Eskişehir İllerinde Yapılan Yüzey Araştırmaları. XI. *Araştırma Sonuçları Toplantısı*:571–592. Ankara.

Efe, T., and D. Ş. M. Ay-Efe 2007 The Küllüoba Excavations and the Cultural/Political Development of Western Anatolia before the Second Millennium B.C. In *Belkıs Dinçol ve Ali Dinçol' a Armağan*, edited by M. Doğan-Alparslan, M. Alparslan, and H. Peker, pp. 251–268. Ege Yayınları, Istanbul.

Efe, T., and M. Türkteki 2011 İçbatı Anadolu erken Tunç Çağı Pişmiş Toprak Figürinleri ve İdolleri. In *Karşıdan Karşıya M.Ö. 3, Binde Kiklad Adaları ve Batı Anadolu*, edited by V. Şahoğlu and P. Sotiakopoulou, pp. 228–231. Sabancý Müzesi, Istanbul.

French, H. D. 1969 *Anatolia and the Aegean in the Third Millennium B.C.*, Vol. 1–2. Unpublished PhD Thesis, Cambridge University.

Goetze, A. 1957 *Kleinasien*. Beck, München.

Günel, S. 2007 Çine—Tepecik Höyüğü 2005 Yılı Kazıları. *Kazı Sonuçları Toplantısı* 28(1):231–246. Ankara.

Günel, S. 2008 Çine—Tepecik Höyükte Bulunan Mermer İdoller. In *Muhibbe Darga Armağanı*, edited by T. Tahran, A. Tibet, and E. Konyar, pp. 251–260. Sadberk Hanım Müzesi Yayını, Istanbul.

Hüryılmaz, H. 1999 Eine Gruppe frühbronzezeitlicher Menschenfigurinenaus Yenibademli auf Gökçeada (Imbros). *Studio Troica* 10:475–488.

Jokowsky, M. S. 1986 *Prehistoric Aphrodisias. An Account of the Excavations and Artifact Studies*. Center for Old World Archaeology and Art, Brown University, Providence.

Lamb, W. 1936 *Excavations at Thermi in Lesbos*. Cambridge University Press, Cambridge.

Lamb, W. 1937 Ecavations at Kusura Near Afyon Karahisar I. *Archaeologia* 86:1–64.

Lamb, W. 1938 Ecavations at Kusura near Afyon Karahisar II. *Archaeologia* 87:217–273.

Lloyd, S., and J. Mellaart 1962 *Beycesultan Vol. 1*. British Institute of Archaeology at Ankara, London.

Mellink, M. J. 1964 Excavations at Karataş-Semayük in Lycia, 1963. *American Journal of Archaeology* 68:269–278.

Mellink, M. J. 1967 Excavations at Karataş Semayük in Lycia, 1966. *American Journal of Archaeology* 71:251–267.
Obladen-Kauder, J. 1996 *Demircihüyük IV: Die Kleinfunde B*. Von Zabern, Mainz am Rhein.
Özkan, T., and H. Erkanal 1999 *Tahtalı Barajı Kurtarma Kazısı Projesi*. T. C. Kültür Bakanlığı Anıtlar ve Müzeler Genel Müdürlüğü İzmir Arkeoloji Müzesi Müdürlüğü, İzmir.
Özsait, M. 2000 1998 Yılı Harmanören (Göndürle Höyük) Mezarlık Kazısı. *Kazı Sonuçları Toplantısı* 21:371–380. Ankara.
Peet, T. E. 1909 Two Prehistoric Figurines from Asia Minor. *Annals of Archaeology and Anthropology*:145–147.
Renfrew, C. 1969 The Development and Chronology of the Early Cycladic Figurines. *American Journal of Archaeology* 73(1):1–32.
Sarı, D. 2012 İlk Tunç Çağı ve Orta Tunç Çağı'nda Batı Anadolu'nun Kültürel ve Siyasal Gelişimi. *MASROP E-Dergi* 7:112–249.
Takaoğlu, T. 2005 A Chalcolithic Marble Workshop at Kulaksızlar in Western Anatolia: An Analysis of Production and Craft Specialization. British Archaeological Reports—International Series, Oxford.
Topbaş, A., T. Efe, and A. İlaslı 1998 Salvage Excavations of The Afyon Archaeology Museum, Part 2: The Settlement of Karaoğlan Mevkii and The Early Bronze Age Cemetery of Kaklık Mevkii. *Anatolia Antiqua* VI:21–94.
Schliemann, H. 1875 *Troy and Its Remains*. J. Murray, London.
Seeher, J. 2000 Die Bronzezeitliche Nekropole von Demircihöyük-Sarıket. Ernst Wasmuth, Tübingen.

CHAPTER NINE

Distribution and Characteristics of the Beycesultan Early Bronze Age I Pottery

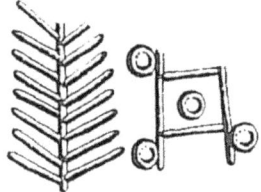

*Sinem Üstün Türkteki**

Introduction

For the periods that predate the advent of writing, pottery is one of the most important find groups for the establishment of regional chronologies and distribution areas of the cultures, and for determining the relationships between settlements. This is due to the variety of manufacturing techniques and wares, as well as countless pottery forms and decoration styles (Özdoğan 1997:380).

During the Early Bronze Age 1A (EBA IA), which is also defined as "Transitional Period into the EBA," characteristic elements of the West Anatolian EBA pottery emerge and in the succeeding period, subgroups with local characteristics become more and more apparent. It was K. Bittel who mentioned these groups for the first time in the early 1940s. In the 1960s, in light of new excavations and surface surveys, J. Mellaart and D. French determined the borders of these groups more precisely. However, based on the results of the recent research, T. Efe has brought a new perspective on the subject. Efe suggests that, in EBA Anatolia, there are Culture Regions that cover wider areas and pottery zones in every cultural region, which might indirectly point to the influential areas of the local authorities. Beycesultan EBA 1 Culture Region, which covers a wide geographical area in the middle part of Inland Western Anatolia, has its own pottery characteristics.

Beycesultan, which was excavated between the years 1954–1959 under the co-directorship of S. Lloyd and J. Mellaart, is one of the most important mounds in Western Anatolia. The pottery recovered at the site makes an important contribution to the

---

*Dr. Sinem Üstün Türkteki, Department of Archaeology, Bilecik Şeyh Edebali University, Bilecik, 11210, Türkiye

establishment of the regional chronology. Beycesultan still maintains its position as the key site for evaluating the EBA pottery groups of Elmalı Plain in which Karataş-Semayük is situated (west of Antalya) and Physidia/Lakes District where sufficient research has not yet been carried out.

Chronology Problems in Relation with the Beycesultan EBA 1 Pottery

J. Mellaart states that, even though there are significant differences between pottery groups of the Late Chalcolithic Period and the EBA 1, the EBA 1 pottery has particularly developed from the Late Chalcolithic 4 (which is the top layer of the Late Chalcolithic) and has no association with the arrival of a new ethnic group (Lloyd and Mellaart 1962:117).

Since Beycesultan is one of the sites excavated many years ago, certain chronological problems exist, especially in connection with the EB 1 period. Scientists who have been carrying out recent investigations and excavations in the region and the immediate surroundings bring new suggestions to this chronology problem.

E. Akdeniz, one of the researchers who carried out investigations in the area, supports Mellaart's thesis and suggests that the pottery in question has absolutely developed from that of the Late Chalcolithic locality, specifically of the Late Chalcolithic 4-Culture. Furthermore, E. Akdeniz is of the opinion that the pottery of Beycesultan layers XX/XIX displays characteristics of the Transitional Period into the EBA and these layers must be considered "transitional" from the Late Chalcolithic into the EBA 1 (Akdeniz 1999:321).

J. Mellaart states that the EBA 1 pottery is much more developed and more skilled when compared to that of the Late Chalcolithic in terms of both ware groups and vessel forms. The thin-walled, brilliantly burnished, and shallow-fluted ware group, which is characteristic of the Beycesultan EBA 1, is not encountered in the preceding Late Chalcolithic Period (Lloyd and Mellaart 1962:117). Taking this view of J. Mellaart into consideration, T. Efe is of the opinion that there is a gap between the Late Chalcolithic and the EBA 1 (Efe 1988:117), and Kaklık Place and Kusura finds fill this gap (Efe et al. 1995:374).

T. Efe explains the existence of the gap as following: The shallow-grooved and brilliantly burnished pottery of the Beycesultan EB 1, which has been recovered in small numbers at Kusura, should be dated between Kusura A and B. Two arguments that lead him to date this group to an earlier period are as follows:

1. The pottery of Kusura Cemetery is not represented in Kusura A-Group.

2. The graveyard pottery is less developed than that of Kusura A-Group pottery in terms of ware groups and forms. (Efe et al. 1995:374)

Efe further states that Kaklık Mevkii pottery, with its bowls with incurving rim, anti-splash bowls, and beak-spouted jugs as well as the thin-walled, brilliantly burnished, and shallow-fluted group, should fill the gap at Beycesultan as in Kusura (Efe et al. 1995:373).

Thin-walled, brilliantly burnished, and shallow-fluted pottery, most of which is represented in black ware, has been recovered at the Küllüoba excavations that have been carried out under the tutelage of T. Efe and is of utmost importance for comparisons with the Beycesultan EB1 settlement (Efe et al. 1995:25).

This period in which new architecture and pottery traditions emerged has been designated "EBA 1A" by M. Mellink (1992) and "Transitional Period into the EBA" by T. Efe (Efe and Ay Efe 2000). According to M. Mellink, the last layers of Beycesultan Late Chalcolithic should be dated earlier than 3000 B.C. She dates Beycesultan XX Layer to the EBA 1A, which corresponds roughly to the timespan between 3400 and 3000 B.C., and she proposes a time span stretching from 3000 to 2700 B.C. for the EBA 1B (1992:172).

In conclusion, J. Mellaart states that certain new forms, which are characteristic for the succeeding EBA 1, appear already in Late Chalcolithic 4, especially in layer XX. These forms are bowls with incurving rim, single-handled bowls, two-handled pots (amphora), and pots with sharply outturning necks and possible round bodies (Figure 9.1). No white-on-dark painted pottery, which is very characteristic for the Late Chalcolithic layers of Beycesultan, is encountered in layer XX. However, in the later phases a small number of white painted pottery are found. Beak-spouted jugs and black-burnished vessels with incrustation begin to appear (Figure 9.2: 7, 8), for the first time, in Layer XIX dated to the EBA 1 by J. Mellaart. Bowls with incurving rim, single-handled bowls, and pots with sharply outturning necks are among the forms continuing from the preceding period. Thin-walled vessels with shallow fluting, which are characteristic in the Beycesultan EBA 1, appear from layer XVIII on.

According to the reassessment made above on the pottery groups of the Late Chalcolithic and the EBA 1 period at Beycesultan, it would be suitable to date the layers XX and XIX at the site to the Transitional Period into the EBA, based especially on the following arguments:

- In Layers XX and XIX, pottery characteristics of both Late Chalcolithic and the EB 1 appear together.

- The characteristic white-painted pottery of the Late Chalcolithic Period appears rarely from the end layers of the Late Chalcolithic.

- The amphora, the characteristic form of the EB1, appears from the Layer XX on at Beycesultan.

CHARACTERISTICS AND CHRONOLOGY OF THE BEYCESULTAN EBA1 POTTERY

Pottery of Western Anatolia displays more and more local characteristics from the EBA 1B on. Pottery belonging to "Beycesultan EBA1 Cultural Region" has been recovered at Beycesultan layers XIX, XVIII and XVIIc,b,a. This cultural region has distinctive pottery groups in terms of wares, forms, and decorations in comparison with those of the neighboring regions (Efe and Türkteki 2011:216).

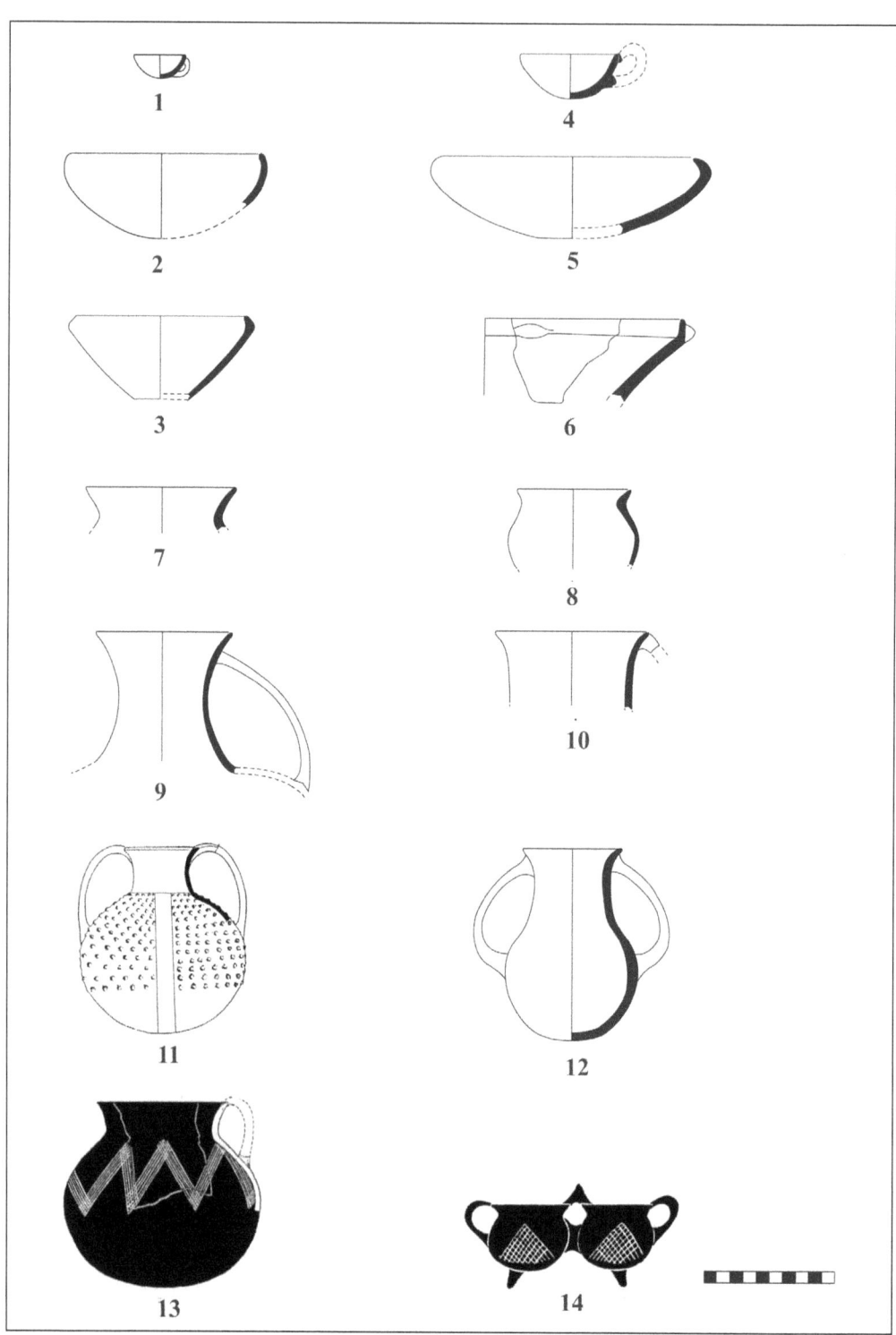

FIGURE 9.1. 1, 2, 7, 10, 12 (Level XX), 6 (Level XXX), 13 (Level XXII)—LC 4; 3, 4, 5, 8, 10 (Level XIX), 11, 14 (Level XVIIb)—EBA I.

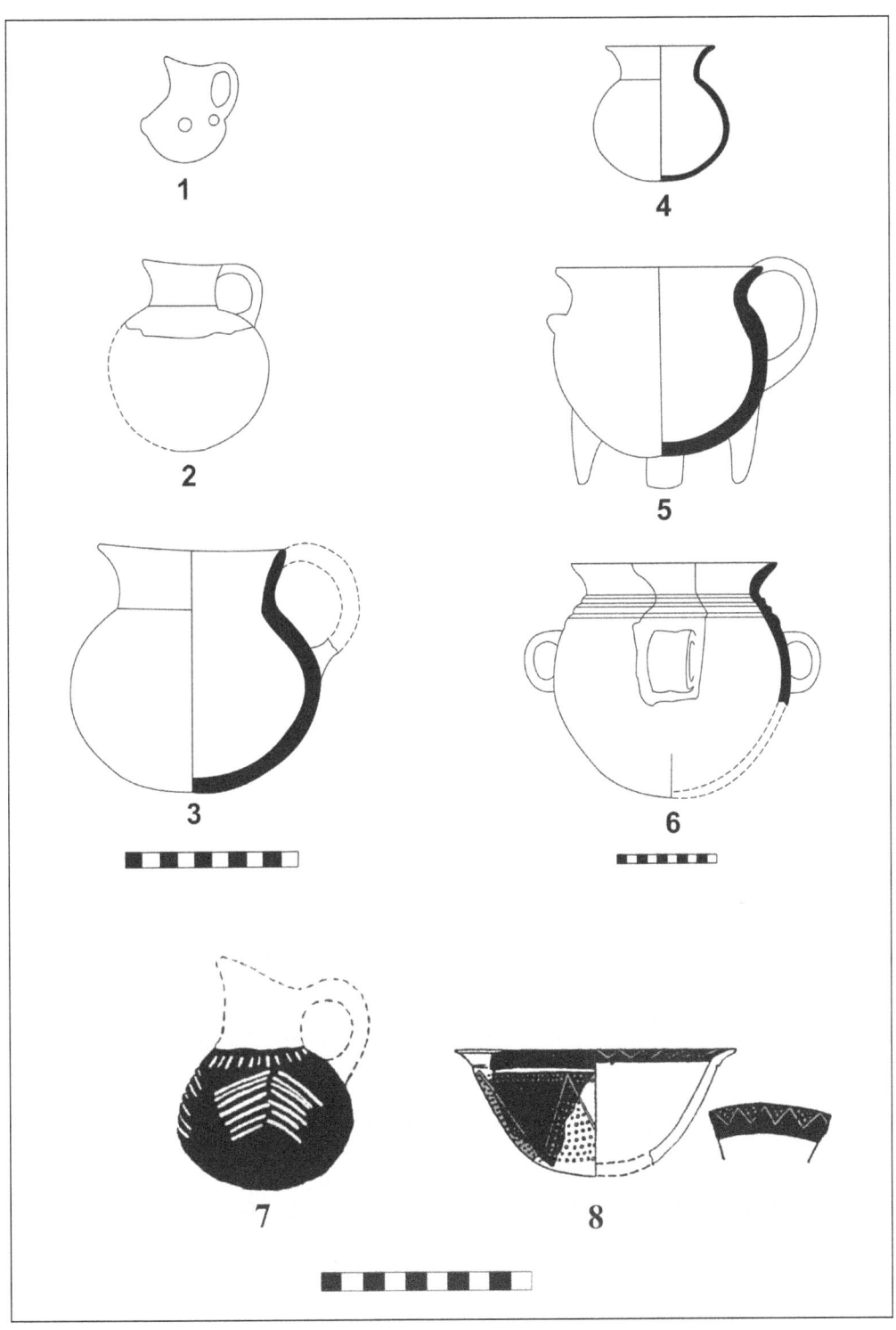

FIGURE 9.2. 1–3 Beak-spouted jugs; 4–6 jars; 7, 8 pots with incrusted decoration.

J. Mellaart classified the ware groups represented in the Beycesultan EBA1 layers as *"Fine Ware"* and *"Coarse Ware."* Coarse ware continues from the earlier period with no visible change. Fine Ware, on the other hand, is represented with a few examples already present in the earlier period (Lloyd and Mellaart 1962:117). Black/red burnished and thin-walled vessels of Fine Ware, which first appear in EBA 1 layers, are more predominantly represented than the other ware groups at Beycesultan. Brilliant burnishing and shallow fluting on the bodies of the vessels are among the most typical characteristics of this pottery. This decoration is mostly applied on the round bodies of cups, jugs, and necked pots (Lloyd and Mellaart 1962). The insides of the vessels are frequently wet-smoothed by a cloth (Figure 9.3).

The fine Ware of J. Mellaart is represented by vessels, the surfaces of which are in various tones of black, grey, bluish black, olive gray, salmon pink, orange-red, light brown, and brown. Beycesultan is the only center where we can see all these surface colors

Figure 9.3. EBA 1 Red-black slipped and brilliant burnished ware with fluted decoration.

together (Lloyd and Mellaart 1962). In addition, *"Plum-Red Slipped Burnished Ware"* of Physidia/Lakes District, and Konya Region appears to have also been represented according to the samples seen in the Collection of Beycesultan kept at the British Institute of Archaeology at Ankara (Üstün-Türkteki 2012:55).

Many forms are in close relation with those of the preceding Late Chalcolithic 4. Carinated bowls (anti-splash) or bowls with incurving rims, which appear in Layer XIX at Beycesultan for the first time, increase in number in the succeeding layers (Lloyd and Mellaart 1962). The examples of these bowls with single- or double-holed horizontal handles are encountered in Beycesultan EBA1 layers (Figure 9.4:5, 6; Lloyd and Mellart 1962).

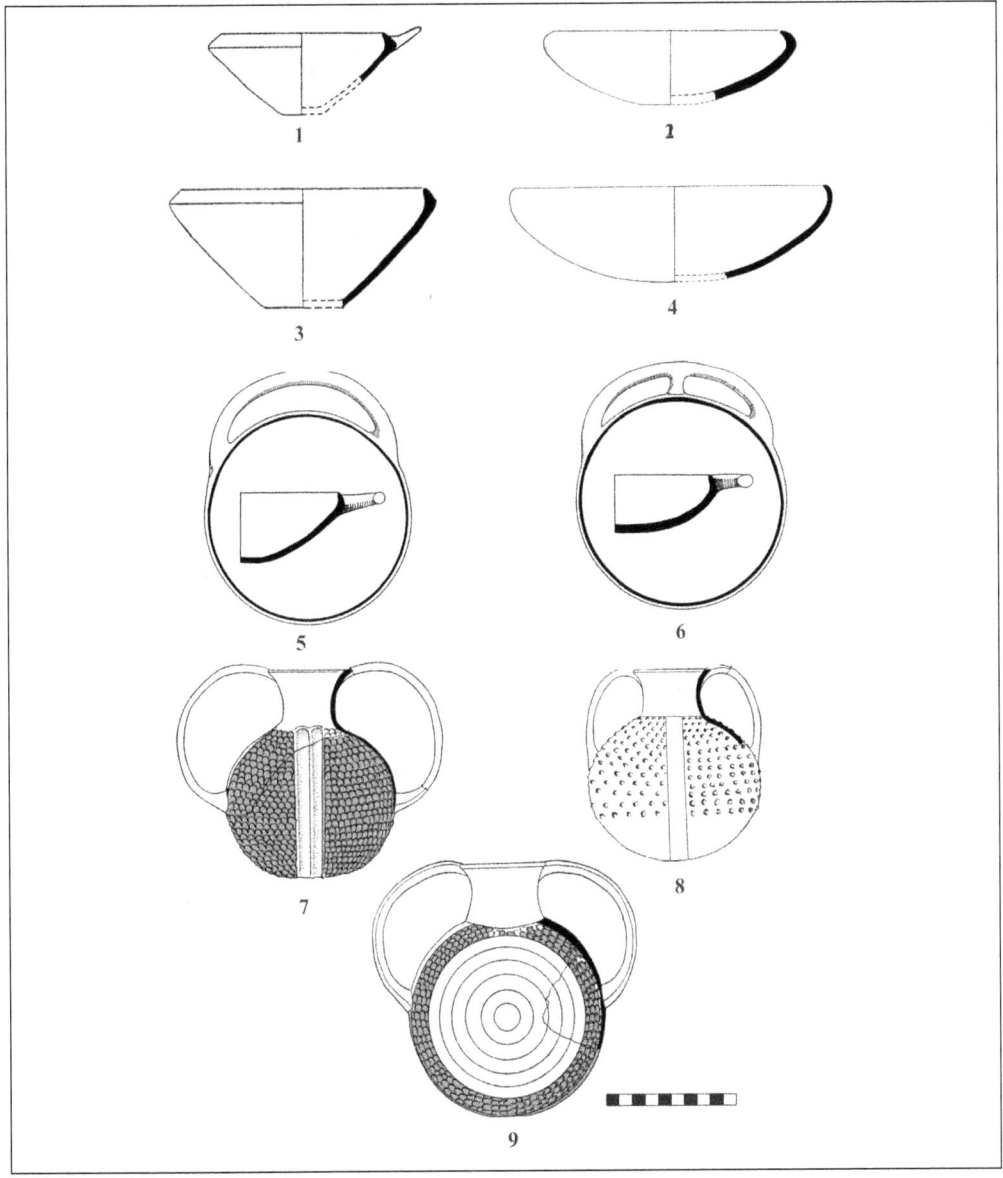

FIGURE 9.4. Characteristic pottery forms of EBA 1.

The amphora form, typical for the entire Western Anatolian EBA 1, appears from the Beycesultan Late Chalcolithic on. The amphorae show differences in both form and decoration from those of the preceding Late Chalcolithic. Those recovered in layers XVIII and XVIIb at Beycesultan are defined as rare forms and they have bold handles reaching from the rim down the middle part of the body. For these black-burnished vessels the fish-scale decoration applied in reserved bands is very characteristic. Sometimes the necks and the handles of amphorae are slipped and the body has a barbotin decoration on an unslipped surface (Figure 9.4:7, 8, 9; Lloyd and Mellaart 1962). Beak-spouted jugs of the Beycesultan EBA1 are quite different from those of the EBA 2. The slender ribbon handles on beak-spouted jugs are very characteristic (Figure 9.2:1, 3).

Pots that appear for the first time at the end of the Late Chalcolithic have globular bodies; their necks flare out sharply (Figure 9.2:4) and they frequently have vertical lug-handles on the body (Figure 9.2:6). Tripod-cooking pots seldom occur in the EBA 1—except Troy-Yortan Cultural Region—around Beycesultan and the immediate regions (Figure 9.2:5; Sarı 2012:150).

Beycesultan EBA 1 pottery has a rich variety of decorations. However, its percentage within the total ceramic count is quite low. Besides the vertical, horizontal (Figure 9.3), and concentric applied fluting (Figure 9.4:9), barbotine (Figure 9.4:8) and fish-scale motifs in reserved bands (Figure 9.4:7) and knobs (Figure 9.2:1) are very characteristic for this group. The white-on-black painted pottery tradition continues from the Late Chalcolithic, decreasing gradually (Efe and Türkteki 2011:216). Incrustation (Figure 9.2:7, 8) and relief decoration are rarely represented in this group.

The Coarse Ware continues from the Late Chalcolithic without much change. It has a red or brown unslipped surface; the paste often has straw and stone tempering. This ware is represented by bowls, cooking-pots, pots, and baking platters. Large vessels are commonly used for child burials as in the Late Chalcolithic (Lloyd and Mellaart 1962:117). The last layer (XVII) of the Beycesultan EBA 1 ends with a conflagration. This marks the end of "Beycesultan EBA 1 Cultural Region," and many local pottery zones of the EBA 2 emerge within its distribution area (Lloyd and Mellaart 1962:136).

Suggestions of the Distribution Area of Beycesultan EBA1 Cultural Region

J. Mellaart states that we are not well informed on the distribution area of this culture, as is the case for the Late Chalcolithic, since the EBA I layers are often sealed under thick EBA 2 deposits. And on the borders of the culture, J. Mellart discusses the existence of the orange-red groove-decorated jug forms as the proof of this culture in Upper Büyük Menderes Valley and in Beycesultan and Kocayaka in Denizli. Analyzing the vertical groove–decorated pots captured in Yenice, in the northwest of Afyon, he determines the farthest distance in the east where this culture has reached. And J. Mellaart considers Aslanapa, which is to the south of Kütahya, within the Beycesultan Group on the distribution map of the Culture Regions. In this case the northernmost border of the Culture Group is Aslanapa settlement according to J. Mellaart (Lloyd and Mellaart 1962:133, Map III).

According to Mellaart, the distribution area of the Beycesultan EBA 1 Cultural Region encompasses the Upper Büyük Menderes Valley, northwestern part of the Afyon province, and Burdur, Yeşilova, Tefenni, and Korkuteli regions, situated within the boundaries of Physidia/Lakes District (Figure 9.5; Lloyd and Mellaart 1962:129, 133).

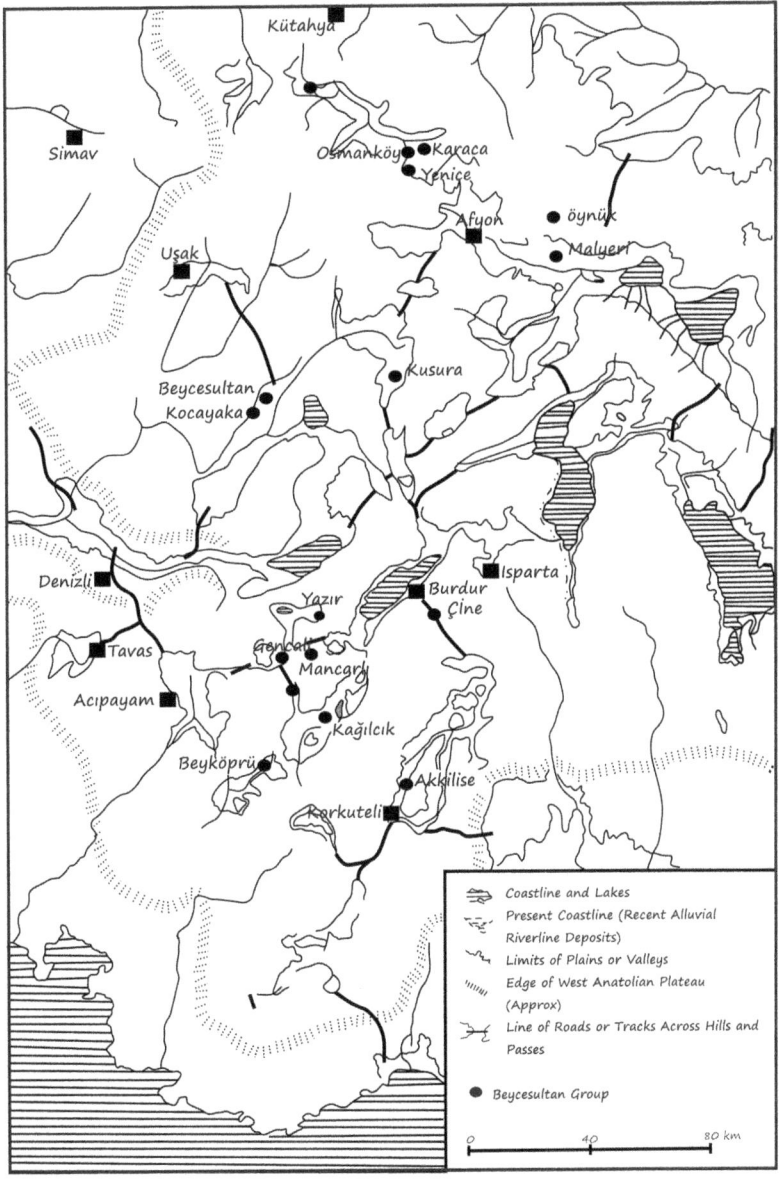

FIGURE 9.5. Distribution area of the Beycesultan EBA 1 cultural region; adapted from J. Mellaart.

In his doctoral thesis, D. French extended the borders of distribution of Beycesultan EBA 1 pottery starting from Beycesultan and Kocayaka settlements, as J. Mellaart suggested, up to a region covering all settlements within Acıpayam, Burdur, Kusura, Altıntaş, Afyon, Hoyran, Beyşehir, Akşehir, and Konya Regions (1969: Figure 9.6).

After his surface surveys carried out in the provinces of Kütahya, Bilecik, and Eskişehir, T. Efe redrew more precisely the northern border of the "Beycesultan EBA I Cultural Region." The northernmost sites with the typical pottery of the "Beycesultan EBA I Cultural Region" are Aslanapa near Altıntaş and Aizonoi (Çavdarhisar) in the Örencik Plain. The other sites with this pottery in the Altıntaş area are Hacıhamza, Tatarmuhat, and Karataş II. The typical characteristics of this pottery fade out in the Tavşanlı Plain farther to the north, as seen at Tepecik situated in the NW of Tavşanlı. T. Efe lists the Beycesultan EBA 1 pottery characteristics at the site as follows: bowls with incurving rim, reserved slip, and shallow fluting. However, red burnished fine ware, which is characteristic for the Beycesultan EBA 1 pottery group, is not encountered at Tepecik. In the light of all this new evidence T. Efe extends the borders of this group as far north as the Tavşanlı Plain (Figure 9.7; Efe and Ay Efe 2000:34–35).

E. Akdeniz states that the pottery of the Late Chalcolithic exhibits quite a homogenous character throughout the entire basin of Büyük Menderes. However, this situation gradually changes during the EBA 1 and local pottery zones begin to emerge. He named

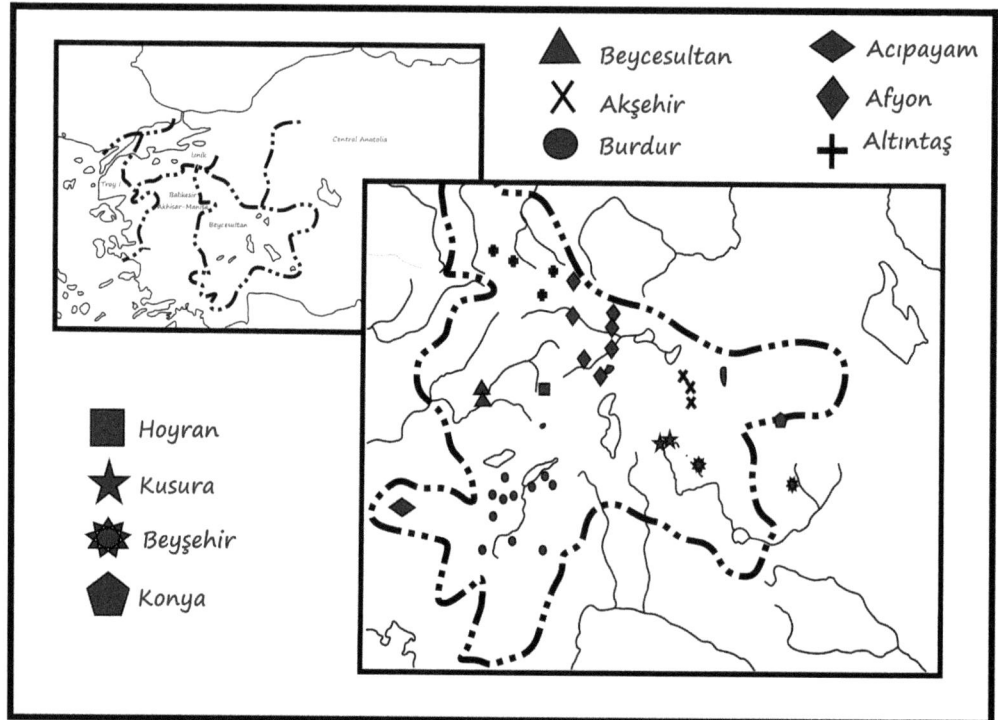

Figure 9.6. Distribution area of the Beycesultan EBA 1 cultural region; adapted from D. French.

FIGURE 9.7A. Distribution area of the Beycesultan EBA 1 cultural region, around Kütahya; adapted from T. Efe.

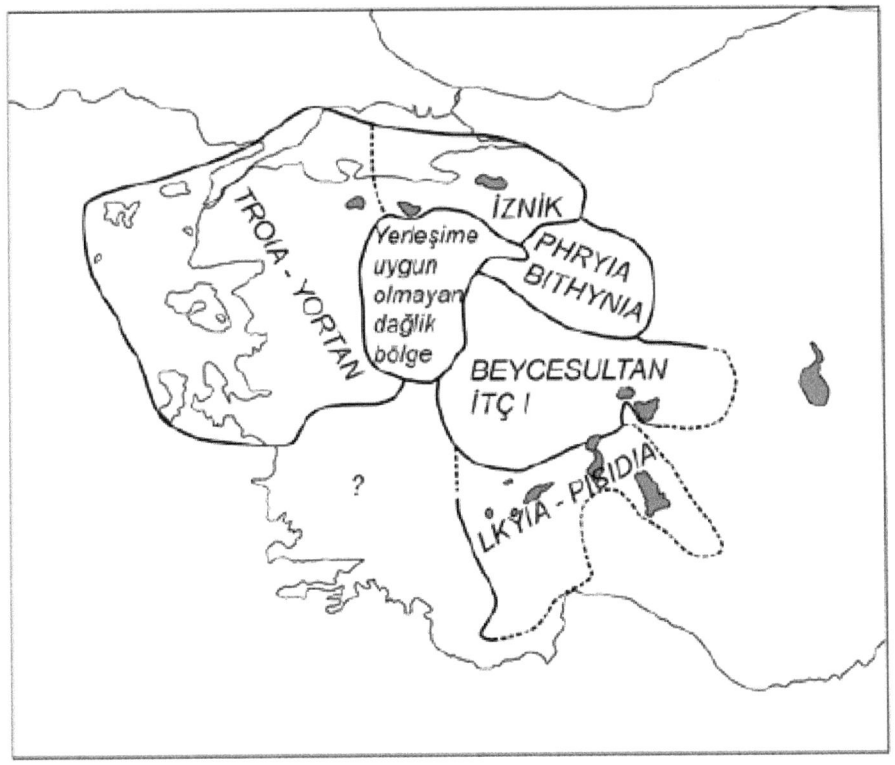

FIGURE 9.7B. Distribution area of the Beycesultan EBA 1 cultural region in Western Anatolia; adapted from T. Efe.

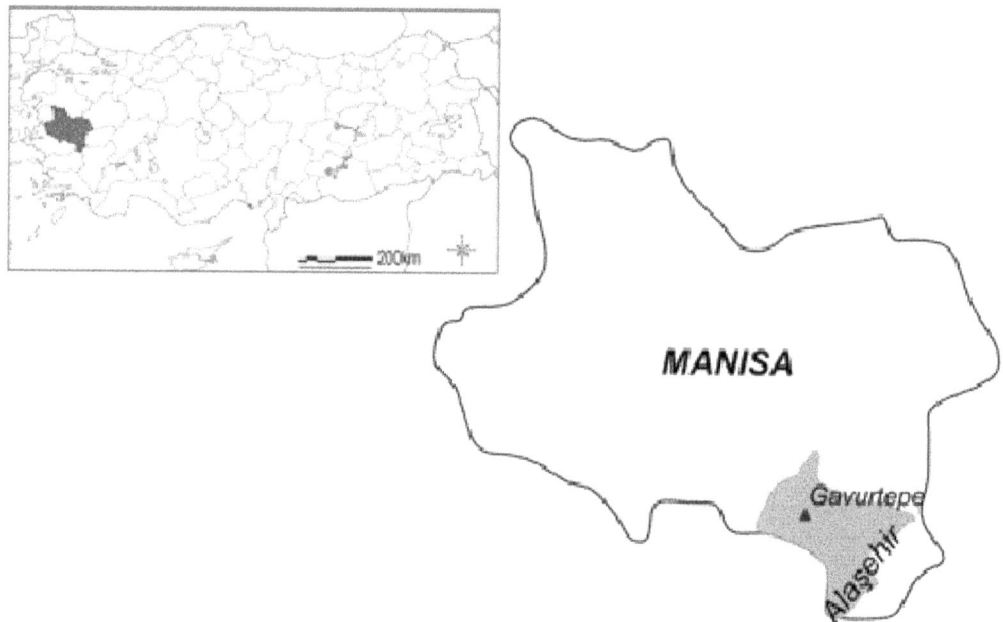

FIGURE 9.7C. Distribution area of the Beycesultan EBA 1 cultural region, around Manisa; adapted from T. Efe.

this new culture "Büyük Menderes Basin EBA 1 Culture." According to him, this culture originated in the area around Beycesultan and Kocayaka and from here, dispersed to the entire basin, as J. Mellaart and D. French already emphasized (Akdeniz 1999). He thinks that two other cultures (Kusura and Aphrodisias) were formed under the influence of this culture. However, all the characteristic elements of this culture are not represented at these sites.

J. Mellaart (Lloyd and Mellaart 1962) and D. French (1969) evaluated Physidia/Lakes District under "Beycesultan EBA 1 Cultural Region," based on the sherds with fish-scale and barbotine decorations collected from the surface of the Burdur Mound and the pottery of Beycesultan EBA 1 style found on the surface of many other mounds in the region. However, no fish-scale or barbotine decoration has been encountered among the pottery recovered from the Kuruçay, Harmanören-Göndürle, and Bademağacı excavations and collected from many mounds during the surface surveys that lasted almost 40 years in the Lakes District. This doesn't accord with what D. French and J. Mellaart suggest for the southern border of the culture.[1]

Based on the results of new excavations, surface surveys carried out in the region by J. Mellaart and D. French,[2] and current research, it became possible to redraw the southern border of the "Beycesultan EBA1 Culture Region." As stated before, very few pottery samples of "Beycesultan EBA1 Cultural Region" have been found in Physidia/Lakes District. The Beycesultan EBA1 characteristics are designated by thin-walled, brilliantly burnished and fluted pottery. This pottery is represented by red-slipped pottery in the Isparta Region and black-burnished pottery in the Burdur region (Figure 9.8). The simple bowls, bowls with incurving rims and pots with sharply outturning necks of the Physidia/Lakes District display parallels with those of Beycesultan. Since this pottery is represented by few examples in the Lakes District, all of it can be considered as imports in the region.

FIGURE 9.8. Pisidia/Lake District EBA 1 Local Wares.

Physidia/Lakes District during the EBA 1 period harbors a separate cultural region with its own local wares and forms (Figure 9.9). The two cultural regions are separated geographically by mountain ranges of Söğüt, Karakuş, and Sultan.

In the light of new excavations and surface surveys it has become clear once more that there is a separate culture in the region (Üstün Türkteki 2012:123) in the south

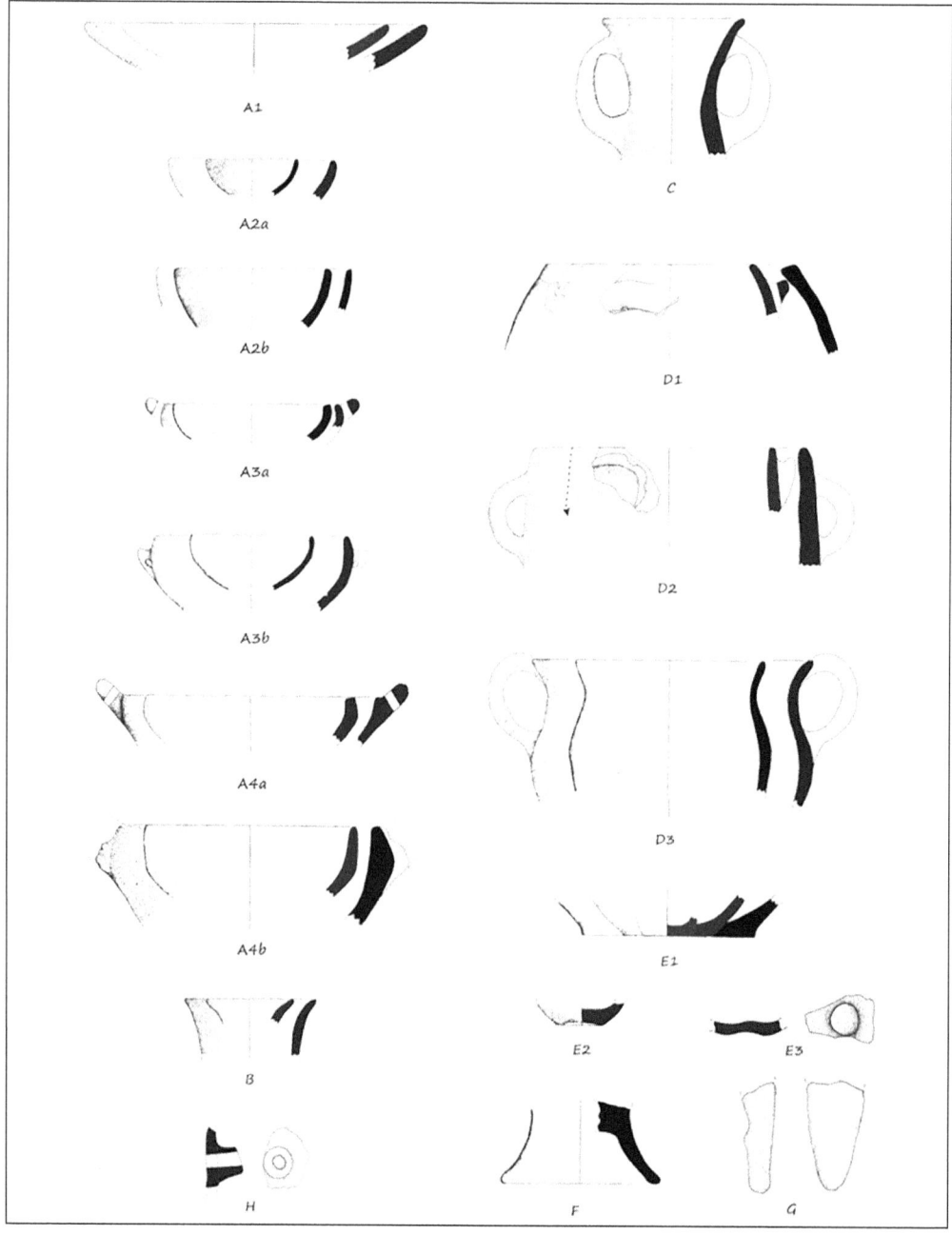

Figure 9.9. Pisidia/Lake District EBA 1 Form Table.

of "Beycesultan EBA1 Cultural Region" named as "Lycia-Physidia/Lakes District EBA 1 Cultural Region."[3]

Based on the new research, the borders of "Beycesultan EBAI Cultural Region" can be redefined roughly as the following: The northern limit of the cultural region should be delineated by the Kütahya Plateau. Farther to the northeast, the border crosses the central part of the Phrygian Highlands all the way down to Emirdağ. In the north of this borderline takes place the Phrygian Cultural Region. Typical pottery of the Beycesultan EBA 1 Cultural Region has been recovered in small numbers at Küllüoba EBA 1 layers. These all must be imports at the site from the southern neighboring areas (Efe and Ay Efe 2000:25).

The Akşehir Plain is the easternmost region into which the characteristic pottery of the cultural region dispersed. As for the western limits of the culture, certain characteristic pottery elements of the culture have been recovered at Gavurtepe near Alaşehir situated 90 kilometers west of Beycesultan. As mentioned above, the mountain ranges of Sultan, Karakuş, and Söğüt constitute a natural border between "Beycesultan EBA 1 Cultural Region" and "Lycia-Physidia/Lakes District EBA1 Cultural Region" (Figure 9.10).

New investigations in the region and the neighboring areas which shall be carried out in the future may change—to a certain extent—the borders of "Beycesultan EBAI

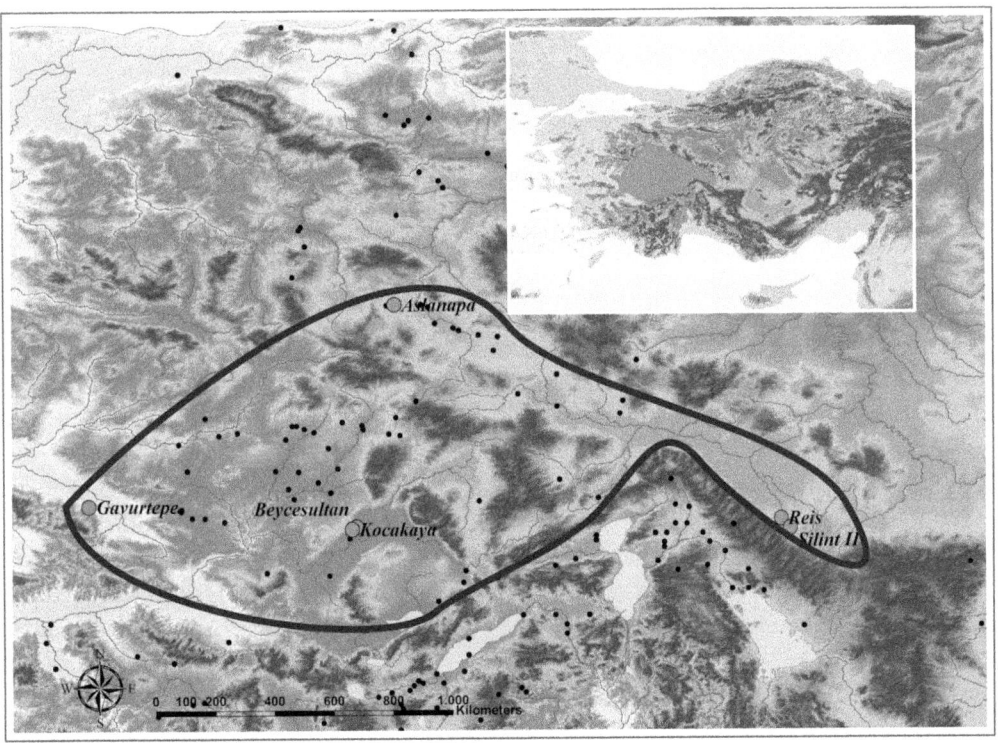

FIGURE 9.10. Distribution of area of the Beycesultan EBA 1 Cultural Region in light of recent research, adapted from Akdeniz.

Cultural Region" as drawn in this paper. This important cultural region with its own distinct pottery covers a vast geographical area in the middle part of Inland Western Anatolia and, without a doubt, it had an important role in the cultural development and interregional trade relations of Western Anatolia.

NOTES

1. The EBA pottery of the Physidia/Lakes District collected during the surface surveys carried out under the aupices of M. Özsait constituted the main body of my thesis completed in 2012. This pottery is evaluated with a new perspective in terms of its characteristics, pottery zones, and its comparisons with the neighboring regions. It is a note of interest that not a single piece of pottery with fish scale and barbotine decoration is encountered in the studied material.
2. M. Özsait conducted surface surveys in the region between 1972 and 2010, and excavated Harmanören Göndürle cemetery between 1995 and 2005. Kuruçay, Höyücek, and Bademağacı excavations are carried out from 1978 on under the auspices of R. Duru. Finally, Hacılar II Mound (Büyük Höyük) situated in the immediate vicinity of Hacılar is under excavation since 2011.
3. K. Bittel first introduces Physidian Cultural Group. Kurt Bittel, Gründgzuge der Vor-und Frügeschichte Kleinasiens, 1945; Afterward, A. Goetze shows a local group which he named as "Physidia Group." Goetze, A., Kleinasien, Munich, 1957, p. 20; Furthermore, Likya/Pisidya Cultural Region was named by T. Efe, 2003 *Pottery Distribution within the Bronze Age of Western Anatolia and Its Implications upon Cultural, Political (and Ethnic?) Entities, Archaeological Essays in Honour of Homo Amatus: Güven Arsebük için Armağan Yazılar*, p. 91.

REFERENCES CITED

Akdeniz, E. 1999 Büyük Menderes Havzası'nda Demir Çağı Öncesi Kültürleri. Ege Üniversitesi, İzmir.

Duru, R. 1994 Kuruçay I: 1978–1988 Kazılarının Sonuçları, Neolitik ve Erken Kalkolitik Çağ Yerleşmeleri. Türk Tarih Kurumu Yayınları, Ankara.

Efe, T. 1986 Patterned Reserve-slip Decoration in the Early Bronze Age of Western Anatolia. *Anatolica* 13:1–17.

Efe, T. 1988 Demircihüyük. Band III, Die Keramik 2, Die Frühebronzezeitliche Keramik der Jüngeren Phasen (ab Phase H). Verlag von Philipp von Zabern, Mainz am Rhein.

Efe, T. 2003 Pottery Distribution within the Bronze Age of Western Anatolia and Its Implications upon Cultural, Political (and Ethnic?) Entities. In *Archaeological Essays in Honour of Homo amatus: Güven Arsebük için Armağan Yazılar*, edited by. M. Özbaşaran, O. Tanındı, and A. Boratav, pp. 87–105. Ege Yayınları, İstanbul.

Efe, T., and D. Ş. M. Ay Efe 2000 Early Bronze Age I Pottery from Küllüoba near Seyitgazi, Eskisehir. *Anatolia Antiqua* 8:1–87.

Efe, T., A. İlaslı, and A.Topbaş 1995 Salvage Excavations of the Afyon Archaeological Museum, Part I: Kaklık Mevkii, A Site Transitional to the Early Bronze Age. *Studia Troica* 5:357–399.

Efe, T., and M. Türkteki 2011 İç Batı Anadolu Bölgesi Erken Tunç Çağı Seramiği. In *MÖ 3. Bin'de Kiklad Adaları ve Batı,* edited by V. Şahoğlu and K. Karşıya, pp. 214–224. Anadolu, Sabancı Üniversitesi Sakıp Sabancı Müzesi, İstanbul.

French, D. 1969a *Anatolia and the Aegean in the Third Millennium B.C.* Yayınlanmamış Doktora Tezi. University of Cambridge.

French, D. 1969b *Anatolia and the Aegean in the Third Millennium B.C.* Yayınlanmamış Doktora Tezi, Cilt 2. University of Cambridge.

French, D. 1969c Prehistoric Sites in Northwest Anatolia, II. The Balıkesir and Akhisar/Manisa Areas. *Anatolian Studies* XIX:41–98.

Lloyd, S., and J. Mellaart 1962 *Beycesultan I. The Chalcolithic and Early Bronze Age Levels.* British Institute of Archaeology at Ankara, London.

Mellaart, J. 1954 Preliminary Report on a Survey of Pre-Classical Remains in Southern Turkey. *Anatolian Studies* 4:175–240.

Mellart, J. 1963 Early Cultures of the South Anatolian Plateau, II: The Late Chalcolithic and Early Bronze Agesin the Konya Plain. *Anatolian Studies* 13:199–236.

Mellink, M. J. 1992 Anatolian Chronology. In *Chronologies in Old World Archaeology,* edited by R. Ehrlich, pp. 102–132. The University of Chicago Press, Chicago.

Özdoğan, M. 1997 *Çanak-Çömlek.* Eczacıbaşı Sanat Ansiklopedisi, Cilt: 1, Yapı Endüstri Merkezi Yayınları, İstanbul.

Sarı, D. 2012 İTÇ ve OTÇ'de Batı Anadolu'nun Kültürel ve Siyasal Gelişimi. *M.A.S.R.O.P.* 7:112–249.

Üstün-Türkteki, S. 2012 Pisidya/Göller Bölgesi İlk Tunç Çağı 1–2 Çanak Çömleği. İstanbul Üniversitesi, Sosyal Bilimler Enstitüsü, Protohistorya ve Önasya Arkeolojisi Anabilim Dalı, Yayımlanmamış Doktora Tezi, İstanbul.

PART II

Architecture, Settlement, and Sociopolitical Organization

CHAPTER TEN

Urbanism in the Western Anatolian Early Bronze Age

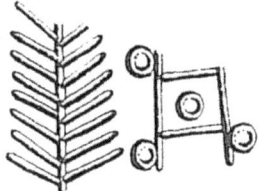

*Erkan Fidan**

Urban/city is defined in the city sciences dictionary by Ruşen Keleş as "the residential unit of continuous social development in which the requirements of society such as residence, sheltering, transportation, working, resting, entertainment are met. So, few people are busy with agricultural activity; population is more dense compared to villages which consists of small neighborhood units" (Keleş 1980). Surely, this definition is mainly valid for today's city settlements. Regarding urbanization in the prehistoric times, a variety of interpretations have been delivered and some ideas have been put forward (Çevik 2005). The most extensively debated among these are doubtless the opinions expressed by V. G. Childe in the 1950s (Childe 1950:3–17; 1979:12–17). Childe sorted the criteria needed for a settlement to be considered urban into 10 articles as follows:

1. Size and population density of the settlement
2. Skilled labor force working full-time
3. Central storage
4. Monumental public buildings
5. Class society
6. Writing
7. Science
8. Art
9. Long-distance commerce
10. Governmental organization

---

*Associate Prof. Dr. Erkan Fidan. Bilecik Şeyh Edebali University, Department of Archaeology. erkan fidan@gmail.com

More than a half-century has passed since Childe put forward those ten basic rules, and in the meantime new ideas have come up and discussions have begun in terms of definition, arising, and development of urbanization. It is possible to find all of Childe's criteria for urbanism in the Uruk settlement located in Southern Mesopotamia during the Uruk Period in the Near East. With the impetus of the previous Ubaid Culture, by which Mesopotamia reached cultural unity for the first time in its history, urbanism reached its climax in the Uruk period. However, in the remaining significant part of the Near East the emergence of urbanism was realized over a longer period of time, in comparison to Mesopotamia, due to the geographical, cultural, and political reasons specific to the regions; on the other hand, it is seen that some of the criteria for urbanism were not met or determined. Therefore, it is wrong to accept the criteria of Mesopotamian urbanism as a benchmark for the other geographies in the Near East. M. Özdoğan has tried to explain the situation with the following remarks: "The environmental diversity of Anatolia within itself and formation of different cultural developmental process in each region as well as the cultural accumulations of the regions surrounding Anatolia make it impossible to create a single theory to explain the development all around this geography" (Özdoğan 2006:572). It doesn't seem possible to make generalizations for the whole region with regard to urbanism since different general settlement layouts could be present according to the size and the importance of the settlements. For this reason, the criteria for urbanism can be evaluated in Anatolia separately for each region.

Criteria for Urbanism in Western Anatolia

Western Anatolia had a unique sociopolitical structure and showed a different cultural developmental trajectory, in many aspects, from that of Mesopotamia. Recent excavations, carried out especially in the last two decades, have provided us with new information about the transition into urbanism (Figure 10.1). However, the number of excavations should be increased and large-sized settlements especially need to be excavated in order to make a more concrete generalization, assessment, and comparisons. Excavation of centrally located large settlements in the region may cause some alterations in our opinions and assessments on this issue.

The following four topics should be taken into consideration in order to define a settlement as a "city" in Western Anatolia (Figure 10.2).

1. Existence of a ruling class
2. Establishment of Upper and Lower Town which can be taken as proof of the existence of social classes
3. Storing of surplus product
4. Craftsmanship

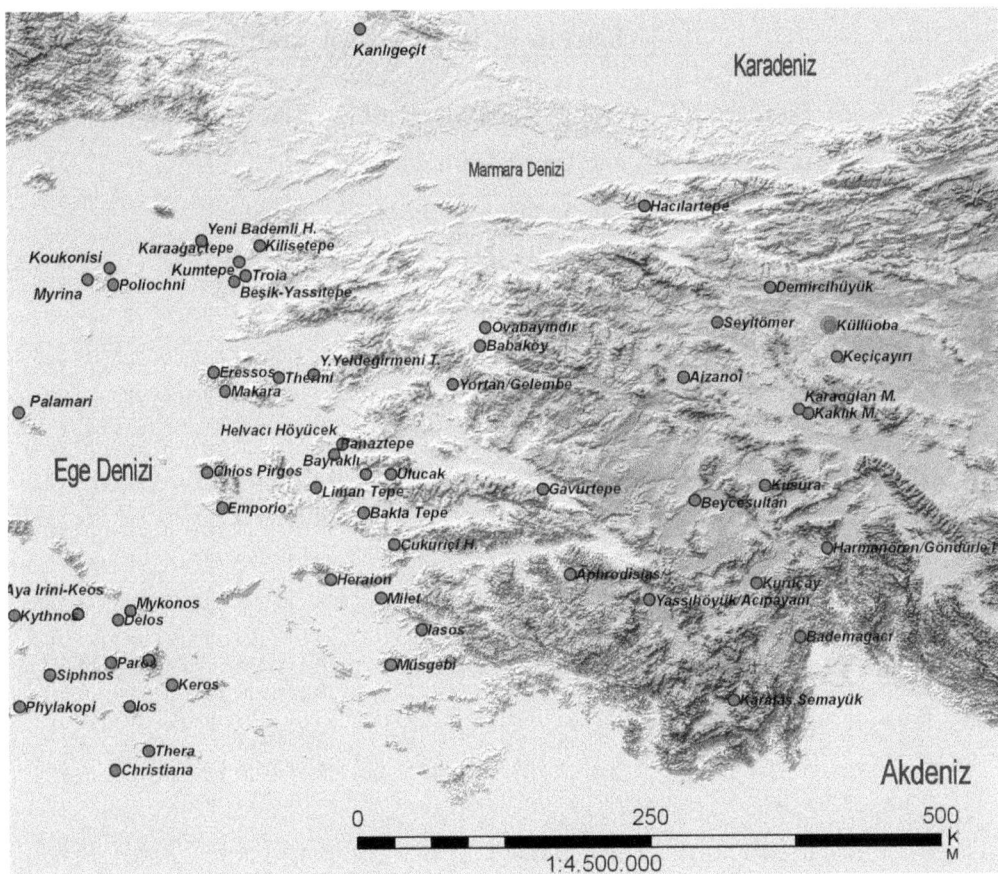

FIGURE 10.1. Early Bronze Age sites in Western Anatolia.

EXISTENCE OF A RULING CLASS

The emergence of a ruling class may be considered the most important criterion of urbanization in Western Anatolia. The existence of this class can be indirectly determined by the existence of buildings that have a special and central location in the settlements. They are constructed more monumentally and with different plan characteristics.

The centrally located Complex in the EBA I and EBA II of the Karataş-Semayük in the Elmalı plain is the first example of a structure that might have belonged to the ruler (Figure 10.3).[1] The independent rectangular building, which is thought to be two-storied, had been constructed on a natural hill and surrounded with courtyards, ramparts, and defense walls. The fact that it is encircled by earthen ramparts and courtyards and constructed with rather thick walls gives the impression that the building has a special position in the settlement.

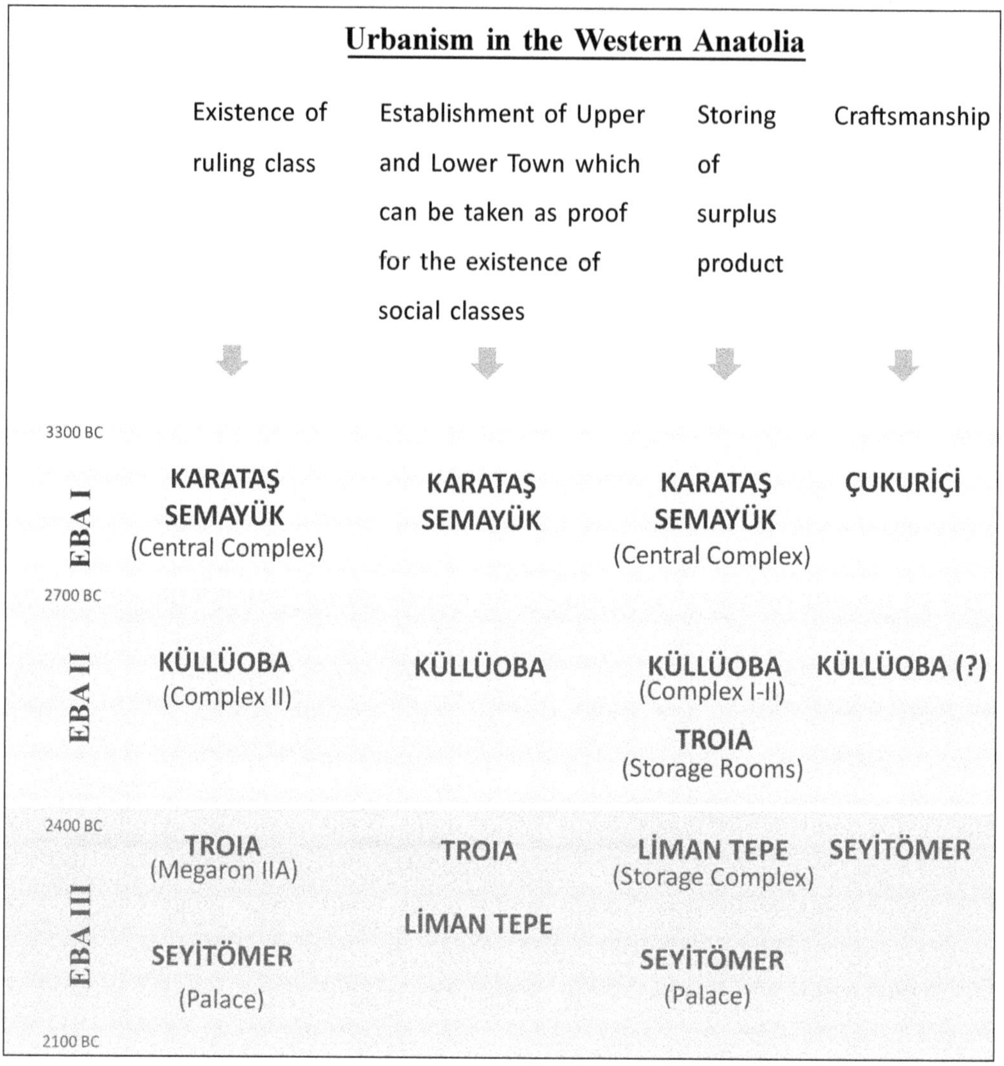

	Existence of ruling class	Establishment of Upper and Lower Town which can be taken as proof for the existence of social classes	Storing of surplus product	Craftsmanship
EBA I (3300 BC – 2700 BC)	KARATAŞ SEMAYÜK (Central Complex)	KARATAŞ SEMAYÜK	KARATAŞ SEMAYÜK (Central Complex)	ÇUKURİÇİ
EBA II (2700 BC – 2400 BC)	KÜLLÜOBA (Complex II)	KÜLLÜOBA	KÜLLÜOBA (Complex I-II) TROIA (Storage Rooms)	KÜLLÜOBA (?)
EBA III (2400 BC – 2100 BC)	TROIA (Megaron IIA) SEYİTÖMER (Palace)	TROIA LİMAN TEPE	LİMAN TEPE (Storage Complex) SEYİTÖMER (Palace)	SEYİTÖMER

FIGURE 10.2. Criteria for Urbanism in Western Anatolia.

Central and independent structures, having been constructed at least in the middle of EBA II Period in Küllüoba, located in the the Upper Sakarya Plain, east of Eskişehir, demonstrate the existence of a ruling class. In this regard, the building called Complex II is highly important (Efe and Fidan 2008). The complex in question was a simple structure consisting of one or two row-houses in its early phases. Then it became a complex following the additions applied in time. It is also shown that a "Multi-Roomed Building" in Bademağacı dated to this period and a complex defined as "Palace" in EBA III Period in Seyitömer settlement might have belonged to the rulers.[2]

FIGURE 10.3. 3D plan of Karataş Semayük Central Complex (Drawing by S. Kuşu and E. Fidan).

Unlike Inland Western Anatolia, structures of administrative function from the EBA I and II periods in the Coastal Region of Western Anatolia are not yet known. The earliest administrative structure in the aforementioned region is the monumental II A megaron of Troy IIc, dated to the beginning of the EBA III Period (Blegen et al. 1950:261; Mellaart 1959: Figure 6; Naumann 1998:162; Ünlüsoy 2006:140). Other adjacent megara might also have similar functions. The function of the Central Complex located in Liman Tepe, which was identified as "public building," is not fully understood. The appearance of administrative buildings in centers such as Kanlıgeçit in Thrace, and Kolonna and Lerna in Greece, along with the EBA III Period—according to the Anatolian chronology—can be interpreted as indicating that either the ruling class in the Inland Western Anatolia had emerged earlier or this development had been reflected on architecture in the region before (Arı et al. 2010:Figure 1; Walter and Felten 1981:12).

Lower and Upper Town (Social Class Differences)

One of the other criteria required to define a settlement as an urban site in Western Anatolia is the existence of lower and upper towns. In this new social organization, the area where the rulers live becomes more defined and better protected; the dense population in the

Lower Town increases the labor force. In this system, in a way so similar to the feudalism in Middle Ages Europe, only the ruler and the relatives and their servants live in the Upper Town, while the ordinary people who lived in the more densely populated Lower Town were engaged in agriculture, livestock, mining, and pottery (due to the division of labor).

Outside the modest EB I settlement of Karataş-Semayük, the concept of Lower Town and Upper Town in Inland Western Anatolia is known earliest from the beginning of the EB II on at Küllüoba (Figures 10.3–10.5).

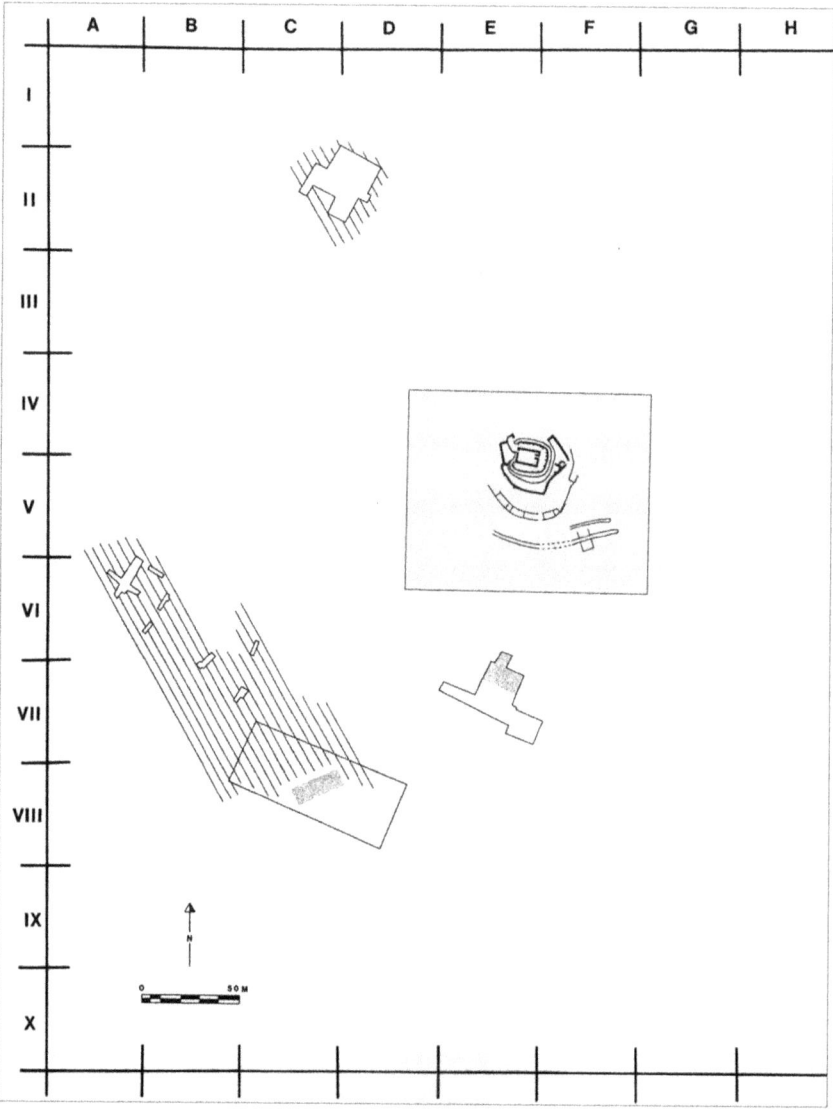

FIGURE 10.4. Karataş Semayük EBA I Settlement Plan (Mellink 1974: Fig. 1; Warner 1994: Plan 8).

In the Coastal Region of Western Anatolia, we can say that this settlement concept in centers such as Troy and Liman Tepe becomes apparent during the EBA III Period (Figures 10.6–10.7; Erkanal et al. 2003:432; Jablonka 2001:Figure 437, 439). Although remnants of the defense systems that are supposed to have encircled the Lower Town were exposed in these settlements, remains from the houses are hardly known. Remnants of the Lower Town at Troy must have been destroyed during the Classical Periods.

The remains unearthed 600 meters away from the Upper Town at Liman Tepe may belong to a defense system surrounding the Lower Town (Figure 10.7).[3] In Greece, on the other hand, Lower Towns have only been documented for certain in Tiryns (Harrison 1995:36). However, this model in question in Tiryns seems to have emerged during the EBA III Period, according to the Anatolian chronology.

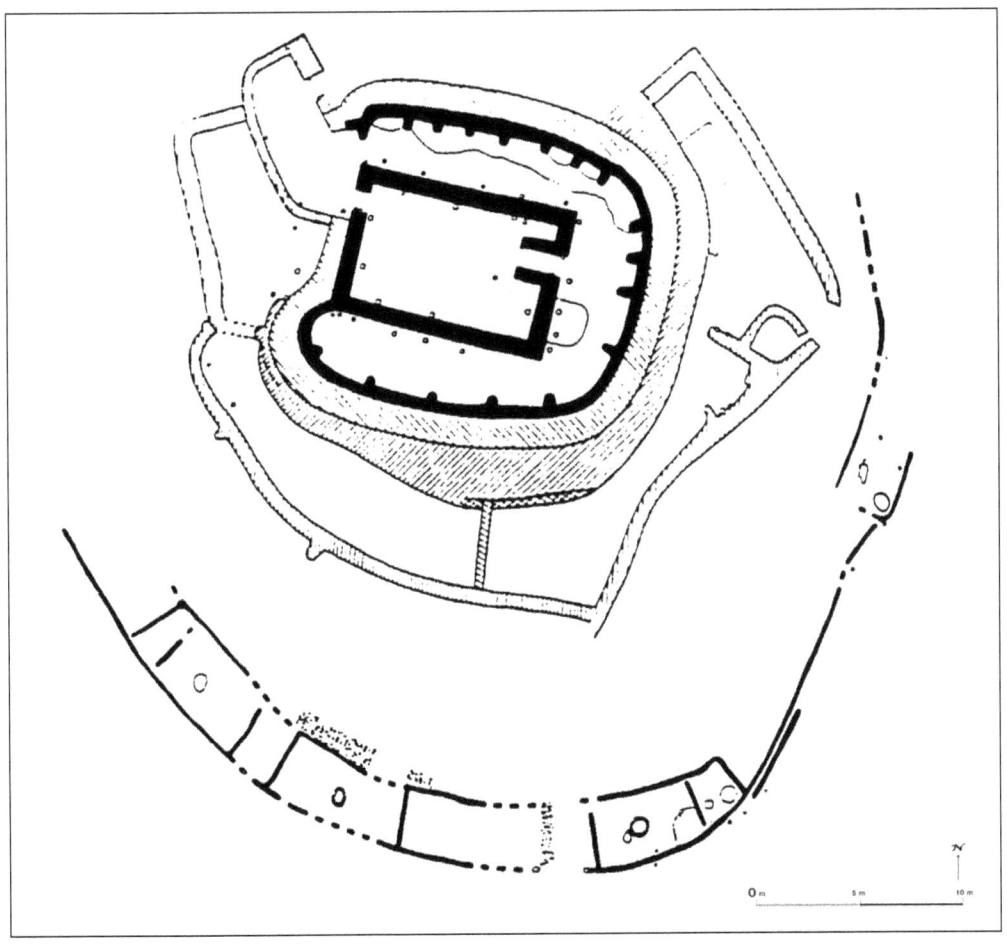

FIGURE 10.4. Continued.

FIGURE 10.5. Küllüoba EBA II Settlement Plan.

STORING OF SURPLUS PRODUCT

In Western Anatolia, due to the population increase during the Early Bronze Age, accommodation of sufficient product or the need to be prepared for a possible famine or aridity gain importance. The ruler managing to store the surplus product and distribute it fairly comes, no doubt, to a stronger position in the society. In this regard, it should be no coincidence that the majority of the storage facilities are hidden inside the administrative buildings or in the protected areas of Upper Towns in the settlements of Early Bronze Age Western Anatolian. While the basement of the Central Complex in Karataş-Semayük appears to have functioned as a storage room, three of the five units of Complex II at Küllüoba were used for storage purposes. In the Coastal Region of Western Anatolia, special buildings for storage were constructed in Liman Tepe and Troy during the EBA III Period (Mellart 1959:Figure 10.5; Şahoğlu 2005:Figure 3).

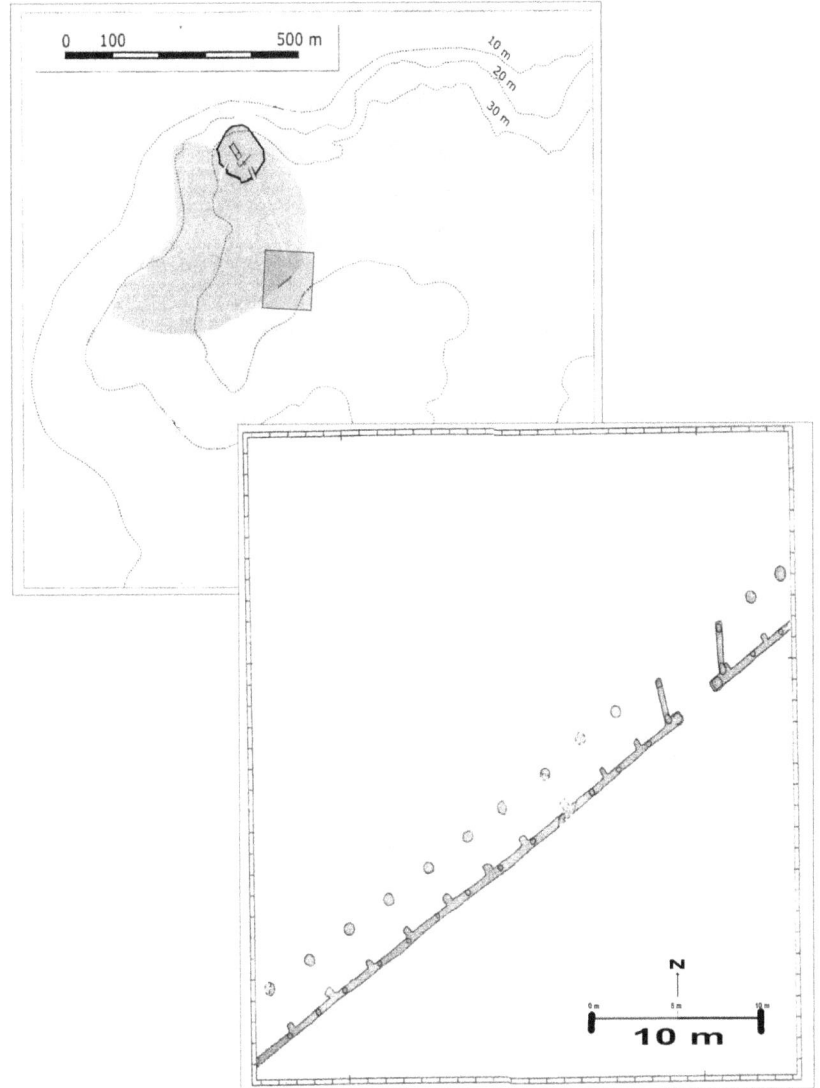

FIGURE 10.6. Settlement Plan of Troia IIc, Early Bronze Age III (Jablonka 2001: Fig. 437 and 439).

CRAFTSMANSHIP

The dictionary defines *craftsman* as an artisan producing goods to meet materialistic or aesthetic needs. It is possible that the majority of people were used as labor in agriculture and livestock during the EBA Period. Additionally, it is possible that the other section of the population might have occupied other areas according to their skills or under the

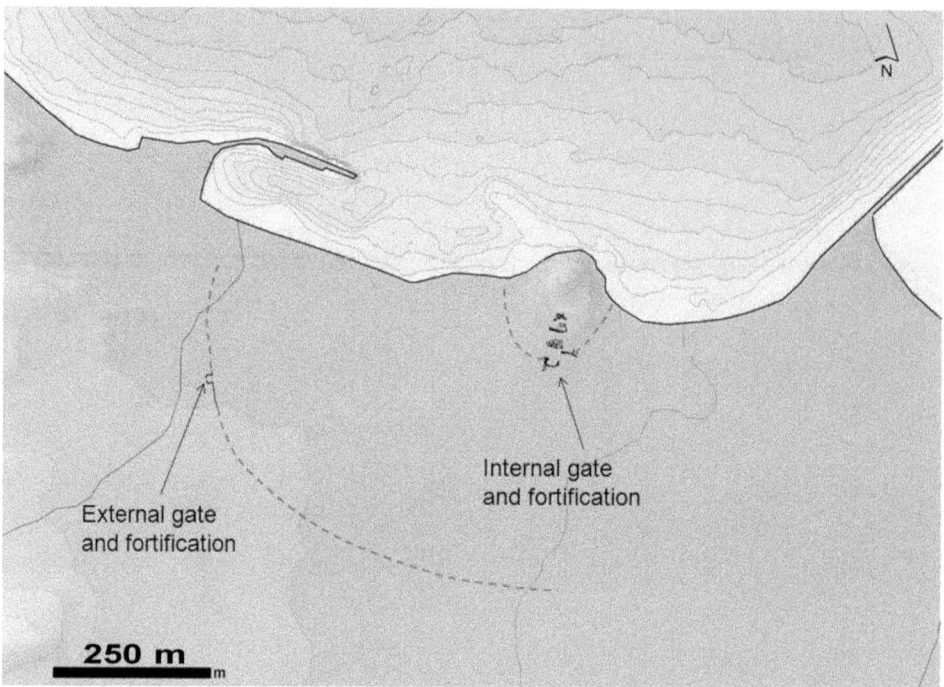

FIGURE 10.7. Topographical map of Liman Tepe (Drawing by M. Massa).

direction of rulers. It can be supposed that these craftsmen earned products cultivated by the farmers in the Lower Town and stored by the ruler living in the Upper Town; in return they produced jewelry, tools, and weapons out of metal, clay, and stone. It is most likely that this occupation was under the control of the ruler. Thus, in return for the ordered product, the ruler must have determined the share the craftsman would take.

The workshops that supported the production in question in Western Anatolia have not yet been found. However, metal workshops in Çukuriçi Mound from the EB I Period and pottery workshops in Seyitömer from the EB III Period are well known (Bilgen 2011; 2012; Horejs 2009). It is likely that certain partially excavated single-roomed structures exposed in the Lower Town at Küllüoba might have functioned as workshops (Figure 10.5). A few Lower Town houses excavated during 2011 and 2012 campaigns at Küllüoba support this premise.

Conclusion

We have clues for the gradual emergence of urbanism in certain settlements during the Early Bronze Age in Western Anatolia where a simpler architectural arrangement prevailed in pre-third millennium B.C. However, excavation of only a few settlements which would give information on urbanism in the entirety of Western Anatolia is the most important hindrance to making generalizations on the subject. On the other hand, we should emphasize that Western Anatolia went through important developmental phases sociopolitically during the Early Bronze Age. An administrative building and possible Lower Settlement with megara or long-houses in the EB I settlement of Karataş-Semayük can be interpreted as the first reflections of new political order on the architecture.

EB II is the period in which investigations have been conducted most and thereby we have the most information. It is possible to divide the region in two sections based on the development of architecture in this period: Inland Western Anatolia and the Aegean coastline. Settlements such as Demircihüyük, Keçiçayırı, Karaoğlan, and Bademağacı in Inland Western Anatolia can be characterized as modest villages or towns. At both Karataş-Semayük and especially Küllüoba continuing uninterrupted from the EB I period, the emergence of Lower and Upper Towns as well as administrative buildings in the succeeding EB II indicate the existence of a ruler. Social stratification can be considered a very important step in terms of urbanization. Hence, Küllüoba can be specified as an administrative center controlling at least some part of the Upper Sakarya Plain in which it is located. We can say that the ruler's building in the Upper Town was constructed at least in the middle of the Late EB II and remained in use for three to four generations until it went out of use in the Late EB II Period. We shouldn't forget that that a large settlement such as Beycesultan, which has been recently reexcavated in Inland Western Anatolia, shall provide us with important data in relation to urbanism in the future. Unlike Inland Western Anatolia, it is difficult to talk about urbanism on the Aegean coastline of Anatolia. The two important settlements in the region, Troy and Liman Tepe, were encircled by impressive defensive walls, as was the case on many other Aegean settlements. However, no public buildings have been recovered and the concept of Upper and Lower Town has not yet developed in both settlements. Hence, it would be reasonable to define these settlements as towns during the EBA II Period.

EBA III is the period in which an important breaking point occurred (Efe 2007). The investigations demonstrate that the settlements decreased in number, whereas the size of settlements got bigger (Dedeoğlu 2014:Figure 7–8; Sarı 2012:228, Figure 177). This brings centralization and thereby city-states concepts into mind. Unfortunately, investigations over this period in Inland Western Anatolia are so insufficient that our knowledge is practically limited to Seyitömer, which served as an important production center. On the coast, the earliest evidence of Lower Town in Troy comes from IIc dated to the beginning of this period. The settlement of this layer, the diameter of which appears to have reached 500 meters, has a ruler's building/public building (II A Megaron) which is the first of its kind at Troy. The excavations carried out in the last years at Liman Tepe provided clues for both Lower Town and the Central Complex that possibly functioned as a public building.

In conclusion, for the urbanism of the Western Anatolian Early Bronze Age, the following criteria can be put forth: existence of ruling class, emergence of Lower and Upper Town, storage of surplus product, and existence of craftsmanship/division of labor. In this regard, the concept of urbanism, the earliest simple reflections of which we see in the EB I settlement of Karataş-Semayük, further developed in the EB II settlement of Küllüoba in Inland Western Anatolia and in the EB III settlements of Troy and Liman Tepe situated on the Aegean coastline of Anatolia. Unfortunately, we cannot trace the development of urbanism through the Late EB III in the region. We need more research and excavations particularly of large-sized settlements in order to reach more concrete and lasting conclusions regarding the developmental phases of urbanization in Western Anatolia.

Notes

1. The Central Complex hasn't been published completely yet. Most important parts of the pre reports of excavations are: Mellink 1964:269–278; Mellink 1965:241–251; Mellink 1969:293–307.
2. Duru 2008:150; Duru/Umurtak 2009:Plan 1; Bilgen 2012. However, it is still in dispute that the structure in Bademağacı has an administrative function, since it exhibits an irregular plan and has no distinctive characteristics in comparison to normal houses. Furthermore, the middle part of the settlement was ruined by erosion, especially in the north. Therefore, we shouldn't rule out the possibility that there are other houses inside the settlement in addition to the row houses.
3. My sincere thanks go to V. Şahoğlu and M. Massa for giving me the permission to publish the drawing. The studies on the pottery in relation with the dating of the inner and outer fortification walls have not yet been completed (pers com. with Vasıf Şahoğlu). The dating (Late EB II or EB III) and the contemporaneity of these walls will be more precisely determined only after this evaluation.

References Cited

Arı, İ., Z. Eres, and A. Demirtaş 2010 Kanlıgeçit Açık Hava Müzesi: Trakya'da Bir İlk Tunç Çağ İç Kalesi. *TÜBA-Kültür Envanteri Dergisi* 8:229–240.

Bilgen, N. 2011 *Seyitömer Höyük Kazısı Ön Raporu (2006–2010)*. Dumlupınar Üniversitesi-TKİ, Kütahya.

Bilgen, N. 2012 *Seyitömer Höyük Kazısı Ön Raporu (2011–2012)*. Dumlupınar Üniversitesi-TKİ, Kütahya.

Blegen, C. W., L. J. Caskey, M. Rawson, and J. Sperling 1950 *Troy I General Introduction The First and Second Settlements*. Princeton University Press, Princeton.

Çevik, Ö. 2005 Arkeolojik Kanıtlar Işığında Tarihte İlk Kentler ve Kentleşme Süreci Kurumsal Bir Değerlendirme. Arkeoloji ve Sanat Yayınları, İstanbul.

Childe, G. 1950 The Urban Revolution. *Town Planning Review* 21(1):3–17.

Childe, G. 1979 The Urban Revolution. In *Ancient Cities of the Indus*, edited by G. L. Possehl, pp. 12–17. Vikas Publishing House, New Delhi.

Dedeoğlu, F. 2014 Yukarı Menderes Havzası Bölgesel Yerleşim Analizi: Erken Tunç Çağı'nda Sosyo-Ekonomik Örgütlenmedeki Değişim ve Dönüşüm Süreçleri. In *Tematik Arkeoloji Serisi 1—Yerleşim Sistemleri ve Mekan Analizi*, edited by Ö. Çevik, B. Erdoğu, pp. 19–42. Ege Yayınları, Istanbul.

Duru, R. 2008 *MÖ 8000'den MÖ 2000'e Burdur–Antalya Bölgesi'nin Altıbin Yılı*. Suna-İnan Kıraç Akdeniz Medeniyetleri Araştırma Enstitüsü, Monografi Dizisi 4, Antalya.

Duru, R., and G. Umurtak 2009 Bademağacı 2008 yılı Kazıları. *ANMED Anadolu Akdenizi Araştırma Haberleri* 7:15–21.

Efe, T. 2007 The Theories of the "Great Caravan Route" between Cilicia and Troy: The Early Bronze Age III Period in Inland Western Anatolia. *Anatolian Studies* 57:47–64.

Efe, T. and E. Fidan 2008 Complex II In the Early Bronze II Upper Town of Küllüoba Near Eskişehir. *Anatolica XXXIV*:67–102.

Erkanal, H., M. Artzy, and O. Kouka 2003 2001 Yılı Liman Tepe Kazıları. 24. *Kazı Sonuçları Toplantısı* 1:423–437. Ankara.

Fidan, E. 2012 Küllüoba İlk Tunç Çağı Mimarisi. *MASROP/ E-Dergi* 7:1–41.

Harrison, S. 1995 Domestic Architecture in Early Helladic II: Some Observation on the Form of Non Monumental Houses. *The Annual of the British School at Athens* 90:23–40.

Horejs, B. 2009 Metalworkers at the Çukuriçi Höyük? An Early Bronze Age Mould and a "Near Eastern Weight" from Western Anatolia. In *Metals and Societies. Studies in honour of Barbara S. Ottaway*, edited by T. L. Kienlin and B. Roberts, pp. 358–368. R. Habelt, Bonn.

Jablonka, P. 2001 Şehrin Tahta Surları Troia II Aşağı Şehrinin Savunması. In *Troia: Düş ve Gerçek*, edited by M. Korfmann, pp. 391–394. Homer Publications, Istanbul.

Keleş, R. 1980 *Kentbilimleri Sözlüğü*. Türk Dil Kurumu Yayınları, Ankara.

Mellaart, J. 1959 Notes on the Architectural Remains of Troy I and II. *Anatolian Studies* 9:131–162.

Mellink, M. J. 1964 Excavations at Karataş-Semayük in Lycia, 1963. *American Journal of Archeology* 68:269–278.

Mellink, M. J. 1965 Excavations at Karataş-Semayük in Lycia, 1964. *American Journal of Archeology* 69:241–251.

Mellink, M. J. 1969 Excavations at Karataş-Semayük and Elmalı. *American Journal of Archeology* 73:293–307.

Mellink, M. J. 1974 Excavations at Karataş-Semayük and Elmalı, Lycia, 1973. *American Journal of Archaeology* 78:351–359.

Naumann, R. 1998 *Eski Anadolu Mimarlığı*. Türk Tarih Kurumu, Istanbul.

Özdoğan, M. 2006 Yakın Doğu Kentleri ve Batı Anadolu'da Kentleşme Süreci. In *Hayat Erkanal'a Armağan, Kültürlerin Yansıması. Studies in Honor of Hayat Erkanal, Cultural Reflections*, pp. 571–576, edited by A. Erkanal-Öktü, E. Özgen et al. Homer Publications, Istanbul.

Şahoğlu, V. 2005 The Anatolian Trade Network and the Izmir Region during the Early Bronze Age. *Oxford Journal of Archaeology* 24:339–361.

Sarı, D. 2012 İlk Tunç Çağı ve Orta Tunç Çağı'nda Batı Anadolu'nun Kültürel ve Siyasal Gelişimi. *MASROP/E-Dergi* 7:112–249.

Ünlüsoy, S. 2006 Vom Reihenhaus zum Megaron-Troia I bis Troia III. In *Troia Archaologie Siedlungshügels und Seiner Landschaft*, edited by M. Korfmann, pp. 133–144. Verlag Philipp von Zabern, Mainz am Rhein.

Walter, H., and F. Felten 1981 *Alt-Agina III. Die Vorgeschıchtlıche Stad*. Verlag Philipp Von Zabern, Mainz am Rhein.

Warner, J. L. 1994 *Elmalı-Karataş II, The Early Bronze Age Village of Karataş*. Bryn Mawr, Pennsylvania.

CHAPTER ELEVEN

Seyitömer Mound during the Early Bronze Age

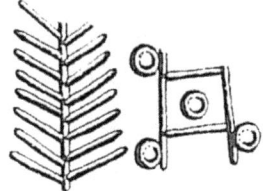

A. Nejat Bilgen*

Seyitömer Mound is located in the Çelikler Seyitömer Electricity Production Company's reserve zone situated 26 kilometers northwest of the province of Kütahya within the borders of the old town of Seyitömer. The original height of the mound was 23.5 meters, with an area of 150 × 140 meters (Figure 11.1).

Excavations at Seyitömer Mound began with the aim of mining the 12 million tons of exploitable coal reserve underneath the mound. The excavations on the site initiated by the Directorate of Eskişehir Museum were continued until 1990 and then excavations were undertaken by the Directorate of Afyon Museum from 1990 to 1995. The excavations, then interrupted, were reinitiated by the staff of DPU-Department of Archaeology under the direction of Prof. Dr. A. Nejat Bilgen, through a protocol signed on February 27, 2006, between Dumlupınar University (DPÜ) and General Directorate of Coal Enterprises of Turkey (TKİ) for a duration of 5+1 years. The protocol was extended for three years in 2011. Seyitömer Lignite Company was privatized in 2013 by the Turkish Privatization Administration and the excavations were continued under Çelikler Seyitömer Electric Production Company.

The architectural stratigraphy of the mound that was determined after the archaeological excavations is as follows:

Layer I (Roman Period: A.D. 255–363)

Layer II (Hellenistic Period: 334–30 B.C.)
  II-A: Late Phase
  II-B: Early Phase

---

*Prof. Dr. A. Nejat Bilgen, Dumlupınar Üniversitesi, Fen-Edebiyat Fakültesi, Arkeoloji Bölümü, nejat.bilgen@dpu.edu.tr

FIGURE 11.1. Aerial view of Seyitömer Höyük.

Layer III (Achaemenid Period: 500–334 B.C.)
  III-A: 4th century BC (400–334 B.C.)
  III-B: 5th century BC (500–400 B.C.)

Layer IV (Middle Bronze Age: 20th–18th centuries B.C.)
  IV-A: Late Phase (1750–1700 B.C.)
  IV-B: Middle Phase (1790–1750 B.C.)
  IV-C: Early Phase (20th–19th centuries B.C.)

Layer V (Early Bronze Age: 3000–2000 B.C.)
  V-A: Late Phase (2150–2000 B.C.)
  V-B: Middle Phase (2250–2150 B.C.)
  V-C: Early Phase (2350–2250 B.C.)

Layer I (Roman Period)

The archaeological remains pertaining to this period were encountered in the upper platform of the mound. The remains at the center of the mound include foundations of a sanctuary and a sacred canal and a bothros associated with this building. These were the only architectural remains dated to the Roman Period in the upper platform of the mound. Buildings, courtyards, a water canal, and water wells were excavated on the southwestern slope of the mound (Figure 11.2). A large number of roof tile fragments, coins, and other small finds were also discovered here. This indicates that the upper

FIGURE 11.2. Roman period remains from Seyitömer Höyük.

platform of the mound was used as a sacred area and the main settlement was located around and on the slopes of the mound.

Layer II (Hellenistic Period)

The remains belonging to this period were unearthed during 2007 and 2008 excavations and they are represented in the complex buildings and individual buildings located at the top of the mound. The scientifically documented Hellenistic Period architectural remains were removed.

Layer III (Achaemenid Period)

This layer, which included two architectural phases, is comprised of individual buildings. The settlement was surrounded with a terrace wall during the fourth century B.C. The one-sided terrace wall leans on the slope and they were built forming a step-like glacis. The significant findings discovered in this layer include terracotta figurines, a marl die, Attic pottery, and a sword.

Layer IV (Middle Bronze Age)

Three architectural phases, A, B and C, were distinguished in the Middle Bronze Age layer. Earthquake cracks were discovered in the B and C phases. The aforementioned cracks point at the oldest known earthquake in the region and many architectural remains and small finds affected by the earthquake were discovered. A large number of skeletons were discovered inside the buildings that collapsed during the earthquake and it was also determined that some of these skeletons had their brains preserved inside the skulls (Figure 11.3, 11.4a, 11.4b).

The architectural elements discovered in all three phases share the same building technique. All the phases belonging to the Middle Bronze Age do not display an organized settlement pattern. The buildings, which were built using two-sided walls, might

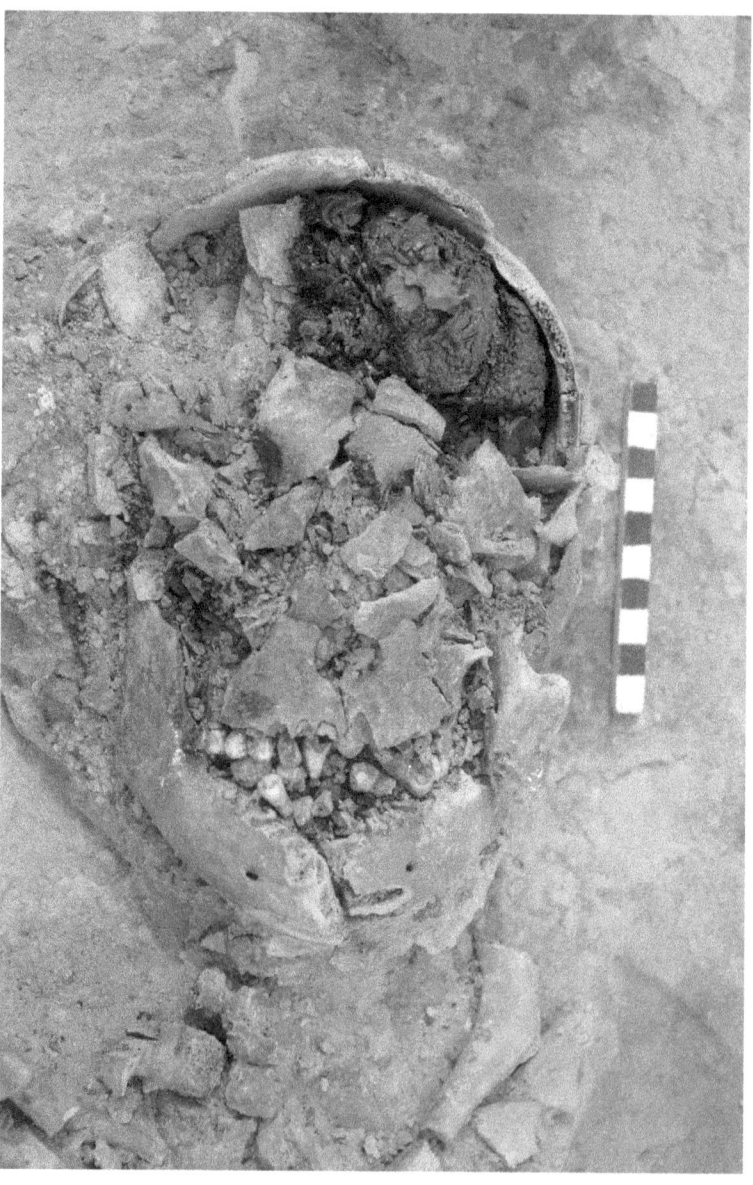

FIGURE 11.3. Carbonized brain tissue from the Middle Bronze Age at Seyitömer Höyük.

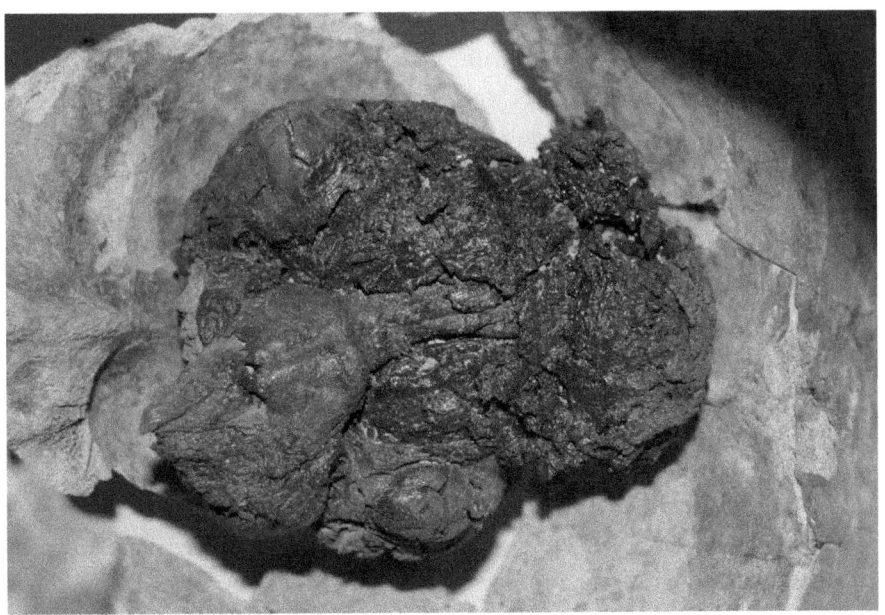

FIGURE 11.4A. Detail of carbonized brain tissue from the Middle Bronze Age at Seyitömer Höyük.

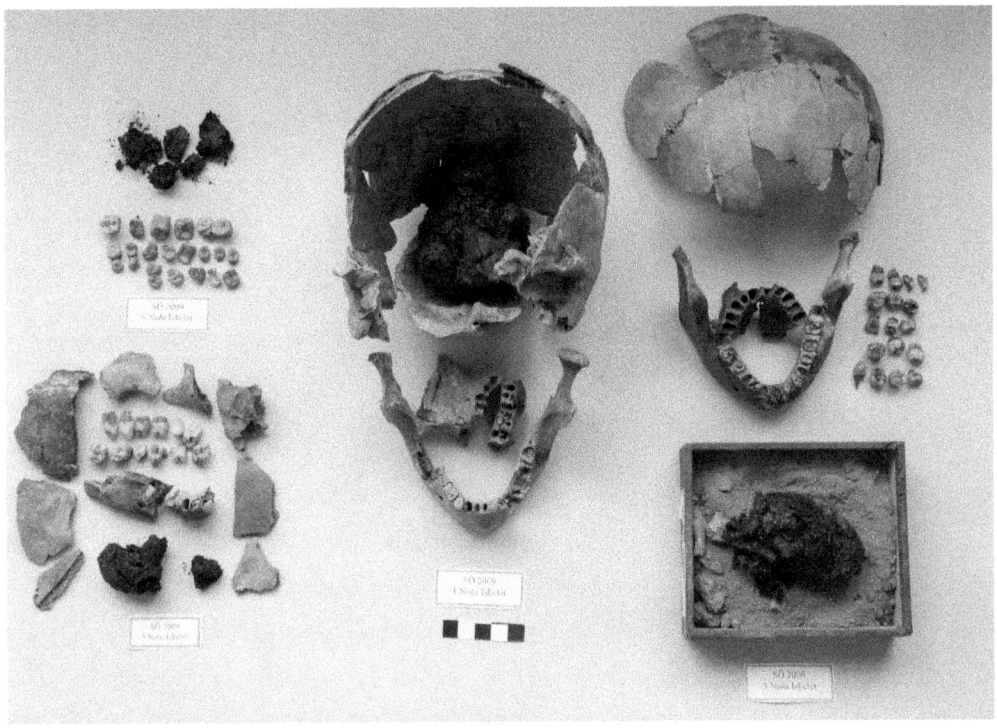

FIGURE 11.4B. Detail of carbonized brain tissue from the Middle Bronze Age at Seyitömer Höyük.

contain ovens, compartments, workshops, platforms, and kilns. It was determined that the Mound was surrounded by a tough fortification wall during the Middle Bronze Age, C Phase. However, the fortification wall was not entirely preserved and the total preserved length of this wall was measured at 182 meters (Figure 11.5). Moreover, it would be appropriate to assert that a settlement also existed outside the fortification as indicated by the buildings discovered outside the fortification walls.

The findings dated to this phase include pithoi, pitchers, bowls, spindle whorls, loom weights, bronze axes, bronze pins, a lead figurine (Figure 11.6), rythons (Figure 11.7), and seals (Figure 11.8). These findings are significant as they affirm the existence of the trade relations of Seyitömer Mound with Central Anatolia and Mesopotamia.

Layer V (Early Bronze Age)

The Early Bronze Age is represented at Seyitömer Mound in two phases that are referred to as Early Bronze Age II (EBA II) and Early Bronze Age III (EBA III) in archaeological literature. Those settlements pertaining to the EBA III weren't unearthed until the present time and EBA II layers have not been excavated yet. However, the sounding excavations

FIGURE 11.5. Location of Middle Bronze Age circuit wall at Seyitömer Höyük.

FIGURE 11.6. Middle Bronze Age lead figurine.

FIGURE 11.7. Middle Bronze Age foot rhyton.

FIGURE 11.8. Selection of seals from Seyitömer Höyük.

carried out confirm the existence of further remains that belong to the aforementioned period. The EBA III layer referred to in our study as Layer V is architecturally divided into phases, that is, the collapsed settlement was built again and again. Three phases were categorically determined and these were identified in the stratigraphy of the mound from top to bottom as V-A, V-B, and V-C phases.

A significant building was encountered among the architectural remains of V-A phase (Plan 11.1). This is the megaron planned sanctuary located at the center of the Mound. In addition to this, other megaron buildings that were used either as dwellings, storage houses, or workshops were aligned along the western and northern boundaries of the upper platform of the Mound (Figure 11.9, 11.10).

It was determined that the sanctuary that collapsed during V-B phase provided the foundations of the sanctuary at this phase. It was also determined that the sanctuary was renovated three times after its construction during the V-A phase. During the last phase the intermediate room was closed and filled to form a platform. Many in-situ finds that provide clues about the use of the building were discovered over the last phase floor of the sanctuary. Among these were rhytons, libation vessels, and various other pottery finds (Figure 11.11).

The workshops, kilns, and pottery moulds discovered during this phase indicate that Seyitömer Mound was an important production center (Figure 11.12).

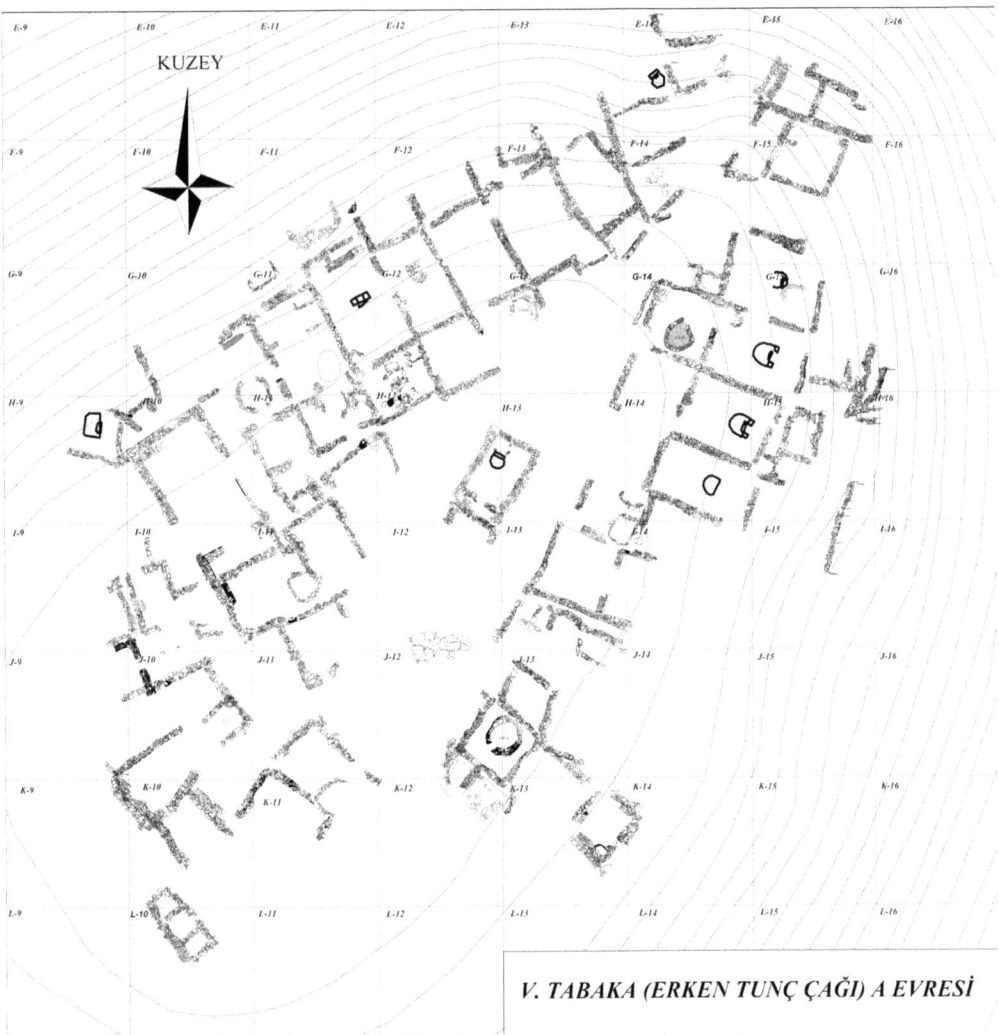

PLAN 11.1. Early Bronze Age Phase V-A settlement at Seyitömer Höyük.

All of the kilns inside the buildings have the same plan. They were built using clay and stones. The kilns are located inside the largest room of the building, named the main room. The kilns are built over a slightly elevated round platform and backed by two connected horn-shaped ridges. It is believed that these ridges were not functional but had sacred value.

It was determined that the well-planned V-A phase settlement underwent a large fire that spread to the entire settlement and caused the buildings to collapse.

It is possible to presume that the V-B phase settlement was practically almost the same as V-A phase settlement (Plan 11.2). The overall plan of the settlement is similar to the V-A phase settlement. In many buildings the plans were preserved and similar

FIGURE 11.9. Sanctuary building at center of mound from Early Bronze Age Phase V-A.

FIGURE 11.10. Detail of sanctuary building at center of mound from Early Bronze Age Phase V-A.

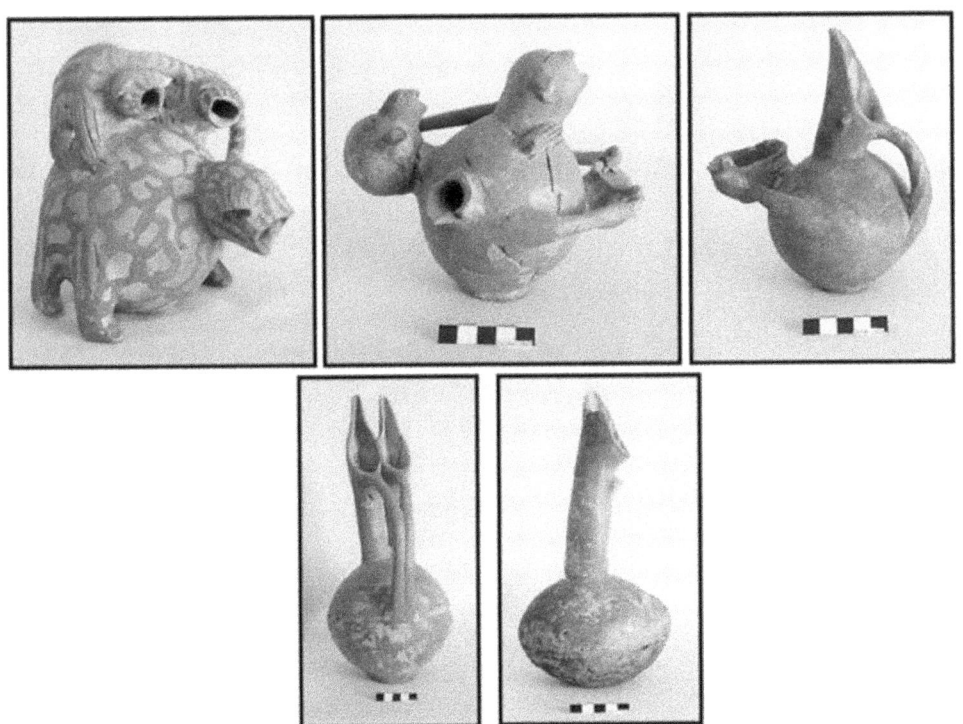

FIGURE 11.11. Libation vessels from sanctuary building in Early Bronze Age Phase V-A.

FIGURE 11.12. Evidence for use pottery production, including pottery kilns in houses and moulds for shaping pottery.

156   A. Nejat Bilgen

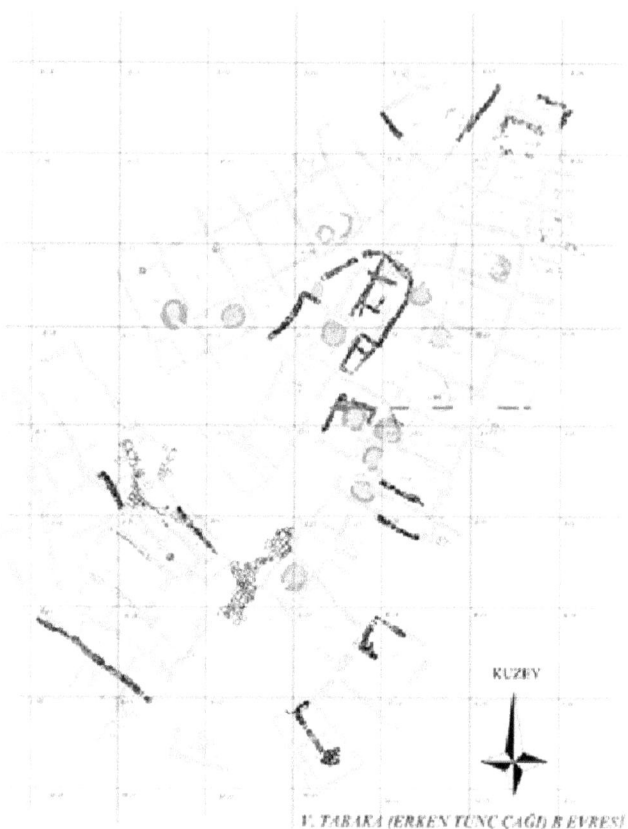

PLAN 11.2. Early Bronze Age Phase V-A settlement at Seyitömer Höyük.

buildings were erected over the remains of the former phase. Some buildings have minor changes in the building plans. This phase also has buildings that were used as dwellings, storage houses, and workshops similar to V-A phase. The V-B phase settlement also underwent a large fire.

The architectural remains of V-B phase include two significant buildings. One of these buildings is the megaron-planned sanctuary located at the center of the mound. The other is the palace complex located on the southwest area of the mound. In addition to these, other megaron buildings that were used either as dwellings, storage houses, or workshops were aligned along the western and northern boundaries of the upper platform of the Mound. Moreover, an alleyway that stretches from the north of the sanctuary to the northeast of the Mound was unearthed.

It was observed that the sanctuary was independently built, while all other buildings shared common walls. During this phase the building had a main room, a front room, and a courtyard before this. In addition to these, there are two rooms adjacent to the megaron on the northwestern part sharing this wall. There is a hearth with horn-like ridges at the back in the middle of the main room. The various pottery forms discovered in situ over the floor of the main room along with the rhytons used as libation pottery are significant as they also verify that the building was a sanctuary.

A large palace complex was unearthed on the southwestern part of the upper platform of the mound in the layer that belongs to V-B phase. The palace is composed of a main room at the center accompanied by a front room and several storage rooms. The main room measures 8.304 × .90 meters, and there is a large kiln inside. The kiln has horn-shaped ridges, which were observed in all other buildings of the layer. The main room connects to the storage rooms through a passage at the back corner. The finds encountered inside the main room were especially significant. Among the abundant finds encountered, these significant finds include golden, silver, and bronze hairpins, pendants and rosettes, and thousands of beads alongside pottery. Ten Akkadian cylinder seals from Mesopotamia are also among the significant findings.

V-B and V-A phases appear similar in both the settlement plan and architectural techniques. There are no cultural differences between these phases, as also supported by other findings. As a result, the general properties of the two phases were determined as follows:

All of the hearths inside the buildings have the same plan. The hearths were built using clay and stones. The hearths are located inside the largest room of the building named the main room. The hearths are built over a slightly elevated round platform and backed by two connected horn-shaped ridges.

The pottery kilns are found both indoors and outdoors. Most of the kilns lean on the walls of the buildings they were built in. In some examples the kiln completely occupies the building, which might be interpreted as instances wherein which the walls were later built in order to prevent heat loss. There are kilns inside the buildings which were probable pottery workshops. It can be presumed that dwellings, workshops and storage rooms might exist side by side or inside one another. Many pottery vessels, cups, weights, spindle whorls, and pottery moulds were discovered inside some of the workshops which suggest that these places were also used for storage purposes. All the pottery kilns have either round or oval plans. Pottery moulds and moulded pottery were discovered inside the workshops which suggest that moulding technique was used. These moulds were made of clay or stone and are spherical or semi-spherical.

The largest group of finds discovered from the Early Bronze Age layers is the pottery. The pottery findings include bowls, depata and similar drinking vessels, pithoi, pots and various pitchers, lids, tripod cups, and similar finds (Figure 11.13). Another group of finds are the loom weights and spindle whorls, which may be grouped under weaving materials. The terracotta finds also include brushes (Figure 11.14). Metal findings include jewelry, axes and other sharp objects, and various pins (Figure 11.15). The stone finds include axes, burnishing stones, blades, whetstones and pestles, various beads, and stone idols (Figure 11.16, 11.17). Bone objects include various handles, handle rivets, awls and pins, spatula, and similar tools (Figure 11.18).

FIGURE 11.13. Early Bronze Age pottery from Seyitömer Höyük.

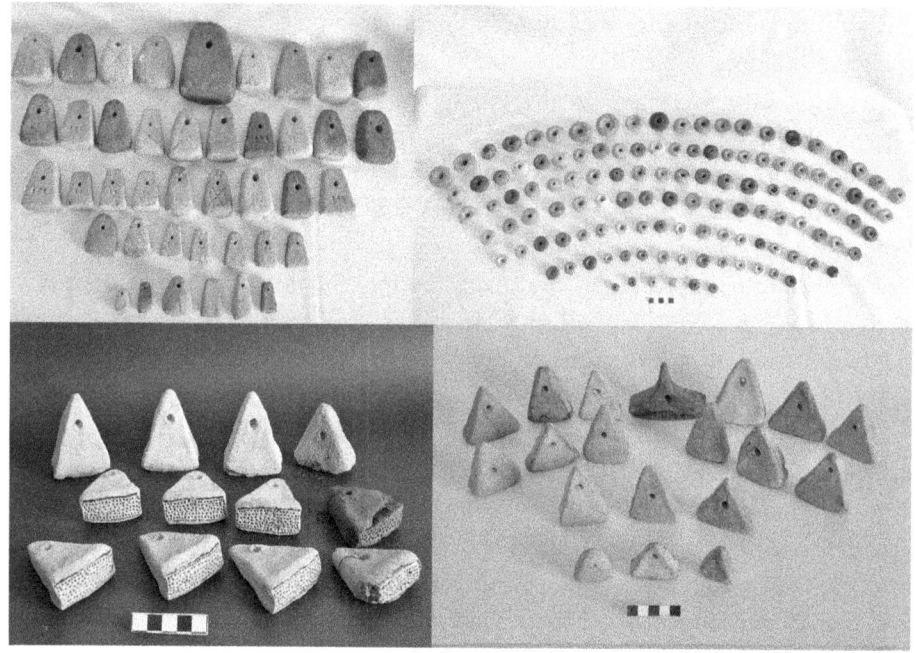

FIGURE 11.14. Terracotta brushes from the Early Bronze Age.

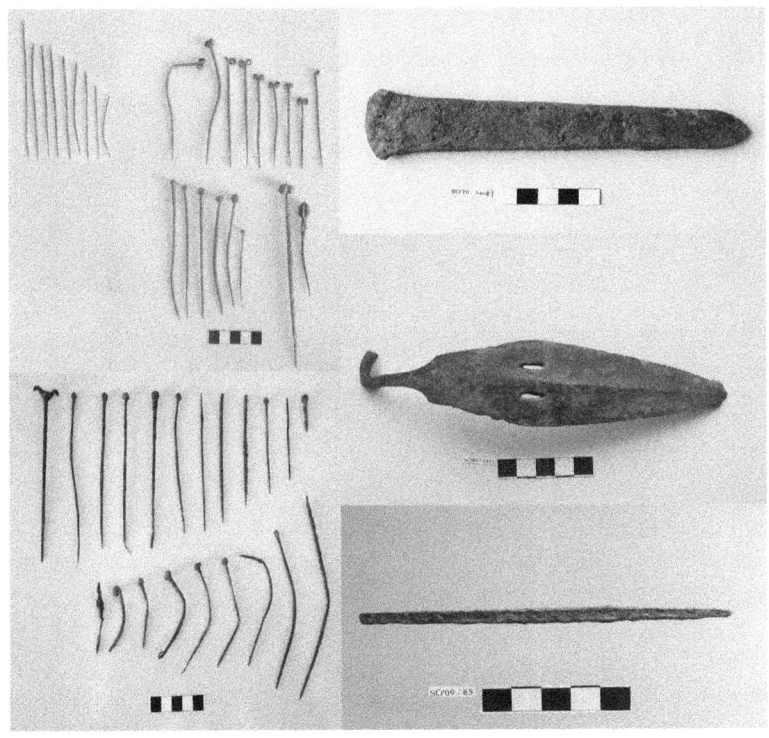

FIGURE 11.15. Metal finds from the Early Bronze Age.

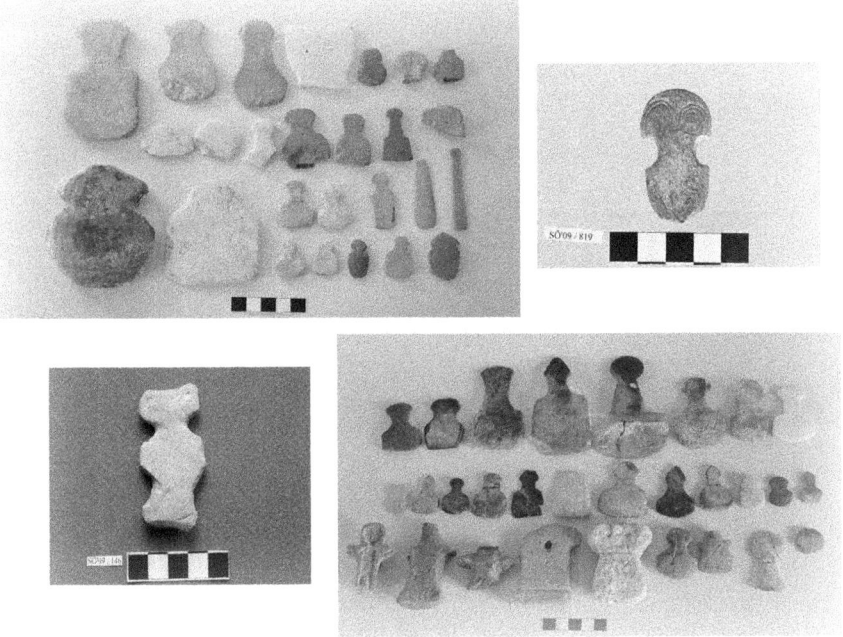

FIGURE 11.16. Figurines and idols from the Early Bronze Age.

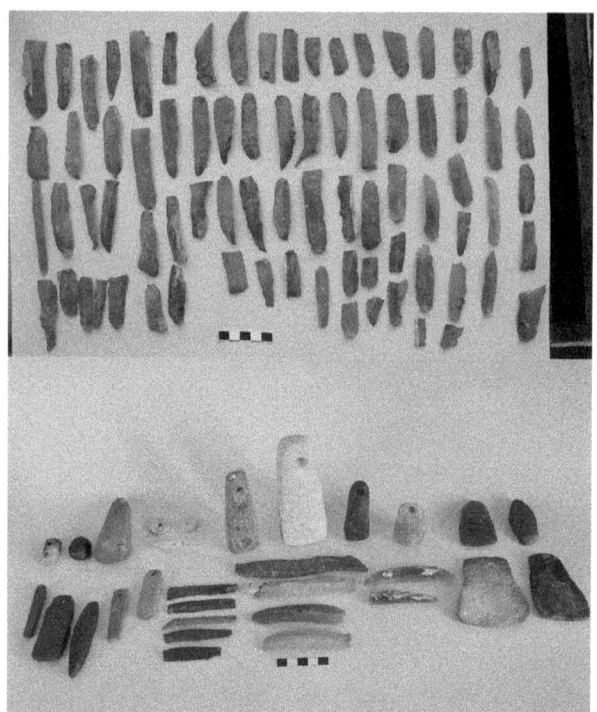

FIGURE 11.17. Stone objects from the Early Bronze Age.

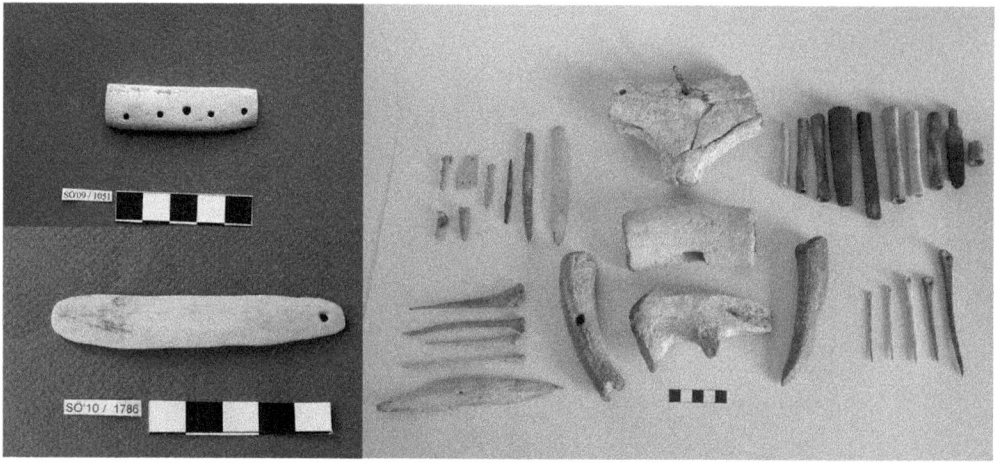

FIGURE 11.18. Bone objects from the Early Bronze Age.

The excavations concerning the V-C phase settlement are continuing; however, the unearthed sections suggest an extensive use of mud bricks during this period compared to later phases.

General Evaluation of the Early Bronze Age

Important conclusions were reached about the Early Bronze Age settlement considering the present data obtained through the Seyitömer Mound excavations. An organized pattern of settlement was observed in all phases of the Early Bronze Age. In short, the Early Bronze Age settlement was planned at a single time and the buildings were constructed accordingly, resulting in an organized settlement plan. Moreover, a similar city-planning mentality was not observed during the Middle Bronze Age settlement, suggesting the inhabitants of the Mound during these separate ages were members of different cultures.

A transition from the Early Bronze Age to the Middle Bronze Age was not encountered at the Mound, also suggesting that the Mound was peopled by different, unconnected tribes during these eras.

The present findings suggest that a cult of the bull existed alongside the cult of the mother goddess. Religious objects include original zoomorphic rhytons, bull figurines, and long-necked trefoil cups together with idols.

Moulded pottery dominated pottery production during the Early Bronze Age. Moulds, kilns, and the large number of pottery finds suggest that the art of shaping clay and making pottery that started during 3000 B.C. transformed into the art of tile making through time, which is one of the leading industries in present-day Kütahya.

Architectural remains that belong to the Early Bronze Age C Phase were excavated during the 2013 excavations. After the excavations, it was determined that C phase was similar to A and B phases in terms of pottery and small finds, while it was completely different in terms of architecture. However, different pottery forms and finds were also obtained despite similarities. For instance, stone moulds were not encountered during previous phases. The ongoing excavations on the C phase are going to be finalized by the end of the 2014 excavation season.

More than 7,000 inventoried items and 20,000 studied items were delivered to the Kütahya Archaeological Museum during 2006–2013 excavations, and 1,381 items are exhibited at Private Dumlupınar University Museum. Seyitömer Mound excavations emerged as one of the leading excavation projects with regard to its budget and the large spectrum of finds, especially considering the period of excavations (six months every year), the number of staff (300 workers), and the number of finds.

References Cited

Altınöz, M. A., B. İnce, A. Sav, A. Dinçer, S. Cengiz, Z. Yazıcı, H. Altuncul, and A. N. Bilgen
    2010 Could a 3800-yr Old Brain Still Exert Traces of Life? Analysis on the Bases of Organic Lipids, DNA, and trace elements. *Archaeological Research in Western Central Anatolia* (The IIIrd International Symposium of Archaeology, Kütahya 8th–9th March 2010), pp. 232–252. Üçmart Press, Kütahya.

Altınöz, M. A., A. Sav, B. İnce, A. Dinçer, S. Cengiz, Z. Yazıcı, H. Altuncul, and A. N. Bilgen
    2010 A 3800 Yr Old Brain: Looking to the History in the Light of Macroscopical and

Microscopical Anatomy and Computer Tomograpy. *Archaeological Research in Western Central Anatolia* (The IIIrd International Symposium of Archaeology, Kütahya 8th–9th March 2010), pp. 212–231. Üçmart Press, Kütahya.

Aydın, N. 1991 Seyitömer Höyük Kurtarma Kazısı 1989. In *Müze Kurtarma Kazıları Semineri, 19–20 Nisan 1990 Ankara*, pp. 191–204. T.C. Kültür Bakanlığı, Anıtlar ve Müzeler Genel Müdürlüğü, Ankara.

Bilgen, N. A. 2008 Seyitömer Höyüğü 2006 Yılı Kazısı. *29. Kazı Sonuçları Toplantısı, 28 Mayıs–1 Haziran 2007*, pp. 321–323. Kültür ve Turizm Bakanlığı, Ankara.

Bilgen, N. A. 2009 Seyitömer Höyüğü 2007 Yılı Kazısı. *30. Kazı Sonuçları Toplantısı, 26–30 Mayıs 2008*, pp. 71–88. Kültür ve Turizm Bakanlığı, Ankara.

Bilgen, N. A., C. Brixhe, and G. Coşkun 2011 Un nouveau site épigraphique paleo-phrygien: Seyitömer Höyük. *KADMOS* 50:141–150.

Bilgen, N. A., G. Coşkun, and Z. Bilgen 2010 Seyitömer Höyüğü 2008 Yılı Kazısı. *31. Kazı Sonuçları Toplantısı, 25–29 Mayıs 2009, Denizli, (1. Cilt)*, pp. 341–354. Kültür ve Turizm Bakanlığı, Ankara.

Bilgen, N. A., G. Coşkun, N. Yüzbaşıoğlu, and A. Kuru 2011a Seyitömer Höyüğü 2009 Yılı Kazısı. *32. Kazı Sonuçları Toplantısı, 24–28 Mayıs 2010, İstanbul, (1. Cilt)*, pp. 367–380. Kültür ve Turizm Bakanlığı, Ankara.

Bilgen, N. A., ed. 2011b *Seyitömer Höyük Kazısı Ön Raporu (2006–2010)*. Dumlupınar Üniversitesi Fen-Edebiyat Fakültesi Arkeoloji Bölümü, Kütahya.

Bilgen, N. A., G. Coşkun, Z. Bilgen, A. Kuru, N. Yüzbaşıoğlu, F. Ç. Özcan, S. Çırakoğlu, and S. Silek 2012 Seyitömer Höyük 2010 Yılı Kazısı. *33. Kazı Sonuçları Toplantısı, 23–28 Mayıs 2011, Malatya, (1. Cilt)*, pp. 233–255. Kültür ve Turizm Bakanlığı, Ankara.

Bilgen, A. N., G. Coşkun, Z. Bilgen, N. Yüzbaşıoğlu, A. Kuru, S. Silek, S. Çırakoğlu, F. Ç. Özcan, M. B. Akalın, and B. Dikmen 2013a *Seyitömer Höyük Kazısı Ön Raporu (2011–2012)*. Dumlupınar Üniversitesi, Kütahya.

Bilgen, A. N., G. Coşkun, Z. Bilgen, N. Ünan, S. Silek, S. Çırakoğlu, F. Ç. Özcan, A. Kuru, and Z. Kuzu 2013b Seyitömer Höyük 2011 Yılı Kazısı *34. Kazı Sonuçları Toplantısı, 28 Mayıs–1 Haziran 2012, Çorum, (1. Cilt)*, pp. 201–216. Kültür ve Turizm Bakanlığı, Ankara.

Coşkun, G. 2010 Attic Pottery from Seyitömer Höyük. *TÜBA-AR* 13:61–76.

Coşkun, G. 2011a Achaemenid Bowls from Seyitömer Höyük. *OLBA* XIX:57–79.

Coşkun, G. 2011b Achaemenid Period Architectural Remains at Seyitömer Mound. *Archaeological Research in Western Central Anatolia* (The IIIrd International Symposium of Archaeology, Kütahya 8th–9th March 2010), pp. 81–93. Üçmart Press, Kütahya.

İlaslı, A. 1996 Seyitömer Höyüğü 1993 Yılı Kurtarma Kazısı. *VI. Müze Kurtarma Kazıları Semineri, 24–26 Nisan 1995 Didim*, pp. 1–20. Kültür ve Turizm Bakanlığı, Ankara.

Topbaş, A. 1992 Kütahya Seyitömer Höyüğü 1990 Yılı Kurtarma Kazısı. *II. Müze Kurtarma Kazıları Semineri, 29–30 Nisan 1991 Ankara*, pp. 11–34. TC Kültür Bakanlığı Millî Kütüphane Basımevi, Ankara.

Topbaş, A. 1993 Seyitömer Höyüğü 1991 Yılı Kurtarma Kazısı. *III. Müze Kurtarma Kazıları Semineri, 27–30 Nisan 1992 Efes*, pp. 1–30. TC Kültür Bakanlığı Millî Kütüphane Basımevi, Ankara.

Topbaş, A. 1994 Seyitömer Höyüğü 1992 Yılı Kurtarma Kazısı. *IV. Müze Kurtarma Kazıları Semineri, 26–29 Nisan 1993 Marmaris*, pp. 296–310. T.C. Kültür Bakanlığı, Anıtlar ve Müzeler Genel Müdürlüğü, Ankara.

CHAPTER TWELVE

Power and Ritual Practice in the Early Bronze III Period at Seyitömer Höyük

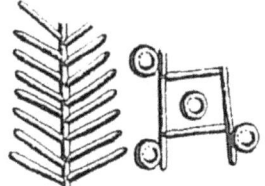

An Integrative Analysis of Movement, Interaction, and Visual Perception

Laura K. Harrison*

INTRODUCTION

In Early Bronze Age (EBA) Western Anatolia, societies became increasingly complex and social and political hierarchies expanded. Elites and ritual leaders hosted public occasions and gatherings in ritual spaces, which were intentionally designed to direct pedestrian movement, shape social interaction, and control visual perception. The architecture and spatial layout of ritual buildings establishes the relative accessibility and exclusivity of particular rooms, along a continuum from public to private. It also creates viewsheds through interior space that aid in surveillance and draw attention to public occasions. Building size, shape, and architectural elaboration create settings that establish focal points for ritual action, or signal exclusivity. In addition, building layout can also impact the duration of social interaction, by encouraging directional movement forward and brief encounters, or promoting sustained interactions in place. Placing guards or inspectors at entrances and passageways works in concert with spatial controls in the built environment and limits the ability of visitors to move through buildings and access private spaces; an elite legitimation strategy that reinforces hierarchical social relations. Architectural and spatial contexts are thus meaningfully constructed and can be mobilized as instruments of power. Therefore, the built environment is not merely a passive setting or backdrop, but an active participant in social production (Moore 1996).

This chapter investigates the interplay between symbol-laden material remains and past behaviors in ritual contexts. I apply an integrative approach to architecture and social organization (modified from Fisher 2009) that incorporates observations about visual perception and nonverbal cues in the built environment of a ritual at the Early Bronze

---

*Dr. Laura K. Harrison, Access 3D Lab, University of South Florida, 4202 E. Fowler Ave., Tampa, Florida 33620, USA. harrisonl@usf.edu.

III settlement of Seyitömer Höyük, in Western Anatolia. This approach draws on a body of theory that stresses the recursive and mutually constituting relationship between social organization, meaning, and the built environment (i.e., Ashmore 2002; O'Donovan 2002; Parker Pearson and Richards 1994; Rapoport 1982; Smith 2003). It identifies three different settings for ritual practice, which range from informal and public to private and exclusive. These settings are located on a pedestrian route through a ritual building. Nonverbal cues along this route aid in a process of social filtering that limits the ability of certain individuals to reach the most symbolically important space in the complex.

Household and Community Rituals in the Early Bronze Age

Ritual practice in the Early Bronze Age in Western Anatolia is characterized by the emergence of community symbolism and shrines used for supra-household ritual practice (Kouka 2011:44–45; Lamb 1956). The coexistence of household and community shrines in the Early Bronze Age is evident at Western Anatolian sites including Demircihöyük (Korfmann 1983), Karataş (Bachhuber 2015:76–78); Poliochni Blue (Bernabo-Brea 1964:186–200); Küllüoba (Efe and Ay-Efe 2007:256; Efe and Fidan 2008:79) and Seyitömer Höyük (N. Bilgen, this volume; Bilgen 2011:495, 498, 501, 504). Ritual furniture, such as bull-shaped hearths and platforms, is also found in both Late Chalcolithic household shrines and Early Bronze Age community shrines (Fidan et al. 2015:71; Steadman 2000:181). This suggests the existence of a deeply rooted shared belief system that shifted in scale from household to community in the Early Bronze Age, as society became increasingly complex (Frangipane 2010:83; Yakar 1974:156–157). Control over the accessibility of these ritual spaces reflects a growing desire to organize and order encounters between different factions of society. These changes occurred during a period of urbanization and increasing sociopolitical complexity in which public events, feasting, and conspicuous consumption became important settings for the negotiation of social roles among elites and nonelites.

The Central Megaron Complex at Seyitömer Höyük

Seyitömer Höyük is one of the best-preserved examples of an Early Bronze III urban settlement in Inland Western Anatolia (Harrison et al. this volume, Figure 1; Bilgen 2011; Harrison 2016; Harrison and Bilgen 2019). Its EBA occupation is subdivided into three subphases: Phase V-A, Phase V-B, and Phase V-C. A Bayesian analysis of radiocarbon dates estimates the start of the V-C period between 3008 and 2255 B.C. (95.4% accuracy), with a median date of 2367 B.C. The date range for this transition is long and rather imprecise, because of a lack of data about the preceding phase (which is unexcavated), and the relatively small number of successful radiocarbon determinations from Phase V-C in the model.

The Bayesian model offers high-resolution results for Phase V-B and V-A. It suggests that the Phase V-C to V-B transition falls between 2297 and 2226 B.C. (95.4% accuracy), with a median date of 2272 B.C. The Phase V-B to V-A transition falls between 2281 and 2218 B.C. (95.4% accuracy), with a median date of 2259 B.C., and the Phase

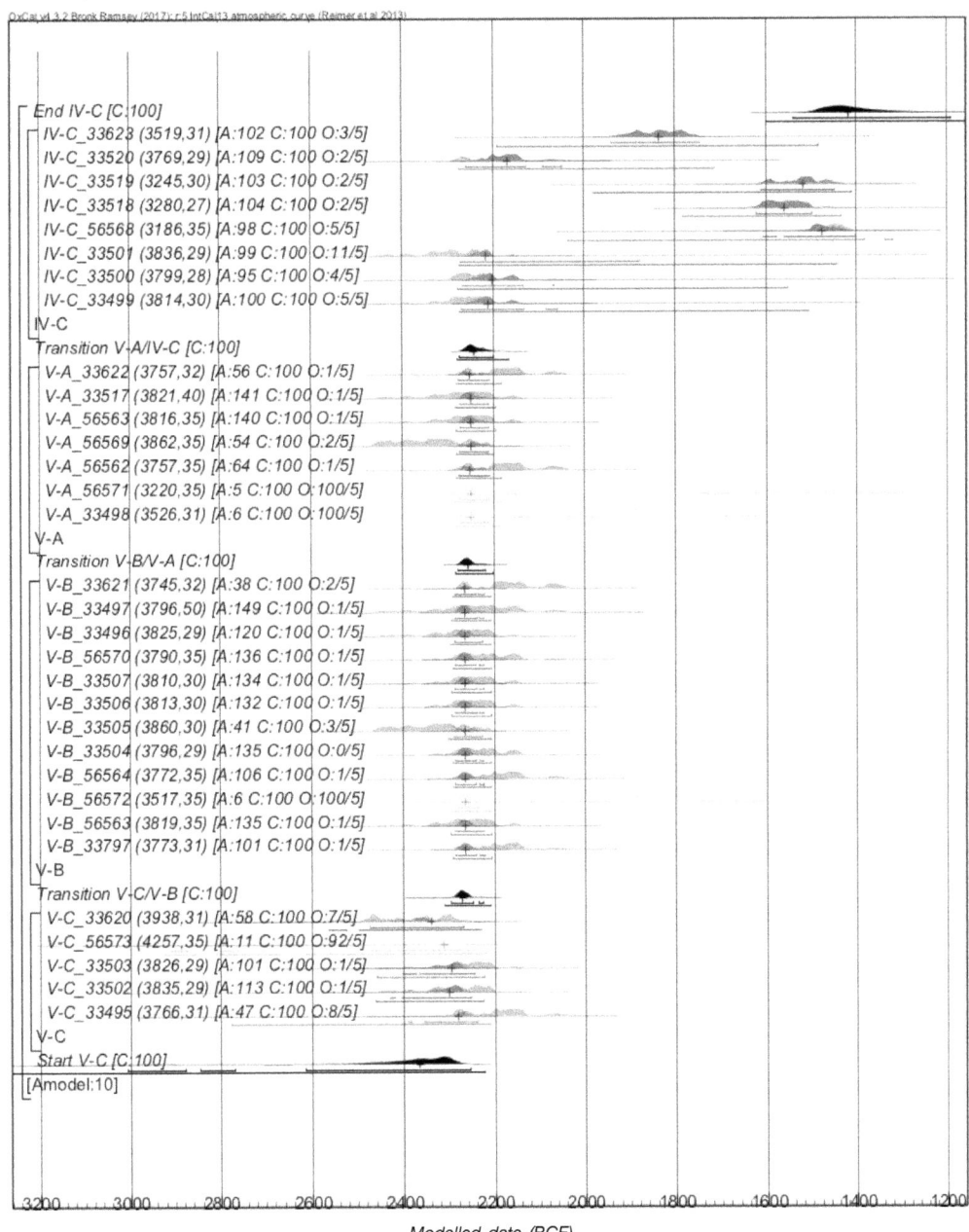

FIGURE 12.1A. Calibrated C14 dates from Phase V-A, V-B and V-C plotted in a Bayesian sequence. Credit: Laura K. Harrison.

V-A to IV-C transition falls between 2274–2200 B.C. (95.4% accuracy), with a median date of 2245 B.C.

Bayesian phases

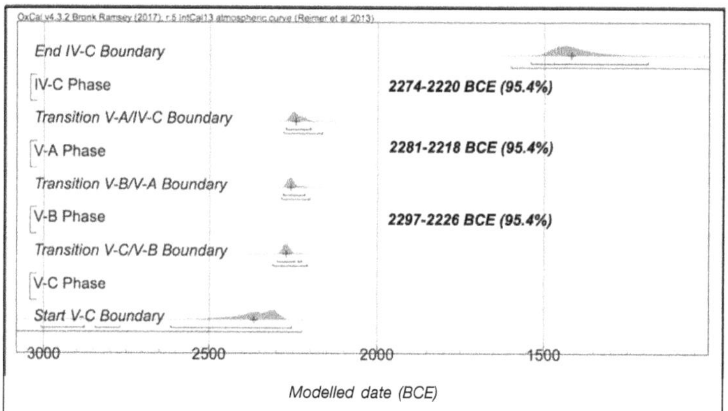

Phase	Interval length (years)	Percentage certainty
IV-C	687-1047	95.4%
V-C	0-46	95.4%
V-B	0-44	95.4%
V-C	0-737	95.4%

Bayesian sequence interval length

Phase	Interval length (years)	Percentage certainty
IV-C	687-1047	95.4%
V-C	0-46	95.4%
V-B	0-44	95.4%
V-C	0-737	95.4%

Figure 12.1b. Bayesian phases and interval length from Phase V-A, V-B and V-C. Credit: Laura K. Harrison.

These results suggest that Phase V-C was a relatively long period of about 100 years, and that V-A and V-B were much shorter (less than 50 years each). The transition from one phase to the next in the EBIII period appears to have occurred rapidly, without any gaps. The model struggled to determine the length of Phase IV-C. Detailed information about the Bayesian chronological model and each C14 sample context is available online in open access, in Harrison (2017).

The well-preserved architectural remains of Phase V-B contain approximately 30 interconnected buildings that serve administrative, religious, industrial, and residential functions, and are linked together with a simple network of streets and public spaces (Harrison 2016; Harrison and Bilgen 2019). A circuit wall surrounds the settlement, and there is an entrance to the southeast. The presence of shared party walls and common building orientation provides physical evidence to organize the buildings into four distinct groups: the Rowhouses West, Rowhouses East, Central Megaron Complex, and Administrative Complex (Figure 12.2, Figure 12.3; Harrison 2016; Harrison and Bilgen 2019). The focus of this chapter is the Phase V-B Central Megaron Complex, which is a freestanding, four- to five-room structure used for various types of formalized rituals. Its architectural characteristics, fixed features, and in situ deposits work together to shape ritual practice, by controlling access to the most private and exclusive space in the complex, the main room.

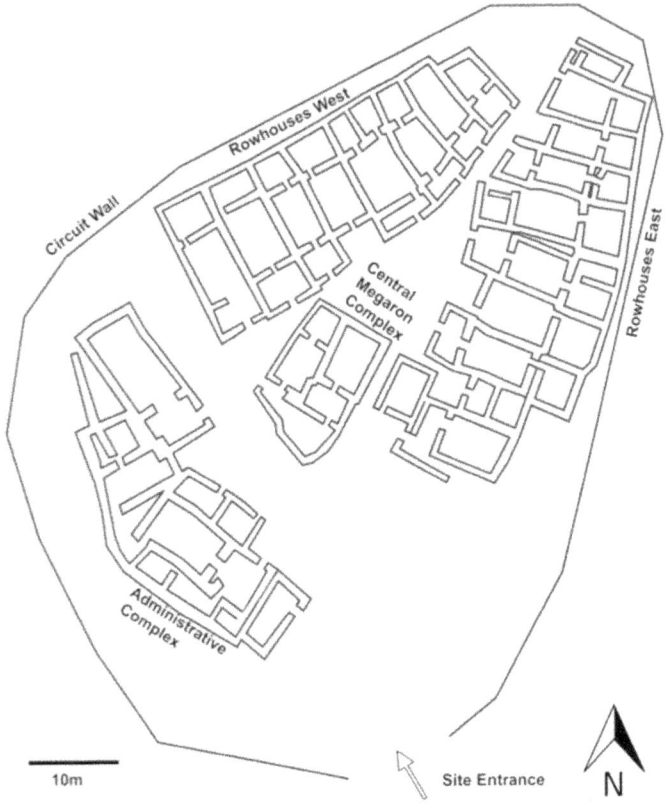

FIGURE 12.2. Plan of Seyitömer Höyük Phase B settlement showing analytical sections. Credit: Laura K. Harrison.

FIGURE 12.3. Aerial photo of Seyitömer Höyük. Credit: A. Nejat Bilgen.

The Central Megaron Complex is a centrally located megaron-style building with a front room, a main room, two attached storage rooms, and a courtyard (Figure 12.4). The front room and the main room are used for formalized social occasions, and they

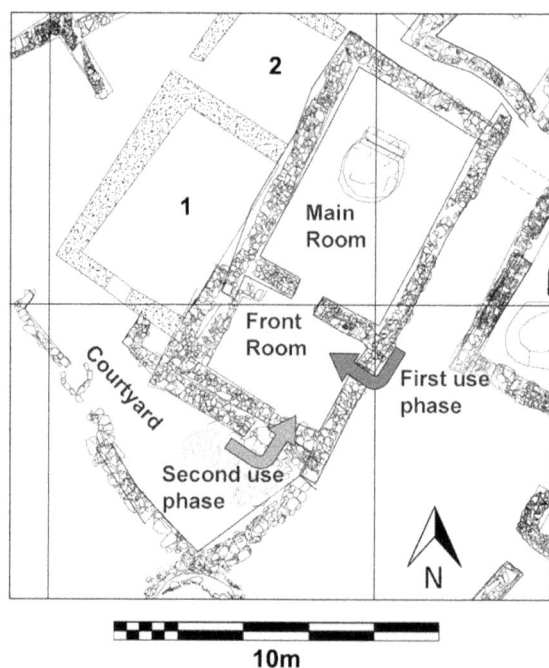

FIGURE 12.4A. Drawing of offset entrances in first use phase and second use phase of Central Megaron Complex. Credit: Laura K. Harrison.

FIGURE 12.4B. Photo of offset entrances in first use phase and second use phase of Central Megaron Complex. Credit: Laura K. Harrison.

each support different kinds of activities. Although the building was in use throughout Phase V-B, patterns of accessibility changed over time. In the first use phase, the entrance from the street to the front room is on the building's long southeast wall, and in the second use phase this entrance is closed and a new, stepped entrance is constructed in the short southwest wall, providing passage from the courtyard to the front room (Figure 18.4). The entrances in both use phases require a pedestrian to shift direction, which contrasts with the linear paths of movement found in Phase V-B residential buildings in the Rowhouses East and Rowhouses West areas.

ARCHITECTURE AND CONSTRUCTION TECHNIQUE

The formal properties of walls are instrumental in communicating meaning about a building's function, the status of its inhabitants, and the type of interactions that it is intended to host. In addition, the choice of wall construction technique is deeply embedded within a context of available resources, time, and building expertise, as well as cultural preferences. Wall construction technique is therefore deeply intertwined with the "middle-level" expression of status, power, and identity (Rapoport 1988; 1990). A recent study of the architecture and construction technique carried out by the author identified eight different types of walls in Phase V-B (Harrison 2016; 2017; Harrison and Bilgen 2019). Each type of wall represents a combination of a particular set of formal

FIGURE 12.5. Megaron Front Room and Main Room showing key architectural features: plastered, semi-coursed rubble walls, interior and exterior wall plaster, and yellow clay floor. Credit: Laura K. Harrison.

building techniques that encompasses wall construction material, coursing, cross-section or bonding technique, dry or wet masonry, and surface dressing. For a full discussion of the typology, see Harrison (2016:167–171; Harrison and Bilgen 2019).

In the Central Megaron Complex, there are three distinctive types of wall construction: uncoursed, unplastered single stone (Type 1), mudbrick (Type 6), and semi-coursed, plastered rubble (Type 5; Figure 12.6). This is the only building in Phase V-B that incorporates such a wide range of different building techniques. Uncoursed, single stone rubble is used in the courtyard, as a hastily constructed solution to flooding. The mudbrick walls (Room 1 and Room 2) demonstrate enduring links with the earlier Phase V-C settlement, in which mudbrick architecture is commonplace. The plastered, semi-coursed rubble walls used in the front room and main room are a form of architectural elaboration that requires an added labor investment. This construction technique is not used elsewhere in Phase V-B, which heightens the distinctiveness of the Central Megaron Complex.

The Central Megaron Complex is the only freestanding building in Phase V-B, and it is also the only building with exterior wall plaster (Figure 12.6). This creates a marked contrast with surrounding buildings—especially those in the Rowhouses West and Rowhouses East—which are constructed out of uncoursed, unplastered rubble and mudbrick, and share party walls. The heightened visual impact of the Central Megaron Complex can be thought of in terms of singularity and dominance, which are "form

Figure 12.6. Artists' reconstruction of Central Megaron Complex, showing construction technique. Credit: Kristin Donner.

qualities" of the built environment that foster the expression of symbolic importance (Lynch 1960). Singularity refers to figure-background clarity: a building's visual contrast with its immediate surroundings. This visual contrast is the result of the way a building's formal properties make it stand out, by rendering it more remarkable, vivid, or recognizable (Lynch 1960:105). Dominance refers to the domination of one part over others in an urban context by means of size, intensity, or visual interest (Lynch 1960:106). This results in the perception of the building as the principal feature within a group of buildings (Lynch 1960:106).

The built features in the Central Megaron Complex also aid in the communication of a symbolic message, by establishing focal points that structure social interaction, formalizing the process of entering the main room, and limiting the accessibility of certain interior spaces (Figure 12.7). For example, in the front room, a stone bench is attached to the northwest wall. This bench plays an important role in mediating social interactions by creating a context for formalized waiting prior to entering the more inaccessible main room. In the center of the main room is a hearth with a rectangular rear platform with hornlike protrusions attached to a larger circular platform. The rear platform of the hearth measures .45 × 1.40 meters, and the circular platform measures 1.87 × 1.77 meters.

This hearth has formal similarities with other Early Bronze Age hearths at sites such as Thermi Level VI (Erkanal and Şahoglu 2016:159), Beycesultan (Lloyd and Mellaart

FIGURE 12.7. Photo of Central Megaron Complex with features and in situ deposits labeled. Credit: Laura K. Harrison.

1967:152–154); Troy (Ivanova 2013) Demircihöyük (Düring 2011:253; Korfmann 1983), and Karataş-Semayük (Mellink 1965:258; Warner 1979:138). This form is thought to emulate bulls' horns and represent a bull cult (Mellaart 1967). It is the center of attention for ritual practice in the Central Megaron Complex, and its symbolism is heightened through its location at the center of the deepest and most inaccessible part of the building.

Material culture deposits offer further evidence that the main room was an important ritual context in Phase V-B. The in situ deposit from the floor of the main room contains a group of anthropomorphic and zoomorphic rhytons that were used for ritualized pouring, and a preliminary analysis suggests they were produced locally at Seyitömer Höyük, using a mould-based technique (Figure 12.8; Z. Bilgen, this volume). Their closest stylistic parallel is the Hedgehog vessel from Chalandriani, on Syros in the Aegean (see Broodbank 2000:216). Because the Central Megaron Complex is the only Phase V-B context in which anthropomorphic and/or zoomorphic vessels are found, it appears that they were intentionally restricted to this symbolically important space.

The courtyard is an irregularly shaped space that was added to the southwest of the Central Megaron Complex in its second use phase and used for informal social gatherings. The entrance is located in the northwest wall, and is perpendicular to the axis of movement through the front room and the main room. Unlike the architecturally elaborate front room and main room, the courtyard is constructed out of single stone, dry-laid rubble masonry, and neither the interior nor exterior wall faces are plastered. Given the

FIGURE 12.8. In situ ritual vessel deposit from northeast corner of Megaron main room. Credit: A. Nejat Bilgen.

topography of the mound, and the location of the Central Megaron Complex downslope from the Administrative Complex, it is likely that the courtyard was hastily constructed in order to prevent runoff from higher elevations from damaging the front room and main room (Bilgen 2011). The paved stone floor in the courtyard may also have functioned to improve drainage and stabilize the area, a practice that has parallels at Küllüoba (Efe and Fidan 2008:69) and Poliochni (Cultraro 2007:61). Other than the paved floor, the most notable feature of the courtyard space is the presence of a bench near the entrance to the front room, which (like the bench inside the front room) formalizes the process of waiting and controls the flow of visitors into the more private main room (Figure 12.8). At 9.60 × 3.15 meters, the courtyard is also one of the largest interior spaces in Phase V-B, and its shape encourages directional movement from the street toward the entrance of the front room. No in situ finds were recovered from this space.

Room 1 and Room 2 are storage spaces that were used to provide support for more formalized activities taking place in the front room and the main room, similar to the rooms surrounding the twin shrines at Beycesultan (Yakar 1974:152). Unlike the other rooms in the Central Megaron Complex, Room 1 and Room 2 are constructed of mudbrick, they lack architectural elaboration, and they do not have any built features or material culture that suggests symbolic importance or directly relates to ritual practice. In addition, neither Room 1 nor Room 2 provides direct access to the ritual core of the complex (the front room and the main room), and the only in situ deposit is a modest assemblage of two loom weights and a bone hammer found in Room 1 (Figure 12.9). It is likely that Room 1 and Room 2 were initially built in Phase V-C, when mudbrick construction was common, and then incorporated into the Central Megaron Complex later in Phase V-B. They probably functioned as storage or waiting rooms.

FIGURE 12.9. Loomweight found in Room 1 of Central Megaron Complex. Credit: A. Nejat Bilgen.

An Integrative Approach to Understanding Ritual Space

As the foregoing discussion illustrates, the construction technique, layout, built features, and in situ deposits of the Central Megaron Complex nonverbally communicate a message that this building was an important context for ritual practice in Phase V-B. But this generalization leaves many questions unanswered: Who participated in these rituals, and which people/groups were included or excluded? Were different spaces used for different types of ritual practice? And how, specifically, were social relations communicated through the built environment?

The integrative approach presented in this chapter attempts to develop an understanding of these key questions, by combining insights about the construction technique and fixed features of the Central Megaron Complex with analyses of movement, interaction, and visual perception in the built environment. This mixed-methods research design, which is modified from Fisher (2009), combines quantitative and qualitative analyses to better understand the recursive relationship between ritual action and the built environment.

Space Syntax Analysis and the Formality of Social Interaction

Space syntax analysis is a quantitative methodology that operates under the premise that all settlements contain a highly unique combination of a recurring set of topological spatial relations, which can be quantified in mathematical terms (Hillier and Hanson 1984). Different spatial configurations encourage or restrict certain kinds of social interactions between inhabitants and visitors, and structure patterns of social interaction by shaping accessibility, control, and movement.

Access analysis is a type of space syntax analysis that quantifies the relative accessibility and spatial relationships of interior spaces within buildings. Buildings are represented as nodes, and paths of movement between them are represented as lines. Once the convex spaces and the location of entrances in a particular building or settlement are known, access graphs can be created (Figure 12.10)—for a full discussion of the space syntax methodology, see Harrison (2016:124–133). The process is relatively straightforward: architectural spaces in the settlement are illustrated graphically as nodes, linked by the paths of access drawn from an entrance (the carrier space or root) to all successively accessible spaces (Hillier and Hanson 1984:148–149; VanDyke 1999:466).

Access graphs make the basic syntactic properties of symmetry and distributedness (which are technical terms for accessibility and circulation) much more obvious than in a basic architectural plan. They also allow for simple visual comparisons of different access patterns (Hillier and Hanson 1984:149; Moore 1996:185). Access graphs can be justified by placing all nodes in horizontal rows above the carrier to show how many steps away from the starting point each space is (Figure 12.10). Hillier and Hanson liken the creation of access graphs to "dissection," because "the premises are 'sliced' down the middle and 'pinned out' so that their internal structure is visible" (Hillier and Hanson 1984:149).

Access analysis allows the social implications of depth, integration, and control to be examined with reference to numerical values, which are more nuanced than simple

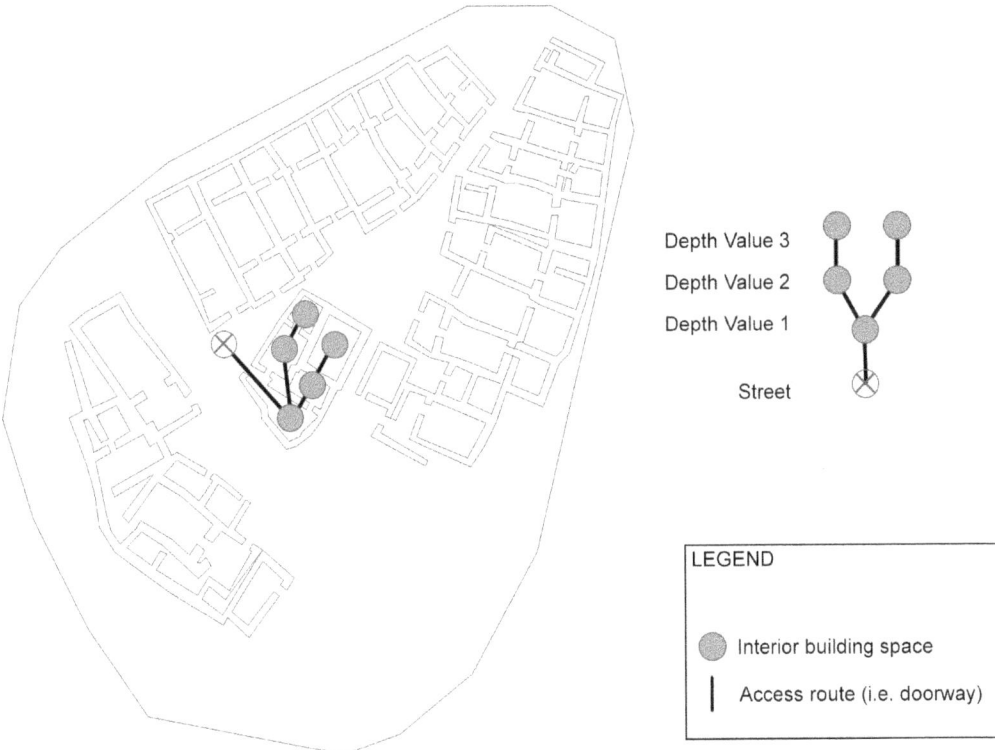

FIGURE 12.10. Diagrammatic representation of access analysis. On the left, convex interior spaces are represented as nodes, and pathways between them are represented as lines. The graph on the right is justified, and shows the depth of each room from the street. Space syntax analysis quantifies the spatial relationships of these access graphs, in order to reveal how the building configuration shapes movement and interaction. Credit: Laura K. Harrison.

observations of building layout or site plans (Shapiro 2005:49). For this reason, space syntax analysis is gaining traction as a methodology for the analysis of past urban settlements, and has been used to investigate a wide range of archaeological topics. For instance, Letesson (2014) investigates the emergence of configurational principles in Minoan Neopalatial architecture through access graphs and visual integration analyses (Letesson 2014), and Moore (1996) studies the changing relationship between power and public architecture by investigating monumentality, the architecture of ritual, and the architecture of social control with visibility analyses and access graphs. Other key space syntax analyses in archaeology are Fisher (2009), Letesson and Vansteenhuyse (2006), Matney (2002), Osborne (2012), Shapiro (2005), and Spence-Morrow (2009).

While individual space syntax measures (such as control, depth, and relative asymmetry) are useful in revealing the underlying topology of urban spatial arrangements, considering multiple measures in tandem generates greater insight into complex human social behaviors. Particular combinations of space syntax values are indicative of certain types of social interactions, and can be integrated with further observations about the size, relative convexity (squareness), and the architectural elaboration of interior spaces. This chapter employs such an approach to identify spaces used for informal gatherings, public/inclusive occasions, and private/exclusive occasions in the Central Megaron Complex at Seyitömer Höyük (Table 12.1). These are categories originally defined by Goffman (1963), and applied to archaeological contexts by Fisher (2009; 2014).

Gatherings are informal encounters that involve unfocused or unsustained actions. They often occur in spaces of movement, such as streets or courtyards, in which there is a high potential for chance encounters. Public/inclusive occasions are formal, sustained social interactions that occur within a well-defined spatial context. They are more for-

TABLE 12.1
SPACE SYNTAX MEASURES AND THEIR SIGNIFICANCE

	Measure	Formula	Significance
RA	Relative Asymmetry	The Relative Asymmetry (RA) describes the integration of a node by a value between (or equal to) 0 and 1, where a low value describes high integration. RA is calculated by the formula RA=2*(MD-1)/(k-2).	Global measure of integration that reveals the relative accessibility of spaces; highlighting likely patterns of social interaction, such as differential access for visitors and inhabitants, or the interfacing of different social groups.
i	Integration	A parameter that (contrary to RA) describes integration by a high RA. number when a node is highly integrated is the "integration value" (i). The integration value is found by inverting the RA, i=1/RA.	Global measure that is the inverse of Reveals how how well integrated or segregated a particular space is to the entire spatial system. Integrated spaces promote movement and encounter; segregated spaces restrict and control movement.
C	Control	The Control Values (CV) are found by letting each node give the total value of 1 equally distributed to its connected nodes. The Control Value of node n, CV(n), is the total value received by node n during this operation.	Local measure that expresses the influence a particular space has in controlling movement between its neighbors. Reveals unequal power relations as expressed in space.
MD	Mean Depth	Mean Depth for a node n is the average depth (or average shortest distance) from node n to all the other nodes. If k is the total number of nodes in the system, then MD(n)=TD(n)/(k-1).	Local measure that reveals the total number of spaces, on average, that one must pass through to travel from any space in the system to the outside. Measures the privacy and exclusivity of a particular space with relation to the entire spatial system.
TD(n)	Total Depth	Total Depth of a node n, TD(n), is the total of the shortest distances from node n to the other nodes in the system.	Global measure that captures the depth of a particular space in relation to the other spaces in the system; measures the closeness of spaces to each other.

Credit: Laura Harrison, adapted from Hillier and Hanson, 1984.

mal than casual gatherings, and often take place in large, architecturally elaborate, and relatively integrated spaces. Public/inclusive occasions tend to occur in highly convex (square) spaces, which support continued social interactions, rather than directional movement forward. Private/exclusive occasions tend to involve a more exclusive group of participants than public/inclusive occasions. They can occur in rooms of any size, and involve formal, sustained meetings between individuals or people with a high degree of social status. These occasions encourage private discussions between leaders and smaller groups of powerful individuals, rather than the active negotiation of power relations among large groups (Goffman 1963; Fisher 2009).

Table 12.2 reveals that the main room of the Central Megaron Complex is a context for private/exclusive occasions; the front room is a context for public/inclusive occasions, and the courtyard is a context for informal gatherings. Room 1 and Room 2 do not contain a meaningful combination of space syntax measures, and they were not as important for the staging of social gatherings and occasions as the other spaces in the Central Megaron Complex.

Isovist Viewsheds and Power Relations

We can gain further insight into the role of the built environment in shaping ritual practice by considering how visibility within buildings encourages or discourages participation in certain activities. Vision is one of the primary ways that human actors gain information about their surroundings, and this ultimately impacts perception and behavior. A key historical example of this phenomenon is Jeremy Bentham's model of the *Critchef Panopticon* 1748 prison design, in which prisoners' cells are arranged radially around an inspector's rotunda, allowing for constant, invisible surveillance and ensuring an "automatic functioning of power" (Foucault 1977:201).

Isovists, isovist fields, and viewsheds are particularly useful when constructed from vantage points with important syntactical and architectural characteristics, such as spaces of power and symbolically charged spaces, which draw attention to certain locales and actions and shield others. *Isovists* capture the set of points visible from a specific vantage point, and can be used to reconstruct the visual experience of being in a landscape or a space (Lake and Woodman 2003; Moore 1996:106–107, 109–116). An *isovist field* broadens the extent of an isovist by including all points visible from a particular space (Benedict 1979:54–57). A *viewshed* is a subset of the isovist that represents a directional field of vision, showing the full 200-degree extent of human binocular vision, as well as the 10-degree arc of detailed (foveal, macular) vision (Fisher 2009:449–450). In this chapter, the hearth in the main room, which was used for private/exclusive occasions, and the entrance to the front room, which was used for public/inclusive occasions, represent two powerful locales for social action.

Figure 12.11 shows a viewshed from the entrance to the front room of the megaron toward the main room. From this vantage point, the central hearth is partially visible, but most of the room is shielded from view. This could communicate a message to

TABLE 12.2
Space Syntax Values for the Central Megaron Complex, Second Use Phase

Room Number	Depth from Street	CV rank	RA	RRA	i	MD	Relative Convexity	Room Capacity Seated	Room Capacity Standing
1	2	1	0.40	1.15	0.87	1.8	0.68	39	70
2	3	1	0.80	2.29	0.44	2.6	0.97	21	38
Courtyard	1	2	0.20	0.57	1.75	1.4	0.33	57	103
Megaron Front	2	1	0.40	1.15	0.87	1.8	0.78	25	44
Megaron Main	3	1	0.80	2.29	0.44	2.6	0.67	54	97

Room Number	Control Value	CV Rank	RRA	RRA Rank	Room Number	Depth Value	Depth Value Rank	Room Number	Relative Convexity	Relative Convexity Rank
1	1.04	Medium	0.534	Low	1	2	Medium	1	0.68	Medium
2	0.5	Low	0.810	Medium	2	3	High	2	0.97	Medium
Courtyard	1.04	Medium	0.514	Low	Courtyard	1	Low	Courtyard	0.33	Low
Megaron Front	1.04	Medium	0.534	Low	Megaron Front	2	Medium	Megaron Front	0.78	Medium
Megaron Main	50	Low	0.810	Medium	Megaron Main	3	High	Megaron Main	0.67	Medium

☐ Gatherings (Medium to high CV; low RRA; low depth; low convexity; may be a narrow space)
▨ Public/Inclusive Occasions (Medium to high CV; low RRA; low to medium depth; med. to high convexity; 12m² or larger)
▧ Private/Exclusive Occasions (Low CV; medium to high RRA; high depth; high convexity; size not important)

Credit: Laura K. Harrison.

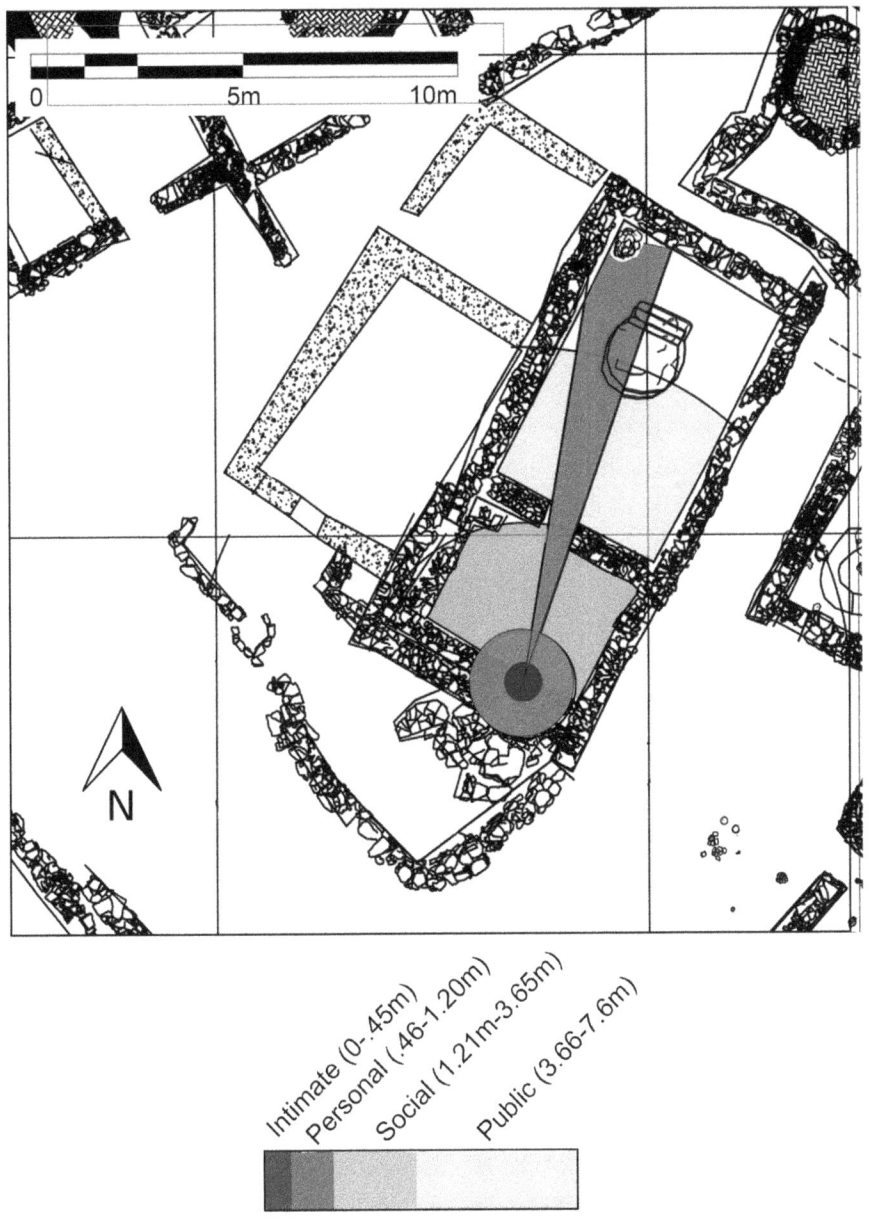

FIGURE 12.11. Viewshed coded for proxemic distance from the entrance to the front room Credit: Laura K. Harrison.

visitors that they are approaching a sacred space, but they have not yet fully entered it. This viewshed reinforces the message of privacy and exclusivity that is embedded in the spatial arrangement and architecture of the complex, because people inside the front room are made aware of activities occurring in the main room, but are unable to actively participate in them.

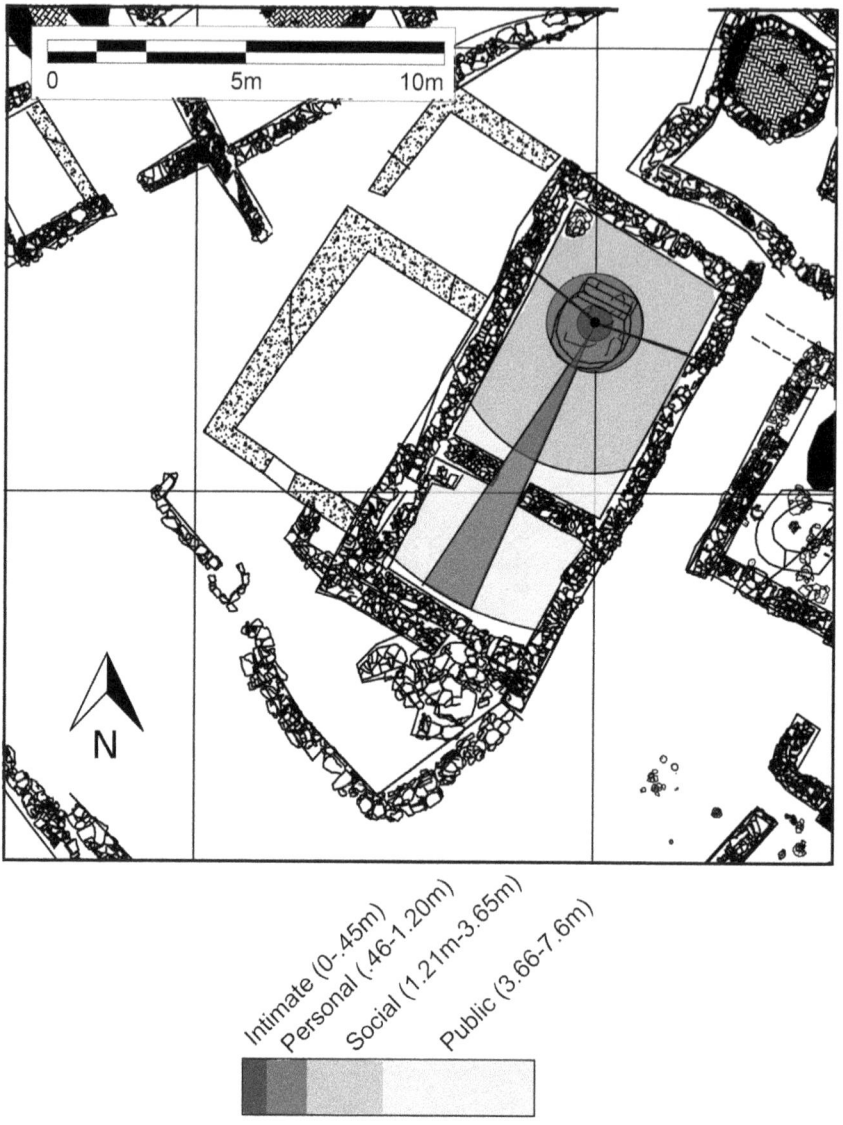

FIGURE 12.12. Viewshed coded for proxemic distance from the hearth in the main room. Credit: Laura K. Harrison.

Figure 12.12 illustrates the viewshed from the hearth toward the entrance of the main room, on the southern wall. From this vantage point, peripheral vision is limited to the main room, but the 10-degree arc of detailed vision makes it is possible to see through the doorway into the front room, when looking straight ahead. This doorway is a crucial liminal zone between the inclusive front room and the exclusive main room, and this viewshed from the hearth toward this entrance would have been essential in controlling the passage of visitors into the main room. A person near the entrance could directly observe rituals taking place in the main room, and use this information to mediate activities between the two rooms, such as the entrance and exit of visitors at appropriate times.

Isovists and viewsheds can be coded for proxemics to gain further information about the relationship between the built environment and human behavior. Proxemics is a field of study developed by Edward T. Hall that explores how peoples' use of space is an aspect of culture, which enables and constrains certain behaviors (Hall 1966; Fisher 2009:442; Lawrence and Low 1990:478). Hall's research identifies four categories of proxemic distance: intimate, private, social, and public, each of which affects patterns of likely human social interaction. Although the spatial extents of each category have been debated, and social and environmental factors such as room shape affect proxemic distances, Hall's observations are generally accepted (See Altman 1975; Altman and Vinsel 1977; Fisher 2013) and add a further dimension to our understanding of architecture and behavior in the megaron building.

Figure 12.11 demonstrates that the main room was well suited to interactions at a social distance of up to three meters. At a social distance, two people can reach each other by stretching, and it is possible to see facial features, hair, and clothing clearly with detailed (foveal) vision, upper body gestures with 60-degree scanning vision, and the head and shoulders are visible with 200-degree peripheral vision. Communication tends to be of a casual or consultive style, using a conventional modified voice (Hall 1966:116–129; Fisher 2009:443). While proxemic distances indicate that the main room could have accommodated small-scale public interactions (in which a loud voice is necessary and facial expressions are not seen clearly) the long and narrow shape of the space would likely have been a deterrent to these larger-scale interactions.

Discussion: Movement, Interaction, and Visibility in a Ritual Context

The primary route of movement through the Central Megaron Complex leads through the courtyard to the front room, and then the main room. This pathway contains a rich milieu of features that create very specific contexts for social interaction; and the way in which the built environment communicates meaning can be thought of in terms of what Rapoport calls a "system of settings" (Rapoport 1990). These contexts are expressed through a convergence of nonverbal cues derived from construction technique, built features, and distinctive artifacts. One of the key functions of this message is to aid in a process of social filtering, by discouraging certain members of society from reaching the most exclusive and symbolically important space in the complex, the main room, while simultaneously encouraging others to do so.

First, a visitor enters the courtyard from the street (Figure 12.13). The simple wall construction signals that this is not an exclusive space, and its syntactical properties indicate it was used for informal gatherings. The courtyard controls access to the front room, and contributes to a process of social filtering, by limiting the ability of certain individuals to proceed to the front room, which is used for more formal public/inclusive

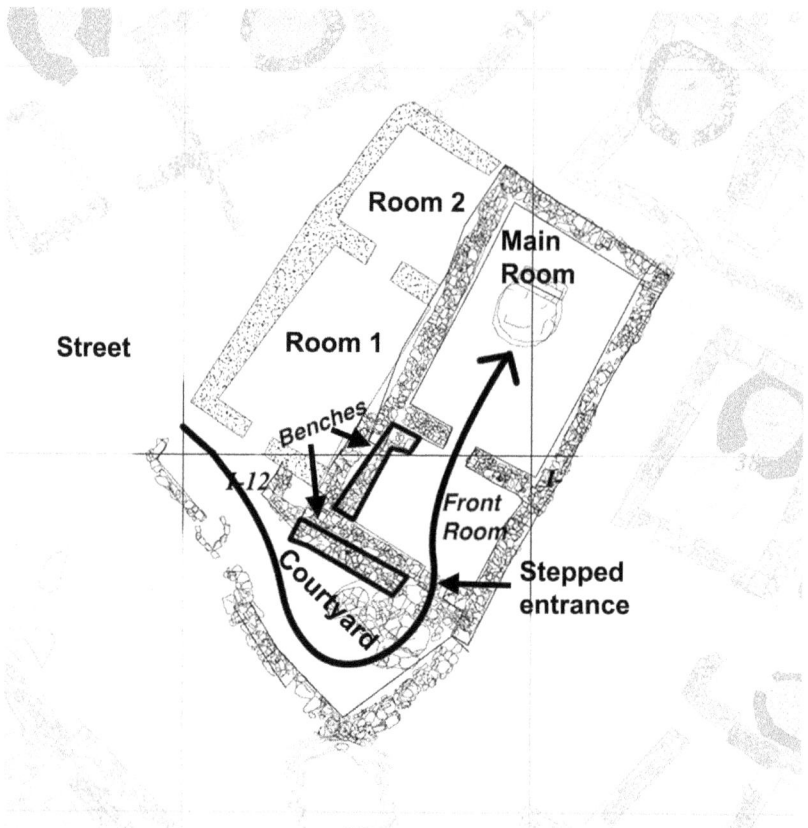

FIGURE 12.13. Pedestrian route through Central Megaron Complex. Credit: Laura K. Harrison.

occasions. In addition, the courtyard's irregular shape has a disorienting effect, which is enhanced by the space's lack of a focal point. Therefore, sustained, formal social interactions would not have taken place here.

As one passes through the courtyard and approaches the entrance to the front room, a suite of nonverbal cues comes into view: the presence of wall plaster on the exterior face of the front room, and a bench alongside its outer wall. The bench is particularly important, because it is the first feature a visitor encounters that formalizes the process of waiting to enter a restricted area. This bench, moreover, is not oriented toward the entrance of the front room, but in a perpendicular direction. This subtle cue has strong effect on social interaction in two key ways: it limits spatial perception by preventing visitors from visually engaging with the more private activities taking place inside the front room, and the size of the bench limits the number of individuals formally involved with the waiting process.

The process of passing from the courtyard to the front room involves navigating a step up and a 90-degree change in direction. Once inside the front room, visitors perceive an interior space fully dressed with a thick layer of yellow clay plaster, as well as a stone bench, on which they would be directed to wait. As seen in Table 12.2, the front room has a high control value. This indicates that it is an important space for mediating the passage from one room to another (in this case, from the courtyard to the main room). The presence of a bench in this room supports this interpretation because, like the high control value, it interrupts the flow of visitors from one room to the next. In addition, the architectural elaboration and fixed features of this space communicate a message of increased formality and social distinction.

As the final stage in a process of social filtering, the built environment of the main room does not include benches for formalized waiting, but a well-defined context for ritual action. If allowed to enter the main room, visitors would notice the elaborate plastered walls, and their attention would be drawn to a hearth at the center of the room. This hearth would have been the focus of attention for private/exclusive social occasions, because it is only accessible to individuals allowed to pass through the courtyard and front room. In the southeast corner of the room is a platform that is only visible to individuals fully inside the main room. While this platform is not found in association with any artifacts, it was probably used in the performance of private rituals, and is imperceptible to individuals in the front room. The combination of architectural elaboration, features, and a distinctive deposit of anthropomorphic and zoomorphic rhytons communicates a message of exclusivity that is unique in Phase V-B. The inaccessibility of this space further reinforces its identity as an elite locale. In this context, the performance of repeated activities within the megaron locale contributes to a process of urban "placemaking" (see Rubertone 2008) that ascribes symbolic on the megaron building itself. The concept of placemaking examines the various physical elements of urban environments, their spatial arrangement, and the way in which they intersect and work together to create and transform social practices (Rubertone 2008:13). In other words, human actions within the Central Megaron Complex transform it from a neutral *space* into a meaningful *place*.

Conclusion

The integrative analysis of the Central Megaron Complex at Seyitömer Höyük reveals that movement, interaction, and visibility worked in tandem to shape ritual practice in the Early Bronze III period. The freestanding location of the Central Megaron Complex, and the conspicuous exterior wall plaster, draw attention and create a highly imageable environment. This communicates a nonverbal message of symbolic importance to the entire settlement (Lynch 1960). Interior spaces are also symbol-laden. The spatial arrangement of the five rooms in this complex encourages a nonlinear pedestrian route through space, which is an intentional choice that is designed to periodically interrupt forward motion. The strategic placement of benches, doorways, stepped entrances, and offset paths reinforce this message. These barriers impact the movement of visitors, and limit the accessibility of the front room and the main room. Control over movement is thus one of the primary channels through which elites oversee a process of social filtering, and express hierarchical power over nonelites. The quantitative measures of space syntax further reinforce this concept by drawing attention to different types of social interaction likely to occur in each space, that range from informal gatherings in the courtyard, to public/inclusive occasions in the front room, and private/exclusive occasions in the rear room. Together, these observations demonstrate that the Central Megaron Complex was an active participant in the production of social relations at a community scale in the Early Bronze Age.

Acknowledgments

I would like to warmly thank Prof. Dr. A. Nejat Bilgen and the faculty of the Dumlupinar University Department of Archaeology for inviting me to participate in the Fourth International Archaeology Symposium on Early Bronze Age in Western Anatolia. Peter F. Biehl offered valuable comments on an earlier version of this paper. Thanks are also due to the National Science Foundation for supporting research into the absolute dating at Seyitömer Höyük (Award #1523389).

References Cited

Altman, I. 1975 *The Environment and Social Behavior: Privacy, Personal Space, Territory, Crowding.* Brooks/Cole, Monterey.

Altman, I., and A. M. Vinsel 1977 Personal Space: An Analysis of E.T. Hall's Proxemics Framework. In *Human Behavior and Environment: Advances in Theory and Research. Volume 2*, edited by I. Altman and J. F. Wohlwill, pp. 181–260. Plenum Press, New York.

Ashmore, W. 2002 "Decisions and Dispositions": Socializing Spatial Archaeology. *American Anthropologist* 104(4):1172–1183.

Bachhuber, C. 2015 *Citadel and Cemetery in Early Bronze Age Anatolia.* Equinox, London.

Benedikt, M. L. 1979 To Take Hold of Space: Isovists and Isovist View Fields. *Environment and Planning B: Planning and Design* 6(1):47–65.

Bilgen, A. N., and Dumlupinar Universitesi 2011 *Seyitömer Höyük Kazisi on Raporu, 2006–2010.* Kutahya: Dumlupinar Universitesi Fen-Edebiyat Fakultesi Arkeoloji Bolumu.

Bilgen, A. N. 2013 *Seyitomer Hoyuk 2013 Yili Kazi Raporu.* Kutahya: Fen-Edebiyat Fakultesi, Arkeoloji Bolumu.

Bourdieu, P. 1977 *Outline of a Theory of Practice.* Cambridge University Press, Cambridge.

Brea, B. 1964 Poliochni, Citta Preistorica Nell'isola Di Lemnos. L'erma di Bretschneider, Rome.

Broodbank, C. 2000 *An Island Archaeology of the Early Cyclades.* Cambridge University Press, Cambridge.

Cultraro, M. 2007 Domestic Architecture and Public Space in Early Bronze Age Poliochni (Lemnos). *British School at Athens Studies* 15 (January). British School at Athens: 55–64.

Düring, B. S. 2011 *Elites and Commoners. In Correlates of Complexity: Essays in Archaeology and Assyriology Dedicated to Diederik J. W. Meijer in Honour of His 65th Birthday*, edited by B. S. Düring, A. Wossink, and P. M. M. G. Akkermans, pp. 257–304. Nederlands Instituut voor het Nabije Oosten, Leiden.

Efe, T., and D. S. M. Ay Efe 2007 The Kulluoba Excavations and the Cultural/political Development of Western Anatolia before the Second Millennium B.C. In *Ali Dinçol—Belkıs Dinçol Anı Kitabı*, edited by M. Doğan-Alparslan, M. Alparslan, and H. Peker, pp. 251–267. Ege Yayınları, Istanbul.

Efe, T., and E. Fidan 2008 Complex Two in the Early Bronze II Upper Town of Kulluoba Near Eskisehir. *Anatolica* 34:67–102.

Erkanal, H., and V. Sahoglu 2016 Liman Tepe, an Early Bronze Age Trade Center in Western Anatolia: Recent Investigations. In *Early Bronze Age Troy: Chronology, Cultural Development, and Interregional Contacts: Proceedings of an International Conference Held at the University of Tubingen May 8–10, 2009*, edited by E. Pernicka, C. B. Rose, and P. Jablonka, pp. 157–166. Herausgeber, Bonn.

Fidan, E., D. Sari, and M. Turkteki 2015 An Overview of the Western Anatolian Early Bronze Age. *European Journal of Archaeology* 18:60–89.

Fisher, K. D. 2013 Investigating Monumental Social Space in Late Bronze Age Cyprus: An Integrative Approach. In *Spatial Analysis and Social Spaces: Interdisciplinary Approaches to the Interpretation of Prehistoric and Historic Built Environments*, edited by E. Paliou, U. Lieberwirth, and S. Polla pp. 167–202. Walter de Gruyter, Berlin.

Fisher, K. D. 2009 Placing Social Interaction: An Integrative Approach to Analyzing Past Built Environments. *Journal of Anthropological Archaeology* 28(4):439–57.

Foucault, M. 1977 *Discipline and Punish: The Birth of the Prison*. Pantheon Books, New York.

Frangipane, M. 2010 Different Models of Power Structuring at the Rise of Hierarchical Societies in the Near East: Primary Economy versus Luxury and Defence Management. In *Development of Pre-State Communities in the Near East*, edited by D. Bolger and L. C. Maguire, pp. 79–86. Oxbow Books, Oxford.

Goffman, E. 1963 *Behavior in Public Places: Notes on the Social Organization of Gatherings*. Free Press of Glencoe, New York.

Hall, E. T. 1966 *The Hidden Dimension*. Doubleday, Garden City.

Harrison, L. K. 2016 Living Spaces: Urbanism as a Social Process at Seyitömer Höyük in Early Bronze Age Western Anatolia. PhD dissertation University at Buffalo.

Harrison, L. K., and A. N. Bilgen 2019 Emergent Urbanism: Trade, Settlement, and Society at Seyitömer Höyük in Early Bronze Age Western Anatolia. In *Coming Together: Comparative Approaches to Population Aggregation and Early Urbanization*, edited by Attila Gyucha, pp. 189–214.

Harrison, L. K. 2017 Architecture, Urbanism, and Radiocarbon Dating at Seyitömer Höyük, Turkey. Edited by L. K. Harrison. Released: 2017-05-05. Open Context. http://opencontext.org/projects/347286db-b6c6-4fd2-b3bd-b50316b0cb9f. DOI: http://dx.doi.org/10.6078/M76W980X.

Hillier, B., and J. Hanson 1984 *The Social Logic of Space*. Cambridge University Press, Cambridge.

Ivanova, M. 2013 Domestic Architecture in the Early Bronze Age of Western Anatolia: The Row Houses of Troy 1. *Anatolian Studies* 63:17–33.

Kouka, O. 2011 Symbolism, Ritual Feasting and Ethnicity in Early Bronze Age Cyprus and Anatolia. In *On Cooking Pots, Drinking Cups, Loomweights and Ethnicity in Bronze Age Cyprus and Neighbouring Regions: An International Archaeological Symposium Held in Nicosia, November 6th–7th 2010*, edited by V. Karageorghis, pp. 43–56. A. G. Leventis Foundation, Nicosia.

Lake, M. W., and P. E. Woodman 2003 Visibility Studies in Archaeology: A Review and Case Study. *Environment and Planning B: Planning and Design* 30(5):689–707.

Lamb, W. 1956 Some Early Anatolian Shrines. *Anatolian Studies* 6:87–94.

Lawrence, D. L., and S. M. Low 1990 The Built Environment and Spatial Form. *Annual Review of Anthropology* 19:453–505.

Letesson, Q. 2014 From Building to Architecture: The Rise of Configurational Thinking in Bronze Age Crete. In *Spatial Analysis and Social Spaces: Interdisciplinary Approaches to the Interpretation of Prehistoric and Historic Built Environment*, edited by E. Paliou, U. Lieberwirth, S. Polla, pp. 49–90. De Gruyter, Berlin.

Letesson, Q., and K. Vansteenhuyse 2006 Towards an Archaeology of Perception: "Looking" at the Minoan Palaces. *Journal of Mediterranean Archaeology* 19(1):91–119.

Lloyd, S., and J. Mellaart 1955 Beycesultan Excavations: Second Preliminary Report, 1955. *Anatolian Studies* 6:101–135.

Lynch, K. 1960 City Form. In *The Image of the City*, pp. 91–118. MIT Press, Cambridge.

Matney, T. 2002 Urban Planning and the Archaeology of Society at Early Bronze Age Titris Hoyuk. In *Across the Anatolian Plateau: Readings in the Archaeology of Ancient Turkey*, edited by D. C. Hopkins, pp. 19–34. American Schools of Oriental Research, Boston.

Mellaart, J. 1967 *Çatal Höyük: A Neolithic Town in Anatolia*. Thames and Hudson, London.

Mellaart, J. 1970 *Excavations at Hacilar*. Published for British Institute of Archaeology at Ankara, Edinburgh University Press, Edinburgh.

Mellink, M. J. 1965 Excavations at Karataş Semayük in Lycia. *American Journal of Archaeology* 69(3):241–251.

Moore, J. D. 1996 *Architecture and Power in the Ancient Andes: The Archaeology of Public Buildings*. Cambridge University Press, Cambridge.

O'Donovan, M. 2002 Grasping Power: A Question of Relations and Scales. In *The Dynamics of Power*, edited by M. O'Donovan, Occassiona, pp. 19–34. Center for Archaeological Investigations, Southern Illinois University, Carbondale.

Osborne, J. 2012 Communicating Power in the Bit Hilani Palace. *Bulletin of the American Schools of Oriental Research* 368:29–66.

Parker Pearson, M., and C. Richards 1994 *Architecture and Order: Approaches to Social Space*. Routledge, London.

Rapoport, A. 1988 Levels of Meaning in the Built Environment. In *Cross-Cultural Perspectives in Nonverbal Communication*, edited by F. Poyatos, pp. 317–336. Hogrefe, Toronto.

Rapoport, A. 1990 Systems of Activities and Systems of Settings. In *Domestic Architecture and the Use of Space: An Interdisciplinary Cross-Cultural Study*, pp. 9–20. Cambridge University Press, Cambridge.

Rapoport, A. 1982 *The Meaning of the Built Environment: A Nonverbal Communication Approach*. Sage, Beverly Hills.

Rubertone, P. E. 2008 *Archaeologies of Placemaking Monuments, Memories, and Engagement in Native North America*. Left Coast Press, Walnut Creek, CA.

Sagona, A., and P. Zimansky 2009 *Ancient Turkey*. Routledge, New York.

Shapiro, J. S. 2005 *A Space Syntax Analysis of Arroyo Hondo Pueblo, New Mexico: Community Formation in the Northern Rio Grande*. School of American Research Press, Sante Fe.

Smith, M. L. 2003 Introduction: The Social Construction of Ancient Cities. In *The Social Construction of Ancient Cities*, edited by M. L. Smith, pp. 1–36. Smithsonian Institution Press, Washington, DC.

Spence-Morrow, G. 2009 Analyzing the Invisible: Syntactic Interpretation of Archaeological Remains through Geophysical Prospection. In *Proceedings of the 7th International Space Syntax Symposium*, edited by D. Koch, L. Marcus, and J. Steen, pp. 1–10. Stockholm.

Steadman, S. R. 2000 Spatial Patterning and Social Complexity on Prehistoric Anatolian Tell Sites: Models for Mounds. *Journal of Anthropological Archaeology* 1(2):164–199.

Van Dyke, R. M. 1999 Space Syntax Analysis at the Chacoan Outlier of Guadalupe. *American Antiquity* 64(3):461–473.

Warner, J. 1979 The Megaron and Apsidal House in Early Bronze Age Western Anatolia: New Evidence from Karatas. *American Journal of Archaeology* 83(2):369–385.

Yakar, J. 1974 The Twin Shrines of Beycesultan. *Anatolian Studies* 24:151–161.

Zeynep B. 2017 A Pre-Evaluation of Libation Vessels Discovered at Seyitömer Mound Early Bronze Age Layer III Sanctuaries. In *Early Bronze Age in Western Anatolia*, edited by L. K. Harrison, A. N. Bilgen, and A. Kuru. State University of New York Press, Albany.

CHAPTER THIRTEEN

On the Perceptions of Sacred Space during the Early Bronze Age

The Case of Beycesultan

Fulya Dedeoğlu*

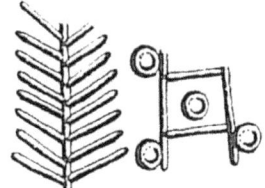

INTRODUCTION

In his 1956 article entitled *"Some Early Anatolian Shrines,"* W. Lamb preferred using the term *shrine* rather than *temple* for the buildings related to ritual or cult in Western Anatolia during the Early Bronze Age. Nonetheless, the reason underlying the preference rests on the fact that he identified the *shrines* at Kusura Höyük and Beycesultan as domestic shrines rather than public ones (Lamb 1956:84). Further, S. Lloyd and J. Mellaart continued using the word *shrine* for the buildings at Beycesultan Höyük corresponding to their view that these spaces were entirely dedicated to rituals (Lloyd and Mellaart 1957). J. Yakar has also considered these buildings in a similar sense to that of S. Lloyd and J. Mellaart (Yakar 1974; 1968). Although definitions may vary, it is clear that rituals or cults related to the household existed in Western Anatolia during the Early Bronze Age and this tradition was widespread before construction of independent temple buildings. Such a development was also observed across the Aegean coast; it was determined that domestic shrines coexisted with independent temples in Minoan and Mycenaean settlements (Wightman 2007:923). In this article, which reevaluates relatively congeneric domestic cult spaces located in Southwestern Anatolia, the primary focus will be on the sacredness of living spaces, starting as a tradition during the early Bronze Age and continuing thereafter, with particular emphasis on Beycesultan Höyük. The article will also investigate whether the "shrines" at Beycesultan Höyük were domestic or public spaces.

How cult and ritual applications are determined in the archaeological context has been intensely debated since the end of the 1980s, especially through post-processual and

---

*Associate Professor Dr. Fulya Dedeoğlu, Ege University, Faculty of Letters, Department of Archaeology, Division of Protohistory and Archaeology of Asia Minor, dedeoglufulya@hotmail.com.

cognitive approaches (Hodder 1982a; 1982b; 1986; Price 2001:7; Renfrew 1985; 1994). These approaches, which foreground symbolism and the context of material culture, hardly find a place and significance among archaeological data. C. Renfrew's formative study, which lists the questions to be asked in order to determine the existence of a cult or ritual in a given space, represents one of the earliest examples (Renfrew 1985). C. Renfrew's study, which is concerned with the sacred spaces of the Phylakopi settlement on the island of Melos, has identified some aspects of worship and cult in terms of archaeology. Stressing the inadequacy of archaeological deductions based solely on material culture (Renfrew 1985:1), C. Renfrew's eighteen-item list that provides clues about identifying ritual spaces in archaeological settlements (Renfrew 1985:19–20) has also been simplified and used by many other scientists for other settlements in the region (Marakas 2010:7–14; Pilafidis-Williams 1998:121–125.) The aforementioned criteria, either original or reorganized, basically include some findings or symbolic items that are expected to be discovered at the ritual site: among these one might include internal structures such as an altar, bench, libation pit, or oven and movable assets such as candles, libation vessels, or votive offerings alongside figurative objects that could be associated with gods (Marakas 2010:9; Pilafidis-Williams 1998:124–125; Renfrew 1985:19). C. Renfrew's approach presents some perspective for the definition of sacred places; however, it has been criticized: providing a single set of criteria for almost all settlements "as a rule" would not be acceptable (Bertemes and Biehl 2001:13). Thus, it is considered that the findings that might be related to cults or rituals should be evaluated within their own archaeological contexts (Bertemes and Biehl 2001:17–20).

The second step should be to determine whether the ritual or cult applications were carried out at the domestic level or public level. Nevertheless, it is extremely challenging to distinguish domestic worship from small-scale common worship. It is necessary to investigate the exact locations and concentrations of finds that might be related to cult or ritual: for instance, in order to label an entire building as a ritual space it would be valuable to know whether the finds related to cult or ritual are concentrated at a single point of the building or are dispersed throughout. In addition, it would be helpful to consider the number of finds in order to establish whether the attendance at the ritual went beyond a domestic extent. Another aspect to be determined is whether everyday finds, those items that are not related to the cult, exist inside the building labeled as a "shrine."

Early Bronze Age "Shrines" at Beycesultan Höyük

Beycesultan Höyük Early Bronze Age shrines were unearthed at an excavation site named SX sounding, which had a dimension of 25 × 14 meters. Three phases of Early Bronze Age (EBA 1–3) layers were identified at the site and the earliest sacred building was encountered at Level XVII, which was dated to the Early Bronze Age 1 period (Figure 13.1a). This two-room megaron building, which has a pentice, was approximately 5.3 × 11.5 meters and was built of mudbricks over a stone foundation. The main room, which measures 4.5 × 5.0 meters was entirely unearthed, while the back room was only partially unearthed. There is an aperture connecting the two rooms on the dividing wall of the building. Another door at the side wall of the back room opens to further rooms (Lloyd and Mellaart 1962:29–33). There are many architectural elements inside the main room of the building. On the north of the room there is a clay structure which probably is an altar and next to this is a pit filled with ashes. There is a clay bench in the northwestern corner and there is a grain storage opposite this bench. Moreover, the additional room to the north of the main room was named as a "priest's room" since the findings inside the room were identified as votive items (Lloyd and Mellaart 1962:29; Yakar 1968:86).

It is considered that the sacred buildings continued during the succeeding three layers (XVI–XIV) above layer XVII (Lloyd and Mellaart 1962:36–55; Yakar 1974:152–154). The earliest of these layers dated to Early Bronze Age II, layer XVI, is characterized by two buildings that were built using mudbricks over a stone foundation sharing a common wall (Figure 13.1b; Lloyd and Mellaart 1962:36–38). The building to the west was entirely unearthed (A) while part of the building to the east remains in the unexcavated site. It is thought that both of these tetragonal buildings have the same size (7.5 × 12 meters). Both buildings were designed with a pentice before the main room. Moreover, the main room of Building A was designed as a two-roomed structure (rooms 1 and 2).

The rooms are linked to each other by an opening and both rooms have an opening to the pentice on the south. Room 1, which is located to the east, has a mudbrick granary next to the entrance and a platform on the northwest. There is a stela altar at the center of the building. These stela rise above a 30–40 centimeters high clay foot and they are surrounded by a round platform. There is an oven at the center of Room 2, which is located to the west of Room 1, and there is a storage compartment contiguous to the western wall. Nine whole cups were unearthed over the floor of Room 1, between the entrance and the oven. There is a two-compartment storage room contiguous to the western wall of the front pentice, which serves as a common space for both rooms. The main room of Building B, which was built contiguous to building A, was designed as a single room. There is a stela altar at the center of the building which has two apertures: one on the northern part and another that opens to the pentice. The other structures inside the building are an oven before the western wall and a hearth adjacent to the northern wall.

The excavators have identified the aforementioned buildings as special structures with religious functions (Lloyd and Mellaart 1962:38). Two adjacent structures with separate walls were discovered in layer XV (Figure 13.1c) which is located right above layer XVI (Lloyd and Mellaart 1962:40–49; Yakar 1964:90–94). Building A has a size of 5.4 × 12.7 meters and it was almost entirely unearthed. Part of Building B, which is located at the immediate east of Building A, remains outside the excavation boundaries. These buildings, which were built over a stone foundation using mudbricks, follow a plan that comprises a main room and a back room located to the north of this room and a front pentice on the south. There is a semicircular granary on the left of the pentice of the building on the west, which was named House A, and there are two ovens and a bench opposite this grain storage. There is a stela altar inside the main room of the building.

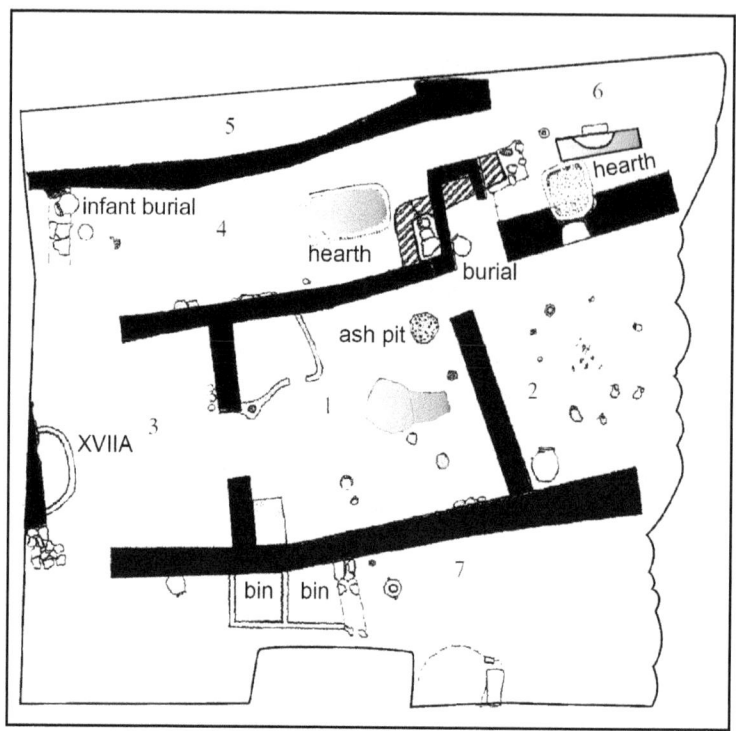

Figure 13.1A. Early Bronze age "shrines" from Beycesultan Höyük. Layer XVII (adapted by Yakar 1978: Fig. 91).

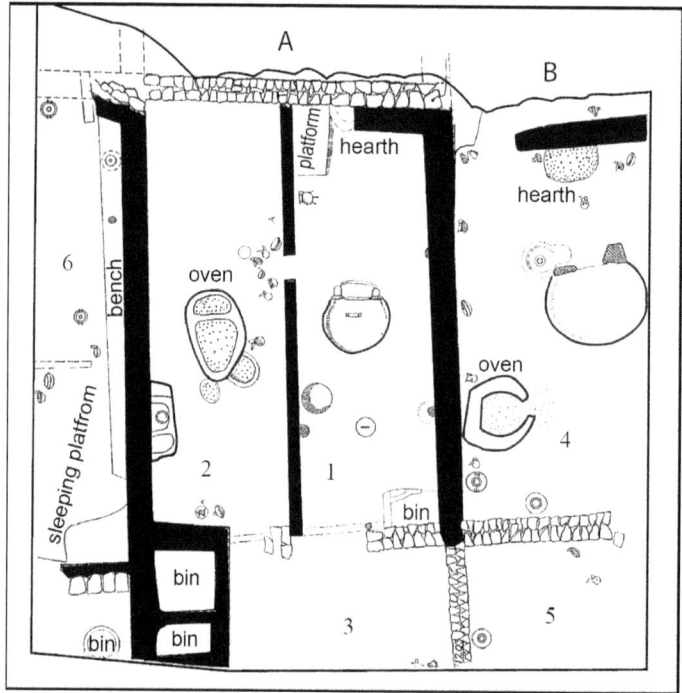

Figure 13.1B. Early Bronze age "shrines" from Beycesultan Höyük. Layer XVI (adapted by Lloyd/Mellaart 1962: Fig. 10).

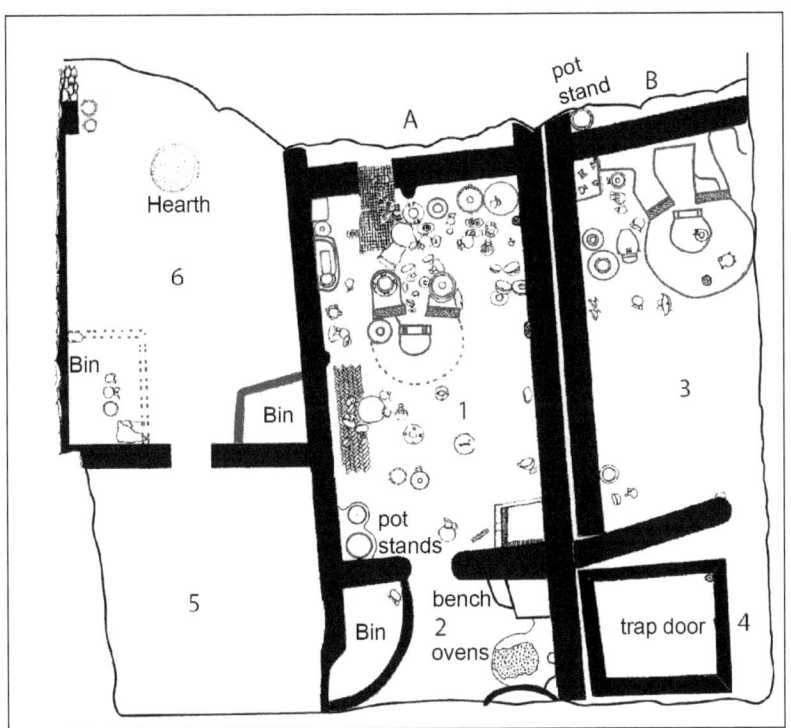

FIGURE 13.1C. Early Bronze age "shrines" from Beycesultan Höyük. Layer XV (adapted by Lloyd/Mellaart 1962: Fig. 13).

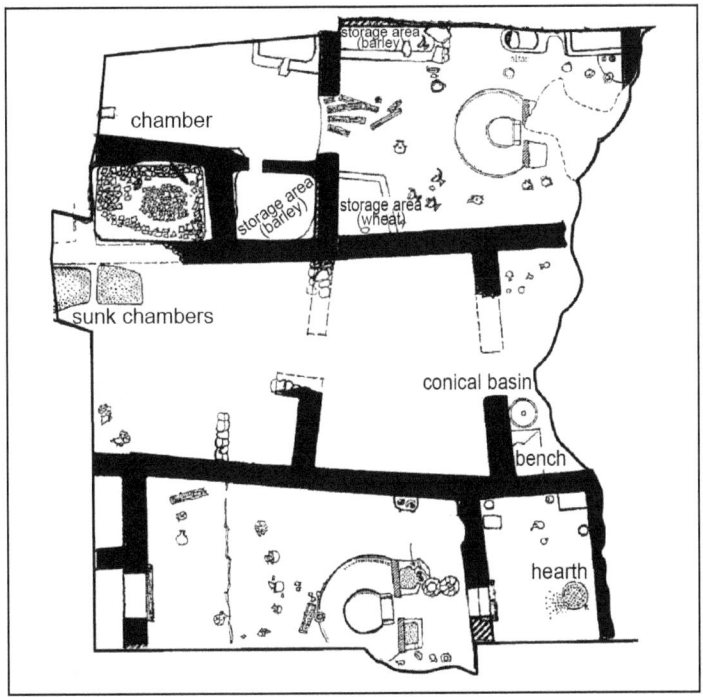

FIGURE 13.1D. Early Bronze age "shrines" from Beycesultan Höyük. Layer XVI (adapted by Lloyd/Mellaart 1962: Fig. 17).

There is a 20 centimeters high, double-compartment clay one, which the excavators named a blood altar, at the northwestern corner of the building, a square storage pit at the southeastern corner, and a clay platform at the southwestern corner. A large portion of the front pentice of Building B is occupied by a grain storage. There is a stela altar inside the main room which is similar to the one in Building A. There is a platform between the walls and the stela. There is a horn-shaped item before the stela. There was a bench on the northwestern corner of the building on which the excavators discovered twenty complete cups; probable fragments of a pithos were discovered inside the back room, which is located at the north end.

Another sacred space at Beycesultan Höyük was unearthed at layer XIV (Lloyd and Mellaart 1962:49–55; Yakar 1968:94–98; 1974:152–154). This layer architecturally resembles layers XVI and XV, and is characterized by three buildings that share a joint wall (Figure 13.1d). Unlike in other layers, the buildings identified as sacred spaces at the building complex at layer XIV were not placed contiguously but a three-roomed building (buildings 4, 5, and 6) existed between them. These buildings that were connected to each other contain not only architectural structures made of clay but also a large number of pottery items. The buildings surrounding this building were also excavated and two rooms of a building and four rooms of another were unearthed. The northern room of the building to the west (numbered 7) has a stela altar near the center and there is a "blood altar" and a bench contiguous to the wall to the west of the altar. Other architectural elements observed inside the building include two grain storages—one on the southwestern section, the other on the southeastern. The building to the south (Building 8) has two grain storages placed opposite each other and a compartment on the southeastern corner. There is a stela altar and abundant complete vessels around the altar inside the main room of the building on the east (Building 1). Inside the northern room of the building (Building 2) there is an oven and bench together with several complete vessels. No architectural elements were encountered in the southern section of the central building which only partially remains within the excavation boundaries.

Generally, it is understood that these buildings, which are considered as "shrines," solely served religious functions. All of the mentioned buildings have spaces such as "adyton" and "priest's room," which are characteristic of places of worship in addition to storages for votive offerings or some architectural elements that can be considered as cult objects. The definitions discussed point to the fact that these buildings were completely reserved for rituals and those rituals went beyond a domestic scale. This necessitates a detailed study of the findings and architectural elements inside such buildings that are accepted as "shrines."

Beycesultan Höyük "Shrines" from a Different Point of View

When the overall architectural plans of the "shrines" at Beycesultan Höyük are considered, it is observed that the buildings are generally rectangular. Though observed in a very limited space, these buildings were formed either of adjoining (layer XVI) or independently built (layer XV) houses (Figure 13.1b-c). Hence, the mentioned architectural plan was known in other settlements in Western Anatolia during the Early Bronze Age including Bademağacı (Duru and Umurtak 2010: Res. 2), Küllüoba (Fidan 2012: Res. 9), and Seyitömer (Bilgen 2010:547, Plan 4). It can be said that the buildings are formed of a main room and spaces annexed to the front or back side of this room. It was determined that some of these buildings were formed of two adjacent rooms, as observed in layer XV. A similar plan was also partially detected in the building at layer XVII. It was determined that the buildings named as twin temples were not connected to each other through a passage (Figure 13.1c). Thus, these buildings might be interpreted as adjacently built independent buildings, as well (Figure 13.2). Yet, earlier examples of buildings with similar plans were encountered in the Late Chalcolithic layer of Beycesultan Höyük (Figure 13.3). In particular, the building unearthed at layer XXXIA of the Late Chalcolithic, which has a bench that extends along the northern and eastern walls and a circular oven, resembles Early Bronze Age buildings both in terms of architectural plan and inner elements (Lloyd-Mellaart 1962:23; Figure 13.5).

When we consider the findings from the "shrines" of Beycesultan Höyük it is not possible to talk about a rigid standardization (Table 13.1). The architectural element observed in almost every layer is the clay structure referred to as a "stela altar" by S. Lloyd and J. Mellaart (Figure 13.1). However, there are some views which assert that the structures accepted as altars at Beycesultan might well be ovens (Diamant and Ruther 1969:152). Nevertheless, parallels of these buildings were observed among the dwellings of the Early Bronze Age II layer at Tarsus (Diamant and Ruther 1969: Figure 4–5; Goldman 1956: Figure 108). The horn-shaped form of these structures that were defined as ovens is similar to those at Beycesultan. During recent years ovens similar to those

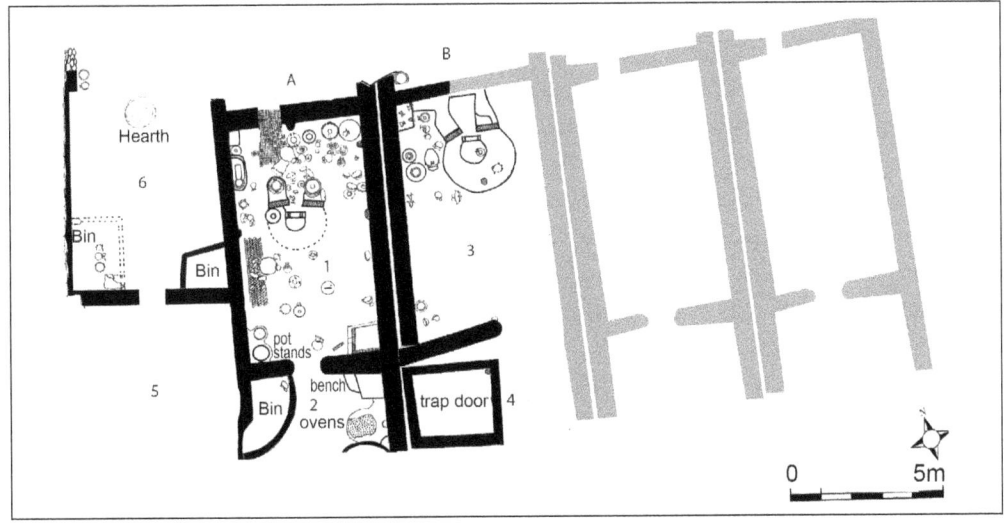

FIGURE 13.2. A different interpretation for architecture of "twin shrines" from Beycesultan Höyük.

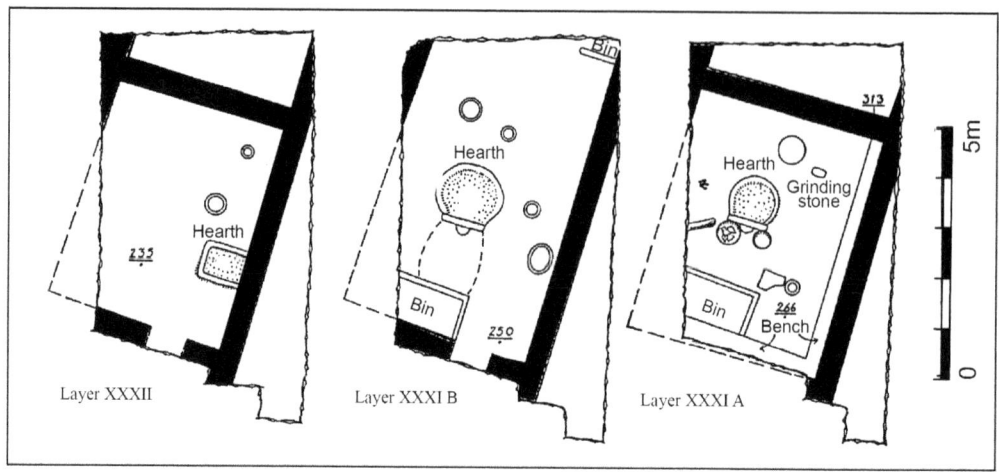

FIGURE 13.3. Architectural remains at XXXII-XXXIA-B of Late Chalcolithic from Beycesultan (adapted by Lloyd/Mellaart 1962: Fig. 5).

at Beycesultan and Tarsus were also discovered inside domestic structures at Seyitömer (Bilgen 2010:548) Almost every house at the Seyitömer Höyük VA layer that was dated to Early Bronze Age III has horn-shaped, clay ovens. All these findings confirm that the structures determined at Beycesultan Höyük and named "stela altars" might be ovens. Other common architectural elements among these buildings are platforms and grain bins (Figure 13.1). However, these architectural elements are not limited to sacred places but are observed mostly in domestic buildings. The largest group of finds contains the various forms of vessels discovered. It has to be noted that these vessels include both fine pottery and everyday cups (Lloyd and Mellaart 1957:31–36; Lloyd and Mellaart 1962:34, 38–39, 46–49, 54–55). It is also observed that objects other than pottery finds were also discovered inside the buildings. In this context, the most fruitful building in terms of objects discovered is on layer XVII. The abundance of figurines inside this building is noteworthy (Figure 13.1a; Lloyd and Mellaart 1962:34–35, 266, Figure F.1.1–14, 17).

On the other hand, figurines are more frequently discovered at other layers and no figurines, even fragments, were discovered at layer XV (Lloyd and Mellaart 1962:46–49). Except for these, the small finds repertoire contains finds that might be related to domestic or personal use. For instance, the objects discovered include personal finds such as necklace (Lloyd and Mellaart 1962:35, Pl.XXXIIIb), dagger-blade (Lloyd and Mellaart 1962:35, Figure 9), and pin (Lloyd and Mellaart 1962:35, 39, 55, Figure 11), and household objects such as pestle and mortar (Lloyd and Mellaart 1962:35, Pl.XXXII), brush-handle (Lloyd and Mellaart 1962:39, 48, Pl.XXXIIIa), or needle. All the present data suggest that the buildings labeled as "shrines" at Beycesultan Höyük could be living spaces in real life. The oven and bull cult at the center of almost every living space might be considered as elements of domestic worship, which shows the sacredness of living spaces.

TABLE 13.1
DISTRIBUTION OF FINDS FROM BEYCESULTAN "SHRINES"

		Beycesultan Höyük "Shrines"			
		Layer XVII	Layer XVI	Layer XVI	Layer XV
Architectural Units	Stela altar/Horn-shaped ovens	√	√	√	√
	Oven	√	√		√
	Hearth		√	√	
	Platform/Bench	√	√	√	√
	Grain Bin	√	√	√	√
	Ash Pit	√			
	Wooden post			√	
Pottery	Jug	√	√	√	√
	Bow	√	√	√	√
	Storage Jar		√	√	√
	Quadruple vassel	√			
	Jar	√	√	√	√
	Miniature jar		√	√	√
	Bottle	√	√		
Small Finds	Figurine	√	√		√
	Copper needle	√	√		√
	Copper pin	√	√		√
	Dagger blade	√			
	Necklace	√			
	Pestle and mortal	√			
	Clay brush			√	√
	Child Burial	√			

THE OVEN AND BULL CULT IN DOMESTIC WORSHIP

It is apparent that the oven and bull cult that was observed at Seyitömer and Karataş settlements alongside Beycesultan during the Early Bronze Age continued in later periods. Data concerning this situation were reached during both first- and second-phase excavations at Beycesultan Höyük. During the excavations supervised by S. Lloyd and J. Mellaart, buildings that could be associated with domestic worship with regard to the ovens that are similar to Early Bronze Age ovens were encountered. The second period of excavations undertaken by E. Abay presents some data on the issue (Abay 2014:177–178.) Horn-shaped ovens were discovered inside the domestic structures unearthed at the layer labeled Layer II during the first phase of excavation, which is currently named layer 5b (Figure 13.4–5). E. Abay notes that the buildings where these ovens were detected were dwellings constituting a living space connected to a storage room (Abay and Dedeoğlu 2013:219). The oven right opposite the entrance of this rectangular living space is built over a large platform and it has two horn-shaped wings at the upper part, which is connected to a rectangular platform (Figure 13.5). The wings are ornamented using butterfly

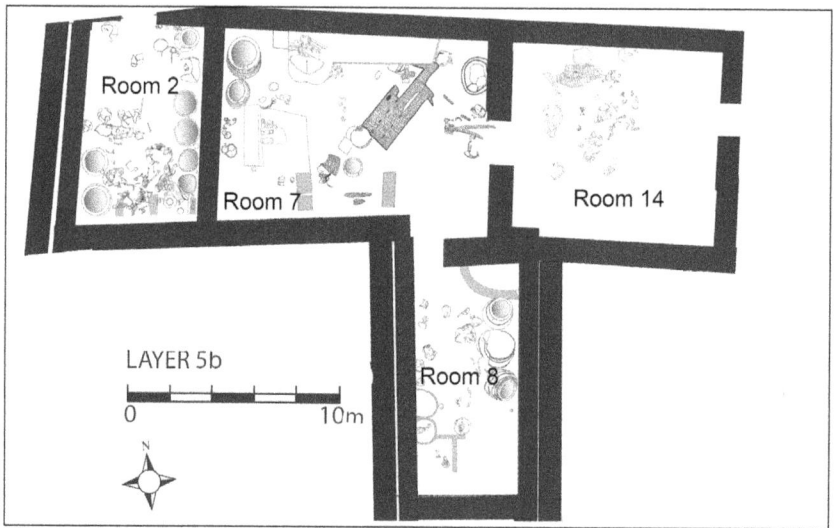

FIGURE 13.4. The architectural remains of domestic structures at Layer 5b from Beycesultan Höyük.

FIGURE 13.5. Details of horn-shaped ovens and domestic structures at Layer 5b from Beycesultan Höyük.

motifs and they lie over an oval firepan. A similar building was discovered at that layer of Kusura Höyük, another settlement in the Upper Meander Basin, which was a contemporary of the layer at Beycesultan (Lamb 1956). Exploring the similarities, it can be asserted that this structure is also an oven (Diamant and Rutter 1969:152–153) which is located at the center of a rectangular room. W. Lamb indicated that sherds of pottery and seeds that might be related to ritual were encountered on the platform where this structure rises (Diamant and Rutter 1969:152–153; Lamb 1936:12.)

It can be asserted that the oven and bull images foregrounded in the domestic worship objects of the mentioned settlements found their meanings in the religious understandings of many other cultures, because the sacredness of fire and oven is generally represented as the acceptance of fire or oven as gods or symbols of a god's power (Uhri 2003:28). A classic example of this is the sacredness of the oven in Early Transcaucasia Culture (Işıklı 2011:103–104; Takaoğlu 2000:11–14). It is known from the ritual texts that gods of the oven existed in the Hittite religion and offerings were made to the oven (Taş 2011:9–11). It is also considered that fire and oven represent continuation of the bloodline and might be related to the cult of the ancestors (Taş 2011:12). This close relationship between the family and the oven is later embodied in Hestia, the goddess of family and the hearth in Greek mythology. Hestia is known in Roman mythology as Vesta and she represents the cult of the oven and the sacredness of home (Uhri 2003:32–35).

The bull image has been observed in many cultures since the Pre-pottery Neolithic Age (Karul 2011:179–180; Hodder 2006:142–143; Twiss and Russell 2009:19–20). Particularly, bull symbolism is not only seen on ovens but also on some cups at Beycesultan Höyük (Lloyd and Mellaart 1962: Figure 27–28).

As a result, the sacredness assigned to the family in Western Anatolia through the cult of the bull and oven since Early Bronze Age I has been archaeologically defined in many settlements in Southwestern Anatolia. It is concluded that domestic worship played an important role in the religious system during this process when religious structures were not yet well organized in Western Anatolia during the Early Bronze Age.

References Cited

Abay, E. 2014 Kazı Verileri Işığında Arkeolojik Mekân Analizleri, Beycesultan Örneği. In *Yerleşim Sistemleri ve Mekan Analizi, Tematik Arkeoloji Serisi*, edited by Ö. Çevik and B. Erdoğu, pp. 177–178. Tematik Arkeoloji Serisi, İstanbul.

Abay, E., and F. Dedeoğlu 2013 Beycesultan 2007–2010 Yılları Kazı Çalışmaları Raporu. *KST* 34(1):217–229.

Bertemes, F., and P. F. Biehl 2001 The Archaeology of Cult and Religion: An Introduction. In *The Archaeology of Cult and Religion*, edited by F. Bertemes, P. F. Biehl, and H. Meller, pp. 11–26. Archaeolingua, Budapest.

Bilgen, N. 2010 *Seyitömer Höyük Kazısı Ön Raporu (2006–2010)*. Dumlupınar Üniversitesi Fen-Edebiyat Fakültesi Arkeoloji Bölümü, Kütahya.

Diamant, S., and J. Ruther 1969 Horned Objects in Anatolia and the Near East and Possible Connexions with the Minoan Horns of Consecration. *Anatolian Studies* 19:147–177.

Duru, R. and G. Umurtak 2010 Bademağacı Kazıları, 2008. *31. Kazı Sonuçları Toplantısı* 3:261–268. Ankara.

Fidan, E. 2012 Küllüoba İlk Tunç Çağı Mimarisi. Küllüoba Kazıları ve Batı Anadolu Tunç Çağları Üzerine Yapılan Araştırmalar, MASROP e-dergi:1–44.

Goldman, H. 1956 *Excavations at Gözlü Kule, Tarsus. Volume II: From the Neolithic through the Bronze Age*. Princeton University Press, Princeton.

Hodder, I. 1982a *Symbols in Action. Ethnoarchaeological Studies of Material Culture*. Cambridge University Press, Cambridge.

Hodder, I. 1982b *The Present Past. An Introduction to Anthropology for Archaeologists*. Batsford, London.

Hodder, I. 1986 *Reading the Past. Current Approaches to Interpretation in Archaeology*. Cambridge University Press, Cambridge.

Hodder, I. 2006 *Çatalhöyük, Leoparın Öyküsü*. Yapı Kredi Yayınları, İstanbul.

Işıklı, M. 2011 *Doğu Anadolu Erken Transkafkasya Kültürü. Çok Bileşenli Gelişkin Bir Kültürün Analizi*. Arkeoloji ve Sanay Yayınları, İstanbul.

Karul, N. 2011 Anadolu'da Boğa Sembolü ve Batıya Transferi. In *Işın Yalçınkaya'ya Armağan/ Studies in Honour of Işın Yalçınkaya*, edited by H. Taşkıran, M. Kartal, K. Özçelik, M. B. Kösem, and G. Kartal, pp. 179–184. Bilgin Kültür Sanat Yayınları, Ankara.

Lamb, W. 1956 Some Early Anatolian Shrines. *Anatolian Studies* 6:87–94.

Lloyd, S., and J. Mellaart 1957 An Early Bronze Age Shrine at Beycesultan. *Anatolian Studies* 7:27–36.

Lloyd, S., and J. Mellaart 1962 *Beycesultan I: The Chalcholithic and Early Bronze Age Levels*. British Institute of Archaeology at Ankara, London.

Marakas, G. 2010 *Ritual Practice between the Late Bronze Age and Protogeometric Periods of Greece*. BAR International Series 2145.

Pilafidis-Williams, K. 1998 *The Sanctuary of Aphaia on Aigina in the Bronze Age*. Hirmer Verlag, Munich.

Price, N. 2001 *The Archaeology of Shamanism*. Routledge, London.

Renfrew, C. 1985 *The Archaeology of Cult: The Sanctuary Philakopi*. British School of Archaeology at Athens Suppl. Vol. 18, London.

Renfrew, C. 1994 The Archaeology of Religion. In *The Ancient Minds: Elements of Cognitive Archaeology*, edited by C. Renfrew and E. B. W. Zubrow, pp. 3–12. Cambridge University Press, Cambridge.

Taş, İ. 2011 Hititçe Çivi Yazılı Belgelere Göre Ocak Kültü ve Ocağın Kutsallığı Üzerine Bazı Gözlemler. *Kubaba Arkeoloji-Sanat Tarihi-Tarih Dergisi* Sayı 17:7–18.

Takaoğlu, T. 2000 Hearth Structures in the Religious Pattern of Early Bronze Age Northeast Anatolia. *Anatolian Studies* 50:11–16.

Twiss, K. C., and N. Russell 2009 Taking the Bull by the Horns: Ideology, Masculinity, and Cattle Horns at Çatalhöyük (Turkey). *Paléorient* 35(2):19–32.

Uhri, A. 2003 *Ateşin Kültür Tarihi*. Dost Kitabevi Yayınları, Ankara.

Wightman, G. J. 2007 *Sacred Spaces. Religious Architecture in the Ancient World*. Ancient Near Eastern Studies Suppl. 22, Belgium.

Yakar, J. 1968 *The Religious Architecture and Art of Early Anatolia*. PhD thesis, Brandeis University.

Yakar, J. 1974 The Twin Shrines of Beycesultan. *Anatolian Studies* 24:151–161.

CHAPTER FOURTEEN

Defense Systems Dated to the Early Bronze Age at Liman Tepe

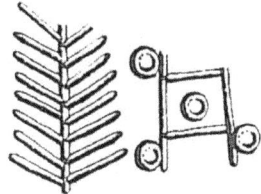

Ayşegül Aykurt,* Hayat Erkanal**

Liman Tepe is located on the southern coast of the Bay of İzmir, in the district of İskele at Urla, across Karantina Island. Before the İzmir-Çeşmealtı road reaches the center of the İskele neighborhood, it cuts through Liman Tepe in the east-west direction (Figure 14.1). Owing to the high rocky terrain on the north of the site, the settlement is relatively protected from the north winds. In the Archaic ages the two bays located at the east and west of the site had characterized Liman Tepe as a peninsula with a rocky north end (Erkanal and Hüryılmaz 1994:361). These bays, particularly the one on the east of the settlement that was larger than the other one, had first turned into a marsh due to the creeks in the area and eventually became completely filled. In connection with these changes that occurred on the coastline, the settlement located just on the south of the rocky terrain had developed toward the southwest, and in due course established the ancient city of Klazomenai.

The Prehistoric period materials at Liman Tepe had first been identified by Ekrem Akurgal with his research in 1950. Excavations had been carried out in the settlement, headed by Çetin Anlağan between 1979 and 1980, and by Güven Bakır in 1980. After a long break, excavations commenced again in 1992 under the directorship of Hayat Erkanal (Erkanal and Hüryılmaz 1994:361–362), and still continue today. During the excavations executed at Liman Tepe since 1992, layers that range from the Chalcolithic to the Roman Period have been studied, and a settlement stratigraphy has been established.

---

*Assoc. Prof. Dr. Ayşegül AYKURT, Hacettepe University, Faculty of Letters, Department of Archaeology, 06800 Beytepe-ANKARA. aysegulaykurt@gmail.com

**Prof. Dr. Hayat ERKANAL, Presidency of Liman Tepe Excavations, Denizli Mahallesi, Harbiye Caddesi, No: 2 Çeşmealtı Urla-İZMİR. hayaterkanal@gmail.com

FIGURE 14.1. A general view of Liman Tepe (Photo: Hakan Çetinkaya).

EARLY BRONZE AGE I DEFENSE SYSTEM

The Chalcolithic Period settlement comprises the earliest settlement of Liman Tepe. The layers belonging to this period have been studied extensively only in the north of the north excavation site. In addition to this, remains belonging to the Chalcolithic Period have been identified in the drillings performed at the floor of the Classical Age wells located on the north excavation site. Due to the level of the groundwater, the size of this period's settlement has not been precisely determined. Following the Chalcolithic Period, it has been observed that the settlement was surrounded by a fortification wall in the Early Bronze Age I Period. While the settlement extends to an approximate area of 125 meters in the north-south direction, its dimensions in the east-west direction are not yet known.

The fortification wall surrounding the Early Bronze Age I settlement has been uncovered to the south of the north excavation site. The uncovered fraction of this fortification wall outstretching in the east-west direction is 26.70 meters long. Having a thickness of 0.90 meters, the height of the identified part of the wall is 3.42 meters. The foundation of the fortification wall had been built with large field stones. It has been observed that this part which is 0.72 meters in height continues in the ground water. Built with rough field stones, the foundation wall had tilted inward because of the weight of the upper defense wall. Moreover, some of the stones had protruded out of the wall due to this deformation. The lower stones of the foundation wall have not been affected by the weight and were preserved their original positions. Above the foundation stones, two different materials had been used in the construction of the wall. The part of the wall that is 25.55 meters in length had been built with thick slab stones over the foundation made of field stones (Figure 14.3). There are tooth-like buttresses with 1.5 meter intervals on the southern side of this part of the wall facing the outer side of the settlement. Probably, these buttresses had been built in order to increase the strength of the wall, and yet there is a possibility that they may be the pedestals of the wooden beams that had been used to reinforce the mud-brick superstructure of the fortification wall. The outer façade of this defense system had been surrounded by a ramp-shaped construction comprised of mid-size field stones. The fortification wall built with the slab stones and the ramp ends neatly at the west. From this point, the fortification wall continues toward the west with a mud-brick structure built over the foundation made of field stones (Figure 14.2, 14.3). Thirty-three rows of the mud-brick fortification wall that

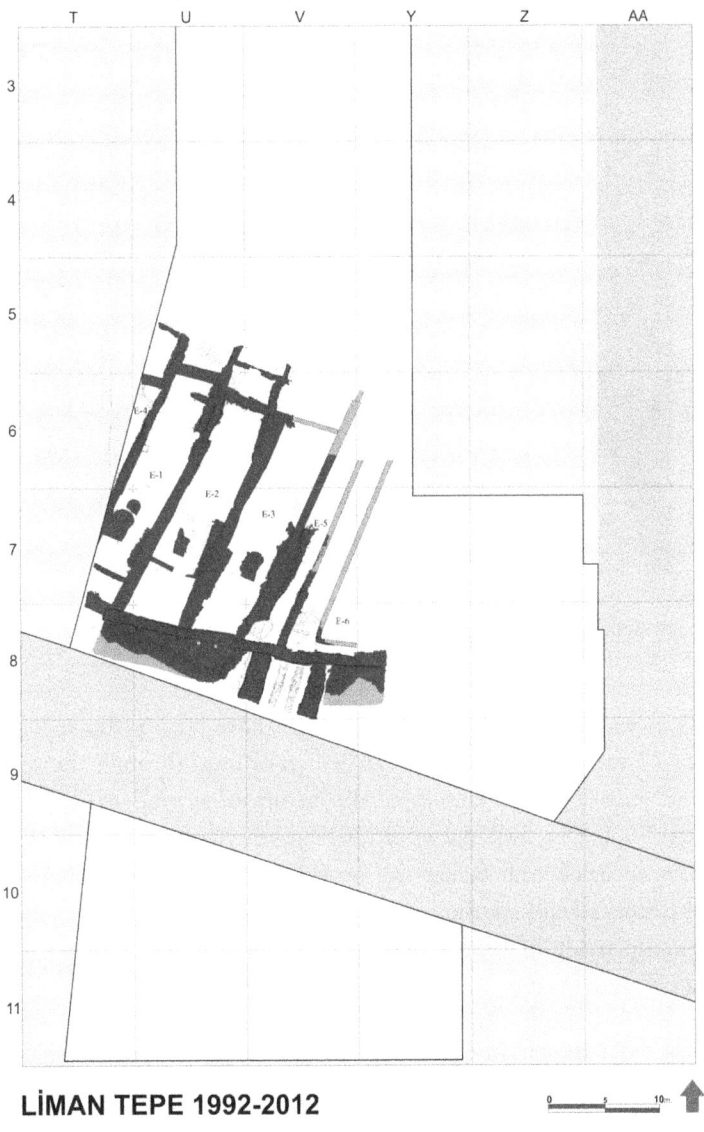

FIGURE 14.2. Plan of the Early Bronze Age I settlement (LMT VI).

FIGURE 14.3. Early Bronze Age I defensive system (LMT VI).

are 1.15 meters in width and 2.65 meters in height have been preserved. The mud-brick wall, of which 1.13 meters have been unearthed, continues through the unexcavated area in the west, and with a little bend joins the fortification wall made of slab stones in the east (Erkanal 2000:254; Erkanal et al. 2012:470). At the excavations carried out on the side of the mud-brick wall facing the outside the settlement, it has been seen that a pile of fist-size stones replaces the ramp made of field stones. This pile of stones also leans onto the ramp made of field stones.

There is a city gate (Figure 14.4), 2.80 meters wide, situated on the eastern extension of the fortification wall built with slab stones. On the exterior side of the gate facing outside the settlement, there are two thick walls 1.37–1.90 meters wide built on each side of the gate, showing tower-like features. The southern extensions of these walls run under the İzmir-Çeşmealtı road. In time, the wall gate had lost its function, and had been closed with a wall but, over time, collapsed due to the gap below.

FIGURE 14.4. Early Bronze Age I city gate (LMT VI).

At the excavations carried out to date at Liman Tepe, there have been six structures unearthed outstretching in the northeast-southwest direction within the interior of the settlement surrounded by the fortification wall (Figures 14.4, 14.5). Five of these structures (E-1–5) are located on the west side of the road that runs toward the city gate, and one (E-6) is located on the east side of the road. Unlike the structures on the west, the one on the east does not connect to the fortification wall. The western and the southern walls of this structure have partially been uncovered. The gap, 0.75–0.80 meters wide, between the southern wall of the structure and the fortification wall must

FIGURE 14.5. Early Bronze Age I houses (LMT VI).

have been used as a passageway. The structures on the west side lean on the fortification wall. The fortification wall also comprises the southern wall of these structures. Out of these structures, E-1, E-2, and E-3 have been completely unearthed. As for the other two, the east part of the structure E-4 and the undamaged south part of the structure E-5 have also been uncovered. Structures E-1, E-2, and E-3 are on average 23.30 meters long and 4.00 meters wide, and structure E-5, located just on the roadside, is narrower than the others with a width of 1.14–1.40 meters. During their long-term use, these structures with stone foundations and white plastered mud-brick walls had been divided into large and small spaces by partitions. It has been understood that in the middle of the inner large space, earth used for pottery and cooking, with a workshop next to it, had been built. At the latest phase of the structures, each structure had a kiln right next to the rear walls. Although different arrangements had been made in the structures at different phases, the main entrances located on the north side of the structures had not been changed (Erkanal et al. 2012:465–468). These structures have been defined as "workshop houses" (Erkanal et al. 2003:425).

The "long houses" that had been used for a long time in the Early Bronze Age I were destroyed because of an earthquake that occurred at the end of the period. The settlement had collapsed toward the sea during the earthquake and due to this, the "long houses" had leaned from south to north and become unusable.

Comparison and Evaluation

It has been observed that in the Early Bronze Age I in Western Anatolia, settlements were surrounded by fortification walls in order to protect their ever-increasing wealth. In addition to Liman Tepe, remains belonging to defense systems have been uncovered at the excavations carried out in Poliochni (Tiné 1997), Troy (Blegen et al. 1950), Bakla Tepe (Erkanal and Özkan 1998; 1999), Beycesultan (Lloyd and Mellaart 1962) and Demircihöyük (Korfmann 1987) of West Anatolia, and in the Aegean Islands, as well. The Early Bronze Age I defense system of Liman Tepe does not bear a resemblance to the aforementioned sites technically. As stated above, a part of the fortification wall surrounding the Early Bronze Age I settlement of Liman Tepe had been built with thick slab stones laid over the foundation made of field stones, and supported from the outside by a ramp made from field stones. The reason why this part of the fortification wall had been built differently must be because the people of the Early Bronze Age I Liman Tepe wanted to provide a monumental look for this part of the wall where the city gate stood. Thus, the city entrance was able to attain an impressive appearance.

Early Bronze Age II Defense System

In the Early Bronze Age II period of Liman Tepe, the organization of the settlement had changed. While the settlement continued inside the fortification wall, it had also started outside the wall. At the beginning of this period, first, the fortification wall that had surrounded the Early Bronze Age I settlement had been dropped out of use, and a stronger defense system had been built 14 meters south of the old fortification wall (Figure 14.6). The gap between the Early Bronze Age I and the Early Bronze Age II fortification walls had been filled with bulk mud-brick. At the excavations carried thus far, the southeast corner of the defense system surrounding the Early Bronze Age II settlement has been uncovered in the south excavation area and in the southeast corner of the north excavation area. This monumental defense system dated to the beginning of the Early Bronze Age II reflects the magnificence of Liman Tepe during this period.

The fortification wall outstretching in the east-west direction had been built with thick slab stones (Figure 14.7). The uncovered fraction of the wall is 6.00 meters in

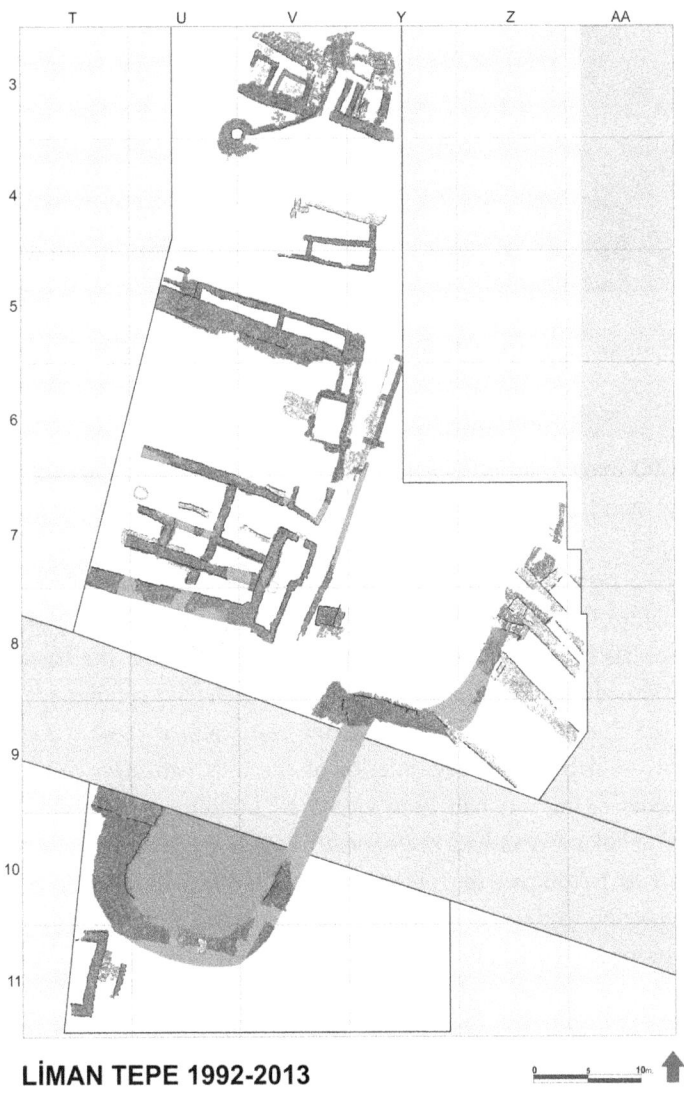

FIGURE 14.6. Plan of the Early Bronze Age II settlement (LMT V.2).

FIGURE 14.7. Early Bronze Age II defensive system (LMT V.2).

length, about 1.00 meters in width, and 5.60 meters in height. The west extension of the fortification wall stands within the unexcavated area where the east extension connects to a horseshoe-shaped bastion (Figure 14.6, 14.7). The horseshoe-shaped bastion is 12 meters in length and 19.5 meters in width. The outer face of the tower built with slab stones is inclined like a ramp. During the excavations carried out at the destroyed part of the bastion, information has been obtained about the inner structure of the bastion. In the inner part of the bastion, there are trapezoid- or semicircle-shaped cellular spaces on the sides (Figure 14.8). The three walls (two side and one rear wall) of these spaces had been built with a single row of slab stones. The interior of the cells had been filled with stones and earth, and the sides facing out had been closed by building a ramp-shaped construction. Thus, a chain of cellular spaces had been constructed at the inner part of the tower's outer face. Owing to this technique, the pressure of the interior mud-brick fill and the upper structure of the bastion to the outer structure had decreased (Erkanal 1999:240; 2001:263). The bastion has a preserved height of at least five meters. The east side of the bastion that had been built with a steeper inclination continues under the İzmir-Çeşmealtı road, and appears again on the north excavation area. The east side of the bastion is 24 meters long.

A second bastion connects from the east to this extension of the bastion that is located on the north excavation. This bastion had also been built in the shape of a ramp with thick slab stones. The bastion is 10.10 meters in length. The south wall

FIGURE 14.8. The cell in Early Bronze Age II bastion (LMT V.2).

of this bastion turns north with a bend in the east. At the northern extension of the bastion there is a narrow entrance. Five stairs have been located at the entrance, which is 0.74–0.95 meters wide. At the north and south of the entrance a buttress was partly uncovered. The bastion had been destroyed beginning with the buttress on the north (Erkanal et al. in press).

Just on the inner side of the magnificent defense system surrounding the Early Bronze Age II settlement of Liman Tepe, topographically in the lowest level of the settlement, there is a central building complex built at the second architectural layer. This building complex is comprised of a rectangular construction outstretching in the east-west direction, and a court and storerooms at the south. The northern part of the construction outstretching in the east-west direction has not yet been uncovered. Considering the portion of the structure unearthed, there is one long and one short room in the interior at the south, and at the north of these rooms, two big rooms built parallel to each other. The entrance of this building is at the west. At the south of this central structure, a big court and at the south of this court, a set of storerooms outstretching in the east-west direction have been uncovered (Şahoğlu 2005:350, Figure 3). The three narrow interconnecting storerooms had been bordered with a thick wall at the south. While the western extension of these storerooms continue in the unexcavated area, the eastern extension joins a slab-paved small area.

At the east of this set of rooms, there is a road in the northeast-southwest direction reaching the defense system at the south. On the west side of the road, there are rectangular interconnecting spaces, and on the east side of the road, there is a temenos wall outstretching in the northeast-southwest direction. The structure or the group of structures surrounded by this buttressed temenos wall will be uncovered in future excavations.

In addition to the above-mentioned remains belonging to the Early Bronze Age II, remains of the defense system that surrounded the lower city have also been found approximately 500 meters southwest of the settlement. A horseshoe-shaped bastion has been uncovered at the excavations carried out by the Klazomenai excavation team (Ersoy et al. 2011:169–170). It has been seen that this bastion is smaller when compared with the Early Bronze Age II bastion. The aforementioned example is significant in order to show the dimensions of the Early Bronze Age II settlement.

The defense system built at the beginning of the Early Bronze Age II was destroyed at the end of the second architectural layer of the Early Bronze Age II. There are rectangular colossal structures built on the destroyed defense system that were dated to the late part of the same level.

Comparison and Evaluation

During the Early Bronze Age II in Anatolia, where trading had long intensified and the number of prestige articles increased, close settlements had come together and united in one center. Accordingly, the number of settlements had decreased, and some centers had come into prominence. It has been seen that, beginning from the Early Bronze Age II, the settlements in the Aegean started to grow economically stronger, and a ruling class had emerged. An example very similar to the defense system of Liman Tepe that is supported by the horseshoe-shaped bastions is seen in an earlier period at Kuruçay in Anatolia. In the eleventh layer of Kuruçay dated to the Late Neolithic Period, a fortification wall, 1.10–1.20 meters in width, built with field stones and horseshoe-shaped towers connected to this fortification wall have been uncovered. Five meters in width, the towers project 3.5 meters out of the fortification wall. Some of the towers have one-meter-wide passageways (Duru 1994:11).

The contemporary examples similar to the Early Bronze Age defense system of Liman Tepe are seen in the Western Aegean. Defense systems with horseshoe-shaped bastions have been unearthed at Syros-Kastri (Bossert 1967:57–59), Naxos-Panarmos (Doumas 1972:161–163), Skyros-Palamari (Theochari and Parlama 1997: Figure 1–2), Aigina (Felten 1986:21–28), and Lerna (Caskey 1957:154, 157) in the Western Aegean. Out of these sites, 71.5 meters of a fortification wall made of stones dated to the Early Helladic II have been explored at Kastri located on the north side of a hill on Syros. The fortification wall, 1.30–1.80 meters wide, had been preserved to a height of 1.34 meters in some places. There are six bastions on the fortification wall varying in measures of 3.70–5 meters. Entry to the settlement is made through the two or three gates that are located on the fortification wall and some bastions. One of the gates located on the bastion is 1.15 meters in width. During the excavations carried out at Syros-Kastri on the outer side of the fortification wall, a second fortification wall, which was weaker, has been uncovered. This wall had been built to make the access to the settlement difficult (Bossert 1967:57–58; Doumas 1972:159; Marthari 1998: Figure 15–16, 26–27). As it is seen, although the bastions on the fortification wall of Syros-Kastri are similar to that of Liman Tepe, they are only one-third the size of the Liman Tepe bastion. In addition to this, while the entrance on the bastion resembles that of Liman Tepe in size, it differs in form, as Liman Tepe has staircases. Naxos-Panarmos is a citadel settlement situated on a low hill. The settlement dated to the Early Cycladic IIB is surrounded by a fortification wall between one and two meters thick. There are horseshoe-shaped bastions, 2.70–3.70 meters wide on the fortification wall. There are towers on both sides of the entrance 0.80 meters in width located on the east of the settlement (Doumas 1990:90; Renfrew 1972:177–178). Another site that shows a similarity to the defense system of Liman Tepe with its horseshoe-shaped bastions is Skyros-Palamari. Three horseshoe-shaped bastions have been unearthed on the fortification wall, which average 1.35 meters in thickness at Skyros-Palamari. Built with 7.70–8.50 meter intervals, the bastions have widths varying between 4.20 and 7.14 meters (Tartaron et al. 2006:148; Theochari and Parlama 1997: Figure 1-2). At Lerna, a horseshoe-shaped tower stands on the fortification wall comprised of a set of interconnecting spaces. The Lerna bastion, which is four meters wide is also smaller than the Liman Tepe examples (Caskey 1958:132–136). At the V settlement of Aigina dated to the end of 3000 B.C., later than that of Liman Tepe, there is a fortification wall with horseshoe and semi-horseshoe-shaped bastions. Eighty meters of the stone-built fortification wall has been uncovered. There are entrances on the semi-horseshoe-shaped bastions (Felten 1986:21–28, 12–13; Walter 1981:28–32).

When the aforementioned fortification walls with horseshoe-shaped bastions were examined, it was observed that the earliest examples of this type of defense systems are found in Anatolia during the Late Neolithic Period of Kuruçay. Such systems appear in the beginning of the Early Bronze Age II of Liman Tepe, in the Early Cycladic IIB of the Cyclades, and in the Early Helladic II of Greece.[1] The excavations carried out on early settlements of West Anatolia in the last 10 years have suggested that the settlements of Southwest Anatolia—where Kuruçay is also located—and West Anatolia had been in connection with each other. In this context, it may be suggested that this type of defense system had spread to the west from Anatolia. Among these settlements, the site in the Cyclades displays small structures of a disorganized settlement inside the defense system, whereas Liman Tepe and Lerna show organized settlements, which included buildings for a central authority inside the defense systems.

Early Bronze Age IIIA Defense System

In this period, a new citadel surrounded by a kind of a boundary wall was built at the center of the settlement. Due to the topography of the mound reaching its highest point, the important constructions of this period inside the citadel had been completely destroyed because of the activities carried out in the ensuing periods. Numerous pits used for garbage or special purposes have been found at the south of the citadel. Besides the characteristic pottery forms such as depas cups, tankards, and wheel-made dishes, a large quantity of tortoise shell was discovered in the pits. At the excavations carried out to the east of these pits, a slab paved road has been unearthed with a water channel located under it.

In the Early Bronze Age III, a ramp had been built in the south excavation area with large field stones (Figure 14.9). Having an inclination from the north to the south the ramp has an entrance comprised of stairs in the middle. The connection between these and the other architectural remains has not yet been determined.

In conclusion, since the early periods, İzmir, as the most important port city of Western Anatolia, has always acted as a bridge between Anatolia and the Aegean due to its strategic and geographical position. With its stratigraphy ranging from the Chalcolithic to the Roman Period, Liman Tepe located on the southern coast of the Bay of İzmir, has been one of the long-inhabited centers of the Aegean. The architectural remains and the finds uncovered in the Early Bronze Age layers of the settlement that have been thoroughly explored have proven that Liman Tepe served as one of the biggest port cities of its time.

Note

1. Arguments continue on Aigina defense system.

Figure 14.9. Early Bronze Age IIIA ramp (LMT IV.2).

References Cited

Blegen, C., J. L. Caskey, M. Rawson, and J. Sperling 1950 *Troy I: The First and Second Settlements*. Princeton University Press, Princeton.
Bossert, E. 1967 Kastri auf Syros. *Archaeologikon Deltion* 22:53–76.
Caskey, J. L. 1957 Excavations at Lerna. *Hesperia* 26:142–162.
Caskey, J. L. 1958 Excavations at Lerna 1957. *Hesperia* 27:125–144.
Doumas, C. 1972 Notes on Early Cycladic Architecture. *Archaologischer Anzeiger* 87:151–170.
Doumas, C. 1990 Weapons and Fortifications. In *Cycladic Culture: Naxos in the 3rd Millennium B.C.*, edited by L. Marangou, pp. 90–92. Nicholas P. Goulandris Foundation, Museum of Cycladic Art, Athens.
Duru, R. 1994 Kuruçay Höyük I. 1978–1988 Kazılarının Sonuçları Neolitik ve Erken Kalkolitik Çağ Yerleşmeleri. Türk Tarih Kurumu Basımevi, Ankara.
Erkanal, H. 1999 Early Bronze Age Fortification Systems in Izmir Region. In *Meletemata. Studies in Aegean Archaeology Presented to Malcolm H. Wiener as he enters his 65th Year. Aegaeum 20*. Vol. 1, edited by P. Betancourt, V. Karageorghis, R. Laffineur, and W.-D. Niemeier, pp. 237–242. Univ. de Liège, Liége.
Erkanal, H. 2000 1998 Liman Tepe Kazıları. *Kazı Sonuçları Toplantısı* 21(1):251–262.
Erkanal, H. 2001 1999 Liman Tepe Kazıları. *Kazı Sonuçları Toplantısı* 22(1): 259–268.
Erkanal, H., and H. Hüryılmaz 1992 1992 Liman Tepe Kazılar. *Kazı Sonuçları Toplantısı* 15:361–373.
Erkanal, H., and T. Özkan 1996 Bakla Tepe Kazıları. *Kazı Sonuçları Toplantısı* 19:399–425.
Erkanal, H., M. Artzy, and O. Kuoka 2003 2001 Yılı Liman Tepe Kazıları. *Kazı Sonuçları Toplantısı* 24:423–436.
Erkanal, H., V. Şahoğlu, A. Aykurt, O. Kouka, and İ. Tuğcu 2012 Liman Tepe 2010 Yılı Kara Kazıları. *Kazı Sonuçları Toplantısı* 33(4):463–478.
Erkanal, H., A. Aykurt, K. Böyükulusoy, V. Şahoğlu, and İ. Tuğcu In press Liman Tepe 2012 Yılı Kazıları. *Kazı Sonuçları Toplantısı* 35.
Ersoy, Y. E., Ü. Güngör, and H. Cevizoğlu 2011 200 Yılı Klazomenai Kazısı. *Kazı Sonuçları Toplantısı* 32(4):169–182.
Felten, F. 1986 Early Urban History and Architecture of Ancient Aegina. In *Early Helladic Architecture and Urbanization*. Studies in Mediterranean Archaeology vol. LXXVI, edited by R. Hägg and D. Konsola, pp. 21–28. Paul Astroms Forlag, Göteborg.
Korfmann, M. 1987 Demircihüyük: die Ergebnisse der Ausgrabungen 1975–1978. P. von Zabern, Mainz.
Lloyd, S., and J. Mellaart 1962 *Beycesultan I: The Chalcholithic and Early Bronze Age Levels*. British Institute of Archaeology at Ankara, London.
Marthari, M. 1998 Syros Chalandriani, Kastri: From the Investigation and Protection to the Presentation of an Archaeological Site. Ministry of the Aegean, Athens.
Özkan, T., and H. Erkanal 1999 Tahtalı Barajı Kurtarma Kazısı Projesi/ Tahtalı Dam Area Salvage Project. T.C. Kültür Bakanlığı, İzmir.
Renfrew, C. 1972 *The Emergence of Civilisation: The Cyclades and the Aegean in the Third Millenium B.C.* Methuen, London.
Şahoğlu, V. 2005 The Anatolian Trade Network and the Izmir Region during the Early Bronze Age. *Oxford Journal of Archaeology* 24(4):339–361.

Tartaron, T. F., D. J. Pullen, and J. S. Noller 2006 Rillenkarren at Vayia: Geomorphology and a New Class of Early Bronze Age Fortified Settlement in Southern Greece. *Antiquity* 80:145–160.

Theochari, M., and L. Parlama 1997 Palamari Sykyros: The Early Bronze Age Fortified Settlement. In *Poliochni e L'Antica età del Bronzo Nell' Egeo Settentrionale*, edited by C. Doumas and V. La Rosa, pp. 344–356. Scuola Archeologica Italiana di Atene et Université d'Athènes, Athens.

Tiné, S. 1997 Poliochni: Problemi di urbanistica e demografia. *Poliochne kai e Proïme Epoche tou Chalkou sto Boreio Aigaio 1991*, edited by C. G. Doumas and V. La Rosa, pp. 226–227. Atina.

Walter, H. 1981 *Alt Ägina. Band II,1*. Philipp von Zabern, Mainz/Rhein.

Chapter Fifteen

Sociopolitical Organization and Territories in Western Anatolia during the Early Bronze Age

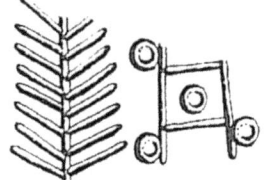

*Ralf Becks**

Introduction

Bronze Age Western Anatolia can be described as a distinct cultural region with its own characteristics and traditions. Due to its specific geographical position, being located at the western end of the Anatolian peninsula and surrounded by the sea on three sides, Western Anatolia absorbed cultural influences from all directions at various times and with different intensities, but never became fully part of any of the neighboring cultures. Instead, Western Anatolia always kept its own cultural traditions, which can be traced back to the Chalcolithic Age and possibly even beyond. The characteristics of Western Anatolia's culture and its homogeneity, especially during the Early Bronze Age, are well attested in the material culture and social organization, for example in the general layout of the settlements according to the Anatolian settlement scheme after M. Korfmann (Korfmann 1983:222–241), in the architecture with the megaron as the common house-form (Efe and Türkteki 2011a; Naumann 1971:483–489), in burial customs (Massa and Şahoğlu 2011; Stech-Wheeler 1974), in metallurgy (Efe 2002:51–61; Efe and Türkteki 2011c), and also in pottery traditions (Efe 2003; Efe and Türkteki 2011b; Lloyd and Mellaart 1962:103–115, 129–134, 136–139, 179–194, 199–200, 243–258, Maps II–VIII). Although some regional differences clearly exist, which are visible especially in different pottery styles that have led to a differentiation of several cultural groups (Efe 2003:89–92, Figs. 1, 5; Efe and Türkteki 2011b:214–219, Figs. 1, 2; Llyod and Mellaart:183–194, Map V), their common cultural roots are the same.

---

*Ralf Becks, Mehmet Akif Ersoy Üniversitesi, Fen-Edebiyat Fakültesi, Arkeoloji Bölümü, TR-15030 Burdur.

In this paper, another aspect of the sociopolitical organization in Western Anatolia during the Early Bronze Age is presented that deals with the analysis of the physical size of the settlements themselves. A geo-archaeological approach is used in order to analyze the existence and type of settlement system as well as possible settlement hierarchies.[1]

In regional settlement analysis, several theoretical models have been developed in which either the size of a settlement (e.g., the rank-size rule [Smith 1976:29–30; Haggett 1965:100–107]) or the specific functions of a settlement (e.g., the central place theory [Smith 1976:10–28]) are used as a measure to establish settlement hierarchies. Different modes of settlement hierarchies can be interpreted as representing different types or stages of sociopolitical organization (e.g., Johnson 1980; Johnson 1987). With some modifications, these geographical models can be used for archaeological purposes as well (Bernbeck 1997:151–180).

Data Collection and Analysis

This geo-archaeological research project is solely based on information from published reports about the many archaeological excavations and especially survey projects conducted in Western Anatolia and on analysis of satellite images. The survey reports usually contain information about the general localization of a site and a dating of its habitation periods based on the collected surface finds, which mainly consists of ceramic sherds. Information about the exact size of a settlement is often missing, especially in older reports. In order to compensate for these shortcomings and to establish a solid basis for comparison, satellite images have been used here to calculate the overall size of all sites. Only a few sites in Western Anatolia have been excavated completely or to such an extent as to establish securely their absolute sizes for a known time period. Nonetheless, what has become apparent in excavated sites such as Demircihüyük, Seyitömer and Bademağacı Höyük is the fact that the maximum size of a settlement mound clearly corresponds with the maximum extent of the settled area covered with buildings. Changes in settlement size and density of buildings may well occur at any settlement in the course of time which of course can only be detected in excavations. Again, in the above-mentioned excavated sites only minor changes, if any at all, were revealed for the successive phases of the Early Bronze Age. Therefore, the overall dimension of an unexcavated mound corresponds well with the actual size of the settlement, which is used here as a standard for calculation.

Whereas settlement mounds are usually easy to identify in the field, flat settlements or hilltop settlements are more difficult to detect. In EBA Western Anatolia the number of known hilltop settlements (139 sites) is much smaller than the more frequent mounds (691 sites), which were the preferred type of settlement (Figure 15.1). The existence of a lower town next to a settlement mound is usually also difficult to detect, especially when they lie hidden under later habitation deposits. Lower towns are rarely identified in field-surveys, for example, at Tavşanlı (Efe 1990:407). The size of a lower town is of course crucial for the calculation of the overall size of a settlement. Also, the size of a lower town may change in the course of time. These issues can be resolved only in

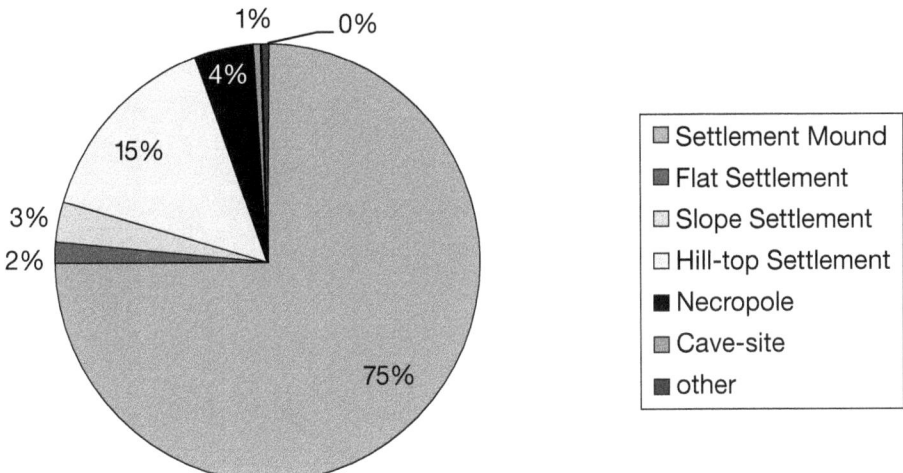

FIGURE 15.1. Frequency of Bronze Age settlement types in Western Anatolia (prepared by the author).

excavations or with systematic intensive surveys. Even in excavations it is sometimes only due to chance discoveries that reveal the existence and dimensions of a lower town, for instance, at Troia and Liman Tepe (Erkanal 2011:132, Figure 5; Jablonka 2001:391–394, Figure 439). Information about existing lower towns has been included in the data collection, their sizes were calculated approximately based on excavation results and topographic conditions.

Distribution of Bronze Age Sites in Western Anatolia

In the last three decades, archaeological research in Western Anatolia has greatly intensified, mainly in the form of field-surveys but also with a growing number of excavations. Nearly 1,000 Bronze Age sites of different kinds are known today in the region between the Aegean coast to the west and the Central Anatolian Plateau to the east (Figure 15.2). The distribution of these sites is rather unbalanced and shows two main clusters: one in the west where Bronze Age sites are concentrated along the Aegean coast and especially in the broad river valleys of the western lowlands; the other in the east on the highland plateau where a vast number of Bronze Age sites are clustered in the numerous alluvial plains and river valleys. Between these two regions lies a broad area which is almost void of settlements. Some of these regions are archaeologically still unexplored. Here, mountains and hilly country prevail, making these areas less suitable for settlement. This is also reflected in the modern low settlement density. About 45 excavated sites in Western Anatolia revealed cultural remains of the third millennium B.C. These sites are rather evenly distributed all over Western Anatolia, with some concentrations along the Aegean coast, in the regions of Eskişehir and Kütahya, and in Southwestern Anatolia (Figure 15.3).

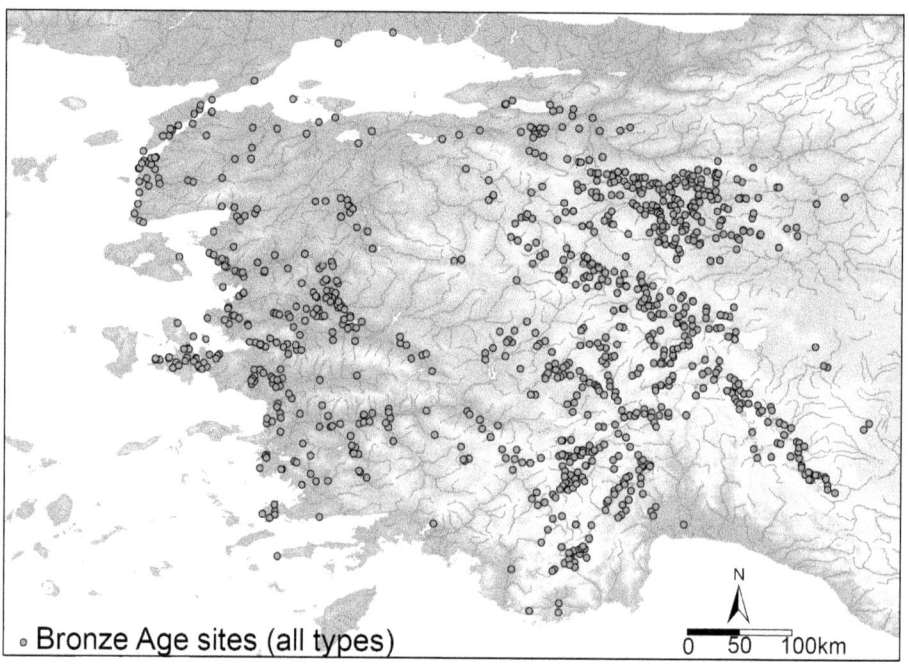

FIGURE 15.2. Distribution of Bronze Age sites (all types) in Western Anatolia (map prepared by the author).

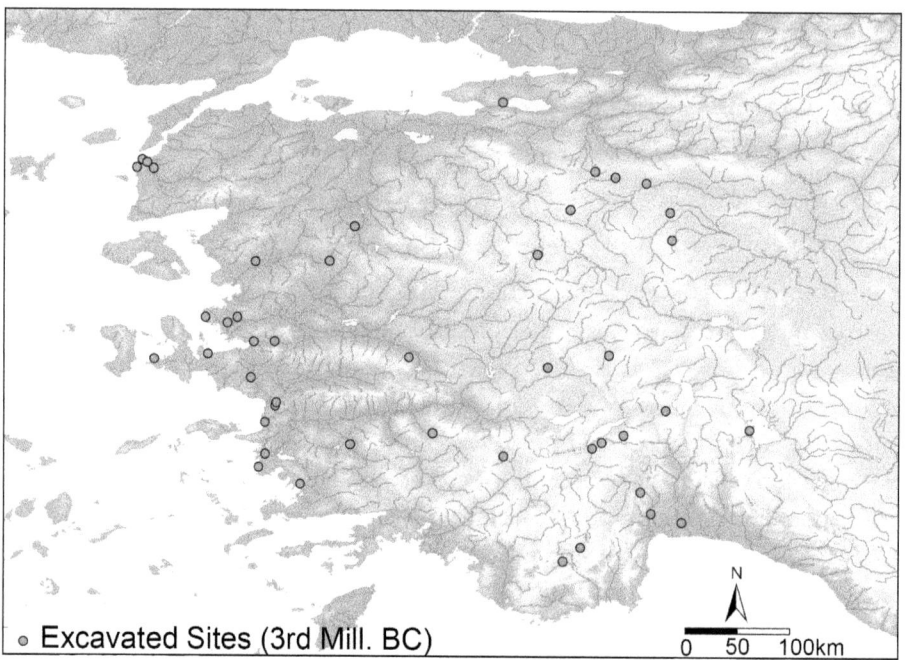

FIGURE 15.3. Excavated sites of the Early Bronze Age in Western Anatolia (map prepared by the author).

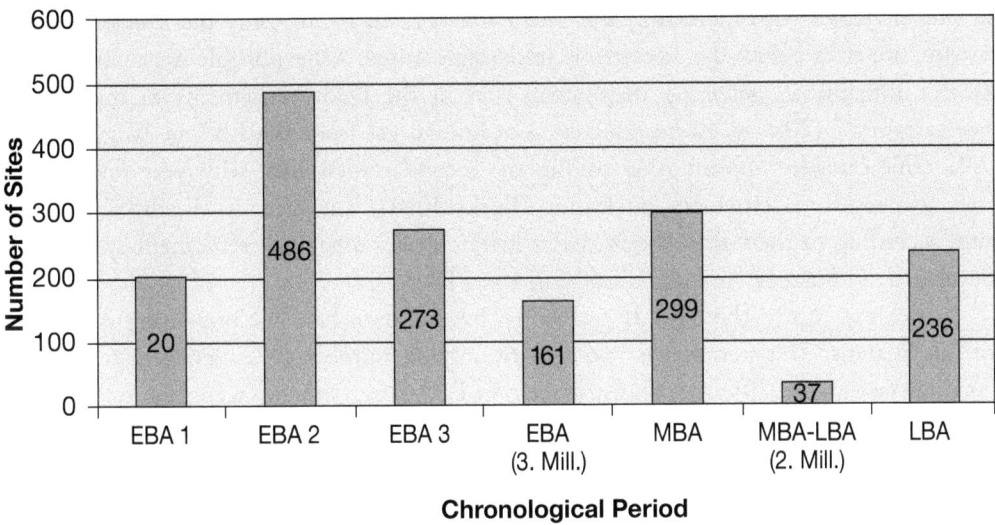

FIGURE 15.4. Chronological frequency of Bronze Age sites in Western Anatolia (prepared by the author).

The chronological distribution of these settlements shows some strong fluctuations (Figure 15.4): 204 sites have produced finds dating to the EBA 1 period, 486 sites belong to the EBA 2 period, and 273 sites were inhabited during the EBA 3 period; 161 sites were generally dated to the third millennium B.C. (EBA). For the Middle Bronze Age, 299 sites are attested and for the Late Bronze Age 236; 37 sites have been assigned generally to the second millennium B.C.

Settlement Patterns and Settlement Hierarchies in Western Anatolia

According to the collected data, the sizes of settlements in Western Anatolia range from 1,500 sqm to 40,000 sqm. Even the largest settlements in Western Anatolia are much smaller than the urban centers in Central Anatolia (e.g., Boğazköy-Hattuša with 181 hectares) or in Mesopotamia. The collected data has been analyzed using the rank-size rule as theoretical approach. This model is based on the observation that the rank of a settlement correlates with its size in a closed system (Bernbeck 1997:175; Haggett 1965:100–107). According to this rule, the largest site is double the size as the second-largest site, the third-largest site is half the size of the second-largest, and so on. Ideally, each closed settlement system should be analysed individually.[2] For comparative purposes, the sizes of all known settlements in Western Anatolia are considered here together. Based on the existing settlement sizes, a ranking order with seven categories has been determined. With the largest site of 40 hectares as the upper limit, the settlement size in the next lower category is half the size of the former category. There is an obvious correspondence between the size of settlements and their quantities, that is, the number of sites decreases with increasing settlement size (Figure 15.5). Only the lowest category 1 with site sizes below 0.5 hectares is underrepresented. One possible explanation may be the difficulty in detecting these small sites in the field. Settlements of the highest size category 7 (20.1 to 40 hectares) are not known yet from the EBA in Western Anatolia. This category appears only during the second millennium with very few known sites as a result of settlement nucleation (Becks 2014). The quantitative distribution of sites according to their sizes shows that a hierarchically organized settlement system had developed in Western Anatolia already in the EBA.

As a case study, the EBA II period has been chosen here for presenting the results of this analysis. This period has revealed the highest number of settlements in Western Anatolia (see above). The spatial distribution of EBA II settlements according to these size categories shows many distinct clusters which correspond in general to the geographical preconditions of Western Anatolia, namely, the alluvial plains are the preferred areas for habitation (Figure 15.6). This becomes especially obvious in the eastern part of Western Anatolia with its many alluvial plains separated by mountain ranges. Nearly all these plains are densely settled. The largest settlement cluster is located in the Eskişehir plain and south of it in the region of the upper Sakarya River. There is a large number of sites of the small and middle-sized settlements of categories 1–5 and two settlements of the second largest category 6: Bahçehisar (10.6 hectares) located at the western end of the plain and Karahöyük-Midaion (14.5 hectares) as the largest site in the center of the Eskişehir plain. A smaller concentration of settlements is located farther to the north in the İznik region with settlements of size categories 1–5 with İnegöl-Cuma Tepe (9.6 hectares) and Orhangazi-Ilıpınar (9.6 hectares) as the largest sites. To the south

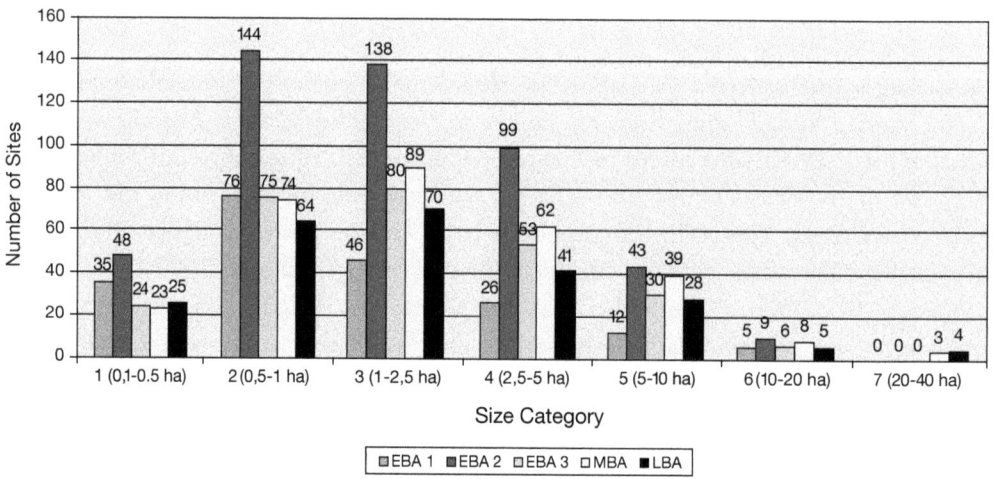

FIGURE 15.5. Frequency of Bronze Age sites according to size categories (prepared by the author).

and southeast, a series of settlement clusters are to be found in the alluvial plains of the Akçay river valley. The first cluster is around modern Kütayha with settlements of size categories 1–6 with Hacıkebir (10.5 hectares) as the largest site, the second cluster is near Afyon also with categories 1–6 with Küçükhüyük-Kidiesos (16.2 hectares) at the top, and the third cluster is located in the vicinity of Lake Akşehir with categories 1–5 with Kocaoğuz (7.5 hectares) as the largest site. Farther to the west in the alluvial plains of the Upper Menderes River are settlement concentrations with size categories 1–6, with Beycesultan (12.5 hectares) as the largest site. Farther south and southeast, several settlement clusters can be observed in various parts of the Lake District with size categories 1–6. Besides a rather high number of settlements of size category 5, there are only two sites of category 6: Şeref Höyük (11.8 hectares) in the Bucak-Korkuteli plain and Yalıhüyük (16.6 hectares) at Lake Suğla.

In the western part of the Anatolian peninsula, the density of settlements is much lower compared to the east. In the west, the river plains are the preferred areas for habitation. The largest concentration of settlements is located in the central Hermos river valley with many sites of categories 1–5; the largest EBA site here is Maltepe Höyük (7.3 hectares). Several smaller settlement clusters are located along the Aegean coast and its immediate hinterland. In the northwest, the peninsula of the Troad shows a scatter

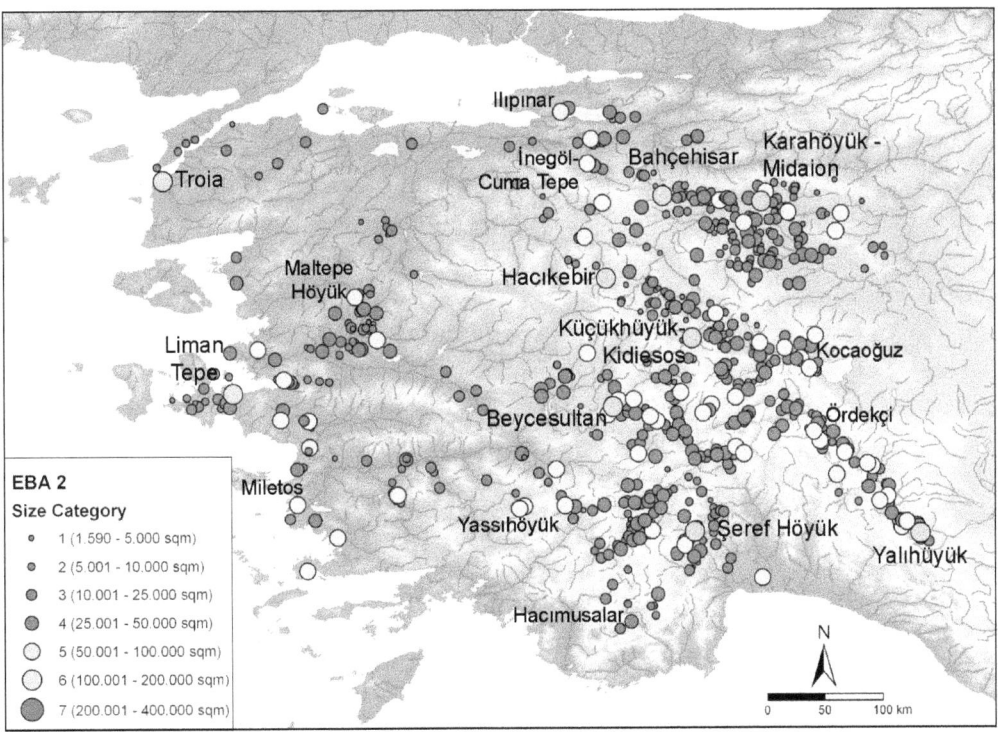

FIGURE 15.6. Distribution of Early Bronze Age II settlements according to size categories (map prepared by the author).

of settlements of categories 1–6 with the site of Troia (estimated 13.5 hectares, including lower town) as the regional center. Farther south, a larger cluster of settlements is located around the Izmir Bay with the delta of the Hermos River to the north and the Çeşme-Peninsula to the south. Here, settlement sizes of categories 1–6 are present, with Liman Tepe (estimated 15.2 hectares including lower town) as the largest site. Farther south along the Aegean coast habitation is concentrated mainly in a few sites of categories 1–5. The largest site in this region is Miletos (8 hectares).

In the EBA II period, each settlement cluster with one large site of category 6 represents a distinct settlement system. These systems are organized hierarchically in three levels. The largest settlements of category 6 (altogether nine sites) are at the top of the hierarchical system, they function as political and economic center of each region. Each center is surrounded by settlements of the lower categories, which sometimes even build smaller clusters as well. The sites of category 6 are quite evenly distributed with similar distances between them, especially in the central-western highland region (about 75 kilometers). Settlements of the next lower category 5 (altogether 43 sites) are more frequent than sites of category 6, but are less numerous than the other smaller-sized categories. The second level in this hierarchical system consists of size categories 5 and 4 with functions as subregional and local centers. Settlements of category 5 show also a quite even distribution and are surrounded by many settlements of the lower categories, too. Some of the larger sites of category 5 may actually have functioned as a regional center as well, especially when the rather equal distances between sites of category 6 are taken into consideration. Possible further regional centers could be located among the clusters in the Lake District, for example, Kocaoğuz (5.9 hectares) at Lake Eber and Ördekçi (8.5 hectares) in the Beyşehir cluster. Also Ilıpınar or İnegöl-Cuma Tepe in the İznik region, or Maltepe in the Hermos valley would suit as candidates for such regional centers. Other sites of category 5 may have functioned as centers on a subregional level, such as Yassıhöyük (7.1 hectares) in the Acıpayam plain. Even some sites of category 4 such as Hacımusalar (4.8 hectares) in the Elmalı plain would fit for a subregional center. On the lowest level of the hierarchical system are the smaller settlements of categories 3–1. They consist of medium- and small-sized villages and hamlets.

Geographically, each settlement cluster with a site of category 6 at the top of the settlement hierarchy represents a closed settlement system. Each of these systems also represents a distinct territorial unit under the control of one center. Archaeologically, these territories have been identified as distinct cultural regions according to characteristic pottery finds by J. Mellaart and T. Efe (Efe 2003:89–94, Figs. 1, 5; Lloyd and Mellaart 1952:136–139, 183–194, Maps IV, V). The combination of the results from the geographical settlement analysis and from the archaeological pottery regions is shown in Figure 15.7. Both approaches have been developed independently using different methods. The territories defined by the geographical settlement systems fit almost perfectly into the archaeologically defined regions of pottery groups. This result shows that the geo-archaeological analysis of settlements is an effective tool to investigate settlement systems and settlement hierarchies at different levels in order to reveal the sociopolitical

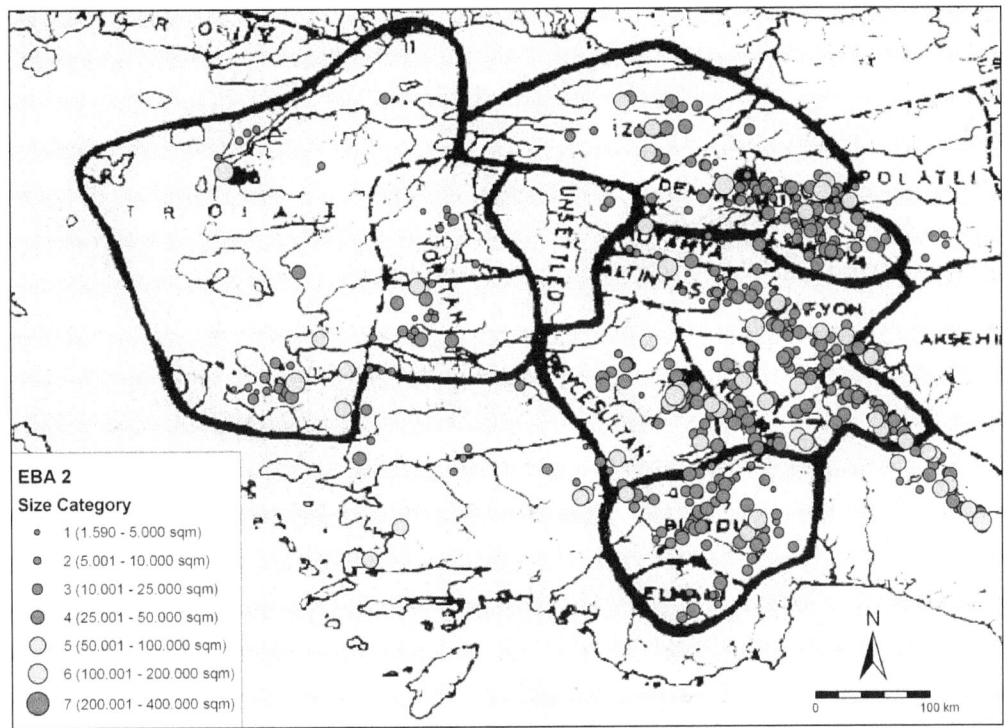

FIGURE 15.7. Cultural pottery groups of the Early Bronze Age II period in Western Anatolia (map after Efe 2003, Figure 5) combined with Early Bronze Age II settlements according to size categories (prepared by the author).

organization that is lying underneath. In Western Anatolia, regional territories began to emerge during the Early Bronze Age as a result of growing social stratification. This process continued through the EBA III period with increasing developments toward urbanization. Obviously, the sociopolitical situation of Western Anatolia being split up into many regional chiefdoms and smaller kingdoms did not change during the first half of the second millennium B.C. This is reflected in the earliest Hittite sources about Western Anatolia from I. Tudhaliya's report on military campaigns against Arzawa and the so-called Assuwa coalition that consisted of some 20 countries (Bryce 2005:124–127). Concerning the long duration of the prevailing settlement systems in Western Anatolia from the EBA through the LBA, it represents just another cultural tradition that lasted for more than 1,000 years.

Notes

1. The results presented here are part of a research project entitled "Settlement Systems in Western Anatolia during the Bronze Age," conducted from 2008 to 2011 as a research fellow at the German Archaeological Institute in Istanbul (Becks forthcoming). For the

second millennium B.C. in Western Anatolia, some results of this research project are presented in Becks 2014.
2. The analysis of each individual settlement system in Western Anatolia would lie beyond the scope of this paper; the results will be published separately (Becks forthcoming).

REFERENCES CITED

Becks, R. forthcoming *Siedlungsstrukturen des zweiten Jahrtausends v.Chr. im westlichen Kleinasien.*

Becks, R. 2014 Settlement Patterns and Socio-political Landscape of Western Anatolia in the Middle and Late Bronze Age—A Geoarchaeological View. In *NOSTOI—Indigenous Culture, Migration, and Integration in the Aegean Islands and Western Anatolia during the Late Bronze and Early Iron Age*, edited by N. Stampolidis et al., pp. 115–130. Koç University Press, Istanbul.

Bernbeck, R. 1997 *Theorien in der Archäologie*. UTB, Stuttgart.

Bryce, T. 2005 *The Kingdom of the Hittites*. 2nd edition. Oxford University Press, Oxford.

Efe, T. 1990 1988 Yılı Kütahya, Bilecik ve Eskişehir İllerinde Yapılan Yüzey Araştırmaları. VII. *Araştırma Sonuçları Toplantısı*: 405–424. Ankara.

Efe, T. 2002 The Interaction between Cultural/Political Entities and Metalworking in Western Anatolia during the Chalcolithic and Early Bronze Ages. In *Anatolian Metal II*, edited by Ü. Yalçın, pp. 49–65. Bergbau Museum, Bochum.

Efe, T. 2003 Pottery Distribution within the Early Bronze Age of Western Anatolia and Its Implications upon Cultural, Political (and Ethnic?) Entities. In *Homo Amatus. Archaeological Essays in Honour of Güven Arsebük*, edited by M. Özbaşaran et al., pp. 87–103. Ege Yayınları, Istanbul.

Efe, T., and E. Fidan 2006 Pre-Middle Bronze Age Metal Objects from Inland Western Anatolia: A Typological and Chronological Evaluation. *Anatolia Antiqua* 14:15–43.

Efe, T., and M. Türkteki 2011a Early Bronze Age Architecture in the Inland Western Anatolian Region. In *Across. The Cyclades and Western Anatolia during the 3rd Millennium B.C.*, edited by A. Anadol, pp. 198–207. Sakip Sabanci Muzesi, Istanbul.

Efe, T., and M. Türkteki 2011b Early Bronze Age Pottery in the Inland Western Anatolian Region. In *Across. The Cyclades and Western Anatolia during the 3rd Millennium B.C.*, edited by A. Anadol, pp. 214–222. Sakip Sabanci Muzesi, Istanbul.

Efe, T. and M. Türkteki 2011c Metalworking in Inland Western Anatolia (3rd Millennium B.C. In *Across. The Cyclades and Western Anatolia during the 3rd Millennium B.C.*, edited by A. Anadol, pp. 224–226. Sakip Sabanci Muzesi, Istanbul.

Erkanal, H. 2011 Early Bronze Age Settlement Models and Domestic Architecture in the Coastal Region of Western Anatolia. In *Across. The Cyclades and Western Anatolia during the 3rd Millennium B.C.*, edited by A. Anadol, pp. 130–135. Sakip Sabanci Muzesi, Istanbul.

Jablonka, P. 2001 Eine Stadtmauer aus Holz. Das Bollwerk der Unterstadt von Troia II. In *Troia—Traum und Wirklichkeit*, edited by Archäologisches Landesmuseum Baden-Württemberg, pp. 391–394. Konrad Theiss Verlag, Stuttgart.

Johnson, G. A. 1980 Spatial Organization of Early Uruk Settlement Systems. In *L'Archéologie de l'Iraq*, edited by M. T. Barrelet, pp. 233–264. Éditions du Centre National de la Recherche Scientifique, Paris.

Johnson, G. A. 1987 The Changing Organization of Uruk Administration on the Susiana Plain. In *The Archaeology of Western Iran*, edited by F. Hole, pp. 107–139. Smithsonian Institution Press, Washington, DC.

Korfmann, M. 1983 *Demircihüyük. Die Ergebnisse der Ausgrabungen 1975–1978, Bd. I. Architektur, Stratigraphie und Befunde*. P. von Zabern, Mainz am Rhein.

Lloyd, S., and J. Mellaart 1962 *Beycesultan, Vol. I*. British Institute of Archaeology at Ankara, London.

Massa, M., and V. Şahoğlu 2011 Western Anatolian Burial Customs during the Early Bronze Age. In *Across. The Cyclades and Western Anatolia during the 3rd Millennium B.C.*, edited by A. Anadol, pp. 164–171. Sakip Sabanci Muzesi, Istanbul.

Naumann, R. 1971 *Architektur Kleinasiens*. E. Wasmuth, Tübingen.

Smith, C. A. 1976 Regional Economic Systems: Linking Geographical Models and Socioeconomic Problems. *Regional Analysis (Vol. I): Economic Systems*, edited by C. A. Smith, pp. 3–63. Academic Press, New York.

Stech-Wheeler, T. 1974 Early Bronze Age Burial Customs in Western Anatolia. *American Journal of Archaeology* 78:415–425.

Steponaitis, V. P. 1981 Settlement Hierarchies and Political Complexity in Nonmarket Societies: The Formative Period of the Valley of Mexico. *American Anthropologist* 83:320–363.

CHAPTER SIXTEEN

Early Bronze Age Graves from Kubad Abad (Toprak Tol Höyük)

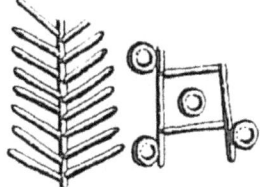

Derya Yalçıklı*

Toprak Tol Höyük is situated on the southwest side of Beyşehir Lake, 27 kilometers west of Beyşehir town center northeast of the Anamas Mountains, which constitutes one of the northern branches of Toros Mountains (Figure 16.1). The höyük has an oval low-hill shape with dimensions of 280 × 250 meters and is situated at four meters above the present level of the plain, which is filled with alluvion deposit carried by the Hızar River generated from the Anamas Mountains. On its east slope, there is a water source called Gürlevi. The rocky hill on the northern side of the höyük has dimensions of 340 × 280 meters. There are structures on this hill situated on the edge of the lake that belonged to Seljuk times. In prehistoric times, this ridge (650 × 280 meters) consisted of höyük and rocks should have been in the shape of a peninsula surrounded by alluvion deposit (Figure 16.2).

As the excavations progressed, we were able to obtain more and more information on the topography of the land on which Sultan Alaaddin Keykubad first started to build the city of Kubad Abad nearly 1231 years ago (Kuniholm 1996:182). We started to come across information on Kubad Abad from the early twentieth century. This city became prominent with its castles that belonged to the Seljuk period and has been visited by travelers and scholars at different times (Arık 2000:44–48).

When we analyze the studies conducted on pre–Middle Ages periods, it is seen that our höyük is mentioned under the names "Topraktol/Toprak Tol Höyük," "Hoyran Höyük," or "Kubadabad" in archeological literature (Lloyd and Mellaart 1962:197 Map I and VI; Mellaart 1954:181, Map 2; 1961: Map 1; 1963: 209 Map 1, 5). It had been visited by J. Mellaart between 1951 and 1952 during surface surveys undertaken toward

---

*Associate Prof. Dr. Derya YALÇIKLI, Çanakkale Onsekiz Mart University, Çanakkale, Turkey, e-mail: dyalcikli@comu.edu.tr.

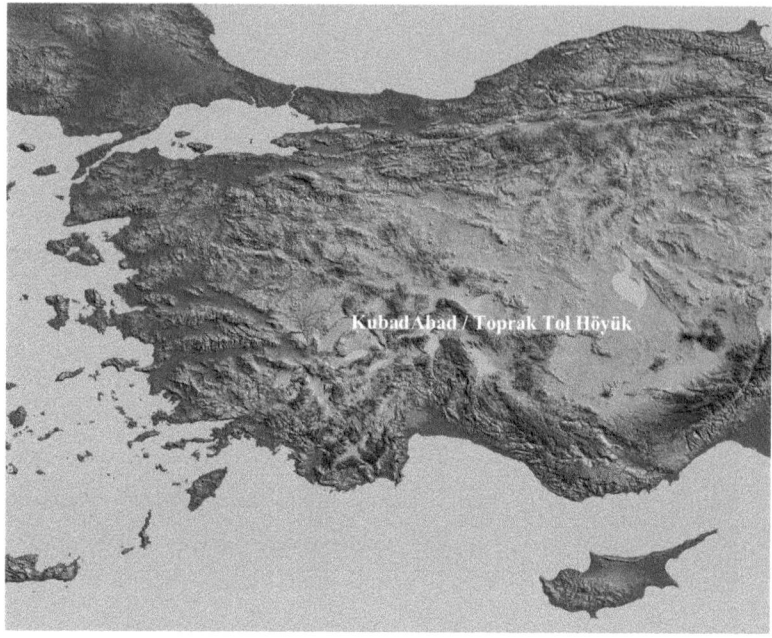

FIGURE 16.1. Map showing the location of Kubad Abad.

FIGURE 16.2. KubadAbad is situated on the southwest side of Beyşehir Lake.

exploring the cultures in the pre-Classical Period in Southern Anatolia (Mellaart 1954:181, Map 2). Information given about Toprak Tol Höyük in studies published afterward are just repetitions of material already presented in Mellaart's work (Thissen 2002:346; Yakar 1985:102 Map VA-VB; 1991: Map VI).

The very first aim of the 1980 excavations undertaken in Kubad Abad was research on the Seljuk Period. Toward this aim, the social complex of the castle on the rocky hill on the edge of the lake was chosen as the central focus for the research. Due to the increasing amount of data accumulated in recent years on the pre–Middle Ages, research concentrated on the layers belonging to the Prehistoric Period of Kubad Abad, conducted by myself starting in 2008.[1]

Distribution of the Ruins from the Prehistoric Period

It is possible to see ceramic pieces belonging to the Prehistoric Period dispersed around the excavation area in Kubad Abad. The prehistoric findings unearthed in Seljuk structures were mostly preserved by chance. According to the evolution of the findings, two cultural levels, the Early Bronze Age and the Chalcolitic Age, have been determined. The findings belonging to the Chalcolitic Age have also been separated into two different phases, Middle and Late Chalcolitic Ages.

In Kubad Abad, various ceramic pieces from the Early Bronze Age found dispersed in certain excavation areas belonged to the Prehistoric Period. Among these ceramic pieces, some pieces belonged to mugs, which we are already familiar with. Similar items coming from Central Anatolian centers such as Ahlatlıbel (Bittel 1936–37: Figure 3; Koşay 1934:35, A.B.142) and Alişar (Schmidt 1933:44 Figure 48), with single handles decorated with red or black linings and glaze constituting an important group (Figure 16.3a,b). Also, a damaged piece of depas cup has also been captured in a pit (Figure 16.3c). This piece of depas is made of dark grey pulp with linings and a glaze and is

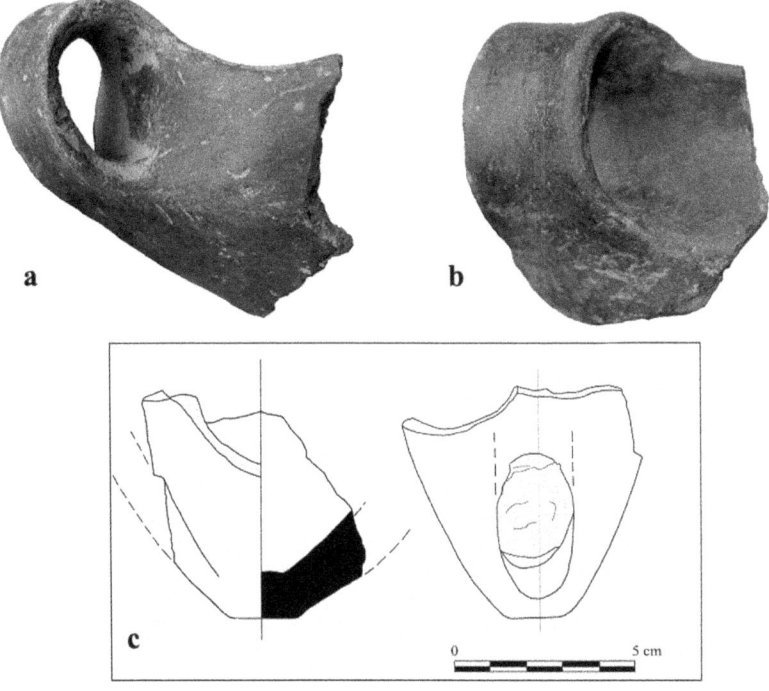

Figure 16.3. Ceramic finds.

among the examples of the Pisidia region (Hüryılmaz 1995:184; Schachner and Schachner 1995:309–310; Spanos 1972:47–52).

Graves belonging to the Early Bronze Age have been discovered in two separate areas. They are Building VIII and the courtyard of the Küçük Palace (Figure 16.4).

FINDINGS IN BUILDING VIII

As a result of excavations undertaken in Building VIII, which is situated on the rocky slope of the hill that stands on the north of Toprak Tol Höyük, a terrace set approximately three meters wide and placed in the middle of the building was found (Arık 2009:474–475). In the inner side of this terrace set, at the low level, there were five cubic graves, some of them partially destroyed. These graves are lined in north-south direction with distances between them ranging from 0.50 centimeters to one meter. Two of these graves could not be excavated because they were trapped under the wall of the terrace set.

Among these graves, the grave M5 consisted of a jar with two vertical handles whose rim is aligned in the west-east direction, and a pot was positioned at its head (Figure 16.5). It was not possible to determine the lying position of the skeleton from the remaining pieces of bone dispersed in the grave and there were no articles in the grave, either.

The grave M6 is situated at the north side of the terrace and a part of it is buried under a terrace wall (Figure 16.6a). It consists of two jars laid down head to head in the northwest-southeast direction and supported with stones placed around it. Both jars are smashed as a result of pressure. There is a skull situated toward the north by the side of

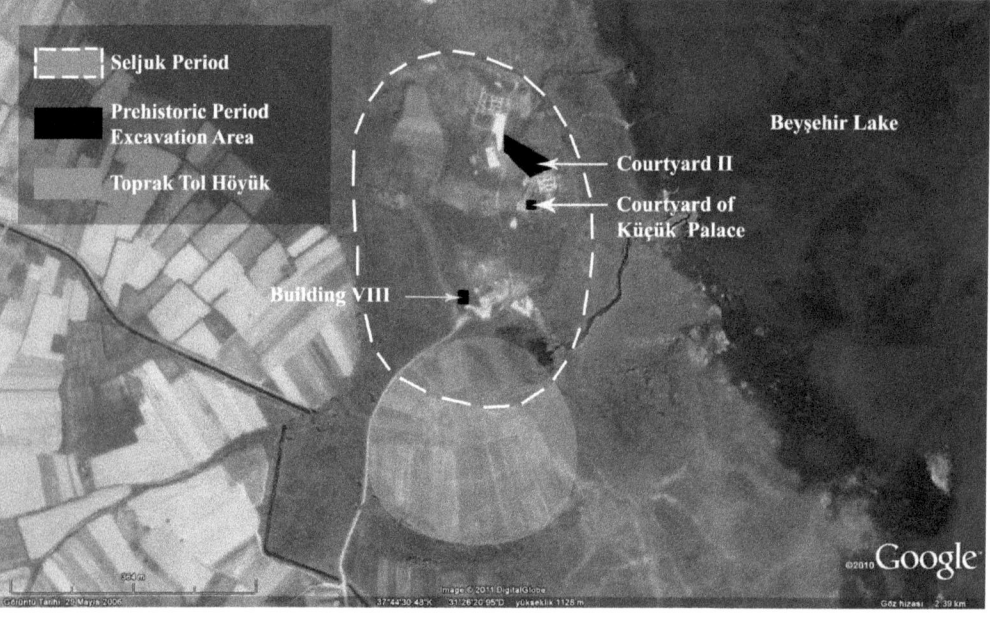

FIGURE 16.4. Topographical map of Kubad Abad and Toptak Tol Höyük.

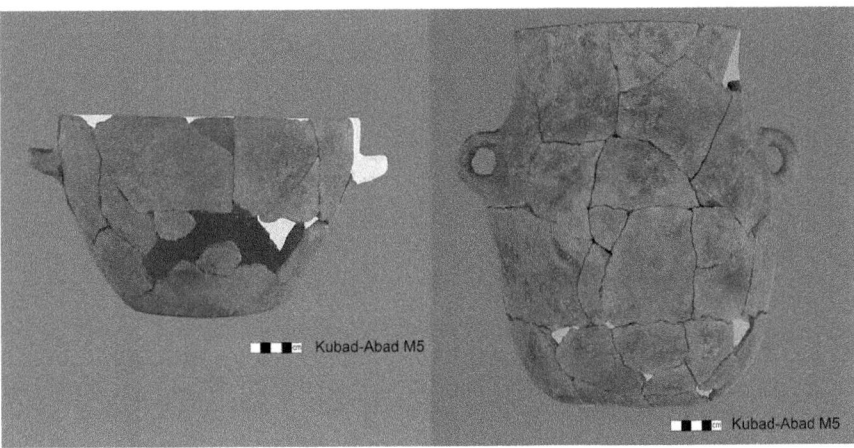

FIGURE 16.5. Ceramic finds from Grave M5.

a big jar's rim, which is trapped under the terrace. This individual has been laid toward north in a *hocker* position. Behind this skull, there is a black-lined, glazed, miniature-like beak-shaped jug with a broken rim (Figure 16.8a) and handles, and a little farther on a combined pot with basket handles (Figure 16.7). A jug, which is black lined and glazed, is decorated with incised zigzag lines. On the north of the skull, a bracelet produced with two thin bronze sheets, one of them in half and other in full size (Figure 16.8e), is found on the chest as well as a piece of a bronze knife whose cutting edge is destroyed (Figure 16.8b) and a bronze hollow pin (Figure 16.8c). Similar findings of this miniature-like beak-shaped jug found in the grave are known from Kuruçay (Duru 1996:74 Pl. 132.1) and Karataş (Mellink 1965: Pl. 59 Figure 4). Similar examples of combined pots are found in other Early Bronze Age centers such as Bağdemağacı (Duru 2008: Figure 349), Karataş-Semayük (Mellink 1966:252 Pl. 61 Figure 30), Yortan (Kâmil 1982: Pl. XV. 238, 239 Figure 98.380, Beycesultan (Lloyd and Mellaart 1962:127, Figure 14.32, 20.3), and Gözlü Kule (Goldman 1956:260.360, 278.620–623).

The M7 grave is made up with a jar and a good-sized pot placed in reverse direction at its mouth (Figure 16.6b). There are stones lined in a single file around the jar. Due to the fact that the bone fragments found at the bottom of the jar are heavily dispersed and in bad shape, it is not possible to determine the angle of the skeleton. Alongside these bones, a bronze sliced-headed pin (Figure 16.8d) and a black-lined, glazed, beak-shaped jug with a broken rim have also been found. Also, outside the jar, there is a bracelet made of a thin and spiral-shaped bronze sheet (Figure 16.8e). Similar artifacts made of different metals and stones to sliced-headed pins have also been found in various locations such as Alaca Höyük (Arık 1937: Pl. CLXVII.Al.240), Seyitömer Höyük (Bilgen 2013:98 Figure 263) and Merzifon (Sipahi 1995:702 Pl. IV.4–6) dated back to the end of the third millennium B.C., as well as in Yanarlar (Emre 1978:47, 53 Figure 118,119), Demircihüyük-Sarıket (Seher 2000: Figure 63.G133.a,b), Gordion (Mellink 1956:33–34 Pl.18.m, 19.o), Kültepe (Özgüç 2005: Figure 275,279), Kazankaya

FIGURE 16.6. Graves, M6, 7, 3.

(Özgüç 1978:25 Pl. 59.6), Alaca Höyük (Arık 1937: Pl. LXI.Al.33; Koşay/Akok 1973: 37 Pl. LXXXIII.Al.t.33), and İkiztepe (Bilgi 1984: Figure 16.199) that were dated to the second millennium B.C.

The direction of these jars were determined to be northwest-southeast and east-west. It was determined that the mouths of the jars in the graves were closed with pots or bulky bowls. Although it has been observed in many centers or graveyards in Anatolia, the tradition of sealing the mouths of the jars with flat stones was not seen in Kubad Abad. It was clear that graves are lined with stones in order to support the structure. The practice of covering the mouths of the jugs with a second cover and surrounding it with stones is known from the graveyards of Harmanören Mezarlığı (Özsait 1998:610–611; 1999:470; 2002: 327, 330), Karataş-Semayük (Mellink 1965:243–244 Pl. 59 Figure 4)

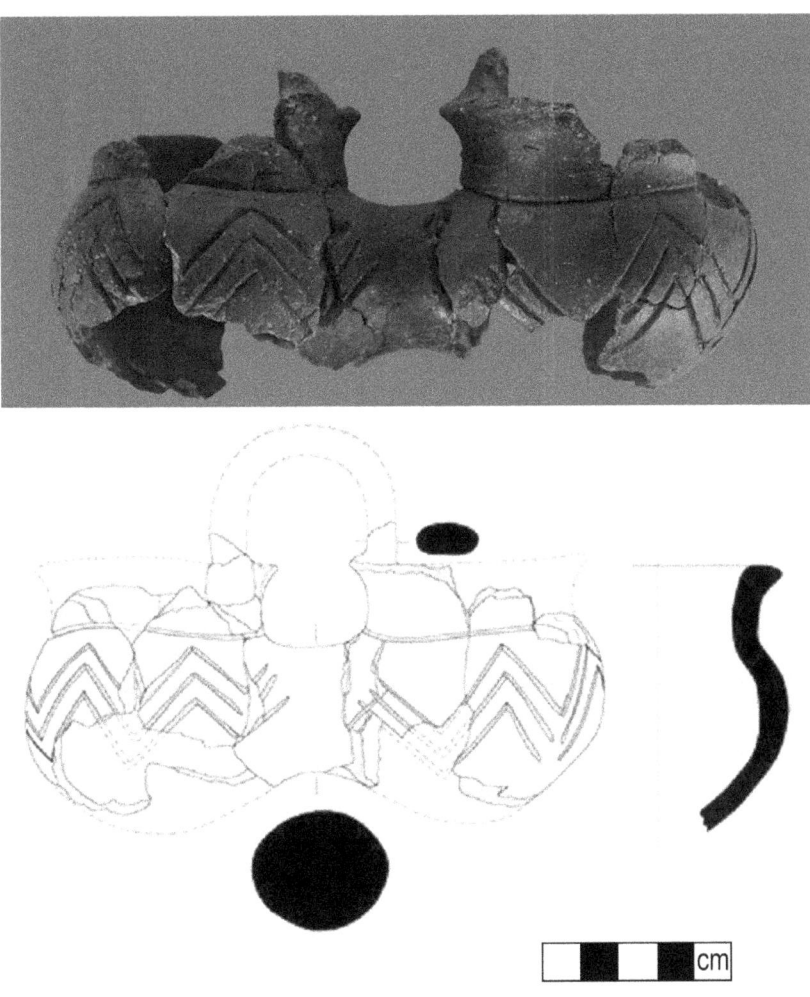

FIGURE 16.7. Ceramic find from Grave M6.

and Resuloğlu (Yıldırım 2006: Figure 10), which are dated to the Early Bronze Age II and III.

Two or three horizontal relief bands hiding under the handles of some jugs in Kubad Abad remind us of those grave jugs in Harmanören graveyard (Özsait 1999:468; 2000: Figure 3; 2002: Figure 11; 2005: 319 Figure 9; 2006: 313 Figure 9; 2007: 615 Figure 5; Özsait and Özsait 2007: 131–132 Figure 2–4). Examples with different designs embossed on jugs which were used for burial purposes have been captured in Karataş-Semayük graveyards (Mellink 1965:249 Pl. 66 Figure 41–44). Similar horizontal relief bands have also been found on jugs with single handles in Karataş-Semayük graveyards (Mellink 1965: Pl. 62 Figure 19–22). Özsait thinks that such decorations are exclusively from this particular region (Özsait 2006:313).

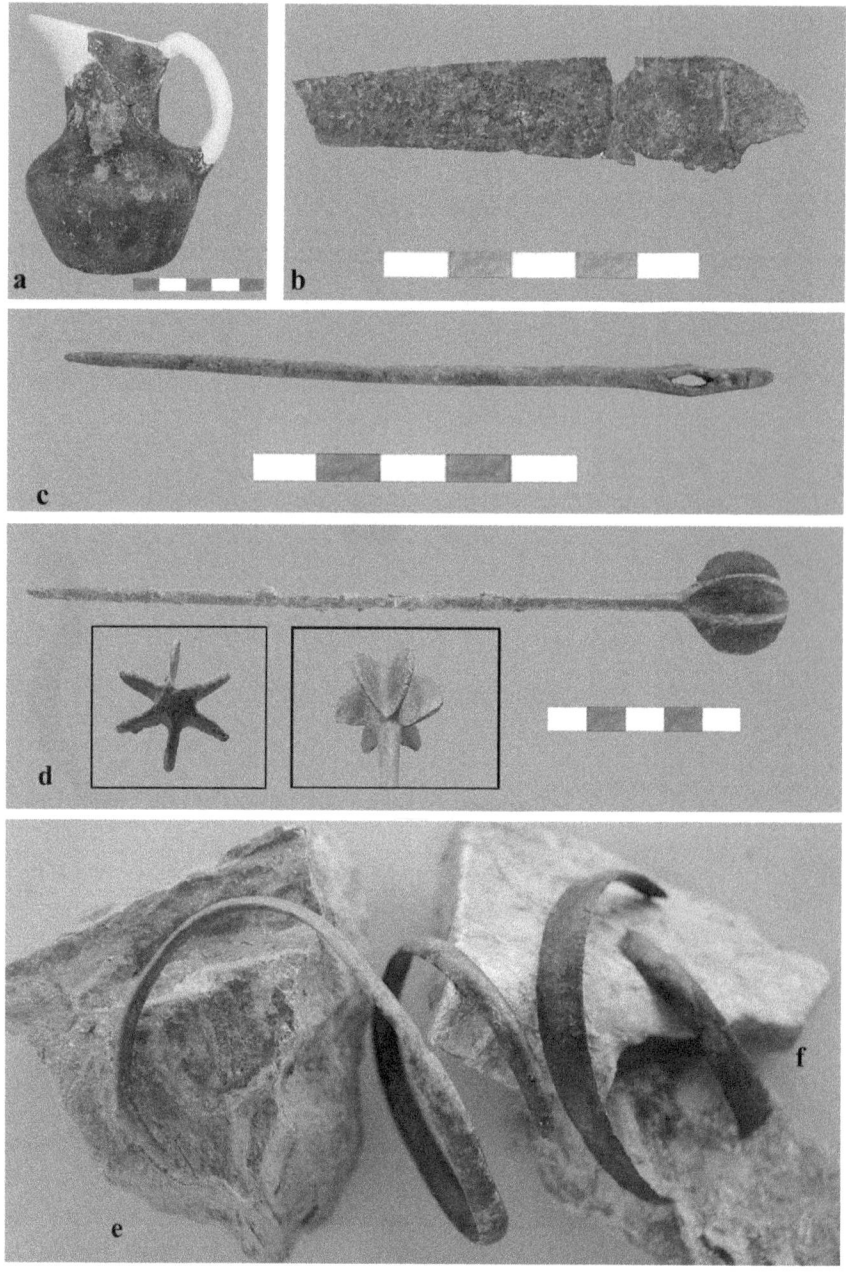

FIGURE 16.8. Finds from the graves.

The bones unearthed in cube graves of Kubad Abad are in such a bad shape that it was not possible to determine the angle of the skeletons. Pots were found near the skull while items such as a knife, needle, and bracelets were placed on the chest and close to neck. A bracelet that was left outside the grave M7 after it was closed shows us that there was a tradition of leaving items outside the graves. Some other bracelets, similar to those we've unearthed in Kubad Abad, dated to Early Bronze Age III are also found in the Harmanören graveyard (Özsait 1998: Figure 12, 22).

FINDINGS IN THE COURTYARD OF KÜÇÜK PALACE

A grave was unearthed in 1993 at the entrance of the courtyard that was situated at the southwest of the Küçük Palace (Figure 16.6c).[2] The discovery reflected a simple soil grave and there were no other findings around it that might be connected to this particular grave. The front side of the skeleton, which was laid down in *hocker* position, is toward northwest-southeast direction.[3] The lower side of this skeleton was destroyed during the settlements of the Seljuk period.

Retrieved articles from the grave consisted of personal ornaments found on the skeleton. Apart from two silver bracelets on the wrists of the skeleton (Figure 16.9b), a total of 1,605 beads with 21 gold (Figure 16.9c), 1,180 silver (Figure 16.9d), 7 bronze or copper, 8 onyx (Figure 16.9e), and 389 black jasper (Figure 16.9f) have also been

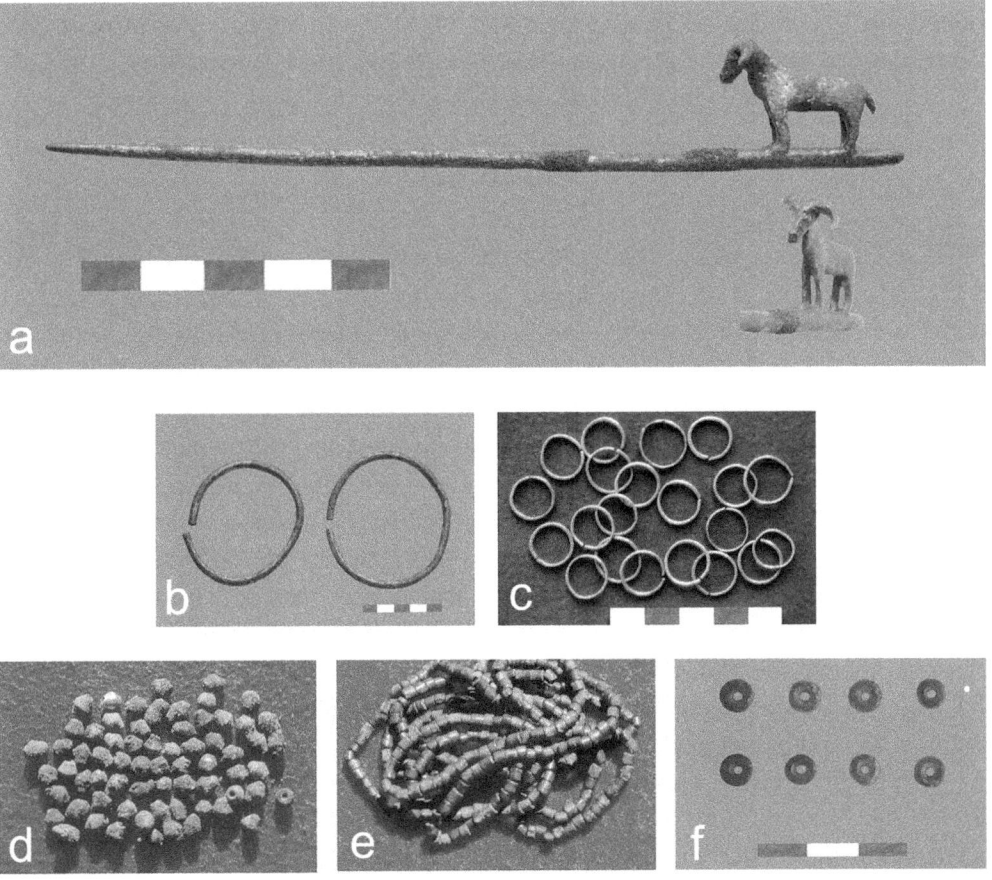

FIGURE 16.9. Ceramic finds from Grave M7.

recovered. A majority of beads have been collected from the neck and the nape of the neck. Among the findings, two bronze headless needles and another bronze needle in the shape of a bull are especially noteworthy (Figure 16.9a). The bull figure standing on its four legs is pointed toward the tip of the needle. This particular needle is an example of the artistic approach and the technical ability of the period as well as being a realistic representation.

This figure of the bull is the only example of its specific group. In this group, needles with different animal figures have been unearthed in regions such Karataş (Mellink 1970:128, Pl. 57 Figure 16a,b), a silver pig head (Early Bronze Age) or a lion's head in bronze found in Girnavaz (*Early Dynastic* II; Erkanal 1991:283, Figure 14–15). Other examples of needles with bull and bird heads have been found at Kültepe (Özgüç 1955: Figure 86; 1986:119, Figure 29; 1999: 29–30 Pl. 86.1a-b; 2005: 224 Pl. 237), a ram head from Çavlum graveyard (Bilgen 2005:28, 120 Pl. XXXIX.2a-c, LXXVIII.11.a-d), and another bird head from Alişar (Schmidt 1933:83 Figure 130.b409). Similar items to those silver round bracelets found on the arms of the skeleton have also been found both in Baklatepe (Early Bronze Age I; Erkanal and Özkan 1999:30–31 Figure 29, 30) and Aphrodisias (Joukowsky 1986:519, Figure 372.3, 374.15–16) and Eskiyapar (Early Bronze Age III; Özgüç and Temizer 1993:619, Pl. 119.1–2). Similar items to those onyx beads captured among the ornaments have been found Alaca Höyük (Koşay 1951: Pl. CC, CCVII) and Resuloğlu (Yıldırım and Ediz 2005:195, Figure 13) graveyards.

Conclusion

The five cube graves, which were incidentally preserved in a small area within Building VIII, and other pieces of cubes scattered nearby gave rise to the idea that some cube graves were destroyed during the construction work undertaken during the Seljuk era. During the excavations, there were no traces of layers of settlement belonging to the Prehistoric Period. Those cube graves and pieces of cubes indicate that the residents of Toprak Tol Höyük might have used this particular slope as an extramural grave area.

The shapes and relief bands on those grave cubes found in Kubad Abad are reminiscent of those found in Harmanören graveyard, which was in use during the Early Bronze Age III. It is possible to date those graves to the last phase of the Early Bronze Age when we take into consideration the fact that similar items of headed needles with animal figures and a bronze sliced headed pin were concentrated in many centers in Anatolia around the end of the third millennium B.C. and the second millennium B.C., as well as some other small findings and the production technology of ornaments captured in inhumation graves.

Although layers of settlements in Toprak Tol Höyük that belonged to the Early Bronze Age have yet to be excavated, already-opened graves prove to us that this region was an important place for settlement. A high number of ornaments produced from precious metals recovered in inhumation graves show us that the dead persons were rich individuals. But the question of why such a wealthy person was laid in such a simple grave still remains unanswered. The first question to be asked is this: Does the place of this inhumation grave—160 meters away from the cube graves—show us that the graveyard had extended to this point? Other questions are: Was the graveyard architecture around it destroyed? Did inhumation graves coexist with cube graves within the same period? The answers to these questions—whether an inhumation grave was in a separate place or not, as well as whether it was contemporary with cube graves—are not available as of today. Future excavations would probably shed some light on these issues.

These findings show us that Kubad Abad had strong connections with Central and Western Anatolia as well as the Cilicia region during the Early Bronze Age III and, as a result of its geographical position, was regarded as an important crossroads. Findings at the graves in Kubad Abad show us the economic strength of a society that lived in a center, and its importance in that period. When we take the findings related to silver mining in the Bolkar Mountains located by Yener (1986; 2013; Yener and Özbal 1986) into consideration, it would be possible to assume that the nearby Kubad Abad might have easily benefited from this staple.

Notes

1. I would like to extend my gratitude to Prof. Dr. Rüçhan Arık who provided this opportunity to me.
2. The M3 grave has been introduced by Prof. Dr. R. Arık in his preliminary report and excavation report (see footnote 9). The information presented in this article has been gathered from the data obtained from excavation archive. The findings from the grave have been studied by myself at the Konya Karatay Museum in 2010.
3. Anthropological studies on these skeletons are being conducted by Assist. Prof. Dr. Arzu Demirel, the Department of Anthropology, Mehmet Akif Ersoy University, Burdur.

References Cited

Arık, R. O. 1937 *Les Fouilles D'Alaca Höyük, Entreprises par la Société d'Histoire Turque, Rapport Prèliminaire sur les Travaux en 1935*. Ankara.

Arık, R. 2000 *Kubad Abad, Saray ve Çinileri*. Türkiye İş Bankası Kültür Yayınları, İstanbul.

Arık, R. 2009 Kubad Abad 2006–2007 Yılı Kazı Çalışmaları Raporu. XXX. *Kazı Sonuçları Toplantısı* 2:471–478.

Bilgen, N. 2005 *Çavlum, Eskişehir Alpu Ovası'nda Bir Orta Tunç Çağı Mezarlığı*. Anadolu Üniversitesi, Eskişehir.

Bilgen, N. 2013 Seyitömer Höyük 2011 Kazı Raporu. Seyitömer Höyük Kazısı Ön Raporu, Kütahya:1–199.

Bilgi, Ö. 1984 Metal Objects from İkiztepe-Turkey. *Beiträge zur Allgemeinen und Vergleichenden Archäologie* 6:31–99.

Bittel, K. 1936–37 Orientalistik Beiträge zur kleinasiatischen. *Archiv für Orientforschung* 11:38–56.

Duru, R. 1996 *Kuruçay Höyük II*. Turkish Historical Society Publications, Ankara.

Duru, R. 2008 *M.Ö. 8000'den M.Ö. 2000'e Burdur-Antalya Bölgesi'nin Altıbin Yılı*. The Suna-İnan Kıraç Mediterranean Civilizations Research Institute, İstanbul.

Emre, K. 1978 *Yanarlar, Afyon Yöresinde Bir Hitit Mezarlığı*. Türk Tarih Kurumu Yayınları, Ankara.

Erkanal, H. 1991 1989 Girnavaz Kazıları. XII. *Kazı Sonuçları Toplantısı* 1:277–284.

Erkanal, H., and T. Özkan 1999 Bakla Tepe Kazıları. In *Tahtalı Barajı Kurtarma Kazısı Projesi*, edited by T. Özkan ve H. Erkanal, pp. 12–42. Kültür ve Turizm Bakanlığı Yayınları, İzmir.

Goldman, H. 1956 *Excavations at Gözlü Kule, Tarsus II, From the Neolithic through the Bronze Age*. Princeton University Press, Princeton.

Hüryılmaz, H. 1995 Uşak Arkeoloji Müzesinde Bir Grup Depas Amphikypellon. In *Memoriam İ. Metin Akyurt ve Bahattin Devam, Eski Yakındoğu Kültürleri Üzerine İncelemeler/Studies for Ancient Near Eastern Cultures*, edited by A. Erkanal et al., pp. 177–188. Arkeoloji ve Sanat Yayınları, İstanbul.

Joukowsky, M. S. 1986 *Prehistoric Aphrodisias, An Account of the Excavations and Artifact Studies*. Brown University Center for Old World Archaeology and Art, Providence.

Kâmil, T. 1982 *Yortan Cemetery in the Early Bronze Age of Western Anatolia*. BAR International Series 145, Oxford.

Koşay, H. Z. 1934 Türkiye: Cumhuriyeti Maarif Vekâletince Yaptırılan Ahlatlıbel Hafriyatı. *Türk Tarih Arkeoloğya ve Etnografya Dergisi* II:3–100.

Koşay, H. Z. 1951 *T.T.K. Tarafından Yapılan Alaca Höyük Kazısı. 1937–39 daki Çalışmalara ve Keşiflere Ait İlk Rapor*. Turkish Historical Society Publications, Ankara.

Koşay, H. Z., and M. Akok 1973 *T.T.K. Tarafından Yapılan Alaca Höyük Kazısı. 1963–67 Çalışmaları ve Keşiflere Ait İlk Rapor*. Turkish Historical Society Publications, Ankara.

Kuniholm, P. L. 1996 Aegean Dendrochronology Project:1993–1994. XI. *Arkeometri Sonuçları Toplantısı*:181–187.

Lloyd, S., and J. Mellaart 1962 *Beycesultan I, The Chalcolithic and Early Bronze Age Levels*. British Institute of Archaeology at Ankara, London.

Mellaart, J. 1954 Preliminary Report on a Survey of Pre-Classical Remains in Southern Turkey. *Anatolian Studies* 4:175–240.

Mellart, J. 1961 Early Cultures of the South Anatolian Plateau. *Anatolian Studies* 11:159–184.

Mellart, J. 1963 Early Cultures of the South Anatolian Plateau, II: The Late Chalcolithic and Early Bronze Ages in the Konya Plain. *Anatolian Studies* 13:199–236.

Mellink, M. J. 1956 *A Hittite Cemetery at Gordion*. University Museum, University of Pennsylvania, Philadelphia.

Mellink, M. J. 1965 Excavations at Karataş-Semayük in Lycia, 1964. *American Journal of Archaeology* 69(3):241–251.

Mellink, M. J. 1966 Excavations at Karataş-Semayük in Lycia, 1965. *American Journal of Archaeology* 70(3):245–257.

Mellink, M. J. 1970 Excavations at Karataş-Semayük and Elmalı, Lycia, 1969. *American Journal of Archaeology* 74(3):245–259.

Özgüç, T. 1955 Kültepe Hafriyatı 1954 Ib Katı Eserleri. *Belleten* XIX/73:55–62.

Özgüç, T. 1978 *Maşat Höyük Kazıları ve Çevresindeki Araştırmalar*. Türk Tarih Kurumu Yayınları, Ankara.

Özgüç, T. 1986 *Kültepe-Kaniş II, Eski Yakındoğu'nun Ticaret Merkezinde Yeni Araştırmalar*. Türk Tarih Kurumu Yayınları, Ankara.

Özgüç, T. 1999 *Kültepe-Kaniš/Neša Sarayları ve Mabetleri*. Türk Tarih Kurumu Yayınları, Ankara.

Özgüç, T. 2005 *Kültepe, Kaniş/Neša*. Yapı Kredi Yayınları, İstanbul.

Özgüç, T., and R. Temizer 1993 The Eskiyapar Treasure. In *Aspects of Art and Iconography: Anatolia and Its Neighbours. Studies in Honor of Nimet Özgüç,* edited by M. Mellink, E. Porada, and T. Özgüç, pp. 613–628. Türk Tarih Kurumu Yayınları, Ankara.

Özsait, M. 1998 1996 Yılı Harmanören Mezarlık Kazısı. XIX. *Kazı Sonuçları Toplantısı* 1:607–612.

Özsait, M. 1999 1997 Yılı Harmanören (Göndürle) Mezarlık Kazısı. XX. *Kazı Sonuçları Toplantısı* 1:467–470.

Özsait, M. 2000 1998 Yılı Harmanören (Göndürle Höyük) Mezarlık Kazısı. XXI. *Kazı Sonuçları Toplantısı* 1:371–374.

Özsait, M. 2002 1999–2000 Yılları (Göndürle Höyük) Harmanören Mezarlık Kazısı. XXIII. *Kazı Sonuçları Toplantısı* 1:327–333.

Özsait, M. 2005 2003 Yılı Harmanören-Göndürle Höyük Mezarlık Kazısı. XXVI. *Kazı Sonuçları Toplantısı* 2:319–322.

Özsait, M. 2006 2004 Yılı Harmanören-Göndürle Höyük Mezarlık Kazısı. XXVII. *Kazı Sonuçları Toplantısı* 2:311–314.

Özsait, M. 2007 2005 Yılı Harmanören (Göndürle Höyük) Mezarlık Kazısı. XXVIII. *Kazı Sonuçları Toplantısı* 2:613–617.

Özsait, M., and N. Özsait 2007 Harmanören İçten Tutamaklı Küpleri. In *Refik Duru'ya Armağan/ Studies in Honour of Refik Duru,* edited by G. Umurtak, Ş. Dönmez, and A. Yurtsever, pp. 131–132. Ege Yayınları, İstanbul.

Schachner, Ş., and A. Schachner 1995 Ürgüp ve Nevşehir Müzelerindeki "Depas Amphikypellon" ve "Tankart" Tipli Kaplar ve Düşündürdükleri. In *Memoriam İ. Metin Akyurt ve Bahattin Devam, Eski Yakındoğu Kültürleri Üzerine İncelemeler / Studies for Ancient Near Eastern Cultures,* edited by A. Erkanal et al., pp. 307–315. Arkeoloji ve Sanat Yayınları, İstanbul.

Schmidt, E. F. 1933 *The Alishar Hüyük: Seasons of 1928 and 1929.* Part. I–II. The University of Chicago Press, Chicago.

Seeher, J. 2000 *Die Bronzezeitliche Nekropole von Demircihüyük-Sariket: Ausgrabungen des Deutschen Archäologischen Instituts in Zusammenarbeit mit dem Museum* Bursa 1990–1991. E. Wasmuth, Tübingen.

Sipahi, T. 1995 Eski Tunç Çağında Orta Anadolu Bölgesi Madeni İğneleri. *Dil ve Tarih-Coğrafya Fakültesi Dergisi* XXXVII.1–2:693–710.

Spanos, P. Z. 1972 Untersuchungen über den bei Homer "depas amphikypellon" genannten Gefästypus. E. Wasmuth, Berlin.Thissen, L. 2002 CANeW Archaeological Sites Database, Central Anatolia, 10.000–5.000 cal. BC. In *The Neolithic of Central Anatolia, Internal Developments and External Relation during the 9th–6th Millennia cal BC,* edited by F. Gérard and L. Thissen, pp. 339–348. Ege Yayınları, İstanbul.

Yakar, J. 1985 *The Later Prehistory of Anatolia, The Late Chalcolithic and Early Bronze Age.* BAR International Series 268, Oxford.

Yakar, J. 1991 *Prehistoric Anatolia, The Neolithic Transformation and the Early Chalcolithic Period.* Tel-Aviv University Press, Tel-Aviv.

Yener, A. 1986 The Archaeometry of Silver in Anatolia: The Bolkardağ Mining District. *American Journal of Archaeology* 90:469–472.

Yener, A. 2013 Negotiating Changing Landscapes: Trojan Silver and the Taurus Mountains. In *İlhan Kayan Anı Kitabı,* edited by E. Öner, pp. 291–298. Ege Üniversitesi Yayınları, İzmir.

Yener, A., and H. Özbal 1986 The Bolkardağ Mining District Survey of Silver and Lead Metals in Ancient Anatolia. In *Proceedings of the 24th International Archaeometry Symposium*, edited by J. S. Olin and M. J. Blackman, pp. 309–320. Smithsonian Institution Press, Washington, DC.

Yıldırım, T. 2006 An Early Bronze Age Cemetery at Resuloglu, Near Ugurludağ, Çorum. A Preliminary Report of the Archaeological Work Carried out Between Years 2003–2005. *Anatolia Antiqua* XIV:1–14.

Yıldırım, T., and I. Ediz 2005 2003 Yılı Resuloğlu Mezarlık Kazısı. XXVI. *Kazı Sonuçları Toplantısı* 2:193–196.

CHAPTER SEVENTEEN

An Early Bronze Age Cemetery in the Caria Region

Kumyeri

*Onur Kara**

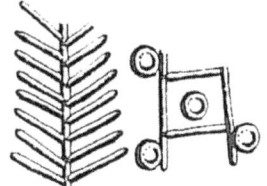

INTRODUCTION

Among all living creatures, only mankind has been conceptually involved in specific postmortem practices or arrangements. Such data essentially act as a mirror and are significant for explaining a tradition, not only assisting us to interpret the religious world of societies but also integrally casting light upon prehistoric periods.

Recent research has proven that, rather than being known only by cities of the Late Period, the prehistoric background of Caria dates from the Mesolithic Age to the Chalcolithic Age (Peschlow 1998:379; Günel 2004:2; Yaylalı 2006:3). In particular, the ecological corridor created by the Büyük Menderes River and the mounds on the bottom lands of fertile plains formed by stream systems feeding that corridor demonstrate that contrary to popular opinion, the cultural background of the region is not weak. In this sense, the Kumyeri Cemetery, providing reference to a cultural history of around 5,000 years, is a witness not only to regional but also to periodic innovations and rare practices visible through the data of burial customs as well as rich assemblages of material culture.

Different parameters derived from the necropolises enable a greater understanding of social life, socioeconomic level, and the cultural and ethnic identity of Caria residents in the Early Bronze Age. In view of the region in general, extramural pithos graves represent the dominant burial customs. However, intramural burial practices that are indicative of an unexplored extramural cemetery in Aphrodisias (Joukowsky 1986:176) and the four tombs revealed in Iasos (Baldoni and Berti 2004:32) are important to demonstrate that

---

*Dr. Onur Kara, Republic of Turkey Ministry of Culture and Tourism, Directorate of Antalya Museum, Archeology II Service, TR 07050 Antalya. karaonur79@hotmail.com.

this practice was maintained in the southwest of Turkey in the third millennium B.C. Significant burial sites of the Region are Damlıboğaz, Iasos, Yarbaşı, Küpasar, and Kumyeri cemeteries. However, the cemeteries, other than Iasos and Kumyeri, have been substantially destroyed by both natural and human factors. Of these cemeteries, Iasos (Pecorella 1984:91) has stone cist graves dated to EBA I–II, and Küpasar (Tırpan 1997:89) and Yarbaşı (Boysal 1979:389; Tırpan 1997:79) have pits that reflect the EBA II.

Kumyeri Cemetery

Located in the province of Muğla, county of Yatağan, and adjacent to the village of Yesilbağcılar, this center is currently within the decoupage site of Güney Ege Linyit İşletmeleri (GELI) [South Aegean Lignite Pit] (Figure 17.1). In this site, preserved as an island, a large cemetery was identified which is dated to all three phases of the Early Bronze Age during the works in 2009.[1] Nearly all of these graves, which were revealed by brief but active works in Kumyeri, are pithos graves. On the other hand, seven ovens were identified in the northeast of the cemetery, which were located at a close distance to the tombs.[2] The largest one of these immovable features is 3.25 × 2.70 meters in size, which appear in ovoid shape with the top construction made of mudbrick blocks.

The Kumyeri pits typologically fall into two groups in consideration of their rim and body profiles. The samples representing Group I are in ovoid shape or long body,

FIGURE 17.1. Aerial photo of Kumyeri showing the EBA cemetery and decoupage area.

and pointed base [**KYM 01, KYM 03, KYM 13, KYM 14, KYM 15, KYM 18**]. Two, three, four, or five pairs of vertical handles placed on either side of the samples attract attention, and the handles are arranged on a line from the rim to the base (Figure 17.2).[3] Group II is represented by pits with two handles, which have a spherical body and a round base [**KYM 09, KYM 16, KYM 21, KYM 27**] (Figure 17.3). Decorations on several pits that have a local character are rare items [**KYM 03**].[4] Kumyeri appears to have adhered to Anatolian burial customs with graves in an east-west direction[5] of which the rims are covered by thin stone flags. Our sample consists of the Kumyeri pits, with eight of them having capstones except two [**KYM 03, KYM 21**]. This is associated with failure to conserve the existing capstones rather than absence of a covering design [**KYM 02**]. These stones, serving as sort of a surface mark, are measures to prevent mistaking the location of the tomb and damaging it with subsequent burials (Wheeler 1974:417; Şahoğlu 2011a:165).

Archaeological investigations in Kumyeri exhibit that adults and children were buried in the same area; both single burials and multiple burials were performed, and the dominant form of burial was hocker. However, in hocker position, there are individuals left on their back [**KYM 14**] (Figure 17.3), or with their head supported by a stone [**KYM 18**].[6] Multiple burials, which are dated to the Neolithic Age and closely associated with the cult of ancestors, are fundamentally an anthropological concept. This concept relied on the respect and commitment to ancestors and to sharing the same place with them;

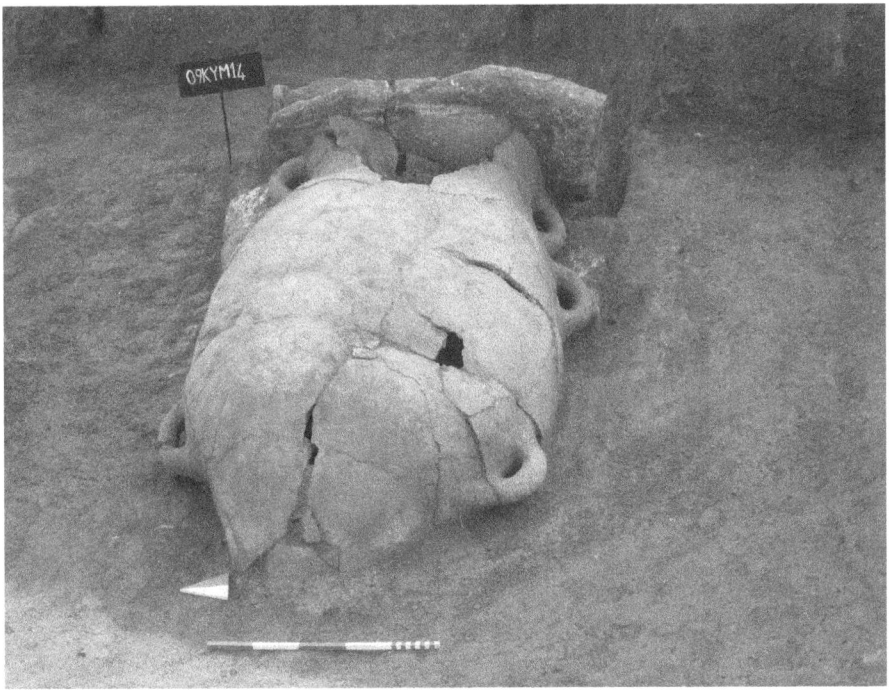

FIGURE 17.2. Grave No [**KYM 14**].

FIGURE 17.3. Pithos burial with burial offering in-sutu, Grave No [KYM 14].

and the graves that we examined based on this concept had two [KYM 16, KYM 27] and even three individuals [KYM 18]. Multiple burials appear to be associated with the bloodline or blood-relation and are suggestive of the desire to be buried with deceased relatives. In these graves of secondary use, the bones of the first burial were carefully put together at one side of the tomb. On the other hand, untouched presents, which were left outside the tomb, are another expression to show respect to spirits of the deceased ones. A pithos with a total of three individuals has a different position from other tombs in the same age [KYM 18]. Due to lack of space in this grave, a concave piece of pithos was used as a capstone to cover the head in order to prevent the adult's head, sticking out of the rim, from being damaged. It is apparent that no difficulty was experienced in producing a large size of the pits for this necropolis. Individuals receiving secondary burials were pressed and put in the already-occupied tombs instead of new pithos, which is significant.

The cemetery of Kumyeri is characterized by pits surrounded by stones (Figure 17.4), uniformly placed pits with one being small and the other large, and the presents left outside the tomb, in addition to the multiple burials mentioned before. Similar behaviors, which are in support of the concept of the family grave and emphasize the sociological aspect of this practice, can be observed in Karataş (Mellink 1969:319) and Baklatepe (Erkanal and Şahoğlu 2012:95) **[KYM 16, KYM 21]** (Figure 17.5).

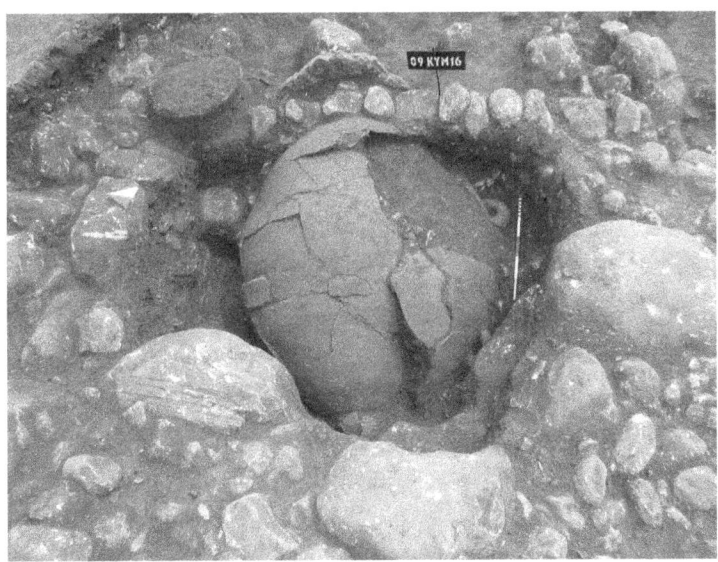

FIGURE 17.4. Grave No [KYM 16].

FIGURE 17.5. EBA II-III graves and architectural remains (EBA III).

FIGURE 17.6. Grave No [KYM 01].

The grave [KYM 01] provides specific data that make Kumyeri special among others of the same age. It is significant as an example of cremation practices in Kumyeri.[7] These types of cremations are known from Aceramic Neolithic Aşıklı Höyük, which is contemporary or earlier than those of Gedikli-Karahöyük,[8] and follow the practice of the Caria Region (Figure 17.6).

Libations that announce the presence of rituals about burial, or pots left on the graves to present a gift, in Kumyeri underline the importance of burial customs in the belief system.[9] Similarly, of ten pits we used as sample, five had presents left inside and outside the grave [KYM 01, KYM 14, KYM 18, KYM 21, KYM 27]. Examination of the presents left on the tomb discloses that the pitchers that represent the dominant form of ceramics (80%) and were found in all of the five graves should be considered cult objects, whose composition was changed as part of ongoing rituals during the funeral. The only concrete religious object identified in Kumyeri is a "Kusura Form" idol made of marble from graves other than those we sampled (Tırpan 2010:366).

Art of Ceramic

The largest group of materials in the Kumyeri Cemetery contains examples of pottery. A rich repertoire of ceramics, indicative of a heavy process of production, were unexceptionally handmade by masters, who were not familiar with a turntable during EBA

I/II and EBA II. These ceramics can be classified into two groups by their quality and production place. Pots from Kumyeri fall into two subgroups based on their quality: fine and rough pots. In addition to this classification, we could further classify the pots as local and imported pots. The repertoire of ceramics include bowls, high-pedestal bowls, jars, mugs, spouted pitchers, cutaway spouted pitchers, tankards, miniature vases, pyxises, and curved tripod miniature vases that vary by form. The paste color of locally produced pots is brown, grey, pink, red, yellowish, brownish, and reddish buff. Dark paste colors of wares known from the Yortan Cemetery Culture include black, grey, and brown tones. Colors of red, brown, grey, black, and buff on the pot surfaces were popular slip colors. In the group of local ceramics, dominance of red slip, representing the tradition of EBA II, is more apparent on the bowls, jars, mugs, and pitchers. The slip color of imported wares is black and grey, which is in harmony with the paste color.

Examples that reflect the repertoire of pots in Kumyeri appear to have introduced typological innovations, perhaps not to the period but to the region. In general, these pots do not exhibit forms that imitate one another. Bowls and pitchers in particular give the impression that masters exerted considerable effort not to identify themselves, by making differences in details such as bases or handles. A good example of this would be the rim and base profiles of the bowls that represent a similar form. For example, the bowls of the early period had a flat rim. By contrast, bowls with flaring rims gained importance toward the mid-period. Only a few inward rims were produced in the EBA II/III.

The pots in Kumyeri, which represent the transition to EBA II, have non-uniformities on their surfaces, and thinning and thickening on their walls. Similarly, skews in round-base bowls or the bases of some pitchers demonstrate that required care was not paid when shaping these pots. But this does not apply to all pots. Spherically bodied jars, spouted pitchers, internally black/externally red polished bowls with or without base, which are specific to the Caria Region, and mugs and tankards made using a similar technique are significant in exhibiting the positive development of ceramic art during the following period.

Similar ceramic forms to those in Kumyeri, which are available in a wide range, can be observed in Turkey as well as on the eastern Aegean islands, the Cyclades, and Greece. The copying of decorations on the imported wares, which can be considered a reflection of Yortan Culture of the Balkans, is seen on the pots of centers of the same age in distant locations such as Bulgaria, Romania, and Serbia (Kara 2013:37).

Small Finds

Among the metal objects, weapons, sockets, and pins of various qualities made of bronze are apparent. In addition, ornaments made of gold, silver, and bronze are also important. Unlike the Chalcolithic Age, metalworking is a significant indicator of prestige and, surely, of trade. In consideration of metallurgic remains, it is apparent that the production that Kumyeri devoted to metallurgy was parallel to its specializing in the production of pottery.

Kumyeri was also prominent in weaving, in addition to pottery and metalworking. Spindle whorls, with or without decoration, of different forms made of terracotta or stone and used to spin thread are exhibited in the Muğla Museum. The repertoire of stone tools includes spindle whorls of simple form and a few hammers. This proves that the community of Kumyeri did incorporate objects whose raw material was metal, particularly bronze (after all, the period named after it), and yet did not fall behind in the stone industry; on the contrary, it closely kept up with developments in technology.

Dating

Of ten graves included in the sample, those in "Group I"[10] were dated to EBA I/II, those in "Group II"[11] were dated to EBA II, and those in "Group III" were dated to EBA II/III.[12] The earliest pottery examples of Kumyeri come from the graves defined as "Group I" [**KYM 14, KYM 16, KYM 18**], which could be synchronized with the Beycesultan XVI and Late Troia I that represent the transition to the EBA II (Kara 2013:194, 195). For example, bowls similar to a typical Kumyeri bowl (Figure 17.7a) from the [**KYM 16**] can be observed in Caria cemeteries such as Iasos (Levi 1986: Pl. 61; Pecorella 1984: 43, Figure 1.2), Damlıboğaz (Gülseven 2002: Lev. 25 a-b, Lev. 27 a), and Yarbaşı (Tırpan 1997: Figure 3) as well as in Karataş III (Warner 1994: Pl. 169 g; 172 c-ç, 174 I, 176 h, 177 a), Bademağacı Höyük (Duru 2008: 164, Figure 333), Kuruçay II (Duru 1996: Lev. 120-1), Harmanören Höyük (Ünlüsoy 1992: 297, Figure 4), Demircihüyük H (Efe 1993: Lev. 2-9, 18), and Chalandriani (Rambach 2000: Pl. 57-3; Hekman 2003: 331) outside Anatolia. Another pot from these tombs with secondary use is a distinguished Kumyeri cup (Figure 17.7b) with a short neck and ring handles that is known from Liman Tepe V (Şahoğlu 2008: 158, Figure 2 d-e), Baklatepe (Şahoğlu 2008: 158, Figure 2 f), Beycesultan XIIIa (Lloyd and Mellaart 1962: 190, Figure 46 3-4), and Karataş III (Warner 1994: Pl. 162 c-g) and that characterizes the EBA II and is considered a "prototype" of tankards (Şahoğlu 2011b:139).

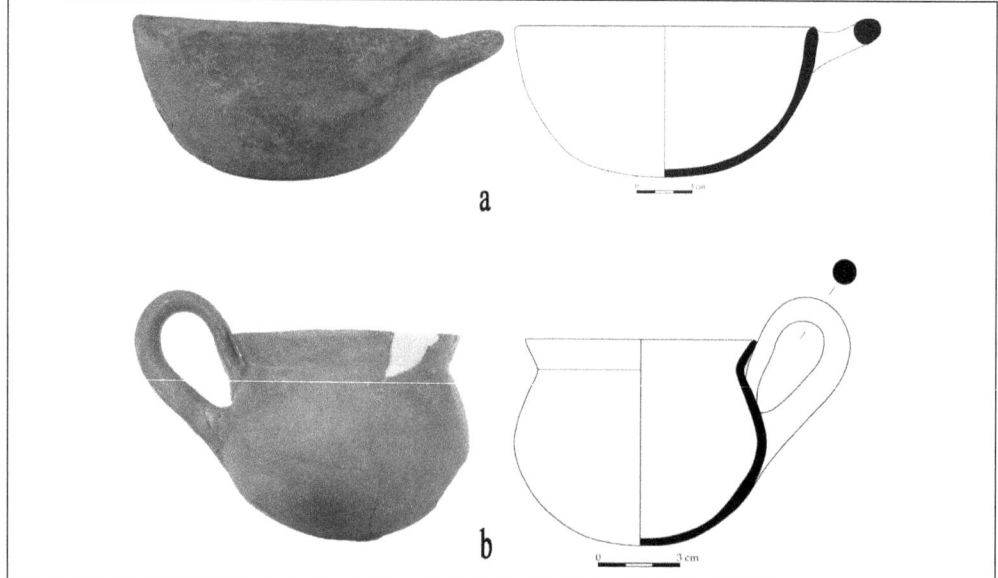

Figure 17.7a–b. Type No: ÇA II.5; Type No: F II.1.

The pots of graves [**KYM 01, KYM 03, KYM 09, KYM 13, KYM 15, KYM 27**] included in Group II have a form that can be dated to Beycesultan XV-XIIIa and Troia II and reflects the EBA II (Kara 2013: 195). A miniature tripod vase of Kumyeri (Figure 17.8) from the [**KYM 01**] that is identical to the products of "Yortan Cemetery Culture" is in perfect consistency with the materials of Troia II (Podzuweit 1979: Pl. 16B. IIa2, Pl. 29 7BIIa29; Mansfeld 2001: Pl. 15 2-4), Yortan (Kâmil 1982: Figure 25-27), Beycesultan XV (Lloyd and Mellaart 1962: 178, Figure 4), Mordoğan (Bossert 1942: 18, Figure 109), and Poliochni *yellow* (Bernabo-Brea 1964: Pl. CXCIX b; CC a-b-d).

The examples, which appeared during the EBA II, evolved in time toward the late period and symbolized the pleasures and preference of the new period, belong to "Group

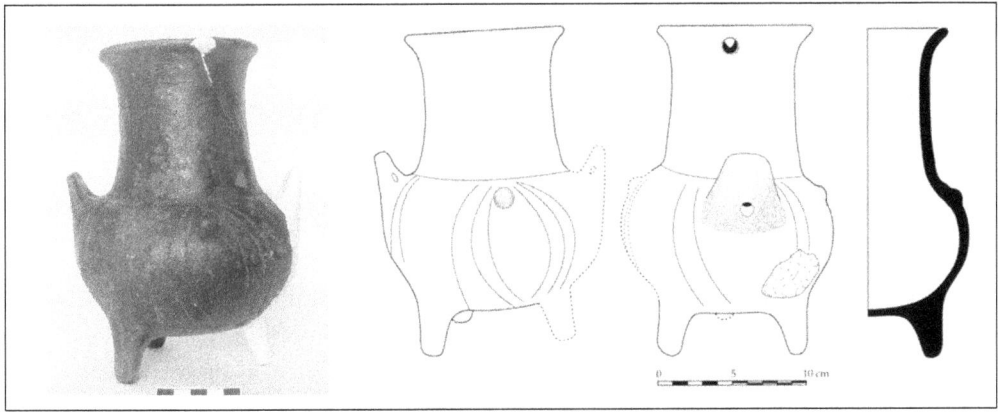

FIGURE 17.8. Type No: KÇ II.1.

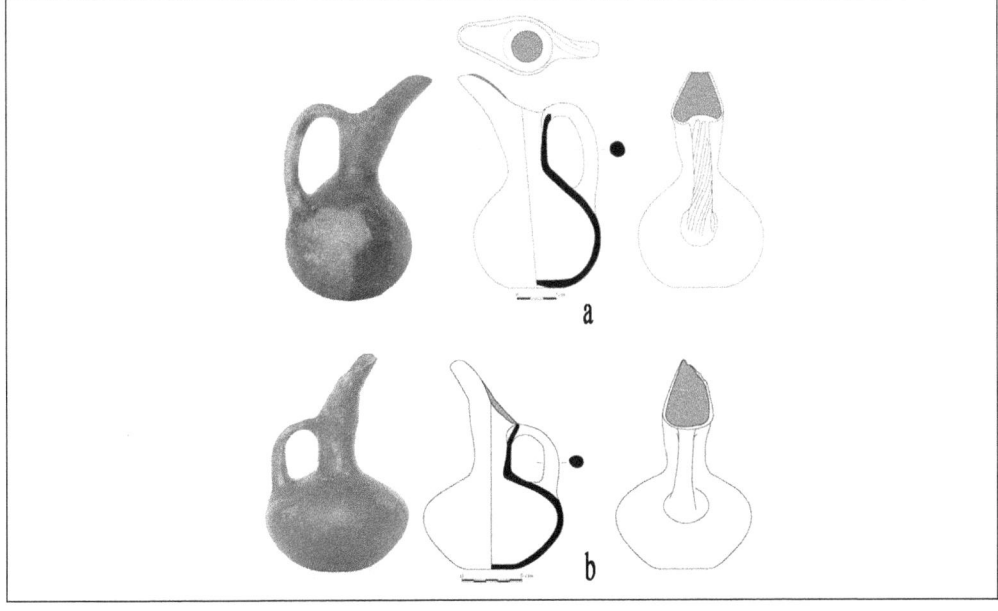

FIGURE 17.9A–B. Type No: TE III. 1; Type No: TE III. 2.

III [**KYM 21**]. Some of these graves that appear to belong to the same age as Beycesultan XIIIa and after, and Late Troia II,[13] have pot forms that represent the transition to the EBA III to some extent. Pitchers similar to two delicate spouted pitchers of Kumyeri (Figure 17.9a, 17.9b) are among the remarkable examples in Group III that represent the "Anatolian Forms," known from Damlıboğaz (Gülseven 2002: Lev. 23 a-b; Lev. 24 a), Karahisar Höyük (Yaylalı and Akdeniz 2002: Lev. 6, Figure 18), Baklatepe (Erkanal 2008:173, Figure 5; Şahoğlu 2011b:275, Figure 144, 145), Küçükhöyük (Gürkan and Seeher 1991:65, Figure 12-3, 5), Phylakopi IB (Renfrew and Evans 2007:168, Figure 5–15.1); equivalents of Kumyeri tankards (Figure 17.10) are known from Liman Tepe V (Şahoğlu 2011a:266, Figure 110, 111, 113), Baklatepe (Şahoğlu 2011a:266, Figure 112), Karaoğlan (Topbaş et al. 1998:84, Figure 64-197), and Heraion II (Milojcic 1961: Pl. 47-12), Aya Irini III (Wilson 1999: Pl. 33-328), and Mount Kynthos (MacGillivary 1980:21, Figure 7-421, 429, 436) in the Aegean.

Evaluation and Conclusion

In light of the above data, it can be concluded that Kumyeri has a developed habitat demographically. Objects made of ceramic, metal, stone, and terracotta indicate that industrial activities based on specialization were performed in this center, in other words, they attest to the presence of a developed professional organization that was dependent on the internal dynamics of the location. However, the finds from the graves that have differences in material culture demonstrate a central authority, which theoretically shaped the social life and collectively organized those activities. In this sense, the stamp seals, among other materials, provide cues about the presence of an administrative class within

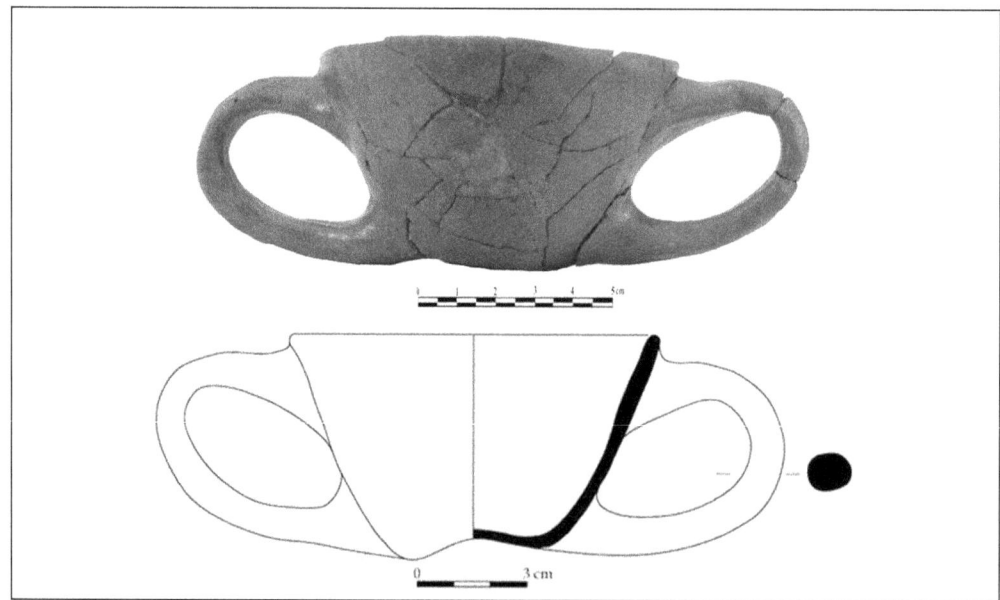

Figure 17.10. Type No: TA I.1.

the sociocultural structure under a hierarchical system in this settlement. The materials of interest, in general, suggest that the living standard of the Kumyeri community was higher than that of communities of the same age, and those people lived well and prosperously. The internal distribution of tomb gifts indicates that they were works of nearly the same level of art and social status. However, the few gold or silver ornaments from several graves as a symbol of wealth and blazon confirm the existence of a coterie that might have had access to such materials in Kumyeri.

In comparison to pottery forms from centers of the same age in different locations, the equivalents of pot types found in Kumyeri have been discovered in neighboring cemeteries, such as Damlıboğaz, Küpasar, Yarbaşı, and Karahisar. In addition to this, similarities to Karataş, a major residential settlement of the Elmalı Plain, are remarkable (Kara 2021). Except for the mentioned regions, several Kumyeri types resemble the types of Liman Tepe and Baklatepe in the Western Anatolia coastline and types of Demircihüyük and Kaklık in Inland Western Anatolia to some extent. As seen, Kumyeri's ceramic art technically adhered to the pottery of Northwest Anatolia, the Coastal Aegean, and the Menderes Basin, and maintained its own cultural development by typologically undergoing a different adaptation than other Caria centers.

As a result, excavations of Kumyeri confirm that the Caria Region, contrary to popular belief, was not isolated from Anatolian prehistory, which has been signified by question marks due to insufficient research and brought to the agenda through Iasos, mentioned in connection with Cycladic Culture in publications about the cultures of Anatolian Early Bronze Age and their spread and influence area. Kumyeri—a special prehistoric center—which completed branching out in professional fields, was capable of producing quality industrial wares, particularly in ceramic art and metalworking. Kumyeri incorporated itself into the trading system, and was able to import qualified wares from distant or nearby geographies thanks to its economic power, and had materials and designs that suggested social class division, in addition to innovations manifesting with burial customs alone.

We believe that Kumyeri excavations have brought a new insight into Caria prehistory and allowed us to become acquainted with different aspects of the southwest of Turkey in the third millennium B.C. Thus, we hope that the data and evaluations we have offered to the scientific world may bring new gains to researchers interested in the archaeology of Anatolia, along with other research to be performed in the region.

Notes

1. We are sincerely indebted to Prof. Dr. Ahmet A. Tırpan, conducting Kumyeri Cemetery excavation, for sharing materials with us and providing a work permit for excavations.
2. Of immovables dated to EBA II, representing the largest ovens of Western Anatolia in terms of their size, only three have been completely excavated (Tırpan 2010:386).
3. Those that are similar to this type of pits recognized in Western Anatolia and the Eastern Aegean to some extent can be found in Baklatepe (Özkan ve Erkanal 1998:423, Figure 7–8; Özkan ve Erkanal 1999:193, Figure 28; Erkanal 2008:175, Figure 10–12), Tepecik, Ahlatlı (Mitten and Yüğrüm 1974:26), Emporio (Hood 1981:528, Figure 231; Figure 2332,

2333), and Aphrodisias (Kadish 1969: Pl. 28 Figure 37; Joukowsky 1986:571, Figure 411: 5; Joukowsky 1996:22, Figure 1: 25).

4. This form of decoration observed in pits of Yortan (Kâmil 1982: Figure 12–17, 19, 21, 22), Küçükhöyük (Gürkan and Seeher 1991:50, 54), Kaklık (Topbaş et al. 1998:33, 37), Karataş (Mellink 1964:275), and Harmanören (Özsait 1995:156) in Western Anatolia is considered to symbolize certain concepts such as power, fertility, welfare, or life cycle (Uhri 2010:193).

5. Our ten samples that we examined have the east west direction but one pithos **[KYM 21]** stands against this design of directions.

6. For similar graves of this form in Inland Western Anatolia, refer to Küçükhöyük (Gürkan and Seeher 1991:44) and Kaklık (Topbaş et al. 1998:35, 69).

7. The grave **[KYM 01]** appears to most likely belong to the late phase of EBA II (The highest data that makes the tomb numbered [KYM 01] special among the other Kumyeri burials is that the cremated bones were placed in a pithos with the characteristics of an urn and placed in a pithos (Kara 2015: 30).

8. A large crematorium was found in Gedikli Karahöyük in Southeastern Anatolia (Alkım 1997:663; Duru 2006: 57, 67). Extensive examinations by R. Duru show that examples of bowls and jars found in the cremation graves belong to EBA II/III.

9. Presents left on the graves known from Baklatepe (Şahoğlu 2011a:167), Yortan (Kâmil 1982:10) and Yarbaşı (Tırpan 1997:80) are a common fact in Kumyeri.

10. In Kumyeri Cemetery, none of the forms from the "Group I" graves appear to decrease to the previous level of Beycesultan XVI, or to the level XVII (Kara 2013:194 et al.). Similarity of pots we examined to the examples of the same age in other centers synchronized with Beycesultan XVI reveals the fact that these tombs must be dated to the Late Troia I; in other words, to the late EBA I and early EBA II. However, several pot forms and burnished ring pedestal miniature vases, which characterize the EBA II, suggest that secondary use of graves **[KYM 16]** and **[KYM 18]** occurred in the early Troia II.

11. Similarity of potteries from Group II to the finds of Beycesultan XV–XIV, Karataş III, Demircihüyük H L, and Aya Arini III indicates that these graves were used in the early and late phases of EBA II (Kara 2013: 196). In addition to centers providing stratigraphy, close similarity of ceramics found in pits in the Group II to the finds of cemeteries of Baklatepe, Kusura B, Kaklık, Harmanören, and Chalandriani, particularly Iasos, Damlıboğaz and Yarbaşı, clears the doubt that "Group II" must be dated to the EBA II.

12. The examples of ceramics representing the Group III include the high pedestal bowls, delicate long neck cutaway spouted pitchers, mugs with one handle, and tankards defined as bell shaped or two handled pots by some researchers, which are known as "Anatolian Forms" (Mellink 1986:146, 150); fully characterize the second half of the third millennium B.C., and reflect the ceramic trend of the new period (Kara 2013:197 et al.).

13. Graves no. **[KYM 49]** and **[KYM 47]** included in the Group III were excluded from this study.

References Cited

Alkım, H. 1997 Gedikli Höyük. In *Eczacıbaşı Sanat Ansiklopedisi*, edited by N. F. Eczacıbaşı. Yapı Endüstri Merkezi Yayınları, İstanbul.

Baldoni, D., and F. Berti 2004 *Iasos Karia'da Bir Liman Kenti*. Homer Kitabevi, İstanbul.
Bernabo-Brea, L. 1964 *Poliochni. Citta Preistorica Nell'isola Di Lemnos*, Vol. II. L'Erma di Bretschneider, Roma.
Bossert, H. 1942 *Altanatolien. Kunst und Handwerk in Kleinasien von den Anfangen bis zum Völligen Aufgehen in der Griechischen Kultur*. Wasmuth, Berlin.
Boysal, Y. 1979 Lagina Kazıları. Türk Tarih *Kongresi* 8:389–391.
Duru, R. 1996 *Kuruçay Höyük I–II. 1978–1988 Kazılarının Sonuçları, Geç Kalkolitik ve İlk Tunç Çağı Yerleşimleri*. Türk Tarih Kurumu Basımevi, Ankara.
Duru, R. 2006 *Gedikli Karahöyük I. Prof. Dr. U. Bahadır Alkım Yönetiminde 1964–1967 Yılları Arasında Yapılan Kazıların Sonuçlar*. Türk Tarih Kurumu Yayınları, Ankara.
Duru, R. 2008 *MÖ 8000'den MÖ 2000'e Burdur-Antalya Bölgesi'nin Altıbin Yılı*. Suna-İnan Kıraç Akdeniz Medeniyetleri Araştırma Enstitüsü: Vehbi Koç Vakfı, Antalya.
Efe, T. 1993 *Demircihüyük. Die Ergebnisse Der Ausgrabungen 1975–1978. Die Frühbronzezeitliche Keramik Der Jüngeren Phasen (bis Phase H). Band III 3 Die Keramik 2*. Verlag Philipp von Zabern, Mainz am Rhein.
Erkanal, H. 2008 Die Neuen Forschungen in Baklatepe bei İzmir. In *The Aegean in the Neolithic, Chalcolithic and the Early Bronze Age*, edited by H. Erkanal, H. Hauptmann, V. Şahoğlu, and R. Tuncel, pp. 165–178. Ankara University Press, Ankara.
Erkanal, H., and V. Şahoğlu 2012 Bakla Tepe (1995–2001). In *DTCF Arkeoloji Bölümü Tarihçesi ve Kazıları (1936–2011) III/2*, edited by O. Bingöl, A. Öztan, and H. Taşkıran, pp. 91–98. Ankara Üniversitesi Dil ve Tarih-Coğrafya Fakültesi, Ankara.
Gülseven, E. 2002 *Milas Müzesi Eski Tunç Çağı Kapları*. Yayınlanmamış Yüksek Lisans Tezi, Muğla Üniversitesi Sosyal Bilimler Enstitüsü, Muğla.
Günel, S. 2004 Aydın Bölgesi'nde Prehistorik Bir Merkez: Köprüova. *OLBA* IX:1–20.
Gürkan, G., and J. Seeher 1991 Die Frühbronzezeitliche Nekropole von Küçükhöyük bei Bozüyük. *IstMitt* 41:39–96.
Hekman, J. J. 2003 *The Early Bronze Age Cemetery at Chalandriani on Syros. Cyclades and Greece*. University Library Groningen, Assen.
Hood, S. 1981 *Excavations in Chios. Prehistoric Emporio and Ayio Gala Vol. II*. British School of Archaeology at Athens, London.
Joukowsky, M. 1986 *Prehistoric Aphrodisias. An Account of the Excavations and Artifact Studies, Vol. I: Excavations and Studie*. Brown/Louvain-La-Neuve, Rhode Island.
Joukowsky, M. 1996 *Early Turkey. An Introduction to the Archaeology of Anatolia from Prehistory through the Lydian Period*. Kendall/Hunt, Iowa.
Kadish, B. 1969 Prehistoric Remains at Aphrodisias 1967. *American Journal of Archaeology* 73:51–65.
Kâmil, T. 1982 *Yortan Cemetery in the Early Bronze Age of Western Anatolia*. BAR 145, Oxford.
Kara, O. 2013 *Karia Bölgesi Tunç Çağı Yerleşimleri*. Yayınlanmamış Doktora Tezi, Selçuk Üniversitesi Sosyal Bilimler Enstitüsü, Konya.
Kara, O. 2015 Erken Tunç Çağı Kumyeri Nekropolü'nde Saptanan Kremasyon Uygulaması ve [KYM 01] No.lu Mezar. In Stratonikeia Çalışmaları I, Stratonikeia ve Çevresi Araştırmaları, edited by B. Söğüt, pp. 29–45. İstanbul.
Kara, O. 2021 Kumyeri Erken Tunç Çağı Nekropolü Buluntuları Işığında Karia-Lykia İlişkileri Üzerine Notlar. (In press).
Levi, D. 1986 *Iasos Kazıları Gli Scavi Di Iasos*. İtalyan Kültür Heyeti, Ankara.

Lloyd, S., and J. Mellaart 1962 *Beycesultan. The Chalcolithic and Early Bronze Age Level.* British Institute of Archaeology at Ankara, London.

MacGillivray, J. A. 1980 Mount Kynthos in Delos. The Early Cycladic Settlement. *Bulletin de correspondance hellénique* 104:3–45.

Mansfled, G. 2001 Die Kontroll Ausgrabung Des "Pinaccle E 4/5" Im Zentrum Der Burg von Troia. *Studia Troica* 11:51–308.

Mellink, M. 1964 Excavation at Karataş-Semayük in Lycia 1963. *American Journal of Archaeology* 68:269–278.

Mellink, M. 1969 Excavation at Karataş-Semayük in Lycia 1968. *American Journal of Archaeology* 73:319–331.

Mellink, M. 1986 The Early Bronze Age in West Anatolia. In *The End of the Early Bronze Age in The Aegean*, edited by G. Cadogan, pp. 139–152. BRILL, Leiden.

Milojcic, V. 1961 *Samos. Die Prähistorische Siedlung Unter Dem Heraion, Grabung 1953 und 1955.* R. Habelt, Bonn.

Mitten, D., and G. Yüğrüm 1974 Ahlatlı Tepecik, Beside the Gygean Lake. *Archaeology* 27:22–29.

Özkan, T., and H. Erkanal 1998 1996 Baklatepe Kazıları. *Kazı Sonuçları Toplantısı* XIX(I):399–425.

Özkan, T., and H. Erkanal 1999 *Tahtalı Barajı Kurtarma Projesi.* T.C. Kültür Bakanlığı Anıtlar ve Müzeler Genel Müdürlüğü İzmir Arkeoloji Müzesi Müdürlüğü, İzmir.

Özsait, M. 1995 1993 Yılı Harmanören Mezarlık Kazısı. *Kazı Sonuçları Toplantısı* XVI(2):153–174.

Pecorella, P. E. 1984 *La Cultura Preistorica Di Iasos in Caria.* G. Bretschneider, Roma.

Peschlow, A. 1998 Die Arbeiten Des Jahres 1995 im Territorium von Herakleia am Latmos (Beşparmak). *Araştırma Sonuçları Toplantısı* XIV(2):141–160.

Podzuweit, C. 1979 *Trojanische Gefäßformen der Frühbronzezeit in Anatolien, der Ägais und angrenzenden Gebieten. Ein Beitrage zur Vergleichen Stratigraphie.* Philip von Zabern, Mainz am Rhein.

Rambach, J. 2000 *Kykladien I. Die Frühe Bronzezeit Grab und Siedlungbefunde. Beiträge zur Urr- und Frühgeschichtlichen Archaologie des Mittelmeer Kulturraumes*, BAM 34. Habelt, Bonn.

Renfrew, C., and R. Evans 2007 The Early Bronze Age Pottery. In *Excavations at Phylakopi in Melos 1974–1977, BSA 42*, edited by C. Renfrew, pp. 129–180. The British School at Athens, London.

Şahoğlu, V. 2008 Crossing Borders: The İzmir Region as a Bridge between the East and West during the Early Bronze Age. In *Trade and Production in Premonetary Greece: Crossing Borders: Proceedings of the 7th, 8th and 9th International Workshops Athens, 1997–1999*, edited by C. Gills and B. Sjöberg, pp. 153–173. Paul Astroms, Savedal.

Şahoğlu, V. 2011a Erken Tunç Çağı'nda Batı Anadolu'da Ölü Gömme Gelenekleri. In *Karşıdan Karşıya. MÖ 3. Bin'de Kiklad Adaları ve Batı Anadolu,* edited by V. Şahoğlu and P. Sotirakopoulou, pp. 164–171. Sakıp Sabancı Museum, İstanbul.

Şahoğlu, V. 2011b Batı Anadolu Sahil Kesiminde Erken Tunç Çağı Seramiği. In *Karşıdan Karşıya. MÖ 3. Bin'de Kiklad Adaları ve Batı Anadolu,* edited by V. Şahoğlu and P. Sotirakopoulou, pp. 136–143. Sakıp Sabancı Museum, İstanbul.

Tırpan, A. 1997 Buluntular Işığında Lagina ve Yakın Çevresi'nin Tarihi Süreci. *Selçuk Üniversitesi Fen-Edebiyat Fakültesi Edebiyat Dergisi* 11:75–98.

Tırpan, A. 2010 Lagina ve Börükçü 2009 Yılı Çalışmaları. *Kazı Sonuçları Toplantısı* XXXII(II): 374–395.

Topbaş, A., A. İlaslı, and T. Efe 1998 Salvage Excavations of the Afyon Archaeological Museum, Part 2: The Settlement of Karaoğlan Mevkii and the Early Bronze Age Cemetery of Kaklık Mevkii. *Anatolia Antiqua* VI:21–94.

Uhri, A. 2010 *Anadolu'da Ölümün Tarihöncesi. Bir Geleneğin Oluşum Süreci*. Ege Yayınları, İstanbul.
Ünlüsoy, I. 1992 Isparta İli Atabey İlçesi Harmanören (Göndürle) Kurtarma Kazısı 1989–1991. *MKKS* III:291–314.
Warner, J. L. 1994 *Elmalı—Karataş II The Early Bronze Age Village of Karataş*. Bryn Mawr, Pennsylvania.
Wheeler, T. 1974 Early Bronze Age Burial Customs in Western Anatolia. *American Journal of Archaeology* 78:415–425.
Wilson, D. 1999 *Keos IX-Aya İrini: Periods I–III. The Neolithic and Early Bronze Age Settlements. Part I: The Pottery and Small Finds*. Philip von Zabern, Mainz am Rhein.
Yaylalı, S. 2006 Muğla Prehistoryası: Paleolitik Dönem'den Erken Tunç Çağı Sonuna Kadar. In *Anadolu Arkeolojisine Katkılar. 65. Yaşında Abdullah Yaylalı'ya Sunulan Yazılar*, edited by T. Takaoğlu, pp. 1–20. Hitit Color, İstanbul.
Yaylalı, S., and E. Akdeniz 2002 Aphrodisias Müzesi'ndeki Karahisar Buluntuları. *OLBA* VI:1–40.

PART III

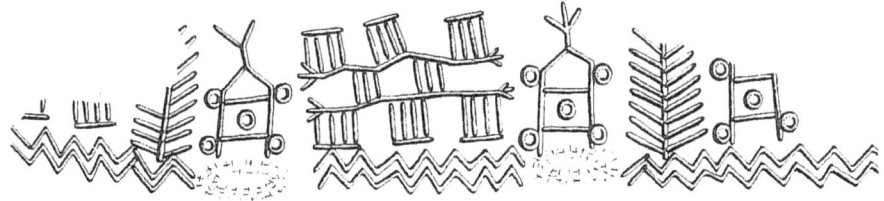

Material Culture

CHAPTER EIGHTEEN

Textile Production and Fishing Technologies at EBA 1 Çukuriçi Höyük

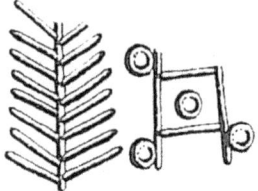

Barbara Horejs,* Christopher Britsch**

INTRODUCTION

Çukuriçi Höyük is situated on the central Aegean coast in Western Anatolia, in the immediate vicinity of the ancient city of Ephesos. Excavations demonstrate that Çukuriçi Höyük is a tell encompassing at least six settlement phases dating to the Pottery Neolithic period (seventh millennium), early Chalcolithic (6200–6000 cal. B.C.), late Chalcolithic (fourth millennium) and Early Bronze Age 1 (2900–2750 B.C.).[1] This paper focuses on the Early Bronze Age 1 phase, consisting of two settlement phases—ÇuHö IV and ÇuHö III. A large number of ovens used for metal production inside the buildings, combined with a high amount of metal artefacts, suggest a strong specialization in metallurgy in the Early Bronze Age occupations. In comparison to other Early Bronze Age sites in Western Anatolia it is possible to assert that Çukuriçi Höyük was a metallurgical center (Horejs 2008; 2009; 2010; Horejs et al. 2011). The small finds inventory indicates that, besides metallurgy, multicrafting households were also contained in the settlement. Two of these—textile production and fishing—are well traceable via clay small finds. Both tasks require distinctive steps and different tools to perform them. This paper explores one of these activities for each of the two crafts—spinning for textile production, and the preparation of bottom gillnets used for fishery. Therefore, the possible function of pierced-clay discs in the Early Bronze Age will be discussed. These discs are sometimes referred to as net weights and in other cases as a spindle whorl type. One aim of this

---

*Prof. Dr. Barbara Horejs Institute for Oriental and European Archaeology, Austrian Academy of Sciences, Hollandstrasse 11–13, 1020 Vienna, Austria; email: barbara.horejs@oeaw.ac.at.

**Christopher Britsch, MA Institute for Oriental and European Archaeology, Austrian Academy of Sciences, Hollandstrasse 11–13, 1020 Vienna, Austria; christopher.britsch@oeaw.ac.at.

paper is to clarify these interpretations by analyzing and comparing the perforated discs and spindle whorls of Çukuriçi Höyük. Additionally, a detailed reconstruction of the spinning process is provided through the analysis of Early Bronze Age spindle whorls from Çukuriçi Höyük. Subsequently, spindle whorl types from other Early Bronze Age sites are also considered and compared to our results.

Spindle Whorls of EBA I Çukuriçi Höyük

For this analysis, only objects that were conclusively produced and used for spinning with a hand spindle were recorded as spindle whorls. At Çukuriçi Höyük, 56 of such pieces were analyzed, representing the largest group within the Early Bronze Age clay small finds (Figure 18.1). The whorls vary in shape, but it is possible to determine four distinct types, each with different variations (Figure 18.2). The general shapes are round to ovoid, flat, conical, and biconical, whereof the biconical ones represent the largest group (32 pieces). Their weight differs between c. 10 g to nearly 80 g. With the present data there was no correlation detectable between weight and settlement phase or weight and type of spindle whorl (Figure 18.3) However, it was noticeable that type III spindle whorls only occurred in phase ÇuHö IV, the older occupation phase (Figure 18.4). Therefore, conical spindle whorls were only produced and used in the older phase

FIGURE 18.1. Selection of spindle whorls of Early Bronze Age Çukuriçi Höyük (Photographer: N. Gail).

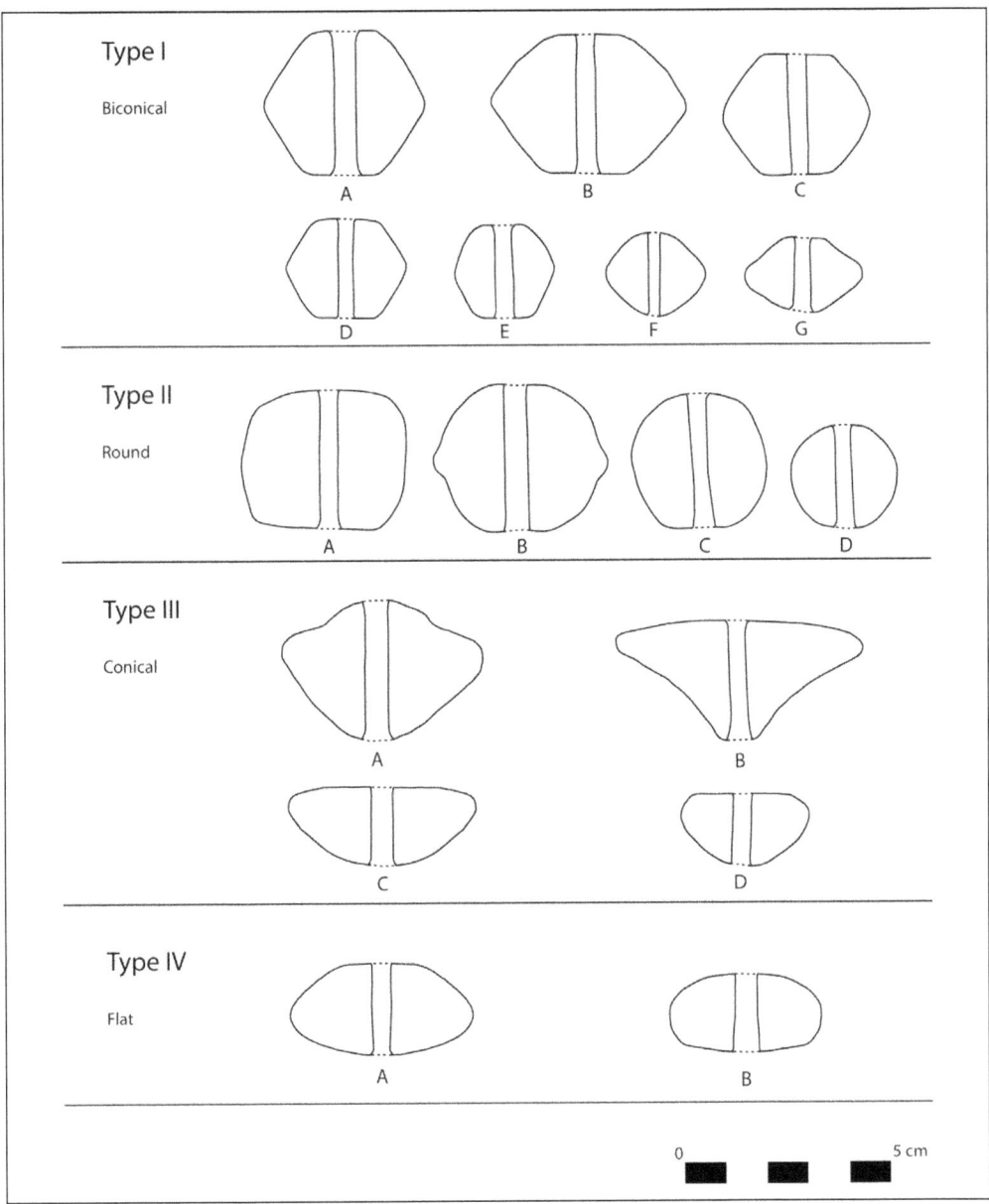

FIGURE 18.2. Typology of spindle whorls of Çukuriçi Höyük phases ÇuHö IV-III (n = 56).

and seem to vanish in the younger settlement. While no preference of a certain clay type was detectable, most spindle whorls were made from finely pored clay, tempered by fine-grained mineral components, with very fine mica inclusions dominating. Nearly all spindle whorls were produced with considerable care. They are often nearly perfectly symmetrical and are in some cases decorated.

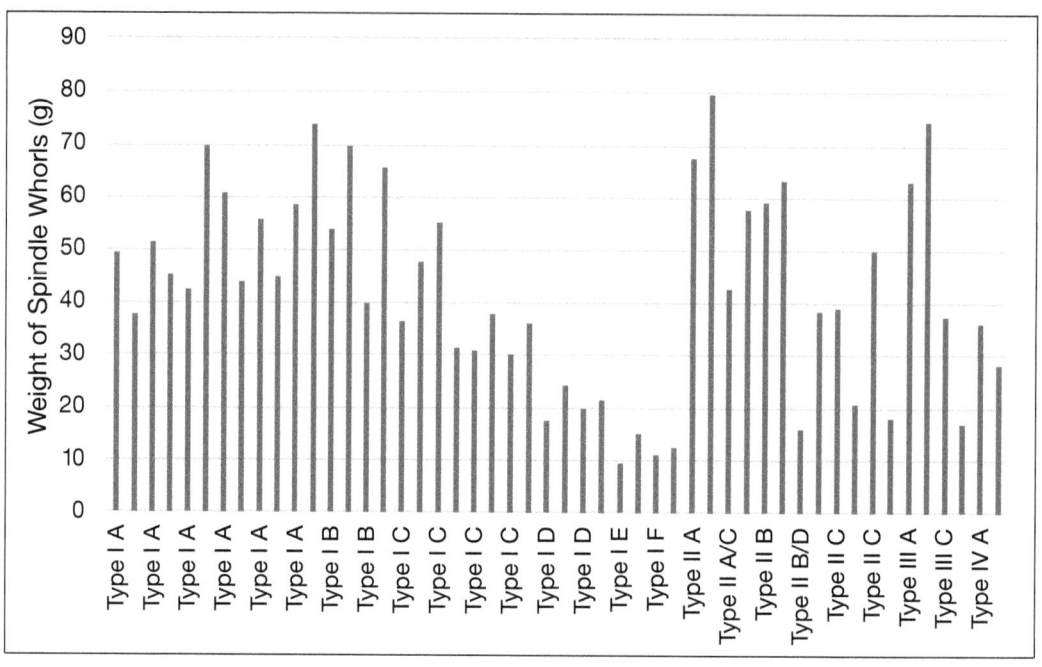

FIGURE 18.3. Weight of individual spindle whorls (exemplary selection, n = 50, n (g) = 2047.9).   000

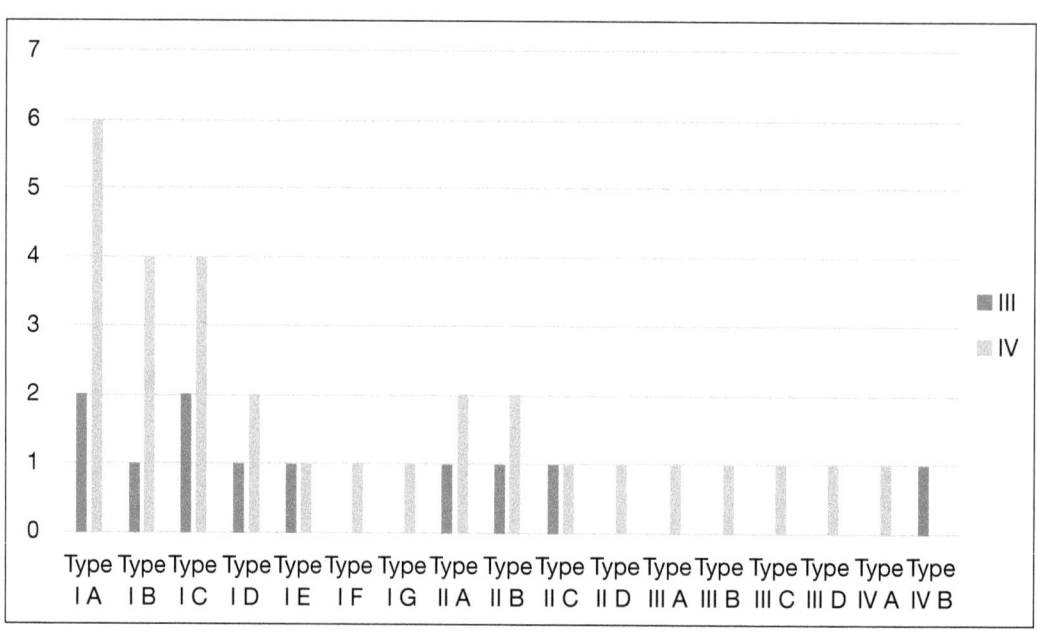

FIGURE 18.4. Distribution of spindle whorl types within phases ÇuHö III and IV (n = 41).   000

Analyzing the Spinning Process

Spinning is the process of manufacturing yarn from previously cleaned and prepared fibers. While there are different techniques to do so, it is commonly assumed that in the Early Bronze Age in Western Anatolia hand spindles where used. Prior to the spinning process, the spinner must form a short starting line by twisting it between the fingers. This starting line is tied onto the spindle, which is also attached to the spindle whorl. The remaining mass of raw fibers can be held under one arm or with a distaff or something similar. The spindle can now be put into rotation. The spindle whorl acts as a swing weight, which—depending on its weight, size, and shape—influences this rotation. During this process, the raw fibers twist into a yarn, which winds on the spindle. Accordingly, the spinning is influenced by the raw material, the size and weight of the spindle and the size, weight, and shape of the spindle whorl. Since, in most cases, spindle whorls are the only artifacts remaining in the archaeological context, approaches in spindle whorl analysis will be demonstrated here. The most important factor is weight. A heavier whorl creates a stronger force on the fibers than a lighter one. Consequently, heavier spindle whorls are better for rough fibers and the production of thicker yarn. This is due to the difficulty in twisting such fibers. A lighter whorl, on the other hand, is necessary for finer fibers, since those are not sturdy enough and would quickly tear during spinning with a whorl that is too heavy (Bohnsack 1981; Schade-Lindig and Schmitt 2003:11–12). Thus, the weight of the spindle whorl will directly affect the thickness and strength of the produced yarn. This was tested in a series of experiments by members of the CTR (Andersson et al. 2008:173; Andersson et al. 2010:164–165; Mårtensson 2007:101; Mårtensson et al. 2009). Their research illustrates that differently sized spindle whorls produced a yarn with a specific thickness and strength. In the test series, spindle whorls weighing 4 g, 8 g, 18 g, and 44 g were tested.[2] A wool variety, most closely resembling ancient and prehistoric characteristics, was used as the raw material. The following relationships between weight and thickness of yarn were observed:

    4 g spindle whorl—yarn thickness thinner than 0.3 mm

    8 g spindle whorl—yarn thickness between 0.3 to 0.4 mm

    18 g spindle whorl—yarn thickness between 0.4 to 0.6 mm

    44 g spindle whorl—yarn thickness between 0.8 to 1.0 mm

In another test series, a further effect of the weight of the spindle whorl could be established. It was shown that a spinner with a heavier whorl is able to work faster, although producing a yarn with reduced length, than someone working with a lighter spindle whorl. The following correlations between the weight of the spindle whorl and operating speed (meter yarn/hour) and yarn length (meter yarn/100 g wool) were observed (Andersson et al. 2008:173; Andersson et al. 2010:164–165; Mårtensson 2007:101):

4 g spindle whorl—35 m/h—1700 m/100 g wool
8 g spindle whorl—40 m/h—1000 m/100 g wool
18 g spindle whorl—50 m/h—625 m/100 g wool

These experiments emphasize the relevance of spindle whorl weight. It has to be mentioned that both experiments were conducted by several individuals under the same conditions and led to the same or similar results. Therefore, it is reasonable to assume that thickness and strength of yarn, as well as the productivity of spinning, primarily depends on the tool, not on the craftswoman or craftsman (Andersson et al. 2010:165).

Such a relationship was not only found for the weight, but also for the shape of the tool. Specific shapes function differently. Biconical-shaped whorls spin faster and in smaller circles, while flat, round, and conical whorls spin more slowly and in larger circles. Faster spinning is an advantage when processing fine, short fibers, while longer, coarser fibers can be processed with both fast and slow spindle whorls. However, for coarse fibers, the latter are sometimes even better (Schade-Lindig and Schmidt 2003). Additionally, a conical whorl will produce a tighter yarn than a biconical one. The spinner must, therefore, consider the kind of spindle whorl and the raw material (s)he chooses, as well as the desired thickness and strength of the yarn. With this information it is possible to give insight into the spinning techniques at Early Bronze Age Çukuriçi Höyük.

As mentioned, the spindle whorls of Çukuriçi Höyük range in weight between c. 10 and 80 g. Referring to the tests of the CTR, yarns with a thickness thinner than 0.4 mm can therefore be ruled out. It is more likely that yarns thicker than 1.0 mm were spun. Since most spindle whorls weigh between c. 20 and 50 g, a general yarn thickness between c. 0.6 and 1.2 mm can be expected.[3] This indicates that Çukuriçi Höyük is within a comparable technological framework with other Early Bronze Age sites, such as Troy I (weights of spindle whorls between 3 and 88 g, mostly between 15 and 35 g) (Balfanz 1995:119) and Demircihüyük (weights of spindle whorls between 2.5 and 60 g, mostly between 5 and 25 g) (Obladen-Kauder 1996). Considering the occurrence and preference of certain shapes there also seems to be a typological connection. In Troy I, biconical spindle whorls make up the largest group of spindle whorls and become more and more predominant through Troy II and III (See Völling 2008). The same is true for Demircihüyük and Aphrodisias.[4]

Biconical spindle whorls are advantageous for spinning wool fibers. While this might be only a slight advantage, it must be considered that a person working daily with such a tool would tend to prefer a more efficient whorl, even if the enhancement is only slightly noticeable. Hoffmann notes, "If there is one thing to be learnt from watching people work in old traditional crafts it is this: The tools and the working procedures are never clumsy, never impractical" (Hoffmann 1988). Of course, individual objects cannot be seen as clear indicators. However, a majority of biconical spindle whorls can imply that a preference for wool over plant fibres was prevalent. Therefore, the change in the spectrum of spindle whorls might mark the moment when wool became the more common raw material for textile production. However, it is important to mention that it does not

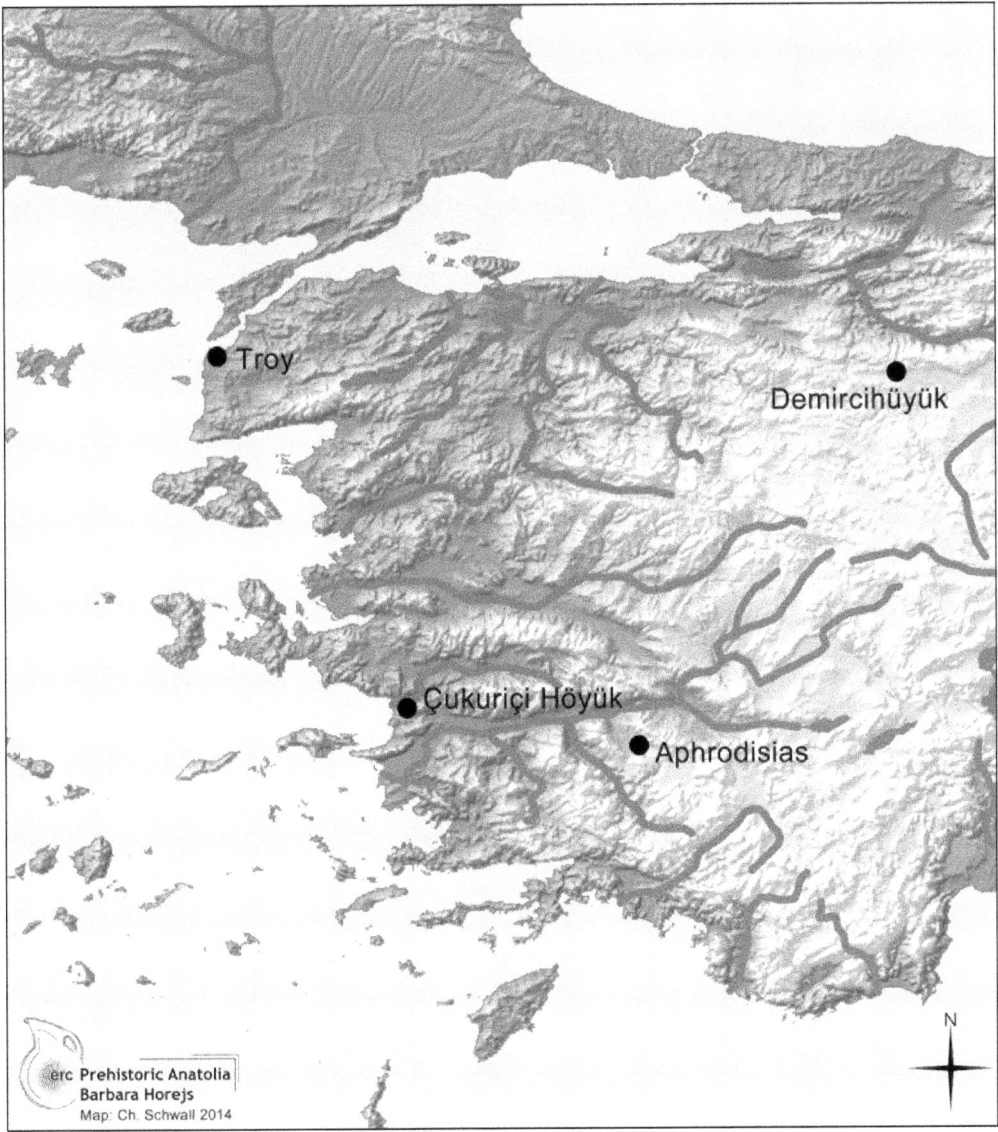

FIGURE 18.5. Sites mentioned in the text.

indicate the beginning of the use of wool. For Çukuriçi Höyük, this hypothesis would mean that a preference for wool over plant fibers is noticeable and probable.

Analyzing the Perforated Discs

Considering the facts and analyses discussed above, it is possible to explore the potential usage of perforated discs at Çukuriçi Höyük. Altogether, 32 objects from the Early Bronze Age small find ensemble can thus far be referred to as pierced or perforated discs. The

FIGURE 18.6. Selection of pierced discs of Early Bronze Age Çukuriçi Höyük (Photographer: N. Gail).

discs are exclusively made from recycled ceramic body sherds with nearly no or only a very slight curvature. The edges are polished and are relatively round in shape. The discs vary in diameter from 2.5 to 10 cm and weigh from c. 6 to 130 g. It was possible to separate the discs into four groups based on their size and weight (Figure 18.6).

As already mentioned, there are two common interpretations for the function of perforated-clay discs, either as net sinkers or spindle whorls (Blegen 1950; Hochstetter 1987; Obladen-Kauder 1996; Rahmstorf 2008; Sharp and Joukowsky 1986). Comparing the weights of the spindle whorls (Figure 18.3) and pierced discs (Table 18.1), one can see that some discs would be lighter than the smallest spindle whorl. Thus, a thread spun with such a pierced disc would create a thinner and finer yarn than could be produced

TABLE 18.1
WEIGHTS AND DIAMETERS OF THE GROUPS OF
NET SINKERS IN PHASES ÇuHö IV-III

	Weight	Diameter
Group 1	c. 6 to 15 g	c. 3 to 5 cm
Group 2	c. 25 to 50 g	c. 5 to 7 cm
Group 3	c. 70 to 80 g	c. 7 to 8 cm
Group 4	c. 100 to 130 g	c. 8 to 10 cm

with any of the spindle whorls. It seems highly unlikely that one would use a recycled potsherd to make a finer product, rather than using a specially made tool for this task. Since a large quantity of spindle whorls was produced at Çukuriçi Höyük, which would definitely have constituted the better tools, it can be decidedly assumed that only these objects were used to spin yarn and the perforated discs served a different function. The function as net sinkers is especially common for the larger pierced discs but is mostly excluded for the smaller ones, because of their low weight. When reconstructing their use, clear indications of function are rare in prehistoric assemblages, however, they can be detected in later periods. The finds of a shipwreck from the seventh century A.D. on the coast of Dor, Israel, for example, demonstrate that discs of such weight certainly could have been used as net sinkers, contradicting the common opinion. One hundred and fifty-nine objects made of lead were found that could clearly be identified as net sinkers on the shipwreck. Out of these, six pieces weighed c. 30 to 60 g, 78 weighed c. 15 g, 39 c. 9 g, and a total of 36 pieces weighed only 5 to 6 g (Galili and Rosen 2008: 69–70). This means that even the smallest pierced discs of Çukuriçi Höyük could have been used as net sinkers. The impetus for using such small weights when fishing with bottom gillnets lies in their adaption to certain types of sea or lake bottoms. For example, if the sea bottom is muddy or sandy, large and heavy net sinkers will sink into the ground and become buried with sediment. This causes the net to rip apart. In such environmental situations, smaller net sinkers appear not only advantageous but necessary for efficient fishing.

Conclusion

This paper demonstrates which considerations and effects are dependent on the spindle whorl used as swing weight when spinning yarn. The main influencing factors are the weight and shape of the spindle whorl. These dictate thickness and strength of the spun yarn. The choice of the spindle whorl thereby fundamentally impinges on the textile end product. With this in mind, a framework can be created that represents the span of probable and possible spindle whorl types. Subsequently, the pierced discs of Early Bronze Age Çukuriçi Höyük were put in contrast to this typology. Referring to these results and the dependency of the produced yarn on the spindle whorl type, it is possible to establish the unlikelihood that the perforated discs were used as swing weights. Although there exist a few discs that could have been used as spindle whorls, it is more probable that all pierced discs possessed the same function since they are all uniformly made. By referring to finds of later periods it was possible to demonstrate that all analyzed pierced discs could have been used as net sinkers. This implies that both the larger pieces, which are often interpreted as net sinkers, and the smallest pieces could have been used as such. Furthermore, it was demonstrated that the small and light pierced discs have advantages when fishing under certain conditions. While this was only attested for the Early Bronze Age finds of Çukuriçi Höyük, it can be assumed that this insight also applies to other Early Bronze Age sites in western Anatolia.

Notes

1. The research for this paper was funded by the START Project nr. Y 528 G19 and the ERC Starting Grant Project no. 263339.
2. See Mårtensson et al. 2009, as well as *Experimental Reports* at http://ctr.hum.ku.dk/tools/.
3. Estimated numbers in comparison to the calculations in Mårtensson et al. 2009: 378.
4. For Troy see Obladen Kauder 1996:231; and Korfmann et al. 1987, XV; for Aphrodisias see Sharp Joukowsky 1986:160 and 372.

References Cited

Andersson, E., L. Mårtensson, M.-L. Nosch, and L. Rahmstorf 2008 New Research on Bronze Age Textile Production. *Bulletin of the Institute of Classical Studies* 51:171–174.

Andersson, E., E. Felluca, M.-L. Nosch, and L. Peyronel 2010 New Perspectives on Bronze Age Textile Production in the Eastern Mediterranean. The First Results with Ebla as a Pilot Study. In *Proceedings of the 6th International Congress on the Archaeology of the Ancient Near East*, edited by P. Matthiae, F. Pinnock, L. Nigro, and N. Marchetti, pp. 159–176. Otto Harrassowitz Verlag, Wiesbaden.

Balfanz, K. 1995 Bronzezeitliche Spinnwirtel aus Troia. *Studia Troica* 5:117–144.

Blegen, C. W., J. L. Caskey, M. Rawson, and J. Sperling 1950 *Troy General Introductions The First and Second Settlements*. Princeton University Press, Princeton.

Bohnsack, A. 1981 *Spinnen und Weben: Entwicklung von Technik und Arbeit im Textilgewerbe*. Rowohlt, München.

Galili, E., and B. Rosen 2008 Fishing Gear from a 7th-Century Shipwreck off Dor, Israel. *The International Journal of Nautical Archaeology* 37:67–76.

Hochstetter, A. 1987 *Kastanas: Ausgrabungen in einem Siedlungshügel der Bronze- und Eisenzeit—6. Die Kleinfunde*. V. Spiess, Berlin.

Hoffmann, M. 1988 Textile Implements: Identification in Archaeological Finds and Interpretation in Pictorial Sources. In *Archaeological Textiles. Report from the 2nd NESAT Symposium*, edited by L. Bender-Jørgensen, B. Magnus, and E. Munksgaard, pp. 232–246. Arkæologisk Institut, København.

Horejs, B. 2008 Erster Grabungsbericht zu den Kampagnen 2006 und 2007 am Çukuriçi Höyük bei Ephesos. *Jahreshefte des Österreichischen Archäologischen Institutes in Wien* 77:91–106.

Horejs, B. 2009 Metalworkers at the Çukuriçi Höyük? An Early Bronze Age Mould and a "Near Eastern Weight" from Western Anatolia. In *Metals and Societies Studies in Honour of Barbara S. Ottaway*, edited by T. L. Kienlin and B. W. Roberts, pp. 358–368. R. Habelt, Bonn.

Horejs, B. 2010 Çukuriçi Höyük Neue Ausgrabungen auf einem Tell bei Ephesos. In *The Land of the Crossroads Essays in Honour of Recep Meriç*, edited by S. Aybek and A. K. Öz, pp. 167–175. Homer Kitabevi, Istanbul.

Horejs, B., A. Galik, U. Thanheiser, and S. Wiesinger 2011 Aktivitäten und Subsistenz in den Siedlungen des Çukuriçi Höyük. Der Forschungsstand nach den Ausgrabungen 2006–2009. *Praehistorische Zeitschrift* 86:31–66.

Korfmann, M., et al. 1987 *Demircihüyük: Die Ergebnisse der Ausgrabungen 1975–1978 2 Naturwissenschaftliche Untersuchungen*. Philip von Zabern, Mainz am Rhein.

Mårtensson, L., M.-L. Nosch, and E. Andersson Strand 2009 Shape of Things: Understanding a Loom Weight. *Oxford Journal of Archaeology* 28:373–398.

Mårtensson, L. 2007 Investigating the Function of Mediterranean Bronze Age textile tool using wool and flax fibers. *Experimentelle Archäologie in Europa Bilanz* 6:97–106.

Obladen-Kauder, J. 1996 *Die Kleinfunde aus Ton, Knochen und Metall, Demircihüyük: Die Ergebnisse der Ausgrabungen 1975–1978 4 Die Kleinfunde*, edited by M. Korfmann. Philipp von Zabern, Mainz am Rhein.

Rahmstorf, L. 2008 *Kleinfunde aus Tiryns: Terrakotta, Stein, Bein und Glas, Fayence vornehmlich aus der Spätbronzezeit*. Dr Ludwig Reichert Verlag, Wiesbaden.

Schade-Lindig, S. and A. Schmitt 2003 Außergewöhnliche Funde aus der bandkeramischen Siedlung Bad Nauheim-Nieder-Mörlen, "Auf dem Hempler" (Wetteraukreis): Spinnwirtel und Webgewichte. *Germania* 81:1–24.

Sharp Joukowsy, M. 1986 *Prehistoric Aphrodisias 1 Excavations and Studies*. Brown University, Rhode Island.

Völling, E. 2008 Die durchlochten Tonobjekte in der Berliner Sammlung. In *Berliner Beiträge zur Vor- und Frühgeschichte, Neue Folge 14*, edited by M. Wemhoff, D. Hertel, and A. Hansel, pp. 227–270. Staatliche Museen zu Berlin, Berlin.

CHAPTER NINETEEN

A Preevaluation of Libation Vessels Discovered at Seyitömer Mound Early Bronze Age Layer III Sanctuaries

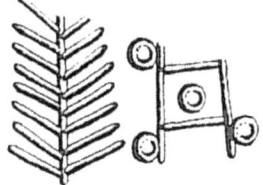

Zeynep Bilgen*

At Seyitömer Mound, the excavations reinitiated by Dumlupınar University, Department of Archaeology, in 2006 show that the architectural stratigraphy of the mound extends from the Roman Period to the Early Bronze Age (Bilgen 2008; 2009; 2011; 2013).

At the mound the EBA III and EBA II phases of the Early Bronze Age were identified. Three architectural phases were defined in the cultural layer EBA III, which was named layer V. These were named from late to early as A, B, and C phases. The Early Bronze Age architecture at Seyitömer Mound was observed over V-A and V-B phases, and the C phase was excavated from 2012 to 2014. It has been determined, with regard to both the architectural remains and the archaeological findings, that this layer of the mound underwent a large fire.

The civic plans of the period were clearly understood as the architectural remains in V-A and V-B phases were completely unearthed. It was observed that the town was well planned when the city plans of the mentioned cultural layers were examined.

The architectural remains present from V-C phase offer clues that suggest differences in both town planning and building materials (Bilgen 2013:102). However, it is too early for a strong evaluation. The V-B and V-A phase settlements have a teardrop-like plan which narrows from southwest to northeast over the mound cone (Bilgen 2013; Bilgen et al. 2013).

In the V-B settlement, which is surrounded by a terrace wall (Figure 19.1, Plan 1), there are adjacently built rectangular buildings that lean on the terrace wall and open to the courtyard. The temple complex, which has a megaron-planned main room, is an independent building located in this courtyard right at the center of the town. A

---

*Lecturer, Zeynep BİLGEN, Dumlupınar University Department of Archaeology, zeynepatar@yahoo.com. I would like to thank archaeologist Dr. Serpil Sandalcı and archaeologist Bayram Uygun for their valuable contributions.

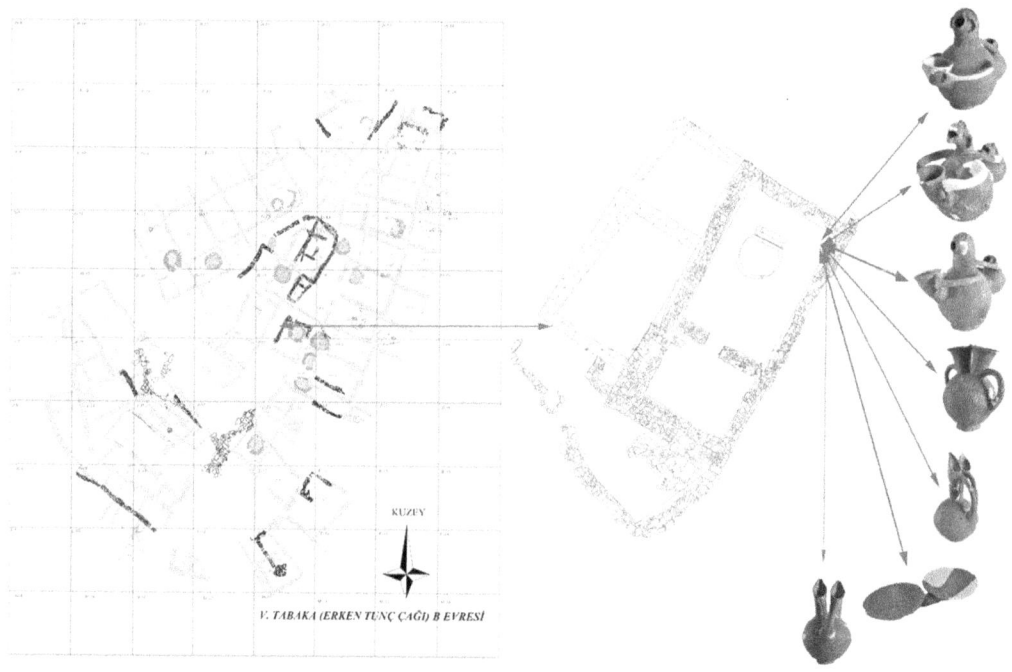

PLAN 19.1. Seyitömer Mound, Early Bronze Age III, Phase V-B, Sanctuary and Palace Complex.

FIGURE 19.1. V-B Phase, Megaron-Planned Sanctuary.

stone-paved alley running from the north of the mound to the northeast and separating the buildings allocated on both sides of the sanctuary has been uncovered. On the south of the sanctuary is an independently and firmly constructed building complex. Considering the dimensions, the nearby storage rooms, its architectural elements, and the findings discovered here, it is believed that this building is a palace complex (Bilgen 2013:96; Bilgen et al. 2012). The sanctuary and palace complex located at the center of the courtyard are separated by a stone-paved alley. However, it is significant that the entrance of the sanctuary faces the palace.

During the B Phase the sanctuary is a complex that opens to the courtyard and has a megaron-planned main room, a front room before it, and two other rooms adjacent to this (Figure 19.1, Plan 1). In the middle of the main room there is an oven, which has horn-shaped bulges (Bilgen 2013: 103–109). The location of the building within the town, its megaron structure, and most importantly the libation vessels discovered over the floor of the main room, which shed light upon the religious functions of the building, are the major factors that reify the building's peculiarities (Figure 19.2, Bilgen 2011).

In addition to the libation vessels, a number of cups, bowls, jugs, and carbonized grains were also discovered over the floor of the main room; a *pithos* was discovered at the northern corner of the room; a bowl at the threshold; a lid and bowls on the bench in the front room were among the other findings. A bone hammer and terracotta weights were discovered on the floor of Room 1, which is contemporary with the main room (Bilgen 2013:105–109).

FIGURE 19.2. V-B Phase, libation vessels.

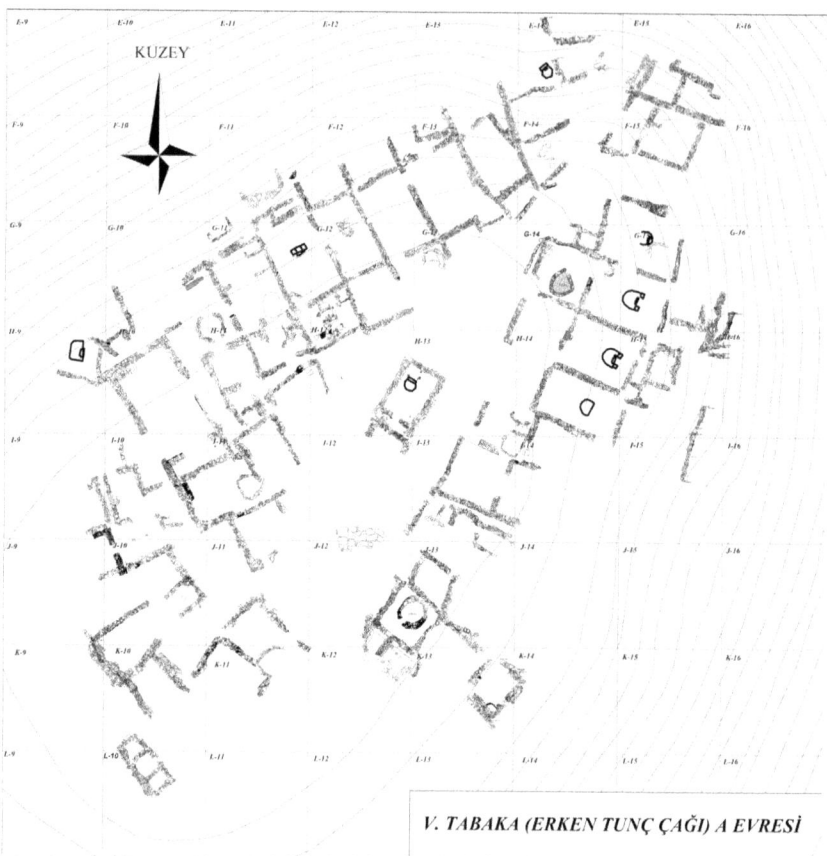

PLAN 19.2. Seyitömer Mound, Early Bronze Age III, Phase V-A, Sanctuary.

It was understood that the sanctuary was rebuilt during Phase A with some changes in its plan (Plan 19.2, Figure 19.3). It was recognized that the sanctuary was renovated four times after its construction during the A phase (Bilgen 2013:91), and during the first phase of use it had a main room, an entrance with ante walls, and a middle room between the two. It was interesting that the door that connects the front entrance to the middle room and the door that connects the middle room and the main room were not on the same axis. Such a preference was probably aimed at preventing the ritual taking place in the main room from being seen by outsiders and was not continued during the second use phase. During this phase the middle entrance room was raised and transformed into a platform. The last plan of the sanctuary presented a megaron-planned building which has a main room that has an oven with horn-shaped bulges and a front room (Bilgen 2011:355–357).

During the fifth phase, alongside libation vessels several bowls, jugs, pots, and a bone awl were discovered over the floor of the main room. Over the platform which was built on the former middle entrance were bowls, jugs, deep bowls, pots, a stamp seal,

FIGURE 19.3. V-A Phase, Megaron-Planned Sanctuary.

and libation vessels (Bilgen 2011:357). No findings pertaining to the fourth and third use phases were discovered. The findings related to the second phase are represented by a wheel-made bowl discovered under the floor of the main room and bowls, jugs, and pots discovered over the floor of the front room (Bilgen 2013:93–94).

Alongside libation vessels, various forms of vessels, tools, and carbonized grains were discovered from the A and B phases of the sanctuary. Such findings indicate that this sanctuary was also a probable dwelling, which might have housed the religious authority as well.

LIBATION VESSELS

The libation vessels were unearthed at Early Bronze Age III B and A layers inside the sanctuary, which continued its religious functions after all renovations.[1] The vessels were classified as libations based on both the locations in which they were discovered and the forms of the vessels. Some of these vessels that have unique forms were not encountered at contemporary settlements around the mound, thus we cannot comment on which cult the libation vessels and the buildings were related to. However, it might be asserted that the cults of both God and Mother Goddess were observed at the mound with reference to the idols and figurines and the ovens with horn-shaped bulges encountered in all types of buildings, including houses, workshops, and silos. Aside from the libation vessels, there is only one religious element inside the sanctuary: an oven with horn-shaped bulges. However, no idols or figurines related to the cult of the mother goddess were encountered inside the aforementioned building. This study aims to introduce only the libation vessels that were discovered at the sanctuaries with regard to their unique forms, though there are no specific data on the cult they represent, yet.

The libation vessels unearthed at the B and A layers of the sanctuary are represented by twelve samples. These libation vessels include a double-plate; double-round mouthed double-necked pitcher; double-necked double-spouted pitchers and a spouted pitcher; a rython shaped in the form of a spouted pitcher carrying a cup; anthropomorphic pitcher-shaped rythons, and zoomorphic (turtle?) rythons.

DOUBLE PLATE

The double plate was discovered in the B phase of the sanctuary over the floor of the main room on the east corner (Bilgen 2013:105). Two flaring-rimmed, conical-bodied, and concave-based plates were connected to each other from their sides through a bridge (Figure 19.4). The double plate connected to both ends of a thick handle unearthed at Seyitömer has not been encountered elsewhere.

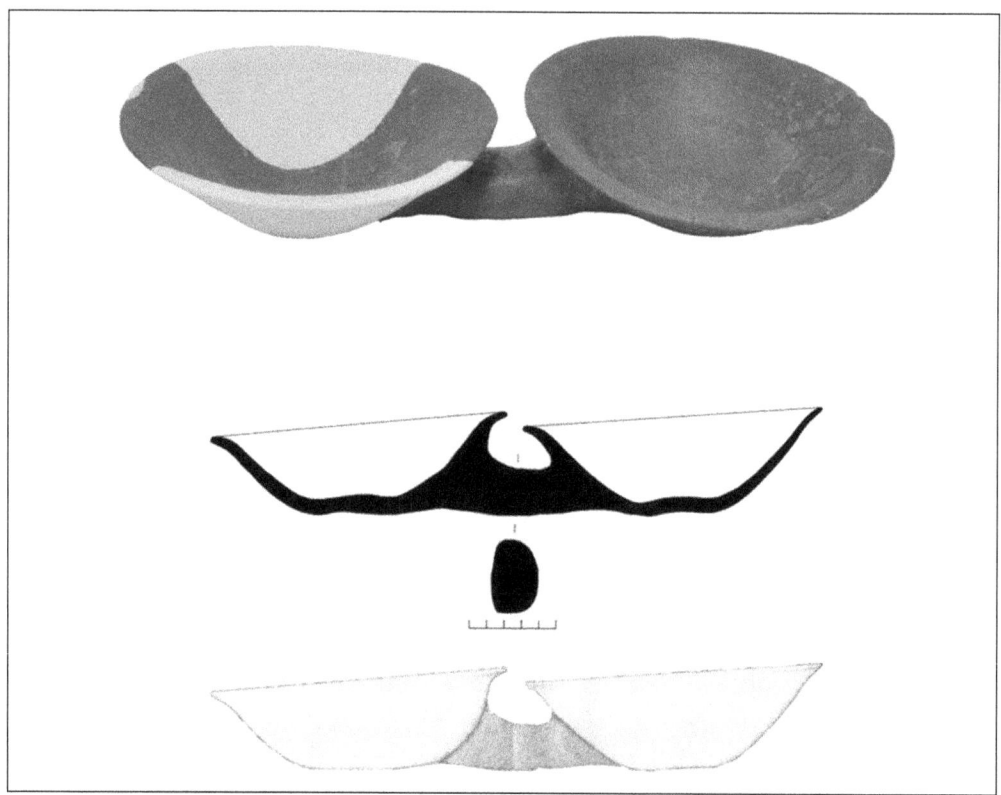

FIGURE 19.4. Double plate from Sanctuary Complex B Phase.

Beakers and Spouted Pitchers

This group is composed of double-round-mouthed and double-necked beakers and spouted pitchers. The spouted pitchers are represented by both double-round-mouthed and double-necked pitchers and single-necked spouted pitchers. These were made using orange, red, and light brown paste; and their surfaces are orange, orange-red, and red washed. The paste contains marl, sand, grit, mica, and chamotte. The body was formed using two horizontally connected semispherical moulded parts.

The double-round-mouthed double-necked beaker and the double-spouted double-necked pitchers that belong to the B phase were discovered inside the sanctuary on the east corner of the megaron-planned main room behind the oven. The double-round-mouthed double-necked pitcher (Figure 19.5) has a flaring rim, double cylindrical necks narrowing toward the body, a spherical body, two twisted handles that connect the neck to the body, and a round base. The necks that widen toward the mouth are separately made and connect at the mouth. There is a horn-shaped bulge at the point of connection. The end of the neck is incised, while the upper body and the handles are chamfered.[2] No parallels of this vessel were encountered.

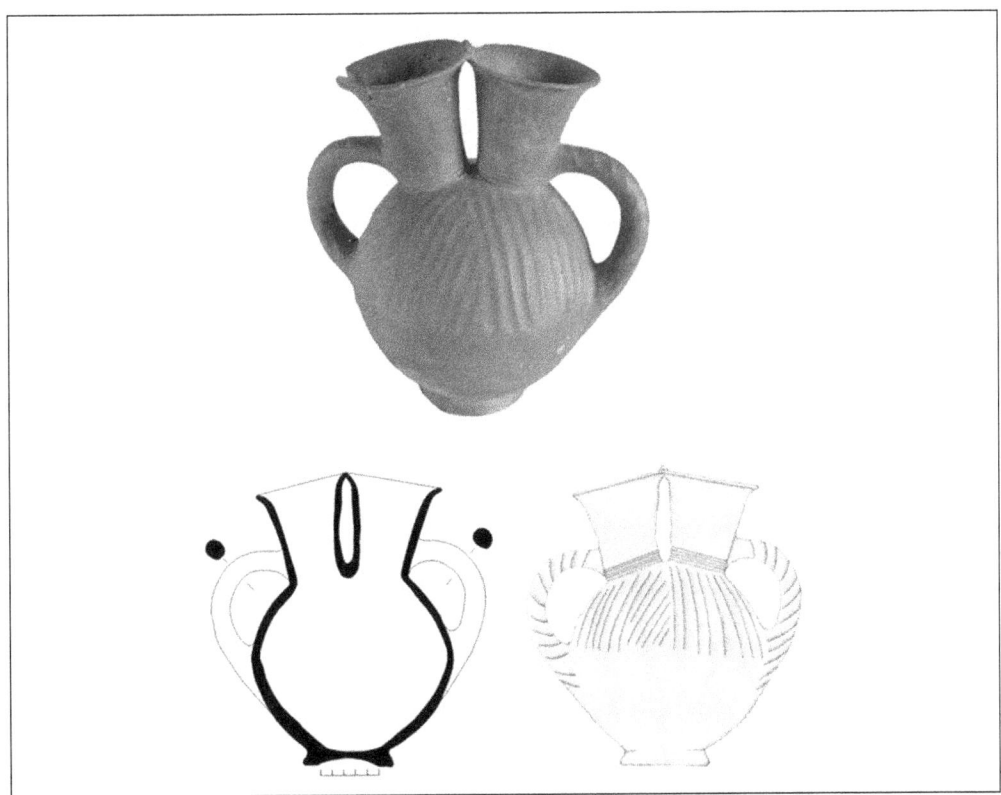

FIGURE 19.5. Sanctuary Complex B Phase. Double-necked double-spouted pitcher.

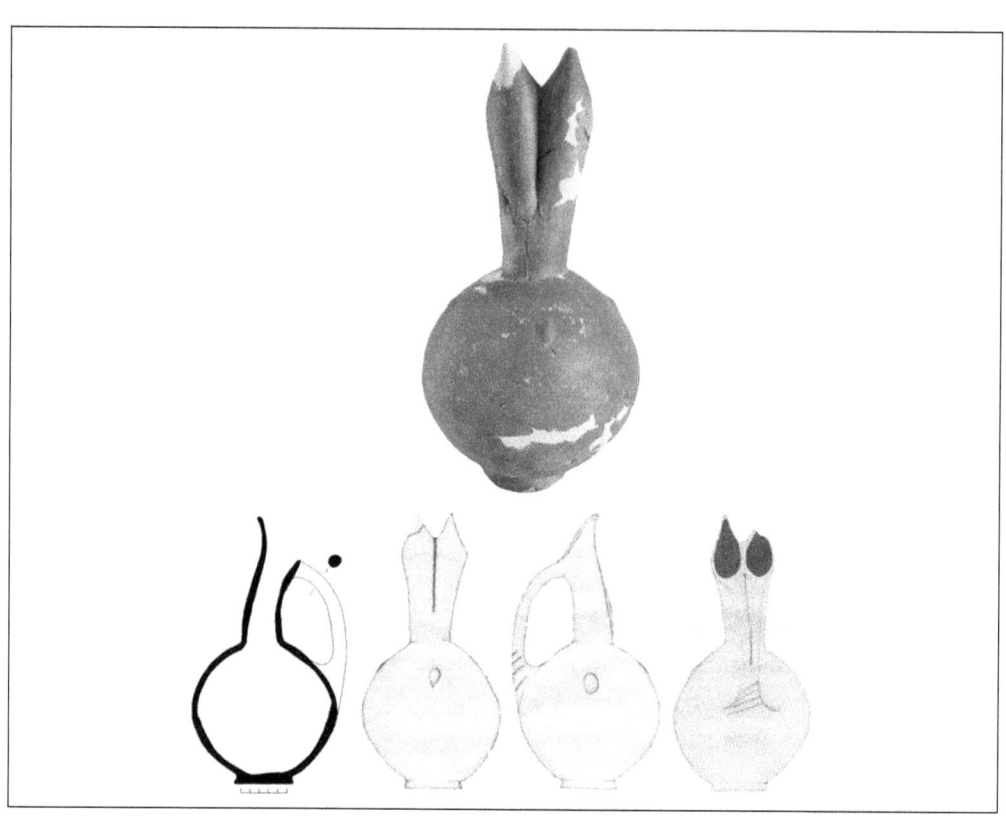

FIGURE 19.6. Sanctuary Complex B Phase. Double-necked double-spouted pitcher.

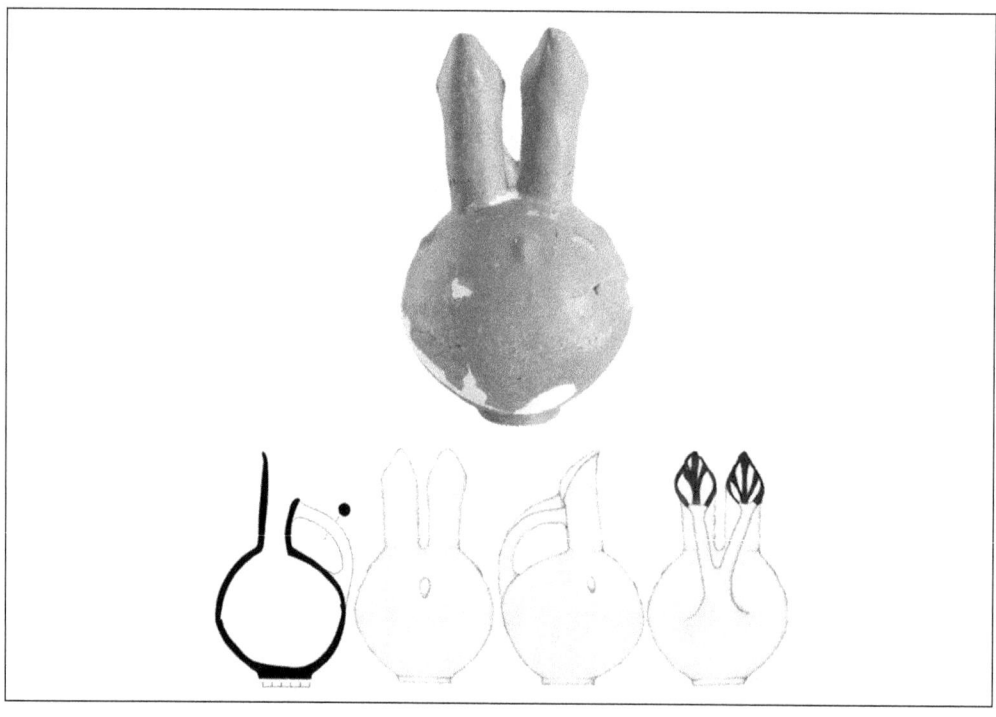

FIGURE 19.7. Sanctuary Complex B Phase. Double-necked double-spouted pitcher.

The double-spouted double-necked beakers have sharp beaks, spherical bodies, and raised flat bases (Figure 19.6, Figure 19.7). There are three knobs over their body. One of the samples has connected necks and the handles that start at the mouth end near the body. The end point of the handle is chamfered. The inner side of the spout is washed.[3] The other sample has separate necks with handles running toward the body (Figure 19.7). Both samples have poured adornments made using slip-colored wash inside the spout.[4]

There are two samples discovered at the A phase; one of them is double-necked (Figure 19.8) the other is single-necked (Figure 19.9). The double-spouted double-necked beaker was discovered at the northeast of the main room of the sanctuary; the single-necked beaker was discovered on the east of the platform on the south (Bilgen 2011:357).

The pitchers have straight, long cylindrical necks and sharp spouts with squat and carinated bodies. The handle of the double-necked pitcher starts in the form of two handles at the rim that instantly join each others' ends as a single handle over the body. It has a shallow ring base.[5] The handle of the single-necked pitcher starts at the neck and extends to the body. The base is slightly concave. The end of the handle is ornamented with shallow chamfers.[6] Both samples have orange-red colored poured-wash adornments inside the spout.

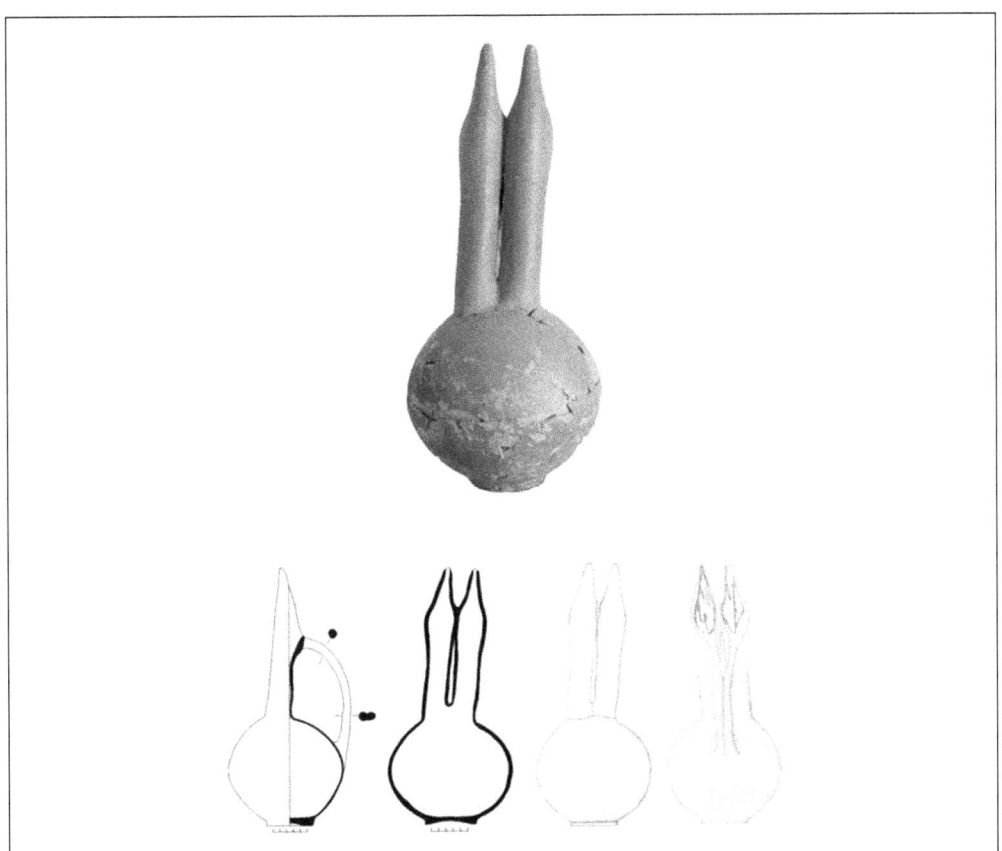

FIGURE 19.8. Sanctuary Complex A Phase. Double-necked double-spouted pitcher.

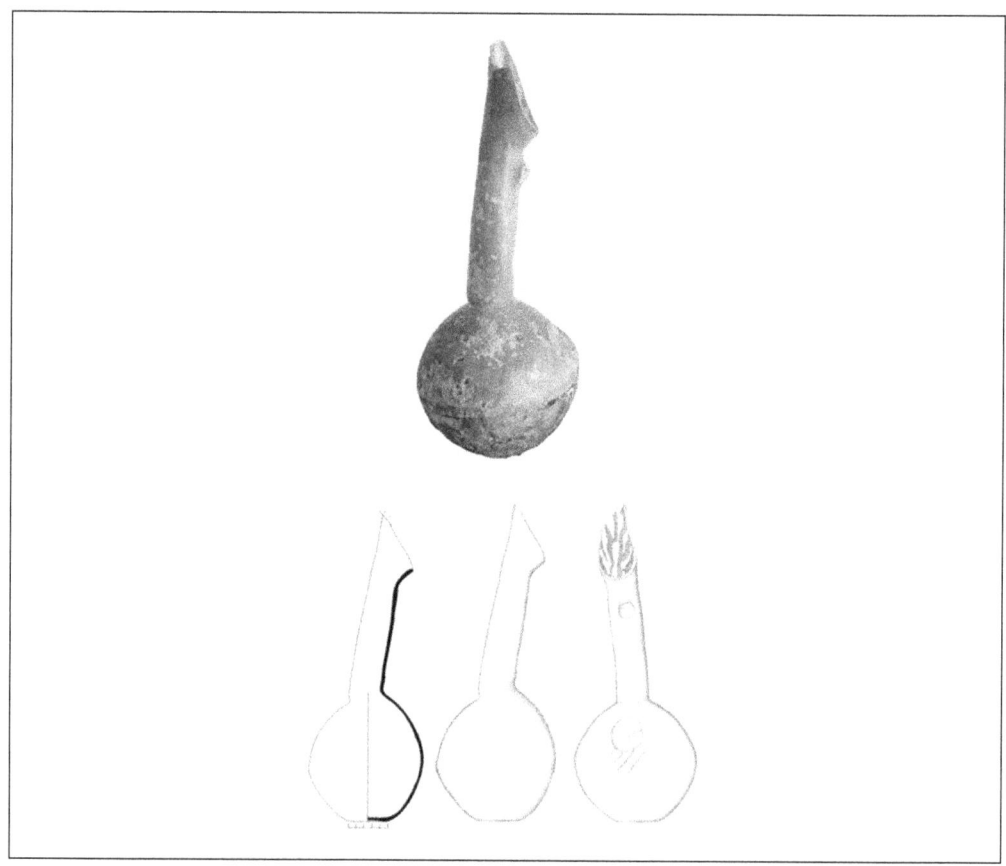

FIGURE 19.9. Sanctuary Complex A Phase. Single necked spouted pitcher.

The closest parallels of double-spouted double-necked pitchers in terms of form were discovered at Kilise Tepe Mound (Jackson et al. 2013:6, 12). Further double-necked spouted pitcher samples were encountered at Yortan (Kamil 1982:48, Figure 75), Troia (Kamil 1982:48), and EBA 3b phase of Beycesultan (Lloyd and Mellaart 1962:233, 242), though they have differences in form and technical properties. There is another sample at Sadberk Hanım Museum (Türkteki and Hürmüzlü 2007:20, 45). Another grave-gift discovered at Karataş-Semayük (Mellink 1969:321) with three spouts is considered a parallel, as it has multiple spouts.

A SPOUTED-PITCHER-SHAPED RYTHON CARRYING A VESSEL

A spouted pitcher connected to a double-handled cup was discovered at the A phase of the sanctuary on the northwest of the main room, behind the oven (Figure 19.10, Bilgen 2011:357). It has a sharp spout, a backswept short cylindrical neck, a spherical body, a twisted handle that extends from the rim to the body, and a shallow ring.

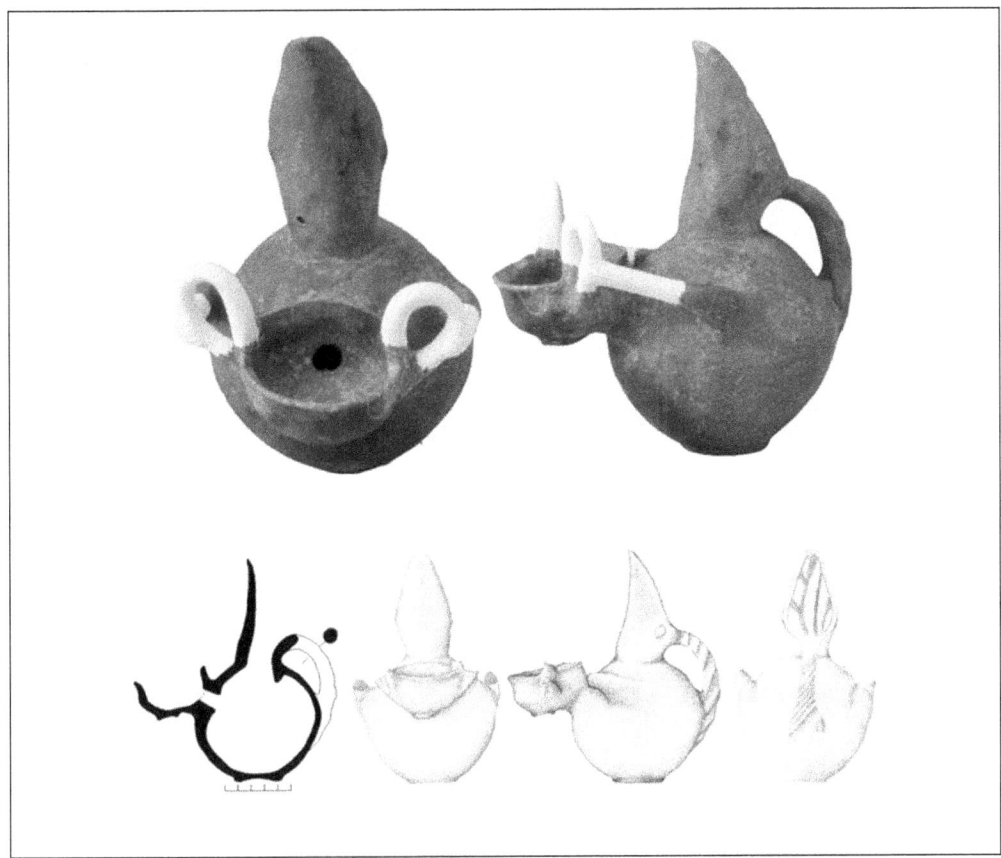

FIGURE 19.10. Sanctuary Building A phase. A spouted-pitcher shaped rython carrying a vessel.

There are eye-shaped bulges on both sides of the spout. The inner side of the spout is poured-red-wash decorated. It has two arms extending to the front above its belly; the hands hold an s-profile cup that has two twisted handles. There is a gap for pouring at the joint of the body and the cup.[7] No samples of this type of pitcher were encountered in the B phase, nor does it have parallels elsewhere.

Human-Faced Pitcher-Shaped Rythons and Zoomorphic (Turtle?) Rythons

There are five samples of human-faced pitcher-shaped rythons and zoomorphic rythons (Figure 19.11, Figure 19.12, Figure 19.13, Figure 19.14, Figure 19.15). The human-faced vessels comprise three pitchers discovered at the B phase of the sanctuary. Three remaining zoomorphic samples were discovered at B and A phases of the sanctuary.

The mentioned libation vessels have reddish paste and they are orange-red or red washed. Only the zoomorphic rython discovered at B phase of the sanctuary has dark grey paste and surface (Figure 19.13). The paste includes sand, grit, mica, lime, and

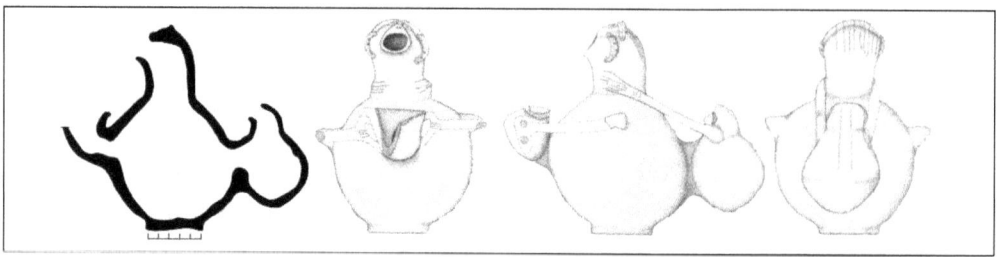

Figure 19.11. Sanctuary Complex B Phase. Human-faced pitcher-shaped rhyton.

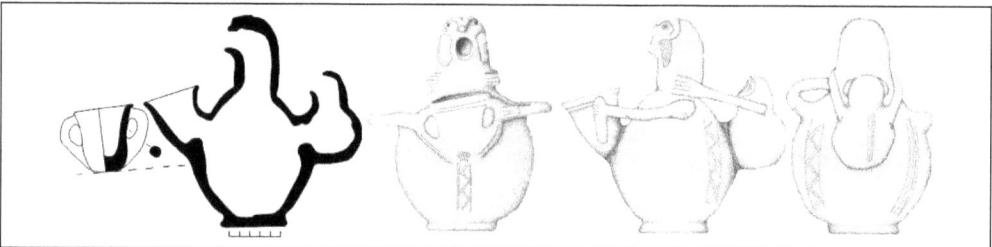

Figure 19.12. Sanctuary Complex B Phase. Human-faced pitcher-shaped rhyton.

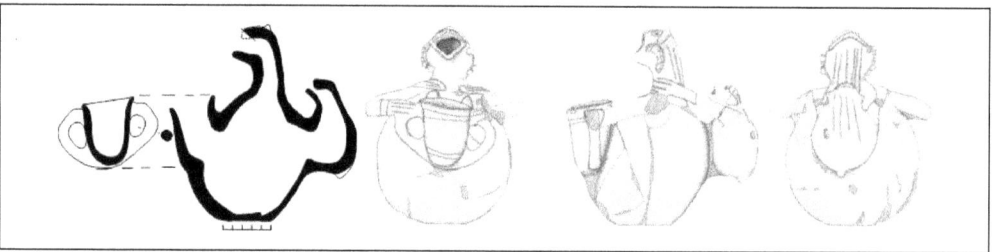

Figure 19.13. Sanctuary Complex B Phase. Human-faced pitcher-shaped rhyton.

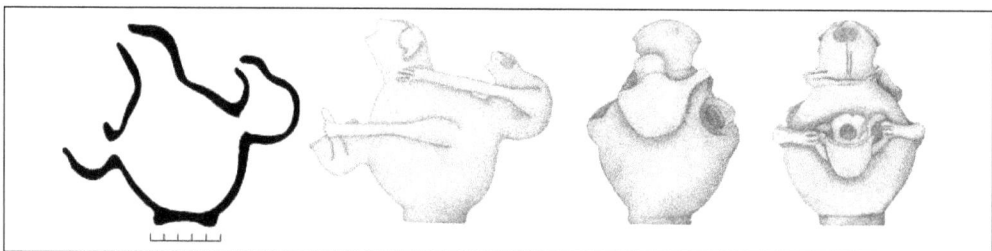

Figure 19.14. Sanctuary Building A Phase. Zoomorphic rhyton.

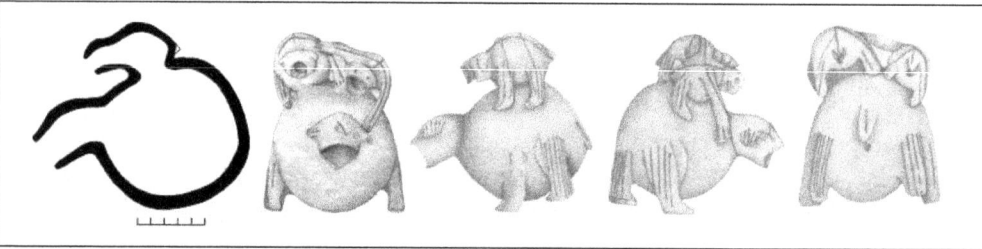

Figure 19.15. Sanctuary Building A Phase. Zoomorphic rython and Zoomorphic/Turtle (?) rython.

chamotte. The bodies are formed of two moulded halves joined together either horizontally or vertically.

The human-faced pitcher-shaped rythons have spherical bodies, cylindrical necks, round heads, ring, and flat bases (Figure 19.11, Figure 19.12, Figure 19.13). They have arms stemming from the shoulders and stretching forward. They hold depas-shaped cups over their belly and have pouring holes at the joint. They carry on their back smaller cups which are almost technically and physically identical. These smaller cups are also made horizontally connecting two moulded spherical miniature halves. These cups are connected to the main cup from their center and there is a gap at the joint that allows liquid/libation to flow. At the same time they hug the main cup with their uneven arms. The open-mouthed rythons, which carry human face traits, are different especially in terms of the faces depicted. This type of rython is represented by three samples discovered at the east corner of the B phase main room (Bilgen 2013:105, 106).

There is a crescent-shaped and notched coronet on the upper part of the head of the first sample (Figure 19.11). There are vertically scraped lines on the back of the head which we believe represent hair. The eyeholes are surrounded with embossed circles. The tip of the nose is upturned and the nostrils are discernible. The round mouth is open and it is connected to the nose. The spoon-shaped ears are decorated with horizontal holes. The arms stretch forward like a bow. It holds a depas-like cup. Only the ears and open oval mouth of the twin it carries on its back are distinguishable. Wrist and finger details are scraped on its arms, which embrace the neck of the main cup. Two rows of scraped lines run from the head to the middle of the body on the back of the cup.

The second sample discovered at the B phase (Figure 19.12) has highly embossed horseshoe-shaped eyebrows. It has a long, pointed nose with discernible nostrils. The ears are missing. However, it can be said that it had spoon-like ears in view of its smaller twin. It has carved round eyeholes with surrounding embossed sides. It has a round and open mouth. The arms stretch forward like a bow and it holds a depas with both hands. The grooves on the arms probably stress the shoulders, elbows, and wrists. The fingers are marked with horizontal, deeply scraped lines. Unlike other samples it has vertical deeply scraped bands on both the front and the back of the cup. The bands are ornamented with scraped zigzag motifs and vertical lines. The twin noticeably only has spoon-like ears and an open, round mouth. The details of the arms and hands extending to the neck are similar to those of the main figure. There are three rows of vertical scraped lines on its back.[8]

The closest parallels of the human-faced pitcher-shaped rythons were dated to EBA II. One of these is the human-shaped vessel discovered at Troia (Blegen 1950), which holds a cup in its hands; the other is the disk-faced figurine-headed pitcher discovered at Afyon-Bavurdu (Bilgi 2012:309). There is a spouted pitcher on the shoulder of this vessel. Another similar sample at Afyon Museum is a disk-faced figurine-headed pitcher, the findspot of this item is not known (Bilgi 2012:309). In the aforementioned sample the embossed bow-like arms are connected to the body. However, the shoulders and wrists and the fingers are stressed with scraped lines, which are identical with Seyitömer samples.

The zoomorphic rythons are represented with two samples and they were discovered on the east corner of the main room of the sanctuary at the B phase; at the A phase, they were discovered on the east of the platform that lay on the south of the sanctuary (Bilgen 2011; 2013).

The sample discovered at the B phase (Figure 19.13) has a flat base. There is a crescent-shaped high coronet over the head, the midpoint of this coronet has been sharpened, and the hair is marked with vertical lines at the back of the head. It has round carved eyes with embossed sides and a slightly roman nose. The jawbone is pointed. The mouth is open with a diamond shape. Large half-moon-shaped ears are appliqued with paste fragments. There are two embossed breasts on the body. The bow-like arms stretch forward. It holds a depas-like cup which has horizontal incised ornaments on the base. The two-row incisions on the arms stress the shoulders, elbows, and wrists. The fingers are represented with horizontal, deep, scraped lines. The twin it carries on its back has a steeple head with round carved eyeholes and a roman nose with visible nostrils. It has an open oval mouth. It has crescent-shaped embossed ears. It has a tail at the end of its body.[9]

The first sample discovered at the A phase (Figure 19.14) has a spherical body and a ring base. The head is round with beetle brows, the oval mouth is open, and the ears are low-set. The upper and lower jawbones are pointed. Unlike other samples the tongue is appliqued inside the mouth. There are two deep scraped lines on the neck that run from the jaw to the end of the neck. Its arms are stretched forward at the shoulder level and it holds a two-handled cup. The fingers are marked with deep scraped lines. The cup has two smaller twins mounted on its back. One of the twins with similar technical and form properties is present. The rython is similar to human-faced pitcher-shaped rythons in terms of its general form and structural properties. However, it is similar to the turtle (?) rython with regard to its facial makeup and the two twins it carries on its back.[10]

The animal/turtle (?) rython discovered at A phase (Figure 19.15) has a spherical body formed of two vertically connected moulded halves. There is a cylindrical neck stemming from the middle of the body with an oval head on the end. The beetle brows are deeply incised and the eyes are depicted as concentric circles. The diamond-shaped mouth is open. The ears are low-set. There are two twins over the main body which are structurally and ornamentally identical with it. They are connected to the main cup by their bellies and feet. One of these has a foot on the back of the other twin. Its ornamentation and structural properties distinguish this rython from the rest. Its entire surface—both the main cup and the twins—is orange washed over beige slip and looks like a shell.[11] The legs of the main body are also vertically incised. A vertical groove runs on the bodies of the twins and this groove is marked with horizontal lines at certain intervals. The legs and the feet are similarly incised with vertical lines. Another distinguishing structural feature is the four legs over which the cup stands. The twins that stand over the main cup also have four legs. The quadrangular prism legs have flat-based feet that are slightly pulled forward. The nails are visible on the front feet with deep incisions. Another difference is the drop-like tail that exists on all figurines. Below the tails are pressed circular holes. The Seyitömer animal/turtle (?) rythons that depict a mother and her twins are unique and no parallels were observed.

Evaluation

Unique libation vessels discovered inside the sanctuary show that it is an integral part of the city at Seyitömer Mound EBA III-B and -A layers with its location, plan, and the findings discovered. These vessels were not encountered over all the settlement, however, their technical features endorse that they are indigenous to the settlement.

The studies at the site show that Seyitömer Mound was a pottery production center during the period discussed. However, the most significant feature of the settlement is the production of almost all the pottery with mould technique. Thus, it is possible to assert that the libation vessels are locally produced, since they were also moulded.

The libation vessels were evaluated in relation to both the vessels they were found with and also the pottery discovered in the entire settlement, and it was observed that they were similar in terms of paste colors and material. The surface wash, ornamentation styles, and motifs are peculiar to Seyitömer EBA III pottery. These include eyes on the spouts, breasts on the body, poured wash inside the spout, grooves over the bodies and handles of the cups. Moreover, the horizontal and vertical grooves observed on the bodies and the motifs inside these grooves are also observed on double-necked double-spouted rythons. A large number of washed samples exist among Seyitömer EBA III pottery. These vessels are ornamented with orange, red, and brown motifs. The turtle (?) rythons[12] are considered to be rather functional and related to the corresponding animal.

Considering the libation vessels as a whole it might be concluded that they exist in all sanctuary phases without disruption. The necks grow in length and the bodies get smaller in double-necked double-spouted pitchers from early (B) phase to late (A) phase. It might be asserted that A phase vessels are more elegant in form. Another important feature is the existence of double or triple pouring holes in almost all vessels.[13] It is considered that the libation that flows between the mouths was filled in spouted rythons with connected cups from the mouth section and from the depas and cup in human-faced and zoomorphic two-handled rythons. The pouring was probably made from the mouths of the main figure and the twins and the cup at the front. All vessels except the double-plate and the single-necked spouted pitcher were considered as joint cups due to the mentioned properties. The existence of multiple filling and pouring holes in both rythons and double-necked double-spouted pitchers might also have symbolic meanings.

The surface surveys conducted at Kütahya province, which is in the Northwestern Anatolia, Aegean shore, and Central Anatolia triangle show that the region has a rich historical heritage (Efe 1990; 1991; 1992; 1993a; 1993b; 1994; 1995; 1995b). The architectural texture and rich repertory of pottery findings discovered during Seyitömer Mound excavations present important data about the Bronze Ages in Inland Western Anatolia.

In this context, the unique rythons discovered during the excavations that laid bare the EBA III culture at the mound in its entirety have local properties, but when also taking into consideration the building in which they were discovered they are expected to form a distinctive group in Anatolian archaeology.

Notes

1. Vessels that could be identified as libations were also discovered at different buildings in A, B, and C phases, although very rarely. At the C phase a double spouted double necked pitcher and a spouted pitcher with a depas like cup attached below the handle, at the B phase two askos, and at the A phase three spouted pitchers linked together on a ring and an askos were discovered.
2. Orange paste washed the same color. The paste contains mica, sand, grit, and chamotte. Rim diameter: 8.4-8.1 cm, Height: 25.3 cm, Base diameter: 7.4 cm.
3. Light red paste washed red. The paste contains sand, mica, and grit. Height: 29.4 cm, Base diameter: 6.2 cm.
4. Light brown paste washed orange red. The paste contains mica, sand, grit, chamotte, and marn. Height: 23.3 cm, Base diameter: 5.2 cm.
5. Light pink orange paste washed orange red. The paste contains mica, sand, grit, chamotte, and marn. Height: 37.1 cm, Base diameter: 6.8 cm.
6. Light pink orange paste washed orange red. The paste contains mica, sand, grit, chamotte, and marn. Height: 36.1 cm, base diameter: 4.4cm.
7. Pink brown paste washed red. The paste contains sand and chamotte. Height: 16.1 cm, Base diameter: 3.4 cm.
8. Bilgen 2013:106, Image 278; Pink red paste washed orange red. The paste contains sand, mica, grit, and limestone. Height: 20.2 cm, Base diameter: 6.1 cm.
9. Bilgen 2013:106, Image 279; Dark grey paste greyish camel slipped burnished surface. The paste contains sand, grit, and mica. Height: 19.6 cm, Base diameter: 4.7 cm.
10. Bilgen 2011:357, Image 477; Red paste washed orange red. The paste contains sand, grit, mica, and chamotte. Height: 13.7 cm, Base Diameter: 4.2 cm.
11. Bilgen 2011:357, Image 476; Brownish orange paste with beige slip. The paste contains sand and mica. Height: 13.4 cm.
12. Same slip and wash and similar motifs on a lid fragment discovered around the same location with the rython was significant.
13. All vessels except the double plate and the single necked spouted pitcher share these properties.

References Cited

Bilgen, A. N. 2008 Seyitömer Höyüğü 2006 Yılı Kazısı. *Kazı Sonuçları Toplantısı* 29(1):321–332.

Bilgen, A. N. 2009 Seyitömer Höyüğü 2007 Yılı Kazısı. *Kazı Sonuçları Toplantısı* 30(1):71–88.

Bilgen, A. N., G. Coşkun, and Z. Bilgen 2010 Seyitömer Höyüğü 2008 Yılı Kazısı. *Kazı Sonuçları Toplantısı* 31(1):341–354.

Bilgen, A. N. 2011 *Seyitömer Höyük Kazısı Ön Raporu (2006–2010)*. Dumlupınar Üniversitesi Fen-Edebiyat Fakültesi Arkeoloji Bölümü, Kütahya.

Bilgen, A. N., G. Coşkun, Z. Bilgen, N. Yüzbaşıoğlu, and A. Kuru 2011 Seyitömer Höyüğü, 2009 Yılı Kazısı. *Kazı Sonuçları Toplantısı* 32(1):367–380.

Bilgen, A. N., G. Coşkun, Z. Bilgen, A. Kuru, N. Yüzbaşıoğlu, F. Ç. Özcan, S. Çırakoğlu, and S. Silek 2012 Seyitömer Höyüğü, 2010 Yılı Kazısı *Kazı Sonuçları Toplantısı* 33(1):233–255.

Bilgen, A. N., G. Coşkun, Z. Bilgen, N. Ünan, S. Silek, S. Çırakoğlu, F. Ç. Özcan, A. Kuru, and Z. Kuzu 2013 Seyitömer Höyüğü, 2011 Yılı Kazısı. *Kazı Sonuçları Toplantısı* 34(1):201–216.

Bilgen, A. N. 2013 *Seyitömer Höyük Kazısı Ön Raporu (2011–2012)*. Dumlupınar Üniversitesi Fen-Edebiyat Fakültesi Arkeoloji Bölümü, Kütahya.

Efe, T. 1990 1988 Yılında Kütahya, Bilecik ve Eskişehir İllerinde Yapılan Yüzey Araştırmaları. *Anadolu Araştırmaları* XI:1–19.

Efe, T. 1991 1989 Yılında Kütahya, Bilecik ve Eskişehir İllerinde Yapılan Yüzey Araştırmaları. *Araştırma Sonuçları Toplantısı* VIII:163–177.

Efe, T. 1992 1990 Yılında Kütahya, Bilecik ve Eskişehir İllerinde Yapılan Yüzey Araştırmaları. *IX. Araştırma Sonuçları Toplantısı* IX:561–583.

Efe, T. 1993a 1991 Yılında Kütahya, Bilecik ve Eskişehir İllerinde Yapılan Yüzey Araştırmaları. *Araştırma Sonuçları Toplantısı* X:345–364.

Efe, T. 1993b Chalcolithic Pottery from the Mounds Aslanapa (Kütahya) and Kınık (Bilecik). *Anatolica* XIX:19–31.

Efe, T. 1994 1992 Yılında Kütahya, Bilecik ve Eskişehir İllerinde Yapılan Yüzey Araştırmaları. *Araştırma Sonuçları Toplantısı* XI:571–592.

Efe, T. 1995a 1993 Yılında Kütahya, Bilecik ve Eskişehir İllerinde Yapılan Yüzey Araştırmaları. *Araştırma Sonuçları Toplantısı* XII:245–266.

Efe, T. 1995b İçbatı Anadolu'da İki Neolitik Yerleşme: Fındık Kayabaşı ve Akmakça. In *İ. Metin Akyurt ve Bahattin Devam Anı Kitabı*, edited by A. Erkanal et al., pp. 105–114. Arkeoloji ve Sanat Yayınları, İstanbul.

Jackson, M. P. C., J. N. Postgate, and T. E. Şerifoğlu 2013 Kilise Tepe 2011 Yılı Kazıları. *Kazı Sonuçları Toplantısı* 34 2:5–24.

Kamil, T. 1982 Yortan Cemetery in the Early Bronze Age of Western Anatolia. BAR International Series (145), Oxford.

Mellink, M. J. 1969 Excavations at Karataş-Semayük in Lycia, 1968. *American Journal of Archaeology* 74(3):319–331.

Türkteki, S. Ü. and B. Hürmüzlü 2007 *Sadberk Hanım Müzesi Koleksiyonu, Eski Çağ'da İçki ve Sunu Kapları*. Vehbi Koç Vakfı Sadberk Hanım Müzesi, İstanbul.

Chapter Twenty

Seyitömer Höyük
Early Bronze Age III Platters

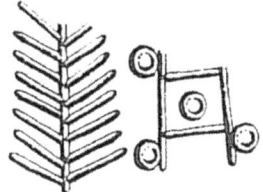

Asuman Kapuci*

Introduction

Seyitömer Höyük is a settlement located in Kütahya province, near the town of Seyitömer. The Early Bronze Age III period, which is called layer V, constitutes our study subject. Within this layer at Seyitömer Höyük, there are three phases: VA, VB, and VC, from youngest to oldest.

Seyitömer Höyük is located in Inland Western Anatolia and has gained an important place in the cultural heritage of Early Bronze Age Anatolia, in terms of architecture and in terms of the pottery characteristics that we evaluate in our study. When considering the relatively poor knowledge of this region, it can be said that the importance of this study is clear in the context of the architecture and artifacts of the Early Bronze Age III period especially in Western Anatolia.

The form studied has been evaluated with specimens found in the period 2008–2012 of the Seyitömer Höyük excavation project. The platters identified in all three phases of the Early Bronze Age III (VA, VB, VC) were investigated considering the slip color groups and typological characteristics.

Surface Properties

In this chapter, operations applied to the surface of the platters of Seyitömer Höyük EBA III are examined. Accordingly, these processes are divided into two subgroups:

---

*Arş. Gör. Asuman Kapuci, Dumlupınar Üniversitesi, Fen-Edebiyat Fakültesi, Arkeoloji Bölümü, asumankuru@gmail.com

1. coated ware surface
2. uncoated ware surface

Almost all of the Seyitömer Höyük EBA III platters are coated ware. There are only four uncoated groups in the study groups.

The burnishing property of surface of the platters found was investigated in two groups:

1. less burnished ware examples
2. unburnished ware examples

Ninety-eight percent of the examined platters were identified as unburnished, and 2 percent as less burnished. The color groups of the less-burnished ware group are as follows: red, orange, grey, and light brown.

ORANGE-SLIPPED GROUP

The earliest phase of Seyitömer Höyük, EBA III, Phase C, was determined to be 8 percent; the second phase, Phase B, was 36 percent; the final phase, Phase A, contained 56 percent. All samples were coated except one of the examples, and some of the samples are less burnished, but most of samples are unburnished. As for the inclusions, they consisted of: sand, mica, small stone; sand, mica, small stone, lime, chamotte; sand, mica, small stone, lime; sand, mica, limestone, chamotte; sand, mica, lime; sand, mica, chamotte; sand, small stone. Paste colors have been identified as brown, pinkish-brown, orange, cream, and light brown.

BROWN-SLIPPED GROUP

The earliest phase of Seyitömer Höyük EBA III, Phase C, was determined to be 6 percent, the second phase, Phase B, contained 54 percent, and the final phase, Phase A, contained 40 percent. All samples were coated and all are unburnished. Inclusion distribution was found to be: sand, mica, small stone; sand, mica, small stone, chamotte, lime; sand, mica, small stone, lime; sand, mica, lime; sand, chamotte, lime; sand, mica, chamotte; sand lime; sand chamotte. Paste colors have been identified as brown, pinkish-brown, light brown, orange, cream, grey, and light grey.

REDDISH-BROWN-SLIPPED GROUP

The earliest phase of Seyitömer Höyük EBA III, Phase C, was determined to be 3 percent, the second phase, Phase B, contains 52 percent, and the final phase, Phase A, contains 45 percent. All samples were coated and all are unburnished. The inclusions consisted of: sand, mica, small stone; sand, lime; sand, small stone, lime, chamotte. Paste colors have been identified as brown, pink coffee, orange, reddish, and light brown.

Light Brown–Slipped Group

In the earliest phase of Seyitömer Höyük EBA III, Phase C, this color group was determined to be 0 percent, in the second phase, Phase B, it was 38 percent, and the final phase, Phase A, contained 62 percent. All samples except two of the group were coated, some samples are less burnished, but most of samples are unburnished. It was found that they had sand, mica, and small stones added. Paste colors have been identified as orange, light brown, pinkish-brown, brown, reddish-brown, and grey.

Dark-Brown-Slipped Group

The earliest phase of Seyitömer Höyük EBA III, Phase C was determined to be 0 percent, the second phase, Phase B, contained 40 percent, and the final phase, Phase A, contained 60 percent. All samples were coated and all are unburnished. It was found that they have sand, mica, small stones added. Paste colors have been identified as brown, pinkish-brown, orange, and dark brown.

Red-Slipped Group

In the earliest phase of Seyitömer Höyük EBA III, Phase C was determined to be 0 percent, the second phase, Phase B, contained 50 percent, and the final phase, Phase A, contained 50 percent. All samples were coated, except one of the examples, and some samples are less burnished, but most of samples are unburnished. It was found that they have sand, mica, and small stone added. Paste colors have been identified as brown and pinkish brown.

Grey-Slipped Group

The earliest phase of Seyitömer Höyük EBA III, the Phase C was determined to be 0 percent, the second phase, Phase B, contained 50 percent, and the final phase, Phase A, contained 50 percent. All samples were coated except one of the examples, and some samples are less burnished, but most of samples are unburnished. It was found that they have sand, mica, small stone added. Paste colors have been identified as brown.

Plain Group

The earliest phase of Seyitömer Höyük EBA III, Phase C, was determined to be 0 percent, the second phase, Phase B, contained 100 percent, and the final phase, Phase A, contained 0 percent. All samples were coated and all of the samples are unburnished. It was found that they have sand, mica, small stone added. Paste colors have been identified as cream.

Inclusions

The inclusions added to the paste of Seyitömer Höyük EBA III platters were placed into six groups:

1. sand, mica, small stone
2. sand, mica, small stone, chamotte, lime
3. sand, mica, small stone, chamotte
4. sand, mica, small stone, lime
5. sand, mica, chamotte
6. sand, mica, and lime

Colors of Pastes

While examining the color groups, typical paste colors for each color group are determined. Paste color was found to be partially correlated with color groups. The common paste color in Seyitömer Höyük EBA III platters was identified as an orange. Paste colors are specified in each color group. Forty-nine percent of the Seyitömer Höyük EBA III platters were found to be orange, 29 percent brown, 11 percent reddish-brown, 5 percent light brown, 3 percent dark brown, 1 percent red, 1 percent grey, 1 percent plain group.

Typological Evaluation

Deep Platters

Everted Rimmed Deep Platters

In this form group, slip groups were 67 percent orange and 33 percent brown. As for the distribution of the said form according to the phases, Phase C is 0 percent, Phase B is 67 percent, and Phase A is 33 percent.

Extroverted Rimmed Deep Platters

In this form group, slip groups were found to be 50 percent orange, 32 percent brown, 8 percent reddish-brown, 6 percent light brown, 3 percent dark brown, 1 percent grey, 1 percent lean. As for the distribution of the said form according to the phases, Phase C is 50 percent, Phase B is 44 percent, and Phase A is 53 percent.

Shallow Platters

Everted Rimmed Shallow Platters

Brown, which is a slip group in this form group, was detected by 100 percent. As for the distribution of the said form according to the phases, Phase C is 50 percent, Phase B is 0 percent, and Phase A is 50 percent.

Extroverted Rimmed Shallow Platters

In this form group, slip groups were found to be 47 percent orange, 21 percent reddish-brown, 19 percent brown, 6 percent dark brown, 4 percent light brown, 2 percent red, 2 percent grey. As for the distribution of the said form according to the phases, Phase C is 13 percent, Phase B is 43 percent, and Phase A is 44 percent.

Flattened Rimmed Shallow Platters

Light brown, which is a color group in this form group, were identified by 100 percent. As for the distribution of the said form according to the phases, Phase C is 0 percent, Phase B is 0 percent, and Phase A is 100 percent.

Platter-Making Techniques

When we look at platter-making techniques of Seyitömer Höyük EBA III platters, we see that they are handmade and wheel-made. Three of the parts and all platters evaluated have been found to be wheel-made and the others are handmade. It is also understood that wheel-made materials belong to the plain color group.

Decorations

When analyzed according to the decoration elements of the Seyitömer Höyük EBA III platters, they can be divided into three groups.

1. incised decoration
2. red-washed decoration
3. relief decoration

Incised Decoration

We see the said decoration mostly at bottom part. Decoration elements which can be considered as a sign of the potter emerge with the mark "+."

RED-WASHED DECORATION

The decoration seen both in the platters and in the bottom parts is applied with primer. In motifs applied to the interior of the platters, points filling between water waves are used. The motifs applied below the bottom are seen as three-, four-, five-point form and "+."

RELIEF DECORATION

The decoration applied to the body portion of the platters consists of spinnerets in relief.

Conclusion

Color groups of the Seyitömer Höyük Early Bronze Age III platters were examined as a form typology. By considering the typological similarity and the geographic proximity, a comparison to Seyitömer Höyük will be made. As a result of the evaluations performed, Seyitömer Höyük Early Bronze Age III platters have been found to show more similarity with the platters in Troia.

It is found that the forms in the deep platters group have similarities with Troia (Blegen et al. 1951: Lev. 62 34.283, Lev. 62 34.305, Lev. 62 37.1101, Lev. 63 34.838, Lev. 63 33.177, Lev. 63 34.275, Lev. 63 33.213.), Beycesultan (Lloyd and Mellaart 1962: Lev. IX 2, 3) and Küllüoba (Türkteki 2004: Lev. 13.2, Lev. 3.4.) settlements. The shallow platters evaluated are found to have similarities with Troia (Blegen et al. 1951: Lev. 62 34.352, Lev. 62 37.1099, Lev. 62 34.340.) Beycesultan (Lloyd and Mellaart 1962: Lev. IX.1) and Küllüoba (Türkteki 2004: Lev. 12 5, 6, Lev. 13, 1, 3; Lev. 33.4.). General conclusions were drawn in the study by typological distinctions by dividing into color groups. These results can be summarized as follows: It is understood that the largest group is orange in the work pieces. In terms of form typology of platters, the largest group is deep platters. The distribution of the dish artifacts was shown to be 54 percent in sites and 46 percent in the landfill in grid squares. It is seen that platters found in the sites are more prevalent in storage and living spaces (Figure 20.4, 20.5, 20.6, 20.7, 20.8; Bilgen et al. 2011:532, 537, 538, 540, 542; Bilgen et al. 2013: 139, 148, 191). They have been seen as stacked in the warehouse, and in earthenware jars. As for the distribution of Seyitömer Höyük EBA III platters according to the phases, Phase A is 50 percent, Phase B is 44 percent, and Phase C is 6 percent (Figure 20.1, 20.2, 20.3). The fact that the Phase C has not yet been fully excavated is a factor.

A factor that should be highlighted finally is that the group called Troia A2 platters and the red-coated ware goods were not uncovered in Seyitömer Höyük. Also, platters showing mostly local elements seem to have served in daily use.

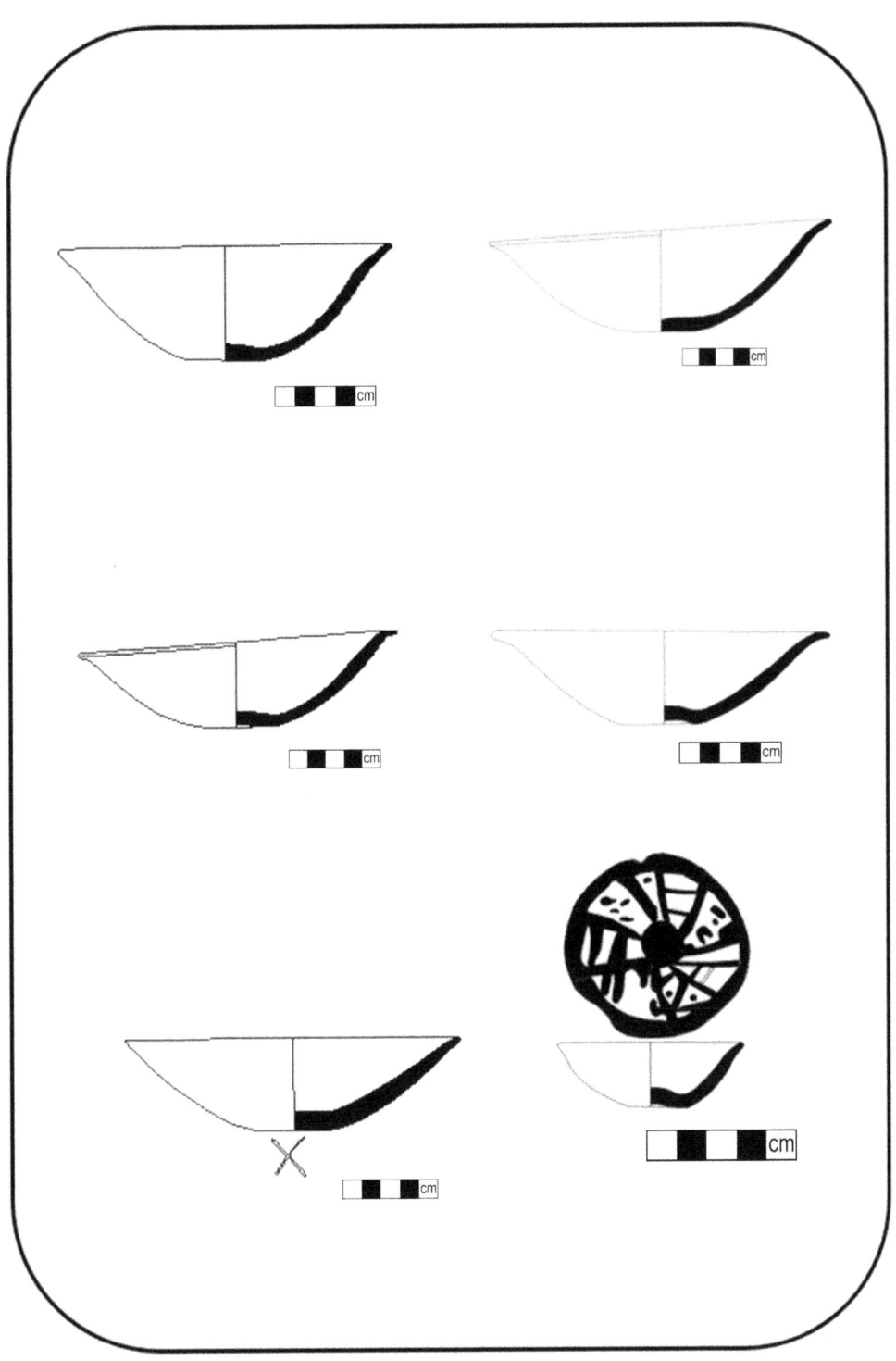

FIGURE 20.1. The Platters—Phase VA (Seyitömer Höyük excavation archive).

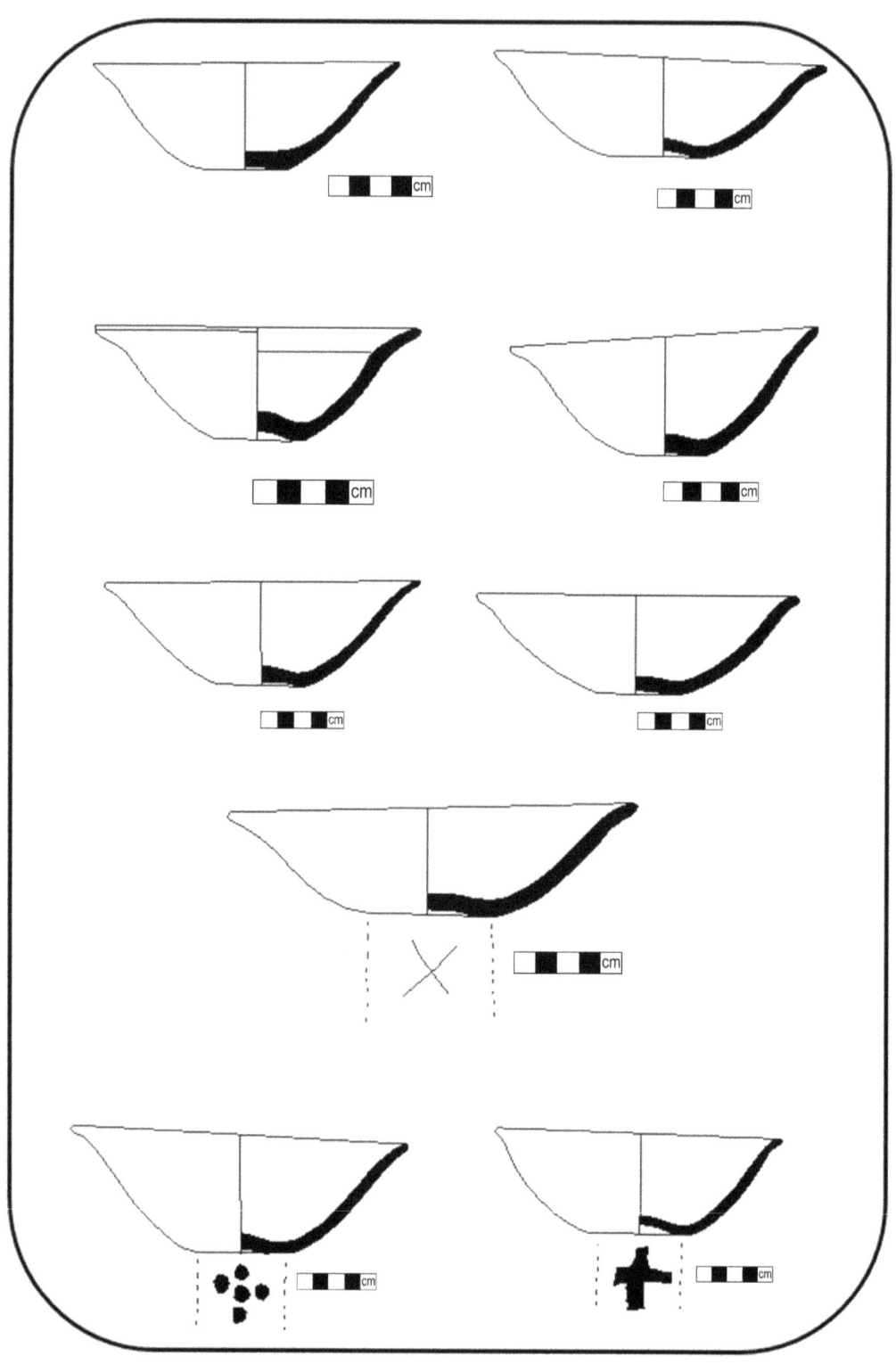

FIGURE 20.2. The Platters—Phase VB (Seyitömer Höyük excavation archive).

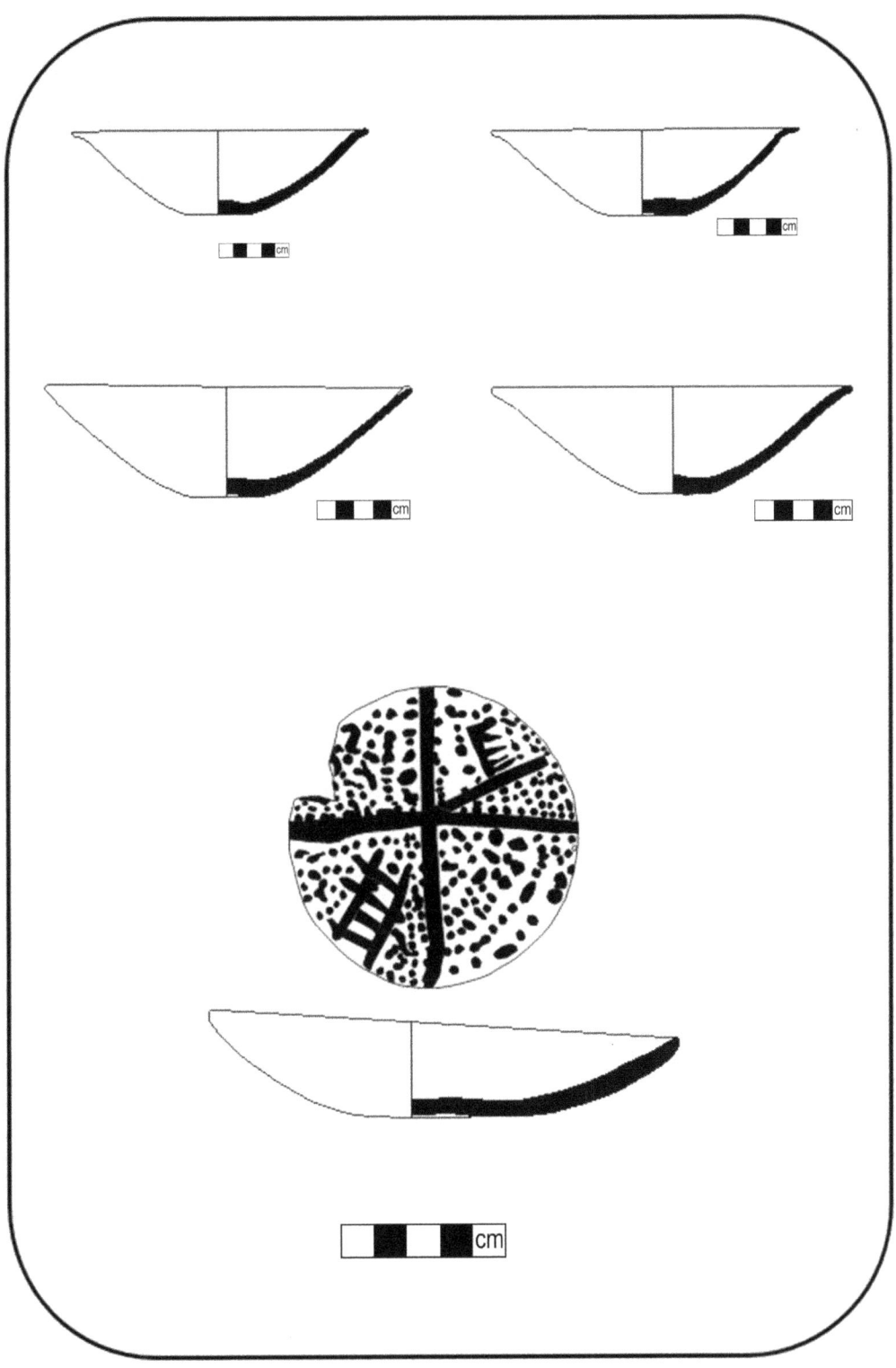

FIGURE 20.3. The Platters—Phase VC (Seyitömer Höyük excavation archive).

FIGURE 20.4. Context of the Platters (Seyitömer Höyük excavation archive).

FIGURE 20.5. Context of the Platters (Seyitömer Höyük excavation archive).

FIGURE 20.6. Context of the Platters (Seyitömer Höyük excavation archive).

FIGURE 20.7. Context of the Platters (Seyitömer Höyük excavation archive).

FIGURE 20.8. Context of the Platters (Seyitömer Höyük excavation archive).

REFERENCES CITED

Bilgen, A. N., G. Coşkun, Z. Bilgen, A. Kapuci (Kuru), N. Yüzbaşıoğlu, S. Silek, S. Çırakoğlu, M. B. Akalın, and B. Dikmen 2011 *Seyitömer Höyük Kazısı Ön Raporu (2006–2010)*. Dumlupınar University, Üç Mart, Kütahya.

Bilgen, A. N., G. Coşkun, Z. Bilgen, N. Ünan, S. Silek, S. Çırakoğlu, F. Ç.Özcan, A. Kapuci (Kuru), Z. Kuzu, M. B. Akalın, and B. Dikmen 2013 *Seyitömer Höyük Kazısı Ön Raporu (2011–2012)*. Dumlupınar University, Üç Mart, Kütahya.

Blegen, C. W., J. L. Caskey, and M. Rawson 1951 *Troy II: The Third, Fourth, and Fifth Settlements*. Princeton University Press, Princeton.

Lloyd, S., and J. Mellaart 1962 *Beycesultan I. The Chalcolithic and Early Bronze Age Levels*. British Institute of Archaeology at Ankara, London.

Türkteki, M. 2004 *Külloba Erken Tunç Çağ III Çanak Çömleği*. Unpublished Master's Dissertation, Istanbul University, Social Sciences Institute.

CHAPTER TWENTY-ONE

A Group of Stamp Seals from the İzmir Archaeology Museum

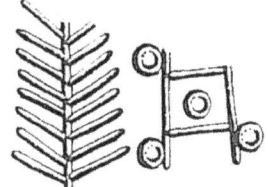

Halil Hamdi Ekiz,*
Neşide Gençer,**
Selma Kaya***

The following is a study of the stamp seals with inventory numbers 3724, 3725, 5586, 21839, 24677, 26315, and 26316 from the İzmir Archeology Museum.[1] The seals with inv. nos. 21839 and 24677 were brought into the museum by purchasing, but the others by means of confiscation. In the inventory registers, there is no information about the locations where these items were unearthed. All of the stamp seals were made of stone.

We can examine the stamp seals from İzmir Archeology Museum under the following groups:

1. the cross-motif separating the imprint side of the seal into four parts;
2. the triangular motif;
3. the motifs consisting of lines;
4. the point motif;
5. the depiction of an antelope;
6. the depiction of a deer;
7. the vegetal decoration resembling a branch and leaf.

---

*Halil Hamdi Ekiz, Arkeolog MA, Çiğli-İzmir, e-posta: halilhamdiekiz@gmail.com.
**Neşide Gençer Arkeolog MA, Kubaba Dergisi Sorumlusu ve Sahibi, e-posta: kubabadergi@hotmail.com.
***Selma Kaya, Arkeolog, İzmir Arkeoloji Müzesi, slmkaya35@hotmail.com.

1. The Cross-Motif Separating the Face of the Seal into Four Parts: The imprint side of the stamp seals with inv. nos. 24677 and 26315 are divided into four parts by two lines cutting each other. This kind of seal appears in Anatolia from the Early Neolithic Period. The imprint sides of some stamp seals from Bademağacı (Early Neolithic period [Umurtak 2000:3] and Early Bronze Age [Duru and Umurtak 2000:644]); Köşk Höyük II (Early Chalcolithic period [Özkan 2001:18, 22]); Yumuktepe XVII (Middle Chalcolithic period, Halaf Phase [Carter et al. 1997:176]), Domuztepe (Halaf phase [Carter et al. 1997:176, Figure 5]); Amuk E (Late Chalcolithic period and Late Uruk-Cemdet Nasr period [Braidwood and Braidwood 1960:130, Figure 101]); Alişar (Late Chalcolithic period [Osten 1937:81, Figure 87] and Early Bronze Age [Osten 1937:183]); Elmalı Karataş (Early Bronze Age II-III [Mellink 1067:71; Warner 1994:204]); Etiyokuşu (Early Bronze Age [Goldman 1956:237, 392]); Gözlükule (Early Bronze Age II [Kansu 1940: Figure 78]); Karaoğlan (Early Bronze Age [Özgüç 1987]); Koçumbeli (Early Bronze Age [Tezcan 1966:7]): Tepecik (Early Bronze Age [Esin 1972:145]); Troya III (Early Bronze Age [Schliemann 1880:415]) and Kuşluca (Early Bronze Age [Çokbanker 1974:34]) are also divided into four parts, and these divisions were decorated with various geometrical motifs. The imprint side of stamp seals from Yarimtepe (Hassuna-Samarra period [Wickede 1990:80]) and Tepe Gawra XIX (Halaf phase [Tobler 1950:179]) are divided into four parts, as well.

2. The Triangular Motif: The seal with inv. no. 26316 has a triangular motif. A number of seals with the triangular motif were unearthed in Arpachiyah (Chalcolithic Halaf Phase [Mallowan and Rose 1935:90–92, 95]), Kusura B (Early Bronze Age [Ekiz 2011:22; Lamb 1938]), and Tepe Hisar (beginning of Early Bronze Age [Yule 1982:11]).

3. The Motifs Consisting of Lines: The seals with inv. nos. 24677 and 26315 were decorated with linear motifs. The stamp seals from Hacılar II (Early Chalcolithic Period [Mellaart 1970:164]); Köşk Höyük II (Early Chalcolithic Period [Özkan 2001:18, 22]); Değirmentepe (Late Chalcolithic Ubeid Period [Wickede 1990:173–174]); Alaca Höyük (Early Bronze Age [Koşay 1951:49]); Alişar (Early Bronze Age [Osten 1937:183]); Elmalı Karataş (Early Bronze Age [Warner 1994:204]); Eti Yokuşu (Early Bronze Age [Kansu 1940:87]); Karaoğlan (Early Bronze Age [Özgüç 1987a:26, 27, 30, 31]); Koçumbeli (Early Bronze Age [Tezcan 1966:7]) and Troya IV (Early Bronze Age [Schliemann 1880:561]); the one that was obtained after the Kusura excavation (Early Bronze Age [Ekiz 2011:23–24]), and the stamp seals from Kuşluca (Early Bronze Age [Çokbanker 1974:34]) were decorated with linear motifs. Furthermore, the seal imprints from Tepe Gawra XIX (Halaf phase [Tobler 1950:179]), Susa (Susa I, beginning fourth millennium B.C. [Amiet 1973:5]), Chagar Bazar (Early Cemdet Nasr Period [Mallowan 1947:132]), the stamp seals from Tepe Hissar (Late Chalcolithic [Yule 1982:11]), and the seal impressions from Lerna (Early Helladic Period [Bıçakçı 2012:79]) also include linear motifs.

4. The Point Motif: The seal with inv. no. 26216 has a pointed decoration. A number of seal stamps from Tepecik-Çiftlik III (Neolithic period [Bıçakçı 2012:79]), Köşk

Höyük III (Late Neolithic period [Özkan 2001:15–16; Silistreli 1986:130]), Samsat (Early Chalcolithic Period [Özgüç 1987b:430]); Karaoğlan (Old Bronze Age [Özgüç 1987a:31]), Koçumbeli (Old Bronze Age [Tezcan 1966:7]), Kusura B (Old Bronze Age [Ekiz 2011:22; Lamb 1937:30]); Troya III (Old Bronze Age [Schliemann 1880:415]), Kuşluca (Old Bronze Age [Çokbanker 1974:34]), Tell Sabi Abyad (Late Neolithic period [Akkermans and Miere 1992:11]), and Geraki (Old Helladic period [Weingarten et al. 1999:366–367]), and also an impression of the seal from Hamoukar'da (M.Ö.4300 [Reichel 2009:85]) were decorated with the point motif.

5. The Depiction of an Antelope: The seal, inv. no. 3725, includes a portrayal of an antelope. However, one each seal impression from Cemdet Nasr (Late Uruk period [Matthews 1992:19]), Değirmentepe (Late Chalcolithic period [Esin 1985:260]), and also a stamp seal from Tilbeşhöyük (Late Chalcolithic period [Fuensanta and Mısır 1990:231]), Tepe Gawra XI/X A and VIII (Early and Middle Uruk period [Rothman 2002]), another seal imprint from Tepe Yahya (third millennium B.C. [Lamberg-Karlovsky 2001]), a stamp seal from Alişar (Old Bronze Age [Osten 1937:183]), and a cylindrical seal from Arslantepe (Old Bronze Age I [Frangipane 2012:251]) were decorated with an animal depiction, interpreted as an antelope.

6. The Depiction of a Deer: On the seals, inv. nos. 5586 and 21839, a depiction of a deer can also be seen clearly. The depiction of a deer also appears on a number of seal impressions from Tell Sabi Abyad (Late Neolithic period [Akkermans and Duistermaat 1996:22]), Cemdet Nasr (Late Uruk Period [Matthews 1992:19]), Değirmentepe (Late Chalcolithic period [Esin 1985:261]), and Norşuntepe (Late Chalcolithic period [Hauptmann 1976:55]). Furthermore, some seal impressions from Tepe Gawra XII and VIII (Late Ubeid–Middle Uruk period [Rothman 2002]) and on a stamp seal from Tell Zeidan (Late Chalcolithic period [Stein 2010:134]) also were decorated with depictions of deer.

7. The Vegetal Decoration Resembling a Branch and Leaf. The seals with inv. nos. 21839 and 3724 have the vegetal decoration resembling a branch and leaf. A seal impression from Değirmentepe (Late Chalcolithic period [Esin 1985:260]) also was decorated with stylized branch and leaf motifs.

CATALOG

A Stamp Seal with Inv. No. 24677 (Figure 21.1): This seal was purchased in 2007 by M. Halil Tatar. It was made of black stone and it was polished, as well. It measures 2.2 cm in length, 1.8 cm in width, and 0.6 cm in depth. The seal has been well preserved. At the point where the short raising handle attaches to the base, a horizontal string hole was opened. The rectangular imprint side of the seal with the slightly rounded corners is divided into four divisions by the intersecting lines in the cross-shape. It seems that there are parallel vertical lines both above and below a horizontal line in one of these divisions; in another division, a short horizontal line cuts one of two vertical lines. Two

FIGURE 21.1. Inv. No. 24677.

parallel vertical lines were placed in another division. And finally, there are two parallel horizontal lines in the last division.

The ones that most resemble this decoration type appear on two stamp seals from Koçumbeli (Early Bronze Age [Tezcan 1966:7]) and Kusura (Early Bronze Age [Ekiz 2011:23–24]). The seal is probably dated to the Early Bronze Age.

A Stamp Seal with Inv. No. 26315 (Figure 21.2): The artifact was brought into the museum by confiscation in 2010. The seal was made of black basalt and it was polished. It measures 3.9 cm in length, 3 cm in width, and 0.6 cm in depth. The seal was slightly rubbed off: one of its sides and the upper side of the string hole is broken and missing. At the point where an elliptical-shaped raising handle attaches to the base, a horizontal string hole is found. The elliptical imprint side of the seal is divided into four parts by two crossing lines, and at the point where these lines cross exactly, a point profile was arranged. Each of these divisions was decorated with lines following each other in a parallel way.

The artifact resembles another seal from Tepecik (Early bronze Age III [Esin 1970:145]). The seal is dated to Early Bronze Age.

A Stamp Seal with Inv. No. 26316 (Figure 21.3): The seal in question was brought into the museum by confiscation in 1959. It was made of dark grey serpentine, and the stone was polished. It has a 2.5 cm length, 1.7 cm. width, and 1.5 cm depth. The seal has been well preserved. A horizontal string hole is found at the point where a thick raising handle attaches to the base. Three intertwined triangle motifs appear on the imprint side of the seal, and a point motif is found in the middle of the inner triangle.

FIGURE 21.2. Inv. No. 26315.

The point motif on the seal in question resembles the one on the seal from Koçumbeli (Early Bronze Age [Tezcan 1966:7]). The seal is probably dated to the Early Bronze Age.

FIGURE 21.3. Inv. No. 26316.

A Stamp Seal with Inv. No. 3725 (Figure 21.4): The artifact was brought into the museum by confiscation in 1959. It was made of dark grey stone, and it was polished, as well. It is 2.5 cm in length, 1.9 cm in width, and 0.9 cm in depth. The seal is well preserved. A horizontal string hole was opened at the point where the roof-shaped short handle attaches to the base. An animal depiction resembling an antelope fills the imprint side of the rectangular seal. The horns of this animal are long; its facial features resembling a rectangle aren't clear; its neck is long and it has a thick tail and thin legs.

The animal depiction decorating the seal resembles the one on the seal impression from Aslantepe (Early Bronze Age I [Frangipane 2012:251]). We think that this seal must be dated to the Early Bronze Age.

A Stamp Seal with Inv. No. 5586 (Figure 21.5): The seal was brought into the museum by confiscation in 1965. It was made of black stone, and the stone was polished. It is 2.4 cm in length, 2.2 cm in width, and 1.6 cm in depth. The seal has been well preserved. At the point where the flattened spherical handle attaches to the base, a horizontal string hole is found. A stylistic portrayal of a deer appears on the rounded imprint side of the seal. The torso and horns of the animal are thin and long, and its legs are long and thin, but it has short and thick tail.

The depiction of a deer on this artifact resembles the figure of a deer on the seal impression from Norşuntepe (Late Chalcolithic Period [Hauptmann 1976:55]).

A Stamp Seal with Inv. No. 21839 (Figure 21.6): This artifact was purchased in 2002. It was made of black stone, and the stone was polished. This stamp seal is 2.5 cm in diameter and 1.1 cm in depth. Its imprint side was rubbed off, and its corners were

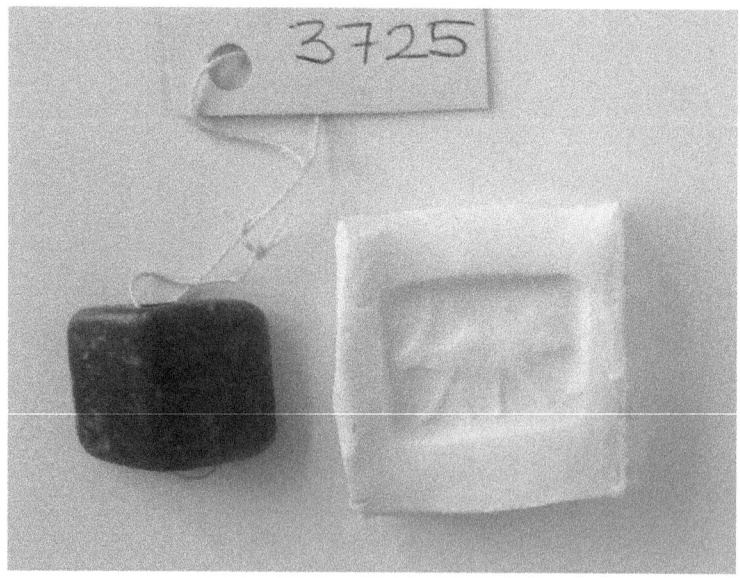

FIGURE 21.4. Inv. No. 3725.

FIGURE 21.5. Inv. No. 5586.

FIGURE 21.6. Inv. No. 21839.

broken slightly. At the point where the flattened spherical handle attaches to the base, a horizontal string hole was opened. A deer under a branch motif decorates the rounded imprint side of the seal. It seems that a star motif also appears just under the legs of deer. The thin and long horns of deer in question are slightly curved. The sharp pointed facial lines of the deer aren't clear enough. Its torso is long, and it has long and thin legs, but its tail is very short.

The depiction of the deer on this artifact resembles the seal impression from Norşuntepe (Late Chalcolithic period [Hauptmann 1976:55]). We suggest that this seal is dated to the Late Chalcolithic period.

A Stamp Seal with Inv. No. 3724 (Figure 21.7): It was made of black stone and the stone was polished. The seal has a 2.2 cm. width, 1.8 cm. length, and 0.9 cm depth. The imprint side of the seal was rubbed off in some degree. The upper side is a little bulged and a string hole is found in the middle of the seal. A decoration including stylized lines resembling a branch and leaf adorns the imprint side of the rectangular seal with slightly rounded corners.

The decoration resembling a branch and leaf on this artifact is reminiscent of the motifs decorating a seal impression from Değirmentepe (Late Chalcolithic period [Esin 1985]). We suggest that this seal must be dated to the Late Chalcolithic period.

However, since the seals as the main theme of this paper were brought to the İzmir Archeology Museum by means of purchasing and confiscation, their findspots haven't been identified exactly.

FIGURE 21.7. Inv. No. 3724.

Discussion

The geometrical motifs that we have examined in this paper are similar in appearance to the motifs on many seals and seal impressions from excavations in Anatolia. These kinds of decorations appear extensively on the seals, and their impressions are dated to the Late Chalcolithic period and Old Bronze age. The animal portrayals and vegetal ornaments are also found extensively in the seals and seal impressions dated to the Late Chalcolithic period.

We suggest that the aforementioned seals with inv. nos. 24677, 26315, 26316, and 3725 must be dated to the Old Bronze Age. In addition to them, since the ones with inv. nos. 3724, 5586, and 21839 resemble the seals dated to the Late Chalcolithic period, we think that they are contemporary with the latter group.

Seals were used in Anatolia from the Neolithic period. A group of seals from the Early Bronze Age were discovered during the archeological surveys and excavations in Central and Central-western Anatolia. In Western Anatolia, the seals decorated with the geometric patterns on their printing areas from the Early Bronze II period were unearthed in Limantepe. Another seal with a circular pattern dated to the same period was found in a grave in Baklatepe recently (Anadol 2011:291).

In Central-western Anatolia, seven seals dated to Early Bronze III period were discovered during the excavations in Küllüoba. The printing areas of these seals were decorated with geometric patterns (Öner 2009:82).

During the excavations in Höyüktepe, Kütahya, a group of seals including the stone and earthen ones from the EBA were unearthed (Türkcan and Beyoğlu 2015:431–445). Earthen seals from the EBA were discovered during the excavations in Çiledir Höyük, near the same town (Türktüzün et al. 2011).

However, since the seals that are the main focus of this paper were brought to the İzmir Archeology Museum by means of purchasing and confiscation, their findspots aren't known exactly.

Note

1. We thank Mrs. Ayşegül Tuğçe Ekiz who took the photographs of these seals.

References Cited

Akkermans, P. M. M. G., and M. L. Miere 1992 The 1988 Excavations at Tell Sabi Abyad, a Later Neolithic Village in Northern Syria. *American Journal of Archaeology* 96:1–22.
Akkermans, P. M. M. G., and K. Duistermaat 1996 Of Storage and Nomads. The Sealings from Late Neolithic, Sabi Abyad, Syria. *Paléorient* 22(2):17–44.
Amiet, P. 1973 Glyptique Élamite, à Propos de Nouveaux Documents. *Arts Asiatiques* 26:3–45.
Anadol, A. 2011 *Karşıdan Karşıya M.Ö.3 Binde Kiklad Adaları ve Batı Anadolu*. Sakıp Sabancı Müzesi, İstanbul.

Bıçakçı, E. 2012 Tepecik-Çiftlik Kazısı 2012 Yılı Çalışmaları. *33. Kazı Sonuçları Toplantısı 1. Cilt,* 69–89.

Braidwood, R. J., and L. S. Braidwood 1960 *Excavations in the Plain of Antioch I: The Earlier Assemblages Phases A-J.* OIP 61, Chicago, Illinois.

Çokbanker, E. 1974 Beyşehir Kuşluca Köyü Buluntuları. *Türk Arkeoloji Dergisi* XXI(2):19–39.

Duru, R., and G. Umurtak 2007 Bademağacı Kazıları 2005. *28. Kazı Sonuçları Toplantısı 1. Cilt,* 639–646.

Ekiz, H. H. 2012 Kusura Mühürleri. Kusura Seals. *Kubaba Yıl 8 Sayı* 18:19–28.

Esin, U. 1972 Tepecik Kazısı, 1970. Tepecik Excavations, 1970. *Keban Projesi 1970 Çalışmaları. Keban Project 1970 Activities,* Orta Doğu Teknik Üniversitesi Keban Projesi Yayınları, Seri I No. 3, Ankara.

Esin, U. 1985 Some Small Finds from Chalcolithic Occupation at Değirmentepe Malatya in Eastern Turkey. *Studi di Palelnologla in Onore di Salvatore M. Puglisi, Univ. di Roma, La Saplenze,* 253–263.

Frangipane, M. 2012 The Collapse of the 4th Millennium Centralised Systemmat Arslantepe and the Far-reaching Changes in 3rd Millennium Societies. *Origini* XXXIV:237–260.

Garstang, J. 1953 *Prehistoric Mersin. Yümük Tepe in Southern Turkey.* Oxford University Press, Oxford.

Goldman, H. 1956 *Excavations at Gözlükule, Tarsus, Vol. 2. From the Neolithic Through the Bronze Age.* Princeton University Press, Princeton.

Hauptmann, H. 1976 Norşun Tepe Kazıları, 1972. Die Grabungen auf dem Norşun-Tepe, 1972, *Keban Projesi 1972 Çalışmaları. Keban Project1972 Activities,* Orta Doğu Teknik Üniversitesi Keban Projesi Yayınları, Ankara 5:42–59, 71–90.

Kansu, Ş. A. 1940 Türk Tarih Kurumu Tarafından Yapılan Etiyokuşu Hafriyatı Raporu (1937). Les Fouilles D'Etiyokuşu (1937). Türk Tarih Kurumu Yayını V. Seri No. 3, Ankara.

Koşay, H. Z. 1951 Türk Tarih Kurumu Tarafından Yapılan Alaca Höyük Kazısı. 1937–1939 daki Çalışmalara ve Keşiflere ait İlk Rapor. Les Fouilles d'Alaca Höyük, Entreprises par la Société d'Histoire Turque. Rapport Préliminaire sur les Travaux en 1937–1939. Türk Tarih Kurumu Yayınları V. Seri No. 5, Ankara.

Lamb, W. 1937 Excavations at Kusura near Afyon Karahisar. *Archaeologia* LXXXVI:1–64.

Lamb, W. 1938 Excavations at Kusura Near Afyon Karahisar: II. *Archaeologia* LXXXVII:218–273.

Lamberg-Karlovsky, C. C. 2001 *Excavations at Tepe Yahya, Iran, 1967–1975, The Third Millenium.* Harvard University Press, Cambridge.

Mallowan, M. E. L. 1947 Excavations at Brak and Chagar Bazar. *Iraq* 9:1–258.

Mallowan, M. E. L. and J. C. Rose 1935 Prehistoric Assyria, The Excavations at Tall Arpachiyah 1933. *Iraq* 2(1):1–178.

Matthews, R. J. 1992 Defining the Style of the Period: Jemdet Nasr 1926–28. *Iraq* 54:1–34.

Mellaart, J. 1970 *Excavations at Hacılar I-II.* The British Institute of Archaeology at Ankara, Edinburgh University Press, Edinburgh.

Mellink, M. J. 1967 Excavations at Karataş-Semayük in Lycia, 1966. *American Journal of Archaeology* 71(3):251–267.

Osten, H. H. von der 1937 *The Alishar Hüyük Seasons of 1930–32, Part I.* The University of Chicago, Oriental Institute Publications XXVIII, Chicago.

Öner B. 2009 Küllüoba Höyüğü Geç Kalkolitik ve İlk Tunç Çağı Küçük Buluntuları (Yontma Taşaletler ve Metal Eserler Hariç) İstanbul Üniversitesi Sosyal Bilimler Enstitüsü Arkeoloji Ana Bilim Dalı Prehistorya ve Önasya Arkeolojisi Bilim Dalı Yayınlanmamış Yüksek Lisans Tezi.

Özgüç, N. 1987a Karaoğlan Mühürleri. *Remzi Oğuz Arık Armağanı,* Ankara Üniversitesi Dil ve Tarih Coğrafya Fakültesi Yayınları No: 360, Ankara.

Özgüç, N. 1987b Samsat Mühürleri. *Belleten* LI/200:429–439.

Özkan, S. 2001 Köşk Höyük Seals. *Anatolica* XXVII:15–22.

Reichel, C. D. 2009 Hamoukar. Oriental Institute 2008–2009 Annual Report:77–87.

Rothman, M. S. 2002 *Tepe Gawra: The Evolution of a Small Prehistoric Center in Northern Iraq.* University Museum Publications 112, Philadelphia.

Schliemann, H. 1880 *Ilios, the City and Country of the Trojans. The Results of Researches and Discoveries on the Site of Troy and throughout the Troad in the Years 1871–72–73–78–79.* New York.

Silistreli, U. 1986 1984 Köşk Höyüğü. *7. Kazı Sonuçları Toplantısı,* 129–141.

Stein, G. J. 2010 Tell Zeidan. 2008–2009 Annual Report of The Oriental Institute, 126–137.

Tezcan, B. 1966 1964 *Koçumbeli Kazısı, Koçumbeli Excavation in 1964.* Orta Doğu Teknik Üniversitesi, Ankara.

Tobler, A. J. 1950 *Excavations at Tepe Gawra Volume 2.* University of Pennsylvania Museum Monograph, Philadelphia.

Türkcan, A. U., and B. Beyoğlu 2015 Höyüktepe 2014 Yılı Erken Tunç Çağı Damga Mühürleri. *Kureyşler Barajı Kurtarma Kazıları* 2014:431–446.

Türktüzün, M., S. Ünan, and S. Ünal 2014 Metin Türktüzün-Serdar Ünan-Semih Ünal "Çiledir Höyük Erken Tunç Çağı II Bulguları. *Tüba-Ar* 17:49–72.

Umurtak, G. 2000 Neolitik ve Erken Kalkolitik Çağlar'da Burdur Antalya Bölgesi Mühürcülüğü Üzerine Bazı Gözlemler. *Adalya* IV:1–19.

Warner, L. J. 1994 *Elmalı-Karataş II, The Early Bronze Age Village of Karataş.* Bryn Mawr College Monographs, Bryn Mawr.

Weingarten, J., J. H. Crouwel, M. Prent, and G. Vogelsang-Eastwood 1999 Early Helladic Sealings from Geraki in Lakonia, Greece. *Oxford Journal of Archaeology* 18(4):358–376.

Wickede, A. von 1990 *Prähistorische Stemppelglyptik in Vorderasien.* Münchener Universitäts-Schriften Philosophische Fakultät 12, Profil Verlag, München.

Wiencke, M. H. 1969 Further Seals and Sealings from Lerna. *Hesperia* 38(4):500–521.

Yule, P. 1982 *Tepe Hissar, Neolithische und Kupferzeitliche Siedlung in Nordostiran.* Materialien zur Allgemeinen und Vergleichenden Archäologie Band 14, München.

Chapter Twenty-Two

Acemhöyük Early Bronze Age Pottery

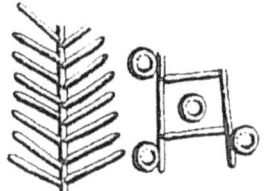

Yalçın Kamış*

Introduction

Acemhöyük is located in the town of Yeşilova, which is 18 kilometers northwest of Aksaray, on the Aksaray Plain lying just south of Tuz Gölü. Acemhöyük is one of the biggest mounds of Anatolia and it extends about 700 meters in the north-south direction and 600 meters in the east-west direction (Figure 22.1, N. Özgüç 1968:3). Acemhöyük attracted scientific interest with the recovery of monumental buildings and rich finds dated to the Assyrian Trading Colonies Period after the beginning of excavations in 1962. These significant findings indicated that the Assyrian Trading Colonies Period city, which dated to the first quarter of the second millennium B.C., had a major role in trade networks and this situation created the ongoing discussion about the name of city (Barjamovic 2011:366; N. Özgüç 1968:2).

The prosperous Assyrian Trading Colonies Period city at Acemhöyük brought about some problems in the third-millennium settlement on the site and its relations with the second-millennium city. Excavations were carried out on different areas of the mound in order to get some answers to these problems (Öztan 2012). These excavations were mainly executed on the southeastern slope, which is very close to Sarıkaya Palace. Although virgin soil was not reached, the stratigraphy of the city from the Early Bronze Age II to the Assyrian Trading Colonies Period was determined in this area (Öztan 2012:60).

The southwestern region of Central Anatolia where Acemhöyük is located is not well known in terms of Early Bronze Age studies. Excluding the Acemhöyük and Konya

---

*Dr. Yalçın Kamış, Nevşehir Hacı Bektaş Veli Üniversitesi Fen-Edebiyat Fakültesi Arkeoloji Bölümü, yalcinkamis@nevsehir.edu.tr.

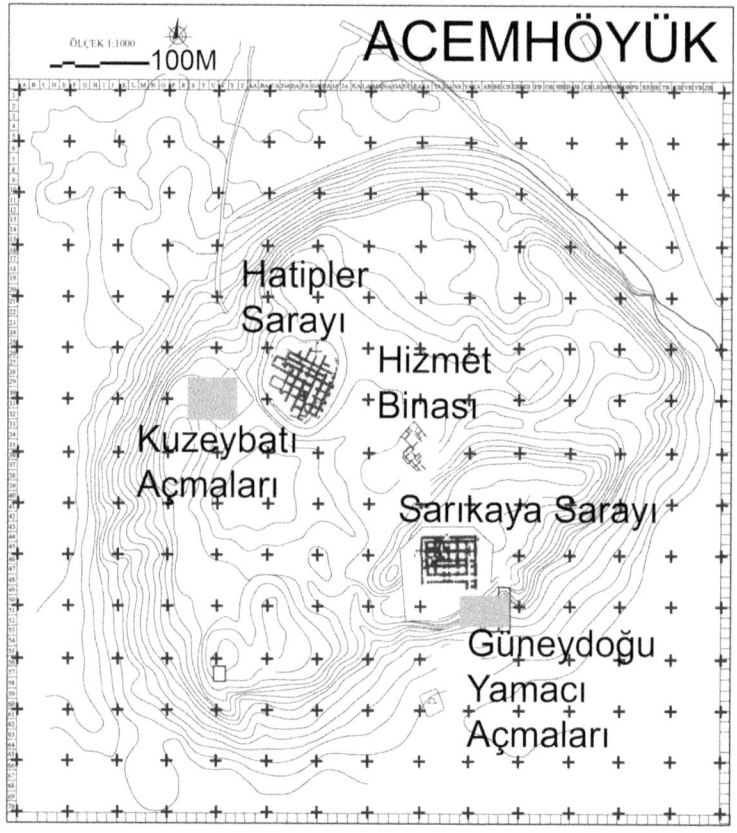

FIGURE 22.1. Topographical map of Acemhöyük.

FIGURE 22.2. Southeastern slope of Acemhöyük.

Karahüyük excavations, this region is roughly known through the surveys, and the Early Bronze Age cultural development of this region is still a problematic issue. At this point, cultural developments recognized at Acemhöyük are essential for giving some explanations and to understand the Cilician and Western Anatolian relations of the region.

Acemhöyük Early Bronze Age Stratigraphy and Pottery

Level V, the latest level of the Early Bronze Age, was excavated in the northwestern and southeastern trenches at Acemhöyük (Figure 22.1). The earlier levels were investigated on the southeastern slope only. The southeastern slope excavations revealed a settlement history with 12 levels beginning from the end of Early Bronze Age II and lasting to the end of the Assyrian Trade Colonies Period.[1] Pottery from the Early Bronze Age levels indicates that level XII dated to the end of Early Bronze Age II, levels XI–VIII to the earlier part of Early Bronze Age III (EBA IIIA), levels VII–V to the later part of Early Bronze Age (EBA IIIB; Kamış 2012:9–12). With all of the Acemhöyük Early Bronze Age pottery, which was the subject of a few previous studies (N. Özgüç 1990; Öztan 1989), it was possible to see the developments reflecting three different periods. It is not possible to present here all of the Early Bronze Age pottery reflecting the various aspects of these periods. For that reason, the main characteristics of the Early Bronze Age II and Early Bronze Age IIIA pottery are discussed below within the framework of local developments and relations with Western Anatolia.

Acemhöyük Early Bronze Age II Pottery

Level XII represents the earliest cultural stratum of Acemhöyük, and it was excavated in a very limited area. In line with this, the number of ceramics recovered from this area is very limited. If the fabric and surface characteristics of this small group of level XII pottery is considered, a homogenous characteristic emerges. All of the pottery is handmade and approximately 60 percent of them are red slipped and burnished. A crackled and abraded thick red slip could be recognized easily on the surfaces of the vessels. White grit, sand, mica, lime, and plant temper are the most common inclusions in the pastes of red-slipped ceramics. The rest of level XII pottery consists of heavy grit–tempered coarse ware and a buff variant of red-slipped ceramics. The form repertory of level XII pottery assemblage is very limited. Shallow conical simple bowls, vertical loop-handled bowls and cups, horizontal-handled large bowls, trays, and simple hole-mouth pots are the main forms of this assemblage.

Shape, fabric, and surface characteristics of level XII pottery could be compared with Early Bronze Age II and III ceramics of Central Anatolian settlements (N. Özgüç N. 1980:621; N. Özgüç 1990:71; Öztan 1989:409). Large-scale similarities with the survey materials also indicate that this type of pottery is widely distributed in the southwestern part of Central Anatolia (French 1969:41; Mellaart 1963:211).

Acemhöyük Early Bronze Age IIIA Pottery

The Early Bronze Age IIIA period, which is the first period of major change in terms of the pottery tradition of Acemhöyük, consists of levels from XI to VIII. This period also indicates significant changes in the settlement layout of Acemhöyük. The strongest sign of this change is the mudbrick fortification wall revealed in the earliest level of this period (Öztan and Arbuckle 2013:280). Another sign of the dynamic settlement history is the level X buildings constructed directly on the fortification wall, which was destroyed at the end of level XI.

Developments observed in ceramic production after level XI at Acemhöyük have also brought significant diversity in the shapes and fabrics of vessels. Red-slipped handmade pottery dominating level XII is also common during this period (Kamış 2012:30). But new groups such as Central Anatolian Metallic Ware, Plain Ware, Red-Slipped Ware, Moiré Painted Ware, and Konya Plain Painted W were introduced in pottery assemblage after level XI.

Metallic ware, which might be defined as the most characteristic pottery of the southwestern part of Central Anatolia, is easily separated from other wares with their thin walls and sharp profiles. Metallic ware sherds have been collected at approximately a hundred sites within the course of different surveys conducted in Central Anatolia and Cilicia (Öztan 1989:407). Despite that, the number of archaeological excavations that yielded metallic ware is limited. Mersin Yümüktepe (Garstang 1953:Figure 122), Tarsus Gözlükule (Mellink 1989:322), Konya Karahöyük (Mellink 1965:114; Mellink 1992:215), Kilisetepe (Symington 2007:298), Göltepe (Yener and Vandiver 1993: Figure 4.4), Kültepe (T. Özgüç 1986: Figure 3–21), and Ovaören Topakhöyük (Şenyurt et al. 2014: Figure 4, 5–7) are the sites where metallic ware was found in archaeological excavations. Central Anatolian metallic ware was mostly recovered from the Early Bronze Age II levels of these sites. But at Acemhöyük Central Anatolian metallic ware was found together with the Western Anatolian shapes such as wheel-made plates and tankards within the same contexts, and this clearly indicates that the production of this ware continued in the earlier period of the Early Bronze Age III (Öztan 1989:410).

The Introduction of plain wares in level XI represents another development in pottery production at Acemhöyük. A small amount of sand and grit inclusions were found in the paste of wheel-made plain ware. Introduction of this ware should be related to the use of the potter's wheel in ceramic production, and the most distinctive shape of this ware at Acemhöyük is the plates (Figure 22.3:5–10). Forty-six diagnostic sherds of wheel-made plates were found in levels XI, X, and IX in addition to a well-preserved one (Figure 22.3:8) recovered from an Early Bronze Age III burial close to the mound (Öztan 1989:409). A few sherds recovered from the levels VIII and VII indicate the continuation of this shape in later Early Bronze Age III levels. Acemhöyük wheel-made plates are the products of the same tradition with plates recovered from the Early Bronze Age III levels of sites like Troy (Blegen et al. 1950:225–226; Blegen et al. 1951:24), Beycesultan (Lloyd and Mellaart 1962: Figure P.47.1), Küllüoba (Efe and Türkteki

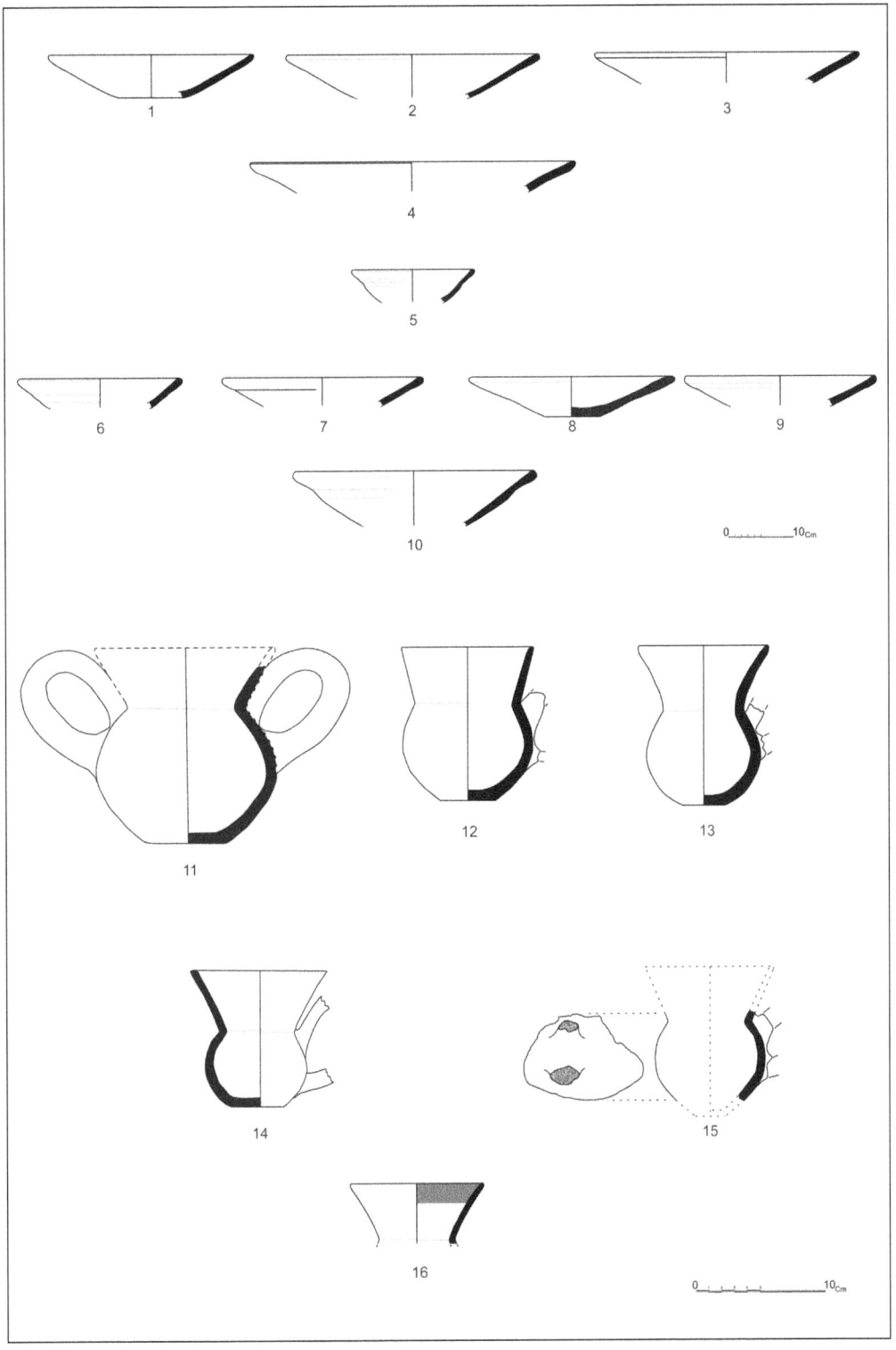

FIGURE 22.3. Western Anatolian related pottery from Acemhöyük.

2011:220), Karataş-Semayük (Eslick 2009:223), Kültepe (T. Özgüç 1986: Figure 3.22-250, Kinethöyük (Gates 2011:184), and Tarsus (Mellink 1989:325).

Red-slipped wares represent another innovation of level XI ceramic repertory. Production technique and better surface and paste treatments distinguish red-slipped ware from the handmade red-slipped ware dominating Acemhöyük Early Bronze Age II and III levels. Red-slipped ware is divided into two groups according to paste and surface characteristics. The first group is related to the red-coated ware of Western Anatolia that appeared at the beginning of Early Bronze III (Türkteki 2012:55). Their buff-colored pastes are fine and do not have inclusions. They are slipped in the various shades of red and the quality of burnishing is not uniform. The first group of Acemhöyük red-slipped ware includes only two shapes. These shapes are wide shallow plates (Figure 22.3:1–4) and tankards (Figure 22.3:11–16). Fourteen sherds of shallow plates were found in levels XI, X, and IX. They are mostly wider than 30 centimeters and the diameter of the widest sample (Figure 22.1:4) is 49 centimeters. The Acemhöyük shallow plates are considered to be within the same category of plates that were found in Troy (Blegen et al. 1950:224, Figure 412, Figure 413, Figure 414), Küllüoba (Sarı 2009:99), Aphrodisias (Joukowsky 1986:452) and Karataş-Semayük (Eslick 2009:220, 223; Warner 1997: Pl.167-c). Single-handled and double-handled types of tankards (Figure 22.3:11–14) were found in Acemhöyük. Two of them were recovered from level X and the remaining two samples were found in the Early Bronze Age burial close to the mound. In addition to these vessels, nine tankard sherds were found in levels X and IX. Red-slipped and burnished tankard sherds, especially body fragments, indicate that wheel-made and handmade tankards were used together in levels X and IX. Rim slip applications of a few sherds (Figure 22.3:16) are another significant issue with the tankards. Tankards were found in a wide geographical area extending from Greece to Southeastern Anatolia in the Early Bronze Age.[2] This vessel is considered a part of new eating and drinking customs that appeared at the beginning of Early Bronze Age III (Mellink 1989:325). The recovery of a significant amount of this vessel at Acemhöyük implies that Acemhöyük adopted new eating and drinking customs.

A second group of red-slipped ware has a small amount of sand and grit temper. Their reddish-orange fabrics are compact and the vessels in this group are well fired. Red slips are not uniform and appear in different shades on the surfaces of the vessels together with dull burnishing. A few sherds of this ware found in level XI but its amount increased in levels X and IX. The shapes observed in the second group of red-slipped ware are limited to bowls (Figure 22.4:1–3) and pots (Figure 22.4:4). Slightly inverted, simple rimmed, and horizontal-handled deep bowls are among the principal shapes of this ware. Most of these bowls have painted bands on their rims (Figure 22.4:3). These painted wide bands are applied to the inside and outside of the rims and their color is usually red. The application of thick slips and burnishing obscures the production techniques of these bowls. The sharp lines of the bowls and wheel marks are visible, especially on the connection points of the rims to the body, which shows that these bowls are wheel formed. Red-slipped pots usually have everted rims with wide rim slips. Wheel marks on interior surfaces clearly indicate their production technique. According to statistical analysis, the second group of the red-slipped ware represents 20 percent of the Early

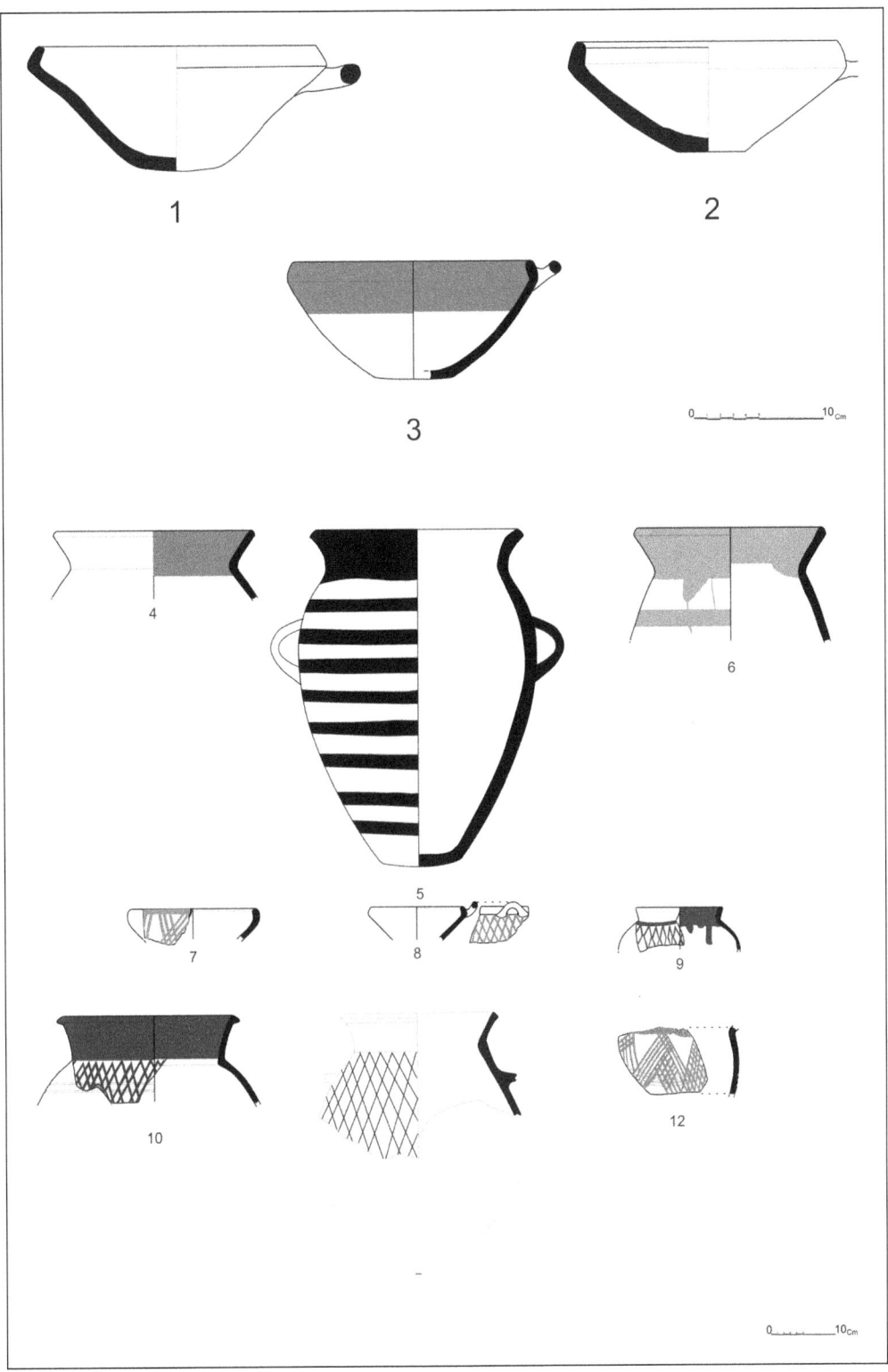

FIGURE 22.4. Local EBA III pottery shapes of Acemhöyük.

Bronze Age IIIA pottery at Acemhöyük.[3] This proportion suggests that the second group of red-slipped ware belongs to the local pottery repertoire of Acemhöyük.

Moiré painted ware, which is one of the painted wares of Acemhöyük's Early Bronze Age III pottery, is mostly light reddish-buff, light buff, or grey slipped. Wide painted bands applied to the rims and bodies characterize the moiré painted ware. The wide painted bands could be red, reddish-brown, or grey. Their fabrics are very similar to the second group of red-slipped ware. Compact fabrics have a small amount grit and sand temper. Vessels in this group are well fired. A few sherds of this ware were found in level XI but their amount increased in levels X and IX. Their amount decreased in Early Bronze Age IIIB levels, but they were in use until the end of this period (N. Özgüç 1990:71). All of the more painted ware samples are wheel made and it is interestingly limited with pot shapes (Figure 22.4:5–6). We do not have sufficient information about the distribution of Acemhöyük moiré painted ware in Central Anatolia. There are no published examples of this ware apart from the a few sherds found in Early Bronze Age III levels of Ovaören Topakhöyük (Şenyurt et al. 2014: Figure 4, 1–2).

A new painted group came in the pottery repertory of Acemhöyük in level IX. This group, which we call Konya Plain Painted Ware, has light buff, light reddish-brown, light brown, or brown-slipped surfaces. Fabrics are usually tempered with small grit, mica, and sand. Firing of the vessels is not uniform but most of them are well fired. The most distinctive feature of this group is the red, reddish-brown, dark red, or grey simple geometrical decorations observed on the surfaces of vessels (Figure 22.4:7–12). Simple motifs are composed of bands, lattice patterns, chevrons, and lattice-patterned triangles. The range of the shapes considered in Konya Plain Painted Ware is not very rich. A few bowl types (Figure 22.4:7–8), pot stands, and various sized pot types are the major forms of this ware (Figure 22.4:9–11). Different production techniques used in the forming of the vessels occurred in this ware group and it was determined that half of them are wheel made. Konya Plain Painted Ware was in use during the Early Bronze Age IIIB levels at Acemhöyük but it disappeared after level IV.

The Konya Plain Painted Ware was related to the "Intermediate" pottery, which was abundantly represented in the Early Bronze Age III layers of Alişar and Kültepe, by N. Özgüç (N. Özgüç 1968:28; N. Özgüç 1990:71). J. Mellaart visited Acemhöyük during his survey in Konya Plain and he published the same type of painted sherds in relation with "Cappadocian Pottery" (Mellaart 1958:323). A similar approach was used also at Konya Karahöyük, which yielded the same type of painted pottery (Alp 1994:16). M. Mellink, who provided brief information about Konya Karahöyük pottery, preferred the same name and she stated that hand- or wheel-made "Intermediate" pottery was found in the Levels 5 and 6 at the mound (Mellink 1962:75). Acemhöyük painted pottery samples have some similarities with the "Intermediate" pottery of Alişar and Kültepe in terms of simple decorative elements, but a significant amount of wheel-made samples create a major difference between these two groups. This difference indicates that these two contemporary wares are the representatives of different regional pottery traditions.

The ware groups briefly introduced above compose approximately 40 percent of Acemhöyük Early Bronze Age IIIA pottery. All of the remaining pottery groups, such as handmade red-slipped ware, are the successors of Early Bronze Age II pottery traditions of the region.

Concluding Remarks

The Early Bronze Age IIIA pottery found in the different excavation areas at Acemhöyük reflects distinct characteristics as compared with the Central Anatolia. Typical monochrome Central Anatolian Pottery dominates late Early Bronze Age II and Early Bronze Age IIIA levels. However, the local and imported wheel-made pottery of level XI denotes a change in the pottery production technique. Wheel-made pottery represents approximately 30 percent of the assemblage in Early Bronze Age IIIA levels and this proportion increased in Early Bronze Age IIIB levels. This position separates Acemhöyük in terms of pottery production technique from the rest of the Central Anatolia, where the wheel-made pottery began to spread at the end of Early Bronze Age III. In addition to this, pottery groups such as Moiré painted ware and Konya Plain Painted Ware indicate that the southwestern part of Central Anatolia should be considered a different pottery region within Central Anatolia.

The beginning of the EBA III period on the Anatolian Plateau is marked by developments such as the emergence of fortified city states, foundation of interregional trade networks, increased international cultural contacts, appearance of the first wheel-made pottery forms, new eating and drinking customs, and a new economic system indicated by rich metal finds (Şahoğlu 2005:340). The appearance of these developments is usually explained by the increased trade relations with Cilicia, Syria, and Mesopotamia. Trade relations between these regions are conceptualized as the "Anatolian Trade Network" (Şahoğlu 2005) or "Great Caravan Route" (Efe 2007), and recovery of similar pottery shapes from the sites on this route is explained by this relationship. Western Anatolian-originated, wheel-made plate and tankard shapes of Acemhöyük Early Bronze Age III levels[4] are typical examples of these pottery shapes. Taking into consideration Western Anatolian pottery shapes recovered in Early Bronze Age levels, it is possible to suggest that Acemhöyük is located within the third millennium B.C. trade routes, and it was one of the sites connecting Western Anatolian cultures to eastern and southern ones.

Acknowledgments

This article is based on my PhD thesis, "Acemhöyük Early Bronze Pottery," which was completed in 2012 under direction of Prof. Aliye Öztan. I would like to express my sincere gratitude to Prof. Nimet Özgüç and Prof. Aliye Öztan who allowed me studying Acemhöyük Early Bronze Age pottery recovered mostly between 1977 and 1982.

Notes

1. For Acemhöyük stratigraphy see, Özgüç, N. 1980:620–621; Özgüç, N. 1990:70–73; Özgüç, N. 1993:517–520; Öztan 1989:407–410.

2. For distribution of tankards in Central and Western Anatolia see Yılmaz 2010: 63, Map 2.
3. Statistical value is given from 1835 samples of EB IIIA levels.
4. The number of Western Anatolian shapes has significantly increased with recent excavations at the southeastern slope of Acemhöyük.

REFERENCES CITED

Alp, S. 1994 *Konya Civarında Karahöyük Kazılarında Bulunan Silindir ve Damga Mühürleri*. Türk Tarih Kurumu Yayınları, Ankara.

Barjamovic, G. 2011 *A Historical Geography of Anatolia in the Old Assyrian Colony Period*. Museum Tusculanum Press, Copenhagen.

Blegen, C., M. Caskey, and M. Rawson 1950 *Troy I, General Introduction, The First and Second Settlements*. Princeton University Press, Princeton.

Blegen, C., M. Caskey, and M. Rawson 1951 *Troy, The Third, Fourth, and Fifth Settlements*. Princeton University Press, Princeton.

Efe, T. 2007 The Theories of the "Great Caravan Route" between Cilicia and Troy. The Early Bronze Age III Period in Inland Western Anatolia. *Anatolian Studies* 57:47–64.

Efe, T., and M. Türkteki 2011 Early Bronze Age Pottery in the Inland Western Anatolian Region. In *Across: The Cyclades and Western Anatolia During the 3rd Millenium B.C.*, edited by V. Şahoğlu and P. Sotirakopoulou, pp. 214–222. Sakıp Sabancı Muzesi, İstanbul.

Eslick, C. 2009 Elmalı Karataş V. *The Early Bronze Age Pottery of Karataş: Habitation Deposits*. Bryn Mawr College Archaeological Monographs, Pennsylvania.

French, D. H. 1969 Anatolia and Aegean in The Third Millennium. Unpublished PhD thesis, Cambridge.

Garstang, J. 1953 *Prehistoric Mersin Yümük Tepe in Southern Turkey*. Clarendon Press, Oxford.

Gates, M. H. 2011 2009 Season at Kinet Höyük (Yeşilköy-Dörtyol-Hatay). *Kazı Sonuçları Toplantısı* 32(3):182–195.

Joukowsky, M. S. 1986 *Prehistoric Aphrodisias. An Account of the Excavations and Artifact Studies Volumes I–II*. Brown University Press, Providence.

Kamış, Y. 2012 Acemhöyük Erken Tunç Çağı Seramiği, Ankara. Unpublished PhD thesis, Gazi Üniversitesi.

Lloyd, S., and J. Mellaart 1962 *Beycesultan I. The Chalcolithic and Early Bronze Age Levels*. British Institute of Archaeology at Ankara, London.

Mellaart, J. 1958 Second Millennium Pottery from the Konya Plain and Neighborhood. *Belleten* XXII.87:311–345.

Mellaart, J. 1963 Early Cultures of the South Anatolian Plateau II: The Late Chalcolithic and Early Bronze Ages in the Konya Plain. *Anatolian Studies* 13:199–236.

Mellink, M. 1962 Archaeology in Asia Minor. *American Journal of Archaeology* 66(1):71–85.

Mellink, M. 1965 Anatolian Chronology. In *Chronologies in Old World Archaeology*, edited by R. W. Ehrich, pp. 101–131.University of Chicago Press, Chicago.

Mellink, M. 1989 Anatolia and Foreign Relations of Tarsus in the Early Bronze Age. In *Anatolia and the Near East, Studies in Honor of Tahsin Özgüç*, edited by K. Emre, M. Mellink, B. Hrouda, and N. Özgüç, pp. 319–332. Türk Tarih Kurumu Basımevi, Ankara.

Mellink, M. 1992 Anatolian Chronology. In *Chronologies in Old World Archaeology*, edited by R. W. Ehrich, pp. 207–221. University of Chicago Press, Chicago.

Özgüç N. 1968 Acemhöyük Kazıları. *Anadolu* X: 1–28.

Özgüç N. 1980 Acemhöyük Kazısı 1979 Çalışmaları. *Belleten* XLIV:619–621.

Özgüç N. 1990 An Early Bronze Age Jar from Acemhöyük. *Eretz-Israel* XXI:70–73.

Özgüç N. 1993 An Early Bronze Age Pot Grave of a Child from Acemhöyük. In *Between the Rivers and Over the Mountains Archaeologica Anatolica et Mesopotamica Alba Palmieri Dedicata*, edited by M. Frangipane, pp. 517–522. Dipartimento di ScienzeStoriche Archeologiche e Antropologiche dell'Antichità, Università di Roma "La Sapienza," Roma.

Özgüç T. 1986 New Observations on the Relationship of Kültepe with Southeast Anatolia and North Syria during the Third Millenium B.C. In *Ancient Anatolia Aspects of Changes and Cultural Development, Essays in Honor of Machteld J. Mellink*, edited by J. V. Canby, pp. 31–47. University of Wisconsin Press, Wisconsin.

Öztan, A. 1989 A Group of Early Bronze age Pottery from the Konya and Niğde Region. In *Anatolia and the Near East, Studies in Honor of Tahsin Özgüç*, edited by K. Emre, M. Mellink, B. Hrouda, and N. Özgüç, pp. 407–418. Türk Tarih Kurumu Basımevi, Ankara.

Öztan, A. 2012 Acemhöyük (1962–1988, 1989–). In *Dil ve Tarih-Coğrafya Fakültesi 75. Yıl Armağanı, Arkeoloji Bölümü Tarihçesi ve Kazıları (1936–2011)*, edited by B. Orhan, A. Öztan, and H. Taşkıran, pp. 59–66. Ankara Üniversitesi Dil ve Tarih-Coğrafya Fakültesi Yayınları, Ankara.

Öztan, A., and B. Arbuckle 2013 2011 Yılı Acemhöyük Kazıları ve Sonuçları. 34. *Kazı Sonuçları Toplantısı* 1:275–294.

Şahoğlu, V. 2005 The Anatolian Trade Network and the İzmir Region During the Early Bronze Age. *Oxford Journal of Archaeology* 24:339–361.

Sarı, D. 2009 Late EB II Pottery Recovered in Complex II of Küllüoba. *Anatolia Antiqua* 17:89–132.

Şenyurt, S. Y., Y. Kamış, and A. Akçay 2014 Ovaören 2012 Yılı Kazıları. 35. *Kazı Sonuçları Toplantısı* 2:62–80.

Symington, D. 2007 The Early Bronze Age Pottery. In *Excavations at Kilisetepe 1994–98 From Bronze Age to Byzantine in Western Cilicia Volume 1–2*, edited by N. Postgate and D. Thomas, pp. 295–318. McDonald Institute for Archaeological Research, London.

Türkteki, M. 2012 Batı ve Orta Anadolu'da ÇarkYapımı Çanak Çömleğin Ortaya Çıkışı veYayılımı. *Küllüoba Kazıları ve Batı Anadolu Tunç Çağları Üzerine Yapılan Araştırmalar. MASROP E-Dergi* 7:45–111.

Warner, J. L. 1997 *Elmalı-Karataş II: The Early Bronze Age Village of Karataş*. Bryn Mawr, Pennsylvania.

Yener, A. and P. B. Vandiver 1993 Tin Processing at Göltepe, an Early Bronze Age Site in Anatolia. *American Journal of Archaeology* 97(2):207–238.

Contributors

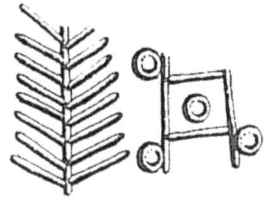

Rabia Akarsu, Rabia AKARSU, Asst. Prof., Faculty of Letters, Department of Archaeology, Atatürk University, Erzurum, 25100, Turkey.

Ayşegül Aykurt, Hacettepe University, Faculty of Letters, Department of Archaeology, 06800 Beytepe-Ankara

Ralf Becks, Mehmet Akif Ersoy Üniversitesi, Fen-Edebiyat Fakültesi, Arkeoloji Bölümü, TR-15030 Burdur

A. Nejat Bilgen, Department of Archaeology, Dumlupınar University, Kütahya 43100, Turkey

Zeynep Bilgen, Department of Archaeology, Dumlupınar University, Kütahya 43100, Turkey

Christopher Britsch, Institute for Oriental and European Archaeology, Austrian Academy of Sciences, Hollandstrasse 11-13, 1020 Vienna

Tayfun Caymaz, Department of Archaeology, Faculty of Arts and Science, Nevşehir Hacı Bektaş Veli University, Nevşehir, 50300, Türkiye

Fulya Dedeoğlu, Ege University, Faculty of Letters, Department of Archaeology, Division of Protohistory and Archaeology of Asia Minor

Turan Efe, Bilecik Şeyh Edebali Üniversitesi, Arkeoloji Bölümü, Bilecik, Turkey

Halil Hamdi Ekiz, Arkeolog M.A., Çiğli-İzmir, Turkey

Hayat Erkanal, Presidency of Liman Tepe Excavations, Denizli Mahallesi, Harbiye Caddesi, No: 2 Çeşmealtı Urla- Izmir

Erkan Fidan, Bilecik Şeyh Edebali University, Department of Archaeology, Turkey

Neşide Gençer Arkeolog M.A., Kubaba Dergisi Sorumlusu ve Sahibi, Turkey

Barbara Horejs, Institute for Oriental and European Archaeology, Austrian Academy of Sciences, Hollandstrasse 11-13, 1020 Vienna, Austria

Laura K. Harrison, Access 3D Lab, University of South Florida, Tampa, FL 33620, USA

Halime Hüryılmaz, Hacettepe Üniversitesi, Edebiyat Fakültesi, Arkeoloji Bölümü, 06800 Beytepe-Ankara / Turkey

Yalçın Kamış, Nevşehir Hacı Bektaş Veli Üniversitesi Fen-Edebiyat Fakültesi Arkeoloji Bölümü, Nevşehir, Turkey

Asuman Kapuci, Department of Archaeology, Dumlupınar University, Kütahya 43100, Turkey

Onur Kara, T.R. Ministry of Culture and Tourism, Directorate of Antalya Museum, Archeology II Service, TR 07050, Antalya

Selma Kaya, Arkeolog, İzmir Arkeoloji Müzesi, Turkey

Deniz Sarı, Bilecik Şeyh Edebali University, Faculty of Science & Letters, Department of Archeology, Gülümbe Campus, Bilecik, Turkey.

Cansu Topal, Anadolu Üniversitesi, Edebiyat Fakültesi, Arkeoloji Bölümü, Yunus Emre Kampusu 26470. Eskişehir, Turkiye

Ali Umut Türkcan, Anadolu Üniversitesi, Edebiyat Fakültesi, Arkeoloji Bölümü, Yunus Emre Kampusu 26470. Eskişehir, Turkiye

Murat Türkteki, Department of Archaeology, Bilecik Şeyh Edebali University, Bilecik, 11210, Türkiye

Sinem Üstün Türkteki, Department of Archaeology, Bilecik Şeyh Edebali University, Bilecik, 11210, Türkiye

Derya Yalçıklı, Çanakkale Onsekiz Mart University, Çanakkale, Turkey

Derya Yilmaz, Ankara University, Faculty of Language, History and Geography, Department of Archaeology, Protohistory and Near Eastern Archaeology, Sıhhiye, Ankara-Turkey, 06100.

Index

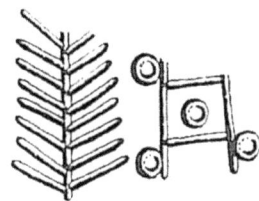

Acemhöyük, 10–11, 315–325
Administrative centers/practices, 1, 9, 11, 23, 27, 30–31, 135, 138, 141–142
Aharköy, 4, 42, 46
Anatolian Settlement Plan, 100
Antelope design, 303–308
Anthropomorphic pottery, 9, 172, 183, 278, 284
Assyrian Trading Colonies period, 10, 315

Bahçehisar, 46, 222
Bakla Tepe, 50–52, 55–56, 59, 80, 94–95 102, 106, 112 –115, 118, 208
Bayesian analysis of C14 dates, 12, 164–166
Beads, 237–238
Beak-spouted jug, 20–21, 55–59, 90, 94, 107–110, 113, 118, 221, 233
Beşik-Yassıtepe, 5, 66, 70–71, 102
Beycesultan, 3–5, 7, 10–11, 19, 21, 25, 27–37, 46, 50–60, 66, 72, 78, 79, 82, 100–106, 111–127, 141, 171, 173, 189–201, 208, 223, 233, 250–254, 282, 296, 318
Boundaries of cultural regions, 1, 5, 95, 97–127
Bronze artifacts, 150, 237, 249–250
Built environment, 7, 163, 174, 177, 181–183
Bull, cult of the, 161, 197, 199

Caria, 9, 243–257
Cemetery, 9, 27, 78, 80, 82, 105, 112, 126, 229–254
Centralization, 11, 89, 95, 141
Cheese pots, 4, 49, 56–59
Childe, V. G, 6, 131–132
Chronology, synchronization of 2, 12, 19–23, 79
Çivril Plain, 4, 25–37
Cross motif, 80
Çukurhisar, 4, 46
Çukuriçi Höyük, 9, 102, 140, 261–271
Cultural regions, 1, 5, 8, 19, 23, 95, 97–110, 111–126, 217, 224

Deer design, 303, 305, 308, 310
Depas cups, 21, 32, 84, 93–93, 214, 231, 285–288
Demircihöyük, 3, 4, 6, 8, 25, 39, 42, 100–101, 103, 164, 172, 208
Dish, 9, 10, 214, 296
Domestic shrine/cult space, 7, 189–227

Elite class, 6, 8, 11, 68, 72, 95, 163–164, 183–184
Erenköy, I 4, 39, 41–42

329

Esnemez's Road mound, 4, 39, 41–42

Figurine, 5, 8, 97–109, 147, 150–151, 159, 161, 196–197, 277–278, 285–286
Fishing, 9, 261–271
Fortifications, 6–8, 142, 150, 204–215, 318
Funerary deposits, 6, 8–9

Geoarchaeology, 8, 218–219, 224
Gold, 95, 157, 237, 249, 253
Grave, 8, 9, 79–80, 82, 112, 229–242, 244–257, 282, 311

Harmanören graveyard, 8, 105, 107, 122, 126, 234, 235, 237–238, 250, 254
Höyran Höyük, 120, 229

Idol, 97–109, 157, 159, 161, 248, 277–278
Imbros, 61–76
Imported goods, 5, 41, 92, 94–96, 123, 125, 249, 253, 323

Kaklık, 21, 51–52, 55–57, 59, 79, 89, 104–105, 112, 253–254
Kanlitaş mound, 39–48
Kepir Höyük, 33
Kubad Abad, 229–242
Küllüoba, 3–6, 10, 20–21, 25, 27, 29, 32, 42, 46, 79, 89–96, 113, 125, 134, 136, 138, 140–142, 164, 173, 195, 296, 311, 318, 320
Kumtepe, 5, 51–52, 55–60, 66–74, 78, 80, 99, 106
Kumyeri, 9, 243–254
Kuzfındık Valley, 4, 39–46

Late Chalcolithic/Early Bronze I transition, 4–5, 11, 21, 49–60, 97, 106, 112–113, 117–118, 120, 164
Libation vessels, 9, 152, 155, 157, 190, 248, 273–289
Liman Tepe, 8, 20, 27, 29, 50–51, 55, 80, 135, 137–143, 203–215, 219, 224, 250, 252–253
Long distance trade routes, 11, 19, 23, 84, 89, 95–96, 105, 323

Map of sites mentioned in the text, 2
Megaron, 6, 30, 135, 141, 152, 156–157, 164–187, 190, 217, 273–279
Metal, 8–9, 23, 27, 77–80, 82, 84, 93, 140, 157, 159, 223, 238, 249–250, 252–253, 261, 323
Metallurgy, 23, 89, 96, 217, 249, 261
Migration, 4, 7, 27
Miniature jugs, 67–68, 72, 197, 233, 249, 251
Mother Goddess, 106, 161, 277–278, 286

Net sinkers, 9, 268–269
Net weights, 261

Palace, 30–31, 134, 156–157, 232, 237, 274–275, 315
Perforated disks, 9, 262, 267–269
Personal adornment, 8, 196, 237
Phrygia, 4, 42, 97, 100, 103–107, 125
Placemaking, 183
Point motif, 303–307
Poliochni, 3, 5–6, 21, 36, 67–73, 78, 80, 82, 164, 173, 208, 251
Population growth, 6, 27, 138
Pottery mould, 9, 152, 155, 157, 161, 172, 279, 285–287
Pottery wheel, 5, 11, 21, 31–32, 64, 80, 82, 87–88, 91–96, 105, 214, 277, 295, 318, 320, 322–323
Proxemics, 179–181

Rank-size rule, 218, 221
Rhyton, 151–152, 157, 161, 172, 183, 281–284

Sanctuary, 9, 146, 152, 154–156, 201, 274–287
Settlement hierarchy, 6, 8, 218, 221, 224
Settlement layout, 1, 6, 63, 99–100, 132, 161, 318
Settlement size, 8, 141, 218, 221–222, 224
Seyitömer, 3–4, 6–7, 9–10, 25, 29, 32, 39, 46, 89, 92, 106, 134, 140–141, 145–162, 163–187, 195–197, 218, 233, 273–290, 291–302
Shrine, 7, 164, 173, 189–196, 194–197

Silver, 95, 157, 237–239, 249, 253
Social filtering, 7, 164, 181–184
Social stratification, 25, 131–137, 141, 163, 184, 225, 252–253
Sociopolitical complexity, 1, 6, 8, 11, 132, 134–135, 141, 164, 217–227, 253
Space syntax, 174–178, 184
Spindle whorl, 9, 33, 36, 150, 157, 249–250, 261–270
Stamp seals, 9–10, 150, 152, 157, 234, 252, 276, 303–313
Stela altar, 191, 194–197

Tankard, 32, 84, 90, 93, 95, 214, 249–250, 252–254, 318, 320, 323–324
Tarsus, 7, 19–20, 21, 27, 36, 78–80, 89, 95, 195–196, 318, 320
Temple, 189, 195, 273
Thermi, 5–6, 36, 64, 66–73, 103, 107, 171
Toprak Tol Höyük, 8, 229–239
Troy/Troia, 3–5, 10, 19, 21–23, 25, 27, 29, 31–32, 36, 50–52, 57–60, 78–85, 89, 91–95, 97, 99, 102–107, 118, 135–142, 172, 208, 266, 304–305, 318, 320
Tubular lugs (pottery), 5, 64–66, 71, 99

Upper Meander Basin, 27–36, 199
Urbanism, 1, 6–7, 11, 23, 131–142
Urbanization, 1, 6, 11–12, 89, 95, 131–133 141–142, 164, 225

Vegetal decoration, 303, 305, 311
Viewshed, 163, 177–181
Volute motif, 5, 77–88

Workshop, 23, 102, 106, 140, 150, 152, 156–157, 208, 277

Yassıtepe, 5, 51–60, 66–71
Yeniköy Mound, 4, 39, 41–42
Yenibademli, 4, 5, 61–74, 104, 107

Zoomorphic pottery, 9, 161, 172, 183, 278, 283–287

www.ingramcontent.com/pod-product-compliance
Ingram Content Group UK Ltd.
Pitfield, Milton Keynes, MK11 3LW, UK
UKHW050543150426
5217IPUK00026B/2055